WITHDRAWN

THE EARLY JOURNALS
AND LETTERS OF
FANNY BURNEY

1. Streatham Park, the estate of Henry Thrale and his wife, Hester Lynch Thrale. From a drawing by Edward Francesco Burney.

THE EARLY JOURNALS
AND LETTERS OF
FANNY BURNEY

VOLUME III
THE STREATHAM YEARS
PART I • 1778–1779

Edited by
LARS E. TROIDE
and
STEWART J. COOKE

McGILL-QUEEN'S UNIVERSITY PRESS
Montreal & Kingston • London • Buffalo
1994

© Lars E. Troide 1994

ISBN 0-7735-1190-3
Legal deposit second quarter 1994
Bibliothèque nationale du Québec

Printed in Canada on acid-free paper

Published simultaneously in Great Britain 1994 by
Oxford University Press
ISBN 0-19-8811267-X

This book has been published with the help of a grant from the Canadian
Federation for the Humanities, using funds provided by the Social Sciences
and Humanities Research Council of Canada.

Canadian Cataloguing in Publication Data
Burney, Fanny, 1752–1840
The early journals and letters of Fanny Burney
Includes index.
Contents: v. 1. 1768–1773 – v. 2. 1774–1777 – v. 3. 1778–1779.
ISBN 0-7735-0538-5 (v. 1) – ISBN 0-7735-0539-3 (v. 2) –
ISBN 0-7735-0527-X (v. 3)

1. Burney, Fanny, 1752–1840 – Correspondence.
2. Burney, Fanny, 1752–1840 – Diaries.
3. Novelists, English – 18th century – Correspondence.
4. Novelists, English – 18th century – Diaries.
I. Troide, Lars E. (Lars Eleon), 1942–   .
II. Cooke, Stewart J. (Stewart Jon), 1954–   . III. Title.
PR3316.A4248 1988   823'.6   c86-094863-3

Typeset in Baskerville 11/12 by Caractéra production graphique inc.,
Quebec City.

ACKNOWLEDGMENTS

FOR HELP with this volume we are especially indebted to the Social Sciences and Humanities Research Council of Canada, which provided grants for the research, and to McGill University, which continued to provide space for the project and also contributed funds for research assistants.

Permissions to publish the manuscripts in their possession have been provided by the Berg Collection at the New York Public Library; the Osborn Collection, Yale University; the British Library (for the Barrett materials); the John Rylands Library at the University of Manchester; the National Library of Wales; the Boston Public Library; and John R. G. Comyn, Esq. Illustrations have been obtained from the Berg Collection and from the Osborn Collection, the Beinecke Rare Book and Manuscript Library, and the Sterling Memorial Library at Yale University.

Graduate student research assistants who helped with this volume in various ways include Ms Nancy Johnson, Ms Cynthia Sugars, Ms Noreen Bider, Ms Elsie Wagner, and Ms Lisa Brown. Ms Ruth Neufeld deciphered some of the obliterated passages in the manuscripts in the Berg Collection.

Prof. Betty Rizzo, who is editing the next volume in this edition, helped us to date some of the manuscripts in this volume, besides making other valuable contributions. For assistance with specific problems (acknowledged at the appropriate points in the text) we are also indebted to: Mrs John R. G. Comyn; Prof. Clive Probyn; Mr J. Hugh C. Reid; Miss E. Silverthorne; Mr J. E. Filmer; Mr Robert J. Barry; Mr John Brett-Smith; and Prof. Antonia Forster.

CONTENTS

LIST OF ILLUSTRATIONS

INTRODUCTION

THE YEAR 1778 was Fanny Burney's *annus mirabilis*. At its beginning she was the virtually unknown second daughter of England's most eminent musicologist, Dr Charles Burney. By its end she had emerged from his shadow as the author of *Evelina*, a universally acclaimed novel that led admirers to place her in the ranks of Fielding and Richardson.

This striking transformation began on the 29th of January. On that date there appeared in the London newspapers the earliest advertisements of *Evelina, or, a Young Lady's Entrance into the World*. The novel appeared anonymously; Burney, fearing the stigma of female authorship, had kept her identity secret even from her publisher, Thomas Lowndes, using first her brother Charles and then her cousin Edward Francesco Burney as her go-betweens with the manuscript. Besides these two, only her sisters Susan, Charlotte, and Esther (Hetty) were initially privy to the secret.

In the ensuing weeks Burney anxiously awaited the appearance of critical reviews of her book. The earliest came in the February issue of William Kenrick's *London Review*. The normally scurrilous Kenrick gave what was, for him, an unusually warm assessment: 'There is much more merit, as well respecting stile, character and Incident, than is usually to be met with among our modern novels' (below, p. 14 and n. 30). On the other hand, the *Monthly Review* (for April) was practically unbounded in its enthusiasm: 'This novel has given us so much pleasure in the perusal, that we do not hesitate to pronounce it one of the most sprightly, entertaining and agreeable productions of this kind which has of late fallen under our notice' (p. 15 and n. 32).

In the meantime praise of the work was spreading by word of mouth through London's literary circles. The earliest important champion seems to have been Mary Cholmondeley, society hostess, who recommended it to

Hester Lynch Thrale, who then gave it to Samuel Johnson. With Dr Johnson's approbation the novel's fame and success were assured; other notable conquests would include Edmund Burke (who stayed up all night to read it), Sir Joshua Reynolds, and Richard Brinsley Sheridan. Before long one of Lowndes' lady customers would complain that she was regarded as out of fashion for not having read *Evelina*, which in epistolary form chronicles the adventures of a beautiful, innocent, and intelligent young girl from the country who keeps her virtue despite a forced education in the follies and vices of London society (exemplified particularly by the duplicitous rake Sir Clement Willoughby and Evelina's vulgar relatives the Branghtons and grandmother Madame Duval).

Burney's journals and letters for 1778 are, as might be expected, preoccupied with the reception of *Evelina*. They also show her obsessive desire to keep her authorship secret. For although Burney was clearly delighted with the critical and public approval her novel received, she was terrified at the prospect of being thrust into the limelight as its author. At the root of her terror was an extreme constitutional shyness compounded by fears of criticism for having transgressed the conventional code of acceptable female behaviour (which held, in effect, that all women ideally should restrict themselves to marriage, childbearing, and homemaking). This terror would result in absurdly unrealistic attempts to limit the knowledge of her authorship, even after her father, Hester Thrale, and Dr Johnson had learned of it.

The most important immediate consequence for Burney of the publication of *Evelina* was her admittance into the illustrious circle at Streatham Park, the country residence of the London brewer and Member of Parliament Henry Thrale and his talented wife Hester Lynch Thrale (later Mrs Piozzi). Streatham was a magnet to the social and literary elite of London largely because it was the second home of Dr Johnson, who had been living with the Thrales since the mid-1760s. Once her authorship of *Evelina* was known, it was inevitable that Burney should be invited to Streatham (where her father, music teacher of the Thrales' daughter 'Queeney', was already a regular visitor), and so it was that in her journal for August 1778 she would 'write an account of the most *Consequential* Day I have spent since my Birth: namely, my Streatham Visit' (p. 66).

Over the next several years (until Hester Thrale's lease of the place in 1782 after the premature death of her husband) Burney would repeatedly return to Streatham, staying there for weeks at a time, until her father would complain about the Thrales' monopolizing her. She would accompany the Thrales on lengthy trips to Brighton and Bath; even a journey to Spa was contemplated, though this had to be cancelled because of the war with France and Spain. At Streatham she became a great favourite of Johnson, whose avuncular affection she returned with a fervour that gave jealous fits to her second 'Daddy', Samuel Crisp of Chessington. Her portraits of Dr Johnson show a rollicking, sportive side to him that is largely missing in other accounts, and constitute a major attraction of the journals for this period of her life.

By the year's end Burney had mostly reconciled herself to the fame brought by *Evelina* (though a harmless reference to her as 'dear little Burney' in a 'low' poem entitled *Warley* practically made her ill). In 1779 she brought to fruition an idea suggested by Hester Thrale and seconded by the playwrights Sheridan and Arthur Murphy, namely that she should write a comedy for the London stage. This suggestion was made because of the evident gift for drama displayed in *Evelina*: Burney's creation of interesting and original characters and situations, her deft mingling of elements of sentiment and satire, and particularly her dialogue, which displayed a keen ear for the varied idioms of the day, convinced Thrale, Murphy, and Sheridan that she could achieve a success in the theatre. Accordingly she set to work on a comedy combining a sentimental love plot (featuring the slightly absurd romantics Cecilia and Beaufort) with a pointed attack on London follies, in particular the ignorance and affectations of would-be female wits.

The result was 'The Witlings', which she had finished by May of 1779. She first showed the play to her father and Hester Thrale, both of whom approved it strongly. Arthur Murphy was also favourably impressed. Then, in early August, Dr Burney read the play at Chessington to an audience that included Samuel 'Daddy' Crisp, Crisp's sister Mrs Sophia Gast, Fanny's sisters Susan and Charlotte, and Crisp's landlady Mrs Sarah Hamilton and her niece Catherine 'Kitty' Cooke. Again the reaction was generally favourable. But then Burney received one of the greatest shocks of her young life. Without warning Dr Burney and Crisp together concocted what she called a 'Hissing, groaning, catcalling Epistle' (missing) in which they advised her to drop the play (below, p. 350).

A number of reasons, genuine or specious, were given for this drastic decision (including the play's resemblance to Molière's *Les Femmes savantes*, and its inferiority to that work). But clearly the central reason for the advice of her 'Daddies' was a fear of offending London's bluestockings, the leader of whom was the prominent and influential Elizabeth Montagu; the comparison would inevitably be made between them and Burney's 'witlings', led by the foolish and pretentious Lady Smatter. Hester Thrale had immediately recognized this danger, commenting in her diary, 'I like [the play] very well for my own part, though none of the scribbling Ladies have a Right to admire its general Tendency' (*Thraliana* i. 381, cited p. 268 n. 18). Burney dutifully agreed to drop the play, though with great pain and regret, feelings which unmistakably underlie the cheerful resignation she expressed in the replies she sent to her Daddies. In later years Thrale added the following note to her account of the episode: '[Fanny's] confidential friend Mr Crisp advised her against bringing it on, for fear of displeasing the female Wits—a formidable Body, & called by those who ridicule them, the *Blue Stocking Club*' (ibid.). This addendum clearly indicates that it was Crisp who had worked upon Dr Burney at Chessington and caused him to change his earlier favourable opinion. In January 1780 Burney wrote to Crisp that Sheridan was upset at her withdrawal of the play and her refusal even to let him see it, adding that her father now urged her to show it to the playwright.

Her observation in the same letter that Dr Burney was
'ever easy to be worked upon' was probably meant as a
broad hint to Crisp that she knew his role in the affair
(Burney to Crisp, 22 Jan. 1780, Berg, printed *DL* i. 313–
20). By this time, however, Burney had had enough pain
and disappointment, and she allowed the play to sink
'down among the Dead Men' (see below, p. 345). It
remains unpublished to this day, though the situation will
be remedied shortly.[1]

The principal 'stars' in this volume, besides Burney
herself, are of course Dr Johnson, as mentioned above,
and Hester Thrale. An interesting counterpoint to these
journals is provided by Thrale's diaries (quoted exten-
sively in our notes). While Burney's journals show Thrale
as a devoted wife terribly distressed by her husband's ill
health (which began in June 1779 with a mild stroke),
Thrale's diaries, although displaying a dutiful concern,
reveal beneath the surface a deeply embittered woman
trapped in a loveless marriage to a philandering husband
(whose latest 'flame' was 'the fair Grecian', Sophie Street-
feild). Similarly, Thrale's kindness to Burney and genuine
liking for her are amply shown by Burney, but Thrale's
own observations indicate an ambivalence unsuspected by
her young guest. For example, upon Burney's return to
Streatham in August 1779, Thrale comments: 'Fanny
Burney has been a long time from me, I was glad to see
her again; yet She makes me miserable too in many
Respects—so restlessly & apparently anxious lest I should
give myself Airs of Patronage, or load her with Shackles
of Dependance—I live with her always in a Degree of
Pain that precludes Friendship—dare not ask her to buy
me a Ribbon, dare not desire her to touch the Bell, lest
She should think herself injured—...' (*Thraliana* i. 400,
cited p. 352 n. 85). While Burney fills her journals with
deprecating remarks about her literary offspring, it is
clear that underneath it all she took great pride in them,

---

[1] Prof. Peter Sabor will be including it in his edition of the complete plays,
to be published by Pickering and Chatto. Dr Clayton Delery, who edited the
play as his dissertation, intends to publish it separately. The holograph is in
the Berg Collection.

and that her defensiveness about her talents was often a
source of irritation and constraint to those around her.

Fanny Burney is unusual in the degree of acclaim she
has received both for her creative writing and for her journals. (Virginia Woolf, an admirer of Burney, provides perhaps the nearest analogy in our own century.) The editor
of the journals and letters of a creative artist must always
be especially alert to the possibility of the author's fancifully
embellishing or altering the bare facts of the narrative.
Among the minor portraits in this volume is Burney's
sketch of Selina Birch, an unusual and precocious young
girl, which she executed with such vividness that Daddy
Crisp suspected her of fictionalizing. Her response to this
charge (in an undated letter to Crisp, Berg, probably
written in early 1780) demonstrates the firm distinction
she always made between the facts of journalizing and the
fictions of creative writing: 'I am extremely gratified by
your approbation of my Journal. Miss Birch, I do assure
you, exists *exactly* such as I have described her. I never mix
Truth & Fiction;—all that I relate in Journalising is *strictly*,
nay *plainly* Fact: I never, in all my Life, have been a sayer
of the Thing that is not, & *now* I should be not *only* a knave,
but a Fool also in so doing, as I have other purposes for
Imaginary Characters than filling Letters with them. Give
me credit, therefore, on the score of Interest & common
sense, if not of Principle!' She goes on to add: 'the World,
& especially the great World, is so filled with absurdity of
various sorts,—now bursting forth in impertinence, now
in pomposity, now giggling in silliness, & now yawning in
dullness, that there is no reason for *invention* to draw what
is striking in every possible species of the ridiculous.' As if
in anticipation of making this point, in Oct. 1779 she comments to her sister Susan on the unconsciously hilarious
conversation of a foolish old Irishman whom she had met
at Brighton: 'Now if I had heard all this *before* I writ my
Play, would you not have thought I had borrowed the hint
of my Witlings from Mr. Blakeney?' (p. 404). Other richly
comic, but, we may presume, 'true' portraits in the volume
include Rose Fuller, with his 'Bow-wow system', the silly
Pitches family (whom Crisp recommended as an alternate

subject for a comedy), and the playwright Richard Cumberland (soon to be satirized as Sir Fretful Plagiary in Sheridan's *The Critic*), whose jealousy of Burney's literary gifts almost chokes him.

While there is no good reason to suspect Burney's basic sincerity when she affirms the veracity of her journals (her accounts more often than not are borne out by contemporary testimony), the reader is reminded that in her moral scheme *strict* veracity is to be eschewed if it shows herself or her family in too unfavourable a light. She devoted the last decades of her long life to mitigating or editing out family scandals or disgraces, such as her brother Charles' dismissal from Cambridge University in 1777 for stealing books, or her brother James' forced retirement from the Navy in 1785 for disobeying orders (see *EJL* i. pp. xxv, 39 n. 13, ii. 289–90). She shared her father's sensitivity about the Burney family's humble beginnings and any 'low' associations, and so in the journals for 1778 and elsewhere she attempted, with only partial success, to eliminate all direct references to Gregg's Coffee House in York Street, which her father probably owned (see Appendix 1). The editors of her journals are continually challenged to remove the lacquer of prudent afterthoughts. The end result continues to be a uniquely revealing picture of the age.

EDITORIAL NOTE

With this volume the editors begin the re-editing of the journals and letters from 1778 through July 1791, which were published very selectively by Burney's niece and literary executrix, Mrs Charlotte Barrett, in the first four and a half volumes of her 7-volume edition of the *Diary and Letters of Madame D'Arblay* (1842–6). We estimate that the restoration of Burney's obliterations and Barrett's deleted passages will more than double the amount of published material in these years. In this volume 35 per cent of Burney's text is new.

The often faulty dating of items in Barrett's edition is corrected. (Some of the letters have been misplaced by a year or more.) Also emended are Barrett's occasional 'corrections' of Burney's language, which do the same disservice to Burney as 19th-century musical editors did to composers when they 'corrected' innovative harmonies. An example is the phrase '*bore* it' (in 'I could not *bore* it again into the Room'). Barrett emended the phrase to 'brave it', assuming it to be a slip. As a result the *Oxford English Dictionary*, which quotes Burney 1,862 times,[2] missed this apparently unique locution (see p. 158 and n. 5).

EDITORIAL SYMBOLS AND ABBREVIATIONS

In this volume the following editorial symbols and abbreviations are employed:

|	A break in the manuscript pages
⟨ ⟩	Uncertain readings
[ ]	Text or information supplied by the editor; also insertions or substitutions by Madame d'Arblay, identified as such by a footnote
⌐ ¬	Matter overscored by Madame d'Arblay but recovered

[xxxxx *3 lines*] Matter overscored by Madame d'Arblay; *not*
[xxxxx *2 words*] recovered

The head-notes use or reproduce the following bibliographic abbreviations and signs:

AJ	Autograph journal
AJLS	Autograph journal letter signed
AL	Autograph letter
ALS	Autograph letter signed
pmks	Postmarks, of which only the essential are abstracted, e.g., 23 IV
⁂	Madame d'Arblay's symbol for manuscripts 'Examined & Amalgamated with others'; also, for manuscripts released for publication in a second category of interest
※ ✕	Other symbols of Madame d'Arblay for manuscripts in a second category of interest

The reader is also referred to the editorial principles outlined in *EJL* i, pp. xxix–xxxiii.

---

[2] Tabulation using *The Original Oxford English Dictionary on Compact Disc*, published by Tri Star Publishing, Fort Washington, Pennsylvania, 1987.

SHORT TITLES AND ABBREVIATIONS

PERSONS

CB	Charles Burney (Mus.Doc.), 1726–1814
CB Jr.	Charles Burney (DD), 1757–1817
EAB	Elizabeth (Allen) Burney, 1728–96
EB	Esther Burney, 1749–1832
EBB	after 1770 Esther (Burney) Burney
FB	Frances Burney, 1752–1840
FBA	after 1793 Madame d'Arblay
HLT	Hester Lynch (Salusbury) Thrale, 1741–1821
HLTP	after 1784 Mrs Piozzi
JB	James Burney (Rear-Admiral), 1750–1821
MA	Maria Allen, 1751–1820
MAR	after 1772 Maria (Allen) Rishton
SC	Samuel Crisp, c.1707–83
SEB	Susanna Elizabeth Burney, 1755–1800
SBP	after 1782 Mrs Phillips
SJ	Samuel Johnson

WORKS, COLLECTIONS, ETC.

Standard encyclopedias, biographical dictionaries, peerages, armorials, baronetages, knightages, school and university lists, medical registers, lists of clergy, town and city directories, court registers, army and navy lists, road guides, almanacs, and catalogues of all kinds have been used but will not be cited unless for a particular reason. Most frequently consulted were the many editions of Burke, Lodge, and Debrett. In all works London is assumed to be the place of publication unless otherwise indicated.

Abbott	John Lawrence Abbott, *John Hawkesworth: Eighteenth-Century Man of Letters*, Madison, Wisconsin, 1982.
Add. MSS	Additional Manuscripts, British Library.
AL	Great Britain, War Office, *A List of the General and Field Officers as They Rank in the Army*, 1740–1841.
AR	*The Annual Register, or a View of the History, Politics, and Literature...*, 1758– .

Barrett   The Barrett Collection of Burney Papers, British
                 Library, 43 vols., Egerton 3690–3708.
Berg   The Henry W. and Albert A. Berg Collection,
                 New York Public Library.
BL   The British Library.
Bowood   Collection of the Marquess of Lansdowne at
                 Bowood House, Calne, Wiltshire.
BUCEM   *The British Union-Catalogue of Early Music*, ed.
                 Edith B. Schnapper, 2 vols., 1957.
CB *Mem.*   *Memoirs of Dr. Charles Burney 1726–1769*, ed.
                 Slava Klima, Garry Bowers, and Kerry S. Grant,
                 Lincoln, Nebraska, 1988.
CJ   *Journals of the House of Commons.*
Clifford   James L. Clifford, *Hester Lynch Piozzi (Mrs.
                 Thrale)*, 2nd edn., Oxford, 1952.
Comyn   The Collection of John R. G. Comyn.
Daily Adv.   *The Daily Advertiser*, 1731–95.
Delany Corr.   *The Autobiography and Correspondence of Mary
                 Granville, Mrs. Delany: with Interesting Reminis-
                 cences of King George the Third and Queen Charlotte*,
                 ed. Lady Llanover, 6 vols., 1861–2.
DL   *Diary and Letters of Madame d'Arblay (1778–1840)*,
                 ed. Austin Dobson, 6 vols., 1904–5.
DNB   *Dictionary of National Biography.*
DSB   *Dictionary of Scientific Biography*, ed. C. C. Gil-
                 lispie, 16 vols., New York, 1970–80.
ED   *The Early Diary of Frances Burney, 1768–1778*, ed.
                 Annie Raine Ellis, 2 vols., 1913.
EDD   *The English Dialect Dictionary*, ed. J. Wright,
                 6 vols., 1898–1905.
EJL   *The Early Journals and Letters of Fanny Burney.*
Frag. Mem.   Fragmentary MS memoirs after 1769 of Charles
                 Burney in the Berg Collection, New York Public
                 Library.
Garrick, *Letters* *The Letters of David Garrick*, ed. David M. Little
                 and George M. Kahrl, 3 vols., Cambridge, Massa-
                 chusetts, 1963.
GEC, *Peerage*   George Edward Cokayne, *The Complete Peerage*,
                 rev. by Vicary Gibbs *et al.*, 13 vols., 1910–
                 59.
German Tour   Charles Burney, *The Present State of Music in
                 Germany, the Netherlands, and United Provinces*,
                 2 vols., 1773; 2nd corrected edn., 1775.
GM   *The Gentleman's Magazine*, 1731–1880.
Graves   A. Graves and W. V. Cronin, *A History of the
                 Works of Sir Joshua Reynolds*, 4 vols., 1899–1901.
HFB   Joyce Hemlow, *The History of Fanny Burney*,
                 Oxford, 1958.

Highfill	Philip H. Highfill, Jr., Kalman A. Burnim, and Edward A. Langhans, *A Biographical Dictionary of Actors, Actresses, Musicians, Dancers, Managers and Other Stage Personnel in London, 1660–1800*, Carbondale, Illinois, 1973– .
Hist. Mus.	Charles Burney, *A General History of Music, from the Earliest Ages to the Present Period*, 4 vols., 1776–89.
Houghton	Houghton Library, Harvard University, Cambridge, Massachusetts.
Hyde	The Hyde Collection, Four Oaks Farm, Somerville, New Jersey.
IGI	International Genealogical Index (formerly the Mormon Computer Index).
JL	*The Journals and Letters of Fanny Burney (Madame d'Arblay), 1791–1840*, ed. Joyce Hemlow *et al.*, 12 vols., Oxford, 1972–84.
LCB	*The Letters of Dr Charles Burney*, ed. Alvaro Ribeiro, SJ, Oxford, 1991– .
LDGL	London Directories from the Guildhall Library (on microfilm reels published by Research Publications, Woodbridge, Connecticut and Reading, England).
Lib.	Leigh and Sotheby, *A Catalogue of the Miscellaneous Library of the Late Charles Burney*, 9 June 1814, priced copy in the Yale University Library.
Life	*Boswell's Life of Johnson*, ed. George Birkbeck Hill, rev. by L. F. Powell, 6 vols., Oxford, 1934–64.
Lonsdale	Roger Lonsdale, *Dr. Charles Burney: A Literary Biography*, Oxford, 1965.
LSJ	*The Letters of Samuel Johnson*, ed. Bruce Redford, Princeton, 1992– .
LS 1, 2, [etc.]	*The London Stage 1660–1800*, Parts 1 to 5 in 11 vols., Carbondale, Illinois, 1960–8. References are to volume and page in each part.
Manwaring	G. E. Manwaring, *My Friend the Admiral: The Life, Letters, and Journals of Rear-Admiral James Burney, F.R.S.*, 1931.
Maxted	Ian Maxted, *The London Book Trades, 1775–1800: A Preliminary Checklist of Members*, Folkestone, Kent, 1977.
Mem.	*Memoirs of Doctor Burney, Arranged from His Own Manuscripts, from Family Papers, and from Personal Recollections*, by his daughter, Madame d'Arblay, 3 vols., 1832.
Mercer	Charles Burney, *A General History of Music*, ed. Frank Mercer, 2 vols., 1935.
MI	Memorial Inscription(s).

ML	Great Britain, War Office, *A List of the Officers of the Militia, 1778–1825.*
Namier	Sir Lewis Namier and John Brooke, *The House of Commons, 1754–1790,* 3 vols., 1964.
New Grove	*The New Grove Dictionary of Music and Musicians,* ed. Stanley Sadie, 20 vols., 1980.
Nichols, *Lit. Anec.*	John Nichols, *Literary Anecdotes of the Eighteenth Century,* 9 vols., 1812–15.
Nichols, *Lit. Ill.*	John Nichols, *Illustrations of the Literary History of the Eighteenth Century,* 8 vols., 1817–58.
OED	*Oxford English Dictionary,* 2nd edn.
Osborn	The James Marshall and Marie-Louise Osborn Collection, Yale University Library, New Haven, Connecticut.
PCC	Prerogative Court of Canterbury.
Piozzi Letters	*The Piozzi Letters,* ed. E. A. and L. D. Bloom, Newark, 1989– .
PRO	Public Record Office, London.
Rees	*The Cyclopaedia; or, Universal Dictionary of Arts, Sciences, and Literature,* ed. Abraham Rees, 45 vols., 1802–20. CB contributed the musical articles in this work.
RHI	The Royal Household Index, the Queen's Archives, Windsor Castle.
Rylands	The John Rylands University Library of Manchester, England.
Scholes	Percy A. Scholes, *The Great Dr. Burney,* 2 vols., 1948.
Sedgwick	Romney Sedgwick, *The House of Commons, 1715–1754,* 2 vols., 1970.
SJ, *Letters*	*The Letters of Samuel Johnson, with Mrs. Thrale's Genuine Letters to Him,* ed. R. W. Chapman, 3 vols., Oxford, 1952.
SND	*The Scottish National Dictionary,* ed. W. Grant and D. D. Murison, 10 vols., Edinburgh, 1931–76.
Stone	George Winchester Stone, Jr. and George M. Kahrl, *David Garrick: A Critical Biography,* Carbondale, Illinois, 1979.
Survey of London	London County Council, *The Survey of London,* 1900– .
Thieme	Ulrich Thieme and Felix Becker, *Allgemeines Lexikon der bildenden Künstler von der Antike bis zur Gegenwart,* 37 vols., Leipzig, 1907–50.
Thorne	R. G. Thorne, *The House of Commons, 1790–1820,* 5 vols., 1986.
Thraliana	*Thraliana: The Diary of Mrs. Hester Lynch Thrale (later Mrs. Piozzi), 1776–1809,* ed. Katharine C. Balderston, 2nd edn., 2 vols., Oxford, 1951.

Tours	*Dr. Burney's Musical Tours in Europe*, ed. Percy A. Scholes, 2 vols., 1959.
TSP	Mary Hyde, *The Thrales of Streatham Park*, Cambridge, Massachusetts, 1977.
'Worcester Mem.'	'Memoranda of the Burney Family, 1603–1845', typescript of a family chronicle in the Osborn Collection, Yale University Library. The MS is untraced.
YW	*The Yale Edition of Horace Walpole's Correspondence*, ed. W. S. Lewis *et al.*, 48 vols., New Haven, 1937–83.

E V E L I N A,

OR, A

YOUNG LADY'S

ENTRANCE

INTO THE

W O R L D.

VOL. I.

LONDON:

Printed for T. LOWNDES, N° 77, in
FLEET-STREET.

M.DCC.LXXVIII.

2. Title page of the first edition of *Evelina*, published 29 Jan. 1778.
Sir Joshua Reynolds' copy.

AJ (Diary MSS I, paginated 635–48, 651–8, 671–4, 685–714, 795–8, 811–14, 819–22, foliated 1–8, 13–19, 23–[41], Berg), Journal for 1778.

39 single sheets 4to, 78 pp. (1 blank), and a fragment of a single sheet 4to. *Entitled (by FBA) 1778 and annotated* DIARY ✣

March is almost over—& not a Word have I bestowed upon my Journal!—N'importe,—I shall now whisk on to the present Time, mentioning whatever occurs to me promiscuously.

This Year was ushered in by a grand & most important Event,—for, at the latter end of January, the Literary World was favoured with the first publication of the ingenious, learned, & most profound Fanny Burney!—I doubt not but this memorable affair will, in future Times, mark the period whence chronologers will date the Zenith of the polite arts in this Island!

This admirable authoress has named her most elaborate Performance '*Evelina, or a Young Lady's Entrance into the World*.'[1]

Perhaps this may seem a rather bold attempt & Title, for a Female whose knowledge of the World is very confined, & whose inclinations, as well as situations, incline her to a private & domestic Life.—all I can urge, is that I have only presumed to trace the accidents & adventures to which a '*young woman*' is liable, I have not pretended to shew the World what it actually *is*, but what it *appears* to a Girl of 17:—& so far as that, | surely any Girl who is

---

[1] The novel was published on Thurs., 29 Jan. '*This day was published*, In three volumes, 12mo. price seven shillings and sixpence sewed, or nine shillings bound, EVELINA; Or, A YOUNG LADY'S ENTRANCE into the WORLD. Printed for T. Lowndes, No 77, in Fleet street' (*London Evening Post*, 27–9 Jan. 1778, s.v. 29 Jan.; see also *General Evening Post* and *London Chronicle* of that date). With the 3rd edn. (1779), the title was changed to *Evelina, or the History of a Young Lady's Entrance into the World*. FBA later wrote that she learned of the book's publication when her stepmother read the advertisement 'accidentally, aloud at breakfast-time' (*Mem.* ii. 131).

past 17, may safely do? The motto of my excuse, shall be taken from Pope's Temple of Fame,—

None ⌜ere⌝ can compass more than they intend.[2]

About the middle of January, my Cousin Edward brought me a private message from my Aunts, that a Parcel was come for me, under the name of Grafton.[3]

I had, some little Time before, acquainted both my Aunts of my *frolic*: They will, I am sure, be discreet;—indeed, I exacted a *vow* from them of strict secresy;—& they love me with such partial kindness, that I have a pleasure in reposing much confidence in them. & the more so, as their connections in Life are so very confined, that almost all their concerns centre in our, & my Uncle's Family.

I immediately conjectured what the Parcel was, ⌜opened it &⌝ [xxxxx ½ *line*] found the following Letter.[4]

To Mr. Grafton
     to be left at ⌜Gregg's⌝ Coffee House.
                                    ⌜York street⌝

Mʳ Grafton,
   Sir,
      I take the liberty to send you a Novel, which a Gentleman your acquaintance, said you would Hand to him. I beg with Expedition, as 'tis Time it should be

---

[2] FBA actually adapts slightly l. 256 of *An Essay on Criticism*.

[3] The pseudonym adopted by Edward Francesco Burney as FB's courier in her transactions with Thomas Lowndes. See *EJL* ii. 288 n. 75 and below, p. 32.

[4] The original (without the address) is in the Barrett Collection. In the address in the Journal FBA attempted to obliterate 'York street' and 'Gregg's', substituting 'the Orange' for the latter. Later this year, however, FB wrote to Lowndes that 'I sent to Gregg's to enquire if any parcel had been left there for Mʳ Grafton' (below, p. 33), thus confirming our reading of the obliterations.

This later letter escaped the elderly FBA's censorship, and as a result contains the only untouched mention by name in her papers of Gregg's Coffee House, York Street, Covent Garden. It now appears, from an examination of the rate books for York Street (Westminster Reference Library) and other evidence, that the house of FB's aunts and Gregg's Coffee House were identical. Presumably the aunts lived above or behind the Coffee House. The Coffee House may in fact have been owned by CB. See Appendix 1.

published, & 'tis requisite he should first revise it or the Reviewers may ¹ find a flaw. I am sir,⁵

Your obed^t serv^t

Fleet street, Jan. 7. 1778.   Thos. Lowndes

My Aunts, now, would take no denial to my reading to *them*, in order to make Errata; &—to cut the matter short, I was compelled to communicate the affair to my Cousin Edward,—& then to obey their Commands.

Of course, they were all prodigiously charmed with it.

My Cousin, now, became my Agent with Mr. Lowndes, &, when I had made the Errata, carried it to him.⁶

49   [St Martin's Street, *post* 10 January 1778]

To Thomas Lowndes

AL (Comyn), Jan. 1778
Single sheet 4to, 1 p.
Addressed: Mr. Lowndes | Fleet Street
The MS is in vol. 1 of a grangerized copy of *DL*.

Sir,

I am extremely sorry to have kept the press waiting, but I did not receive yours of the 10th⁷ till this Instant. I hope you have not gone on with the 2^d volume, without the corrections:

I will send you the conclusion before the End of the week: but I must beg you to let me have a waste sheet of the last of the 3^d volume as the set from which I correct is incomplete. You will be so good as to give it to the bearer.

I am,

    sr,

       yr. ob^d ser^t

_____   _____

⁵ 'sir,' not in the original.
⁶ Despite what FB writes here, it appears that cousin Edward had already been her agent since the preceding Nov. See *EJL* ii. 288.   ⁷ Missing.

Pray let the sheet you had be put in a cover, & wafered, & without any direction.[8]

[*The Journal for 1778 resumes.*]

The Book, however, was not published till the latter End of the month. A thousand little incidents happened about this Time, but I am not in a humour to recollect them: however, they were none of them productive of a discovery either to my Father or Mother.

My Cousins Richard & James past thro' Town this Christmas, in their way to Dover, & they spent 6 weeks in France: on their return, poor Richard was taken extremely ill, and obliged to continue in ⌐York Street⌐,[9] & be attended by Dr. Jebb.[10] James is gone to Worcester, & Miss Humphries is come hither by way of Nurse. He is now very much recovered, thank God, & gone to Brumpton,[11] for a little change of air, there he is to continue till he is able to return to Worcester. | |[12]

March 26ᵗʰ

I have now to trace some curious anecdotes for about a fortnight past.

My Cousin Richard has continued *gaining* strength & Health with a Daily rapidity of recovery, that has almost as much astonished as it has *delighted* us. & that is saying very much, for his truly amiable behaviour during his

---

[8] FB did not receive a complete set of *Evelina* from Lowndes until July (see below, p. 54). He inserted her errata at the beginning of the 1st vol.

[9] In the home of Aunts Ann and Rebecca. 'Near the Christmas Hollidays in December Richard Gustavus, & James Adolphus put their plan into execution of visiting Paris, for the sake of improving themselves in their profession, which plan answered the fullest expectations of themselves & friends. But the journey back had very nearly proved fatal to the former, who was seized with such a violent attack of Low Fever on his return to London, that his life was almost dispair'd of' ('Worcester Mem.', p. 15).

[10] Richard Jebb (1729–87), MD (Aberdeen), 1751; FRS, 1765; FRCP, 1771. In Sept. of this year, he was created a baronet, and he later became physician to the Prince of Wales (1780) and to George III (1786). He was the Thrales' family physician and had subscribed to *Hist. Mus.*

[11] Brompton, a hamlet of Kensington, noted for its salubrious air. Richard Gustavus presumably rented a suite of rooms there.

[12] A page has been left blank here.

residence here, has so much encreased the regard I *always* had for him, that I have never in my life been more heartily rejoiced than upon his restoration to his Friends.

On Friday se'night [13 Mar.], my mother accompanied my Father to Streatham, on a visit to Mrs. Thrale for 4 or 5 Days. We invited Edward to Drink Tea with us, &, upon the plan of a *frolic*, determined upon going to Bell's circulating Library,[13] at which my Father subscribes for new Books, in order to ask some questions about Evelina, however, when we got to the shop, I was ashamed to speak about it, & only enquired for some magazines, at the back of which I saw it advertised. But Edward, the moment I walked off, asked the shop man if he had ⌐Evelina.—yes, he said, but not at ⟨Home⟩⌐ [xxxxx *1½ lines*] heard of my name or Existence;—I have an exceeding odd ¦ *sensation*, when I consider that it is in the power of *any* & *every* body to read what I so· carefully hoarded even from my best Friends, till this last month or two,—& that a Work which was so lately Lodged, in all privacy, in my Bureau, may now be seen by every Butcher & Baker, Cobler & Tinker, throughout the 3 kingdoms, for the small tribute of 3 pence.

The next morning, Edward Breakfasted here, & we were very ⌐cheerful⌐. Charlotte, afterwards, accompanied him to Brumpton, & Susan & I settled that we would go thither about noon.

But, when Charlotte returned, *my* plan altered; for she acquainted me that they were then employed in reading Evelina. My sister had recommended it to Miss Humphries, & my Aunts & Edward agreed that they would save it,[14] without mentioning any thing of the author! Edward, therefore, bought, & took it to Brumpton! This intelligence gave me the utmost uneasiness,—I foresaw a thousand dangers of a Discovery,—I dreaded the indiscreet warmth of all my Confidents; & I would almost as soon have told the *Morning Post* Editor, as Miss Humphries, In truth, I was quite sick from my apprehensions,

---

[13] Bell's British Library, 132 Strand, owned by John Bell (1745–1831), bookseller, printer, and newspaper publisher (Maxted).

[14] i.e., the secret of FB's authorship.

⌐& seriously regretted that I | had ever entrusted any body with my secret.⌐

I was too uncomfortable to go to Br⌐u⌐mpton, & ⌐so⌐ Susan went by herself. Upon her return, however, I was somewhat tranquillised, for she assured me that there was not the smallest suspicion of the author, & that they had concluded it to be the Work of a *man*! & Miss Humphries, who read it aloud to Richard, said [xxxxx *1 word*] things in its commendation, & concluded them by exclaiming 'It's a thousand pities the author should lie concealed!'

Finding myself more safe than I had apprehended, I ventured to go to Br⌐u⌐mpton [xxxxx *1 word*] In my way up stairs, I heard Miss Humphries reading, she was in the midst of Mr. Villars' Letter of Consolation upon Sir John Belmont's rejection of his Daughter,[15] &, just as I entered the Room, she cried out 'How pretty that is!'—

How much in luck would she have thought herself, had she known *who* heard her!—In a private *confabulation* which I had with my aunt Anne, she told me a thousand things that had been said in its praise, & assured me they had not for a moment doubted that the Work was a *man's*.

Comforted & made easy by these assurances, I longed for the Diversion of *hearing* their observations, & therefore, though rather mal *à propos*, after I had been near 2 Hours in the Room, I told Miss | Humphries that I was afraid I had interrupted her, & begged she would go on with what she was reading. 'Why, cried she, taking up the Book, We have been prodigiously entertained—' &, very readily, she continued. I must own I suffered great difficulty in refraining from Laughing upon several occasions,—& several Times, when they praised what they read, I was upon the point of saying '*You are very good!*' & so forth, & I could scarce keep myself from making Acknowledgements, & Bowing my Head involuntarily.

However, I got *off perfectly* safely.

Monday [16 Mar.], Susan & I went to Tea at Br⌐u⌐mpton. We met Miss Humphries coming to Town. She told us she had just finished 'Evelina,' & gave us to understand

[15] Vol. ii, letter 6.

that she could not get away till she had done it. We heard,
afterwards, from my aunt, the most flattering praises,—
& Richard could talk of nothing else! His Encomiums
gave me double pleasure, from being wholly unexpected:
for I had prepared myself to hear that he held it extremely
cheap. And I was yet more satisfied, because I was sure
they were sincere, as he convinced me that he had not
the most distant idea of suspicion, by finding great fault
with Evelina herself for her bashfulness with such a man
as Lord Orville: 'a man, continued he, whose politeness
is ¦ so extraordinary,—who is so elegant, so refined,—so—
so—*unaccountably* polite,—for I can think of no Word,—I
never read, never heard such Language in my life!—&
then, just as he is speaking to her, she is *so confused*,—that
she runs out of the Room!'

I *could* have answered him, that he ought to consider
the original Character of Evelina,—that she had been
brought up in the strictest retirement, that she knew
nothing of the World, & only acted from the impulses of
Nature; & that her timidity always prevented her from
daring to hope that Lord Orville really was seriously
attached to her. In short, I *could* have bid him read
the Preface again, where she is called 'the offspring of
Nature, & of Nature in her simplest attire:' but I *feared*
appearing too well acquainted with the Book, & I *rejoiced*
that an *unprejudiced* Reader should make no weightier
objection.

Edward walked Home with us; I railed at him violently
for having bought the Book, & charged him to consult
with me before he again put it into any body's Hands:
but he told me he hoped that, as it had gone off so well,
I should not regret it. Indeed he seems quite delighted
at the approbation it has met with. He was extremely
desirous that his Brother should be made acquainted with
the Author, telling me that he wished to plead for him,
but did not know how. ¦

The next Day [17 Mar.], my Father & mother returned
to Town. On Thursday morning [19 Mar.], we went to a
delightful Concert at Mr. Harris's. The sweet Rauzini was
there, & sung 4 Duets with Miss Louisa Harris; He has

now left the opera, where he is succeeded by Roncaglia.[16]
I was extremely delighted at meeting with him again, &
again hearing him sing. La Motte,[17] Cervetto,[18] played
several Quartettos divinely, & the morning afforded me
the greatest Entertainment. There was nobody we knew,
but Lady Hales[19] & Miss Coussmaker, who were, as usual,
very civil.

Friday [20 Mar.]; Miss Humphries, Charlotte, Edward
& I went to the Oratorio of Judas Maccabeus.[20] Oratorios
I don't love, so I shall say nothing of the performance.
We were, also, a few night's since, at Giardini's Benefit,[21]
& heard a most charming Concert. This was the first
Public place to which we went, after Our long, melancholy,
voluntary confinement to the House.[22]

Edward talked only of Evelina, & frequently ʺhinted
his desire that Richard could be of the select party—ʺ It
seems,—to my utter amazement, Miss Humphries has
guessed the Author to be *Anstey*, who wrote the Bath
Guide!—Good God, how improbable,—& how extraordi-

[16] Francesco Roncaglia (*c*.1750-*c*.1800), Italian soprano castrato, was one of
the principal singers at the Opera during the 1777–8 and 1780–1 seasons. He
made his London debut at the King's Theatre on 8 Nov. 1777. See *LS 5* i. 126;
Mercer ii. 885–6; Rees, s.v. Roncaglia, Francesco; A. Heriot, *The Castrati in
London* (1956), pp. 177–8.

[17] Franz Lamotte (?1753–80), violinist and composer. A member of the Court
chapel at Vienna from 1772 until his death, he was in London from 1776 to
1779. See *New Grove*; Highfill; *Tours* ii. 125; *LS 4* iii. 1952.

[18] Despite his great age, probably the elder Cervetto, Giaccobe Basevi
(*c*.1682–1783), cellist, who was a featured performer at the Opera on 4 Apr.
1778 (Highfill; *LS 5* i. 161). After Cervetto's name, FB has left about half a line
blank. Presumably, she meant to fill in the names of the rest of the quartet.

[19] Mary Hayward (*c*.1741–1803), only daughter and heiress of Gervas Hayward (d. 1779), brewer of Sandwich, Kent; m. 1 (1758) Evert George Coussmaker (d. 1763), brewer in London; m. 2 (1764) Sir Thomas Pym Hales
(*c*.1726–73), 4th Bt (*GM* lxxiii[1] (1803), 485–6; IGI; SEB to FB 3–27 Nov. 1779,
Barrett). Miss Coussmaker was her daughter by her first husband (see *EJL* ii.
219 n. 9).

[20] Handel's oratorio, first performed in 1747. FB attended the performance
given at Drury Lane on 20 Mar. See *LS 5* i. 155.

[21] At the Freemasons' Hall, Great Queen Street, Lincoln's Inn Fields, on
Thurs., 12 Mar. The singers were Piozzi, Tenducci, and Signora Balconi, and
the principal instrumentalists included Giardini (violin), Cramer (violin), Fischer
(oboe), Florio (flute), and Crosdill (cello). See the *Public Advertiser* and *Morning
Post* 12 Mar. 1778.

[22] Because of the family disgrace caused by Bessy Allen's elopement and CB
Jr.'s expulsion from Cambridge the preceding Oct. (see *EJL* ii. 289–90).

nary a supposition! But they have both of them done it
so much Honour that, but for Richard's ⌐ anger at Evelina's
bashfulness, I never could believe they did not ⌐smoak⌐
me. I never went to Br⌐u⌐mpton, without finding the 3d
volume in Richard's Hands; ⌐he talks of it eternally⌐; he
speaks of all the Characters as if they were his Acquaintance; & praises different parts perpetually: both he &
Miss H. seem to have it by Heart, for it is always apropos
to whatever is the subject of Discourse, & their whole
conversation almost consists of quotations from it.

As his recovery seemed now confirmed, his Worcester
Friends grew impatient to see him, & he fixed upon
Tuesday [24 Mar.] to leave Town: to the great regret of
us all, glad as we were that he was able to make the
Journey. Sunday, therefore, was settled for his making a
last visit at our House, that he might again see my Father,
& try his own strength.

I now grew very uneasy, lest Miss Humphries & Richard
should speak of the Book to my mother, & lest she should
send for it to read, upon their recommendation;—for
I could not bear to think of the danger I should run,
from my own consciousness, & various other Causes, if
the Book ⌐was⌐ brought into the House: I therefore
went, on Saturday morning, to consult with my aunt at
Br⌐u⌐mpton. She advised, nay, *besought* me ⌐ to tell them
the real state of the Case at once; but I could not endure
to do that, & so, after much pondering, I at last determined to take my chance.

Richard, in Handing me some macaroons, chose to call
them *macaronies*, & said 'Come, Miss Fanny, you *must* have
some of these,—they are all *Sir Clement Willoughby's*,—all
in the highest style,—& I am sure to be like *him* will
recommend them to *you*, for *his* must be a very favourite
Character with you;—a Character in the *first style*, give me
leave to assure you.'

My Aunt could not refrain from Laughing, but he did
not notice it; & then ran on in praise of Lord Orville,
with whom he seemed so struck, that we all fancied he
meant to make him his *model*, as far as his situation would
allow.

Indeed, not only *during* his illness, he ⌜⟨moved⟩ us all by his⌝ patient & most amiable behaviour, but since his recovery he has *more* than kept his Ground, by having wholly discarded all the foibles that formerly tinged his manners, though they *never*, I believe, affected his Heart.

Sunday went off just according to my hopes, for though Richard talked twice or thrice of Lord Orville, calling him 'his favourite Lord, whose Character he studied every Day of his life,' & though Miss H. ⎮ made various applications to the Book, yet they happened, most fortunately, not to be noticed by my Father or Mother.

Miss Humphries stayed to supper, & slept in Town; & Richard begged Susan & me to Breakfast with him the next morning, which we readily promised to do, as it was to be our last visit; for at Night ⌜we⌝ were to go to the Pantheon,[23] & on Tuesday he was to set off for Worcester.

We found him with only aunt Anne & Edward; we were as comfortable as we could be with the thoughts of so soon losing him. My aunt pressed me very much to reveal my secret to Richard;—but I assured her that I could not think of it. Some Time after, I heard her say, in a low voice, to Susan, 'Pray *won't* Fanny tell him?'

'No, I believe not.'

'Why then, if *she* won't,—*I* will!'

This intimation ⌜startled⌝ me at first, & then determined me since I *must* be *blab'd*, to speak *myself*, since I might, at least, make my own conditions: &, in an affair, so important to me, will never trust to *mere* discretion, but bind my confidents by the most solemn promises. Soon after, Edward returned to Town; & I seated myself at a Table, to finish a Letter to Betsy.[24] ⌜Sukey⌝ took up Evelina—which ⌜is⌝ always at Hand,—Richard said to her 'I like that Book better & better; I have read nothing like it, since Fielding's Novels.' ⎮

---

[23] To attend the 11th subscription concert of the season, Mon. evening, 23 Mar. Piozzi, Florio, Giardini, Fischer, and Crosdill were again among the performers (see n. 21); the other principals were the singers Manzoletto and Signor and Signora Giorgi, and the overtures were by Sarti and Van Maldere (*Public Advertiser* and *Morning Post* 23 Mar. 1778).

[24] FB's Worcester cousin Elizabeth Warren Burney. The letter is missing.

⌐Sukey¬ laughed,—so did I, but I wrote on. He asked
with some surprise, what was the Joke? but, as he obtained
no answer, he continued his ⌐favorite topic.¬ 'I think I
can't read it too often,—for you are to know I think it
very *edifying*. The two principal Characters, Lord Orville
& Mr Villars, are so excellent!—& there is something in
the Character, & manners, of Lord Orville so *refined*, &
so polite,—that I *never saw the like* in any Book before:
& all his Compliments are so *new*,—as well as elegant—'

'His Character,' said Susan, 'rises vastly in the 3^d
volume; for he hardly appears in the second, it is almost
filled with the Branghtons.'

'Yes cried he, with warmth, but then how admirable is
all that low humour!—how well done what a mixture of
high & low life throughout.'

'It is pity,' cried I, still writing, 'but you should know
the author,—you like the Book so well.'

'O,' cried he, very unsuspiciously, 'there are a great
num. of authors unknown at present. Several good things
have appeared without any Name to them.

Soon after, Miss Humphries & my aunt Rebecca came.
The former immediately began an ⌐account¬ of a Civility
she had met with from an officer, 'whom, continued she,
I never saw in my life ⌐before¬ but he was so very polite—
no, an Orville could not have been more so!'

'But, cried Richard, pray did not You, like Eve[lina] [*a
line cut away*] │ of writing such a Book!—I am quite lost—
such amazing knowledge of Characters,—such an acquaintance with *high*, & *low* Life,—such universal & extensive
knowledge of the World,—I declare, I know not a man
Breathing who is likely to be the author,—unless it is my
Uncle.'

All this extravagant praise redoubled my difficulties in
making my confession; but he would not let me rest, &
followed me about the Room, till I feared Miss Humphries
would hear the subject of his earnestness. At last, he
brought me a pen & some Paper, & begged me to *write*
the name, promising not to read it till I left him. I am
sure, by his manner, that if he *had* a suspicion, it was of
my Father.

I only wrote, on this Paper, 'No man,'—& then folded it up. He was extremely eager to see it, but I told him he must first make an oath of secresy. He put his Hand on his Heart, & promised, by his Honour, to be faithful.

'But this, cried I, *won't* satisfy me;—you must kiss the Bible,—or kneel down; & make a Vow, that you will never tell *any* body in the World.'

'Good God! cried he, astonished,—what, not a *sister?*'

'No, not a human Being.'

'But, not *Betsy?*—O, pray let me tell *her!*'

'No, no,—not a soul!'

'But—sha'n't I Laugh, when I see them reading it?'

['I] can't recede,—you must tell *Nobody,*—or not hear it.'

'Good God!—Well, I *must* vow, then, to satisfy my curiosity.' |

'Kneel, then,' cried I.—he Laughed, but seemed all amazement; however, he could not kneel, for Miss Humphries looked round; but I made him repeat after me, that he would never communicate what he was to hear, to any human Being, without my leave; & this he protested, by all he held sacred on Earth, or in Heaven.

I then gave up my Paper, & ran to the Window. He read it with the extremest eagerness,—but still did not seem to comprehend how the affair stood, till he came to the Window,—& then, I believe, my Countenance cleared up his doubts.

His surprise was too great for speech; Susan says he Coloured violently,—but I could hardly look at him. Indeed, I believe it utterly impossible for astonishment to be greater, than his was at that moment.

When he recovered somewhat from it he came to me again, & taking my Hand, said 'I believe I must now kneel indeed!—' & drawing me to the Fire, he actually knelt to me,—but I made him rise almost instantly.

After this,—as if he had forgot all the flattering speeches he had made about the Book, or as if he thought them all *inadequate* to what he *should* have said, he *implored* my forgiveness, for what he called his *Criticisms,* & seemed ready to kill himself for having made them. I know his

⌐⟨deference⟩⌐ to be so great, that, had he ever suspected me, I am sure he would offered [*sic*] me nothing short of *Adulation*. |

²⁵ March 30th

I have just received a Letter from ⌐"poor"⌐ Charles, in which he informs me that he has subscribed to a Circulating Library at Reading,—& then he adds 'I am to have Evelina to Day; the man told me that it was spoken very highly of, & very much enquired after; that, as yet, there has been no *critique* upon it; but that it was thought one of the best publications we have had for a long Time.'²⁶

*Ver. pret.*²⁷ upon Honour! Who it is can have recommended it to *Reading*, is to me inexplicable,—&, in all probability, so it will continue to be.

As to a *Critique*,—it is with fear & fidgets I attend it;— next *Wednesday*²⁸ I expect to be in one of the Reviews,— oh Heavens, *what* should I do, if I were *known!*—for I have very little doubt but I shall be horribly mauled.

And—*mauled*, indeed, I have been!—but not by the Reviewers,—no,—with them I have come off with flying Colours,—but I have had a long & a dangerous Illness,— an Inflammation of the Lungs,—which, even when the danger was over, left me so weak & enfeebled, that for a long, long Time I was totally incapacitated from Walking,

²⁵ At the top of this page, foliated 13, FBA has noted: '10. 11. 12. burnt', i.e., 3 leaves or 6 pages.

²⁶ Following his expulsion from Cambridge the previous Oct., CB Jr. had been banished by his father to Shinfield, Berks, 3½ mi. S of Reading. Perhaps Shinfield was chosen because of some connection with the Peter Floyer, Esq. of Shinfield Place, who d. on 4 Dec. 1777 and whose death was commemorated by CB Jr. in MS verses (see *HFB* p. 492 n. D). In any case, the village was suitably remote and obscure for the disgraced scholar. The letter FB quotes is missing. CB Jr. later wrote her that 'I have read Evelina, & like it *vastly much*' (undated fragment, Osborn); so much, that he was inspired to write a 'Sonnet' on the novel (Appendix 2). See Ralph S. Walker, 'Charles Burney's Theft of Books at Cambridge', *Transactions of the Cambridge Bibliographical Society* iii (1962), 314–15.

²⁷ FB may be echoing Omai (see *EJL* ii. 253) or perhaps Canton in Colman and Garrick's *The Clandestine Marriage*: 'O, ver well, dat is good girl—and ver prit too!' (II.i. 82, *The Plays of David Garrick ... Volume 1*, ed. H. W. Pedicord and F. L. Bergmann (Carbondale, 1980), p. 275).

²⁸ 1 Apr., when the monthly magazines would appear.

Reading, Writing, Working, Dressing myself, or even
sitting upright. Dr. Jebb, who ⌐attended my cousin
Richard,¬ has ⌐also¬ been *my* physician, &, I believe, my
preserver. I was equally pleased with him both in regard
to his Profession, & his ⌐behaviour,¬ for he is ǀ or *seems*,
good humoured, gay, arch & very sensible. Had I ever
doubted the kindness & affection of my Friends, this Illness
would have re-assured me: but though I never did, &
never *could*,—the tenderness, concern & attention with
which I have met I shall always recollect as softness &
sweetness of my long & painful Confinement. Susy, Charlotte, Hetty, & my Aunts *vied* in good offices,—& my
beloved Father was hardly himself till my recovery was
out of doubt.—⌐From¬ Worcester & Chesington I have
received the most flattering marks of partial concern,—
&,—but I will not dwell longer upon this grave business:
I will Copy the Monthly Review of my Book; In the
Critical I have not yet appeared.[29]

But hold,—first, in order, comes
The London Review, by W. Kenrick:[30]

For February. 1778.

Evelina.
The History of a Young lady exposed to very critical
situations. There is much more merit, as well respecting
stile, character & Incident, than is usually to be met with
in modern Novels.

---

[29] A laudatory notice appeared in Sept. (*Critical Review* xlvi (1778), 202–4).
A review not mentioned by FB appeared in the *Westminster Magazine* vi (June
1778), 325: 'May prove equally useful and entertaining to the younger part of
our *male* as well as *female* Readers; to the latter of whom we particularly
recommend it, as conveying many practical lessons both on morals and manners.' This notice was missed by J. A. Grau, *Fanny Burney: An Annotated
Bibliography* (New York, 1981). Another review not mentioned by FB but
noticed by Grau is in *GM* xlviii (Sept. 1778), 425.
[30] William Kenrick (?1725–79), miscellaneous writer, inaugurated the *London
Review of English and Foreign Literature* in 1775. The notice is headed: '*Evelina*.
3 vol. 12mo. 7s. 6d. Lowndes.' FB capitalizes 'history', 'young', and 'novels',
substitutes the ampersand for 'and', and alters the conclusion from 'to be met
with among our modern novels' (*London Review* vii (Feb. 1778), 151).

Very genteel, Mr. Kenrick![31]—Now, pour faire bonne bouche!

Monthly Review. For April. 1778[32]

Evelina, or a young Lady's Entrance into the World.

This Novel has given us so much pleasure in the perusal, that we do not hesitate to pronounce it one of the most sprightly, entertaining & agreeable productions of this kind that[33] has of late fallen under our Notice. A great variety of natural Incidents, some, of the Comic stamp, render the Narrative extremely interesting. The Characters, which are agreeably diversified, are conceived & drawn with propriety, & supported with spirit. The Whole is written with great ease & Command of Language. From this commendation we must, however, except[34] the Character of a son of Neptune,[35] whose manners are rather those of a rough, uneducated Country 'squire, than those of a genuine sea Captain. |

50   Chessington, [11–12] May [1778]

To Susanna Elizabeth Burney

AL (Diary MSS I, paginated 649–50, Berg), May 1778
2 single sheets 4to 3 pp. *pmk* 13 MA red wafer
Addressed: Miss Susan Burney, | Dr. Burney's, | St Martin's Street, | Leicester Square | London.
Annotated (by FBA): Edward. May 11th 78

[31] There may be a dry irony intended here; Kenrick was notorious for his scurrilous attacks on writers and personalities.
[32] *Monthly Review* lviii (Apr. 1778), 316. The notice is headed: 'Art. 49. *Evelina*, or a young Lady's Entrance into the World, 12mo. 3 vols. 9 s. Lowndes. 1778.' Besides the verbal discrepancies noted below, FB slightly alters the punctuation, introduces capitalizations, and substitutes the ampersand for 'and'.
[33] 'which'
[34] 'commendation, however, we must except'
[35] Capt. Mirvan.

As she writes below (p. 19), FB had come to Chessington the first week of May to recuperate from her illness. She was accompanied by SEB and their cousin Edward, who then both returned to London.

Chesington,
Monday, May [11]

My dearest Susy,

I thank you a thousand Times for your two most kind Letters:[36] I rejoice to hear you have escaped the Cold that threatened you: I know not how I could bear to hear of your being ill, now that I am out of the way of Nursing you. I miss *you*, my sweet Girl, very much indeed, though my kind Friends here do not suffer me to miss your attendance: but my Eyes continue abominably weak, & I can use them for so short a Time *de suite*, that I can niether read, write, or work 10 minutes together. So that I terribly wish for an *agreeable Trifler*, to saunter about the House with me; some comfortable *Loiterer*,[37] who would forget the value of their *own* Time, while they encreased that of *mine*. Now *you*, my Susy, are the very thing, cut out ⌐for that⌐ purpose, if I could but catch you: but as that ⌐can⌐ not be, I take up with honest Kate, when she is [al]lowed to give me her Time; & we discuss matters & things, & settle the affairs of the Nation, & draw characters, & communicate opinions, with ⌐just the⌐ judgement, delicacy, & caution she manifested in her discourse before coz. Edward, on the day of my arrival; & that *queer soul*, as she is now pleased to call the lady [EAB], is still the favourite Topic of her Conversation. She said this morning 'I fancy your Cousin will think me a strange Country Put, to blurt out things at once so; but I was in *sich* spirits to see that *queer soul* did n't come, that *reely* I hardly know what I said: *howsever*, I dare say *we was* all of a mind, though he looked very demure, ¦ for to be sure

---

[36] SEB to FB *pmk* 9 May 1778 (Berg), printed in *ED* ii. 220–2, and a missing letter. On a detached leaf (Berg), FBA noted that 'The correspondence at large [with SEB] has been committed to the flames, from Family reasons, resulting from its unbounded openness of Confidence.'

[37] '*Trifler*' and '*Loiterer*' may have been epithets directed by the stepmother, EAB, against SEB, while the remainder of the sentence may be a veiled criticism of EAB's self-centredness. See below and *EJL* ii. Appendix 2.

he can never like *sich* an odd soul, no more than any body else,—for all she's a woman of sense; howsever, I see he couldn't keep his Countenance.'

I am extremely concerned at the Invitation from Barborne: pray let me know my Uncle's [Richard Burney's] answer to his [Edward's] remonstrance as soon as possible. Does he [Edward] think, of Mr Crisp's invitation?—you may truly tell him, that I hardly in my life ever heard him give so earnest a one. You know he put it into *your* Hands to *jigg his memory.*[38]

Betsy's guessing the Author of Evelina is abominable![39] yet I always apprehended that she would, from it's being recommended by my sister [presumably EBB], & from the Ode to my Father. I don't know what we can say to her but will think of something to satisfy her before I send this off. It is now Tuesday [May 12], for I can write but very little at a Time.

Your Letter[40] has just been brought to me; this Barborne affair gives me the truest concern;—pray tell my Cousin Edward that if he *must* go, he also *must* spend a few days here first,—tell him he shall not lose all his Time, though *much* of it, for Mr Crisp says he shall have the Closet my Father *conjures* in to himself,—so beg him to bring something to Copy. ⌜&⌝ *all* his Drawings, of all *sorts,* & the old man's | Head that he painted, &c, &c,—

You are *very* good, my dearest Girl, for writing, & sending me off your Letters as they are ready: it is a great indulgence to me.

We have, now, opportunitys of hearing almost Daily, so never mind waiting for Baker's Days.[41] Mrs. Simmons has

---

[38] As FB indicates below, Edward had received a summons from his father, Richard Burney, to visit him at Barborne Lodge, which would cause Edward to miss his studies at the Royal Academy. Also, when he had accompanied FB to Chessington he had received an invitation from SC to return later for a longer visit there.

[39] See *ED* ii. 220–1 and below, p. 22.

[40] Missing.

[41] Baker's days were Tuesday and Thursday, when the local baker from Kingston delivered his goods to Chessington Hall. At the same time he would bring mail to and from the post office. See FB to HLT, 25 Sept. 1780, FB to SEB, 10, 26 Jan. 1781 (Berg), *EJL* iv; W. H. Hutton, *Burford Papers* (1905), pp. 42, 44.

Letters brought whenever they arrive, & mine come at the same Time.

Adieu my dearest Susy. Give my best Love & Duty to my dear Father,—tell him I now stump into the Garden alone, though not yet able to keep pace even with Daddy Crisp.[42]

Tell my kind Hetty I will write very soon. I am glad the poor little Sophia[43] is in so good a way. My best Love to Charlotte & my two Aunts & Mr. B. & remember me very kindly to my cousin Edward: tell him we *must* see him before he goes, *poz koz*,[44] as Kitty would say.

God bless you, my dearest Nurse,—companion, sister—& Friend! I gain some ground every Day, though my recovery by no means equals my expectations, for Mr Devaynes[45] would still call me a *poor thing*, & a *weak Creature*, & a *poor soul*.

[*bottom of leaf cut away*]

[*The Journal for 1778 resumes.*]

Chesington,
June 18th

Here I am, & here I have been this Age; though too weak to think of Journalising; however, as I have never had so many curious anecdotes to record, I will not at least *this Year*,—the first of my *appearing in public*,—give up my favourite old Hobby Horse.

---

[42] Who suffered from the infirmities of old age, compounded by chronic gout.

[43] EBB and Charles Rousseau Burney's infant daughter Sophia Elizabeth, born the preceding Sept. She seems to have suffered from a lengthy ailment or ailments. She was later brought to Chessington for her health (see below, p. 40).

[44] Presumably meaning 'positively, cousin'.

[45] John Devaynes (*c*.1726–1801), apothecary to the Queen and (from 1779) George III. His brother, William Devaynes, MP, banker, and government contractor, had attended a Burney musical party in 1776 (see *EJL* ii. 211). John Devaynes' friendship with CB seems to date from this period. In a codicil (dated 15 Feb. 1798) to his will, he bequeathed to CB 'a ring and Five Guineas' as a token of his regard (*JL* xi. 259 n. 2; see also RHI; *GM* lxxi^1 (1801), 93).

I came hither the first Week in May. Susan & my Cousin Edward accompanied me in a post Chaise. I bore the Journey as far as Kingston extremely well; but when we came into the Cross Road, which leads to this place, nothing but their joint & most affectionate assistance & support, could have enabled me to get on; I was so extremely weak, faint & feeble, that they were obliged to hold me all the way, & apply salts, &c, to my nostrils; — & when at last we stoped [*sic*] at this House, my emotion at the sight of my dear Daddy Crisp, added to my fatigue, almost overpowered me, & it was with the utmost difficulty I was saved from fainting. However, I am now, thank God, almost restored to perfect Health, & therefore I will not dwell upon any further circumstances of my illness. My dear Mr Crisp was almost as much affected as myself at our meeting; for when I recovered, & held out my Hand to him, he took it, & embraced me, but could not *speak*, & hurried out of the way: — a mark of his affectionate regard for me, that I shall never forget.⁴⁶ |

[*The bottom of the page (6 or 7 lines) has been cut away. The following passage contains Kitty Cooke's harangue against EAB, mentioned above, p. 16.*]

at the *Divil*, God forgive me! — but you know, [*3 words effaced*] what a thing it would be for a fine lady to bring a sick person!'

Edward was quite astonished at this unexpected freedom of Discourse, &, I believe, hardly knew what to think of it. I was myself amazed at her, but too weak & wearried to say a Word; & Susy, from surprise at her abruptness, could only Laugh. But honest Catherine, who has no notion of disguise, & who is utterly incapable of art, continued her Harangue.

'To be sure she did well to stay away, for she knows we none of us love her; she could only think of coming to mortify us; for one must be civil to her, for the Doctor's sake. — but she's such a queer fish, — to be sure, for a

---

⁴⁶ Three years earlier FB had used virtually the same expression in describing her father's eyes filling with tears, suggesting how closely the two 'Daddies' were linked in her mind and heart. See *EJL* ii. 147.

sensible woman, as she is, she has a great many oddities; & as to Mr Crisp, he says he's quite sick of her, d—her, he says, I wish she was Dead! for, you know, for such a good soul as the Doctor to have such a Wife,—to be sure there's some thing very disagreeable in her,—Laughing so loud, & hooting, & clapping her Hands,—I can't love her, a nasty old Cat,—yet she's certainly a very sensible Woman.'—

And thus did this unguarded Creature bolt out all her Thoughts, &, in this unconnected manner, she continued to utter all her sentiments, without the slightest *notion* of the impropriety of which she was guilty, till she had quite exhausted the whole stock of her complaints & objections & opinions.

Edward, I believe, was never more highly diverted in his [?Life] ¦

[*bottom of page cut away.*]

[?Edward and Susan] took leave, & returned to Town.

My recovery, from that Time to this, has been *slow & sure*; but, as I could walk hardly 3 yards in a Day at first, I found so much Time to spare, that I could not resist treating myself with a little *private sport* with Evelina,—a young lady whom I think I have some right to make free with. I had promised *Hetty* that *she* should read it to Mr Crisp, at her own particular request; but I wrote my excuses,[47] & introduced it myself.

I told him it was a Book which Hetty had taken to Br⌐u⌐mpton, to divert my Cousin Richard during his Confinement, ⌐& I pretended to know nothing of it myself.⌐ He was so indifferent about it, that I thought he would not give himself the trouble to read it; & often embarrassed me by unlucky Questions; such as, *if it was reckoned clever? & What I thought of it? & Whether folks laughed at it?* ⌐However,⌐ though I always evaded any direct or satisfactory answer he was so totally free from any idea of suspicion, that my perplexity escaped his Notice. At length, he desired me to begin reading to him.

---

[47] The letter is missing.

I dared not trust my voice with the little introductory ode, for as *that* is no romance, but the sincere effusion of my Heart, I could as soon read aloud my own Letters, written in my own Name & Character: I therefore *skipped* it, & have so kept the Book out of his sight, that, to this Day, he knows not it is there. Indeed, I have, since, heartily repented that I read *any* of the Book to him, for I found it a much more awkward thing than I had expected: my voice quite faltered when I began it, which, however, I passed off for the effect of remaining weakness of Lungs; &, in short, from an *invincible* embarrassment, which I could not for a page together repress, the Book, by my reading, lost all manner of spirit.

Nevertheless, though he has by no means treated it with the praise so lavishly bestowed upon it from all other Quarters, I had the satisfaction to observe that he was even *greedily* eager ⌐ to go on with it; so that I flatter myself the *story* caught his attention: &, indeed, allowing for my *mauling* reading, he gave it much ⌐more⌐ credit as [*sic*] I had any reason to expect. But, now that I was sensible of my error in being my own Mistress of the Ceremonies, I determined to leave to Hetty the 3ᵈ Volume, & therefore pretended I had not brought it. He was in a delightful ill humour about it, & I *enjoyed* his impatience far more than I should have done his forbearance.

Hetty, therefore, when she comes, has undertaken to *bring it.*

But though I have so totally Escaped all suspicion from my *Daddy*, I find I have not been equally successful every where; for Susan, just after I came hither transcribed me part of a Letter from my Cousin Betsy,[48] that has very much surprised me; & which I will *re*-transcribe,—as it is *not* very much to my disadvantage.

[*FB's 're-'transcription follows. Verbal discrepancies from SEB's copy are indicated in the notes.*]

I have just finished reading *Evelina*; & I believe I should thank you, or some of your Family, for the great pleasure

[48] In SEB's letter to FB, *pmk* 9 May 1778 (Berg); see *ED* ii. 220–21. The original letter is missing.

I have received from it. It is by far the most *bewitching*
Novel I ever read; I could not leave it, till I came to the
conclusion of it, & now I can't help regretting that I made
such short work of it. I wish it was as long again. However,
I sha'n't[49] content myself with once reading, for 'twill bear
a second & third, & still delight one I am sure. Indeed I
am quite charmed with it; 'tis so interesting! The Characters are so well drawn, so contrasted, so striking, that I
can't help fancying myself perfectly acquainted[50] with
them all: then[51] there is so much elegance in it, too! I
know not how to say enough of it. But now, as you are a
Friend, an *Honest* Friend, too, & I hope will not go to
deceive me, I'll tell you a conjecture of mine, when I had
read about 3 of the Letters, & which has gained strength
every Letter since. I think I know a Person not *100* miles
from Leicester Square | [52]very capable of writing such a
⌐novel⌐: indeed 'tis so clever, & so much in her style, that
I cannot persuade myself to think she is not the authoress.
Any one else would be proud of putting their Name to it.
I have but one reason to doubt about it, which is, that I
never knew her allow any but her most particular & most
intimate Friends to be the better for her uncommon
abilities ⌐in this way, she is so *dividend*[53] of her own
performances.⌐ However, you must tell me, & tell me *truly*,
whether I am or am not mistaken. If I am *not* mistaken
you must pay me the Compliment of owning I[54] have
some penetration. But don't tell Fanny I[55] *smoke* her, if
you think she will be displeased, for I know her to be
extremely delicate in these matters; & probably she may
not like that any of our Family should suspect her: though
she *cannot*, or at least has no *reason* to be in the smallest
degree afraid of any one of us. I have been very snug &

[49] 'shall not'

[50] 'perfectly well acquainted'

[51] 'then' is not in SEB's transcription.

[52] The top of this page (to the end of this paragraph) has been cut away.
The cut-away fragment is in the Barrett Collection and is here 'rejoined'.

[53] So in both FB's and SEB's transcriptions.

[54] 'owning that I'

[55] 'Fanny that I'

quiet ever since I had this notion about Fanny, & I[56] shall not mention it till I have heard from you, nor[57] even then, unless you give me leave.

What a sly ⌜& insinuating⌝ Girl this is!—I sent her an Answer,[58] with a kind of *angry* denial, abusing the *Book*, & expressing my surprise & displeasure at her suspicion. But, at the same Time, I sent *another* of a different kind.

My Cousin Edward, at this Time, received a summons from his Father, to make him a visit at Barborne. We are all very sorry he should be thus taken from the academy, but hope, & have reason to believe, that he will return in a short Time. However, I wrote, to Him & to his Brother Richard, a very ridiculous & whimsical kind of Proclamation,[59] in which, upon certain conditions, I gave them leave to admit Betsy among the select number of my Confidants.

But, to my great surprise, I find, by Letters she has since sent, both to Susette & me,[60] that she is still *in the Dark*: she writes word to the former, that she is much *hurt* to find I will not trust her, as she is *sure* I wrote the Book, & much more to the same effect. & to me, she has sent a *queerish* Letter, begging my pardon for praising a Book *I* dislike,—telling me that *all* her acquaintance admire it beyond | [61]measure, &, in particular, that Mr Biddulph,[62] who is one of the most sensible, gentlemanlike, & well bred men of Worcester, has never seen her, without talking of it very highly;—but, since *I* run it down, she will get the better of *her prejudice in it's favour*. &, in this dry manner, she pours forth at once her flattery & expresses her madness at what she thinks my reserve. However, I shall expect a different sort of Letter from

[56] 'about F. &'
[57] 'you, & not'
[58] Missing.
[59] Missing.
[60] Missing.
[61] See n. 52.
[62] Perhaps Michael Biddulph (d. 1800) of Ledbury, Herefs, and Cofton Hall, Worcs, who was probably brother-in-law of the Mrs Bund who attended the amateur theatrical performance at Barborne Lodge in 1777 (see *EJL* ii. 236).

her soon. The whole Family have written, in the name of my uncle & themselves, a most pressing & affectionate invitation to me, to spend the rest of the summer at Barborne.[63] It is not yet decided what answer is to be sent, but I am extremely pleased & gratified by their kind desire of so soon having me again. The perfect restoration of my Health is the motive on which they ground their urgency.[64]

Since the receipt of this Letter, I have had a visit from my beloved Susy, who, with my mother & little Sally, spent a Day here, to my no small satisfaction.—& yet, I was put into an embarrassment of which I even yet know not what will be the end, during their short stay: for Mr Crisp, before my mother, very innocently, said to Susan 'O, pray Susette do send me the 3^d volume of Evelina; Fanny brought me the two first; on purpose, I believe, to tantalize me.'—

I felt myself in a *ferment*,—& Susan, too, looked foolish, & knew not what to answer: As I sat on the same sopha with him, I gave him a *gentle shove*, as a token, which he could not but understand, that he had said some thing wrong,—though I believe he could not imagine *what*.

My mother, instantly darted forward, & repeated 'Evelina,? what's that, pray?—

Again I *jolted* Mr Crisp, who, very much perplexed, said, in a *boggling* manner, that it was a Novel,—he supposed from the circulating Library,—'only a *trumpery* Novel.—'

Ah, my dear Daddy! thought I, you would have devised some ⏐ other sort of speech, if you knew all!—but he was really, as he well might be, quite at a loss for what I *wanted* him to say.

'You have had it here, then, have you?' continued my mother.

'Hay?—yes,—two of the volumes,—' said Mr Crisp.

'What, had you them from the Library?' asked my mother.

---

[63] The letter of invitation is missing.
[64] FB did not go.

'No,—Ma'am, answered I, horribly frightened,—from my sister.'

The truth is, the Books are Susan's,—who bought them the first Day of Publication; but I did not dare own that, as it would have been almost an acknowledgement of all the rest.

She asked some further questions, to which we made the same sort of answers, & then the matter dropt. Whether it rests upon her mind, or not, I cannot tell.[65]

Susan & I were, next, forced to exert our wits for some excuse to Mr Crisp, for my [checking][66] him: & one offered very pat. It seems, since I came hither, the set which was bought for my Cousin Richard to read at Brumpton, has been *raffled* for in Town, by my aunts, Mr Burney, my sisters' Hetty & Charlotte, & my Cousin Edward; & *Charlotte* won them: we, therefore, let this set which I had borrowed of Susy, pass for the *Raffled* set, & so we told Mr Crisp, that, as Charlotte had entered into that frolic *privately*, we did not wish to make known that she ⌐had⌐ them.

To be sure, the concealment of this affair has cost me no few Inventions, & *must* cost me many, many more; but I am so well satisfied of their innocency, & feel so irresistably [*sic*] their necessity, that I do not find they at all affect my Conscience. And yet, perhaps no body can have a more real & forcible detestation of falsehood ⌐&⌐ of ⌐*Equivocating*⌐ than myself; but in this particular case, I have no alternative, but avowing myself for an authoress, which I cannot bear to *think of*, or exerting all my faculties to ward of [*sic*] suspicion!

But,—two Days after, I received, from Charlotte, a Letter[67] | the most interesting that could be written to me,—for it acquainted me that my dear Father was, at length, reading my Book!!! —

[65] See below, p. 47.

[66] Inserted by FBA for an obliterated word not deciphered.

[67] Missing. See SEB to FB, *pmk* 4 June 1778 (Berg), printed in *ED* ii. 222–3, where SEB mentions Charlotte's letter and CB's first remarks to SEB about *Evelina*.

How this has come to pass, I am yet in the dark; but, it seems, the very moment, almost, that my mother & Susan & Sally left the House, he desired Charlotte to bring him the Monthly Review;—she contrived to look over his shoulder as he opened it, which he did at the account of *Evelina, or a Young lady's Entrance into the World.* He read it with great earnestness,—then put it down; & presently after, snatched it up, & read it again. Doubtless his paternal Heart felt some agitation for his Girl, in reading a review of her Publication!—*how* he got at the *name*, I cannot imagine![68]

Soon after, he turned to Charlotte, ⌐& asked if she could go to Fleet Street? but, immediately after, said she could not be back in Time, as he must go out in half an Hour; then,⌐ bidding her come close to him, he put his Finger on the Word Evelina, &, saying *she knew what it was*, bid her write down the Name, & send the man to Lowndes, as if for herself. This she did, & away went William![69]

He then told Charlotte that he had never known the name of it till the Day before: 'tis strange *how* he got at it!—& added that I had come off vastly well in this Review: except for the *Captain*; Charlotte told him it had also been in Kenrick's review, & he desired her to Copy out for him what was said in *both* of them. He asked her, too, whether I had mentioned, the Work was by *a Lady*? & When William returned, he took the Books from him, & the moment he was gone, opened the 1st Volume,—& opened it upon the *ode*!—

How great must have been his astonishment, at seeing himself so addressed! Indeed, Charlotte says, he looked

---

[68] FB had the year before confided to CB that she was approaching the publisher Lowndes with a 'work' (see *EJL* ii. 233). She wonders how her father had learned at last that *Evelina* was that work. In fact, SEB had told him, as he revealed in a Frag. Mem. written between 1792 and 1806.

[69] William, the Burneys' manservant, is mentioned in SEB's journals *passim* as answerer of doors, carrier of messages, and doer of errands. He was William Hardcastle, who subsequently left the Burneys for the employ of the violinist Wilhelm Cramer (1746–99) and who was suspected by the Burneys of having perpetrated the 1785 robbery of CB (letter of Charlotte Ann Burney to FB, 1785, in BL Add. MSS Egerton 3693; *Mem.* iii. 28 ff.).

all amazement, read a line or 2 with great eagerness,—&
then, stopping short, exclaimed 'Good God!'—&, as he
read on, he seemed quite affected, ⌐again ⟨stopped⟩,¬ &
the Tears started into his Eyes: dear soul! I am sure they
did into *mine*, nay, I even ⌐*slobbered*¬ ¦ as I read the account.
I believe he was obliged to go out, before he advanced
much further.[70] But the next Day, I had a Letter from
Susan,[71] in which I heard that he had begun reading it
with Lady Hales & Miss Coussmaker! & that they *liked it
vastly*!—I was, indeed, a little startled at this intelligence,
but I received, at the same Time, assurances that my
Father niether did, nor would betray me, & had only told
them it was recommended to him by an acquaintance.
Susan, who knew how deeply I should be interested in all
that related to this affair, was very particular in her
accounts: & highly flattering were all the Comments she
transmitted to me.

My Father, she said, was highly pleased with the Dedication & the Preface, & said they were *vastly strong* & well
written, better than he could have expected, though he
did not think he should meet with *Trash*, when he began
it. Mr. Villars' Letters, too, he called pathetic, & well
written, & he declared Lowndes had had a *devilish good
Bargain*; for the Book, as far as he had read, had real
merit, & he was sure it would sell.

Almost all my Letters, from this Time, contained different Comments upon this my highly honoured Book.
My Father expressed himself more & more satisfied as he
proceeded, & Lady Hales spoke of it, very innocently, in
the highest terms, declaring she was sure it was written
by somebody in high Life, & that it had all the marks of
real Genius!—Miss Coussmaker carried her praise still
higher; she was quite *bewitched* with it, & could talk of
nothing else. The Writer, she said, was a great *acquisition*

---

[70] 'I opened the first vol. with fear & trembling not supposing she w^d disgrace
her parentage, but not having the least idea, that without the use of the press,
or knowledge of the world, she c^d write a book worth reading. The dedication
to myself, however, brought tears in my eyes ...' (CB, Frag. Mem.).

[71] SEB to FB *pmk* 4 June 1778, *ED* ii. 222–3. FB here paraphrases the letter
very closely.

to the World, & Lady Hales added *he must be a man of great abilities!*[72]—

How ridiculous! but Miss Coussmaker was a *little* nearer the truth, for she gave it as *her* opinion, that the Writer was a *Woman,* for she said there was such a remarkable delicacy in the conversations & descriptions, notwithstanding the grossness & vulgarity of some of the Characters, & that all Oaths & indelicate Words were so carefully, yet naturally avoided, that she could not but suspect the Writer was a Female, | but, she added, notwithstanding the preface declared the Writer never would be known, she hoped, if the Book circulated as she expected it would, *he,* or *she,* would be tempted to discovery.

Ha! Ha! Ha!—that's my answer. They little think how well they are already acquainted with the Writer they so much honour.

They finished it before Lady Hales left Town; but Susan did not see her Ladyship or Miss Coussmaker after it, as they went to Howletts[73] the next Day. However, Susan begged to have, then, my Father's *real* & *final* opinion;—& it is such as I almost blush to write, even for my own private reading;—but yet is such as I can by no means suffer to pass unrecorded, as my whole Journal contains nothing so grateful to me.—I will copy his own words, according to Susan's solemn declaration of their authenticity.[74]

'Upon my soul I think it the best Novel I know excepting Fieldings,—&, in some respects, *better*[75] than his! I have been *excessively* pleased with it; there are, perhaps, a few things that might[76] have been otherwise,—Mirvan's trick

---

[72] In this and the following paragraph, FB quotes from SEB's letter to her *pmk* 11 June 1778 (Berg), printed *ED* ii. 223–7. See also SEB to FB *post* 11 June 1778 (Berg), *ED* ii. 228–30.

[73] The Hales' country seat, 3 miles ESE of Canterbury, Kent.

[74] FB's concern for 'authenticity' does not prevent her from transcribing rather loosely from SEB's letter of 16 June 1778 (Berg), printed *ED* ii. 230–2. Verbal discrepancies and omissions are noted below.

[75] 'it is better'

[76] 'things might'

upon Lovel is, I think, carried too far,[77] there is something even disgusting[78] in it:[79] however, this Instance excepted, I protest I think it will *scarce bear an Improvement.*[80] I wish I may die, if I do not believe it to be *the very best*[81] *Novel in the Language*, except Fielding's![82] for Smollets, with all their Wit, are quite too gross.[83] The *Language* is as good as *any body* need write, I declare as good as I would *wish* to read.[84] Lord Orville's Character is just what it should be,[85] perfectly benevolent & upright;[86] & there is[87] a *boldness* in it that struck me mightily, for[88] he is a man not *ashamed* of being better than the rest of mankind.[89] Evelina is in a new style too, so perfectly innocent & Natural;[90] & the scene between her & her Father, Sir John Belmont, is a scene for a *Tragedy*! I *blubbered* at it, & Lady Hales & Miss Coussmaker are not yet recovered from hearing it; it made them quite ill; it is, indeed, wrought up in a most extraordinary manner!'[91] |

---

[77] See vol. iii, letter 21. At this point FB omits: 'I don't hate that young man enough, ridiculous as he is, to be pleased or diverted at his having his ear torn by a monkey—'.

[78] 'there's a something disgusting'.

[79] FB omits: '[SEB:] but the Capt. is reckoned a Brute by *everybody* = [CB:] Why, that's true—but in this case 'tis a brutality wch does not make me laugh—Now Mad^e Duval['s] loss of her curls & all that is very Diverting—'.

[80] 'However *except this instance* I declare I think the Book w^d *scarce bear an improvement*—'

[81] 'the best'

[82] 'Fielding's excepted'

[83] 'for Smollett's are so d–d gross that they are not fit reading for women wth all their wit.' After this, FB omits: 'Mr Villars character is admirably supported—& rises upon one in every Letter—'.

[84] 'the language throughout his [Villars'] Letters are *as good as any body need write* (NB. spoken w^th *emphasis* & spirit) I declare as good as I w^d wish to read! & every Letter of his seems to me better & better'

[85] 'ought to be'

[86] FB omits: '[SEB:] And without being *fade*, I think = [CB:] Oh entirely—'

[87] 'there's'; '&' not in the original.

[88] 'for' not in the original.

[89] FB omits: 'indeed I am excessively pleased wth him—'.

[90] 'natural & innocent—'

[91] '& the scene between her & her Father, Sir John Belmont——I protest I think 'tis a scene for a Tragedy—I *blubber'd* = [SEB:] No—did you Sir?—How the *Ladies* must Cry = [CB:] Oh! I don't think they've recovered it yet—It made them quite ill—'tis indeed wrought up in a most extraordinary manner—I laid the Book down—& c^d not for sometime get on with it ='. See vol. iii, letter 19.

After this, Susy asked what *she* could say to Miss Couss-maker, who insisted upon hearing her opinion of it? 'O, speak about it as you would of any other Book, said he; *I* have, &, if it should ever be discovered, I can tell them I had as much *right* either to praise, or to criticise, as they or any body else had, since I knew as little about it.[92] However, some Time hence I should think there would be no kind of impropriety in its being known; on the contrary, it would do poor Fanny great credit, For, as a Young woman's Work, I look upon it to be really Wonderful!'[93]

This account delighted me more than I can express. Good God! How little did I dream of ever being so much honoured! But the approbation of all the World put together, would not bear any competition in my estimation, to that of my beloved Father. He told Susan that Lady Hales had bought his set; & that he heard Lady Radnor[94] had bought another. So Evelina is still *travelling in the Great World*!

Soon after this communication, my sister Hetty came hither to spend a few Days. Mr. Crisp almost immediately asked for the 3ᵈ Volume of Evelina, but, as she had not Time to stay to read it, she pretended that it was lent to Mrs. O'Connor.[95] While she was with us, though, fortunately, when I was not present, he asked her if any body had yet been named, or suspected, for the Author? No, she said, but that it *took vastly*; & praised it very freely, &

---

[92] 'Oh, speak out about it as you wᵈ of another Book—*I have*—& if it was to be discovered I sh. tell them that I was as much at liberty to admire or criticize as them, for I'm sure I knew as little about it.—'

[93] 'However keep snug for poor Fanny's sake—tho' I protest that sometime hence I shᵈ think there wᵈ be no kind of impropriety in its being known—on the contrary it wᵈ do her a great deal of credit—For a Young Woman's work I look upon it to be really WONDERFUL!'

[94] Presumably Lady Hales' sister-in-law, the *Dowager* Lady Radnor, i.e., Anne Hales (1736–95), widow of Anthony Duncombe (c.1695–1763), B. Feversham of Downton, who m. (1765, as his 3rd wife) William Bouverie (1725–76), cr. (1765) E. of Radnor; or possibly the Dowager Lady Radnor's daughter (by Ld. Feversham) Anne Duncombe (1759–1829), who m. (1777) the Dowager Lady Radnor's stepson Jacob Pleydell Bouverie (1750–1828), 2nd E. of Radnor, 1776 (son and heir of the 1st E. by his 1st wife).

[95] An old friend of FB's late grandmother Ann (Cooper) Burney and of her Aunts Ann and Rebecca. See *EJL* ii. 116.

he assented to all she said. Lord! what will all this come to?—Where will it End? & when, & how, shall I wake from the vision of such splendid success? for I hardly know how to believe it real. Lady Hales has written to Susy, that she has been reading Evelina to Madame de Ferre, the Governess,[96] & the Children,[97] & that her meeting with her father made them all *sob* so much, she was obliged to leave it off. She has, since, lent it to a Mrs. Knatchbull, who is a Cousin of her favourite ' Mr. Harris,[98] & a very clever Woman,—& she, too, has been very well pleased with it. Her Ladyship's set is now being perused by a Mr Barret,[99] one of the *Beaux Esprits* of Kent.

Well, I cannot but rejoice that I published the Book, little as I ever imagined how it would fare; but, hitherto, it has occasioned me no small diversion,—& *nothing* of the disagreeable sort,—but I often think a change *will* happen, for I am by no means so sanguine as to suppose such success will be uninterrupted. Indeed, in the midst of the greatest satisfaction that I feel, an inward *something* which I cannot account for, prepares me to expect a reverse! for the more the Book is drawn into notice, the more exposed it becomes to criticism & annotations.

[96] Not further identified. In her letter to FB *pmk* 11 June 1778, SEB reported Lady Hales's remark to Miss Coussmaker that 'I never can hear poor Mad^e de Ferre open her mouth now without its putting me so in mind of that Mad^e Duval, that I am ready to die wth laughing' (cf. *ED* ii. 225).

[97] 5 daughters: Mary Anne Hales (1765–1833); Jane Hales (1766–1848), m. (1795) Revd Brook Henry Bridges (1769–1855); Elizabeth Hales (1769–1815), m. (1790) John Calcraft (1765–1831) of Rempstone, Dorset; Harriet Hales (1770–1858); and Caroline Hales (1772–1853), m. (1798) Hon. William John Gore (1767–1836). See *GM* cxviii^1 (1848), 561; cxxviii^2 (1858), 655.

[98] James 'Hermes' Harris of Salisbury (see *EJL* i and ii). His half-sister, Catherine Harris (1705–41) m. (1730) Sir Wyndham Knatchbull Wyndham (d. 1747), 5th Bt. The 'Cousin' was probably the half-sister's spinster daughter Joan Elizabeth Knatchbull (b. by 1736, d. 1801), whose obituary praises her 'amiable, benevolent temper, unaffected manners, and chearful, entertaining conversation, enlivened by a natural turn of humour, and sprightly sallies of unoffending wit ...' (*GM* lxxi^2 (1801), 1056; will, PCC, of Catherine Knatchbull (Mrs Knatchbull's sister), prob. 12 May 1757; C. T. Probyn, *The Sociable Humanist: The Life and Works of James Harris 1709–1780* (Oxford, 1991), p. xv; additional information courtesy of Professor Probyn).

[99] Thomas Barret (?1743–1803) of Lee, Kent, a well-known connoisseur of the arts, who upon the death of Lady Hales' husband, Sir Thomas, in 1773, had succeeded him as MP for Dover. He is probably the 'Thomas Barrett, Esq.' who subscribed to *Hist. Mus.* See Namier.

June 23d

O not yet,—not yet, at least, is come the reverse! I have had a visit from my beloved, my kindest Father—& he came determined to complete my recovery by his goodness. I was *almost* afraid—& *quite* ashamed to be alone with him—but he soon sent for me to his little Gallery Cabinet—& then, with a significant smile that told me what was coming, & made me glow to my very forehead with anxious expectation, he said 'I have read your Book, Fanny—but you need not blush at it.—it is full of merit—it is really extraordinary.—' I fell upon his Neck with heart-beating emotion, & he folded me in his arms so tenderly that I sobbed upon his shoulder—so delighted was I with his precious approbation.[1] But I soon recovered to a gayer pleasure, more like his own: though the length of my illness, joined to severe mental suffering from a Family calamity which had occurred at that period,[2] had really made me too weak for a joy mixt with such excess of amazement. I had written my little Book simply for my amusement; I printed it, by the means first of my Brother, Charles, next of my Cousin, Edward Burney, merely for a frolic, to see how a production of my own would figure in that Author like form: but as I had never read any thing I had written to any human being but my sisters, I had taken it for granted that They, only, could be partial enough to endure my compositions. My unlooked for success surprized, therefore, my Father as much as my self— |

[1] '[I] thought she w^d have fainted; but I had but to take her by the hand & tell her that I had read part of her book with such pleasure, that instead of being angry, I congratulated her on being able to write so well; this kindness affected her so much, that she threw herself in my arms, & cried *à chaudes larmes*, till she sobbed. The poor humble author I believe never was happier in her life' (CB, Frag. Mem.).

[2] No evidence remains of what this 'calamity' was. Perhaps it was some aftershock of Bessy Meeke's elopement.

51   **[St Martin's Street,**
30 June 1778]

To Thomas Lowndes

AL (Comyn), June 1778
Single sheet 4to, 1 p. *pmks* 7 OC T PENNY POST PAID W wafer
Addressed: Mr Lowndes, | Bookseller, | Fleet Street
The MS is in vol. i of a grangerized copy of *DL*. The letter is dated
by Lowndes' reply (see below, p. 54) and by the postmark 7 OC T,
meaning Tuesday, 7 o'clock. The 'W' with 'PENNY POST PAID'
stands for Westminster.

Sir,

A long & dangerous illness having, for some months
past, confined me in the country, it was not till yesterday
that I sent to Gregg's[3] to enquire if any parcel had been
left there for Mr Grafton.

In the hurry of your Business, & the variety of your
commerce, you have probably forgotten that the set of
Evelina which you sent to me for the Errata, is incomplete
& unbound, & that I begged of you to make it perfect,
by sending the 1st & last sheets.

However, as I have, since, made certain marginal notes
that will make it impossible for me to send it to a Book-
Binder, I now write to beg the favour of you to let me
have a finished set, sent according to the former direction.

I should not give you this trouble, but that I am
informed it is by no means customary for an author to
purchase his own productions, for his own use,—though
their value may, probably, be by no one so readily
acknowledged.

Sh^d the Book pass through another Edition, I sh^d be
glad to have Timely notice, as I have many corrections &
some alterations, to propose. I find that no acc^t has yet
appeared in the Critical Review: I am extremely satisfied
with what is said in the Monthly & London:—& I heartily

---

[3] See above, p. 2 and n. 4, and Appendix 1.

hope that the general sale will somewhat more than answer your Expectations.

I am,
Sir,
Your obed^t & most h^le ser^t

———   ———

52   Chessington
                                     [5 July 1778]

To Susanna Elizabeth Burney

AL incomplete (Diary MSS I, paginated 675–8, Berg), July 1778
2 single sheets 4to, 4 pp.
Annotated (by FBA): 5. July—78 ✳ ✳ rapturous. & most innocent
happiness during anonymous success.

Chesington

My dearest Susy,

Don't you think there must be some wager depending, among the *little Curled Imps* who hover over *us* mortals,[4] of *how much flummery goes to turn the Head of an Authoress?*— Your last communication very near did my business! for, meeting Mr Crisp ere I had composed myself, I *tipt him such a touch of the Heroicks*, as he has not seen since the Time when I was so much celebrated for *Dancing Nancy Dawson*.[5] I absolutely longed to treat him with one of Capt. Mirvan's frolics, & fling his wig out of the Window.—however, I restrained myself from the apprehension that they would imagine I had a *universal spite* to

---

[4] An allusion to the sylphs in Pope's *Rape of the Lock*. FB's father had invoked them in a letter to HLT, 1 Nov. 1777, as did her stepmother in a letter to her, 11 July 1778 (*EJL* ii. 292; see also Lonsdale, pp. 240–1).

[5] A popular air named after the dancer Nancy Dawson (*c*.1730–67), who became famous after dancing a hornpipe to the tune in the *Beggar's Opera* at Covent Garden in 1759 (see Highfill; *YW* xxxix. 3 n. 4). SC later reminded FB of how she 'Used to dance Nancy Dawson on the Grass plot' at Chessington, *c*.1767 (below, p. 238). The tune of Nancy Dawson is still familiar as that of the nursery rhyme 'Here we go round the mulberry bush'.

that harmless piece of Goods, which I have already been known to treat with no little indignity.[6] He would fain have discovered the *reason* of my skittishness,—but as I could not tell it him, I was obliged to assure him 'twould be lost Time to enquire further into my flights, since *True no meaning puzzles more than Wit.*[7]—& therefore, begging the favour of him to *set me down an ass,*[8] I suddenly retreated.

My dear, dear Dr. Johnson!—what a charming man you are![9]—why Cousin Charles could not be more worthy & affable—Mrs. Cholmondely,[10] too, I am not merely *prepared,* but *determined* to admire—for really she has shewn so much penetration & ⌜Judgement⌝ of late, that I think she will bring about a union between Wit & Judgement, though their separation has been so long, & though their meetings have been so few.[11]—But,—Mrs. Thrale!— She, she is the Goddess of my Idolatry!—*What* an *eloge* is hers!—an *eloge* that not only delights at *first,* but that proves more & more flattering every Time it is considered![12]—⌐

---

[6] Alluding to a childhood incident. See below, p. 49.

[7] Pope, *Epistle to a Lady,* l. 114.

[8] Cf. *Much Ado about Nothing* IV.ii: 'O that he were here to write me down an ass!'

[9] FB is reacting to SJ's report of Mrs Cholmondeley's praise of *Evelina,* spoken by SJ to CB and HLT and relayed by CB to SEB, who enclosed it in a letter to FB (undated fragment, Berg, printed *ED* ii. 233–5).

[10] Mary Woffington (*c.*1729–1811), m. (1746) the Hon. Robert Cholmondeley (1727–1804); society hostess; younger sister of the actress Margaret 'Peg' Woffington (*c.*1718–60).

[11] '"Madam," cried Johnson *see sawing* on his Chair—Mʳˢ Chol'mley was talking to me last night of a new Novel, wᶜʰ she says has a very uncommon share of Merit—*Evelina*—she says she has not been so much entertained this great while as in reading it—... Mʳˢ Chol'mley says she never met so much modesty with so much merit before in any literary performance ... she says everybody ought to read it!"' (SEB to FB, n.d., Berg, *ED* ii. 233–4).

[12] SEB to FB *pmk* 4 July 1778 (Berg), *ED* ii. 236–7: '"Mʳˢ Thrale," sᵈ my Dear Father ... "likes it VASTLY—is EXTREMELY pleas'd with it... sᵈ she ... "tis *very* clever I assure you ... there's a vast deal of humour & entertainment in it ... there's a great deal of human *Life* in this Book, & of the Manners of the present time. It's writ by somebody that knows *the top & the bottom*—the *highest & lowest* of Mankind—..."'". HLT's comments in her diary, after she had learned that FB was the author, were rather more restrained: 'I was shewed a little Novel t'other Day which I thought pretty enough & set Burney to read it, little dreaming it was written by his second Daughter Fanny, who must certainly

I often think, when I am counting my Laurels, what pity it would have been had I *popt off* in my last Illness, without knowing what a *person of Consequence* I was!—& I sometimes think, that, were I *now* to have a relapse, I could never *go off* with so much *Eclat!*—I am now at the *summit* of a high Hill,—my prospects, on one side, are bright, glowing, & invitingly beautiful;—but when I turn round, I perceive, on the other side, sundry Caverns, Gulphs, pits & precipices, that to *look at*, make my Head giddy, & my Heart sick!—I see about me, indeed, many Hills of far greater height & sublimity;—but I have not the strength to attempt climbing them;—if *I* move, it must be in *descending*! I have already, I fear, reached the *pinnacle* of my Abilities, & therefore to *stand still* will be my best policy:—but there is nothing under Heaven so difficult to do!—Creatures who are formed for motion, *must* move, however great their inducements to forbear. The Wisest Course I could take, would be to bid an eternal adieu to Writing; then would the Cry be "'Tis pity she does not go on!—she might do something better by & by;—' &c, &c, *Evelina*, as a First, & a youthful publication, has been received with the utmost favour & lenity,—but would a future attempt be treated with the same mercy?—No, my dear Susy, quite the contrary,—there would not, indeed, be the same *plea* to save it,—it would no longer be a *Young Lady's first appearance* in public;—those who have met with less indulgence, would all *peck* at any new Book,—& even those who most encouraged the 1st offspring, might prove Enemies to the 2d, by receiving it with Expectations which it could not answer—& so, between either the Friends or the Foes of the *Eldest*, the *2d* would stand an equally bad chance, & a million of *flaws* which were overlooked in the former, would be ridiculed as villainous & intolerable *Blunders* in the latter.—But, though my Eyes Ache as I strain them to look forward,—the temptations before me

be a Girl of good Parts & some Knowledge of the World too, or She could not be the Author of Evelina—flimzy as it is, compar'd with the Books I've just mentioned [by Richardson, Rousseau, Charlotte Lennox, Smollett, and Fielding]' (*Thraliana* i. 328–9).

are *almost* irresistible,—& what you have transcribed from *Mrs. Thrale*—may, perhaps, prove my destruction!—

So You wish to have some of the sayings of the Folks here about *the Book*? I am sure I *owe* you all the communications I can possibly give you,—but I have nothing *new* to offer,—for, ⌐O Lord!¬ the same strain prevails *here*, as in *Town*;—& no one will be so obliging to me as to put in a little abuse,—so that I fear you will be *satiated* with the sameness of people's remarks. Yet what can I do—if they *will* be so disagreeable & tiresome as to be all of one mind, how is it to be helpt? I can only advise you to follow *my* example,—which is, to accommodate *my* philosophy to *their* insipidity;—&, in this I have so wonderfully succeeded, that I hear their commendations not merely with *patience*, but even with a degree of pleasure! Such, my dear Susy, is the effect of true philanthropy.

You desire *Kitty Cooke's* remarks in particular.—I have *none* to give you, for none can I get.—to the *serious* part, she, indeed, *listens*, & seems to think it may possibly be *very fine*,—but she is quite *lost* when the Branghtons & Mad^e Duval are mentioned;—she hears their speeches very composedly, & as words of course;—but when she hears them followed by loud bursts of Laughter ⎮ from Hetty, Mr Crisp, Mrs Gast & Mr Burney, she stares with the gravest amazement; & looks so aghast, & so distressed to know *where the Joke can be*, that I never dare trust myself to look at her for more than an Instant. Were she to *speak* her thoughts, I am sure she would ask why such common things, that pass every Day, should be *printed*? And all the Derision with which the party in general treat the *Branghtons*, I can see she feels herself with a plentiful addition of astonishment, for the Author.

By the way, not a human Being here has the most remote suspicion of the *Fact*;—I could not be more secure, were I *literally* unknown here. And there is no end to the ridiculous speeches perpetually made to me, by *all* of them in turn, though quite by accident. 'A'n't you sorry *this sweet Book* is done?' said Mrs Gast,—A silly little Laugh was the answer. 'Lord, said Patty Payne, 'tis the sweetest Book! don't you think so, Miss Burney?'—NB. answer as

above. 'Pray, Miss Fan', says Mrs. Hamilton, 'who wrote
it?' 'Really I never *heard*.'—cute enough, that, Miss
Sukey!—

I desired Hetty to *miss* the Verses,—for I can't *sit* them:
& I have been obliged to hide the Book ever since, for
fear of a discovery.—but I don't know how it will end, for
Mrs. Gast has declared she shall *Buy* it, to take to Burford
with her: ⌜though Daddy ⟨has⟩ advised her to get it from
the Library ⟨—well,⟩ thought I, my dear Daddy, you would
be most *astonished* if you ⟨knew⟩ who you spoke before!—
however, I don't believe she will be presented to the
⟨author⟩ [xxxxx ¾ *line*] she ⟨is *too* modest⟩ & ⟨shy⟩ to
express herself—as I remember⌝ |

[*The rest of the letter is missing.*]

53   Chessington, [5]-6 July [1778]

To Susanna Elizabeth Burney

AL incomplete (Diary MSS I, paginated 670, Berg), 6 July 1778
Single sheet 4to 2 pp. *pmk* 6 IY red wafer
Addressed: Miss Susan Burney, | Sᵗ Martin's Street, | Leicester
Fields, | London.
Annotated (by FBA): ⁘ ⁘

Sunday, Chesington
July 6 [*sic*]

Your Letter,[13] my dearest Susan; & the inclosed one
from Lowndes,[14] have flung me into such a *vehement*
perturbation, that I hardly can tell whether I wake or
Dream,—& it is even with difficulty that I can fetch my
Breath.—I have been strolling round the Garden 3 or 4
Times, in hopes of regaining a little quietness;—however,
I am not *very* angry at my inward disturbance, though it

---

[13] SEB to FB *pmk* 4 July 1778 (Berg), *ED* ii. 235–7.
[14] See below, p. 54.

even exceeds what I experienced from the Monthly
Review.

┌Good God┐! My dear Susy!—what a wonderful affair
has this been!—& how extraordinary is this *torrent* of
success, which sweeps down all before it!—I often think
it *too much*, nay, almost *wish* it happenned [*sic*] to some
other person, who had more native ambition, whose hopes
were more sanguine, & who could less have borne to be
Buried in the oblivion which *I* even sought.—But tho' it
might have been better bestowed, it could by no one be
more gratefully received.

Indeed, I can't help being *grave* upon the subject, for a
success ┌so prodigious, &┐ so *really* unexpected, almost
over powers me. I wonder at *myself*, that my spirits are
not more elated,—but I believe *half* the flattery I have
had, would have made me *madly merry*; but *all* serves only
to almost *depress* me, by the *fullness of Heart* it occasions.

Lowndes Letter is *so* civil!—he had a set *Bound for me*,
immediately, but waited a Direction.—He says *all the polite
World* send to him to *Buy* my Book;—& that a Lady of
Fashion told him to send it her, for she was reckoned
quite unfashionable for not having read it:—The Whole
Impression, he says, will be sold by Christmas, so that it
will go through a 2^d Edition in the 1st Year!—he shall be
proud of my commands, & signs himself my *obliged servant*!

Did you ever know the like?—pray tell my dear Father
all this.—no, don't mention it, for I'll write to him my-
self.[15] | Pray let me *hear* the comments, I sha'n't *mind them*,
I promise you! Nothing of that sort will disturb me from
that quarter.

We shall be extremely full: Mrs. Gast comes on Tuesday
[14 July]. If my dear Father means to be here during the
Time *both* the Paynes are, I hope Hetty & M^r B do *not*,
for there will not be room when *Sally* P. returns, I must
sleep with Patty, & then, Mrs H. & Mr Crisp hope Charles
& Hetty will excuse laying up stairs in Kitty's Room, till
the House clears a little. As the Paynes are to pay the *full*
price, they cannot propose to them a worse room than

[15] See next letter.

the Chintz,—&, they have not a better. I am quite sorry they don't come sooner, for we shall not be half so comfortable. & I am sorry Charles & Hetty are so slow in their motions. Pray let them know the little Baby[16] continues mending.

┌And I must beg _one_ more Letter [xxxxx _½ line_] about┐ _Business_, at Mrs H.'s request. She wishes, for family reasons, to know the _certain_ Day of the Paynes' coming; & whether morning or afternoon. She wants also to know, as near as you can gather, when my Father & mother come?—&, likewise, the same of Mr B. & Hetty. Many things are to be settled according to the information she receives, & she wishes, if possible, an answer by return of Post.

I shall hope for a _Badget_[16a] by the Paynes. Pray give my kind Love to them, & tell Sally I rejoice much that she is to be of our party. Prepare Patty not to expect _I_ shall stay long. I prepare these folks not to expect _she_ will, for I am sure |

[_The rest of the letter is missing._]

54   [Chessington,
pmk 6 July 1778]

To Charles Burney

ALS (paginated 663–6, Berg), July 1778
2 single sheets 4to, 4 pp. _pmks_ 6 IY K[IN]GS[T]ON red wafer
Addressed: Dr. Burney, | St Martin's Street, | London.
Annotated (by FBA): ✗· 20 [_sic_] July. — 1778 On scenes relative to Evelina. From Miss Fa [_sic_] Burney to Doctor Burney These Letters to my dearest Father that I have kept from the flames—I have Numbered chronologically, though there are chasms continual.

16 Presumably Sophia Elizabeth Burney (see above, p. 18). 'Dr Burney ... told me t'other day that his little Grandaughter had got the hooping Cough; I replied She must change the Air—Ay said he so the Doctors tell us Madam ... ' (_Thraliana_ i. 343, s.v. 'Aug. 1778'; the date and 't'other day' must be taken as approximate).
16a Probably Kitty Cooke's mispronunciation of _budget_.

Endorsed (by CB): Fanny
Originally part of Diary MSS I (as indicated by the pagination), the letter was subsequently pulled out and enclosed with other letters to CB in a folder *entitled (by FBA)*: Letters to Dr. Burney—From F—B. of 1778 1779 1780.

My dearest Sir,

I have *just* received from Susan an account of a little *Embarras* You have been in, upon the affair of my *schtoff*,[17] & I know not how to thank you for the kind manner in which you guard my secret:[18]—indeed, every soul, but yourself, who is acquainted with it, I have made take a solemn ⌐Oath, *by all they hold most sacred*, [xxxxx *2 words*],¬ never to reveal it, without my consent. I was sure it would be impossible for me to be too cautious.

But with *you*, the matter has not merely the constrained difference of Duty, but the voluntary one of Inclination,[19] & I should be *ashamed* if I thought *you* had any restriction, but your own Judgement; for *my* Honour, Interest & Welfare I know are yours, & to you, therefore, (though to *you only*,) I willingly commit the same unlimited liberty of concealment or discovery which, of course, I reserve for myself.

Believe me, my dearest Father, I don't *puff* when I tell you it has always been as much upon *your* account as my own, that I have so earnestly desired to continue *incog*; for *I*, as *myself*, am nobody; but as *your* ⌐spawn¬, I could easily make myself *known*, & have power to *disgrace*,

---

[17] FB explains this term later in her journal as 'the *German* pronunciation of *stuff* (below, p. 57). In sending CB her verse translation of a Latin epigram by Salmasius, HLT had cautioned: 'I *think* you have too much regard for me to let any Nonsense of mine go among People less partial to me than yourself, so I will say no more of the *Schtoffe*' (letter of 27 Feb. 1778, collection of H. L. Platnauer, Edgbaston, Birmingham). Evidently the term was used among the Streathamites to deprecate any 'Germanically' heavy or pretentious literary effort. CB may have invented the joke.

[18] In her letter to FB *pmk* 4 July (Berg), SEB quoted her father as saying to her, 'I think I've almost got over yʳ Mother's Suspicions about it [*Evelina*]. ... she told me that by something that had pass'd at Chesington, she *thought Fanny and Sukey had written it together*!' (*ED* ii. 236–7).

[19] Cf. Kate Hardcastle to her father Mr Hardcastle in *She Stoops to Conquer*: 'I hope, sir, you have ever found that I considered your commands as my pride; for your kindness is such, that my duty as yet has been inclination' (Act III, conclusion).

though not to *credit* you, as I have said already, with *truth*,
though not with the *Flowers of poetry*, in the foolish Lines
I ventured to insert in my so highly honoured *wollums*,—
& which cost ¦ me more Time in deliberating whether or
not to *Print* than they did to *write* them,—but I hope their
sincerity will make you accept them as *meant*, for I may
truly say they *flowed from the Heart*, since I wrote them, in
the very fullness of it, in the Dead of the very Night that
I owned to you my secret, & my views & intentions relative
to it,[20]—all which you took so kindly that I could not resist
making the attempt, as soon as I had *de tort*,[21]—& the
very next Day,—as I parted with all power of retreat, by
giving up my M.S.

How you would have *smoked the author*,[22] had you seen
the anxiety I have been in for some Days past, on account
of Mrs. Thrale!—I can't express how painful my suspence
was! for I had *no* expectations, & only just so much Hope
as to give Birth & strength to my Fears.—& now, since
You have read the Book, I am become even uneasily
sollicitous that it should not be *run down* to you:—& yet,
Mr Twining never wished half so much that the Letter he
directed to you might miscarry,[23] as *I* did that the Book I
inscribed to you, might escape your notice,—however,
⌐*God's above all!*[24] &¬ I'm heartily glad it's over. And I
think that, now *you* & *Mrs. Thrale* have Honoured it with
a *partial* reading, not all the severity of all the Critics
under Heaven, can give me so much ¦ mortification, as to
counter-ballance my satisfaction.

---

[20] See *EJL* ii. 233.

[21] i.e., 'the thought'. FB may be echoing the accent of a foreign visitor to St
Martin's St., or she may mean a far-fetched pun on the French *tort* ('wrong',
'error').

[22] Made fun of her. As HLT records in *Thraliana* i. 145 and 251, CB thought
that *smoke* in this now archaic sense derived from the French *se moquer*.

[23] Thomas Twining, writing in 1773 to renew his acquaintance with CB but
fearful of being thought a '*pushing* man', confessed that he had 'half wish'd ...
when I put my letter [of 7 Apr. 1773] in the post, that it might miscarry'
(Twining to CB 28 May 1773, BL).

[24] Cf. *Othello* II. iii. 106–7: 'Well, God's above all, and there be souls must
be saved and there be souls must not be saved.'

I have had *such* a Letter from Lowndes!²⁵—he tells me he had a set Bound purposely for me, as soon as the Book came out, but hoped to *hear* from me, whither to send it: all the *Great World*, he says, send to him, to *Buy* it,—& a most *polite Lady* charged him to let her have it, for she was reckoned quite *unfashionable* for not having read it:—the sale is so great, that, though I know from my Cousin Edward he printed a vast quantity,²⁶ he yet tells me it will go through a *second Edition* in the *First Year!*—he shall be *proud* of my Commands, & signs [him]self my *Obliged Servant!*—

I am so much astonished at this flow of success, that I sometimes think I have taken as long a Nap as the *Sleeping Princess in the Wood*,²⁷ & that, when I wake from my reverie, I shall, like her, find all things just as they were before I was beguiled by such visions.

I am very sorry it will be quite impossible for you to have a better Room, as Mrs. Gast comes next Tuesday [14 July], & stays some months. ⌐Miss Payne can only have the Chintz Room, which you would not like near so well as your old apartment.⌐

I have been sometime in Daily expectation of a recall,— I am ⌐really well⌐ & very near as strong as ever. I have heard again ⌐from Bʸ²⁸ but nothing particular.⌐ |

Adieu, my dearest Sir; pray give my Duty to my Mother, & believe me,

Your most affectionate
& dutiful Daughter
Frances Burney

---

²⁵ See below, p. 54.

²⁶ In 1782 Lowndes claimed to have printed a first edition of 500 copies, while FBA in 1796 gave the figure as 800 (*DL* ii. 481; *JL* iii. 206).

²⁷ The traditional tale of 'Sleeping Beauty', given classic form by Charles Perrault (1628–1703) as 'La Belle au bois dormant', in *Histoires ou Contes du temps passé* (1697). Beauty sleeps 100 years.

²⁸ Perhaps Rebecca ('Becky') Burney, FB's Worcester cousin.

Chessington,
6–[8] July [1778]

With Samuel Crisp to Susanna Elizabeth Burney

ALS (Diary MSS I, paginated [681–4], Berg), 6 July 1778
2 single sheets 4to, 4 pp. *pmk* 8 IY red wax seal
Addressed: Miss Susanna Burney, | St Martin's Street, | Leicester Fields, | London.
Annotated (by FBA): ✳ 1778 written *pendant* the secret of Evelina [*sic*]—Authorship. a very *young* Letter of honest buoyancy of delight at wholly unthought of *Success*

Pray Suzettikin go to a Colour Shop in little Newport Street—I think the Man's Name was Decker formerly—& there buy me, two little Ermine Points, the shortest & stiffest You can get—I believe they are 3 Pence apiece, perhaps more but I must have them[29]—I'll pay Fannikin in mony, & You in Love—your honoured Daddy

S. Crisp—

Chesington July 6

[*FB continues*:]

'*Honoured*, quoth a?' says I.—
'Why *a'n't* I?—' says he.
'Suppose you *are*, says I, it don't become *You* to say it.'
'Oh yes, it does,—& to think it, too!'
And so much for the above.

I have been serving *him* [SC] a pretty trick this morning; ⌜Lord⌝ how he would rail, if he found it all out!—I had a fancy to dive pretty deeply into the real *rank* in which he held my Book: so I told him that your last Letter acquainted me, who was *reported* to be the author of Evelina. I added that it was a *profound secret*, & he ᐟ must

---

[29] SC evidently dabbled in painting. The shopowner Decker has not been further traced.

by no means mention it to a human Being. He bid me *tell him directly*, according to his usual style of Command: but I insisted upon his Guessing. 'I can't guess, said he—may be it's *You*.'

Oddso! thought I, what do you mean by that?—'Pho, nonsense! cried I, what should make you think of me?'

'Why You look guilty.' answered he.

This was a horrible Home stroke;—deuce take my looks! thought I, I shall owe them a Grudge for this!—however, I found it was a mere random shot, &, without much difficulty, I *Laughed it to scorn*.[29a]

And who do you think he guessed next?—

My Father! there's for You!—& several questions he asked me; whether he had lately been *shut up much*, & so on.

And this was not all;—for he afterwards guessed *Mrs. Thrale*,—& *Mrs. Greville*:

There's Honour & Glory for you!—I'll assure you, I Grinned prodigiously.

He then would guess no more.

So I served him another trick for his laziness.

I read a paragraph, *in your last Letter*, (which perhaps You may not perfectly remember,)[30] in which ⌐ You say the *private report* is, that the author is a son of the late Dr. Friend,[31] *my likeness*.

Now this son is a *Darling* of my Daddy's, who reckons him the most sensible & intelligent Young man of his acquaintance: so I trembled *a few*,[32] for I thought ten to one but he'd say '*He? not he*, I promise You!'—but no such thing,—his immediate answer was 'Well, he's *very capable*,—of that, or any thing else.'

⌐God!⌐ I Grinned broader than before!—

[29a] Cf. Handel's *Messiah* 27.   [30] Because FB invented it.

[31] William Freind (1715–66), DD (Oxon.), 1748, Dean of Canterbury, 1760–6. The son who was FB's '*likeness*' presumably resembled her in being 'sensible & intelligent' (below). Of Dr Freind's 3 sons, the 2 nearest in age to FB, either of whom may be meant, were William Maximilian Freind (c.1749–1804), MA (Oxon.), 1771, Rector of Chinnor, Oxon, and John Freind (later Robinson) (1754–1832), cr. (1819) Bt.

[32] i.e., 'a good bit'; an ironic colloquialism (*OED* s.v. few 4b).

And here the matter rests! I sha'n't undeceive him, at least till he has finished the Book.

Friday July.[33] I have received Your Letter, my dearest Girl,—& I think, if possible, I have received yet more delight from it, than from all that went before. I am, indeed, gratified past all words by finding my dear Father can bear to give it, & so soon, a 2ᵈ reading:[34] & the *particulars*, how things take, & go off, are delicious.—Does he go *alone* to Streatham?[35]—How fortunate for me that I was not returned to Town before the last Journey thither! I should never have stood all those confusing questions, the next morning.—I was in a *twitter* for you, when I read them.—&, indeed, I shᵈ have been prodigiously at a *nonplus* with Miss Coussmaker. I am much pleased Mrs Knatchbull approves, because she is one of yʳ Favourites.[36] |

ᵣMy love to Charlotte & tell her I hope to have a ⟨Covy⟩ of her *Inventions*.[37] Mr C. enjoys her Imperence Extremely [xxxxx *1 line*] I took a *Day or two* to think of it. Are you not, *honestly*, quite astonished at its ⟨sale⟩?—so

---

[33] This date is so in the MS, but may have been inserted later. 'Friday' would presumably be 10 July, whereas FB's letter is postmarked 8 July and the letter she here acknowledges is SEB to FB 5–6 July 1778 (Berg), printed *ED* ii. 237–40.

[34] This time to his wife.

[35] 'He goes to Streatham the latter end of the week' (SEB to FB 5–6 July 1778, *ED* ii. 240). CB went with his wife (EAB to FB, postscript by SEB, 11 July 1778, Berg).

[36] CB and EAB had gone to Streatham on Fri., 3 July, but had not stayed since HLT was expecting a 'great deal of Company' on Sat. (SEB to FB *pmk* 4 July 1778, *ED* ii. 235). The 'confusing questions' came from EAB, who suspected that FB and SEB had written *Evelina* together: 'Charlotte says I turn'd as pale as ashes, & I felt my voice so unsteady I was frighten'd at speaking—luckily she did not look at me—& I soon assumed a *firmer tone*' (SEB to FB. n.d., Berg, *ED* ii. 241). SEB's mentions of Miss Coussmaker and of Mrs Knatchbull in her letter of 5–6 July are presumably in the obliterated passages that have not been recovered.

[37] Probably an allusion to Charlotte's fondness for puns and neologisms, which she indulged in her journals and letters, some of which are published in *ED* ii. 277–320. 'Imperence' is a vulgar corruption of *impudence*, perhaps associated with *impertinence*; *OED* cites the earliest occurrence in Colman and Garrick's *Clandestine Marriage* (1766).

unpromoted, so left to itself![38]—[xxxxx *4 lines*] adieu, my ⟨sweet⟩ Girl [xxxxx *7 lines*] ⟨your F.—⟩[n]

56   Chessington
                                          [8 July 1778]

To Charles Burney

ALS (Diary MSS I, paginated 667–70), Berg), July 1778
2 single sheets 4to, 4 pp. *pmk* 8 IY wafer
Addressed: Dr. Burney, | St Martin's Street, | London.
Annotated (by FBA): ✷ 1778 Friday, [*sic*]—July 25. [*sic*] the *same to the same* on Dr. Burney's desire to reveal the authorship of Evelina to Mrs. Burney—& to Mrs. Thrale.

Chessington

My dear & most kind Father.—The *request* You have condescended to make me, I *meant* to anticipate in my last Letter.[39] How good you are, to pave the way for my secret's being favourably received, by sparing your *own* Time & Breath, to gain the Book attention & partiality!— I can't express a third part of either the gratitude or pleasure I feel, upon hearing, from Susy, that you are reading it aloud to my mother—because I well know, nothing can give it so good a chance with her, or indeed with *any body*, & I would have given the World you had Read it to Mrs Thrale,—as she *was* to hear it,—for so *Fortune*, in the shape of Mrs Cholmley, seemed to decree.

---

[38] SEB replied: 'you ask me to tell you *honestly* if I am not astonished at the sale of the Book—& I will not scruple to tell you I *am*.—I *never* doubted its success, provided it was *read*—but its being generally read I confess I scarce hoped—as you wd permit nobody to mention it, & wd have suffered the poor Babe to die in oblivion, had it not been miraculously preserved.—the *Monthly Review* I think must have been its recommendation to Mrs Cholmondeley—& since it has fallen into her hands, its subsequent good fortune has nothing in it that seems to me wonderful' (SEB to FB, n.d., *ED* ii. 241).

[39] The request, conveyed by SEB in her letter to FB 5–6 July (Berg), was for permission to reveal the identity of the author of *Evelina* to HLT and to EAB. See *ED* ii. 239–40.

3. The Hotel St Martin's Street, Leicester Fields, formerly the Burney family residence. From an engraving for the *European Magazine*, Nov. 1811. The house previously belonged to Sir Isaac Newton, whose observatory shows on top.

Will you tell,—or shall I write to my mother?—I believe she will not be *all* surprise, for I fancy she is not totally without suspicion.—But pray be so kind as to tell her, that it was not want of confidence in *her*, but in *myself*, that occasioned my reserve & privacy.—She *knows* how severe a Critic I think her, & therefore, I am sure, cannot wonder I should dread a Lash which I had no other hope of escaping from,—but flight or Disguise.—᷉ Indeed, the thoughts of *hot Rolls & Butter in July* could not have a more indelicate effect on my Lord Ogleby,[40] than those had Upon me, which followed the News of Evelina's visit to St Martin's Street. However, Susan comforts me with assurances that things are in a pretty good way; & therefore I am willing to flatter myself, that hearing who is the writer, will rather serve to blunt, than to soften the Edge of Criticism. I am sure it does with *you*, or your patience & precious Time could never wade through 3 volumes of that sort: & I encourage myself, in regard to my mother, with the knowledge that no person's feelings will be so likely to prove infectious to her, as yours.—She must not be angry, if I own I heartily hope she will not escape the contagion.

As soon as I know that *the Wig is wet*,[41]—I will write, & explain how I managed the affair, & at the same Time, entreat her not to reveal it to *any one*: for though I have already rather too many confidants, I am firmly persuaded I have not one on whose discretion I cannot rely.

My mother will the sooner pardon my privacy, when she hears that even from *you I used* every method in my power to keep my Trash concealed, & that I even yet know not in what manner you got at the Name of it.[42] Indeed, I only proposed, like my friends ᷉ the Miss

---

[40] In Colman and Garrick's *The Clandestine Marriage* (1766), Lord Ogleby exclaims: 'Hot rolls and butter in July! I sweat with the thoughts of it' (II.i).

[41] i.e., the damage is done. For the origin of this Burney family catch phrase, see CB *Mem.*, pp. 142–3; *Mem.* ii. 170–1.

[42] SEB had told him (above, p. 26 n. 68).

Branghtons, a little *private fun*,[43] & never once Dreamt of extending my confidence beyond my sisters.

As to Mrs Thrale,—your wish of telling *her* quite *unmans* me—I *shook* so, when I read it, that, had any body been present, I must have betrayed myself,—&, indeed, many of my late Letters have given me such extreme surprise,—& *perturbation*, that I believe nothing could have saved me from Mr Crisp's discernment, had he seen me during my first reading: however, he has not an idea of the kind.—

But,—if you do tell Mrs Thrale,—won't she think it very strange where I can have *kept Company*, to draw such a family as the Branghtons, Mr Brown[44] & some others?—Indeed, (thank Heaven!) I don't myself recollect ever passing half an Hour at a Time with any *one* person *quite* so bad;—so that, I am afraid she will conclude I must have an *innate vulgarity of ideas* to assist me with such coarse colouring for the objects of my Imagination. Not that I suppose the *Book* would be better received by her, for having Characters *very pretty, & all alike*; my only fear, in regard to that particular, is for poor Miss Bayes![45]—If I were able to *insinuate the plot into the Boxes*,[46] I should build my defence upon Swift's maxim, *that a Nice man is a man of Nasty ideas.*[47]—I should certainly have been more finical, had I foreseen what has happened, or had the most *remote* notion | of being known by *Mrs. Thrale* for the scribe, however, 'tis perhaps as well as it is, for these kind of Compositions lose all their spirit, if they are too scrupulously corrected: besides, if I had been very nice, I must have cleared away so much, that, like poor Mr Twiss after his friends had been so obliging as to give his Book a Scourge, nothing but hum drum matter of Fact w^d be

---

[43] The Branghton sisters or their brother at various times declare their desire to have 'a *little pleasure*', 'some *fun*', and 'a little *fun*' (vol. ii, letters 15, 17, 21: *Evelina*, ed. E. A. Bloom (1968), pp. 195, 213, 232).

[44] Polly Branghton's foolish beau.

[45] FB compares herself to Bayes, the hapless dramatist in Buckingham's *The Rehearsal* (1671).

[46] FB quotes Bayes in Act I.

[47] In 'Thoughts on Various Subjects'. See *The Prose Works of Jonathan Swift*, ed. H. Davis (Oxford, 1939–68), iv. 247.

left.[48] Indeed, I never found courage sufficient to ask any advice of the *useful* Confidents I *might* have made,—You & my Daddy Crisp,—& my fear of Discovery was so great, that I never found opportunity to read even to the kind ones I did make, except Esther & Mr. Burney. Edward & my Aunts, Charles, Charlotte—&, far worse, Susan herself never saw it in MSS. ⌐My Daddy Crisp, of *his own accord*, endeavoured to procure Mrs Woodford's[49] room for you; but found it could not be effected, though the reasons are too various & tedious to mention. Mrs. Gast comes next Tuesday [14 July].⌐

Adieu, my dearest Sir,—pray give my duty to my mother, & pray let her know,—after the *great Gun* is gone off,—that I shall anxiously wait to hear her opinion,—& believe me ever & ever

Your Dutiful & most affectionate
Francesca Scriblerus.[50]

I wonder how *my dear Friend* Mrs Cholmley does: a charming woman, that!—ˡ

[*The Journal for 1778 continues. A leaf or leaves at the beginning are missing. In the first paragraph, FB quotes from SEB's letters to her, pmk 4 July and n.d., ED ii. 235–7, 240–1.*]

but repetitions of what I have heard from so many other quarters, *that she* [HLT] *liked it vastly,* & was *extremely* pleased with it. However, there is scarce any Quarter, besides my Father, from whence praise could have a relish at once so delicate, & so high flavoured: & my Father is quite *delighted* at her approbation, & told Sukey that I could not have had a greater compliment than making 2 such women my Friends as Mrs. Thrale & Mrs. Cholmley, for they were *d—d severe,* & *d—d knowing,* & *afraid* of praising *à tort & à travers* as their opinions are liable to be

---

[48] In 1775 FB had written of Richard Twiss and his *Travels through Portugal and Spain* that 'His Travels proved to be very dull and dry, he was so fearful of his natural flightiness being perceived, that he has cut out every thing that could have been entertaining, & left nothing but tame description' (*EJL* ii. 135).

[49] FB mentions Mrs Woodford, 'a Widow', again in 1785 (*EJL* vi). Presumably a boarder at Chessington Hall, she was probably Rebecca, widow of John Woodford of Chessington (IGI).

[50] Recalling, of course, Martinus Scriblerus.

quoted, which makes them extremely shy of speaking favourably. Miss Thrale, too, who is very cold & reserved, my Father says spoke so much of it as he ever heard her speak of any thing, & said it was very *entertaining* & *well written*. Mrs. Thrale said she had only to complain it was too *short*. She recommended it to my mother to read! how droll!—& she told her she would be much entertained with it, for there was a great deal of human Life in it, & of the manners of the present Times: & added that it was written "by somebody who knows the *Top* & *the Bottom, the highest* & *the lowest of mankind.'* She has even *lent* her set to my mother,—who brought it Home with her! She would not, perhaps, have gone so far, had she known that the original M.S. was now in St. Martin's Street! & that, a few months ago, the Book was *no where else*!

My mother, therefore, is, at last, reading it herself. How I rejoice in my absence from home!

My dear Father has sent me a *request*, that I would allow him to tell *Mrs. Thrale* who is the Authoress!—& also my mother![51]—I am quite amazed that *he* should wish to break the seal of my secresy—however, I submit implicitly to his Judgement & his kindness, & have written to beg he will only consult his *own* opinion in future, since I most chearfully commit to *him*, as to myself, of course, all liberty to tell, or conceal my secret, as he thinks proper: though to *all* others, however loved or esteemed, I have insisted upon a most solemn promise, nay oath, never to divulge it without my leave.[52]

The result I know not yet, but long to hear.

My kind Father, who takes the warmest interest in my Book, is now reading it for the 2^d Time, & aloud, to my mother! In my last Letter, I heard they had nearly finished the 2^d Volume. Susan writes me word that my mother spoke of it, to her, at first, in a very slighting manner, but now she only praises it.—My Father has declared he likes it *better* than before, & says such things as astonish as much as they delight me. At the Comic parts, he Laughs

---

[51] See above, p. 47 and n. 39.
[52] See above, p. 41.

himself quite *sore*, & at the serious, his simpathising soul starts into his Eyes: & he declares, in reading some paragraphs of Mr. Villars', 'that Johnson could not have expressed himself better.' & that his Letters have all the appearance of being written by a man who has had a College Education, with a goodness of Heart rarely to be met with—' he quotes from it forever, &, to sum up his opinion, says 'it entertains, it affects, & it interests.'[53]

My mother, too, condescends to join now in its favour,—but she is evidently half crazy to know the Author, & seems to have some queer suspicions, though hardly to know herself upon whom to cast them owing probably, to some little circumstances which, though they have not satisfied her doubts, have not escaped her observation. She owned, at first, to my Father, that, from what had past at Chesington, she had imagined Evelina was written by Susy & me together:[54]—but since she has gone on, she has manifestly wavered: she confesses she would *give something* to know ⏌ who wrote it: & she often seems to *lay traps*, as if to snare Susan into some confession, if she really knows who it is or not: such as saying 'This Evelina is certainly written by a *Woman*; that's a determined thing.' And then 'I suppose Capt. ⌐Simmons¬ might sit for Capt. Mirvan.' Now Capt. Simmons was the Husband of Mrs. Simmons,[55] & only known, by any of our acquaintance, at *Chesington*, consequently, if he set for Capt. Mirvan, he must be *drawn* either by our own Family, or Mr. Crisp. However, the fact is, it never entered my Head, at the Time I wrote, though every body hás, since, pointed him out to me. She once asked my Father if he did not believe it to be the production of a *Woman*? 'I see no particular reason to think so, said he, for in all Villars' Letters, there is as much *sound sense*, & *manly reasoning* as I ever met with in any thing in my Life.' Well, said my mother,

---

[53] See SEB to FB 5–6 July 1778, *ED* ii. 239.

[54] See above, p. 46 n. 36.

[55] See *EJL* ii. 47 and n. 49.

whatever is the sex, it does it Honour, for it may be read with equal Entertainment & Instruction.'[56]

The Fates, have certainly, in some frolic, determined upon encouraging my devices,—for nothing is to go ill for me that relates to my scrawl. By the way, I have again resumed my Correspondance with my friend Mr. Lowndes; when I sent the Errata I desired to have a set, directed to Mr. Grafton, at ⌐Gregg's⌐ Coffee House.[57] For I had no Copy but the one he sent me to make the Errata from, which was incomplete & unbound. However, I heard nothing at all from him; & therefore, after some consideration, & much demur, I determined to make an attempt once more; for my Father told me it was a *shame* that I, the Author, should not have even one set of my own Work!—& I *ought*, he said, to have had *six*: & indeed, he is often quite *enraged* that Lowndes gave no more for the M.S.—but *I* was satisfied,—& that sufficed.[58] |

I therefore wrote him word, that I supposed, in the hurry of his Business, & variety of his Concerns,—he had forgotten my request, which I now repeated. I also added, that, if ever the Book went through another Edition, I should be glad to have timely notice, as I had some corrections & alterations to propose.[59]

I received an immediate answer, & intelligence, from my sisters, that he had sent a set of Evelina [xxxxx *2 words*] most elegantly Bound. The answer I will Copy.[60]

To Mr. Grafton.[61]

Sir,

I Bound up a set[62] for You the first Day I had them,[63] & hoped by some means to hear from you. The Great

---

[56] The passages in SEB's letter from which these quotations have presumably been copied are heavily obliterated.

[57] See above, p. 33.

[58] Lowndes gave 20 guineas.

[59] See above, p. 33.

[60] The original ALS, a single sheet small 4to, is in the Barrett Collection. Verbal and spelling differences are indicated in the notes.

[61] Not in the original.

[62] 'Sett'

[63] 'one'

World send here to Buy Evelina. A polite Lady said Do, Mr Lowndes, give me Evelina, I am[64] treated as unfashionable for not having read it. I think the Impression will be sold by Christmas. If, mean Time, or about that Time, you favour me with any commands, I shall be proud to observe them.

Your[65] obliged servant,[66]

Fleet Street, T. Lowndes.
July 2d[67] 1778.

I can never cease to exclaim—What astonishing success!—good Heaven, a 2d Edition!—& in the 1st year!—how extraordinary!—I can form no idea in the World how the Book has got about; I heard, from my Cousin Edward, who once went to the Printing office for me, that there was a very large Impression taken;[68]—therefore the sale must have been wonderful.

I am now joined by a Young Companion, Patty Payne, who is come hither to spend 2 or 3 months. She has had very bad Health, & her Beauty is faded by it, Young as she is;[69] but I hope the fine air, & the quietness of this retirement, will restore her to her former strength & bloom. She is a ˡ sweet Girl, & I have a real regard for her; but she is rather too inseparably my Companion, & ⌜follows me as my⌝ shadow, in so much that I have scarce one moment in the whole Day to myself.

Mrs. Gast, Mr. Crisp's sister, is also here. She is a very sensible, chatty, agreeable & *good* Woman.

July 20th

Nothing but Laurels do I receive; & about nothing else can I write! very hard!—I had, yesterday, a Letter from my mother herself, written in consequence of my Father's Discovering me to her, as soon as they had finished

---

[64] 'Im'
[65] 'Yr'
[66] 'Servt'
[67] '2'
[68] See above, p. 43.
[69] She was 20 or 21 (she was christened on 20 July 1757; see IGI).

Evelina.[70] She has written purposely 'to Congratulate me,' she says, 'on the merit & success of my 1ˢᵗ publication.' She declares it has given her more pleasure than any Book she has read of a *long, long* while, & that it has *revived* in her both pleasure & sensation, by alternate Tears & Laughter: she owns she had a *whimsical* idea of the Writer, or writers, ere she saw the Book, but protests that every Letter in it tended to remove it,—she then adds 'throughout the serious part, I traced your feelings, but wondered at your powers of delineation. In the sportive way of holding up Ignorance, Conceit & Folly to ridicule, I thought I discovered Your attentive Ear, & observing Eye; but there is[71] a knowledge of the ill manners & absurd conduct of Bon Ton in domestic Life, that almost puzzled me,—till a Leaf I had over looked at the beginning,[72] brought me back, & gave it *all* to you.' She adds many yet more flattering things, promises me her secresy if I wish it, but concludes with saying no one need Blush to be the acknowledged Author.[73]

Good God!—to receive such a panygeric from the quarter from which I *most* dreaded satire!—I have written her[74] my best thanks for such kind encouragement, entreated ᶦ her continued & strict secresy, & promised to acquaint her with all the particulars of my [xxxxx *1 word*] management of the affair, as soon as we meet. I have, ⌐also,⌐ apologized, in the best manner I was able, for my reserve: & *truly* assured her, that when I planned such total concealment, I never imagined she, or any one, whom we should meet with, would ever hear that such a Book as Evelina existed.

---

[70] EAB to FB, 13 July 1778, *pmk* 18 IY (Hyde). FBA annotated it: 'First Letter on the discovery of the Author of Evelina—written from Streatham before ever the said Author had visited that delicious spot.' Verbal differences in the original are noted below.

[71] 'was'

[72] 'at the beginning' added by FB. The 'Leaf' in question contained FB's dedicatory verses to her father.

[73] Actually, EAB goes on to record her impressions of Streatham: 'as to the Luxury of this Place, both to mind & body 'tis not to be described.—Johnson is Chearfull & good humour'd—Mʳˢ Thrale all Alive & Merry—', etc.

[74] Missing.

At the same Time, I had also a Letter from my beloved Father,[75]—the kindest, sweetest Letter in the World!—in which he says 'Thy *schtoff* (for the *German* pronunciation of *stuff*,) reads better the 2ᵈ Time than the first, & thou hast made thy old Father Laugh & Cry at thy pleasure.' All tenderness & goodness is his dear Heart. He tells me, too, that he found Mrs. Thrale 'full of *ma foi's* jokes, the Captain's brutality, Squire Smith's gentility, Sir Clement's outdaciousness,[76] the Branghton's [*sic*] vulgarity, & Mother Selwyn's sharp knife, &c, &c.' He then says that he wishes to tell Lady Hales, though she cannot be made more fond of the Book by a personal partiality for the author. He concludes with—'I never heard of a Novel Writer's statue,—yet who knows?—but above all things take care of your Head, if that should be at all turned out of it's place by all this intoxicating success, what a figure would You cut upon a Pedestal! prenez y bien garde!— —'

Well may he caution me!—but, as I have told him in answer,[77] if I was to make so ungrateful, so *sinful* a return for the favours of Fortune, as to be ridiculously vain,—I should think all this success, charming as it is, bought much too dear!—|

I have also had a Letter from Susanne.[78] She informs me that my Father, when he took the Books back to Streatham, actually acquainted Mrs. Thrale with my secret! He took an opportunity, when they were alone together, of saying that, upon *her recommendation*, he had himself, as well as my mother, been reading Evelina. 'Well, cried she, & is it not a very *pretty* Book? & a very *clever* Book? & a very *comical* Book?' 'Why,' answered he, "tis[79] *well enough*; but I have something to tell you about it.' 'Well? what?—' cried she,[80] 'has Mrs. Cholmley found out the author?—'

---

[75] Missing.
[76] This 'dial. corruption of AUDACIOUS' predates the earliest example in *OED* by 60 years. See also *EDD*.   [77] Missing.
[78] SEB to FB, 16 July 1778 (Berg), *ED* ii. 241–7.
[79] 'it's' in the original.
[80] At this point FB begins to confuse the speakers of the dialogue. The original runs thus: '[HLT:] Well what? = [CB:] Has Mrˢ Cholmly found out the Author? = [HLT:] No—not that I know of = [CB:] Because I believe I have—tho' but *very* lately = [HLT:] Well pray Let's hear' etc.

'No, returned he; not that I know of; but I believe *I* have,
—though but *very* lately.' 'Well, pray let's hear,' cried she
eagerly, 'I want to know him of all things!'

How my Father must Laugh at the *him*!—He then,
however, undeceived her in regard to that particular, by
telling her it was '*our Fanny.*'—for she knows *all about* all
our Family, as my Father talks to her of his Domestic
concerns without any reserve.

A hundred handsome things, of course, followed. And
she afterwards read some of the comic parts to Dr. Johnson,
Mr. Thrale, & whoever came near her.—How I should
have *quivered* had I been there! but they tell me that Dr.
Johnson Laughed as heartily as my Father himself did.

My Father's request of telling Lady Hales has somewhat
startled me; however, I have, as in Duty bound, given
him *Carte Blanche* in regard to Confidents: but I shall be
horribly out of Countenance when I next see her, for
there will be something very awkward in meeting those
who have been informed of my *authorship*.

"Miss Payne" to Day, very innocently, asked Mr. Crisp
if he had got a Book called *Evelina*?—she said she had
long wished to read it, for she had heard such a character
of it!—I ventured to ask from whom?—'Lord, said she,
from *every body*!' I longed to ask more questions, but did
not dare.

Nothing can be more ridiculous than the scenes in
which I am almost perpetually engaged: Mr. Crisp, who
is totally without suspicion, says, almost Daily, something
that has double the meaning he *intends* to convey: for, as
I am often writing, either Letters, Italian, or some of my
own vagaries, he commonly calls me the *scribe*, & the
authoress; asks when I shall *print*? says he will have all my
Works on *royal Paper*, &c—And, the other Day, Mrs. Gast,
who frequently Lectures me about studying too hard, &
injuring my Health, said 'Pray, Miss Burney, now you
write so much, when do you intend to *publish*?

'Publish? cried Mr. Crisp, why she *has* published; she
brought out a Book the other Day, that has made a great
noise, *Evelina*,—& she bribed the Reviewers to speak well
of it, & has set it a going.'

I was almost ready to run out of the Room;—but, though the *hit* was so palpable[80a] in regard to the *Book*, what he said of the *Reviewers* was so much the contrary, that it checked my alarm: Indeed, had he the most remote idea of the truth, he would be the last man to have hinted at it before a room full of people.

'Evelina? repeated Miss Payne, well, I have heard much of it,—I long to read it.'

'O, cried I, as composedly as I could, *that* is but a *small* part of my Authorship: I shall give you a list of my *Folios* soon.' They had all some *Jocularity* Upon the occasion, but I found I was perfectly safe, Indeed, my best security is, that my Daddy *concludes* the Author to be a *man*, &c, | all the rest follow as he leads. These sort of Questions are always abominably embarrassing; but I generally evade any other answer than a little Laugh:—foolish enough, to be sure!—but I have no other resource.

Mr. Crisp said 'Well, certainly, 'tis a cut very much above any thing of the kind we have had lately; we have nothing new that will bear *any* comparison with it.'

I could hardly forbear *thanking* them all. Good God, how they would have stared! Mr. Burney, yesterday after Dinner, said 'Gentleman & Ladies, I'll propose a Toast: Then, filling his Glass, he Drank to 'The Author of Evelina!'

Had they *known* the Author was present, they could not have more civilly accepted the Toast: it was a bold kind of drollery in Mr Burney, for I was fain to Drink my own Health in a Bumper!—

August 3^d

I have an immensity to write!—

Susan has Copied me a Letter which Mrs. Thrale has written to my Father,[81] upon the occasion of returning

---

[80a] Cf. *Hamlet* V. ii. 292.

[81] HLT to CB, 22 July 1778 (Comyn), copy in SEB to FB *pmk* 23 July 1778 (Berg), *ED* ii. 249–50. A facsimile of HLT's original letter is in *DL* i between pp. 48 and 49. Verbal variations from FB's copy are indicated in the notes.

my mother 2 Novels by Mad^e Riccoboni:[82] it is so honourable to *me*, & so sweet in *her*, that I, also, must Copy it for my *faithful* Journal.

To Dr. Burney.[83]   July 22^d Streatham,[84]

Dear Sir,

I forgot to give you the Novels[85] in your Carriage, which I now send by Mr. Abingdon's.[86] Evelina certainly *excels* them far enough, both in probability of story, elegance of sentiment, & general power over the mind, whether exerted in humour or Pathos. Add to this, that Riccoboni is a veteran author, & all she ever can be, but I cannot tell what might not be expected from Evelina, was she to try her Genius at Comedy.—So far had I written of my Letter, when Mr. Johnson returned Home, full of the praises of the *Book* I had lent him, & protesting ∣ there[87] were passages in it which might do Honour to Richardson. We talk of it forever;—& he *feels* ardent after the *denouement*. He could not get *rid* of the Rogue, he said.—I lent him the 2^d Volume,—& he is now busy with the other.[88]—

You must be more a Philosopher, & less a Father than I wish you, not to be pleased with this Letter.—& the giving such pleasure yields to nothing but receiving it. Long, my dear Sir, may you live to enjoy the just praises of your Children! & long may they live to deserve & delight such a Parent! These are Things that you would

---

[82] Marie-Jeanne Laboras de Mézières (1714–92), m. (1735) Antonio Francesco Riccoboni. Her most recent novels were *Lettres d'Elisabeth Sophie de Vallière* (Paris, 1772), English translation, 1772, and *Lettres de My-Lord Rivers à Sir Charles Cardigan* (Paris, 1777), English translation, 1778.

[83] SEB's heading is 'Mrs Thrale to Dr Burney.' There is no such heading in the original.

[84] SEB's dateline is 'Wednesday 22^d Streatham'; HLT's is 'Wednesday 22: Streatham'.

[85] 'the novels home' (SEB); 'the Novels home' (HLT).

[86] Dancing master to the Thrales' daughters. Not further identified. See *Thraliana* i. 50; *TSP*, pp. 113, 182.

[87] 'that there' (SEB; HLT)

[88] 'other two' (HLT). This was probably emended on purpose by SEB, since there were only 3 volumes in all.

say in verse,[89] but poetry implies Fiction, & all this is naked truth.

My Compts. to Mrs. Burney, & kindest[90] wishes to all your Flock.—&c— —[91]

How sweet, how amiable in this charming Woman is her desire of making my dear Father satisfied with his scribbler's attempt! I do, indeed, feel the most grateful love for her.—But *Dr. Johnson's* approbation!—Good God, it almost *Crazed* me with agreeable surprise!—it gave me such a flight of spirits, that I Danced a Jigg to Mr. Crisp,[92] without any preparation, *music*, or explanation, to his no small amazement & diversion. I left him, however, to make his own comments, upon my friskiness, without affording him the smallest assistance.

Susan also writes me word,[93] that, when my Father went last to Streatham,[94] Dr. Johnson was not there, but Mrs. Thrale told him, that, when he gave her the 1st volume of Evelina, which she had lent him, he said 'Why Madam, why what a *charming* Book you lent me!' & eagerly enquired for the rest. He was particularly pleased with the Snow Hill scenes,—& said that Mr. Smith's *vulgar gentility* was *admirably pourtrayed*, | [xxxxx 1/2 *line*] & when Sir *Clement* joins them, he said there was a *shade of Character* prodigiously well marked.—Well may it be said, that the greatest minds are ever the most candid[95] to the inferior set! I *think* I should love Dr. Johnson for such lenity to a poor mere *Worm* in Literature, [even][96] if I were *not* myself the identical Grub he has obliged.

---

[89] An allusion to the occasional verses which CB had been addressing to HLT, most recently in June (on the month of June, beginning 'Thee! Month benign, devoid of ills' (Osborn; variant in Rylands).

[90] 'the kindest' (SEB; HLT). Before this sentence SEB omits: 'Give my Letter to my little Friend and a warm Invitation to come & eat Fruit while the Season lasts.'

[91] FB omits several more lines copied by SEB.

[92] 'around a large old mulberry tree' (*Mem.* ii. 149).

[93] SEB to FB, *c.*26 July 1778 (Barrett), *ED* ii. 251–4.

[94] On Sat. morning, 25 July.

[95] i.e., kindly, generous; an obsolete sense (*OED* s.v. candid 4).

[96] Inserted by FBA.

However, Susan has sent me a little Note which has really been less pleasant to me, because it has alarmed me for my future concealment. It is from Mrs. Williams,[97] an exceeding pretty poetess, who has the misfortune to be Blind, but who has, to make some amends, the honour of residing in the House of Dr. Johnson: for though he lives *almost* wholly at Streatham, he always keeps his Apartments in Town, & this Lady acts as mistress of his House.[98] Now for the Note,[99]

Mrs. Williams sends Compliments to Dr. Burney, & begs he will intercede with Miss Burney to do her the favour to lend her the reading of Evelina.
    July 25th

I was quite confounded at this request,—which proves that Mrs. Thrale has told Dr. Johnson of my secret, & that *he* has told Mrs. Williams, & that *she* has told the person, whoever it be, who she got to write the Note![1] —
    I instantly scrawled a hasty Letter[2] to Town, to entreat my Father would be so good as to write to her, to acquaint her with my earnest & unaffected desire to remain unknown, & so to prevent, at least any *further* propagation of this my poor mauled to pieces secret.
    And yet, though I am frightened at this affair, I am by no means insensible to the Honour which I receive from the certainty that Dr Johnson must have spoken very well of the Book, to have induced Mrs. Williams' to send to our House for it. She has known my Father, indeed, some years, but not with any intimacy:[3] & *I* Never saw

[97] Anna Williams (1706–83), poet. Totally blind since 1752, she took up residence that year in SJ's household. Her *Miscellanies in Prose and Verse* was published in 1766. See J. L. Clifford, *Dictionary Johnson* (New York, 1979), pp. 101, 265, and *passim*.
[98] SJ lived at No. 8 Bolt Court from 1776 until his death.
[99] The original note is missing. SEB did not send the note itself, but copied it in her letter to FB.
[1] Perhaps Miss Owen, who read to her (below, p. 63).
[2] Missing.
[3] CB first met her in 1758 (Lonsdale, p. 52).

her, though the perusal of her poems has often made me wish to be acquainted with her.[4]

I now come to last Saturday Evening [1 Aug.],—when my beloved Father came to Chesington,—in full Health, charming spirits, & all kindness, openness, & entertainment.

As soon as I was alone with him, he presented me a little parcel; it consisted of my new set of Evelina, which Mr. Lowndes sent to *Mr. Grafton*, & which are charmingly Bound.—He then most affectionately congratulated me upon it's great success, & communicated to me a thousand delightful things relative to it.

I enquired what he had done about Mrs. Williams? He told me he *went* to her, himself, at my desire, for if he had *written*, she could not *herself* have *read* a Note: she apologised very much for the liberty she had taken, & spoke highly of the Book, though she had only heard the 1st Volume, as she was dependant upon a Lady's good nature & Time for hearing *any* part of it: but she went so far as to say that 'his Daughter was certainly the first Writer in *that way*, now living:'—My Father then told her how much I was alarmed, & that *my muse was too shy* to bear the light: she promised to be careful & faithful, & assured him that she had not spoken of it to any body but Miss Owen, [5] the Lady who reads to her. In conclusion, she was pleased to express some desire to know me; & my Father told me he would take me to her some morning.

In his way hither, he had stopt ⌐to give Miss Thrale a Lesson⌐[6] at Streatham: & *he* settled with Mrs. Thrale | that he would call on her again in his way to Town, & carry *me* with *him*!—& Mrs. Thrale said 'We all long to know her.'—I have been in a kind of *twitter* ever since, for there seems something very formidable in the idea of Appearing as an *Authoress*! I *ever* dreaded it, as it is a Title which must raise more expectations than I have any chance of

[4] CB's copy of her *Miscellanies* is listed in *Lib.*, p. 63.

[5] Perhaps Margaret Owen, HLT's distant cousin and friend (see *EJL* ii. 224 and n. 26).

[6] This obliteration shows FBA's desire to sink her father's profession, making this visit seem a purely social one.

answering. Yet I am highly flattered by her invitation, & highly delighted in the prospect of being introduced to the Stretham society.

She sent me some very *serious advice* to write for the *Theatre*, as she says, I so naturally run into conversations, that Evelina absolutely & plainly points out that path to me: & she hinted how much she should be pleased to be 'Honoured with my Confidence'.

Oh dear Mrs. Thrale! I am *accablée* with such civilities! I begged to know of my Father if he had given her a hint to be more cautious: 'Why, said he, I told her of my visit to Mrs. Williams, & of your fright, & I think she will take that as an hint: however, she said 'If she does not take the greatest care & pains in the World, she *will* be found out & noticed, in spite of her modesty,—or, indeed, if she *does!*'—

But,—if I *do* go to Stretham, & can muster so much courage, I shall certainly speak earnestly to her not to spread my affair any further. My dear Father communicated all this intelligence, & a great deal more, with a pleasure that almost surpassed that with which I heard it: & he seems quite *eager* for me to make another attempt. He desired to take upon himself the communication to my Daddy Crisp; & as the affair is now in so many Hands, that it is possible *accident* | might discover it to him, I readily consented.

Sunday Evening [2 Aug.], as I was going into my Father's Room, I heard him say, 'the variety of characters,—the variety of scenes, & the *Language*,—why she has had very little Education but what she has given *herself*,— less than any of the others!'—& Mr. Crisp exclaimed 'Wonderful!—it's *wonderful!*'—I now found what was going forward, & therefore deemed it most fitting to decamp.

About an Hour after, as I was passing through the Hall, I met my Daddy.—His Face was all animation & archness,—he doubled his Fist at me, & would have stopt me, but I ran past him, into the Parlour.

Before supper, however, I again met him, & he would not suffer me to escape; he caught both my Hands, &

looked as if he would have looked me through,—& then exclaimed 'Why you little "Hell!"—you young Devil!— a'n't you ashamed to look me in the Face?—you *Evelina* you!—Why what a Dance have you led me about it!— Young Friend, indeed!—O you little "Hell Fire". What tricks have you served me!'—I was obliged to allow of his running on with these gentle appellations for I know not how long ere he could sufficiently compose himself, after his great surprise, to ask or hear any particulars "of the affair".—& then, he broke out every 3 instants with exclammations of astonishment at how I had found *Time* to write so much *unsuspected*, & how & where I had picked up such various materials.—& not a few Times did he, with *me*, as he had with my Father, ⎮ exclaim '*wonderful!*'— He has, since, made me read him all my Letters upon this subject. He said Lowndes would have *made an Estate* had he given me ⟨11⟩oo pounds for it, & that he *ought not* to have given less! 'You have nothing to do now, continued he, but to take your pen in Hand, for your Fame & reputation are made; & any Bookseller will snap at what you write.' I then told him that I could not but, *really*, & *unaffectedly* regret that the affair was spread to Mrs. Williams' & her Friends—'pho, said he, if those who are proper Judges of the affair think it right it should be known, why should you trouble yourself about it? *you* have not spread it, there can be no imputation of vanity fall to *your* share, & it cannot come out more to your Honour than through such a Channel as Mrs. Thrale.'

I found, soon after, that he had acquainted Mrs. Gast of the Transaction: & indeed I very freely told him how little I approved of that measure. 'Pshaw, cried he, it *must* be known,—so why not tell her at once? I bid her keep it secret at present.'

'*Must* be known? repeated I; yes, to be sure it must if every one thinks He has a right to tell one:'

However, it was too late to remonstrate though I charged him to extend his communication no further. & he took me to Mrs. Gast's room, & made me read to her all the Letters I had read to him. Mrs. Gast was quite in raptures at being so trusted, &, indeed, at the whole affair, & I almost thought she would have *worshipped* me, she was so much delighted to find I was authoress of a Book she had been so greatly pleased with ǀ but she has faithfully promised me that, from *her*, at least, it shall go no further.

London. August

I have now to write an account of the most *Consequential* Day I have spent since my Birth: namely, my Streatham Visit.

My good & dear Chesington Friends parted with me in the kindest manner, & with so much reluctance, that I was quite pained to leave them, though my stay had been so long that I grew impatient to return to my dear Father & sisters. Mrs. Gast, while I was Dressing, came into my Room, & told me she had a very great favour to request of me,—& I saw that her Eyes were filled with Tears. 'I *had* a sister,' she said,—'a sister who was one of the best of Women,[7]—she had every good quality under Heaven, & the most lovely, & universal philanthropy:—now for this dear sister I have some Time intended putting up a stone & some memorial of her Worth:—now, my sweet Fannikin, if *you* would write me a few Lines,—no matter *how* few,—to indicate her Character,—You would, indeed, most highly oblige me;—& I know nobody whose delicacy of mind,—so like the dear soul's own,—could so well do her Justice.'

I was both amazed & affected by this request. I was grieved to deny Mrs. Gast, but did not dare make such an attempt; &, to own the truth, as I did not *know* Mr[s.] Crisp, I think it a kind of *prostitution* of writing to give only hear-say praises in so solemn a manner. I was, therefore, obliged to assure her, that though her ǀ request did me infinite Honour, & give me infinite surprise, I could not venture at a Task for which I was so ill qualified.

---

[7] Mrs Gast's spinster sister, Ann Crisp, who had died in 1776 (*EJL* ii. 65 and n. 5).

She was a little disappointed, but told me she could not *quite* give it up.[8]

Our Journey to Streatham was the least pleasant part of the Day: for the Roads were dreadfully dusty,—& I was really *in the Fidgets* from thinking what my reception might be, & from fearing they would expect a less awkward & backward kind of person than I was sure they would find.

Mr. Thrale's House is white, & very pleasantly situated, in a fine Paddock.[9] Mrs. Thrale was strolling about & came to us as we got out of the Chaise. 'Ah, cried she, I hear Dr. Burney's Voice!—& you have brought your Daughter?—well, now you *are* good!' She then received me, taking both my Hands, & with a mixt politeness & cordiality, welcoming me to Streatham.

She led us into the House, & addressed herself almost wholly, for a few minutes, to my Father, as if to give me an assurance she did not mean to regard me as *a shew*, or to distress or frighten me by *drawing me out*. After wards, she took me up stairs, & shewed me the House: & said she had very much wished to see me at Streatham, & should always think herself much obliged to Dr. Burney for his goodness in bringing me, which she looked upon as a very great favour. But, though we were some Time to-gether, & though she was so very civil, she did not *hint* at my Book: & I love her much more than ever for her delicacy in avoiding a subject which she could ⏐ not but see would have greatly embarrassed me.

When we returned to the Music Room, we found Miss Thrale was with my Father. Miss Thrale is a very fine Girl, about 14 years of age, but cold & reserved, though full of knowledge & intelligence. She may, & I doubt not, *will* be as *learned* as her mother, but never half so amiable, *selon apparance*.

[8] She erected no memorial to her sister. Upon her death in 1791, she was buried next to her in Burford Church with a marble tablet commemorating them both as 'blessings to the poor and the ornaments of Society' (W. H. Hutton, *Burford Papers* (1905), p. 12).

[9] See the frontispiece to this vol.

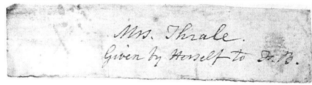

Mrs. Thrale.
Given by Herself to Dr. B.

4. A silhouette of Hester Lynch Thrale, given by her to Fanny Burney.
The identification is in Burney's hand.

Here the subject that was started was *Dick*,[10] who played truant at Winchester, & is now under the displeasure of Dr. Warton. Mrs. Thrale interests herself greatly for Dick, & spoke all sort of comforting things to my Father: &, when he expressed his vexation at the affair, 'Pho, said she, Boys *will* be naughty, there's nothing in that;—but let him be what he will, I sha'n't suffer the man who has such Daughters as Miss Burney to complain.'

'That's aside, said my Father, Laughing; Fanny must not hear that.'

In truth, I was employed in looking at Prints, & therefore affected not to attend.

'Ay, well, said Mrs. Thrale, she often, I doubt not, hears more praise than she believes, though not more than she deserves.

My Father, then, enquired after Mr. Thrale. 'Why, said she, my master is gone out on Horseback, with Mr Seward.'[11]

This Mr. Seward is a Young man of Fortune, who is a great favourite at Streatham. He is handsome, & very sensible & intelligent: but Mrs. Thrale told us, he had a very strange singularity of Disposition, for that, with real goodness of Heart, Benevolence & Generosity of Temper, he ⏑ always affected the utmost sourness, bluntness & moroseness. She added, that there was, at this Time, a poor man in great distress, & that, to her certain knowledge, he had insisted on lending him 100 pounds yearly, till his affairs were retrieved: '&, said she, he can never

[10] FB's half-brother, Richard Thomas Burney, not yet 10 years old. CB had persuaded HLT to encourage SJ to sponsor beautiful little 'Dick' as a candidate for admission to Winchester School, of which Joseph Warton was the headmaster. Warton, in a letter to SJ, 27 Jan. 1778 (Winchester Fellows' Library MS 129, printed Scholes i. 320–1), informed him that there could be no vacancy for Richard till after the next election (22 July), but offered 'to receive Dr Burney's Son into my House till a Vacancy happens.' SJ accompanied CB when he took his son to Winchester to meet Warton. Sometime later Richard had evidently run away, and as a consequence he was never admitted to Winchester. In Sept. CB wrote HLT regarding a new scheme to place Richard in Westminster School, where CB's father had once been a day scholar. This plan also came to naught. See *ED* ii. 286; *Mem.* i p. xii, ii. 81–2; *LCB* i. 241–2, 253–4. Additional information courtesy of Mr J. Hugh C. Reid, Kanata, Ontario.

[11] William Seward (1747–99) (*EJL* ii. 224).

hear the name of this man, without Tears; yet he pretends to a Character the very reverse, & aims at a kind of misanthropy.'

I have had *very* little conversation with this Gentleman, but I have seen him 3 or 4 Times. And I was much rejoiced in finding that no other Company was expected.

Soon after, Mrs. Thrale took me to the Library; ⌐& we left Miss Thrale to take her Lesson. I endeavoured to prevail upon her to return to them, & give me leave to find out some Book for my own amusement: but she would not go.⌐ She talked a little while upon common topics, & then,—at last,—she mentioned Evelina, calling it *'the Book of which I alone was ashamed.'* And ashamed enough I felt, in Conscience! & I began ⌐*poking* among⌐ the Books, in order to turn from her.

'Well, said she, it is a sweet pretty Book indeed! & Yesterday at supper we talked it all over, & discussed all your Characters; but Mr. Johnson's favourite is Mr. Smith!—he is *so* smart!—he declares the *fine Gentleman manqué* was never better drawn: & he acted—him all the Evening, saying *he was 'all for the Ladies! whatever was agreeable to the Ladies,'*[12] & so on; while *I* took up Madame Duval, & told them *I desired I might hear no more of such vulgar pieces of Fun!*[13]—But ⌐ Mr. Johnson repeated whole scenes by Heart!—I declare I was astonished at him!—O you can't imagine how much he is pleased with the Book;—he *'could not get rid of the Rogue'*, he told me.'

I could only Laugh & thank her: & express, though not very *audibly*, my surprise, & assure her I hardly knew *how* to credit flatteries so unexpected & so undeserved.

'But was it not droll, said she, that *I* should *recommend* it to Dr. Burney? & teize him, so innocently, to read it?'

In the midst of this conversation, Mrs. Thrale, from the Window, perceived Mr. Thrale, & called to him;— 'Mr. Thrale,' said she, 'if you will come hither, I can give

---

[12] At various points in the story, Mr Smith says 'I'm never so happy as in obliging the ladies' and 'one place is the same as another to me, so that it be but agreeable to the ladies' (*Evelina*, ed. E. A. Bloom (1968), pp. 179, 190: vol. ii, letters 11, 14).

[13] Ibid., pp. 220–1: vol. ii, letter 19.

you very great pleasure; I have a Young Lady to introduce to you whom you want very much to know.'

So! thought I, what, is he, too, acquainted with my frolic!—And I am sure, by her looks, & the earnest curiosity of her regards, that *Miss* Thrale was not ignorant of it. Heigh ho! how difficult is *secret keeping*!

Mr. Thrale came immediately, & was extremely civil to me. He is a very Tall, well looking man, & very well bred; but shy & reserved: however, he was attentively obliging to me all the Day.

I found, by the enquiries that followed of *if* & *when* they had seen me, that I, as well as my Book, had had the Honour to supply them with conversation the preceding Evening, & they had ⌜told &⌝ recollected all they knew of me. 'But, said Mr. Thrale, to his Wife, who was in a white muslin Jacket, I think you might as well have been better equipped to receive your Guests.' |

'And so I *would*, I assure You, answered she, if I had imagined Miss Burney would have thought at all the better of me for *Dress*; but I had no Notion it would be any recommendation to her.'

When he left us I prevailed upon Mrs. Thrale to let me amuse *myself*, & she went to obey her master's order & Dress. I then *prowled* about, to chuse some Book, & I saw, upon the Reading Table, Evelina;—I had just fixed upon a new Translation of Cicero's Laelius,[14] when the Library Door was opened, & Mr. Seward Entered. I instantly put away my Book, because I dreaded being thought *studious* & affected. He offered his service to find any thing for me, & then, in the same Breath, ran on to speak of the Book with which I had, myself, *favoured the World*! The exact Words he began with I cannot recollect, for I was actually confounded by the attack: I had not any idea that he knew of the affair; & his abrupt manner of letting me know he was *au fait* equally *astonished* & *provoked* me: how different from the delicacy of Mr. & Mrs. Thrale!—I was so much amazed, & so much displeased, that I could not

---

[14] *Laelius: or, an Essay on Friendship*, a translation by William Melmoth (1710–99) of Cicero's *De Amicitia*, was published by James Dodsley in 1777.

speak a word, & he then went on with some general praises, & said that I had hit off the *City manners* wonderfully.

I doubt not but he expected my thanks!—but I only stammered out something of my surprise to find the affair *so spread*, & then, with the coldest gravity, I seated myself, & looked another way.

It could not be very difficult for him, now, to perceive that he had wholly mistaken *his Game*, & that my *Greediness* for praise ˡ was by no means so *gluttonous* as to make me swallow it when so ill Cooked; but I fancy he imagined I should, of course, be delighted to hear my *own* Book mentioned with Compliments, & so he concluded I should, with much eagerness, Enter upon the subject. However, when he discovered his mistake, he spared no endeavours to repair it, for he Changed his Theme, & did not again ever go back to his first topic, notwithstanding he continued with me near 2 Hours, & never once suffered the Conversation to *flag*. Indeed, I was for some Time, so totally disconcerted by his abrupt attack, that I hardly knew what I answered him, but, by degrees I *tranquillised*, as I found he forbore distressing me any further, by such *Home* strokes; And I must do him the justice to own that I believe he was sorry himself that he had started the subject, when he saw how I received it.

He stayed, talking upon divers matters, till he was obliged to go & Dress for Dinner:—& then, before he left me, he offered his service to find me any Book;—I accepted his offer, ⌐& desired him to chuse,¬ as I did not know where to look, or for what. He spent no little Time ere he could satisfy himself, &, at last, he brought me a Book of Poems by Miss Aiken: I Laughed *inwardly* at this Choice, which seemed *a Bob at the Court*,¹⁵ but took it very chearfully, & said I had long wished to read them. ¹⁶

---

¹⁵ i.e., a taunt or jibe at the reigning 'Queen of Literature', FB. Writing poems was considered a more decorous occupation for a woman than writing novels. FB is probably echoing Bayes' line in Buckingham's *Rehearsal*, III.i: 'There's a bob for the court', referring to a jibe about courtiers not paying their debts.

¹⁶ FB mentions these poems in her Journal for 1774 (*EJL* ii. 21).

'But the doubt is, Ma'am, said he, whether they are her own writing.' *Another Bob*, perhaps, thought I! however, I felt too innocent of *that* to be hurt. I asked him who *was* suspected as Author? 'Why her Brother,[17]—they Live ln the same House.' Ah, thought I, how kindly willing ¦ is the World to make charitable constructions!

I then began reading, & he left the Room.

Mrs. Thrale soon after joined me: I wished much to have expostulated with her upon betraying me to Mr. Seward, but could not myself introduce the subject, & *she* never again led to it; I am sure she *spared* me from good nature, as she could not but observe how much more easy I was upon all other Topics.

The rest of the morning was all spent charmingly;—we went into the Music Room, & there joined Mr. & Miss Thrale, Mr. Seward & my Father.

When we were summoned to Dinner, Mrs. Thrale made my Father & me sit each side of her: I said that I hoped I did not take Dr. Johnson's place?—for he had not yet appeared. 'No, answered Mrs. Thrale, he will sit by you,— which I am sure will give him great pleasure.'

Soon after we were seated, this great man entered. I have so ⌐great⌐ a veneration for him, that the very sight of him inspires me with delight & reverence, notwithstanding the cruel infirmities to which he is subject; for he has almost perpetual convulsive ⌐motions⌐, either of his Hands, lips, Feet, knees, & sometimes of all together. However, the sight of them can never excite ridicule, or, indeed, any other than melancholy reflections upon the imperfections of Human Nature; for this ⌐man,⌐ who is the acknowledged ⌐Head of Literature⌐ in this kingdom, & who has the most extensive knowledge, the clearest understanding, & the greatest abilities of any Living Author,—has a Face the most ugly, a Person the most awkward, & manners the most singular, that ¦ ever were, or ever can be seen. But all that is unfortunate in his

---

[17] John Aikin (1747–1822), physician and author. He and his sister had together published *Miscellaneous Pieces in Prose* in 1773 (2nd edn., 1775), which no doubt encouraged the uncharitable rumour that he had ghost written the poems.

exterior, is so greatly compensated for in his *interior*, that I can only, like Desdemona to Othello, '*see his Visage in his mind*.'[18] His Conversation is so replete with instruction & entertainment, his Wit is so ready, & his Language at once so original & so comprehensive, that I hardly know any satisfaction I can receive, that is equal to listening to him.

Mrs. Thrale introduced me to him, & he took his place. We had a Noble Dinner, & a most elegant ⌐& delicious¬ Desert. Dr. Johnson, in the middle of Dinner, asked Mrs. Thrale what was in some little pies that were near him? 'Mutton, answered she, so I don't ask you to Eat any, because I know you despise it.'

'No, Madam, no; cried he, I despise *nothing* ⌐in its way¬ that is good of its sort:—but I am too proud *now* to Eat of it;—sitting by Miss Burney makes me very proud to Day!'

'Miss Burney, said Mrs. Thrale, Laughing, you must take great care of your Heart if Dr. Johnson attacks it!— for I assure you he is not often successless.'

'What's that you say, Madam? cried he, are you making mischief between the young lady & me already?'

A little while after, he Drank Miss Thrale's Health & mine; & then added—''Tis a terrible thing that we cannot wish young Ladies *well*, without wishing them to become Old Women!'

'But some people, said Mr. Seward, are old & young at the same Time, for they ⌐look¬ so well that they never look old.' |

'No, Sir, no; cried the Doctor, Laughing; that never yet was; You might as well say they are at the same Time Tall & short! I remember an Epitaph to that purpose, which is in— — —'

I have quite forgot *what*,—& also the *name* it was made upon; but the *rest* I recollect exactly;—

—— —— lies Buried here;
So *early* wise, so *lasting* fair,

---

[18] Cf. *Othello* I.iii.

That none, unless her Years You told,
Thought her a Child, or thought her Old.[19]

Mrs. Thrale then repeated some Lines in French, & Dr.
Johnson some more in Latin; an Epilogue of Mr. Garrick's
to Bonduca[20] was then mentioned, & Dr. Johnson said it
was a miserable peformance, & every body agreed it was
the worst he had ever made. 'And yet, said Mr. Seward,
it has been very much admired; but it is in praise of
English valour, & so I suppose the *subject* made it popular.'[21]

'I don't know, Sir, said Dr. Johnson, any thing about
the subject, for I could not read on till I came to it: I got
through half a dozen Lines, but I could observe no other
subject than eternal dullness. I don't know what is the
matter with David; I am afraid he is grown superannu-
ated, for his Prologues & Epilogues used to be incompa-
rable.'

'Nothing is so fatiguing, said Mrs. Thrale, as the Life
of a Wit: he & Wilks[22] are the 2 oldest men of their ages
I know, for they have both worn themselves out by being
eternally on the rack to give entertainment to others.'

'David, Madam, said the Doctor, *looks* much older than
he *is*; for his Face has had double the Business of any
other man's,—it is never at rest,—when he speaks one
minute, he has quite a different Countenance to what he
assumes the next; I don't believe he ever kept the same
look for half an Hour to gether in the whole course of
his Life; & such an eternal, restless, fatiguing play of the
muscles, must certainly wear out a man's Face much
before it's real Time.'

---

[19] The source of these lines has not been traced.
[20] George Colman the elder's alteration of Beaumont and Fletcher's tragedy
Bonduca opened at the Theatre Royal, Haymarket, on 30 July 1778 and was
published that day by Thomas Cadell. The text of the prologue (not the
epilogue), which was written by Garrick and spoken by Robert Palmer, can be
found in *GM* xlviii (1778), 432; *AR* xxi (1778), 199–200; and *The Poetical Works
of David Garrick* (1785; rpt. 1968), ii. 354. See *LS* 5, i. 185.
[21] The prologue addresses British fears of a French invasion, with a tribute
to the intrepidity of the late Lord Chatham (the elder William Pitt).
[22] John Wilkes (1725–97), politician and wit.

'O yes, cried Mrs. Thrale, we must certainly make some allowance for such *wear* & *Tear* of a man's Face.'[23]

The next Name that was started, was that of Sir John Hawkins: & Mrs. Thrale said 'Why now, Mr. Johnson, he is another of those whom you suffer nobody to abuse but yourself; why Garrick is one, too,—for if any other person speaks against him, you Brow-beat him in a minute!'

'Why, Madam, answered he, they don't know *when* to abuse him, & *when* to praise him; I will allow no man to speak ill of David that he does not *deserve*; & as to Sir John: why really I believe him to be an honest man at the *bottom*,—but to be sure he is penurious; & he is mean;—& it must be owned he has a degree of brutality, & a tendency to savageness, that cannot easily be defended.—'

We all Laughed, as he *meant* we should, at this curious manner of speaking in his *favour*; & he then related an anecdote that he *knew* to be true in regard to his meanness. He said that Sir John & he once ¦ belonged to the same Club;[24]—but that, as he *Eat no supper*, after the first night of his admission, he desired to be excused *paying his share*!

'And *was* he excused?'

'O yes,—for no man is angry at another for being inferior to himself! we all scorned him,—& admitted his plea. For my part, I was such a fool to pay my share for *Wine*, though I never tasted any. But Sir John was a most *unclubable* man!'[25]

[23] HLT may be alluding to a remark of SJ made to CB and later quoted by Boswell: '"Dr. Burney having remarked that Mr. Garrick was beginning to look old, he said, 'Why, Sir, you are not to wonder at that; no man's face has had more wear and tear'"' (*Life* ii. 410). Samuel Foote is credited with a similar observation (ibid., n. 1).

[24] Actually, Hawkins and SJ were members of both the Ivy Lane Club (founded by SJ in 1749) and the more famous Club (later known as the Literary Club), founded in 1764. SJ seems to be referring to the Ivy Lane Club.

[25] Hawkins's biographer observes: 'Perhaps Hawkins, through long habits of economy, had purposely dined at home to avoid the expense of a tavern dinner' (B. H. Davis, *A Proof of Eminence: The Life of Sir John Hawkins* (Bloomington, 1973), p. 40).

How delighted was I to hear this *master of Languages* so unaffectedly & sociably & good naturedly *make* Words, for the promotion of ⌐sport &⌐ humour!²⁶

'And this, continued he, reminds me of a Gentleman & Lady with whom I travelled once; I suppose I *must* call them so according to form, because they travelled in their own Coach & 4 Horses: But at the first Inn where we stopt, the Lady called for— — —a pint of Ale!—& when it came, quarrelled with the Waiter for not giving full measure!—Now *Madame Duval* could not have done a grosser thing!'

O how every body Laughed!—& to be sure *I* did not *glow* at all! nor *munch fast*,—nor look on my plate,—nor lose any part of my usual composure! But how grateful do I feel to this dear Dr. Johnson for never naming *me* and the *Book* as belonging one to the other, & yet making an allusion that shewed his *thoughts* led to it!—&, at the same Time, that seemed to justify the Character, as being *Natural*! But, indeed, the delicacy I met with from him & from all the Thrales was yet *more* flattering to me than all the praise with which I have ˡ *heard* they have Honoured my Book. And though *I* was displeased with Mr. Seward for his abruptness, which indeed most vilely disconcerted me, perhaps most others would have been *gratified* by it, & therefore –, upon further consideration, he appears less to blame in the affair than he did at first.

After Dinner, when Mrs. Thrale & I left the Gentlemen, we had a Conversation that to *me*, could not [but]²⁷ be delightful, as she was all good humour, spirits, sense & *agreeability*. Surely *I* may make words, when at a loss, if Dr. *Johnson* does.²⁸ However, I shall not attempt to *write* any more particulars of this Day,—than which I have never known a happier,—because the Chief subject that was started & kept up, was an invitation for me to Stretham, & a desire that I might accompany my Father

²⁶ The *OED* cites this famous coinage from FBA's text (Mrs Barrett's edn., 1842).

²⁷ Inserted by FBA.

²⁸ *OED* cites 'agreeability' as a fresh coinage by FB after 400 years of being obsolete. Chaucer had used the form ('agreablete') in his *Boethius, c*.1374.

thither next Week, & stay with them some Time. Now, though no subject could be so highly agreeable to me, it would yet appear to no advantage upon paper, & therefore I shall *abridge* it into saying that Mrs. Thrale was quite *violently* urgent, & assured my Father my *Health* might depend upon my returning again to spend some Time in the Country, for that, after such an illness, London might half kill me,—& a thousand other pleas, all uttered with the most good natured cordiality; & *Mr.* Thrale joined her request with great politeness;—but nothing was absolutely fixed. We left them at about 8 o'clock, & Mr. Seward, who Handed me into the Chaise, added *his* interest to the rest, that my Father would not fail to bring me. In short, I was loaded with civilities from them all. And my ride Home was equally happy with the rest of ¦ the Day, for my kind & most beloved Father was so happy in *my* happiness, & congratulated me so sweetly, that he could, like myself, think on no other subject. & he told me that, after passing through such a House as that, I could have nothing to fear. Meaning for my Book.

My felicity was rendered complete, when I returned Home, by relating all that had passed to my dear sisters, who were equally happy with myself, from their most affectionate simpathy. Indeed, Hetty, Susan & Charlotte take the same animated interest in *my* Affair, that they would do were it their own. Yet my Honours stopt not here;—for Hetty, who, with her sposo, was here to receive us;—told me she had, lately, met Mrs. Reynolds,[29] sister of Sir Joshua, at Mrs. Ord's; & that she talked very much, & very highly, of a new novel called *Evelina* [though without a shadow of suspicion as to the scribbler];[30] &, not contented with her own praise, said that Sir Joshua, who began it one Day when he was too much engaged to go on with it, was so much caught by it, that he could think of nothing else, & was quite *absent* all the Day, not knowing a word that was said to him: &, when he took it

---

[29] Frances Reynolds (1729–1807), painter.
[30] Inserted by FBA.

up again, found himself so much interested in it, that he sat up all night to finish it!—

One thing, however, was much less pleasing to me;—for it seems that to *Miss* Ord; who has bought the Book,—Hetty has betrayed the Writer!—& given her leave to tell her mother! Now though this was in *confidence,* I am quite displeased & concerned at it, as this perpetual spreading *can* have but one End! |

Sir Joshua, it seems, vows he would give 50 pounds to know the Author!—I have, also, heard of a Mr. Taylor,[31] a Gentleman of Reading, by the means of Charles, who has declared he *will* find him out!—This intelligence determined me upon going myself to Mr Lowndes, & finding out what sort of answers he made to such curious Enquirers as, I found, were likely to address him. But, as I did not dare trust *myself* to speak, for I felt that I should not be able to act my part well, I asked my mother to accompany me: ⌐she was pleased with the Task, &⌐ determined, as if from a mere idea, yet earnest curiosity, to *push the matter Home.*

We introduced ourselves by Buying the Book, for which I had a Commission from Mrs. Gast. Fortunately, Mr. Lowndes himself was in the shop; as we found by his air of consequence & authority, as well as his age; for I never saw him before. The moment he had given my mother the Book, she asked if he could tell her who wrote it? 'No. he answered, I don't know myself.'

'Pho, Pho, said she, you mayn't chuse to *tell*, but you *must* know.'

'I don't, indeed, Ma'am, answered he; I have no honour in keeping the secret, for I have never been trusted. All I know of the matter is, that it is a Gentleman of the other End of the Town.'

And *that*, thought I, is *more* than even the *Author* knows! but I took up an old Book, & turned my back, & seemed not to attend. |

---

[31] Perhaps the 'John Vickris Taylor, Esq.' who subscribed to C. Coates, *The History and Antiquities of Reading* (1802). See the list of subscribers, p. viii.

My mother made a thousand other enquiries, to which his answers were to the following effect. That, for a great while, he did not know if it was a man or a Woman; but now, he *knew that much*, & that he was a master of his subject, & well versed in the manners of the Times. 'For some Time, continued he, I thought it had been Horace Walpole's; for *he* once published a Book in this snug manner;[32] but I don't think it is now. I have often people come to enquire of me who it is;—but I suppose he will come out soon, & then, when the rest of the World knows it, *I* shall.—Servants often come for it from the other end of the Town, & I have asked them divers questions myself, to see if I could get at the Author; but I never got any satisfaction.'

Just before we came away, upon my mother's still further pressing him, he said, with a most important Face, 'Why, to tell You the truth, Madam, I have been informed that it is a piece of *secret History*; &, in that case, it will never be known!'

This was too much for me; I grinned irresistably; & was obliged to look out at the shop Door till we came away. How many ridiculous things have I heard upon this subject! I hope that, next, some particular *Family* will be fixed upon, to whom this *secret History* must belong! However, I am delighted to find myself so safe, & that if Sir Joshua, Mr. Taylor, Mrs. Cholmondley, or any other person, enquire of Mr. Lowndes,—they will not be much wiser for his intelligence. |

August.—

Again I have had the pleasure of a short Illness,—but as it lasted not long, I shall not dwell upon it's delights. I could not, therefore, accompany my dear Father to Streatham according to my invite, but as soon as I recovered, I

---

[32] Horace Walpole (1717–97), wit, connoisseur, and writer, published his *Castle of Otranto* (in Dec. 1764, though with the imprint date of 1765) as a supposed translation 'by William Marshal, Gent. from the Original Italian of Onuphrio Muralto' (title page of 1st edn.). As soon as the book succeeded, Walpole revealed his authorship (A. T. Hazen, *A Bibliography of Horace Walpole* (New Haven, 1948), pp. 52–3).

received a Note from Mrs. Thrale to tell me that if I was well enough, & *so forth*, she would call for me ⌐in her vis-a-vis & get me⌐ on Thursday,[33]—& I wrote her word[34] I could not *help* being well enough to have such an Honour.—

Mean Time, my Daddy Crisp wrote me word that he found all *secresy* was needless & therefore, that he had told Kitty, Mrs. Hamilton, ⌐& Patty Payne⌐—I was quite thunderstruck,—& quite provoked,—& wrote him word[35] how little I was pleased with his taking such a step, & that I desired he would, at least, tell them all how earnestly I wished the communication not to be further spread.

But *every body* longs to tell *one* body!—Susy & Charlotte have, indeed, been faithful,—& willingly shall I therefore again trust them;—my dear Father has always asked my *leave* for telling my poor woe begone secret,—but yet the failure of *one* is sufficient to overset all the discretion of all the rest.

As to what passed at Streatham,—I wrote all the Account to Susan,—& shall here insert the original.

[*Before the account to SEB, FBA has inserted the following AL fragment, single sheet 4to, 2 pp., from SC. She dates it '16. Aug. 1778' and annotates it as* 'In Answer to F.B.'s account [*missing*] of her first Streatham visit.']

My dear Fannikin

If I wish to hear the Sequel of the Day?—the Question is injurious—both because I warmly interest myself in whatever concerns a Fannikin; & likewise that I must else be *duller than the Fat Weed, that rots itself at Ease on Lethe's Wharf.*'[36]——there I had ye, *My Lad*[37]—The reception You met with at Streatham, tho' highly flattering, by no means surprizes me—every Article of it is most strictly your Due—You have fairly earn'd it; & if Your Host & Hostess, had given You less, they had defrauded You—

---

[33] Presumably 20 Aug.
[34] Both HLT's note and FB's reply are missing.
[35] This exchange is also missing.
[36] Cf. *Hamlet* I.v.
[37] A pet phrase of Kitty Cooke. See below, p. 172.

Flummery is a Commodity I do not much deal in; but on this Occasion I will subscribe with hand & heart to what I have now written.

After what I had heard of Mʳ Seward, I should not I own have expected such an Attack, as You describe from *him*.—what a Contrast between him, & Mʳˢ Thrale! I was once in a Situation somewhat like Yours, when I supp'd with Quin[38] at Bath, a good many Years ago—There was a *Fade*, Empty Fellow at Table with Us, who thought to be mighty civil to me on a former Occasion—Quin, observing, I did not much relish his insipid Trash, cried out, *Why, he is a Grocer, Man! Prythee, dont choak him with his own Figs!*—Mʳ Seward certainly merited such a rebuff. I desire you to be very minute in the remainder of the Day, particularly with regard to Dʳ Johnson, who, tho single *is himself an Host*.[39]—then I had ye again, my Lad!— Well, the Ice is now broke, & your perturbation ought to be in a great Measure at an end—When You went into the Sea at Tinmouth, did not You shiver & shrink at first, & almost lose your breath when the Water came up to your Chest?[40]—I suppose You afterwards learn'd to plunge in boldly overhead & Ears at once, & then Your pain was over—You must do the like now; & as the Public have thought proper to put You on a Cork Jacket, your Fears of drowning would be unpardonable. ⌐[xxxxx *12 lines*] Hetty & I are agreed on one alteration you must make in the new Edition—the Captain should call the French *Monseers*, the word should be so spelt, & not (as it is printed throughout) *Monsieurs*, as that spelling may mislead some Readers to pronounce it so[41]—As any further Concealment of the Author is ⟨impossible⟩⌐

[*The rest of the letter is missing.*]

---

[38] James Quin (1693–1766), actor.
[39] 'That happy Man whom *Jove* still honours most, / Is more than Armies, and himself an Host' (Pope, *Iliad* ix. 149–50).
[40] See *EJL* i. 302.
[41] This advice was followed. See *Evelina*, ed. E. A. Bloom (1968), pp. 51, 410.

Streatham,
[21] August [1778]
To Susanna Elizabeth Burney

AJL (Diary MSS I, paginated 715–22, foliated 1–4, Berg), Aug.
1778
4 single sheets 4to, 8 pp.
Annotated (by FBA): ✲ ✵ 1778

Streatham,
Augst

Indeed, my dearest Susy, I know not how to express
the *fullness of my contentment* at this sweet place,—All my
best expectations are exceeded, & you know they were not
very *little*;—if, when my dear Father comes, you & Mr.
Crisp were to come too,—I believe it would require at
least a *Day's* pondering, to enable me to form another
wish!

Our Journey was charming. At first, *to be shor*, I did not
fatigue my Lungs,—but the kind ⌐& sweet⌐ Mrs. Thrale
would give courage even to Edward, if she studied so to
do for she did not ask *me* questions, Catechise me upon
what I knew, or use any means to *draw me out*, but made it
her business to *draw herself out*, that is, to start subjects, to
support them herself, & to take all the weight of the
Conversation, as if it *behoved her* to find *me* entertainment.
But I am so much [xxxxx *1 word*] in love with her, [xxxxx
2–3 words] that I shall be obliged to run away from the
subject, or shall write of nothing else.

When we arrived here, Mrs. Thrale shewed me my
Room, which is an exceeding pleasant one, & then conducted me to the Library, there to divert myself while she
Dressed. I found Evelina upon the Reading Table, among
other Books. She is determined Mrs. Cholmondley shall
not out do her! however, I *hid* it under Books, for I
should *Die*, or *Faint* at least, if any body was to pick it up
innocently while I am here.

Miss Thrale soon joined me: & I begin to like her a *little* better, for she lays aside, now, a great deal of reserve which I had imagined *stuck too close* to her for dismission. I cannot say the same for *Mr.* Thrale, for he was neither well nor in spirits all Day. Indeed, he seems not to be a happy man, though he has every means of happiness in his power. ǀ

Dr Johnson was in the utmost good humour; he & Mrs. Thrale act as *of one accord* by me, for they both give me Time to *come to myself*, &, from a refinement of delicacy which is inexpressibly flattering, restrain themselves from speaking of my *Book*, till I am sufficiently *out of my fright* to hear them with more gratitude than embarrassment: for not once did they mention it all Day;—though the Conversation at Breakfast this morning convinced me it was not because they forgot it. Indeed, the *first* Day, forgetfullness *could not* be the case, whether they liked the Book, or only Laughed at it, for the sight of me *must remind* them of it.

There was no Company at the House all Day.

After Dinner, I had a delightful stroll with Mrs. Thrale;—we walked round the Paddock, rested upon Chairs to chat at our ease, & did not return to the House till we had a summons to Tea. She gave me a list of all her *good neighbours* in the *Town* of Streatham, & said she was determined to take me to see Mr. Tattersall,[42] the Clergyman, who was a Character I could not [but][43] be diverted with, for he had so furious, & so absurd a rage for Building, that, in his Garden, he had as many Temples, & summer Houses, & statues, as in the Gardens of Stow,[44] though he had so little Room for them, that they

---

[42] The Revd James Tattersall (*c.*1712–84), MA (Cantab.), 1742; Rector of St Leonard's, Streatham (1755–84) and of St Paul's, Covent Garden (1754–5, 1758–84).

[43] Inserted by FBA.

[44] Stowe, the famous seat of Ld. Temple in Buckinghamshire, praised by Pope in his *Epistle to Burlington.*

all seemed tumbling one upon another.[45] She told me, also, of another curious Family, the master of whom, when my Father accompanied her to his House, said to him—'Dr. Burney, do you know this morning I killed a *wanking Wiper?*'[46] & she regretted that she *had* made her visit to him, & could not *treat* me with seeing him. In short, she was all unaffected drollery, & sweet good humour. And she spoke very *pretty* of *you*,—said she never saw you look so well,—'*Well*, she repeated, I declare she looked quite beautiful!—& Miss Charlotte is vastly like Dick,—she & Dick have no | *London air* in their Faces,— they might either of them sit for the Picture of Health.'

At Tea we all met again, & Dr. Johnson was gaily sociable: He gave a very droll account of the Children of Mr Langton,[47] 'Who, he said, might be very good Children, if they were let alone; but the Father is never easy when he is not making them do some thing which they can *not* do; they must repeat a Fable,—or a speech,—or the Hebrew alphabet;—& they might as well *Count Twenty*, for what they know of the matter: however, the *Father* says *half*, for he *prompts* every other Word. But he could not have chosen a man who would have been less entertained by such means.'

'I believe not! cried Mrs. Thrale; nothing is more ridiculous than ⌐people's⌐ cramming their Children's nonsence down other people's Throats![48] I keep mine as much out of the way as I can.'

---

[45] 'Mr Tattersall ... diverts himself with making absurd Devices to put up in his Garden:—as Root Houses, Harlequins, Shellwork Baubles, & various Follies, till the Place looks like the Spaniard's at Hamstead or Don Saltero's at Chelsey' (*Thraliana* i. 381).

[46] i.e., 'a very large viper'. *Whanking* is a Yorkshire term, while a *w* pronunciation of *v* occurs in other provincial dialects (*EDD*).

[47] Bennet Langton (*c.*1737–1801), Greek scholar and SJ's close friend, m. (1770) Mary née Lloyd (*c.*1743–1820), Dowager Countess of Rothes. By 1778, they had 5 children: George (1772–1819), Mary (1773–96), Diana (1774–1811), Jane (1776–1854), and Elizabeth (1777–1804). See *GM* lxxxi[2] (1811), 593; IGI.

[48] In Aug. 1777 HLT attended a dinner party given by Sir Joshua Reynolds where the 2 eldest Langton children 'playd and prattled and suffer'd nobody to be heard but themselves ... Langton & his Wife with a triumphant Insensibility kissed their Children and listened to nothing with Pleasure but what they said' (*Thraliana* i.108–9). 'Very troublesome' the children were 'with their prattle,

'Your's, Madam, answered he, are in *nobody's* way; no Children can be better managed, or less troublesome; — but *your* fault is, a too great perverseness in [not]⁴⁹ allowing any body to give them any thing. Why should they not have a Cherry, or a Gooseberry ⌐given them?⌐

'Because they are sure to return such Gifts by wiping their Hands upon the Giver's Gown, or ⌐apron,⌐ & nothing makes Children more offensive: People only make the Offer to please the *Parents* & they wish the poor Children at Jerico⁵⁰ when they accept it:'

'But, Madam, it is a great deal *more* offensive to refuse them; let those who make the offer, look to their own Gowns ⌐& Aprons,⌐ for when *you* interpose, they only wish *You* at Jerico.'

'It is difficult, said Mrs. Thrale, to please every body!'

Indeed, the freedom with which Dr. Johnson condemns whatever he disapproves, is astonishing! & the strength of Words he uses would, to most people, be intollerable; but Mrs. Thrale seems to have a sweetness of Disposition that equals All her other excellencies, & far from making a ǀ point of vindicating herself, she generally receives his admonitions with the most respectful silence. But I *fear* to say all I think at present of Mrs. Thrale, — lest some *flaws* should appear by & by, that may make me think differently: — & yet, why should I not indulge the *now*, as well as the *then*, since it will be with so *much* more pleasure? — In short, my dear Susy, I do think her *delightful*: she has *Talents* to create admiration, — *Good humour* to excite Love, *Understanding* to give Entertainment, — & a *Heart* which, like my dear Father's, seems already fitted for another World! My own knowledge of her, indeed, is very little for such a Character — but all I have *heard*, & all I *see*, so well agree, that I *won't* prepare myself for a future disappointment.

every word of which their Papa repeated in order to explain' (HLT to SJ, 13 Aug. 1777, in SJ, *Letters*, ii. 193). See also *Life* iii. 28, 128.

⁴⁹ Inserted by FBA.

⁵⁰ 'A place far distant and out of the way' (*OED*, s.v. Jericho). David bade his servants to tarry at Jericho till their beards were grown (2 Samuel 10:5).

But to return; Mrs. Thrale then asked whether Mr. Langton took any better care of his affairs than formerly?

'No, Madam, cried the Doctor, & never will; he complains of the ill effects of *habit*, & rests contentedly upon a *Confest indolence*. He told his Father[51] himself that he had *no turn to oeconomy*;—but a Thief might as well plead that he *had no turn to Honesty*.

Was not that excellent?

At Night, Mrs. Thrale asked if I would have any thing? I answered *no*: but Dr. Johnson said '*yes*;—she is used, Madam, to suppers;—she would like an Egg or two, & a few slices of Ham,—or a *Rasher*,—a Rasher, I believe, would please her better.'

How ridiculous! however, nothing could persuade Mrs. Thrale not to have the ⌜Cloath⌝ laid: & Dr. Johnson was so facetious, that he challenged Mr. Thrale to get Drunk!—'I wish, said he, my master would say to me, Johnson, if you will oblige *me*; you will call for a Bottle of Toulon, & ᴵ then we will set to it. Glass for Glass, *till* it is done;—& after that, *I* will say, Thrale, if you will oblige *me*, You will call for *another* Bottle of Toulon, & then we will set to it, Glass for Glass, till *that* is done: & by the Time we should have Drunk the 2 Bottles, we should be so happy, & such good Friends, that we should fly into each other's arms, & *both together* call for the Third!'

I Eat nothing, that they might not again use such a Ceremony with me. Indeed their late Dinners *forbid* suppers; especially as Dr. Johnson *made* me Eat cake at Tea, for he held it till I took it, with an odd, or absent complaissance.

He was extremely comical after supper, & would not suffer Mrs. Thrale & me to go to Bed for near a Hour after we made the motion. The Cumberland Family were discussed; Mrs. Thrale said that *Mr.* Cumberland[52] was a very *amiable* man in his own House; but as a *Father* mighty simple; which accounts for the ridiculous conduct &

[51] Bennet Langton (1696–1769), of Langton, nr. Spilsby, Lincs.
[52] Richard Cumberland (1732–1811), dramatist.

manners of his Daughters,[53] concerning whom we had much talk, & were all of a mind, for it seems they used the same rude stare to Mrs. Thrale that so much disgusted *us* at Mrs. Ords:[54] she says that she really concluded something was wrong, & that, in getting out of the Coach, she had given her Cap some *unlucky Cuff,* by their merciless staring. & I told her that *I* had *not* any doubt, when I had met with the same *attention* from them, but that they were Calculating the exact cost of all my Dress. Mrs. Thrale then told me that, about 2 years ago, they were actually *Hissed out of the Play House,* on account of the extreme height of their Feathers!—& we both exclaimed that it must be a disgrace never to be forgotten.

Dr. Johnson instantly composed an *extempore Dialogue* between himself & Mr. Cumberland upon this subject, ' in which *he* was to act the part of a *provoking Condoler;*— 'Mr. Cumberland, I should say, how *monstrously ill bred* is a play House Mob! how I pitied *poor* Miss Cumberlands about that affair!' 'What affair? cries he, for he has tried to forget it: 'Why, says I, that unlucky accident they met with some Time ago.' 'Accident? what accident, Sir?— Why, you know, when they were Hissed out of the Play House,—You remember the Time—Oh, the English mob is most insufferable!—they are Boors,—& have no manner of Taste!'

Mrs. Thrale accompanied me to my Room.

Now for this morning's Breakfast.

Dr. Johnson, as usual, came last into the Library: he was ⌐quite⌐ in high spirits, & full of mirth & ⌐sport⌐. I had the Honour of sitting next to him: & now, all at once, he flung aside his reserve, thinking, perhaps, that it was Time *I* should fling aside mine!

Mrs. Thrale told him that she intended taking me to Mr. Tattersall's: 'So You ought, Madam, cried he, 'tis your Business to be *Cicerone* to her:' Then, suddenly he

---

[53] Elizabeth (*c.*1760–1837), m. (1782) Ld. Edward Charles Cavendish Bentinck (1744–1819); and Sophia, m. 1 (1791) William Badcock (*c.*1773–1802), m. 2 (1802) Mr Reece (*GM* lii (1782), 598; lxxii[1] (1802), 471; lxxii[2] (1802), 1223; cvii[2] (1837), 548; IGI).

[54] This visit is not otherwise recorded.

snatched my Hand, & kissing it;—*true 'pon Honour*! he added, 'Ah! they will little think what a *Tartar* you carry to them!'

'No, that they won't! cried Mrs. Thrale; Miss Burney looks so meek, & so quiet,—nobody would suspect what a comical Girl she is:—but I believe she has a great deal of *malice* at Heart.'

'Oh she's a Toad!—cried the Doctor, Laughing,—a sly Young Rogue! with her Smiths & her Branghtons!'

'Why, Mr. Johnson, said Mrs. Thrale, I hope you are very well this morning! if one may judge by Your spirits & good humour, the Fever you threatened us with is gone off.'

He had complained that he was going to be ill last night. 'Why no, Madam, no, answered he, I am not yet well; I could not sleep at all;—there I lay, restless & uneasy, & thinking | all the Time of Miss Burney!— Perhaps I have offended her, thought I, perhaps she is angry;—I have seen her but once, & I talked to her of a *Rasher*!'—Were You angry?'

I think I need not tell you my answer.

'I have been endeavouring to find some excuse, continued he, so, as I could not sleep, I got up, & looked for some *authority* for the word,—& I find, Madam, it is used by *Dryden*: in one of his Prologues, he says—

'And snatch a homely *Rasher* from the Coals.'[55] So you must not mind me, Madam,—I say strange things, but I mean no harm.'

I was almost afraid he thought I was *really* Ideot enough to have taken him seriously; but, a few minutes after, he put his Hand on my arm, & shaking his Head, exclaimed 'O, You are a sly little Rogue!—What a *Holbourn Beau* have you drawn!'

'Ay, Miss Burney, said Mrs. Thrale, the *Holbourn Beau* is Mr. Johnson's favourite;—& we have *all* your Characters by Heart, from Mr. Smith up to Lady Louisa.'

[55] The prologue to *All for Love*, l. 34 ('the homely' in the original). SJ is facetiously begging FB's pardon for using such a 'low' word on short acquaintance. In his *Dictionary* he cites a similar line by William King, a different passage from Dryden, and Shakespeare (*The Merchant of Venice*).

'O, Mr. Smith, Mr. Smith is the Man! cried he, Laughing violently, Harry Fielding *never* drew so good a Character!—such a fine *varnish* of low politeness!—such a *struggle* to appear a Gentleman!—Madam, there is *no* Character better drawn *any* where—in *any* Book, or by *any* Author.'

⌐Lord,⌐ Susy!—I almost poked myself under the Table: never did I feel so ⌐queer⌐ a confusion since I was Born! But he added a great deal *more*,—only I cannot recollect his exact words, & I do not chuse to give him *mine*.[56]

'Come, come, cried Mrs. Thrale, we'll torment her no more about her Book, for I see it *really* plagues her. I own I thought for a while it was only affectation, for I'm sure if the Book was mine I should wish to hear of nothing else. But we shall teach her in Time how proud she ought to *be* of such a performance.'

'Ah, Madam, cried the Doctor, be in no haste to teach her | *that*,—she'll speak no more to *us* when she knows her own weight.'

'O but, Sir, cried she, if Mr. Thrale has his way, she will become our *Relation*, & then it will be hard if she won't acknowledge us.'

You may think I stared—but she went on.—

'Mr. Thrale says nothing would make him half so happy as giving Miss Burney to Sir John Lade.'[57]

Mercy! what an exclamation did I give! I wonder you did not hear me to St. Martin's Street.

'Mr. Thrale says Miss Burney seems ⌐the most⌐ formed to draw a Husband to herself, by her humour when gay, & her ⌐goodness⌐ when serious, than almost any body he ever saw.'

'He does me much honour, cried I,—though I cannot say I much enjoyed *such* a proof of his good opinion, as giving me to such a wretch as Sir John Lade: but Mr.

[56] Further evidence of the fidelity of FB's reporting (see *EJL* ii. 14 n. 34).

[57] Thrale's spendthrift and profligate nephew Sir John Lade (1759–1838), 2nd Bt, son of Sir John Lade (*c.*1731–59), MP, and Anne, Lady Lade, née Thrale (*c.*1733–1802), Thrale's sister. SJ addressed his satiric 'Short Song of Congratulation' to Sir John on his reaching his majority in 1780. He later married the notorious Laetitia Darby (d. 1825), supposed to have been the mistress of Jack Rann, the highwayman.

Thrale is both his Uncle & his Guardian, & thinks, perhaps, he would do a mutual good office, in securing *me* so much money, & his Nephew a decent Companion,— O if he knew how *little* I require with regard to money, how *much* to even *bear* with a Companion!—But *he* was not brought up with such folks as my Father, my Daddy Crisp & my Susan, & does not know what indifference to all things but good society such people as those inspire.

'My master says a very good speech, cried the Doctor, if Miss Burney's Husband should have any thing in common with herself; but I know not how we can level her with Sir John Lade,—unless she would be content to put her Virtues & Talents in a scale against his thousands: & poor Sir John ⌐must¬ give *cheating weight* even then! However, if we bestow such a prize upon him, he shall settle his whole Fortune on her.'

Ah, thought I, I am *more* mercenary than *you* fancy me, for not even that would bribe me high enough! But the most offensive thing I know of rich people is that they | 58

58   Streatham,
                    23–[30] August [1778]

To Susanna Elizabeth Burney

AJL (Diary MSS I, paginated 723–54, Berg), Aug. 1778
16 single sheets 4to, 32 pp.
Annotated (by FBA): ✲ ✲

Sunday, Aug. 23^d

I was obliged, my dear Susy, to send You a strange unfinished scrawl this morning, for, I have now very little Time to myself, & had not been able to get on with my Journal: however, I will keep one *in Hand*, & write at it as I can.

---

58 FB probably meant to conclude with something like 'always think that everyone has his price'. As she explains in her next to SEB, she had to send this journal unfinished.

To proceed, therefore. Before Dr. Johnson had finished his *Eloge*, I was actually on the *Ground*, for there was no standing it,—or *sitting* it, rather: & Mrs. Thrale seemed delighted for me: 'I assure You, she said, *Nobody* can do your Book more justice than Mr. Johnson does: & yet, do you remember, Sir, how unwilling you were to read it?— he took it up, just looked at the first Letter, & then put it away, & said *I don't think I have any Taste for it!*—but when he was going to Town, I put it into the Coach with him,— & then, when he came Home, the very first words he said to me were Why Madam! This Evelina is a *charming Creature!*—& then he teized me to know who she married, & what became of her,—& I gave him the rest. For my part, I used to read it in Bed, when I laid in,[59] & could not part with it:—I Laughed at the second, & I cried at the Third,—but what a trick was that of Dr. Burney's, never to let me know whose it was till I had read it!— Suppose it had been something I had not liked!—O, it was a vile trick!'

'No, Madam, not at all! cried the Doctor, for, in that case, you would *never* have known;—all would have been safe, for he would niether have told *you* who wrote it, nor Miss Burney what you said of it.'

Some Time after, the Doctor began Laughing to himself, & then, suddenly turning to me, he called out '*Only think! Lord, Polly! Miss has Danced with a Lord!*'[60]

[xxxxx *5 words*] 'Ah, poor Evelina! cried Mrs. Thrale,— I see her *now* by Kensington Gardens,—what she must have suffered! Poor Girl! what *fidgets* she must have been in! | & I *know* Mr. Smith, too, very well;—I always have him before me at the Hampstead Ball, Dressed in a white Coat, & a Tambour waistcoat, worked in Green silk;— poor Mr. Seward! Mr. Johnson made him *so* mad t'other Day!—'Why Seward, said he, how *smart* you are Dressed!— why you only want a *Tambour waistcoat* to look like Mr. Smith!' But *I* am very fond of Lady Louisa; I think her

[59] HLT's 12th and last child, Henrietta Sophia, was born at Streatham on 21 June. Only 4 of her other children were still alive at this time. Henrietta Sophia died less than 5 years later (*TSP*, p. xii).
[60] *Evelina*, vol. ii, letter 23.

as well drawn as any character in the Book; so fine, so affected, so languishing!—&, at the same Time, so insolent!'

She then ran on with several of her speeches.

Some Time after, she gave Dr. Johnson a Letter from Dr. Jebb, concerning one of the Gardeners who is very ill. When he had read it, he grumbled violently to himself, & put it away with marks of displeasure.

'What's the matter, Sir? said Mrs. Thrale?—do you find any fault with the Letter?'

'No, *Madam*,—the Letter's well enough, if the man knew how to write his own name,—but it moves my indignation to see a man take pains to appear a Tradesman. Mr. Branghton would have written his name with just such Beastly flourishes.'

'Ay, well, said Mrs. Thrale, he is a very agreeable man & an excellent physician, & a great favourite of mine & so he is of Miss Burney's.'

'Why I have no objection to the man, Madam, if he would write his name as he ought to do.'

'Well, it does not signify, cried Mrs. Thrale, but the *commercial* fashion of writing gains Ground every Day, for all Miss Burney abuses it with her Smiths & her Branghtons,—does not the great Mr. Pennant[61] write, like a Clerk, without any pronouns?—& does not every body flourish their names till nobody can read them?'

After this, they talked over a large party of Company who are invited to a formal & grand Dinner for next Monday [31 Aug.], & among others, Admiral Montague[62] was mentioned;—the Doctor, turning to me, with a Laugh,

---

[61] Thomas Pennant (1726–98), traveller, naturalist, and writer, was HLT's second cousin once removed (see *Thraliana* ii. 965 n. 4). He does seem to have dropped the occasional pronoun when writing in haste. For example, his letter to John Calder, 27 Apr. 1780, begins: 'It gives me great concern to find my time so taken up in the short stay I make here, as to prevent me thanking you in person for your obliging favour; and am [*sic*] sorry that I can be of no use in your design' (Nichols, *Lit. Ill.* iv. 838).

[62] John Montagu (1719–95), Vice-Adm. (1776), later Adm. of the Blue (1782) and of the White (1787). He was the first captain under whom JB served (as a captain's servant in 1760). See *EJL* i. 39 n. 13.

said: 'You must mark the old sailor, Miss Burney;—he'll be a *Character*.'

'Ah! cried Mrs. Thrale, who was going out of the Room, how I wish You would hatch up a Comedy between you!— do, fall to work!—'

A pretty proposal!—to be sure Dr. Johnson would be very proud of such a fellow Labourer!

As soon as we were alone together, he said 'These are as good people as you can be with!—you can go to no better House,—they are all good nature,—nothing makes them angry.'

As I have always heard, from my Father, that every Individual at Streatham spends the morning *alone*, I took the first opportunity of absconding to my own Room, & there I amused myself in Writing to my dear Susan till I *tired*. About Noon, when I went into the Library *Book Hunting*, Mrs. Thrale came to me; 'O la, cried she, I have been looking for you; how soon did you & Mr. Johnson part?—have you begun your Comedy?'

And then, she proceeded to give me her *serious advice* to actually set about one; she said it was her opinion I *ought* to do it the moment she had finished the Book; she stated the advantages attending Theatrical writing, & promised to *ensure* me success. 'I have asked Mr. *Johnson*, added she if he *did* not think You could write a Comedy,— & *he* said *Yes*!'

'O Ma'am, cried I, think of the *poor* Miss Cumberlands!—it would be *my* turn to be *Hissed*; & to be *condoled* with then!'

However, she has frequently *pressed* me to it since, nay, she declared to me *she should never be at rest till I did*.

Indeed since the Ice *has* been broken, almost every thing that is said has some reference either to Evelina, or to future plans which they have all formed for me:—so that, to enumerate them would be to write every thing that passes. |

We had then a very *nice* confab about various Books;— & exchanged opinions & imitations of Barretti: she told me many excellent Tales of him, & I, in return, related *my* stories, &, I assure you, we were very *jocose*. She is so good humoured & so unaffected, that I begin to cast aside all my fear of her. Indeed, her Behaviour to me is so sweet, that she won't *suffer* me to fear her.

She gave me a long & very interesting account of Dr. Goldsmith, who was intimately known here but, in *speaking* of the Good Natured Man,[63] when I extolled my favourite *Croaker*, I found that admirable Character was a downright Theft from Johnson!—Look at No: [59] Vol. [2] of the Rambler,[64] & you will find *Suspirius* is the man, & that not merely the *idea*, but the *particulars* of the Character, are all stolen thence![65]

While we were yet reading this Rambler, Dr. Johnson came in: We told him what we were about. 'Ah! Madam, cried he, Goldsmith was not *scrupulous*;—but he would have been a great man, had he known the real value of his internal resources.'

'Miss Burney, said Mrs. Thrale, is ⌐very¬ fond of the Vicar of Wakefield: & so am I;—don't *You* like it, Sir?'

'No, Madam; it is very faulty; there is nothing of *real* life in it,—& very little of *Nature*. It is a mere fanciful performance.' He then seated himself upon a sopha, & calling to me, said 'Come,—*Evelina*,—come & sit by me,—' I obeyed;—& he took me almost in his arms,—that is, *one* of his arms, for *one* would go 3 times round me,—&, half laughing, half serious, he charged me *to be a good Girl!*

'But, my dear, continued he, with a very droll look, what makes you so fond of the *Scotch*?—I don't like you

---

[63] Goldsmith's first play, which opened 29 Jan. 1768, at Covent Garden (*EJL* i. 12 n. 31). Croaker, the guardian to the heroine Miss Richland, is a fretful, melancholic humour character, 'always complaining and never sorrowful' (I.i). SJ, who wrote the prologue, praised the play as 'the best comedy that had appeared since "The Provoked Husband"' and added 'that there had not been of late any such character exhibited on the stage as that of Croaker' (*Life* ii. 48).

[64] The issue of 9 Oct. 1750. FB left blank spaces for the number and volume, but did not supply them. Her father owned the 1752 collected 6-vol. edn. (*Lib.*, p. 28), to which she is presumably referring.

[65] To Boswell's observation that Croaker 'was the Suspirius of his Rambler', SJ replied that 'Goldsmith had owned he had borrowed it from thence' (*Life* ii. 48).

for *that*;—I hate the Scotch, & so must you. I wish Branghton had sent the Dog to jail!—[66]

'Why, Sir, said Mrs. Thrale, don't you remember he says he would, but that he should *get* nothing by it?'[67] |

'Why ay, true, cried the Doctor, see-sawing very solemnly, that, indeed, is some palliation for his forbearance.—But I must not have you so fond of the Scotch, my little Burney,—make your Hero what you will, but a *Scotch man*. Besides, You talk Scotch,—you say *the one*,—my dear, that's not English,—Never use that phrase again.'

Now was not this *extremely* good in him? Who would not have concluded the Book must have *abounded* in Errors too widely spread, & too closely weaved into the general work, to allow of his instructing me in any *one*?

'O, cried I, I have written *any* thing that is *ignorant*, but I did not *mean* to be only *Scotch*.'

'Perhaps, said Mrs. Thrale, it may be used in Macartney's Letter,[68] & then it will be a *propriety*.'

'No, Madam, no! cried he, You *can't* make a Beauty of it!—it is in the 3ᵈ Volume;[69]—put it in *Macartney's* Letter & Welcome!—that, or *any thing* that is nonsense.'

'Why surely, cried I, the poor man is used ill enough by the Branghtons!'

'But Branghton, said he, only hates him because of his wretchedness,—poor fellow!—But, my dear love, how *should* he ever have Eaten a good Dinner before he came to England?'

And then he Laughed violently at Young Branghton's idea.[70]

'Well, said Mrs. Thrale, I always liked Macartney,—he is a very pretty Character, & I *took to him*, as the folks say.'

'Why, Madam, answered he, I like Macartney myself!—Yes, poor fellow, I liked the *man*,—but I love not the *Nation*.'

[66] FB added: 'That Scotch Dog, Macartney.'
[67] Vol. ii, letter 13.
[68] Vol. ii, letter 20.
[69] Vol. iii, letter 20. In the 2nd edn. FB emended the phrase from 'the one you had designed' to 'the letter you had designed' (*Evelina*, ed. E. A. Bloom (1968), pp. 387, 420).
[70] Vol. ii, letter 13.

And then he proceeded, in a dry manner, to make at once sarcastic reflections on the Scotch, & flattering speeches to *me*, for ⌐the man's⌐ firing at the National insults of young Branghton, his stubborn resolution in not owning, even to his bosom Friend, his wretchedness of poverty, & his fighting at last for the Honour of his *Nation*,[71] when he resisted all other provocations, he said were all extremely *well marked.* ‖

We stayed with him till just Dinner Time, & then we were obliged to run away & Dress: but Dr. Johnson called out to me, as I went. 'Miss Burney, I must settle that affair of the *Scotch* with You at our leisure!'

At Dinner we had the Company,—or, rather, the *presence*, for he did not speak two words, of Mr. Embry,[72] the Clergyman, I believe, of Streatham. And afterwards, Mrs. Thrale actually took the trouble to go with me to the Tattersalls.[73] Dr. Johnson, who has a love of social converse that nobody, without Living under the same Roof with him would suspect, quite *begged* us not to go till he went to Town; but as we were Hatted & ready, Mrs. Thrale only told him she rejoiced to find him so *Jealous of our Companies*, & then away we whisked,—she, Miss Thrale, & my Ladyship.

I could write some tolerable good Sport concerning this visit, but that I wish to devote all the Time I can snatch for writing, to recording what passes *here*;—Themes of mere ridicule offer *every* where.

We got Home late, & had the Company of Mr. Embry & of Mr. Rose Fuller[74] a Young man who Lives at

---

[71] Vol. ii, letter 20.

[72] Mr Embry was a clergyman who kept a school at Streatham and who was dead by 1821 (*Thraliana* i. 101; *Life* iii. 248, 518; *DL* vi. 398). Since his fellow Streatham divine Mr Tattersall was also Rector of St Paul's, Covent Garden (above, p. 84 n. 42), he is probably to be identified with the Revd Edward Embry (*c.*1745–1817), who was Curate of St Paul's, 1780–1810, and Rector, 1810–17 (*GM* lxxx[1] (1810), 482; lxxxvii[1] (1817), 281).

[73] Mr Tattersall and his 2nd wife (m. 1767) Elizabeth, née Critchlow (*c.*1725–1803) (*GM* xxxvii (1767), 563; lxxiii[1] (1810), 599; *JL* xi. 207 n. 11).

[74] Rose Fuller (1748–1821), younger son of Thomas Fuller (1715–80), London merchant (*GM* l (1780), 103; xci[2] (1821), 478; IGI; W. Berry, *Pedigrees of ... Sussex* (1830), p. 279; will of Thomas Fuller, PCC, dated 15 May 1777, prob. 2 Mar. 1780).

Streatham, & is Nephew of the famous Rose Fuller;[75]—& whether Dr. Johnson did not like *them*, or whether he was displeased that we went out, or whether he was not well, I know not, but he never opened his mouth, except in answer to a question, till he bid us good Night.

Saturday morning [22 Aug.], however, he was again all himself; & *so* civil to me!—even admiring how I *Dressed myself*!—Indeed, it is well I have "brought my *best becomes* here," for, it seems, he always speaks his mind concerning the Dress of Ladies, & all Ladies who are here *obey* his injunctions implicitly, & *alter* whatever he disapproves. This is a part of his Character that much surprises me; but, notwithstanding he is sometimes so absent, & always so near sighted, he *scrutinies*[76] into every part of almost every body's appearance. They tell me of a Miss Brown,[77] who often visits here, & who has a *slovenly* way of Dressing; 'And when she comes down in a morning, says Mrs. Thrale, her hair will be all loose, & her Cap half off; & then Mr. Johnson, who sees *something* is wrong, & does not know where the fault lies, concludes it is in the *Cap*; & says 'My dear, what do you wear such a vile Cap for?' '*I'll change it*, Sir, cries the poor Girl, if you don't like it.'— ay do, he says,—& away runs poor Miss Brown,—but when she gets on another, its the same thing, for the *Cap* has nothing to do with the fault. And then she *wonders* Mr. Johnson should not like the *Cap*, for *she* thinks it very pretty! And so on with her Gown,—which he also makes her change,—but if the poor Girl was to Change through all her wardrobe, unless she would put her Things *on* better, he would still find fault.'

75 Rose Fuller (1708–77), of Rose Hill, Sussex; MP; a wealthy Jamaica planter. His father was John Fuller (1680–1745), of Brightling, Sussex (Namier; IGI; Berry, p. 278).

76 SJ cites this form but gives no example of its use in his *Dictionary*. The *OED* cites the verb form (from the *Dictionary*) but also gives no example since Mrs Barrett normalized the word to 'scrutinize' in her edition of the journals. This is thus apparently the only example in print.

77 Frances ('Fanny') Browne, daughter of Lyde Browne (d. 1787) of Wimbledon, a director of the Bank of England. In Sept. 1779 she eloped with Thomas Gunter Browne (see below, p. 356). Despite her '*slovenly* way of Dressing', HLT rated her 14 out of a possible 20 for 'Person Mien & Manner' in her assessment of her friends. See *Thraliana* i. 331; *GM* lvii[2] (1787), 840.

And when Dr. Johnson was gone, she told me of this affair of *my mother's* being obliged to change her Dress. 'Now, said she, Mrs. Burney had on a very pretty Linen Jacket & Coat, & was going to Church,—but Mr. Johnson, who, I suppose, did not like her in a *Jacket*, saw *something* was the matter, & so found fault with the *Linen*: & he *looked*, & *peered*, & then said, why, Madam, *this won't do*! You must not go to Church so!—So away went poor Mrs. Burney, & changed her Gown!—And when she had *done*, he did not like it!—but he did not know *why*, so he told her she should not wear a Black Hat & Cloak, in summer!—Lord, how he did bother poor Mrs. Burney! & *himself* too, for if the Things had been put *on* to his mind, he would have taken no notice of them.'

'Why, said Mr. Thrale, very drily, I don't think Mrs. Burney a very good *Dresser*.'

'Last Time she came, said Mrs. Thrale, she was in a *white* Cloak, & she told Mr. Johnson she had got her Cloak *scoured* on purpose to oblige him!—*Scoured*!—says he,—ay,—have You, Madam?—So he *see sawed*, for he could not for shame find fault, but he did not seem to like the *scouring*!'

So I think myself [amazingly fortunate][78] to be approved of by him, for if he *dis*liked—alack a Day. ⌐What⌐ could I change!—but, I assure you, he has paid me some very fine *Compliments* upon this subject. However, to be in his good Graces, is to almost ensure his indulgence. I was *very* sorry when he went to Town,—though Mrs. Thrale made him promise to return to Monday's Dinner. And he has, very *affectionately*, invited me to visit him, in the Winter, when he is at Home: & he talked to me a great deal of Mrs. Williams, & gave me a List of her Works, & said I *must* visit them.—which, I am sure, I shall be very proud of doing.

And now let me try to recollect an account he gave us of ⌐the⌐ *celebrated Ladies* of his Acquaintance: an account which, had you heard from *himself*, would have made you *die* with Laughing.

---

[78] Substituted by FBA for an obliterated phrase not recovered.

It was begun, by Mrs. Thrale's apologising to him for troubling him with some Question she thought *trifling*,— O, I remember!—We had been talking of *Colours*, & of the fantastic *names* given to them: & why the palest lilac should be called a *soupire etouffer*—& when Dr. Johnson came in, she applied to him,—'Why, Madam, said he, with wonderful readiness,—it is called a *stifled sigh*, because it is *checked in it's progress*, & only half a Colour.'

I could not help expressing my amazement at his universal readiness upon all subjects, & Mrs. Thrale said to him 'Sir, Miss Burney wonders at your *patience* with such stuff;—but I tell her you are *used* to me, for I believe I torment [|] you with more foolish Questions than any body else *dares* do.'

'No, Madam, said he, you don't *torment* me;—you *teize* me, indeed, sometimes;—'

'Ay, so I do, Mr. Johnson, & I wonder You bear with my nonsense—'

'No, Madam, You never talk nonsense,—you have as much *sense*, & *more Wit* than any woman I know!—'

'Oh ⌐Lord⌐, cried Mrs. Thrale, blushing—it is *my* turn to go under the Table this morning, Miss Burney!'

'And yet, continued the Doctor, with the most comical look; I have known *All* the Wits, from Mrs. Montagu,— down to Bet Flint!'

'Bet Flint! cried Mrs. Thrale, ⌐for God's sake⌐ whose [*sic*] she?'

'O, a fine Character, Madam!—she was *habitually* a slut & a Drunkard, & *occasionally* ⌐a ⟨Whore⟩[79] &⌐ a Thief.'

'And, for Heaven's sake, how came *you* to know her?'

'Why, Madam, she figured in the *Literary* world, too!— Bet Flint wrote her own Life, & called herself Cassandra,—& it was in Verse;—it began

When Nature first ordained my Birth
[A Diminitive][80] I was Born on Earth;

---

[79] FBA has written 'Harlot' over the word beneath, which cannot be seen, but Boswell, who repeats SJ's story of Bet in the *Life* (iv. 103), quotes him as saying 'whore'.

[80] Thus in MS; substituted by FBA for an obliterated phrase not recovered (but see next note).

And then I came from a Dark abode
Into a gay & gaudy World.[81]

So Bet brought me her Verses to correct;[82]—but I gave
her half a Crown, & she liked it as well. Bet had a fine
spirit;—she Advertised for a Husband, but she had no
success, for she told me no man aspired to her!—Then
she hired very handsome Lodgings, & a Foot Boy;—&
she got a Harpsichord, but Bet could not *play*;—however,
she put herself in fine attitudes, & *Drum'd*.[83]

Then he gave an account of another of these Geniuses,
who called herself [some fine Name, I have forgotten
what.][84] She had not quite the same stock of *virtue*,
continued he, nor the same stock of *Honesty* as Bet Flint,
but I suppose she envied her accomplishments, | for she
was so little moved by the power of Harmony, that while
Bet Flint thought she was Drumming very *divinely*, the
other Jade had her indited for a Nuisance!'

'And pray what became of her? Sir!'

'Why, Madam, she stole a Quilt from the man of the
House, & he had her taken up;—but Bet Flint had a spirit
not to be subdued,—so when she found herself obliged
to go to Jail, she ordered a sedan Chair, & bid her Foot
boy ⌐go⌐ before her! However, the Boy proved refractory,
for *he* was ashamed, though his mistress was not.'

'And did she ever get out of Jail again, Sir?'

---

[81] Boswell gives the following version (*Life* iv. 103 n. 2):
  'When first I drew my vital breath,
  A little minikin I came upon earth;
  And then I came from a dark abode,
  Into this gay and gaudy world.'
On a scrap among the Boswell papers Boswell gives the 2nd line as 'a little
diminutive I came upon earth' (*Boswell Laird of Achinleck 1778–1782*, ed. J. W.
Reed and F. A. Pottle (1977), p. 349 n. 7). Reed and Pottle suggest that FB
herself was Boswell's source for the anecdote, which in turn suggests that
FB obliterated 'little' in the present text.

[82] Boswell quotes SJ as saying that she wished he 'would furnish her with a
Preface' (*Life* iv. 103).

[83] *OED* cites this passage as its example of *drum* in the sense of 'to thump ...
as distinguished from playing properly' (s.v. drum, *v.* 2. a.).

[84] FBA's substitution; the obliterated name has not been deciphered.

'Yes, Madam; when she came to her Trial,—the Judge,[85]—who Loved a Wench at his Heart, acquitted her. So now, she said to me, the Quilt is my own!—& now I'll make a petticoat of it.—O,—I Loved Bet Flint!—'

Lord, how we all ⌐hollow⌐ed!—then he gave an account of another Lady, who called herself *Laurinda*, & who also writ verses, & stole furniture, & practised Gallantry: but he had not the same *affection* for her, he said,—though she, too, '*was a Lady who had high notions of Honour.*'

Then followed the History of another, who called herself *Hortensia*, & who walked up & down the park, repeating a Book of Virgil,—'But, said he, though I know her story, I never had the *good fortune to* ⌐*pick her up*⌐.'

After this, he gave us an account of the famous Mrs. Pinkethman,[86] '& she, he said, told me she owed all her misfortunes to her *Wit*, for she was so unhappy as to marry a man who thought *himself*, also, a Wit,—though I believe she gave not implicit credit for it,—but it occasioned much contradiction & ill will: & once, at about 3 o'clock Ⅰ in the morning, the Husband came Home, & found a man in her Room,—& he had the insolence to take it amiss,—though she told him that the man had brought her a Book, & only stayed till she had read it,—

[85] Sir John Willes (1685–1761), Lord Chief Justice of the Common Pleas. Bet's trial at the Old Bailey took place in Sept. 1758. She was accused of stealing not only the counterpane, but five other articles as well out of ready furnished lodgings she had rented from Mary Walthow (b.?1720), spinster, in Mares Court, Dean Street, Soho. Mary Walthow claimed that the articles had been given to her by the former keeper of the lodgings, Capt. Baldwin, who had gone abroad to Germany. In the absence of the Captain she could not prove her claim, and Bet was acquitted. Of Chief Justice Willes, Horace Walpole writes: 'He was not wont to disguise any of his passions: that for gaming, was notorious; for women, unbounded' (*Memoirs of King George II*, ed. J. Brooke (New Haven, 1983), i. 62; see also *Life* iv. 103 and n. 3; *The Proceedings ... in the Old-Bailey* (1758), p. 278; IGI). The Captain may have been Capt.-Lt. John Baldwin of the 51st Ft, which went to Germany in April 1758, not returning until 1763; Baldwin appears to have left the service or died after the embarkation to Germany (see *AL*, 1758, p. 113; 1759, p. 99; R. Savory, *His Britannic Majesty's Army in Germany during the Seven Years War* (Oxford, 1966), p. 65 and *passim*; W. Wheater, *A Record of the Services of the Fifty-First ... Regiment* (1870), pp. 6, 33, 204 and *passim*).

[86] A slip for Laetitia Pilkington (1712–50), née Van Lewen, adventuress and writer.

& Mrs. Pinkethman appealed to all the Literary World if
that was not hard usage!'⁸⁷

'"Lord" bless me, Sir! cried Mrs. Thrale, how can all
these Vagabonds contrive to get at *You*, of all people?'

'O the dear Creatures! cried he, Laughing heartily, I
can't but be glad to see them!'

'Why, I wonder, Sir, You never went to see *Mrs. Rudd*⁸⁸
among the rest?'

'Why, Madam, I believe I *should*, said he, if it was not
for the *News papers*; but I am prevented many frolics, that
I should like very well, since I am become such a Theme
for the papers.'⁸⁹

Now would you ever have imagined *this*?—Bet Flint, it
seems, once took *Kitty Fisher*⁹⁰ to see him; but, to his no
little regret, he was not at Home, 'And *Mrs. Williams*, he
added, did not love Bet Flint,—but Bet Flint made herself
very easy about that!'

How *Mr. Crisp* would have enjoyed this account!—I
declare I Laughed till I was *sore*, for he gave it all with so

⁸⁷ Pilkington's husband, the Revd Matthew Pilkington (*c.*1700–74), author of
The Gentleman's and Connoisseur's Dictionary of Painters (1770), surprised her with
a Mr Adair and sued for divorce in the ecclesiastical court in Dublin in Feb.
1738 (*Dublin Evening Post*, 7–11 Feb. 1738). In the first vol. of her *Memoirs*
(1748), Pilkington admits to being 'very indiscreet in permitting any man to be
at an unseasonable hour in my bed-chamber' but declares that 'it was the
attractive charms of a new book which the gentleman would not lend me but
consented to stay till I read it through—that was the sole motive of my detaining
him' (New York, 1928, pp. 133–4; see also p. 18).

⁸⁸ Margaret Caroline Rudd, née Young or Youngson (*c.*1745–97), adventuress. In 1775 she was tried for forging bonds or promissory notes. Though
certainly guilty, she was acquitted for lack of sufficient evidence. Her lover
Daniel Perreau and his brother Robert were found guilty in a separate trial
and were hanged in Jan. 1776. See *YW* xi. 208 n. 22; xxiv. 152–4 and nn. 15–
19; xxviii. 192 nn. 13–14; xxxii. 261 n. 35; *GM* xlvi (1776), 44–5.

⁸⁹ Although SJ did not meet Mrs Rudd, Boswell, 'induced by the fame of
her talents, address, and irresistible power of fascination' (*Life* iii. 79), visited
her on 22 Apr. 1776. For his account of the visit, see *Boswell: The Ominous Years
1774–1776*, ed. C. Ryskamp and F. A. Pottle (New York, 1963), pp. 355–61. A
decade later Mrs Rudd became his mistress (see F. Brady, *James Boswell: The
Later Years 1769–1795* (New York, 1984), pp. 133–5 and *passim*; *Boswell: The
English Experiment 1785–1789*, ed. I. S. Lustig and F. A. Pottle (New York,
1986), pp. 8, 32–5 and *passim*).

⁹⁰ Catherine Maria ('Kitty') Fisher (*c.*1738–67), courtesan. See the portraits
of her in *Reynolds*, ed. N. Penny (1986), pp. 94, 95, 99.

droll a solemnity, & it was all so unexpected, that Mrs. Thrale & I were both almost equally diverted.

Augst 26th

My opportunities for writing grow less & less, & my materials more & more:—yet I am unwilling, for a thousand reasons, to give over my attempt,—& the *first* is, the Debt I owe my dearest Susan, who so kindly feeds *me*, whenever *I* am hungry, & *she* has abundance. But really, after Breakfast, I have scarce a moment that I can spare all Day. |

Mrs. Thrale I like more and more [xxxxx *1 word*]—And I am sure so would you!—for of all the people I have ever seen, since I came *into this gay & gaudy world*, I never before saw the person who so strongly resembles our dear Father!—I find the likeness perpetually; she has the same natural liveliness, the same general benevolence,—the same rare union of *gaity* & of *feeling* in her Disposition. And so kind is she to *me*, that *I know not what for to do!* She told me, at first, that I should have *all* my mornings to myself;—And therefore I have actually *studied* to avoid her, lest I should be in her way; but, since the first morning, she *seeks* me,—sits with me ⌐while I Dress,¬ saunters with me in the park, or compares Notes over Books in the Library; there is an immediate communication from her Dressing Room to my Bed Room, & when she is up stairs, she flings open the Doors, & enters into Conversation.— And her Conversation is *delightful*; it is so entertaining, so gay, so enlivening, when she is in spirits; & so intelligent & instructive when she is otherwise, that I almost as much wish to record all *she* says, as all Dr. Johnson says. I have told her repeatedly how much I was afraid of her,—but that fear is now quite worn away; she is so perfectly natural & unassuming, & she is so *infinitely* kind to me, that fear, now, would be folly.

You know I told you I was determined not to Court Miss Thrale,—well, we are now wonderous intimate, for *she* Courts me:—I am sure I *owe* her favour to Evelina, which she has quite by Heart, & quotes eternally; & not a

Creature comes to the House, but she *names* them from that Book. Indeed, with all her Coldness, distance & gravity, I find she loves a *titter* as much as any Girl, & when I am *in[cl]ine[d]* to run on in a Rhodomantading manner, she Laughs till she can't stand. I was quite *astonished*, to find how *merrily* she is, at Times, disposed. |

Aug[st]

Proceed—no!—go back, my muse, to Thursday [27 Aug.].

Dr. Johnson came Home to Dinner.

In the Evening, he was as lively & full of wit & sport as I have ever seen him,—& Mrs. Thrale & I had him quite to ourselves, for Mr. Thrale came in from giving an Election Dinner[91] to which he sent 2 Bucks & 6 pine apples so tired, that he niether opened his *Eyes* nor *mouth*, but fell fast asleep. Indeed, after Tea, he generally does.

Dr. Johnson was very communicative concerning his present work of the Lives of the Poets;[92]—*Dryden* is now in the Press; & he told us he had been just writing a Dissertation upon Hudibras.

He gave us an account of *Mrs. Lenox*:[93] her Female Quixote is very justly admired here; indeed, *I* think *all* her Novels far the best of any *Living* Author,—but Mrs. Thrale says that though her *Books* are generally approved, Nobody likes *her*.[94] I find *she*, among others, waited on

[91] As MP for Southwark, Thrale periodically treated his constituents to a dinner. There was no new election until 1780.

[92] This famous last work of SJ, commissioned by the booksellers of London, began to appear in 1779.

[93] Charlotte, née Ramsay (*c.*1729–1804), m. (1747) Alexander Lennox; novelist and miscellaneous writer. *The Female Quixote* (1752) is the most acclaimed of her works. SJ, who wrote the novel's dedication to the E. of Middlesex, praised its 'most entertaining series of circumstances and events' (*GM* xxii (1752), 146); Henry Fielding recommended it 'as a most extraordinary and most excellent Performance' (*Covent Garden Journal*, 24 Mar. 1752, ed. G.E. Jensen (1915; rpt. 1964), i. 282); and HLT thought it 'far before Tom Jones or Joseph Andrews with regard to Body of Story, Height of Colouring, or General Powers of Thinking' (*Thraliana* i. 329).

[94] SJ, however, always admired and supported Charlotte Lennox. He told the members of the Essex Head Club on 15 May 1784: 'I dined yesterday at Mrs. Garrick's, with Mrs. Carter, Miss Hannah More, and Miss Fanny Burney. Three such women are not to be found: I know not where I could find a fourth, except Mrs. Lennox, who is superiour to them all' (*Life* iv. 275).

Dr. Johnson, upon her commencing writer: & he told us that, at her request, he carried her to *Richardson*: 'Poor Charlotte Lenox! continued he;—when we came to the House, she desired *me* to leave her, "for, says she, I am under great restraint in your presence, but if you leave me *alone* with Richardson, I'll give you a very good account of him:" however, I fear poor Charlotte was disappointed, for she gave me no account at all!'[95]

He then told us of 2 little productions of our Mr. Harris, which we read;—they are very short, & very clever: one is called *Fashion*, the other *Much ado*,[96] & they both of them full of sportive humour, that I had not suspected to belong to Mr. Harris [the learned Grammarian].[97]

Some Time after, turning suddenly to me, he said 'Miss Burney, what sort of Reading do you delight in?—History?—Travels?—Poetry?—or Romances?—'

'O Sir! cried I, I dread being Catechised by *You*!—I dare not make *any* answer, for I ⌐am sure⌐ whatever I should say would be wrong!—'

'*Whatever* you should say?—how's that?'

'Why not whatever I *should*,—but whatever I *could* say.'

He Laughed, &, to my great relief, spared me any further questions upon the subject. Indeed, I was very happy I had the presence of mind to *evade* him as I did, for I am sure the examination which would have followed, had I made any direct answer, would have turned out sorely to my discredit.

---

[95] Richardson, who printed the 1st edn. of *The Female Quixote*, gave Mrs Lennox criticisms of the novel and persuaded Andrew Millar to publish it. For their efforts on her behalf, she included in the 2nd vol. a compliment to Richardson and to SJ: 'Truth is not always injured by Fiction. An admirable Writer of our own Time has found the Way to convey the most solid Instructions, the noblest Sentiments, and the most exalted Piety, in the pleasing Dress of a Novel [*Clarissa*], and, to use the Words of the greatest Genius in the present Age, "Has taught the Passions to move at the Command of Virtue"' (p. 314). See T. C. D. Eaves, 'Dr. Johnson's Letters to Richardson', *PMLA* lxxv (1960), 377–81; T. C. D. Eaves and B. D. Kimpel, *Samuel Richardson: A Biography* (Oxford, 1971), p. 461.

[96] Both were printed in Sarah Fielding's *Familiar Letters between the Principal Characters in David Simple* (1747), ii. 277–93, where they are identified as 'A kind Present to the Author by a Friend' (ii. 276).

[97] Inserted by FBA.

'Do you remember, Sir, said Mrs. Thrale, how you tormented poor Miss Brown about reading?'

'She might soon be tormented, Madam, answered he, for I am not yet quite clear she knows what a Book is.'

'O for shame! cried Mrs. Thrale; she reads not only English, but French & Italian. She was in Italy a great while.'

'Pho,—exclaimed he,—*Italian* indeed!—Do you think she knows as much Italian as Rose Fuller does English?'

'Well, well, said Mrs. Thrale, Rose Fuller is a very good young man, for all he has not much command of Language; & though he is silly enough, yet I like him *very well*, for there is no manner of harm in him.'

Then she told me, that he once said 'Dr. Johnson's conversation is so instructive, that I'll ask him a question. 'Pray, Sir, what is *Palmyra*? I have often heard of it but never knew what it was.' 'Palmyra, Sir? said the | Doctor; why it is a Hill in *Ireland*, situated in a Bog, & has Palm Trees at the Top, whence it is called *Palm-mire.*' And whether or not he *swallowed* this account, they know not yet.[98]

'But Miss Brown, continued she, is by no means such a simpleton as Mr. Johnson supposes her to be; she is not very *deep*, indeed, but she is a sweet, & a very ingenuous Girl, & nobody admired Miss Stretfield[99] more;—Miss Stretfield was *universally* admired, for her Learning, her beauty, & her manners; & poor Fanny Brown was so far from being hurt at her superiority, when they were here together, that she almost *adored* her, & was always pointing out her excellence. But she made a more foolish speech

[98] Palmyra is an ancient city in Syria. In her *Anecdotes of the Late Samuel Johnson* (1786), HLTP adds: 'Seeing however that the lad thought him serious, and thanked him for the information, he undeceived him very gently indeed; told him the history, geography, and chronology of Tadmor [Palmyra] in the wilderness, with every incident that literature could furnish I think, or eloquence express, from the building of Solomon's palace to the voyage of Dawkins and Wood' (ed. A. Sherbo (1974), p. 92).

[99] Sophia Streatfeild (1754–1835), daughter of Henry Streatfeild (1706–62), of Chiddingstone, Kent, and Anne, née Sidney (1732–1812). Educated by Dr Arthur Collier (1707–77), HLT's former tutor, she was noted for her scholarship and her beauty. HLT would soon rue her friendship, since Mr Thrale fell in love with her. See below, *passim*.

to Mr. Johnson than she would have done to any body else, because she was so frightened & embarrassed that she knew not *what* she said. He asked her some Question about *reading*, & she did, to be sure, make a very silly answer,—but she was so perplexed & bewildered, that she hardly knew where she was, & so she said the *beginning* of a Book was as good as the *End*, or the *End* was as good as the *beginning*, or some such stuff;—& Dr. Johnson told her of it so often, saying well, my dear, *which* part of a Book do you like best *now?*—that poor Fanny Brown burst into Tears!—'

'I am sure *I* should have compassion for her, cried I, for Nobody would be more likely to have blundered out such, or any such speech, from fright & terror.'

'*You?* cried Dr. Johnson,—no; *you* are another Thing; she who could draw Smiths & Branghtons, is quite another Thing.' |

O Susy,—how happy for such a poor sheepish wretch as I am among strangers *whom* I *fear*, is this *prevention* in my favour.

Mrs. Thrale then told some other stories of his degrading opinion of *us poor Fair sex*;—I mean in *general*, ⌜though,⌝ for in *particular*, he does them noble justice. Among others, was a Mrs. Somebody who spent a Day here once, & of whom he asked '*Can she Read?*' 'Yes, to be sure; answered Mrs. Thrale, we have been reading together this Afternoon.' 'And what Book did you get for her?'—'Why what happened to lie in the way,—Hogarth's analysis of Beauty.'[1]—'Hogarth's analysis of Beauty! ⌜for God's sake⌝ what made you chuse that?' 'Why, Sir, what would you have had me take!' 'What she could have understood, Cow hide,[2] or Cinderella!'—

---

[1] A treatise on aesthetics, with two explanatory plates, by William Hogarth (1697–1764), published in 1753.

[2] Obviously a children's tale. John Chute, in a letter to Horace Walpole, 29 July 1742 NS, mentions 'Cow's-skin' in company with 'Tom Thumb', 'Jack the Giantkiller', and 'Pilgrim's Progress' (*YW* xxxv. 33). The story in question (or a version thereof) may be that of the farmer whose three cows are eaten by pixies but magically restored to life, though all that is left of them is literally the skin hanging on the bones. This story was first collected in the 19th c. from the peasantry of Devonshire by the folklorist Sabine Baring-Gould and contributed

'O Dr. Johnson! cried I,—'tis not *for Nothing* you are feared!'

'O you're a Rogue! cried he, Laughing, & they would fear *you* if they knew you!'

'That they would! said Mrs. Thrale, but she's so shy they don't suspect her. Miss Pitches[3] gave her an account of all her *Dress*, to entertain her, t'other Night!—to be sure she was very *lucky* to fix on *Miss Burney* for such conversation!—But I have been telling her she *must* write a Comedy;—I am sure nobody could do it better,—is it not true, Mr. Johnson?'

I would fain have stopt her,—but she was not to be stopt,—& ran on saying *such* fine things!—though we had almost a *struggle* together:—& she said, at last, 'Well, authors may say what they will of *modesty & modesty* [uncredited][4]—but I believe ˡ Miss Burney is *really* modest about her Book, for her Colour comes & goes every Time it is mentioned.'

I then ⌐rose⌐ to look for a Book which we had been talking of, & Dr. Johnson ⌐said most civil things of me *the while*,—but I did not distinctly hear them. However,⌐ when I returned to my seat, ⌐he⌐ said he wished Richardson had been alive, 'And then, he added, you should have been Introduced to him,—though, I don't know, niether;—Richardson would have been afraid of her!'

'O yes!—that's a likely matter!' quoth I.

'It's very true, continued he; Richardson would have been really *afraid* of her;—there is merit in Evelina which he could not have borne.—No, it would not have done!—unless, indeed, she would have flattered him prodigiously.—Harry Fielding, too, would have been afraid of

---

as an appendix to William Henderson's *Notes on the Folk Lore of the Northern Counties of England and the Borders* (1866), pp. 321–4. See also J. Jacobs, *English Fairy Tales* (3rd edn., 1898; rpt. 1968), pp. 198–9, 289, 329.

[3] Sophia Pitches (1761–79), daughter of Abraham Pitches (*c*.1733–92), cr. (1782) Kt, of Bedford House, Streatham, an eminent brandy merchant and later sheriff of Surrey (1782). Her mother was Jane, née Hassel (d. 1797), daughter of Robert Prowse Hassel, of Wraysbury, Bucks. She died the following year, probably of lead or mercury poisoning from cosmetics used to whiten the skin. See *Thraliana* i. 393; *GM* lxii[1] (1792), 390; below, p. 332.

[4] Inserted by FBA.

her,—there is nothing so delicately finished in *all* Harry
Fielding's Works, as in Evelina;—(Then, shaking his Head
at me, he exclaimed) O, you little *Character-monger,* you!'

Mrs. Thrale then returned to her charge, & again urged
me about a Comedy,—& again I tried to silence her,—&
we had a *fine fight* together;—till she called upon Dr.
Johnson to *back* her,—'Why, Madam, said he, Laughing,—
she *is* Writing one!—What a rout is here, indeed!—She is
writing one up stairs all the Time.—Who ever knew when
she began Evelina?

'True, true Oh King!'[5] thought I.

'Well, that *will* be a sly trick! cried Mrs. Thrale;—
however, you know best, I believe, about That, as well as
about every other Thing.'

Friday [28 Aug.],—was a very *full* Day.—

In the morning, we began talking of 'Irene,'[6] & Mrs.
Thrale made Dr. Johnson read some Passages which I
had been remarking [|] as uncommonly applicable to the
present Times. And he read several speeches, & told us
he had not ever Read so much of it before since it was
first printed.

'Why there is no making you read a play, said Mrs.
Thrale, either of your own, or any other Person. What
trouble had I to make you hear Murphy's 'Know your
own Mind!'[7] '*Read rapidly, read rapidly*! you cried, & then
took out your Watch to see how long I was about it!—
Well, we won't serve *Miss Burney* so, Sir;—when we have
her Comedy we will do it all justice.'

Murphy, it seems, is a ⌜very great⌝ favourite here; he
has been acquainted intimately with Mr. Thrale from both
their *Boyhoods,* & Mrs. Thrale is very partial to him. She
told me, therefore, *in a merry way,* that though she wished
me to excell *Cumberland,* & all other Dramatic writers,—

---

[5] Cf. Daniel 3: 24. This unspoken tribute to SJ's perspicacity alludes in the
first place to his intuition about the totally secret beginnings of *Evelina.* But it
also suggests that he may in addition have hit the mark in the present case, i.e.,
that FB had in fact already begun secretly writing a play, or at least toying with
ideas for one.

[6] SJ's tragedy, produced and published in 1749.

[7] A comedy, which opened at Covent Garden on 22 Feb. 1777, and which
was published the following year.

yet she would not wish me better than her old Friend Murphy.—I begged her, however, to be perfectly easy, & *assured* her I *would take care* not to Eclipse him!

Soon after Dr. Johnson began Laughing very Heartily to himself, & when upon repeated entreaty, he confessed the subject of his mirth, what should it be but an idea that had struck him ⌐that I should write *Stretham, a Farce*— Lord, how I laughed, & he carried on the notion, &⌐ said I should have *them all* in it & give a touch of the Pitches[8] & Tattersalls![9]

'O if she does! cried Mrs. Thrale, if she *inserts* us in a *Coomedy*[10]—we'll serve her trick for trick—she is a young Authoress, & very delicate,—say it will be hard if we can't frighten her into order.' |

Many more things were said, all of the most high seasoned flattery,—but I have not Time to write them.

At Noon Mrs. Thrale took me with her to Kensington, to see her little Daughters Susan & Sophia,[11] who are at school there. They are sweet little Girls.

When we were Dressed for Dinner, & went into the Parlour, I had the agreable [*sic*] surprise of seeing Mr. Seward there. I say *agreeable*, for notwithstanding our acquaintance began in a manner so extremely unpleasant to me, there is some thing of *drollery*, good sense, intelligence, & *archness* in this Young man, that have not merely reconciled me to him, but brought me over to liking him vastly.

There was also Mr. Lort,[12] who is reckoned one of the most learned men alive;—he is also a Collector of

---

[8] A family of 'silly' parents and 'foolish', 'extravagant' daughters (below, pp. 123, 338, 357; *EJL* iv).

[9] Besides Mr Tattersall's 'rage for Building' (above, p. 84), the Tattersall family eccentricities included (or would later include) his wife's being a vegetarian, regarded as a far greater oddity in the 18th century than now (see FB to HLT, 1 July 1780, *EJL* iv).

[10] Presumably, HLT is mimicking SJ's Staffordshire accent.

[11] Susanna Arabella (1770–1858) and Sophia (1771–1824), who m. (1807) Henry Merrik Hoare (1770–1856). They were attending a boarding school in Kensington Square run by Elizabeth Cumyns, née Thornton (1741–?82), a childhood friend of HLT. See *TSP*, p. 88 and *passim*; *Thraliana* i. 291 and n. 2.

[12] The Revd Michael Lort (1725–90), antiquary; FSA, 1755; FRS, 1766; DD (Cantab.), 1780.

Curiosities, alike in Literature & natural History: his manners are somewhat blunt & odd, & he is, all together, out of the *common Road*, without having chosen a *better path.*

The Day was passed most agreeably; in the Evening we had, as usual, a *Literary conversation*; — I say *we*, only because Mrs. Thrale *will* make me take some share, by perpetually applying to me, — &, indeed, there can be no better House for rubbing up the memory, — as I hardly ever Read, saw, or heard of *any* Book that by some means or other, has not been mentioned here:

Mr. Lort produced several curious M.S.S. of the famous Bristol Chatterton;[13] among others, his *Will*,[14] & divers Verses written against Dr. Johnson, as a *place man* & *Pensioner*;[15] all which he Read aloud, with a steady voice & unmoved Countenance! — *I* was astonished at him; Mrs. Thrale not much pleased; Mr. Thrale silent & attentive; & Mr. Seward was slyly Laughing. Dr. Johnson himself listened profoundly, & Laughed openly. Indeed, I believe he wishes his abusers no other Thing than a *good Dinner* [like Pope].[16]

Just as we had got our Biscuits & Toast & Water, — which makes the Streatham supper; — & which, indeed, is all there is any chance of Eating after our late & great Dinners, — Mr. Lort suddenly said 'Pray, Ma'am, have you heard any thing of a Novel that runs about a good deal, called Evelina?'

---

[13] Thomas Chatterton (1752–70), poet.

[14] Lort actually possessed a *copy* of Chatterton's will. The original belonged to John Lambert, to whom Chatterton had been apprenticed, and is now in the Bristol Museum. The will is printed in E. H. W. Meyerstein, *A Life of Thomas Chatterton* (1930), pp. 340–3. See also *YW* xvi. 178–9 and nn. 6–7.

[15] For example: 'The pension'd muse of Johnson is no more! / Drown'd in a butt of wine his genius lies:' ('February. An Elegy', ll. 69–70); 'When Bute the Ministry and People's head, / With royal favour pension'd Johnson dead;' ('Kew Gardens', ll. 807–8); 'No, North is strictly virtuous, pious, wise, / As every pension'd Johnson testifies' (ibid., ll. 939–40). Besides ridiculing SJ as a pensioner and an alcoholic, Chatterton accuses him of critical rigidity, satirizes *Irene's* soporific qualities, and implies that he has 'Massacred' Shakespeare. See *The Complete Works of Thomas Chatterton*, ed. D. S. Taylor (Oxford, 1971), i. 362, 449, 460–4, 497, 520–2, 534–8.

[16] Inserted by FBA. 'Yet then did *Gildon* draw his venal quill; / I wish'd the man a dinner, and sate still' (*Epistle to Dr. Arbuthnot*, ll. 151–2).

⌐Good God,¬ what a ferment did this question, before such a set, put me in!—I did not know whether he spoke to *me*, or Mrs. Thrale; & Mrs. Thrale was in the same doubt, &, as she owned, felt herself in a little palpitation for me, not knowing *what* might come next.

Between us both, therefore, he had *no* answer.

'It has been recommended to me, continued he, but I have no great desire to see it, because it has such a foolish Name. Yet I have heard a great deal of it, too.'

My Heart beat so quick against my stays, that I almost *panted* with extreme agitation, ⌐at¬ the dread either of hearing some ⌐cruel¬ criticism, or of being betrayed: & I munched my Biscuit as if I had not Eaten for a fortnight. I believe the whole party were in some little consternation;—Dr. Johnson began *see-sawing*; Mr. Thrale awoke; Mr. Embry, who I fear has picked up some Notion of the affair from being so much in the House, *Grinned* amazingly; & Mr. Seward, biting his Nails, & flinging himself back in his Chair, I am sure had wickedness enough to enjoy the whole scene. Mrs. Thrale was really a little fluttered, but, without looking at me, said 'And *what*, Mr. Lort, pray *what* have you | heard of it?'

Now, had Mrs. Thrale *not* been flurried, this was the last Question she should have ventured to ask before *me*. Only suppose what *I* must feel when I heard it!

'Why they say, answered he, that it's an account of a Young lady's first Entrance into Company, & of the scrapes she gets into: & they say there's a great deal of *Character* in it: but I have not cared to look in it, because the *Name* is so foolish: Evelina!'

'*Why* foolish, Sir? cried Dr. Johnson, Where's the folly of it?'

⌐Lord,¬ Susy, I could have kissed him!

'Why I won't say much for the Name myself, said Mrs. Thrale, to those who don't know the *reason* of it, which *I* found out, but which nobody else seems to know.'

She then explained the Name from *Evelyn*, according to my own meaning.

'Well, said Dr. Johnson, if that was the reason, it is a very good one.'

'Why have you had the Book *here?*' cried Mr. Lort.

'Ay, indeed, have we! said Mrs. Thrale, I read it when I was last confined, & I *Laughed* over it, & I *cried* over it!—

'O ho! said Mr. Lort, this is another thing! if you have had it *here*, I will certainly read it.'

'Had it? ay, returned she, & Dr. Johnson, who would not *look* at it at first, was so *caught* by it, when I put it in the Coach with him, that he has sung it's praises ever since,—& he says Richardson would have been *proud* to have written it.'

'O ho! this is a good hearing! cried Mr. Lort;—if *Dr. Johnson* can read it, I shall get it with all speed.'

'You need not go far for it, said Mrs. Thrale, for it's now upon yonder Table.'

I could sit still no longer; there was some thing so awkward; so uncommon, so strange in my then situation, that I wished myself 100 miles off;—& indeed, I had almost Choaked myself with the Biscuit, for I could not for my life *swallow* it,—& so, before I could consider the embarrassment of *returning* I got up, &, as Mr. Lort went to the Table to look for Evelina, I left the Room.—& was forced to call for Water, to wash down the Biscuit which stuck in my Throat.

I heartily wished Mr. Lort at Jerusalem![17]—I assure you, notwithstanding all this may *read* as nothing, because all that was said was in my favour, yet at the *Time*, when I knew not *what* might be said, I suffered the most severe *trepidation.*

I did not much like going back, but, the moment I recovered *Breath*, resolved not to make bad worse by staying longer away: but, at the Door of the Room, I met Mrs. Thrale, who, asking me if I would have some water, took me into a back Room,—& burst into a hearty fit of Laughter. 'This is very good sport! cried she; the man is as innocent about the matter as a Child, & we shall hear

---

[17] FB's variation on the proverbial expression, 'to wish (someone) at Jericho'. Cf. above, p. 86, below, p. 341, and see *EJL* i. 146.

what he says to it to-morrow at Breakfast: I made a sign to Mr. Johnson & Seward not to tell him.'

When she found I was not in a humour to think it such good sport as she did, she grew more serious, & taking my Hand, kindly said 'May you never, Miss Burney, know any other pain than that of hearing yourself praised!—& I am sure *that* you must often feel.' |

But when I told her how much I dreaded being discovered, & besought her not to betray me any further, she again began Laughing, & openly declared she should not consult me about the matter. I was really uneasy,—nay, quite uncomfortable,—for the *first* Time I have been so since I came hither;—but as we were obliged soon to return, I could not then press my request with the earnestness I wished.—But she told me that, as soon as I was gone when Mr. Lort took up Evelina, he exclaimed contemptuously 'Why it's printed for *Lowndes*!—' & that Dr. Johnson then told him there were things & Characters in it *more* than worthy of Fielding! 'Oho! cried Mr. Lort, what, is it better than *Fielding*?' 'Harry Fielding, answered Dr. Johnson, knew nothing but the shell of Life.' 'So *You*, Ma'am, added the flattering Mrs. Thrale, have found the *kernel*!'[18]

When we returned, to my great joy they were talking of other subjects,—yet I could not sufficiently recover myself the whole Evening to Speak one word but in *answer*; for the dread of the Criticisms which Mr. Lort might, innocently, make the next Day, kept me in a most uncomfortable state of agitation.

When Mrs. Thrale & I retired, she not only, as usual, accompanied me to my Room, but stayed with me at least an Hour, talking over the affair. I seized, with eagerness, this favourable opportunity of conjuring her not merely not to tell Mr. *Lort* my secret, but ever after never to tell *any* body. For a great while she only *Laughed*, saying 'Poor Miss Burney!—so you thought just to have played & sported with your sisters & Cousins, | & had it all your

---

[18] Cf. *Anecdotes of the Late Samuel Johnson*: 'Richardson had picked the kernel of life (he [SJ] said), while Fielding was contented with the husk' (p. 127).

own way!—but now you are *in for* it!——but if you *will* be
an Author & a Wit,—you must take the Consequence!'

ꟛ'⟨Indeed⟩! cried I, yes, in such a ⟨manner as⟩ Bet
Flint—ꟛ

But, when she found me seriously urgent, & really
frightened,—she changed her Note, & said 'O,—if I find
you are in *earnest* in desiring concealment, I shall quite
scold you!—for if such a desire does not proceed from
Affectation,—'tis from something *Worse.*'

'No, indeed, cried I, not from *Affectation,*—for my
conduct has been as uniform in trying to keep snug as my
words: & I *never* have wavered: I *never* have told *any body*
out of my own Family; nor half the Bodies in it.—And I
have so long forborne making this request to you, for no
other reason in the World but for *fear* you should think
me affected.'

'Well, I *won't* suspect you of affectation,—returned
she,—nay, I *can't*, for you have looked, like your name
sake in the Clandestine Marriage, all this Evening, of *50
Colours, I wow & purtest*;[19]—but—when I clear you of *that*,
I leave something *worse.*'

'And what,—dear Madam, *what* can be worse?'

'Why an over-delicacy that may make you unhappy all
your Life!—Indeed you must *check* it,—you must get the
better of it:—for *why* should you *write* a Book, *Print* a
Book, & have every Body *Read* & *like* your Book,—& then
sneak in a Corner & disown it!'

'My *printing* it, indeed, said I, tells terribly against ǀ me,
to all who are unacquainted with the circumstances that
belonged to it: but I had so little notion of being *discovered*,
& was so well persuaded that the Book would never be
heard of, that I really *thought* myself as safe, & *meant* to be
as private, when the Book was at Mr. Lowndes', as when
it was in my own Bureau.'

---

[19] In Act I, scene ii of Colman and Garrick's comedy, Mrs Heidelberg says
to her niece Fanny Sterling: 'Bless me, why, your face is as pale and black and
yellow—of fifty colors, I pertest.' Before and after this speech, she uses the
expression 'I vow and pertest' (*The Plays of David Garrick ... Volume 1*, ed. H. W.
Pedicord and F. L. Bergmann (Carbondale, 1980), pp. 269–70).

'Well,—I don't know what we shall do with you! it is a *sweet* Book, & it *will* make it's way, but indeed you must blunt a little of this delicacy,—for the Book has such success, that if *you* don't own it—somebody else will!'

I then told her that I had never, in the course of my life, been so much confounded as at Mr. Seward's attack; as I had not had any idea he was *au fait*; she Laughed, & said 'Poor Seward!—I am sure *he* would be hurt, if he found he had done wrong! but I told him myself.'

Again I entreated her to rest, at least, contented with the communications she had already made, & to promise not to tell Mr. Lort, nor any others.

'O, cried she, with quickness, you must excuse me!—*You* did not tell it me,—*Dr. Burney* did, & he made no conditions: so I have told it to all the people I have *seen*, if I have *liked* them, & thought they would have a *taste* for the Book.'

'O Mrs. Thrale!—' was all I could exclaim,—for I had not had any *idea* her communications had been so general, or that my Case was so desperate.

'No, no, continued she, You must *blunt* your feelings, & learn to bear, & to hear, the praises you deserve: if *I* had written the Book, I should have been proud to own it.'

'O Mrs. Thrale! this is going too far indeed!'

'Not at all; *any body* would be proud of it.'

You will not wonder I should be ashamed to hear such Words at the Time, when I assure you I am ashamed of *writing* them now.

Yet notwithstanding all her advice, & all her encouragement, I was so much *worked*[20] by the certainty of being *blown* so much more than I had apprehended, & by seeing that, in spite of all my efforts at *snugship*,[21] I was in so foul, I won't say *fair*, a way of becoming a *downright* & *known* scribler,—that I was really ill all night & I could not sleep,—&, at 4 in the morning, found myself so very unwell, that I was obliged to get up, & take a dose of nastiness with which Mr. Devaynes had furnished me, but which I had, hitherto, despised & rejected.

[20] i.e., agitated; more commonly *worked up*.
[21] This formation is not in *OED*, which missed it since it occurs in a deletion not previously published.

When Mrs. Thrale came to me the next morning [29 Aug.], she was quite concerned to find I had *really* suffered from my panics;—'O Miss Burney, cried she, what shall we do with you?—this *must* be conquered, indeed; this delicacy *must* be got over.'

'Don't call it *delicacy*, cried I, when I know you only think it folly.'

'Why indeed, said she, Laughing, it is not very *wise!*'

'Well, cried I, if, indeed, I *am* in for it,—why I must seriously set about reconciling myself—yet I never can!'

'We all Love you, said the sweet woman,—we all Love you *dearly* already,—but the Time will come when we shall all be *proud* of you;—so proud we shall not know where to place you!—you must | set about a *Comedy*,—& set about it openly; it is the true style of writing for you,—but you must give up all these fears & this shyness,—you must do it without any disadvantages,—& we will have no more of such sly, sneaking, private ways!'

I told her of my fright, while at Chesington, concerning Mrs. Williams, & of the Letter I wrote to beg my Father would hasten to caution her.[22]

'And did he?' said she.

'O yes, directly.'

'O fie!—I am ashamed of him! how can he think of humouring you in such maggots![23] If the Book had not been *liked*, I would have said *nothing* to it.—But it is a sweet Book,—& the great beauty of it is, that it reflects back all our own ideas & observations: for every body must have seen *something* similar to almost all the incidents.

In short, had I been the *Child* of this delightful woman; she could not have taken more pains [to][24] reconcile me to my situation: even when she *Laughed*, she continued, by her manner, still to *Assure*, or to *sooth* me.

We went down together. My Heart was in my mouth as we got to the Library, where all the Gentlemen were waiting. I made Mrs. Thrale go in before me;—Mr. Lort was seated close to the Door, Evelina in his Hand,—Mrs.

---

[22] See above, pp. 62, 63.
[23] Whimsical or perverse fancies.   [24] Inserted by FBA.

Thrale began asking how he found it?—I could not, if my life had depended on it,—I am *sure* I could not at that moment have followed her in,—& therefore,—I skipt into the Music Room.

However foolish all this may seem, the foolery occasioned *me* no manner of *fun*,—for I was quite in ¦ an agony. However, as I met with Miss Thrale, in a few minutes, we went into the Library together.

Because I was in a hurry to sneak to my seat, nobody would let me pass without speaking to me: we had exactly the same party as the Night before. However, to my great relief, though not a little to my surprise, not a syllable was said by *any* body of, or relative to my Book.

Dr. Johnson was later than usual this morning, & did not come down till our Breakfast was over, & Mrs. Thrale had risen to give some orders, I believe: I, too, rose, & took a Book at another End of the Room. Some Time after,—before he had yet appeared, Mr. Thrale called out to me 'so, Miss Burney, you have a mind to feel your legs before the Doctor comes?'

'Why so?' cried Mr. Lort.

'Why because when he comes she will be confined.'

'Ay?—how is that?'

'Why he never lets her leave him, but keeps her prisoner till he goes to his own Room.'

'O ho! cried Mr. Lort, she is in great favour with him.'

'Yes, said Mr. Seward, & I think he shews his Taste.'

'I did not know, said Mr. Lort, but he might keep her to help him in his Lives of the Poets.'

'And yet, said Mrs. Thrale, Miss Burney never flatters him, though she is such a favourite with him;—but the Tables are turned,—for *he* sits & flatters *her*!

'*I* don't flatter him, said I, because nothing *I* could say *would* flatter him.'

Mrs. Thrale then told a story of Hannah More,[25] which I think exceeds, in its severity, *all* the severe things I have yet heard of Dr. Johnson's saying.

---

[25] Hannah More (1745–1833), religious writer.

When she was introduced to him,—not long a go,[26]—
she ¦ began singing his praises in the warmest manner: &
talking of the pleasure & the instruction she had received
from his writings, with the highest encomiums. For some
Time, he heard her with that quietness which a long
use of praise has given him: she then redoubled her
⌐charges¬ &, as Mr. Seward calls it, *peppered* her flattery
still more highly:[27] till, at length, he turned suddenly to
her, with a stern & angry Countenance, & said 'Madam,
before you flatter a man so grossly to his Face, you should
consider whether or not your flattery is worth his
having.'![28]

⌐Good God,¬ how the poor Creature must have been
confounded! Yet she deserved *some* rebuke for laying it
on so thick & clumsily.

Mr. Seward then told another instance of his determination not to *mince the matter*, when he thought reproof at
all deserved. During a Visit of Miss Brown to Streatham,
he was enquiring of her several things she could not
answer;—&, as he held her so cheap in regard to *Books*,
he began to question her concerning *domestic* affairs,—
puddings, pies, plain work, & so forth: Miss Brown, not
at all more able to give a Good account of herself in these
articles, than in the others, began all her answers with
'Why Sir, one *need not* be obliged to *do so,—or so,*' what
ever was the thing in question: & when he had finished

---

[26] Actually, in June 1774 (*Life* iv. 341 n. 6).

[27] Cf. Goldsmith's *Retaliation*, l. 112: 'Who peppered the highest were surest
to please' (with reference to Garrick's hunger for praise). See *The Poems of
Thomas Gray, William Collins, Oliver Goldsmith*, ed. R. Lonsdale (1969), p. 754.

[28] HLT's version in *Anecdotes* (p. 122) is still more severe: ' ... he once bade
a very celebrated lady, who praised him with too much zeal perhaps, or perhaps
too strong an emphasis (which always offended him), "consider what her
flattery was worth before she choaked *him* with it."' She softens the anecdote,
though, by adding that 'A few more winters passed in the talking world shewed
him the value of that friend's commendations however; and he was very sorry
for the disgusting speech he made her.' Boswell, in the *Life* (iv. 341–2), attacks
HLT's 'inaccuracy'. He cites Edmond Malone's account of the meeting, according to which SJ's reproof was a milder 'Dearest lady, consider with yourself
what your flattery is worth, before you bestow it so freely.' Miss More herself
merely records that SJ met her 'with good humour in his countenance, and
continued in the same pleasant humour the whole of the evening' (*Memoirs*, ed.
W. Roberts (1834), i. 48, cited in *Life* iv. 341 n. 6).

his interrogotaries, & she had finished her *need nots*,—he
ended the Discourse with saying 'As to your *needs*, my
dear, they are so very many, that you would be frightened
yourself if you knew half of them.'

O horrid, horrible, & horridest horror! What a speech!
I think I should never have recovered from it. ⎮

When Mrs. Thrale & I returned down stairs from our
Toilettes, we found Mr. Seward & Mr. Lort in close *confab*.
I had a French Translation of 'The Prince of Abyssinia'[29]
in my Hand, which Mrs. Thrale had just given me to look
at:—but I saw the 2 Gentlemen were employed with
another Book.

'Mr. Lort, said Mrs. Thrale, I fancy you have never
seen the Book Miss Burney has in her Hand.'

'Book? cried he,—ay, Miss Burney!—*your* Book, I am
sure, has made me both Laugh & Cry![30]—

'O! so I suppose!' cried I, stalking away, in much
vexation to be thus eternally betrayed.

Mr. Seward followed me,—& said he was very sorry to
see me so uneasy the Night before; & added 'I wanted to
have told Lort immediately,—but they would not let me.'

'O,—you are vastly good! cried I; but pray who has told
him *now?*'

'*I* have;' cried he—'I told him in order to stop him,
because I saw the subject made you uneasy.'

Curious enough! But I am now *certain* that Mr. Seward
has never been made to understand how the affair stood,
or that any secresy was wished by me.

'But, Miss Burney, continued he, you must not stop
here,—we all hope for a *Comedy*,—*I* am certain you would
shine particularly in that walk.'

I then contrived to turn off,—& he said no more.

'But pray, Mr. Lort, cried Mrs. Thrale, who ⎮ first told
you of this Book?'

---

[29] *Histoire de Rasselas, prince d'Abissinie*, trans. Octavie Belot, née Guichard
(1719–1804), Amsterdam and Paris, 1760; reprinted 1768.

[30] See above, p. 57.

'The anatomy professor at Cambridge,[31] answered he. He recommended it to me,—but I told him I never read Novels,—No more do I, cried he, but, for all that, you must read *this*,—every body does. But how could I suspect it to be Miss Burney's? I declare I shall always ask if the author of a Book is in the Room, before I mention one again.'

Sunday morning [30 Aug.], when I went into the Library, Mr. Thrale called out 'Why, Miss Burney, this will never do!'

'What, Sir?' cried I.

'Why You grow Thinner & Thinner! You have hardly any *waist* left already! What account can I give of you to Dr. Burney?'

'Ay, well, cried Mr. Lort, drily,—she will be *all* spirit, & *no* substance, by & by, for she *Eats* nothing;—however, it will be all the better for the *World*, one way or other!'

'Yes,—cried Mr. Seward, in a low voice,—I hope it will be all the better for our Comedy!'

After Breakfast,

[*FB's original journal letter breaks off abruptly here. As with her previous journal, she was probably obliged to send to SEB 'a strange unfinished scrawl' by the Sunday morning post (see above, p. 91). Editing this journal letter a half-century later, FBA took advantage of a page and 4 lines left blank at the end to append an embroidered account of SJ's joke that FB should write 'Stretham, a Farce'. (The original account above, p. 111, is deleted in the MS.) FBA's revision is notable only for its pomposity and for rendering SJ pompous; it is written in the grotesquely inflated style of her* Memoirs of Doctor Burney.]

---

[31] Charles Collignon (1725–85), MD (Cantab.), 1754; FRS, 1770; professor of anatomy at Cambridge, 1753–85. Lort later was a subscriber to Collignon's posthumous *Miscellaneous Works* (Cambridge, 1786).

59

[Streatham,
3 September 1778]

To Susanna Elizabeth Burney

AJL (Diary MSS I, paginated 799–810, Berg), Oct. [*sic*] 1778
6 single sheets 4to, 12 pp.
Annotated (by FBA): ❋·
In editing this letter, FBA shifted it out of its proper chronological
sequence and paginated it accordingly. At the beginning FB backtracks
to an account of Sat. evening and then skips ahead to church attendance on Sun. It is probable that a leaf or more is missing at the start
since there is no salutation or account of Sat. afternoon.

Saturday Evening [29 Aug.], Mr. & Mrs. Thrale took
me quite round the Paddock, & shewed me their Hot
Houses, kitchen Gardens, &c. Their size & their Contents
are astonishing: but we have not *once* missed a pine apple
since I came, & therefore you may imagine their abundance: besides Grapes, melons, peaches, nectarines, &
Ices.

Sunday [30 Aug.] we went to Streatham Church: &
afterwards to visit the Family of the Pitches, who now
Live in Bedford House, which is about ½ a mile off. The
Papa I did not see; the *mama* is a civil simple woman, &
the Daughters[32] are pretty, well Dressed, trifling, & *furiously* extravagant: While Mrs. Thrale & I were Dressing,
&, as usual, *confabing*, a Chaise drove into the Park, &
word was brought that Mr. Seward was arrived. 'You
don't know much of Mr. Seward, Miss Burney?' said Mrs.
Thrale.

[32] There were 6 daughters: Jane (the eldest, living 1808), m. (29 Sept. 1779)
William Boyce (*c.*1742–1808), later Lt-Col. of the 16th or Queen's (Light)
Dragoons; Margaret ('Peggy') (1760–1840), m. (1783) George William Coventry
(1758–1831), Visc. Deerhurst, 7th E. of Coventry (1809); Sophia (1761–79)
(above, p. 109); Emily (living 1792); Penelope (d. 1787), m. (1783) Revd Robert
Sheffield (*c.*1758–1815), 3rd Bt (1815); and Julia (1774–1854), m. (1799) Revd
William John Jolliffe (1774–1835). See *DL* vi. 398; *GM* cxxiv[1] (1854), 555; O.
Manning and W. Bray, *History and Antiquities of ... Surrey* (1804–14), iii. 394;
will of Sir Abraham Pitches, PCC, dated 12 Jan., prob. 27 Apr. 1792.

I *could* have told her I wished he had not known much of *me*; but her maid was in my way, & I only said *no*.

'But I hope you *will* know more of him, said she, for I want you to take to him. He is a charming young man, though not without oddities. Few people do him justice, because, as Mr. Johnson calls him, he is an *abrupt* young man; but he has excellent qualities, & an excellent understanding. He has the misfortune to be an *Hypochondriac*, so he runs *about* the World, to *borrow spirits*, & to forget himself. But, after all, if his disorders *are* merely imaginary, the *Imagination* is Disorder sufficient, & therefore I am sorry for him.' The Day past very agreeably, but I have no Time for particulars. I fight very shy[33] with Mr. Seward, &, as he has a great share of sense & penetration, & not a *little* one of pride & reserve, he takes the hint, & I believe he would as soon *bite off his own Nose* as mention Evelina again. And, indeed, now that the propriety of his *after* conduct I has softened me in his favour, I begin to think of him much in the same way Mrs. Thrale does, for he is very sensible, very intelligent, & very well bred.

Monday [31 Aug.] was the Day for our great party,—& the Doctor came Home, at Mrs. Thrale's request, to meet them.

The Party consisted of Mr. Cator,[34] who was formerly a Timber Merchant, but, having amassed a Fortune of 1.00:0000 [*sic*] pounds, he has left off Business. He is a good natured, busy sort of man.

Mrs. Cator,[35] his Lady;—a sort of Mrs. Nobody.

Mr. Norman,[36] another Rich Business *leaver* off.

Mrs. Norman,[37] his Lady; a pretty sort of woman, who was formerly a Pupil of Dr. Hawkesworth: I had a great

---

[33] The earliest instance of the expression in *OED* (s.v. fight, *v*. 9).

[34] John Cator (1728–1806), of Bank Side, Southwark, and Beckenham, Kent; timber merchant; MP (Namier). 'Rough in his manners, acute in his Judgement, skilful in Trade, and solid in Property' (*Thraliana*, i. 418), he was one of the executors of Henry Thrale's will.

[35] Mary Collinson (1733–1804), daughter of Peter Collinson (1694–1768), naturalist, antiquary, and friend of Benjamin Franklin; m. (1753) John Cator.

[36] James Norman (d. 1787), of Bromley, Kent (*GM* xlvii² (1787), 840).

[37] Eleanora Innocent (d. 1819), m. (8 Jan. 1761, at Bromley, as his 2nd wife) James Norman (IGI). She was presumably Dr Hawkesworth's pupil in the girl's school run by his wife at Bromley (see Abbott, pp. 12–13).

deal of Talk with her about him, & about my favourite
Miss Kinnaird,[38] whom she knew very well.

Mr. George   her sons in Law, 2 youths
      Norman,[39]   whom Miss Thrale has, not
Mr Thom^s   [i]naptly, named Mr. Smiths.

Mr. Rice.[40]—of whom I know nothing but that he
married into Mr. Thrale's Family.

Lady Ladd [Lade];—I ought to have *begun* with her![41]—
I beg her Ladyship a thousand pardons,—though if she
knew my offence, I am sure I should not obtain *one*. She
is own sister to Mr. Thrale. She is a Tall & stout Woman,
has an air of mingled dignity & haughtiness, both of
which wear off in Conversation. She Dresses very gaily,
& attends to her person with no little complacency: she
appears to me quite uncultivated, in knowledge, though
an adept in the manners of the World, & *all that*. She
chuses to be much more lively than her Brother, but
liveliness sits as awkwardly upon her as her pink Ribbons.
In talking her over with Mrs. Thrale, who has a very
proper regard for her, but who, I am *sure*, cannot be *blind*
to her, she gave me another proof to those I [have]
already had, of the uncontrolled ‖ freedom of speech
which Dr. Johnson exercises to *every* body, & which *every*
body receives quietly from *him*! Lady Ladd *has* been very
handsome, but is now, I think, quite ugly,—at least, she
has a *sort* of Face I like not. Well, she was, a little while
ago, Dressed in so showy a manner as to attract the

[38] Margaret Kinnaird (d. 1800), later Mrs Wiggens (*EJL* i. 250 n. 66).

[39] George Norman (1756–1830), merchant in the Norway timber trade;
sheriff of Kent (1793). 'Thom^s' is probably an error for George's brother
Richard Norman (1757/8–1847), MP for Bramber (1804–6). They were James
Norman's sons by his 1st wife, Henrietta née Wroughton (d.?1759/60) of
Woodford, Essex, daughter of James Wroughton (IGI; *GM* cxvii¹ (1847), 331;
additional information kindly supplied by Miss E. Silverthorne, Archivist,
Bromley Civic Centre, and Mr J. L. Filmer).

[40] John ('Jack') Rice (1751–1801), who had eloped in 1773 with Frances
('Fanny') Plumbe (1758–90), daughter of Samuel Plumbe (1717–84), Alderman,
Ld. Mayor of London (1778–9), and Frances, née Thrale (1726–1811), sister
of Henry Thrale (*TSP*, pp. 61–2 and *passim*; *GM* lxxxi¹ (1811), 596; A. Beaven,
The Aldermen of the City of London (1908), ii. 133; O. Manning and W. Bray,
History and Antiquities of ... Surrey (1804–14), iii. 376–7).

[41] Because of her rank.

Doctor's regard,—&, when he had looked at her some Time, he broke out aloud into this quotation.

> With Patches, Paint, & Jewels on,
> Sure Phillis is not Twenty one!—
> —But if at *Night* you Phillis see—
> —The Dame, at least, is Forty Three![42]—

I don't recollect the Verses *exactly*, but such was their purport. 'However, said Mrs. Thrale, Lady Ladd took it very good naturedly, & only said, Lord, I know enough of that *43*,—I don't desire to hear any more of it!'—

Miss Moss,[43]—a pretty Girl, who *played & sung*, to the great fatigue of Mrs. Thrale.

Mr. Rose Fuller, Mr. Embry, Mr. Seward, Dr. Johnson, the 3 Thrales & myself close the party.

We had a sumptuous Dinner, of 3 Courses, & a most superb Desert [*sic*]. I shall give no account of the Day, because our *Common* Days are so much more worth recounting. But I must mention that Mrs. Thrale was, if possible, ⌜more attentive to me than ever for the ⟨praises⟩ of these rich folks, & that they all took the hint, & I was made so much of, as you never *saw the like*—& I have⌝ such a load of Invitations!—such a one, by the way, as I would not be bound to *accept* for any *small* bribery.

The *sailor*,[44] who Dr. Johnson bid me *mark*, did not come. |

I had the Honour of making Tea & Coffee for all this set, & upon my Word I was pretty well tired of it. But, since the first 2 Days, I have always made Tea, & now I am also the *Break fast woman*. I am by no means passionately fond of the Task, but I am very glad to do any thing that is ⌜a⌝ sort of relief to Mrs. T.

In the Evening, the Company divided pretty much into Parties, & almost every body walked upon the Gravel

[42] SJ's lines, inexactly recalled by FB, were probably his own Swiftian improvisation. He reverses the situation of Swift's Celia, whom the Dean advises 'to shine by Night' ('The Progress of Beauty', l. 72; *The Poems of Jonathan Swift*, ed. H. Williams (2nd edn., Oxford, 1958), i. 228).

[43] Perhaps Harriot Margaret Moss (*c.*1766–1841), m. (1792) John King (1760–1830), brother of Walter King (below, p. 201).

[44] Admiral Montagu (above, p. 93).

Walk before the Windows. I was going to have joined
some of them, when Dr. Johnson stopt me, & asked how
I did, ⸢& so forth, for⸣ 'I was afraid, Sir, cried I, You did
not intend to *know* me again, for you have not spoken to
me before, since your return from Town.'

'My dear, cried he, taking both my Hands, I was not
sure of you, I am so near sighted, & I apprehended
making some mistake.' Then, drawing me, very unex-
pectedly, towards him, he actually kissed me!—

To be sure I was a little *surprised*, having no idea of
such *facetiousness* from him, however, I was glad nobody
was in the Room but Mrs. Thrale, who stood close to us,
& Mr. Embry, who was lounging on a sopha at the furthest
End of the Room. Mrs. Thrale Laughed heartily, & said
she hoped I was *contented with his amends* for not knowing
me sooner!

A little after, she said she would go & Walk with the
rest, if she did not fear for my reputation, in being left,
almost in the Dark, with the Doctor.—'However, as Mr.
Embry is yonder, I think he'll take some [care]⁴⁵ of you,'
she added:—'Ay, Madam, said the Doctor, we ǀ shall do
very well;—but I assure you I sha'n't part with Miss
Burney!' And he held me by both Hands; & when Mrs.
Thrale went, he drew me a sopha facing the Window,
close to his own;—& thus, Tête à Tete, we continued
almost all the Evening! I say *Tête à Tete* because Mr.
Embry kept an humble distance, & offered us no interruption. And though Mr. Seward soon after came in, he,
also, seated himself in a distant Corner, not presuming,
he said, to break in upon us!—

Our Conversation chiefly was upon the Hebrides, for
he always talks to me of Scotland ⸢for *sport*⸣: & he *wished*
I had been of that Tour!⁴⁶—quite *gravely*, I assure you!—
[xxxxx ½ *line*]

By degrees, however, our party encreased;—Mr. Thrale
came in; Mr. Embry ventured to approach us nearer;—&
then Mr. Seward came & flung himself upon the back of

---

⁴⁵ Inserted by FBA.
⁴⁶ With Boswell in 1773.

my sopha: The Company being now all gone, except these Gentlemen & Lady Ladd, who were to stay all Night, Mrs. Thrale accepted my invite from the Window, & came & sat by me, & we had a *most nice* general conversation, till Mrs. Thrale said she must see after Lady Ladd.—I rose, to accompany her, but Mr. Seward, taking advantage of the *Dark*, for we have no Candles at Streatham till we go into the Library, *held* me, saying 'No, no, we must not lose *you* too!'—

I fancy the folks had all drunk too much Champagne!—for Mr. Seward is, commonly, as shy as any *Girl* can be. So here I was held a Prisoner till Mrs. Thrale called me away—& we went into the Library,—& the Evening was concluded with very serious & sad reflections upon the present dreadful prospect of public affairs;[47]—& Rose Fuller began moralising upon our luxuries, & seemed half angry we had had so fine a *Dinner*, for he *raved* at our feasting on *veneson* [*sic*] & *pine apples*, &c, when *poor old England* was in such danger!—however, he took care to ensure his *own* share before he preached. However, though I *affect not* writing upon politics, which I am sure you would be the last person to wish to read, I must own I am made very soberly melancholy whenever I think upon this subject.—& no other occurs so often.

Tuesday morning [1 Sept.] our Breakfast was delightful. We had Mr. Seward, Mr. Embry, & Lady Ladd added to our usual party, & Dr. Johnson was quite in a sportive humour.—but I can only write some few disjointed speeches, wanting *Time* to be prolix, not *inclination*.

'Sir, said Mrs. Thrale, to Dr. John[son][48] Why did you not sooner leave your Wine Yesterday, & come to *us?*—we had a *Miss* who *sung*, & *played like any thing*!'

'Ay, had you? said he, drolly, & why did you not call me to the rapturous Entertainment?'

'Why I was afraid you would not have *praised* her, for I sat thinking all the Time myself, whether it was better to sing & play as *she* sung & played,—or to do *nothing*! And

---

[47] France had joined the Americans in their war against Great Britain, leading to fears of a French invasion. See below, p. 146 n. 76.

[48] Added by FBA.

at *first*, I thought *she* had the best of it, for we were but stupid before she began;—but *after*wards,—she made it so *long*, that I thought *nothing* ⎹ had all the advantage. But, Sir,—Lady Ladd has had the same misfortune *you* had, for she has fallen down & hurt herself wofully.'

'How did that happen, Madam?'

'Why, Sir, the Heel of her shoe caught in something.'

'*Heel?* repeated he;—nay, then, if her Ladyship, *who walks six foot high*, (N.B. this is a *fact*) will wear a *Heel*,— I think she almost *deserves* a fall!'

'⌐Lord⌐, Sir, my Heel was not high!' cried Lady Ladd.

'But, Madam, why should you wear *any*? That for which there is no occasion, had always better be dispensed with. However, a fall to your *Ladyship* is nothing, continued he, Laughing,—*you*, who are light & little, can soon recover: but *I*, who am a gross man, might suffer severely: with your Ladyship the case is different, for

Airy substance soon unites again.[49]

Poor Lady Ladd, who is quite a *strapper*, made no answer,—but she was not *offended*,—no, Mrs. Thrale & I afterwards settled, that, not knowing his *allusion* from the Rape of the Lock, she only thought he had made a *stupid* speech, & did not trouble herself to find a meaning to it.

'However, continued he, if *my* fall *does* confine me, I will make my confinement pleasant, for Miss Burney shall Nurse me,—*possitively* [*sic*]!—(& he slapt his Hand on the Table,) & then,—she shall *sing* to me, & sooth my cares,— she shall sing me a song, Of 2 Days long,

The Woodcock & the sparrow;
Our little Dog has bit his Tail,
And he'll be Hang'd to-morrow!' ⎹ [50]

---

[49] *Rape of the Lock* iii. 152.

[50] FB's MS is the earliest written source of this nursery rhyme, which was first printed in *Gammer Gurtons's Garland* (1784). The version here differs from all other recorded examples. Mrs Barrett omitted it from her edition, presumably to protect SJ's dignity. Joyce Hemlow published it in *HFB*, p. 114. E. L. McAdam, Jr., and G. Milne ascribe it to SJ in their edition of his *Poems* (New Haven, 1964), p. 300. See also the *Oxford Dictionary of Nursery Rhymes*, ed. I. and P. Opie (Oxford, 1973), pp. 393–4.

'Lady Ladd, said Mrs. Thrale, You are so fine you quite shame *me*,—your Hair is so beautifully Dressed. (Her *Hair Dresser* was ordered to attend her *here*—think of that, Master Brook!)[51] But what will your Ladyship do if you should out-live wearing *Pink?*'

'I don't know,—I believe I should wear lilac.'

'Lilac? repeated Mr. Seward, 'I think *that* is yet Younger;—I am *sure* it is more elegant.'

By the way, when I was next alone with Mrs. Thrale, she said she really believed Lady Ladd would wear *Pink* in her Coffin! 'I'm sure, she added, if any Captain ran away with *her* Cap, she could not say it was the *only* one that *had pink Ribbon in it*, like Mᶜ Duval,[52] for I don't think she has a Cap in the World with any other Colour.'

When public News was started, Mr. Thrale desired the subject might be waved till my *Father* came, & let us know what *part* of the late accounts were true.[53]

'But Dr. Burney is not to take *you* away from us, is he?' said Dr. Johnson, taking my Hand.

'No, no; cried Mrs. Thrale, *I* sha'n't suffer that,—besides, Dr. Burney loves us too well to do us such an injury.'

'Were he *two* Dr. Burneys, exclaimed he, he *should* not take her away, if I could help it!'

There's Honour & Glory!

Mr. Thrale then offered to carry Mr. Seward, who was obliged to go, to Town in ⌐his⌐ Coach—& Mr. Embry also left us. But Dr. Johnson sat with Mrs. Thrale, Lady Ladd & me for an Hour or two.

The *subject* was given by Lady Ladd; it was *The Respect due from the lower Class of the people*. 'I know my place, said

[51] A Burney family catch-phrase taken from *The Merry Wives of Windsor*, III. v. See *EJL* i. 81 n. 3.

[52] *Evelina*, vol. ii, letter 3.

[53] At this time, in home waters, Admiral Keppel's fleet was fruitlessly chasing the French fleet under the Comte d'Orvilliers, while a squadron under the Comte d'Estaing was menacing the British forces in New York and Rhode Island. The Streatham set probably assumed that CB would know the true state of affairs from his friend Ld. Sandwich, First Lord of the Admiralty. See *The Private Papers of John, Earl of Sandwich*, ed. G. R. Barnes and J. H. Owen (1932–8), ii. 10–13, 285–8 and *passim*; also, *YW* xxiv. 405–7, 410–11.

Lady Ladd, & I always *take* it: & I've no notion of *not* taking it. But Mrs. Thrale let's [*sic*] all sort of people do just as they've a mind by her.'

'Lord, said Mrs. Thrale, why should I torment & worry my self about all the paltry marks of *respect* that consist in Bows & Courtsies?—I have no idea of troubling myself about the *manners* of all the people I mix with.'

'No, said Lady Ladd, & so they will take all sort of liberties with you. I remember, when you were at my House, how the Hair Dresser flung down the Comb, as soon as you were Dressed, & went out of the Room without making a Bow.'

'Well, all the better, said Mrs. Thrale, for if he *had* made one, Ten thousand to one if I had seen it! I was in as great haste to have done with *him*, as he could be to have done with *me*. I was glad enough to get him out of the Room; I did not want him to stay Bowing & Cringing.'

'If any man had behaved so insolently to *me*, answered she, I would never again have suffered him in my House.'

'Well, said Mrs. Thrale, your Ladyship has a great deal more dignity than I have!—Mr. Johnson, we are talking of the *respect* due from inferiors;—& Lady Ladd is of the same side *you* are.'

'Why, Madam, said he, subordination is always necessary to the preservation of order & decorum.'

'I protest, said Lady Ladd, I have no notion of submitting to any kind of impertinence: & I never will bear either to have any person *Nod* to me, or enter a Room where I am, without Bowing.'

'But, Madam, said Dr. Johnson, what if they *will* Nod; & what if they *won't* Bow?—how then?'

'Why I always tell them of it.' said she.

'O, commend me to that! cried Mrs. Thrale, I'd sooner never see another Bow in my life, than turn Dancing master to Hair Dressers!'

The Doctor Laughed his approbation,—but said that every man had a right to a *certain degree* of respect, & no man liked to be defrauded of that right.

'Well, Sir, said Mrs. Thrale, I hope *you* meet with Respect enough!'

'Yes, Madam, answered he, I am very well contented.'

'Nay, if *you* a'n't, I don't know who should be!—for I believe there is no man in the World so *greatly* respected.'

Soon after *he* went,—*I* went,—& shut myself up in a sweet cool summer House to read *Irene*:—which, indeed, though not a good *play*, is a beautiful *Poem*.

As my dear Father spent the rest of the Day here, I will not further particularize, but leave accounts to his better communication.—He probably told you that the *Pitches* Family came in to Tea;—&, as he *knows* Mrs. Pitches, pray tell him what Dr. Johnson says of ¹ her:—When they were gone, Mrs. Thrale complained that she was quite *worn out* with that tiresome, silly woman; ⌐& that⌐ she had talked of her Family & affairs till she was sick to Death of hearing her. 'Madam, said he, why do you blame the Woman for the only sensible thing she could do?—talking of her Family & her affairs? For how should a Woman who is as empty as a Drum, talk upon any other subject?—If you speak to her of the *sun*,—she does not know it rises in the East;—if you speak to her of the *moon*, she does not know it changes at the full;—if you speak to her of the *Queen*, she does not know she is the King's wife,—how then, can you blame her for talking of her Family & affairs?'

Yesterday morning [2 Sept.], to my great regret, he went to Town.—but we expect him again to Day. Lady Ladd also went yesterday, to my *no* regret,—nor yet to my *Joy*, for she was most extremely civil & gracious to me,—only I should be glad to know who would *dare* be otherwise at the House of Mrs. Thrale? Her Ladyship Honoured me, also, with a very particular invitation to accompany Mrs. Thrale to see her when in Town.

When they were gone,—O Susy, I had *such* a Conversation with Mrs. Thrale!—We were alone in the Library for I believe 3 Hours;—& though I shall only give you 2 or 3 of the *principal speeches*, I am sure you will not wonder that the extraordinary good opinion she professes of me should have quite overpowered me with gratitude & surprise.

Our Tete à Tête began by comparing Notes about Irene & picking out favourite passages, & agreeing that, though the Language & sentiments are equally Noble, there was not any reason to wonder that the play all together had no success on the stage. Thence we talked over all the Plays we could recollect & discussed their several merits according to our particular Notions,—& when we had mentioned a great number, approving some for *This thing*, & disliking others for *that*,—Mrs. | Thrale suddenly said 'Now, Miss Burney, if *you* would write a Play, I have a Notion it would hit *my* Taste in *all* things;—do,—you *must* write one;—a *play* will be something *worth* your Time, it is the Road both to Honour & Profit,—& *why* should you have it in your power to gain ⌐⟨these rewards⟩⌐ & not do it?'

'O Ma'am—how *can* you—' But I won't write the Answers, or, rather, *exclammations* with which I interrupted her,—for they *make no effect upon paper!*—

'I declare, continued she, I *mean*, & *think* what I say with all my Heart & soul!—You seem to me to have the right & true talents for writing a Comedy,—you would give us all the fun & humour we could wish, & you would give us a scene or 2 of the pathetic kind that would set all the rest off. If you would but *try*, I am *sure* you would succeed, & give us such a Play as would be an Honour to all your Family. And, in the *grave* parts, all your sentiments would be Edifying, & such as would *do good*,—& I am sure *that* would be real pleasure to you.'—My dear Susy, I *assure* you I recollect her words as exactly as my memory will allow. 'Hannah More, added she, got near 400 pounds for her foolish play,[54]—& if *you* did not write a better than *hers*, I say you deserve to be *whipped!*—Your Father, I know, thinks the same,—but we will *allow* that *he* may be partial but what can make *me* think it?—& *Dr. Johnson*;—*he*, of all men, would not say it if he did not think it.

---

[54] Hannah More's tragedy of *Percy* was produced at Covent Garden on 10 Dec. 1777 and performed 19 times. The author's benefit nights of 12, 17, and 22 Dec. 1777 gave her net receipts (after house charges) of £273. 14s. 6d. 4,117 copies of the 1st edn. of her play were sold in 2 weeks; the publisher, Thomas Cadell, gave her £150. See *LS* 5 i. 133–58 *passim*; Stone, p. 435.

She then rejoiced I had published Evelina as I did, without shewing it to any body; 'Because You have proved what are your own real resources, she said, & now,—you have nothing to do but to write a *Play*, ⌐& both Fame & Profit will attend you.¬ Mr. Johnson, *I* am sure, will be at your service in any thing in his power,—we'll make him write your Prologue,—we'll make him carry your play to the manag[ers;] we'll do *any* thing for you, & so, I am sure, he readily will! As to *Plot, situation,* & *Character,*— *Nobody* shall assist you in *them*, for nobody *can!*'—In short, my dear Susy, I was ready to *greet*[55] at the kind things she said, & the sweet manner in which she said them: but I will write no more of them, as these *Heads* will give a notion of all the [rest.][56]

[*The Journal for 1778 resumes. FB evidently wrote this entry, on a single leaf, between her return from Streatham and her going back there, on 12 Sept.*]

St Martin's Street, London.

Yesterday morning Mr. Lort called. My Father was not at Home, but he enquired for *me*,—& came into the Parlour,—only Charlotte & me being there.

We talked over Streatham,—& it's charming Inhabitants, & our opinions could not but co-incidè. He stated very highly the singular favour I have met with from Dr. Johnson, said *Mrs. Thrale* might be jealous of me, & was *vast* civil in his implications. He told me he had a very ingenious & entertaining Book, called Memoirs of—I forget who—which he had promised to send Mrs. Thrale,—but he gave me the offer of first reading it, if I had any curiosity to see it. I thanked him, & *all that*, but prefered having it *after* Mrs. Thrale, as being more decorus [*sic*] & seemly.

---

[55] Weep (for joy); Scottish or northern dialect. The term no doubt recurred in the conversation of the Burneys' many Scottish friends and acquaintances. See *OED* s.v. greet *v.*²; *EDD*; *SND*.

[56] The last sentence is squeezed into the bottom of the leaf; presumably the letter ended here.

He sat about a quarter of an Hour,—& left me well pleased with his Visit, because he never mentioned Evelina,—& I cannot bear to be *palavered* upon that subject;—the flattery I met with at Streatham, would, indeed, have spoilt me for almost all other, by the delicacy of it's texture, had I been ever so greedy of it naturally: but Mr. Lort saw my *Father* the Day before, & to *him* was less scrupulous, but expressed great wonder *where & how* I could have picked up such materials,—& the more so, as I seemed so silent & so quiet.

Thus it is, that an *Authoress* must always be supposed to be flippant, assuming & loquacious!—And, indeed, the dread of these kind of censures I have been my principal motives for wishing *snugship*.[57]

Snugship, however, is now, I fear, all over!—for the fear of *accident* betraying me, since the affair is in so many Hands, has occasioned still *further* spreading even with my *Consent*, which *now* I know not how to withhold, lest I *disoblige* my Friends, merely to gain a *few Weeks* privacy,— for longer I know not how to *hope*, as things are now situated, & as all quarters are blabbing away.

Susan, therefore, with my concurrence, has written the state of the Case to *Lady Hales*:[58]—my Father, almost at my *desire*, has told my uncle, who now I think has a *right* to the information; & my mother, of her own accord, has written it to Miss Young.

Heigh ho!—I part with this my dear, long loved, long cherished *snugship* with more regret than any body will believe, except my dear sisters who *Live with* me, & know me too well & too closely to doubt me: but yet, I am niether insensible to the *Honours* which have wrested my secret from my Friends, nor Cold to the *pleasures* attending a success so unhoped for: yet my fears for the *future*—& my dread of getting into *Print*, & thence into *Public*

---

[57] This formation is not in *OED*, since this journal entry has not been previously published. Cf. above, p. 117.

[58] The letter is missing. Lady Hales replied to SEB on 7 Sept. (Barrett), thanking her for the intelligence and promising to keep the secret even from her daughter Miss Coussmaker, who 'is a good & sensible girl, but young, & sometimes rather too unthinking.' The letter from EAB to Dorothy Young is also missing. The 'uncle' is Richard Burney of Barborne Lodge.

Notice,— — — I niether now can,—or believe I ever shall, wholly Conquer! |

60
Streatham,
[*post* 15] September [1778]
To Susanna Elizabeth Burney

AJL (Diary MSS I, paginated 755–66, Berg), Sept. 1778
6 single sheets 4to, 12 pp.
Addressed: Miss Susan Burney | St Martin's Street, | Leicester Fields. | London
The journal is dated by its content, which covers the period from Sat., 12 Sept., when FB returned to Streatham for another visit, to Tues., 15 Sept.

Streatham.
Sept^r

I must now *begin* a Journal to you, my dearest Girl, in spite of your *leave* that I might forbear,—for I am too deeply in arrears with you to feel comfortable without making, at least, some *effort* at payment.[59] I shall keep *Notes* of all that passes, & write *at length* as Time & opportunity will allow.

Our Journey hither [12 Sept.] proved, as it promised, most sociably chearful: & Mrs. Thrale opened still further upon the subject she began in St. Martin's Street, of Dr. Johnson's kindness towards me: to be sure she saw it was not *totally* disagreeable to me; though I was really *astound* [*sic*] when she hinted at my becoming a Rival to *Miss Stretfield* in the Doctor's good graces! 'I had a long Letter, she said, from Sophy Stretfield t'other Day, & she sent Mr. Johnson her elegant Edition of the Classics:[60] but,

---

[59] SEB's journal to FB, implied here, is missing.

[60] 'It was a Greek Demosthene, given her by Dr. Collier' (HLTP's annotation in a copy of *Letters to and from the Late Samuel Johnson, LL.D.* (1788), cited *LSJ* iii. 127 n. 4). SJ wrote to HLT on 15 Oct. (the letter HLTP annotates): 'I hope you let Miss Stratfield [*sic*] know how safe you keep her book. It was too fine for a Scholar's talons' (ibid. iii. 127). For SJ's rough handling of books, see *EJL* ii. 96–7.

when he had read the Letter, he said 'she is a sweet Creature, & I love her much,—but my little Burney writes a better Letter. Now, continued she, *that* is just what I *wished* him to say of you both.'

When we came within sight of the House, & I was congratulating myself on so soon re-entering it, & expressing some part of my fondness for its walls,—'This, said she, I am sure is among its good things,—that it brings *you* within them.'

In short, she is never tired of saying, or of doing, sweet things. Mr. Thrale came out to the Door, & received me with more civility than ever: indeed, we are *beginning* to grow a little acquainted. With *Miss* Thrale, I had all the business to do over again, for she has such a natural propensity to silence, coldness & reserve, that, I believe, who ever she has not seen for *3 Days*, she meets as a *stranger.*

We had no Company all Day; but Mr. Thrale, being in much better spirits than when I was here last, joined in the conversation, & we were *mighty agreeable*. But he has taken it into his Head to insist upon it that I am a *spouter*:[61]—to be sure, I can't absolutely deny the *Fact*, but yet I am certain *he* never had any reason to take such a Notion:—however, he has repeatedly asked me to read a *Tragedy* to him; & insists upon it that I should do it marvellous well!—& when I ask him *why*, he says I have such a *marking Face*:—however, I told him I would as soon *act* to Mr. Garrick, or *try attitudes* to Sir Joshua Reynolds, as *Read* to *any* body at Streatham.

I have the same Room I had before, &, consequently, I get the same delightful *confabs* with my sweet Mrs. Thrale, at our Dressing, & our *un*dressing Times, exclusive of odd visits.

The next morning [13 Sept.], after Church the Pitches called. After they were gone, I took a stroll round the Grounds,—& was followed by Miss Thrale, with a summons into the Parlour, to see Miss Brown. I willingly obeyed it, for I wished much to have a peep at her.

---

[61] i.e., a reciter, or amateur actor (*OED* s.v. spouter 2.a).

She is very like the Duchess of Devonshire, only less handsome:, &, as I expected, seems a gay, careless, lively, good humoured Girl. She came on Horse back, & stayed but a short Time. She is also very pretty.

The rest of the Day we spent in a Family way, without any visitors.

Our Monday's party [14 Sept.] was very small: for people are so dispersed at present, in various parts, that nothing is more difficult than to get them together: in the List of invitations were included Mr Garrick, Dr Richard Jebb, Mr. Lort, Mr. Seward, Miss Brown, & Mr. Murphy,—*all* of whom were absent from Town. We had therefore only Sir Joshua Reynolds, the 2 Miss Palmers,[62] Dr. Calvert[63] & Mr. Rose Fuller—Dr. Johnson did not return. |

You may easily suppose, that my sister's[64] intelligence of Sir Joshua's curiosity concerning Evelina, made me somewhat apprehend a possibility that that subject might be started: however, when I went into the parlour, I found them all busied in examining the Merlin;[65] Mrs. Thrale introduced me to Sir Joshua & the Eldest Miss Palmer, I renewed my acquaintance with the Youngest,[66] & all things went as quietly & calmly as I could wish.

---

[62] Sir Joshua's nieces: Mary (*c*.1750–1820), who m. (1792, as his 2nd wife) Murrough O'Brien (1726–1808), 5th E. of Inchiquin, cr. (1800) M. of Thomond (Ire.) and (1801) B. Thomond of Taplow (UK); and her sister Theophila ('Offy') (1757–1848), who m. (1781) Robert Lovell Gwatkin (1757–1843). They were the daughters of John Palmer (1708–79), attorney, Great Torrington, Devon, and Mary, née Reynolds (1716–94), sister of Sir Joshua. See *GM* cxiii[1] (1843), 549; Graves i. 406, iv. 1676.

[63] Presumably Peter Calvert (1730–88), LL.D (Cantab.), 1757; Dean of the Court of Arches, 1778; FRS, 1781. Dr Calvert was a member of the Calvert brewing family, Henry Thrale's competitors. See *GM* lviii[2] (1788), 757; IGI.

[64] It is not clear whether EBB or Charlotte is meant.

[65] Probably a combined pianoforte-harpsichord, designed by Merlin and purchased by the Thrales a few months earlier. HLT described the instrument as a 'fine Harpsichord' (SJ, *Letters*, ii. 248; see also below, p. 142), but to FB, 4 Jan. 1781, she writes: 'Merlin has been here to tune the Fortepianos' (Berg; *DL* i. 458). CB, writing to HLT on 29 June 1778, calls it 'the grand new Instrum^t' and informs her that it 'is ready to be sent home upon very short Notice' (*LCB* i. 251). See also A. French, M. Wright, and F. Palmer, *John Joseph Merlin: The Ingenious Mechanick* (1985), pp. 97–100.

[66] FB's earlier meeting (or meetings) with Theophila Palmer is not recorded.

Sir Joshua I am much pleased with: I like his Countenance, & I like his manners: the former I think expressive, soft, & sensible; the latter gentle, unassuming & engaging. I am afraid, my dear Susy, *you* do not like him so well; yet I am sure as far as *I* saw of him, I think you would have joined with me.

The Eldest Miss Palmer seems to have a better understanding than Offy; but Offy has the most pleasing Face.[67] Dr. Calvert I did not see enough of to think about.

The Dinner,—in quantity as well as quality—would have sufficed for 40 people: Sir Joshua said, when the Dessert appeared,—'Now if *all* the Company should take a fancy to the same Dish,—there would be *sufficient* for *all* the Company from any one.'

After Dinner, as usual, we *womells* [*sic*][68] strolled out:— I ran first into the Hall, for my Cloak, & Mrs. Thrale, running after me, said in a low voice 'If you are taxed with Evelina don't own it;—I intend to say it is *mine*, for sport's sake.'

You may think how much I was surprised,—& how readily I agreed not to *own* it: but I could ask no questions, for the two Miss Palmers followed close, saying 'Now *pray*, Ma'am, tell us who it is?—'

'No, no, cried Mrs. Thrale, *who* it is you must find out; *I have* told you that you *Dined* with the Author,—but the rest you must make out as you can.'

Miss Thrale began tittering violently, but I entreated her not to betray me; &, as soon as I could, I got Mrs. Thrale to tell me what all this *meant*? She then acquainted me, that, when she first came into the Parlour, she found them all busy in talking of Evelina; & heard that Sir Joshua had declared he would give 50 pounds to know the Author! 'Well, said Mrs. Thrale; thus much, then, I will tell you;—the Author will *Dine* with you to Day:' They were then all *distracted* to know the Party;—'Why, said I,

---

[67] For portraits by Reynolds of his nieces, see D. Hudson, *Sir Joshua Reynolds: A Personal Study* (1958), facing p. 172.

[68] Perhaps a humorous portmanteau word, combining *women* and *females*. *Womell* is an obsolete form of *wimble*, a boring tool; if such an outrageous pun was intended, it may have originated with Charlotte Ann Burney (see p. 46, n. 37).

we shall have Dr. Calvert,—Lady Ladd, Rose Fuller, & Miss Burney.—'Miss Burney? quoth they; *which* Miss Burney?—'Why the *Eldest*, Miss *Fanny* Burney;—& so out of this List, you must make out the Author.'

I shook my Head at her,—but begged her, at least, to go no further: 'No, no, cried she, Laughing, leave me alone;—the *fun* will be to make them think it *mine*.'

However,—as I learnt at *night*, when they were gone, Sir Joshua was so very importunate with Mr. Thrale, & attacked him with such eagerness, that he *made* him confess who it was, as soon as the ⌐women⌐ retired.—so I find I am *blown* with a vengeance!

Well,—to return to our Walk. The Miss Palmer's grew more & more urgent, 'Did we *indeed*, said the Eldest, Dine with the Author of Evelina?'

'Yes, in good truth did you.'

'Why, then, Ma'am, it was *yourself*!'

'I sha'n't tell you whether it was or not;—but were there not other people at Dinner besides *me*? What think you of Dr. Calvert?'

'Dr. Calvert?—no, no; I am sure it was not *him*: besides, they say it was certainly writ by a *woman*.'

'By a woman?—nay, then,—is not here Lady Ladd, Miss Burney, & Hester?'

'Lady Ladd I am *sure* it was not,—nor could it be Miss Thrale's—O Ma'am,—I begin to think it was really yours!—Now was it not, Mrs. Thrale?'

Mrs. Thrale only Laughed. Lady Ladd, coming suddenly behind me, put her Hands on my shoulders, & whispered 'shall *I* tell?'

'Tell?—tell *what*?' cried I, amazed.

'Why *whose* it is?'

'O Ma'am cried I—*who* has been so wicked as to tell your Ladyship?'

'O, no matter for that;—I have known it some Time.'

I entreated her, however, to keep counsel, though I could not forbear expressing my surprise & chagrin.

'A Lady of our acquaintance, said Miss Palmer, Mrs. Cholmondeley, went herself to the Printer;—but he would not tell.'

'Would he not? cried Mrs. Thrale; Why then he's an honest man.'

'O,—is he so?—nay, then, it is *certainly* Mrs. Thrales!'

'Well, well,—I told you before I should not deny it.'

'Miss Burney, said she [Miss Palmer],—pray do *you* deny it?' [in a voice that seemed to say I *must* ask round—though rather from civility than suspicion.][69]

'Me?—cried I, o no,—if nobody else will deny it, why should I?—it does not seem the *fashion* to deny it.'

'No, in truth! cried she, I believe nobody would think of *denying* it, for it is the sweetest Book in the World!—My uncle could not go to Bed till he had finished it,—& he says he is *sure* he shall make Love to the Author, if ever he meets with her—'

A droll speech enough to make before *me*!—

'Dear Madam, cried Miss Offy, I am *sure* it was you;—*but* why will you not own it at once?'

'I shall neither own nor deny any thing about it.'

'A Gentleman whom we know very well, said Miss Palmer, when he could learn nothing at the *Printers*, took the trouble to go all about *Snow Hill*, to see if he could find any *silversmith's*.'[70]

'Well, *he was* a Cunning Creature! said Mrs. Thrale. But Mr. Johnson's favourite is Mr. Smith.'

'So he is of every body, answered she; he & all that Family; every body says such a Family never was Drawn before. But Mrs. Cholmondely's favourite is Madame Duval; she *acts* her from morning to night, & *ma-fois* every body she sees. But though we all want so much to know the Author, both Mrs. Cholmondeley, & my uncle himself, say they should be frightened to Death to be in her Company, because she must be such a very nice observer, that there would be no escaping her with safety.'

Good God, my dear Susy,—what strange ideas are taken from mere *Book-reading*!—But what follows gave me the highest delight I can feel.

---

[69] Inserted by FBA.

[70] In *Evelina*, Mr Branghton, Mme Duval's nephew, keeps a silversmith's shop in Snow Hill (see vol. i, letter 17).

'Mr. Burke,[71] she continued, *doats* on it: he began it one morning at 7 o'clock, & could not leave it a moment, he sat up *all* night reading it. He says he has not seen such a Book he can't tell when.'

O Susy!—*when* are my Laurels to be *all* collected? Mrs. Thrale gave me, involuntarily, a look of congratulation, & could not forbear *exclaiming* how glad she was Mr. *Burke* approved it. This served to *confirm* the Palmers in their mistake, & they now, without further questioning, quietly & unaffectedly concluded the Book to be really Mrs. Thrales. And Miss Palmer said 'Indeed, Ma'am, you *ought* to write a Novel every year! Nobody can [write][72] like you.'

I was both delighted & diverted at this mistake,—& they grew so easy, & so satisfied under it, that the conversation dropt, & Offy went to the Harpsichord.

When the Gentlemen came in to Tea, not a word was hinted at of my affair, which I truly rejoiced at. But, some Time after, while I was talking with Lady Ladd & Miss Thrale, Rose Fuller, who sat on the other side of me, began a conversation with the Miss Palmers' in a very low voice, & they listened with a most profound attention.— But presently, hearing Miss Palmer say 'How astonishing!—what an extraordinary performance!—Good God, what a nice observer she must be!' I begged Lady Ladd to let me be silent, in hopes of hearing what went on: for I now began to fear Rose Fuller was himself *au fait.* However, they all spoke so low, I could only now & then gather a word,—but I found the tenour of the Conversation to be all commendation, mixed with expressions of surprise: Lady Ladd would not *let* me listen as I wished to do, for she interrupted me to ask,—almost killing herself with Laughter as she spoke,—whether I was ever at Vauxhall the *last night*? I knew what she

71 Edmund Burke (1730–97), the famous politician and writer, was a close friend of Reynolds and his nieces. FB first met him at Sir Joshua's house at Richmond in 1782 (*EJL* v).
72 Inserted by FBA.

meant, & wished Young Branghton over Head & Ears in a kennel for drawing me into such a scrape.[73]

Not long after, the party broke up, & they took leave. Lady Ladd stayed all night, & Rose Fuller till 11 o'clock.

I had no *conversation* with Sir Joshua all Day; but I found myself much more an object of *attention* to him than I wished to be: & he several Times spoke to me,— though he did not *make Love*! but my answers always prevented any further *confab.*—for the truth is, I am frightened out of my wits from the terror of being attacked *as an author*, & therefore *shirk*, instead of *seeking*, all occasion of being drawn into notice.

When they rose to take leave, Miss Palmer, with the air of asking the *greatest* of favours, hoped to see me when I returned to Town:—& Sir Joshua, approaching me with the most profound respect, enquired how long I should remain at Streatham? A week, I believed:—& then, he hoped, when I left it, ⌐to⌐ have the Honour of seeing me in Leicester ⌐Fields.⌐

In short, the *Joke is*, the people speak as if *they* were afraid instead of *my* being such a sneaker.

It seems, when they got to the Door, Miss Palmer said to Mrs. Thrale 'Lord, Ma'am, so it's *Miss Burney* after all!' 'Ay, sure, answered she, who should it be'? 'Ah, Lord, said Offy, why did not you tell us sooner, that we might have had a little talk about it?'

I am heartily glad, however, that that was not the case.— But I had not much *cause* for being in such horrible fidgets about Mr. *Lort*, since he, I find, is only one among a Hundred!

Here, therefore,—End all my Hopes of secresy! I take leave of them with the utmost regret,—& though never yet did any scribler draw more Honourably, more cred-itably, more partially into Notice, I nevertheless can *not* persuade myself to rejoice in the loss of my dear old obscurity.

When they were gone, we went to Cards: & they made me play at whist,—which I did most shockingly, but Rose

---

[73] See *Evelina*, vol. ii, letter 15.

Fuller forced me;—for he said 'We ought to pay all sort
of attention to Miss Burney,—I am sure, for that sort of
system, & things of that sort, we can't do too much.' This
Young man has a cant set ǀ of words, which he makes use
of, most absurdly & indiscriminately, upon all occasions.—
As for example, 'upon my Word, said he, I did not like
my situation at all,—the Miss Palmers kept pumping me,
in such a sort of way,—& I, having Miss Burney at t'other
side, did not know what to say in such a sort of system,—
& they said so much of her being such a nice observer, &
things of that sort, that really I did not know what to do.'
Now this, I assure you, is not *outrée,*—& so Mrs. Thrale
would herself tell you.

Tuesday morning [15 Sept.] Mrs. Thrale asked me if
I should like to see Mrs. Montagu? *Wants,* I truly said, I
had *none* at Streatham, but I should be the most insensible
of all animals not to *like* to see our sex's Glory.—'Well,
said she, we'll try to make you see her;—Sir Joshua says
she is in Town, & I will write & ask her here. I wish you
to see her of all things. But, Mr. Thrale, who can we have
by way of party, to meet her?'

'Who?—said he,—why have you not Miss Burney?—
who would you have?'

So then we all *He He'd*!

Mrs. Thrale wrote her note before Breakfast.[74]

I had a great deal of private confab., afterwards, with
Lady Ladd & Miss Thrale concerning Miss Streatfield: I
find she is by no means a favourite with either of them,
though she is half adored by Mr. & Mrs. Thrale, & by
Dr. Johnson. And Lady Ladd, among other things, mentioned her being here once when Mrs. Montagu came, &

---

[74] She also wrote a note inviting Reynolds, to which Sir Joshua replied the
same day: 'I would (to use Dr Goldsmith's mode) give five pounds to dine with
you tomorrow ... but I have unluckily above a dozen people dine with me
tomorrow on venison which Lord Granby has sent me.

'If Mrs Montagu has read Evelina she will tomorrow receive the same
satisfaction that we have received in seeing the Author of which pleasure
anxious as I was I begun to despair, and little expected to find the Author
correspond to our romantic imaginations. She seems to be herself the *great
sublime she draws'* (*Letters of Sir Joshua Reynolds,* ed. F. W. Hilles (Cambridge,
1929), pp. 61–2; see also the facsimile of p. 1 of the MS in C. B. Tinker, *Dr.
Johnson and Fanny Burney* (1911; rpt. Westport, 1970), facing p. 96).

blamed Mrs. Thrale for *making much* of her *before* Mrs. Montagu, 'Who, she added, has no notion of any *Girl* acquaintance, &, indeed, makes ǀ a point of only cultivating with people of Consequence. I determined, in my own mind, to make use of this hint, & keep myself as much out of the way as I could. Indeed, at *any* rate, a woman of such celebrity in the Literary world, would be the *last* I should covet to converse with, though one of the *first* I should wish to listen to.

Lady Ladd went to Town before Dinner. Her Ladyship is immensely civil to me, & we are mighty facetious together. I find she has really some drollery about her, when she lays aside her *dignity* & stateliness, & is very fond of *Jocoseness*, to which she contributes her part much better than I at first imagined she could.

An answer came from Mrs. Montagu at noon. Mrs. Thrale gave it me to read: it was in a high strain of *politesse*, expressed equal admiration & regard for Mrs. Thrale, & accepted her invitation for the *next Day*. But what was my surprise to read, at the bottom of the Letter 'I have not yet seen Evelina, but will certainly get it: &, if it should not happen to please me, the Disgrace must be mine, not the Author's.'

'Lord, Ma'am, cried I, what does this mean?'

'Why only, said she, that, in my Letter this morning, I said have you seen the new ⌈Novel⌉ called Evelina? It was written by an amiable young Friend of mine, & I wish much to know your opinion of it; for if *you* should not approve it,—what signifies the approbation of a Johnson, a Burke, &c.?—'

O what a Woman is this Mrs. Thrale!—since she *will* make the Book known,—how sweet a *method* ǀ was this, of letting Mrs. Montagu know the Honour it has received![75]

---

[75] FB seems not (or pretends not) to notice that HLT's words also contain a sly dig at Mrs Montagu, who, despite their friendship, was her rival as a hostess and wit and a would-be rival of SJ as an arbiter of literary taste.

Before Dinner, to my great Joy, Dr. Johnson returned Home from Warley Common.[76] I followed Mrs. Thrale into the Library to see him,—& he is so near sighted, that he took me for Miss Stretfield: but he did not welcome me less kindly when he found his mistake, which Mrs. Thrale made known by saying 'No, 'tis Miss Stretfield's *Rival*, Miss Burney.'

All Dinner Time, the Conversation was upon the Camp,[77] but I must skip to *Tea*, when, & till we parted, he was in most excellent spirits.

The subject turned upon the Domestic oeconomy of his own Houshold [*sic*]: Mrs. Thrale has often acquainted me that his House is quite filled & overrun with *all* sort of strange Creatures, whom he admits for mere Charity, & because nobody else *will* admit them,—for his Charity is unbounded,—or, rather, bounded *only* by his circumstances. But the account he gave of the adventures, & the absurdities of the set, was highly diverting,—but too *diffused* for writing.—Though one or 2 speeches I *must* give. I think I shall, occasionally *Theatricalise*[78] my Dialogues.

Mrs. Thrale Pray, Sir, how does Mrs. Williams like all this tribe.

Dr. J. Madam, she does *not* like them at all; but their fondness for *her* is not greater. She & De Mullin[79] Quarrel incessantly; but as they can both be occasionally of service

---

[76] Where he had gone to visit Bennet Langton. Langton was a captain in the Lincolnshire militia, which were training at the camp at Warley Common, Essex. This camp was one of many where the militia were preparing that year for a threatened invasion by France.

[77] SJ later wrote to HLT (15 Oct. 1778): 'A Camp, however familiarly we may speak of it, is one of the great scenes of human life' (*LSJ* iii. 128; see also ibid. iii. 129). For Langton's account of SJ's activities while at the camp, see *Life* iii. 360–2.

[78] Presumably FB's coinage. This is the earliest instance in *OED*.

[79] Elizabeth Desmoulins (1716–?86), the daughter of SJ's godfather Samuel Swynfen, MD, of Lichfield, and widow of Mr Desmoulins, a Huguenot writing master. She, who had earlier been a companion to SJ's wife, left Bolt Court in May 1783, occasioning 'more peace in the house' (SJ, *Letters* iii. 25), but she returned sometime during the following winter. See L. Larsen, *Dr. Johnson's Household* (Hamden, 1985), pp. 27, 66–7, 95, 100, 113–14 and *passim*; *LCB* i. 464 and n. 10.

to each other, & as niether of them have any other place to go to, their animosity does not force them to separate. Mrs. T. And pray, Sir, what is Mr. Macbean?'[80] Dr. J. Madam, he is a Scotch man: he is a man of great learning, & for his learning I respect him, & I wish to serve him; he knows many Languages, & knows them well: but he knows nothing of *Life*: he could draw niether Smiths nor Branghtons; I advised him to write a Geographical Dictionary;—but I have lost all hopes of his ever doing any ⏐ thing *properly*, since I found he gave as much labour to Capua as to Rome.[81] ⏐

[*The letter ends here; the rest of the last page contains the address. FB evidently broke off, as with previous journal letters, in order to catch the post. She continues the dialogue in the next letter.*]

61   [Streatham, *post* 16–21 September 1778]
To Susanna Elizabeth Burney

AJL (Diary MSS I, paginated 767–86, Berg), Sept. 1778
10 single sheets, 4to, 20 pp.

I shall proceed, my Susy, without prelude.
Mr. T. And pray who is clerk of your kitchen, Sir?
Dr. J. Why, Sir, I am afraid there is none; a general anarchy prevails in my kitchen, as I am told by Mr. Levat,[82] who says it is not now what it *used* to be!

---

[80] Alexander Macbean (d. 1784), 'a very learned Highlander' (*Life* iii. 106), had been one of the amanuenses employed on SJ's *Dictionary*. SJ contributed a preface to Macbean's *Dictionary of Ancient Geography* (1773) and was instrumental in obtaining his admission as 'a poor brother of the Charterhouse' in 1780 (*Life* i. 187).

[81] SJ presumably refers to the amount of time Macbean spent in researching the 2 cities and writing them up. Macbean's article on Capua is 31 lines long, as compared to 54 lines for Rome. SJ probably felt that the article on Rome should have been proportionately much longer.

[82] Robert Levett *or* Levet (*c*.1705–82), of West Ella near Hull, Yorks. 'An obscure practiser in physick amongst the lower people' (*Life* i. 243), he was loved by SJ for his charity, humanity, and honesty. SJ's elegy on his death is one of his best poems. See Larsen, pp. 36–8, 44, 93–5, and *passim*.

Mrs. T. Mr. Levat, I suppose, Sir, has the office of keeping the *Hospital in Health?* for he is an apothecary.[83]

Dr. J. Levat, Madam, is a brutal fellow, but I have a good regard for him; for his brutality is in his manners, not his mind.

Mr. T. But how do you get your Dinners Drest?

Dr. J. Why De Mullen has the chief management of the kitchen; but our *Roasting* is not magnificent, for we have no Jack.[84]

Mr. T. No Jack? Why how do they manage without?

Dr. J. Small joints I believe they manage with a string, & larger are done at the Tavern. I have some Thoughts (with a profound gravity) of *buying* a Jack,—because I think a Jack is some *Credit* to a House.

Mr. T. Well, but you'll have a *spit*, too?

Dr. J. No, Sir, no; that would be superfluous;—for we shall never use it; & if a *Jack* is seen, a *spit* will be presumed!

Did you ever hear such comical stuff?—

Mrs. T. But pray, Sir, who is the *Poll*[85] you talk of?—She that you used to abet in her quarrels with Mrs. Williams, & call out, *at her again, Poll! Never flinch, Poll!*?

Dr. J. Why I took to Poll very well at first, but she won't do upon a nearer examination.

Mrs. T How came she among you, Sir?

Dr. J. Why I don't rightly remember, but we could spare her very well from us;—Poll is a stupid slut; I had some hopes of her, at first; but when I talked to her tightly &

---

[83] Actually an unlicensed practitioner whose patients were too poor to pay even an apothecary, let alone a physician or surgeon (Larsen, p. 36). HLT, in calling SJ's house a 'Hospital', alludes of course to the precarious health of its aging inmates.

[84] A machine for turning the spit in roasting meat (*OED*, s.v. Jack *sb.*[1], II. 7).

[85] Poll Carmichael, whom HLT refers to variously as 'a Scotch Wench' and 'a Thing that he [SJ] called Poll' (*Thraliana* i. 184, 532). She was probably the prostitute whom SJ found lying exhausted in the street one night and carried to his house where, Boswell writes, on the testimony of Mrs Desmoulins, 'he had her taken care of with all tenderness for a long time, at considerable expence, till she was restored to health, and endeavoured to put her into a virtuous way of living' (*Life* iv. 321–2). If this account is accurate, it is little wonder that SJ avoids answering HLT's next question. Poll remained with SJ until 1783 (see Larsen, pp. 60–1, 67, 95–6).

closely, I could make nothing of her;—she was wiggle waggle,—& I could never persuade her to be categorical. I wish Miss Burney would come among us; if she would only give us a *week*, we should furnish her with ample materials for a new scene in her next work.[86]

A little while after, he asked Mrs. Thrale who had Read Evelina in his absence?

'Who? cried she;—why *Burke*!—Burke sat up all night to finish it;—& Sir Joshua Reynolds is *mad* about it, & said he would give 50 pounds to know the Author. But our *fun* was with his Nieces,—we made them believe *I* wrote the Book,—& the Girls gave me the credit of it at once.

'I am sorry for it, Madam, cried he, quite angrily,—you were much to blame; deceits of that kind ought never to be practised; they have a worse tendency than you are aware of.

Mrs. T. Why don't *frighten* yourself, Sir,—Miss Burney will have all the credit she has a right to, for I told them whose it was before they went.

Dr. J. But you were very wrong for misleading them a moment: such Jests are extremely blamable: they are *foolish* in the very *act*, & they are *wrong*, because they always leave a doubt upon the mind. What *first* past will be always recollected by those Girls, & they will never feel clearly convinced *which* wrote the Book, Mrs. Thrale or Miss Burney.

Mrs. T. Well, ⌐God knows,¬ I am ready to take my *Bible oath* it was not *me*; & if *that* won't do, Miss Burney must take *her's* too.

She then told him that Mrs. Cholmondeley was *acting* Madame Duval all over the Town.

'Mrs. Cholmondeley, said he, was the first I ever heard mention the Book; she used to talk to me forever of Evelina & Evelina,—but I never heeded her,—I had no intention to read it, till I fell upon it that Day in the Coach;—& a delightful thing it is!—

---

[86] SJ summed up the turmoil in his house in a letter to HLT, 14 Nov. 1778, thus: 'We have tolerable concord at home, but no love. Williams hates every body. Levet hates Desmoulins and does not love Williams. Desmoulins hates them both. Poll loves none of them' (*LSJ* iii. 140).

There! Susy, there was a pretty phrase!

Mrs. T. Ay, Mrs. Cholmondeley has all the *real* merit of making that Book known, for she was the *first* to speak,—

> Be thou the *first* true merit to defend,
> His praise is lost, who waits till all commend.[87]

I am sure I have thought of those Lines a thousand Times upon this occasion.

Dr. J. I have not, yet, read the Book *fairly* through,—but I shall *at it* again,—for I will know every word of it.'

I was then looking over the Life of Cowley, which he had himself given me to Read, at the same Time that he gave to Mrs. Thrale that of Waller.—They are now *printed*, though they will not be *published* for some Time. But he bid me put it away,—'Do, cried he, put away that now, & *prattle* with us;—I can't make this little Burney prattle,—& I am *sure* she prattles well.—but I shall teach her another Lesson than to sit thus silent, before I have done with her.

'To *Talk*, cried I, is the *only* Lesson I shall be backward to learn from you, Sir.'

'You shall give me, cried he, a Discourse 'pon the Passions,—come, begin!—tell us the necessity of regulating them, watching over, & curbing them!—Did you ever read Norris's Theory of Love?[88]

F.B. No, Sir.

Dr. J. Well, it is worth your Reading. He will make you see that *inordinate* Love is the root of all Evil: inordinate Love of *Wealth*, brings on Avarice; of *Wine*, brings on intemperance;—of *Power*, brings on Cruelty;—& so on,—he deduces from *inordinate Love* all human frailty.

Mrs. T. To morrow, Sir, Mrs. Montagu Dines here! & then you will have Talk enough.

Dr. Johnson began to see-saw, with a Countenance strongly expressive of *inward fun*,—&, after enjoying it

---

[87] Cf. Pope's *Essay on Criticism*, ll. 474–5.

[88] *The Theory and Regulation of Love … to which are Added Letters Philosophical and Moral between the Author and Dr. Henry More* (Oxford, 1688), by the Revd John Norris (1657–1711), Rector of Bemerton, Wilts.

some Time in silence, he suddenly, & with great animation, turned to me, & cried '*Down* with her, Burney!—
down with her!—spare her not! attack her, fight her, &
down with her at once!—*You* are a *rising* Wit,—*she* is at the
Top,—& when *I* was beginning the World, & was nothing
& nobody, the Joy of my Life was to fire at all the
established Wits!—& then, every body ˈ loved to hallow
me on;—but there is no Game *now*, & *now*, every body
would be glad to see me *conquered*: but *then*, when I was
new,—to vanquish the Great ones was all the delight of
my poor little dear soul!—So at her, Burney!—at her, &
down with her!'

O how we ⌐all hollow'd!⌐ By the way, I must tell you
that Mrs. Montagu is in very great estimation here, even
with Dr. Johnson himself, when others do not praise her
improperly: Mrs. Thrale ranks her as the *first of Women*, in
the Literary way.

I should have told you, that Miss Gregory,[89] Daughter
of the Gregory who wrote the Letters, or *Legacy* of Advice,
Lives with Mrs. Montagu, & was invited to accompany
her.

'Mark, now, said Dr. Johnson, if I *contradict* her to
morrow; I am determined, let her say what she will, that
I will *not* contradict her.

Mrs. T. Why, to be sure, Sir, you *did* put her a little out
of countenance last Time she came,—yet you were niether
rough, nor cruel, nor ill-natured,—but still, when a lady
changes Colour, we imagine her feelings are not quite
composed.

Dr. J. Why, Madam, I won't answer that I sha'n't contradict her again, if she provokes me as she did then; but a
less provocation I will withstand. I believe I am not high
in her good graces already, & I begin (added he, Laughing

---

[89] Dorothea Gregory (1754–1830), elder daughter of John Gregory (1724–
73), MD (Aberdeen), professor of medicine in Edinburgh University (1766),
whose *A Father's Legacy to his Daughters* was published posthumously in 1774.
She was a companion to Mrs Montagu from *c.*1772 until her marriage, in 1784,
over Mrs Montagu's objections, to the Revd Archibald Alison (*c.*1757–1839).
See R. Blunt, ed., *Mrs. Montagu: 'Queen of the Blues'* (Boston [?1923]), i. 258 and
passim.

heartily) to tremble for my admission into her new House! I doubt I shall never see the inside of it!

Mrs. Montagu is Building a most superb House.[90]

Mrs. T. O, I warrant you! she *fears* you, indeed, but that, you know, is nothing uncommon: & dearly I love to hear your *disquisitions*,—for certainly she is the first woman, for Literary knowledge, in England,—& if in *England* I I hope I may say in the *World*!

Dr. J. I believe you may, Madam. She diffuses more knowledge in her Conversation than any Woman I know,—or, indeed, *almost* any man.

Mrs. T. I declare *I* know *no* man equal to her, take away yourself & Burke, for *that* art.—And *you*, who love magnificence, won't quarrel with her, as every body else does, for her love of finery.

Dr. J. No, I shall not quarrel with her upon that topic. (then, looking earnestly at *me*) Nay, he added, it's very handsome.

'What, sir?' cried I, amazed.

'Why your Cap:—I have looked at it some Time, & I like it much. It has not that vile *Bandeau* a cross it, which I have so often curst.'

Did you ever hear any thing so strange? *Nothing* escapes him. My Daddy Crisp is not more minute in his attentions: nay, I think he is even *less* so.

Mrs. T. Well, Sir, that Bandeau you quarrelled with was worn by every Woman at Court the last Birth Day,[91]—& I observed that *all* the men found fault with it.

Dr. J. The Truth is,—women,—take them in general,— have *no* idea of Grace!—Fashion is *all* they think of;—I don't mean Mrs. Thrale & Miss Burney, when I talk of *women*!—*they* are Goddesses!—& therefore I except them.

Mrs. T. Lady Ladd never wore the Bandeau, & said she never would, because it is unbecoming.

---

[90] Montagu House, on the NW corner of Portman Square, London, was designed by James 'Athenian' Stuart (1713–88). The house was begun in 1777, and Mrs Montagu moved into it in Dec. 1781. See Blunt, ii. 13, 61, 112, and *passim*.

[91] King George III's birthday, 4 June.

Dr. J. (*Laughing*) Did not she? then is Lady Ladd a charming Woman, & I have yet hopes of entering into engagements with her!

Mrs. T. Well, as to that, I can't say,—but, to be sure, the only similitude *I* have yet discovered in you, *is* in *size: there* you agree mighty well. |

Dr. J. Why if *any* body could have worn the Bandeau, it must have been Lady Ladd, for there is *enough* of her to carry it off; but *you* are too *little* for any thing ridiculous; that which seems *nothing* upon a Patagonian,[92] will become very *conspicuous* upon a Lilliputian; & of *you* there is so little in *all*, that one single absurdity would swallow up *half* of you.

Some Time after,—when we had all been a few minutes wholly silent, he turned to me, & said 'Come, Burney,— shall you & I *study our parts* against Mrs. Montagu comes?'

How would you be entertained, my dear Susy, if I could give you the *manner*, as well as *matter*, of the Conversation of this greatest of men.

Wednesday [16 Sept.]—at Breakfast, Dr. Johnson asked me if I had been reading his Life of Cowley?—'O yes!' cried I. 'And what do you think of it?'

'I am delighted with it,' cried I;—& if I was *somebody*, instead of *Nobody*, I should not have read it without telling you sooner how ᵣ⟨highly I⟩ᵀ think of it.' 'Miss Burney, cried Mr. Thrale, you must get up your Courage for this encounter! I think you should *begin* with Miss Gregory; & *down* with *her* first.

Dr. J. No, no,—fly at the *Eagle!*—*down* with Mrs. Montagu herself!—I hope she will come *full* of Evelina!

Again, when I took up Cowley's Life, he made me put it away, to *talk*. I could not help remarking how very like Dr. Johnson is to his writing; & how much the same thing it was to *hear*, or to *read* him.—but that nobody could tell that, without coming to Streatham, for his Language was

---

[92] i.e., a giant. The dominant Indian tribe of Patagonia, the Tehuelches, averaged over 6 ft. in height and were broad in proportion. Reports of their discovery by Capt. John Byron reached England in 1766, and their stature was exaggerated until they were commonly believed to average 7 or 8 ft. tall. See *OED*; *YW* xxii. 420–1 and nn. 9–11, xlii. 182. |

generally imagined to be laboured & studied, instead of the nice common flow of his Thoughts. 'Very true, said Mrs. Thrale, he *writes* & *talks* with ˡ the same ease, & in the same manner;—but, Sir, (to him) if *this Rogue* is like her Book;—how will she *trim* all of us by & by!—*Now*, she *daintys us up*[93] with all the meekness in the World,—but when we are away, I suppose she pays us off finely!'

'*My* paying off, cried I, is like the Latin of Hudibras, who never scanted—His Learning unto such as wanted,—[94] for I can figure *like any thing* when I am with those who can't figure at all.'

Mrs. T. O, if you have any *Mag.*[95] in you, we'll draw it out!

Dr. J. A Rogue!—she told me that if she was *somebody* instead of *Nobody*, she would praise my Book!—

F.B. Why, Sir, I am *sure* you would *scoff* my praise!

Dr. J. If you think that, you think very ill of *me*!——but you *don't* think it!

Mrs. T. We have told her what you said to Miss More, & I believe *that* makes her afraid.

Dr. J. Well, & if *she* was to serve me as Miss More did, I should say the same thing to *her*. But I think she will not. Hannah More has very good intellects, too;—but she has by no means the elegance of Miss Burney.

ʺLord:ʺ Susy!—did you ever hear the like?

'Well, cried I, there are folks that *are* to be spoilt, & folks that are *not* to be spoilt, as well as *souls* that *are* to be saved, & *souls* that are *not* to be saved![96]—but what will become of *me*, I know not!'

Mrs. T. Well,—if you *are* spoilt,—we can only say nothing in the World is so *pleasant* as being spoilt.

Dr. J. No, no, Burney will not be spoilt! She knows too well what praise she has a *claim* to, & what *not*, to be in any danger of spoiling.'

[93] The *OED*, citing this sentence, classifies *dainty up*, meaning 'to pamper or indulge with dainties', as an obsolete rare expression. The only other example dates from 1622.

[94] Cf. *Hudibras* I.i.55–6.

[95] Talk, chatter; the earliest instance of the substantive form in this sense in *OED*.

[96] Cf. *Othello* II. iii. 106–7 (and see below, p. 349).

F.B. I do, indeed, believe I shall never be spoilt at *Streatham*,—for it is the *last* place where I can feel of any consequence.

Mrs. T. Well, Sir, she is *our* Miss Burney, however; we were the first to catch her, & now we have *got*, we will keep her. Mrs. Cholmondeley has the best *claim* to her, I acknowledge, but ⌐ her Conduct has *forfeited* that claim, & so she is all our own.

Dr. J. Yes, I hope she is; I should be *very* sorry to lose Miss Burney.

F.B. O ⌐Lord⌐!—how *can* 2 *such* people sit & talk such—

Mrs. T. Such *stuff* you think?—but Mr. Johnson's Love—

Dr. J. Love?—no,—I don't entirely *Love* her yet,—I must see *more* of her first; I have much too high an opinion of her to flatter her;—I have, indeed, seen nothing of her but what is *fit* to be loved, but I must know her *more*. I *admire* her, & *greatly*, too.

F.B. Well,—this is ⌐in⌐ a very *new* style to *me*!—I have long enough had reason to think myself *loved*,—but *admiration* is perfectly new to me!

Dr. J. I admire her for her observations,—for her good sense,—for her humour,—for her Discernment,—for her manner of expressing them,—& for *all* her *Writing* Talents.'

I quite *sigh* beneath the weight of *such* praise from *such* persons! *sigh* with mixed *gratitude* for the *present*, & *fear* for the *future*,—for I think I shall never, never be able to support myself long so well with them!

We could not prevail with him to stay till Mrs. Montagu arrived, though, by appointment, she came very early. There was no party to meet her. She & Miss Gregory came by one o'clock.

Now don't you want to hear a vast deal about her?——She is middle sized, very thin, & looks infirm. She has a sensible & penetrating Countenance & the air & manner of a Woman [accustomed to being distinguished, & of great parts.]⁹⁷ Dr. Johnson, who agrees in this, says that

---

⁹⁷ Substituted by FBA for an obliterated passage not recovered.

a Mrs. Hervey[98] of his acquaintance, says she can remember Mrs. Montagu *trying* for this same air & manner;—Mr. Crisp has said the same;—however, Nobody can *now* impartially see her, & not confess that she has extremely well *succeeded*. | *My expectations*, which were *compounded* of the praise of Mrs. Thrale, & the abuse of Mr. Crisp,[99] were most exactly answered, for I thought her in a *medium* way.

Miss Gregory is a fine young woman, & seems gentle & well bred.

A Bustle with the Dog Presto,—Mrs. Thrale's favourite,[1]—at the Entrance of these Ladies into the Library, prevented any formal reception, & *all that*; but as soon as Mrs. Montagu heard my Name, she enquired very civilly after my Father, & made many speeches concerning a volume of Linguet, which she has lost;[2]—but she hopes soon to be able to replace it: I am *sure* he is very high in her favour, because she did *me* the Honour of addressing herself to me 3 or 4 Times.—

But—*my ease & tranquility* were soon disturbed: for she had not been in the Room more than 10 minutes, ere, turning to Mrs. Thrale, she said 'O—Ma'am,—but Your Evelina,—I have not yet got it,—I sent for it, but the Bookseller had it not. However, I will certainly have it.'

'Ay, I hope so, answered Mrs. Thrale, & I hope you will like it, too; for 'tis a Book to *be* liked.'

---

[98] Elizabeth Hervey (1730–1803), daughter of the Hon. William Hervey (1699–1776), Capt., RN. See Blunt i. 125–6.

[99] SC had formed his opinion of Mrs Montagu *c.*1750, when the Duchess of Portland showed him some letters of hers, 'so full of affectation, refinement, attempts to Philosophise, talking metaphysics ... that ... I set her down for a vain empty, conceited pretender, & little else!' (SC to FB 27 Apr. 1780, Berg, printed *DL* i. 343). In letters to his sister Mrs Gast, he sneers at her piety (she holds a house-warming on Monday instead of Easter Sunday, 'for she is a mighty good Woman') and her vanity ('Mrs. Montagu, who holds herself up in the Clouds'). See W. H. Hutton, *Burford Papers* (1905), pp. 29, 46.

[1] HLT's '*little favourite Terrier Presto*' had belonged to her elder son Henry ('Harry') Thrale (1767–76) and died at Brighton sometime after 1784 (*TSP*, p. 179).

[2] Perhaps *Histoire des révolutions de l'Empire romain* (1766), by Simon-Nicolas-Henri Linguet (1736–94), listed in *Lib.*, p. 30. CB's friendship with Mrs Montagu dated from the success of his *German Tour* (1773), which caused her to invite him to her blue-stocking parties (Lonsdale, pp. 128–9).

I began, now, a vehement *Nose-blowing*, for the Benefit of *Handkerchiefing*[3] my Face.

'I hope, though, said Mrs. Montagu, drily, it is not in *Verse*? I can read *any* thing in *Prose*, but I have a great dread of a long story in *verse*.'

'No, Ma'am, no; 'tis all in *prose*,—I assure you. 'Tis a Novel; & an exceeding—but it does nothing good to praise too much, so I will say nothing more about it: only *this*,—that Mr. *Burke* sat up *all night* to read it.'

'Indeed?—well, I propose myself great pleasure from it;—& the more I am gratified by hearing it is written by a *woman*.' |

'And Sir Joshua Reynolds, continued Mrs. Thrale, has been offering 50 pounds to know the Author.'

'Well, I will have it to read in my Journey; I am going to Berkshire, & it shall be my Travelling Book.'

'No, Ma'am, if you please, you shall have it *now*,—Queeney, do look it for Mrs. Montagu, & let it be put in her Carriage, & go to Town with her.'

Miss Thrale rose to look [for][4] it,—&, involuntarily, I rose too, intending to walk off, for my situation was inexpressibly awkward; but then I recollected that, if I went away, it might seem like giving Mrs. Thrale *leave* & *opportunity*, to tell my Tale,—& therefore I stopt at a distant window, where I busied myself in contemplating the Poultry.

'And Mr. Johnson, Ma'am, added my kind *Puffer*, says *Fielding* never wrote so *well*,—never wrote *equal* to this Book;—he says it is a better picture of Life & manners than is to be found *any* where in Fielding.'

'Indeed? cried Mrs. Montagu, surprised, *that* I did not expect, for I have been informed it is the work of a Young lady,—& therefore, though I expected a very pretty Book, I imagined it to be a work of mere Imagination;—& the

---

[3] *OED* cites this rare (perhaps unique) use of *handkerchief* as a transitive verb. Richardson used it intransitively in *Sir Charles Grandison* (1754), vol. ii, letter 16.

[4] Inserted by FBA, which indicates that the transitive use of *look* (= *look for*) was already becoming obsolete in the early 19th c.

Name I thought attractive;—but *Life & manners* I never dreamt of finding.'

'Well, Ma'am, what I tell you is literally true;—& for my part, I am never better pleased than when good Girls write clever Books;—& that *this* is clever—But, all this Time, we are *killing* Miss Burney, who wrote the Book herself!'—

Lord, Susan, what a clap of Thunder was this!——the *last* thing in the World I should have expected before my *Face!*—I know not what bewitched Mrs. Thrale, I but *this* was carrying the Jest further than ever:—all *retenue* being now at an End, I fairly & abruptly took to my Heels, & ran out of the Room with the utmost trepidation, amidst astonished exclammations from Mrs. Montagu & Miss Gregory.

I was horribly disconcerted at this affair,—but I am now so irrecoverably *in for it*, that I begin to leave off reproaches & expostulations; indeed, they have very little availed me, while they *might* have been of service, but *now*, they would pass for mere *parade* & affectation, & there-fore, since they *can* do no good, I gulp them down. I find them, indeed, some what hard of digestion, but they must make their own way as well as they can.

I determined not to make my appearance again till Dinner was upon Table; yet I could niether read nor write, nor, indeed, do *any* thing but consider the new situation in Life into which I am thus hurried,—I had almost said *forced*,—& if I *had*, methinks it would be no untruth.

Miss Thrale came Laughing up after me, & tried to persuade me to return; she was mightily diverted all the morning, & came to me with repeated messages of sum-mons to attend the Company; but I could not *bore* it[5] again into the Room, & therefore entreated her to say I was finishing a Letter. Yet I was sorry to lose so much of Mrs. Montagu.

---

[5] i.e., 'penetrate'. Mrs Barrett assumed that FB's phrase was a slip for *brave it* and so emended it (silently). There is apparently no other known instance of this locution.

When Dinner was upon Table, I followed the procession, *in a Tragedy step*, as Mr. Thrale will have it,—into the Dining Parlour. [Dr. Johnson was returned.]⁶

The Conversation was not brilliant, nor do I remember much of it;—but Mrs. Montagu behaved to *me* just as I could have wished, since she spoke to me very little, but spoke that little with the utmost politeness:—but | Miss *Gregory*, though herself a very modest Girl, quite stared me out of Countenance, & never took her Eyes off my Face.

When Mrs. Montagu's new House was talked of, Dr. Johnson, in a jocose manner, desired to know if he should be invited to see it? 'Ay, sure, cried Mrs. Montagu, looking well pleased; or else *I* sha'n't like it: but I invite you *all* to a House warming; I shall hope for the Honour of seeing *all* this Company at my new House next Easter Day: I fix the Day now, that it may be remembered.

Every body Bowed, & accepted the invite but me, & I thought fitting not to hear it; for I have no Notion of *snapping* at invites from the ⌐*Great*:¬ but Dr. Johnson, who sat next me, was determined I *should* be of the party, for he suddenly clapt his Hand on my shoulder, & called out aloud Burney, *you* & *I* will go together!

'Yes, surely; cried Mrs. Montagu, I shall hope for the pleasure of seeing Evelina.'

'Evelina? repeated he, has Mrs. Montagu, then, found out Evelina?'

'Yes, cried she, & I am *proud* of it: I am *proud* that a work *so* commended should be a *woman's*.'

O how my Face burnt!

'Has Mrs. Montagu, asked Dr. Johnson, *read* Evelina?'

'No, Sir, not yet; but I *shall* immediately, for I feel the greatest *eagerness* to read it.'

'I am very sorry, Madam, replied he, that you have not read it already, because you cannot speak of it with a full conviction of it's merit: which, I believe, when you *have* read it, you will find great pleasure in acknowledging.' |

---

⁶ Inserted by FBA.

Never, never, I believe, did any body meet such astonishing kindness as I have! *What* a tribute of Praise was this, so *publicly* given, from Dr. Johnson! Some other things were said, but I remember them not,—for I could hardly keep my place: but my sweet Mrs. Thrale looked *delighted* for me.

I made Tea, as usual, & Mrs. Montagu & Miss Gregory seated themselves on each side of me.

'I can see, said the former, that Miss Burney is very like her Father; & *that* is a good thing, for every body would wish to be like Dr. Burney. Pray, when you see him, give my best respects to him; I am afraid he thinks me a *Thief*, with his Linguet;—but I assure you I am a very *honest woman*, & I spent full 3 Hours in looking for it.'

'I am sure, cried Mrs. Thrale, Dr. Burney would much rather you should have Employed that Time about some *other* Book.'

Some Time after, Mrs. Montagu mentioned her being very short sighted: I forget what led to it, but it was something relative to *me*, for Mrs. Thrale said 'Miss Burney, Ma'am, knows how to allow for that, for she is very near sighted herself.'

'I should be glad, answered Mrs. Montagu, to resemble Miss Burney in *any* thing.'

Upon my Word! methinks I hear you Cry; fine doings!— Miss Gregory was amazing sociable, & began regretting my spending the morning away from them: 'It was very hard upon *me*, cried I, for I was fairly turned out of the Room!'

'It was very hard upon *us*,—& *all that*,' she answered, & so civilities ran about very thick, & very soft. |

They went away very early, because Mrs. Montagu is a great Coward in a Carriage.[7] She repeated her invitation as she left [the][8] Room. So *now*,—that I am invited to Mrs. Montagu's,—I think the measure of my Glory full!

When they were gone, how did Dr. Johnson astonish me by asking if I had observed what an *ugly Cap* Miss

---

[7] Presumably she feared highwaymen after dark.
[8] Inserted by FBA.

Gregory had on? And then, taking both my Hands, &
looking at me with an expression of much kindness, he
said 'Well, Miss Burney, Mrs. Montagu now will read
Evelina.'

To *read* it, he seems to think is *all* that is wanted;—&,
far as I am from being of the same opinion, I dare not,
to *him*, make disqualifying speeches, because it might seem
impertinent to suppose her more difficult to please than
himself.

'You were *very* kind, Sir, cried I, to speak of it with so
much favour & indulgence at Dinner,—yet I hardly knew
how to sit it, *then*,—though I shall be always proud to
remember it here after.'

'Why it is true, said he, kindly, that such things are
disagreeable to sit,—nor do I wonder you were distressed,
yet, sometimes, they are *necessary*.'

Was this not *very* kind?—I am sure he meant that the
sanction of his good opinion, so publicly given to Mrs.
Montagu, would, in a manner *stamp* the success of my
Book: & though, had I been allowed to preserve the
snugshipness[9] I had plan'd, I need not have concerned
myself at all about it's fate, yet now, that I find *myself*
exposed with it, I cannot but wish it ensured from Disgrace.

'Well, Sir, cried I, I don't think I shall mind Mrs.
Montagu herself *now*,—after what *you* have said, I believe
I should not mind *abuse* from any one.' ।

'No; no, never mind them! cried he, *resolve* not to mind
them.'

Mrs. Thrale then told me *such* civil Things!—Mrs.
Montagu, it seems, talked of nothing else, during my
retreat, & enquired very particularly what *kind* of Book it
was? 'And I told her, continued Mrs. Thrale, that it was
a picture of Life, manners, & Characters; But won't she
go on? says she, surely she won't stop here? 'Why, said I,
I ⌐want her to go on in a *new* path,⌐ I want her to write a
Comedy.—'But, said Mrs. Montagu, one thing must be

---

[9] So in the MS, but this humorous formation is not in *OED*. It is misprinted
(or emended) in earlier editions as *snugness*, defined as 'secrecy, reticence' by
OED, which cites this sentence. Cf. *snugship*, above, pp. 117, 135.

considered; Fielding, who was so admirable in Novel writing, *never* succeeded when he wrote for the stage.'

'Very well said, cried Dr Johnson; that was an Answer which showed she considered her subject.'

So you see, Susy, they make nothing of coupling Fielding & me together!—very affronting!—

Mrs. Thrale continued—'Well, but, apropos, said Mrs. Montagu, if Miss Burney *does* write a play, I beg I may know of it, or, if she thinks proper, *see* it;—& all my Influence is at her service;—we shall *all* be glad to assist in spreading the Fame of Miss Burney.'[10]

O dear Susy!—you can't think how I tremble for what all this will *end* in!—I verily think I had best stop where I am, & *never* again attempt writing—for after so much Honour, so much success,—how shall I bear a downfall?—

Mrs. T. I shall never see my set again, I dare say.

Mr. T. Why, what the duce [*sic*] did you give them for?—you are always in such a hurry;—what a foolish business have you made of it, to give away our set?

Mrs. T. Why there is a new Edition coming out,—& then,—Miss Burney, I shall expect a *present*,—for I must have a set of the new Edition.[11]

F:B. O, if you will *accept* them, I shall certainly send ¦ a set, though, without a *hint*, it would be the *last* present I should think of making: & I am sure they can very well be spared here, for you have them quite by Heart.

Nothing can be more true; Mrs. Thrale quotes from them eternally; some or other part of the Book is apropos to every thing that is said or done.

---

[10] As it turned out, Mrs Montagu did *not* like *Evelina*. HLT wrote to SJ, 19 Oct. 1778: 'Mrs Montagu cannot bear Evelina—let not that be published—her Silver-Smiths are Pewterers She says, & her Captains Boatswains' (SJ, *Letters* ii. 259). In his reply, 24 Oct., SJ attributes Mrs Montagu's disapprobation to jealousy: 'I am sorry for Mrs. Montague; ... Montague has got some vanity in her head. Vanity always oversets a Lady's Judgement' (*LSJ* iii. 130–1). Her dislike of the novel may also have stemmed partly from her rivalry with both HLT and SJ. A year later (11 Nov. 1779) SJ wrote to Queeney Thrale: 'The talk was for a while about Burney's book, and the old objection to the Captain's grossness being mentioned, Lady Edgcombe said that she had known such a captain' (below, p. 412 n. 45).

[11] See below, p. 174.

Mr. T. Well,—if you do send us a set, Miss Burney, I desire you will write *from the Author*, in form & order!'

Mrs. T. O,—apropos;—Now you have a new Edition coming out, why should you not put your Name to it?—

F:B. O ⌐Lord⌐ Ma'am,—I would not for the World!

Mrs. T. And why not? come, let us have done, now, with all this *Diddle Daddle*.

F:B. No,—indeed, Ma'am, so long as I live I *never* can consent to that!

Mrs. T Well, but, seriously, Miss Burney, why should you *not? I* advise it with all my Heart; & I'll tell you why,— you want *hardening*,—& how can you get it better than by putting your Name to *this* Book, (to begin with,) which *every* body likes, & against which I have heard *nobody* offer any objection?—You can never write what will please *more* universally.

F:B. But *why*, Ma'am, should I be *hardened?*

Mrs. T. To enable you to bear a little abuse by & by.

F:B. O ⌐God⌐ forbid I should be tried that way!

Mrs. T. O, you must not talk so;—*I* hope to Live to see you trim'd very handsomely.

F:B. ⌐God⌐ forbid, God forbid!—I am sure I should Hang or Drown myself in such a Case!——

Mrs. T. You grieve me to hear you talk so;—is not *every* body abused that meets with success? You must prepare yourself not to mind a few squibs. How is Mr. Johnson abused!—& who thinks the worse of him?

This Comparison made me *Grin*,—& so our Discourse ended. But pray for me, my dear Susy, that Heaven may spare ¦ me the Horror irrecoverable of personal abuse.— Let them Criticise, cut, slash, without mercy my *Book*,—& let them *neglect me*,—but may God [xxxxx *2 words*] avert my becoming a public Theme of Ridicule. In such a Case, how should I wish Evelina had followed her humble predecessors to the all devouring Flames![12]—which, in consuming *her*, would have preserved her Creatress!—

---

[12] On her 15th birthday, FB had burned all her compositions to that time, including 'Caroline Evelyn', the forerunner of *Evelina*. See *EJL* i. p. xv.

Monday,—Septr 21st

I have no Time, my dearest Girl, to Journalise to the present, with any regularity;—for I must make up my Pacquet for my dear Father to carry to Town.

I am more comfortable here than ever; Dr. Johnson Honours me with increasing kindness; Mr. Thrale is much more easy & sociable than when I was here before;—I am quite *jocose*, whenever I please, with Miss Thrale,—& the Charming Head & Life of the House, her mother, stands the Test of the closest examination as well, & as much to her Honour as she does a mere cursory view. She is, indeed, all that is excellent & desirable in Woman.

I have had a thousand delightful Conversations with Dr. Johnson, who, whether he *loves* me or not, I am sure seems to have some opinion of my *discretion*, for he speaks of all this House to me with unbounded confidence, neither diminishing faults, nor exaggerating praise. Whenever he is below stairs, he keeps me a *Prisoner*, for he does not like I should quit the Room a *moment*: if I rise, he constantly calls out 'Don't *you* go, little Burney!—' Last Night, when we were talking of *Compliments*, & of *gross speeches*, Mrs. Thrale most justly said, that Nobody could make *either* like Dr. Johnson. 'Your Compliments, Sir, are made *seldom*, but when they *are* made, they have an elegance unequalled: but then, when you are *angry*, who *dares* make speeches so bitter & so cruel?'

Dr. J. Madam, I am always *sorry* when I make bitter speeches, & I never do it, but when I am insufferably vexed.

Mrs. T. Yes, Sir,—but you do suffer things to vex *you*, that Nobody *else* would vex at. I am sure *I* have had my share of scolding from you!

Dr. J. It is true, you have;—but you have borne it like an Angel—& you have been the *better* for it.

Mrs. T. That I believe, Sir: for I have received more *instruction* from you, than from any *man*, or any *Book*; & the vanity that you should think me *worth* instructing, always overcame the vanity of being found fault with. And so *you* had the scolding, & *I* the improvement.

F.B. And I am sure *both* make for the Honour of both!

Dr. J. I think so, too. But Mrs. Thrale is a sweet Creature, & *never* angry; she has a Temper the most delightful of *any* woman I ever knew.

Mrs. T. *This* I can tell you, Sir, & without any flattery,—I not only bear your reproofs when *present*, but in almost every thing I do in your *absence*, I ask myself whether *you* would like it, & what *you* would say to it. Yet I believe there is Nobody you dispute with oftener than me.

F:B. But you two are so well *established* with one another, that *you* can *bear* a rebuff that would *kill* a stranger.

Dr. J. Yes, but we disputed the same *before* we were so well established with one another.

Mrs. T. O, sometimes I think I shall Die no other Death than *hearing* the bitter things he says to others! what he says to *myself*, I can bear, because I know how sincerely he is my *friend*, & that he means to *mend* me;—but to *others* it is cruel!—

Dr. J. Why, Madam, you often *provoke* me to say severe things, by unseasonable commendation: if you would not call for my *praise*, I would not give you my *Censure*: but it constantly moves my indignation to be applied ˡ to to speak *well* of a thing which I think contemptible.

F.B. Well,—*this* I know,—who ever I may hear complain of Dr. Johnson's *severity*, *I* shall always vouch for his *kindness*, as far as regards *myself*.

Mrs. T. Ay, but I hope he will trim you, yet, too!

Dr. J. *I* hope *not*: I should be very sorry to say any thing that should vex my dear little Burney.

F.B. If you *did*, Sir, it *would* vex me more than you can imagine:—I should sink in a minute!—

Mrs. T. I remember, Sir, when we were Travelling in Wales,[13] how you called me to account for my civility to the people;—Madam, ⌐he'd⌐ said, let me have no more of this idle commendation of *nothing*,—*why* is it, that *what*ever you see, & *who*-ever you see, you are to be so indiscriminately lavish of Praise?—'Why I'll *tell* you, Sir,

[13] SJ visited Wales with Mr Thrale, HLT and Queeney in 1774. For the text of SJ's 'Journey into North Wales', see *Life* v. 427–61. HLT's Welsh Journal is printed in A. M. Broadley, *Dr. Johnson and Mrs. Thrale* (1910), pp. 158–219. See also Clifford, pp. 113–16; *TSP*, pp. 89–105.

said I,—when I am with *you*, & *Mr. Thrale*, & *Queeny*,—I am obliged to be civil for *four*!

There was a Cutter for you!—But this I must say, for the Honour of both;—Mrs. Thrale speaks to Dr. Johnson with equal *sincerity*, (though with greater *softness*,) as he does to her.

Well,—now I have given you so many fine Compliments from Dr. Johnson & Mrs. Thrale,—suppose, by way of contrast & variety, I give you a few of Rose Fuller's?—He called here on Saturday morning [19 Sept.], with his little Dog *Sharp*; who is his constant Companion. When the common salutations were over, & every body had said something to him, & his Dog, he applied to *me*.—

'Well, Miss Burney, & how do *you* do?—Pray how do *you* like my little Dog?

F:B.   —O, very well!—

Mr. Fuller.   —I am very glad to hear it; I shall *pique* myself upon Miss *Burney's* opinion, & that sort of thing: I assure I you, I am quite proud of it.—I have got an Evelina of my own, now, Mrs. Thrale;—we shall break the Book-seller,—for Dr. Calvert sent for it too: I am now in the middle of the second volume:—upon my word, Miss Burney, in that sort of way, 'tis amazing how you've hit off Characters!—upon my word, I never read any thing higher:—I declare I never Laughed so in my Life. And, give me leave to say, for that sort of thing, I think that Captain a very ingenious sort of man; upon my word, he is quite smart in some of his replies: but he is too hard upon the old french woman, too.

In the Evening, he came to Tea, with Mr. Stephen Fuller,[14] his Uncle, a sensible & Gentlemanlike looking man, but who is dreadfully Deaf. Rose Fuller sat by me, & began again upon Evelina; indeed, now the *Ice* is broken, I believe he will talk of nothing else.

'Well, Miss Burney, I must tell you all the secrets, now, in that sort of way,—I put the 1st volume into Mr. Stephen Fuller's Hands,—but I did not *tell* him,—don't be

---

[14] Stephen Fuller (1716–99), MA (Cantab.), 1742; London merchant (*GM* lxix² (1799), 821; IGI).

alarmed,—I kept Counsel,—but, upon my word, you never saw a Man Laugh so!—I could hardly get him to come, in that sort of way,—he says he never saw characters so well hit off, true! upon my word! I was obliged to take the Book from him, & that sort of thing, or we should have been too late. But, upon my word, 'tis amazing.

Adieu, my dearest Susy!—pray let me hear from you as soon as you possibly can: I hate to be so long without Letters.

My best Love to Charlotte: she must excuse my writing separately to her.[15] |

62   Streatham,
                            26 September [1778]
To Susanna Elizabeth Burney

AJL (Diary MSS I, paginated 787–94, Berg), Sept. 1778
4 single sheets, 4to, 8 pp. (the last blank)

Streatham
Septr 26th

I have, from want of Time, neglected my Journal so long, that I cannot now pretend to go on methodically: I must beg you, therefore, my dear Girl, to accept such few *spurts* of conversation as I am able to recollect, & not to be *particular* as to Dates.

My dear Father will doubtless have told you of our Monday's [21 Sept.] Dinner: *Messieurs* Stephen & Rose Fuller stayed very late; the former, talking very rationally upon various subjects, & the latter, *boring* us with his *systems, & those sort of things.* Yet he is something of a favourite, *in that sort of way,* at this House, because of his *invincible* good humour, & Mrs. Thrale says she would not change him, as a *Neighbour,* for a much wiser man. Dr. Johnson says he would make a very good *Mr. Smith*:

---

[15] Missing.

'let him but, he adds, pass a month or two in Holbourne,
& I would desire no better.'

The other Evening, the conversation *fell* upon
Romney,[16] the Painter, who has lately got into great
business, & who was first recommended & patronised by
Mr. Cumberland. 'See, Madam, said Dr. Johnson,
Laughing, what it is to have the favour of a *Literary*
man!—I think *I* have had no Hero a great while; Dr.
Goldsmith was my last: but I have had none since his
Time.— —till my little Burney came!—

'Ay, Sir, said Mrs. Thrale, Miss Burney is the Heroine
now; is it not *really* true, Sir?'

'To be sure it is, my dear! answered he, with a gravity
that made not only *me*, but *Mr. Thrale* ⌐laugh.¬

Another Time, Mr. Thrale ⌐told me¬ he had seen Dr.
Jebb, 'And he told me he was afraid [Miss Burney][17], you
would have gone into a Consumption, said he, but I
informed him how well you are; & he committed you to
my care: so I shall insist, | now, upon being sole Judge of
what Wine you Drink.'

N.B. We had often *disputed* this point.

Dr. J. Why did Dr. Jebb *forbid* her Wine?

F:B. Yes, Sir.

Dr. J. Well,—he was in the right;—he knows how apt Wits
are to transgress that way.

In this sort of ridiculous manner he *Wits*[18] me eternally.
But, the present chief sport with Mrs. Thrale is disposing
of me in the holy state of matrimony—& she *offers* me
who-ever comes to the House: this was begun by Mrs.
Montagu, who, it seems, proposed a match for me, in my
absence, with—Sir Joshua Reynolds!—no less a man, I

---

[16] George Romney (1734–1802), painter. Richard Cumberland's *Odes* (1776)
contains a dedicatory epistle to him. A portrait by him of Cumberland is in the
National Portrait Gallery, London, and another of Mrs Cumberland and their
son Charles is in the Tate. Cumberland wrote of Romney in his *Memoirs* (1807),
ii. 213: 'I sate to him, and was the first, who encouraged him to advance his
terms, by paying him ten guineas for his performance.' See also A. B.
Chamberlain, *George Romney* (New York, 1910), pp. 52–3 and *passim*; S. T.
Williams, *Richard Cumberland* (New Haven, 1917), pp. 115–17, 170, 199–200.

[17] Inserted by FBA.

[18] *OED* cites this nonce-use, in the sense of 'to call (a person) a wit, attribute
wit to.'

assure you!—But, one morning at Break fast, before we were joined by the Gentlemen, Mrs. Thrale was lamenting the Dissipation of Sir John Ladd: & wishing he was *well married*, 'That, alone, she continued, could reclaim him, *if any* thing could: A prudent & sensible wife,—who would Govern him with gentleness & propriety, & whom he loved passionately, might do wonders with him.'

'Not a few, cried I, are the requisites such a Wife must have.'

'Would *to* God *you* were to take him in Hand!' exclaimed she.

'Me?—yes,—*I* should have *all* the requisites!'

'Yes, that you would!—though I don't know whether it is wishing *you* well;—to be wife to a young Baronet of £12:000 a Year is *something*, & *not amiss*,—but to be Wife to a *scoundrel* is *miserable*, & oversets all the good.'

'Well, Ma'am, since *that* is the case—why I won't think of it!'

This *agreeable sally* concluded the confab. in a Grin.

When I was Dressing for Dinner, Mrs. Thrale told me that Mr. Crutchley[19] was expected. 'Who's he?' quoth I.

'A Young man of a very large fortune, said she, who was a Ward of Mr. Thrale. Queeny, what do you say of *him* for Miss Burney?'

'Him? cried she; no, indeed;—what has Miss Burney done to have *him*?'

'Nay, believe me, a man of his fortune may offer himself any where. However, I won't recommend him, for his Fortune is *all* he has to boast.'

'Why then, Ma'am, cried I, with Dignity,—I reject him!'

This Mr. Crutchley stayed till after Breakfast the next morning. I can't tell You any thing of him, because I niether *like* nor *dis*like him;—but that, Mrs. Thrale, after he was gone, said 'What a *popular* Book is this Evelina: Mr. *Crutchley* asked me if I ever read Novels? Yes, said I,

---

[19] Jeremiah Crutchley (1745–1805), of Sunninghill Park, Berks. Crutchley was later elected MP for Horsham, Sussex (in 1784), and was one of the 5 executors of Henry Thrale's will. HLT believed him to be Thrale's natural son, and claimed that Thrale had admitted as much to her (Namier; *Thraliana* i. 497; *TSP*, p. 227).

some times; Have you read Evelina? said he: Yes, sure, I told him, and a very pretty one it is: Do you know the Author? quoth he;—Yes, & *you* do, too, said I:—Do *I?*— why who is it?—Why you won 2 shillings of her last Night at Back Gammon.—Pho, nonsense! said he, but tell me *really*,—& just then you came in.

What a *bloody* determination this is to make me known & noticed in my own despight! However, I now leave off even remonstrances, since I find them so wholly ineffectual.

Mr. Crutchley was scarce gone, ere Mr. Smith[20] arrived. Mr. Smith is a 2^d Cousin[21] of Mr. Thrale, & a modest, pretty sort of Young man; by no means like *my* Mr. Smith: yet I could hardly bear to call him by his Name, for I felt a kind of *conscious Guilt*, as if I had been taking unwarrantable liberties with it.

He stayed till Friday morning [25 Sept.]. When he was gone, 'What say you to *him*, Miss Burney? cried Mrs. Thrale, I am sure I offer you *variety*.'

'Why I like him *better* than Mr. Crutchley—but I don't think I shall *pine* for either of them.'

'Mr. Johnson, said Mrs. Thrale, don't you think Jerry Crutchley very much improved?'

Dr. J. Yes, Madam, I think he is.

Mrs. T. Shall he have Miss Burney?

Dr. J. Why—I think not;—at least, I must know more of him: I must enquire into his connections, his recreations, his employments, & his Character, from his Intimates before I trust Miss Burney with him: And he must come down very handsomely with a *settlement*,—I will not have him left to his *generosity*; for as he will marry *her* for her Wit, & she *him* for his Fortune, he ought to bid well;—& let him come down with what he will, his price will never be equal to her worth.

Mrs. T. She says she likes Mr. Smith better.

---

[20] Henry Smith (1756–89), of New House Farm, near St Albans, Herts, son of Henry Thrale's cousin Henry Smith (1724–65) and his wife Jane (1727–81). The younger Henry Smith was another executor of Thrale's will.

[21] Actually, 1st cousin once removed.

Dr. J. Yes,—but I won't have her like Mr. Smith *without* the money, better than Mr. Crutchley *with* it: besides, if she has Crutchley, he will use her well, to vindicate his Choice: the World, Ma'am, has a reasonable *claim* upon all mankind to account for their Conduct: therefore, if Crutchley, with his great Wealth, marries a woman who has but little, he will be more attentive to display *her* merit, than if she was equally rich, in order to shew that the Woman he has chosen *deserves* from the World all the respect & admiration it can bestow.

Mrs. T. I believe Young Smith is the better man.

F.B. Well,—I won't be *rash* in thinking of *either.* I will take some Time for consideration before I fix.

Dr. J. Why I don't hold it to be *delicate* to offer marriages to Ladies, even in Jest, nor do I approve such sort of jocularity; yet, for once, I must break through the rules of decorum, & propose a match myself for Miss Burney, *I*, therefore, nominate Sir John Ladd.'

Mrs. Thrale: I'll give you my Word, Sir, you are not the *first* to say that; for my master, the other morning, when we were alone, said—What would I give that Sir John Ladd was married to Miss Burney!—it might restore him to our Family!—So spoke his *Uncle* & *Guardian*!

F:B. He! He!—Ha! Ha!—He! He!—Ha! Ha!—

Dr. J. That was elegantly said of my master! & *nobly* said, & not in the *vulgar* way *we* have been saying it. And Where, Madam, will you find another man in *Trade* who will make such a speech? Who will be *capable* of making such a speech?—Well, I am glad my master takes so to Miss Burney; I would have every body take to Miss Burney, so as they allow *me* to take to her *most*!—Yet I don't know whether Sir John Ladd *should* have her, niether! I should be *afraid* for her;—I don't think I would *Hand* her to him.

F:B. Why now what a fine match is here broken off.

A few Days since, at Dinner, Dr. Johnson repeated some verses, & asked Mrs. Thrale whose they were?—She said she knew not: he then asked *me*;—I made the same Answer:—'Miss Burney does not know either, said Mrs. Thrale, yet she is a very good English Classic.' Some Time after, when we were in the Library, he asked me very gravely if I *loved* reading? *Yes,* quoth I:—'Why do you doubt it, Sir?' cried Mrs. Thrale.

'Because, answered he, I never see her with a Book in her Hand. I have taken Notice that she never has been reading whenever I have come into the Room.' | 'Sir, quoth I, courageously, I am always *afraid* of being caught Reading, lest I should pass for being *studious,* or *affected,* & therefore, instead of making a *Display* of Books, I always try to *hide* them,—as is the case at this very Time, for I have now your Life of Waller under my Gloves, behind me!—however, since I am *piqued* to it, I'll boldly produce my voucher.—'

And so saying, I put the Book on the Table, & opened it with a flourishing Air.—And then, the Laugh was on *my* side, for he could not help making a droll Face;—&, if he had known Kitty Cooke, I would have called out 'There I had you, my Lad!'—

'And *now,* quoth Mrs. Thrale, you must be more careful than ever of not being thought Bookish, for *now* you are known for a Wit, & a belle Esprit, you will be *watched,* &, if you are not upon your Guard, all the misses will rise up against you.'

Dr. J. Nay, nay, *now* it is too late! you may read as much as you will now, for you are *in for it,*—you are dipped, over Head & Ears,—in the Castalian Stream,[22]—& so, I hope, you will be *invulnerable.*

Another Time, when we were Talking of the licentiousness of the Newspapers, Dr. Johnson said 'I wonder they have never yet had a touch at little Burney!'

'O *God* forbid! cried I,—I am sure, if they did,—I believe I should try the depth of Mrs. Thrale's *spring pond.*'

---

[22] Castalia, a spring on Mt Parnassus, was sacred to Apollo and the Muses. SJ may have been thinking of the 'slip-shod Sibyl' in Pope's *Dunciad,* who 'never wash'd, but in Castalia's streams' (iii. 15–18; see also Christopher Anstey, *The New Bath Guide,* i. 7). He also seems to be conflating this reference with an allusion to the dipping of Achilles by his mother Thetis in the River Styx, to make him invulnerable.

'No, no, my dear, no! cried he, kindly, you must resolve
not to mind them,—you must set yourself against them,
& not let any such nonsense affect you'.

'There is nobody, said Mrs. Thrale, Tempers the satirist
with so much meekness as Miss Burney!'

Satirist, indeed! is it not a satire upon *words*, Susy, | to
call *me* so?

'I hope to Heaven I shall never be tried, cried I, for I
am sure I should never bear it! Of my *Book*, they may say
what they will, & welcome,—but if they touch [a]t *me*,—I
shall be—O ″Lord″!—I don't know what!'

'Nay, said Mrs. Thrale, if you are not afraid for the
Book, I am sure they can say no harm of the *Author*.

'Never let them know, said Dr. Johnson, *which* way you
shall most mind them, & then they will stick to the *Book*,—
but you must never acknowledge how tender you [a]re
for the *Author*.'

I am so hurried, my dear Girl, that I cannot add another
word. |

[*The letter ends here. The last sentence is scrawled, as if written in
haste, but may have been appended later by FBA. The last 1½ pp. of
the last leaf are blank.*]

63   [St Martin's Street,
                    ante 26 October 1778]

To Thomas Lowndes

AL (Comyn), Oct. 1778
Single sheet 4to, 1 p.
Addressed: Mr. Lowndes | Fleet Street
The MS is in vol. 1 of a grangerized copy of *DL*.

Sir,

I now send you all the sheets of Evelina I have been
able to correct. You shall have the rest in a few Days.
But as I have heard many purchasers of the Work complain of the coarseness of the paper, I hope you will

suffer the 2^d Edition to be printed upon a better. I am, Sir,

Yr. ob^t Ser^t

_____ _____

64   [St Martin's Street,
                        ante 26 October 1778 *bis*]

To Thomas Lowndes

> AL (Comyn), Oct. 1778
> Single sheet 4to, 1 p.
> *Addressed*: Mr. Lowndes
> The MS is in vol. 1 of a grangerized copy of *DL*.

Sir,

I return you my thanks for your attention to my requests.

I now send the rest of the 3^d volume. If the Title-Pages are not yet printed off, I should be very glad to have this addition to them:

Evelina,
or
The History of
A young Lady's &c. &c.[23]

I shall hope that you will favour me with 6 setts of the New Edition, when ready for publication, to be sent according to the former Direction,[24]—for my particular friends: as, hitherto, I have been obliged to purchase whatever I have found necessary to present to them. I am,

Sir

Yr. ob^t h^{le} ser^t

_____ _____

[23] The expanded title was not adopted until the 3rd edn. (1779). The 2nd edn. was published on Mon., 26 Oct. 1778 (though with the imprint date of 1779): '*This day was published*, In Three Volumes 12mo. price 7s. 6d. sewed, or 9s. bound, A NEW EDITION of EVELINA; or, A YOUNG LADY'S

[*See opposite page for n. 23 cont. and n. 24*]

65

[St Martin's Street,
ante 6 November 1778]

To Samuel Crisp

The MS of this letter is now missing, as are the MSS of all FB's letters
to SC in 1778. Mrs Ellis obviously saw the letter, as she quotes the extract
below from it (*ED* i. p. lxxxi n. 1). SC, in an undated letter to FB (Barrett),
had called her 'an Ebrew Jew' for refusing to let him copy part of her
Streatham journals. She then relented and permitted him to send them
to his sister Mrs Gast (the quoted extract here follows),

… as the strongest mark in my power to give her of my
affectionate esteem … I entreat you will enjoin her to
read them quite alone, or, not to be cruel, to poor sick
Mrs. Lenthnall [*sic*],[25] under an oath of secresy and silence.

[*FBA has inserted the following ALS from SC, 2 single sheets 4to, 4
pp.*, pmk 6 NO *and paginated 795–8, into the Journal for 1778. It
is addressed*: Miss Fanny Burney | at Dr Burneys | St Martins
Street | Leicester Feilds [*sic*] | London]

My dear Fannikin
    Since Peace is proclaim'd, & I am got out of my
Hobble,[26] [I] am content; & shall never lose a thought

ENTRANCE into the WORLD. Printed for T. Lowndes, in Fleet-street' (*London
Packet* 23–6 Oct., s.v. 26 Oct.; see also *London Evening Post* 24–7 Oct.). This
edn. was of 500 copies; the 1st had been of 500 or 800 (see *DL* ii. 481; *JL* iii.
206).
    FB's presentation copy to her father of the 2nd edn., inscribed 'Dr. Burney.
From his dutiful scribler', was purchased in 1940 by the late Michael Papantonio
of New York City, afterwards co-founder of the Seven Gables Book Shop, who
probably resold it shortly after buying it. Its present whereabouts is not known.
See *DL* i. 127 n. 1; *Book Auction Records* xxxviii (1940–1), 24; *EJL* i p. xxvi;
additional information courtesy of Mr Robert J. Barry, C. A. Stonehill Rare
Books, New Haven; Mr John Brett-Smith, Princeton Rare Books, Kingston,
New Jersey.
    [24] To 'Mr. Grafton' (Edward Francesco Burney), at Gregg's Coffee House.
    [25] Mary ('Molly') Lenthall (d. 1794), of Burford Priory, Oxon., a good friend
of SC and Mrs Gast who was 'a constant invalid' (W. H. Hutton, *Burford Papers*
(1905), pp. 12, 27).
    [26] 'An awkward or perplexing situation' (*OED*, s.v. hobble, *sb.* 2). Mrs Gast
seems to have broken the 'oath of secresy and silence'. The first sentence of
the next paragraph suggests that Mrs Gast may also have been 'guilty' of
spreading the word of FB's authorship of *Evelina*.

more in considering how I got into it. My Object now, is to reap the fruits of the Accommodation; of which the principal article seem [*sic*] to be, *an open trade* & renewal of Commerce & Confidence together with a strict Observance of former treaties, by which no new Alliances are to be form'd to the prejudice of the Old Family Compact. These preliminaries being acceded to, nothing now remains but, to sing Te Deum, & play off the Fireworks.

I do entirely acquit you of all wish, or design of being known to the World as an Author—I believe it is ever the Case with writers of real Merit & Genius, on the appearance of their first productions: as their powers are finer & keener than other people's, so is their sensibility—on these Occasions they are as nervous as Lady Louisa [in *Evelina*][27] herself; but surely these painful feelings ought to go off, when the salts of general Applause are continually held under their Nose; it is then time to follow your friend Dr Johnson's Advice, & learn *to be a swaggerer* at least so far, as to be able to face the World, & not be asham'd of the Distinction, you have fairly earn'd, especially when it is Apparent You do not court it.

I wish you joy of your second delivery,[28] or rather "the" after-birth [xxxxx *2 words*] tho' I dont see what great Occasion there was for Alteration[29]—the Babe was born a fine, fair fat, healthy Child, as one should see in a Summers day;[30] & its swaddling Cloaths became it very well; & if you have put a Ribband in its Cap & a fine new Sash, its original Features ⏐ will still be the Object to attract Notice, & the little particulars of dress hardly observ'd: however in its new Form I am determin'd & impatient to have it; & as I see by Lowndes' advertisement it is still to

[27] Inserted by FBA. Lady Louisa Larpent, Ld. Orville's sister, is an affected young woman given to displays of nervous agitation.

[28] i.e., the 2nd edn. of *Evelina*.

[29] SC presumably refers to the better quality binding and paper of the 2nd edn. FB had relayed to Lowndes readers' complaints about 'the coarseness of the paper' of the 1st edn., whereas SC himself had suggested at least 1 important change to the *text* (above, pp. 82, 173).

[30] SC is echoing the old English proverb as it appears in Fielding's *Joseph Andrews* (IV. xv): 'As fine a fat thriving Child as you shall see in a Summer's Day' (ed. M. Battestin (Oxford, 1967), p. 337).

be had in Sheets,[31] I wish you would order him to get me a set, bound up in one Volume for You must know, I hate the Idea of breaking off in the midst of a Story, when one has begun it; & this is invariably the Case, because forsooth, Mrs Fiddle, & Mrs Faddle have got the second or third Volume to read, & I must stay till they are returned; besides, these Volumes are so short, they may very well be compriz'd in one, & it is only Booksellers craft to spin out, or split it into three to have a pretence for so many times three Shillings. I shall order Gast, now in town, to pay the Damage. I read to her your kind message, but she has, or will tell you herself in person, how much She loves & esteems a Fannikin.

As you say, your Streatham Journal contains 3 folio Volumes, I must I see give up hope of the Detail; but surely the Contents of the several Chapters of the work, may be had separate; in the mean time, I want to know the Numbers, & the Names of the People, who more particularly lay claim to you; because, as you say, *You wish You could see me* I sigh, & calculate what chance, & what share I may reasonably expect.—Besides, that great Gulph of Streatham & those two Leviathans (Mrs Thrale & Doctor Johnson) that swim about in it, & devour all small Fry, that approach there are, I dare say, ⟨brood⟩ of other Voracious *Fan-eaters*—Your [*Reynolds*], your *Cholmondelys*, your &c's &c's &c—without End—I Molly Chute[32] (an intimate & most infinitely agreable [*sic*] old friend of mine, long since dead) when I us'd to desire her to love me a great deal, would say *Look Ye Sam, I have this Stock of love by me*, putting out her little Finger, *& I can afford You so much*, measuring off perhaps half the length of her Nail—*& I think thats'* [*sic*] *pretty fair*—I thought so too, & was well content—but what shall I do with *You*, who have so many to content?—You have but Your five loaves, & your two fishes, & can You renew the Miracle, & feed

[31] See above, p. 174, n. 23.

[32] Probably the 'Mrs. Chute' who, accompanied by SC's late sister Ann Crisp (*c*.1696–1776), visited Mrs Delany in London in Apr. 1735; perhaps Mary Chute, the spinster sister of John Chute (1701–76) of the Vyne, Horace Walpole's friend. See *Delany Corr.* i. 535; *EJL* ii. 65 n. 5.

five thousand?[33] Well [xxxxx *1 word*] *I must do as I may,*
& that is the very Nuthook humour of it—'[34]

Adieu my Fannikin, I can furnish nothing from this
Place, or this Brain that can ballance our Account, so that
if You dont consider me as entitled by prescription & pay
me on my Pension, because I have been *us'd* to it I can
have no other Claim—in full Confidence of this being
allow'd, I conclude in the Language of the Horseleeche's
two Daughters, *Give, Give*[35] to y^r Loving Daddy

S.C.

Honest Kate, my only Housemate at present, says, I love
Fanny, because she is sincere—

Pray remember me to the Susettikin & *Chùrrlotte*—

[*Here 7 obliterated lines, only partly recovered, contain playful greetings
to the rest of FB's family.*

*Also in the Journal for 1778 is the following AL fragment from SC,
1 single sheet 4to, 2 pp., dated (by FBA) 11* Nov—78 *and annotated
by her on my Journal—on popularity, & old age*—]

My dear Fannikin

[*18 obliterated lines, partly deciphered, evidently concern the pro-
curement of a set of* Evelina *for Mrs Gast.*]

Now then my dear Fanny for the Journal—Gast & I
read it over comfortably together; I shall not tell You
what we said, or what we thought of it—You have been
sufficiently crammd with Sweetmeats already—however,
be it good or bad, if You will give your Consent (for I
will not be so faithless to do it without) I shall be glad to
take a Copy of it, & under the same Oath of Concealment,
as you enjoin'd when You trusted it with Gast—Methinks,
You were pretty well sweated my dear by Mr Lort[36]—Gast
& I really sweated for You—& yet, said I, I owe her a
sort of a Grudge for her Poetical Injustice, & Cruelty to

---

[33] Cf. Matthew 14: 17–21, Mark 6: 38–44, Luke 9: 13–17, John 6: 9–13.

[34] Cf. *Merry Wives of Windsor* I. i. 171. 'Nuthook' was slang for a constable or
beadle. 'Nuthook humour' means, roughly, acting like a constable or 'cop'; SC's
sense seems to be, 'I'll do as I please, like a policeman'.

[35] Cf. Proverbs 30: 15.

[36] See above, p. 112 and *seq.*

poor Lovel, who tho' a compleat Ass, was too harmless to be so crucified—tho' with consummate humour & Sport[37]—You see I dont spare You—however, my Freedom ought to convince You of my strict Sincerity when I approve.

I now proceed to assume the Daddy, & Consequently the Privilege ǀ of giving Counsel—Your kind & judicious Friends are certainly in the right, in wishing You to make your Talents turn to some thing more solid than empty Praise—When You come to know the World half so well as I do,[38] & what Yahoos Mankind are –, you will then be convinc'd, that a State of Independence is the only Basis, on which to rest your future Ease & Comfort—You are now Young, lively, Gay; You please, & the World smiles upon you—this is your time—Years & Wrinkles in their due Season; (perhaps attended with want of health & Spirits,) will succeed—You will then be no longer the same Fanny of 1778, feasted, caress'd, admir'd, with all the soothing circumstances of your present Situation[39]—The Thrales, the Johnsons, the Sewards, Cholmondelys &c &c &c, who are now so high in fashion & might be such powerful protectors as almost to insure Success to any thing that is tolerable, may then themselves be moved off the Stage—I will no longer dwell on so disagreeable a Change of the Scene—: let me only earnestly urge You to act vigorously (what I really believe is in your power) a distinguish'd part in the present one—*now while it is yet to day, & before the night cometh when no man can work; for favour is deceitful, & Beauty is Vain.*[40]

I must again & again repeat my former admonition regarding Your Posture in reading & Writing—it is of infinite Consequence, especially to such lungs, & such a frame as Yours.

[37] SC refers to the pet monkey's tearing the fop Lovel's ear at the end of *Evelina* (vol. iii, letter 21). CB also objected to this episode (above, p. 29).
[38] The unconscious *hubris* of these words is amusing, to say the least.
[39] SC used virtually the same argument in trying to convince FB to marry Thomas Barlow in 1775. See *EJL* ii. 123.
[40] Cf. John 9: 4 and Proverbs 31: 30.

Lastly, if you do resolve to undertake any thing of the Nature your friends recommend, keep it (if possible) an impenetrable Secret that you are about such a Work.— Let it be all your own till it is finish'd intirely in your own Way—it will be time enough then to consult such friends as you think capable of Judging & Advising—if you suffer any one to interfere till then, 'tis ten to one, 'tis the worse for it—it wont be all of a Piece—in these Cases, generally the more Cooks, the worse broth; & I have more than once Observd, those Pieces that have stole privately into the world without Midwives, or Godfathers & Godmothers, like your own, & the Tale of the Tub,[41] & a few others, have far exceeded any that followed— |

[*rest of letter missing*]

66   [St Martin's Street,
                              post 1 December 1778]

To Catherine Coussmaker

ALS (Berg), Dec. 1778
Single sheet folio, 2 pp. red wax seal

Yr kind & most flattering Letter,[42] my dear Miss Coussmaker, claims my best acknowledgements.—Yet, but a few months since, how wd it's subject have startled & confounded me! Little, indeed, did I imagine, when I parted with Evelina, what Honours were in reserve for her! I thought that her only admirers wd be among school girls,

---

[41] Swift's work appeared anonymously in 1704. SC's opinion of it was shared, more famously, by SJ, who believed that, for sheer inventiveness and ingenuity, the *Tale* surpassed any of Swift's later efforts (see *Life* i. 452, ii. 318–19; *Lives of the English Poets*, ed. G. B. Hill (Oxford, 1905), iii. 51).

[42] Catherine Coussmaker to FB, 1 Dec. 1778 (Berg), in which Miss Coussmaker announces her discovery that FB is the author of *Evelina*: 'And could you imagine my dear Miss Burney that the voice of Fame would be as silent on the merits of your Evelina, as you have been yourself? No indeed, it has done you justice in Kent & Wiltshire, whence I had my *first* information, for they resound with your praises—'.

& destined her to no nobler habitation than a Circulating Library.

I cannot express how much I was alarmed when I first received intelligence, ⌐from Susette,¬ of her Introduction to Lady Hales & Miss Coussmaker,[43]—an Honour I dreaded too much to wish;—for I feared the result wd be discovery of the Author—& contempt of the Book. Both these fears, happily for me, proved groundless: the author was, still, obscure & unsuspected,—& the Book was read with the utmost indulgence.

I have a thousand Times congratulated myself upon my absence from Town during Evelina's Examination in Brook Street.[44] I am sure I could never have disguised my solicitude for her reception sufficiently to have escaped observation: yet she cd. not have met with more favour & partiality, had all her connections solicited in her behalf. You saw her as an Orphan, unprotected & unrecommended, & your generous zeal during her obscurity I shall always recollect with the utmost pleasure & satisfaction.

And, indeed, I can not doubt but that both Lady Hales & yourself, in common with many other unsought & unflattered Patronnesses & patrons, will, for the sake of the very cowardly Writer, rejoice at the good nature & lenity shewn to her highly honoured Book. & believe me, had I ever meant to have been found out Lady Hales & Miss Coussmaker wd have been among the very first, out of my own family, to whom my own reserve would have given way. But my Susan will explain how ⌐ the affair has been circumstanced.[45]

---

[43] See above, p. 27.

[44] Lady Hales' London residence.

[45] SEB was visiting Lady Hales and Miss Coussmaker at Howletts. In fact, SEB, with FB's permission, had informed Lady Hales of FB's authorship in early Sept., but Lady Hales had agreed to keep the secret even from her daughter, who because of her youth she thought could not be trusted to stay silent (above, p. 135).

I am very sorry I can not, at present, give you any answer concerning Lusignano.[46] I have never heard of it—but I will certainly make all the enquiries in my power, &, if I can offer any intelligence, communicate it without delay.

I beg my best respects to Lady Hales, & am,
my dear Miss Coussmaker,
Your obliged & faithful servant
Frances Burney.

67   St Martin's Street
[4 December 1778]

To Susanna Elizabeth Burney

AL fragment (Diary MSS I, paginated 815–18, [1]-4, Berg), Dec. 1778

 2 single sheets 4to, 4 pp.
 Annotated (by FBA): ✳ ✳ ✳ 1779 [*sic*] *Pacchierotti. Dr. Franklin.*

St Martin's Street

I was extremely glad, my dearest Susan, to see by Your Letter[47] that your Journey had not totally discomposed the *oeconomy of your Health,*—for the morning proved so cold & damp that I had been a little alarmed for you.

Well but—how will you bear to hear about Pac[48]—*may* I finish the name?—I am almost afraid,—yet think it a

[46] Miss Coussmaker asked if 'you have heard a new Italian Poem, entitled *Lusignano* mentioned by the *Beaux Esprits* & what is the general opinion concerning it. ... Mrs. Carter has spoken very favourably of it.'

No mention of *Lusignano* has been found in Mrs Elizabeth Carter's published works, and no such poem has been otherwise traced. Possibly Miss Coussmaker had heard a garbled report of a new *translation* (by William Julius Mickle, 1776, 2nd edn., 1778) of Luis de Camoens' *Portuguese* epic, *The Lusiads*. Mrs Carter, who read Portuguese, may have praised the poem's merits in the original language.

[47] Missing.

[48] Gasparo Pacchierotti *or* Pacchiarotti (1740–1821), Italian castrato soprano. Pacchierotti's eagerly awaited first appearance in London was in the pasticcio *Demofoonte* at the Opera, Sat. night, 28 Nov. 1778. CB wrote that in Pacchierotti's

miserable compliment to treat you as a Baby, & *hide* from you the play things you must not have in your *own Hand.* So I will only remind you of similar situations in which *I* have been,—&, at the same Time, reminding *myself* of your conduct upon those occasions—the *upshot* of all which will be ... a true account of the transaction.

Well,—last Saturday morning [28 Nov.] mine Fader sent a present of his History to *Timante*,[49]—by way of an incentive to the study of the English Language. At the Opera, at night,—he promised to call here on Sunday. And *so*—on Sunday morning [29 Nov.] he came,—attended by Signor Bertoni.[50]

Well but he did not sing,—*so far* be easy.

I like him of all things. He is perfectly modest, humble, well bred & unassuming. He has a very anxious desire to learn English, which he has studied Grammatically & with much application | & diligence Abroad: & he promised to come hither *frequently*, to take Lessons of Conversation: By way of beginning with *vigour*, he settled to Drink Tea here the next Day [30 Nov.].[51]

Now, Susy, for fortitude!

voice 'there was a perfection so exquisite in tone, taste, knowledge, sensibility, and expression, that my conceptions in the art could not imagine it possible to be surpassed' (Mercer ii. 888). He was arguably, with the castrato Farinelli, one of the two greatest singers of all time, male or female. He became a life-long friend of the Burney family. See also *New Grove*; *LS 5* i. 218; A. Heriot, *The Castrati in Opera* (1956), pp. 163–71; H. C. Schonberg, *The Glorious Ones* (New York, 1985), p. 3; E. R. and R. E. Peschel, 'Medical Insights into the Castrati in Opera', *American Scientist* lxxv (Nov.-Dec. 1987), 578–83; T. W. Culliney, 'Castration for Art's Sake' (letter to editor), ibid. lxxvi (Mar.-Apr. 1988), 124.

[49] Pacchierotti sang the role of Timante in *Demofoonte*, which received a total of 14 performances at the Opera through 26 June 1779 (*LS 5* i. 265 and *passim*).

[50] Ferdinando Gasparo Bertoni (1725–1813), Italian composer. Bertoni, who directed performances of his own music at the Opera in 1778–80 and 1781–83, had brought Pacchierotti to London with him (*New Grove*). Of their collaboration, CB observes: 'Almost every great singer unites himself in interest and friendship with some particular composer, who writes to his peculiar compass of voice, talents, and style of singing. Thus ... Pacchierotti and Bertoni, were closely connected' (Mercer ii. 889).

[51] On 16 Dec. 1778, Pacchierotti wrote to CB (Osborn) that 'The Efficacy of your reasoning, aught [*sic*] to induce me to an extreme application for surmounting all the difficulties that are attach'd to your language' and entreated him 'to continue with me the usual Favours, & the Kind condensension [*sic*], both which, will lead me to my long desir'd End.'

They came early,—& I am more pleased with Pacchier-otti than ever; he seems to be perfectly amiable, gentle & *good*: his Countenance is extremely benevolent; & his manners, infinitely interesting. We are all become very good friends, & talked *English, French & Italian* by *commodious* starts, just as phrases occurred:—an excellent device for *appearing* a good linguist.

He had a very bad Cold,—yet *sung*,—with the utmost good humour, as soon as asked. Bertoni accompanied him. He first sung a rondeau of Artaserse,[52] of Bertoni's—: it is a very fine one, & had it been a very execrable one, he would have made it exquisite: such taste, expression, freedom, fancy & variety never were before joined, but in Agujari. His Voice, however, was by no means *clear*, though extremely *touching*: but his Cold quite tormented him. He afterwards sung a song for a *Tenor* in the same Opera,—& admirably. Then some accompanied recitative to a song in the *Orfeo* of Bertoni:[53]—& lastly the '*che farò senza Euridice.*[54] |

He & I were very sociable: & he said, in English, 'Miss *Borni* give me very much *encourage*:—but, is very troublesome the *difficulties.*'

Bertoni is very much a common sort of Character that admits no delineation.

Piozzi,[55] by invitation, came in the Evening: he did not sing, but was very good humoured.

Giardini—*not* by invitation, came also. We did not, just then, wish for him, but he was very comique.

---

[52] *Artaserse*, libretto by Metastasio. Bertoni's setting was first performed in 1776, in Forlì. He reset it for its London premiere on 23 Jan. 1779 (*LS* 5 i. 230; *New Grove*). FB later celebrated Pacchierotti's performance in *Artaserse* in *Cecilia*, Bk. i, chap. 8, 'An Opera Rehearsal'.

[53] *Orfeo ed Euridice*, libretto by Raniero de Calzabigi, first performed in 1776 in Venice. It was performed once in London, 'in the Manner of an Oratorio', in 1780 (*LS* 5 i. 347).

[54] From *Orfeo*; famous in the setting by Gluck.

[55] Gabriele Mario Piozzi (1740–1809), Italian tenor and composer. CB patronized him on his coming to England in 1776. Through CB he met the Thrales, and after Henry Thrale's death in 1781 he became increasingly intimate with HLT and married her in 1784, to the outrage of her family and friends, including SJ and the Burneys. See *LCB* i. 228 n. 1; *EJL* ii. 293; *New Grove*.

Charlotte desires to write about Etty [EBB][56].

I have seen but 4 folks worth mentioning, these Italians excepted, since you went. The first & second were Mr. Magellan[57] & Mr. Humphreys,[58] who both drank Tea here on Monday senight last [23 Nov.].

Mr. Magellan was just à l'ordinaire.

Mr. Humphreys was almost *insufferable* from curiosity about the *Book writer*,—he *said* not a Word, thank God, but he *looked*, in revenge, all meanning, [*sic*] & actually stared me so much out of Countenance, that I was obliged to contrive myself a seat *out of his way*. He seemed as if he thought to read in my Face at least *half* the Characters he had read in the Book. *Which* half,—whether the '*Wulgar* or the *Genteel part of the Family*'[59] I cannot pretend to say.—but I was not afflicted when he went.[60]

On Thursday [26 Nov.], I had another adventure, & one that I has made me Grin ever since: a Gentleman enquiring for my Father, was asked in to the Parlour. The *then* Inhabitants were only my mother & me: In Entered a square old Gentleman, well wigged, formal,

---

[56] Charlotte probably concluded this letter, the end of which is missing. EBB seems to have been pregnant again at this time, or to have recently given birth, and Charlotte may have wished to write about her condition (see below, p. 191).

[57] Jean Hyacinthe Magellan (João Jacinto de Magalhães (1722–90), Portuguese natural philosopher and writer. His family claimed descent from Ferdinand Magellan, the first circumnavigator of the globe. Magellan was widely known for his research in chemistry and physics and also wrote on scientific instruments. Elected FRS in 1774, he was a good friend of Joseph Priestley and carried on a scientific correspondence with William Bewley. SEB reports another visit of Magellan to the Burneys the previous July. See *DSB*; *DNB*; *GM* lx¹ (1790), 184; *ED* ii. 241–2; William Bewley to CB, [Nov.] 1778 (Osborn); Magellan to CB, 28 Dec. 1778 (Berg).

[58] Ozias Humphry (1742–1810), portrait painter in oils and crayons, but best known for his miniatures; ARA (1779), RA (1791). Humphry painted a miniature of CB, which was engraved by Walker for the *European Magazine* vii (1785), 165. It was misplaced at the time CB wrote his will; he bequeathed it to FBA, 'if it can be found' (Scholes ii. 271). Its present whereabouts is not known. See also D. Foskett, *Collecting Miniatures* (1979), pp. 390–400; B. S. Long, *British Miniaturists* (1966), pp. 229–31.

[59] Apparently a quotation, but not found; not in *Evelina*.

[60] Humphry's staring may have been due in part to his suffering from poor eyesight, which had been aggravated by a fall a number of years earlier. Also, he may have been studying FB's features from a professional point of view. FB is so defensive about being stared at that she seems not to have considered this possibility.

grave, & important. He seated himself;—my mother asked if he had any message for my Father? '—no, none.' Then he regarded *me* with a certain dry kind of attention for some Time,—after which, turning suddenly to my mother, he demanded 'Pray, Ma'am, is this your Daughter?'

'Yes, Sir.' 'O!—This is *Evelina*, is it?—'

'"Lord" no, Sir!' cried I, staring at him, & glad none of you were in the way to say *yes*.

'No? repeated he, incredulous,—is not your Name Evelina, Ma'am?—'

'Dear, no, Sir!' again quoth I, staring harder.

'Ma'am, cried he, dryly, I beg your pardon! I had understood your name was Evelina.'

And, soon after, he went away.

And, when he put down his Card,—who should it prove but Dr. Franklin![61] Was it not queer?—

This morning, while we were at Breakfast,—Mr. *Poore*[62] called. & a *poor* Creature he is, to *look at*! but he behaved *very pretty*, & niether *asked*, nor *stared* Questions.

Mr. Seward is just returned from Bath, he has |

[*rest of letter missing*]

[*The following ALS from SC, inserted in the Journal for 1778, is 2 single sheets 4to, 4 pp., dated 8 Dec. 1778, and paginated 811–14.*]

Chesington, Decr 8. 1778.

My dear Fannikin

Exclusive of the High entertainment Your Susannitical letter[63] afforded me, I was much delighted with it on

---

61 Thomas Francklin (1721–84), classical scholar and miscellaneous writer; DD, 1770 (Cantab.); Regius Professor of Greek, Cambridge, 1750–9; King's Chaplain, 1767. A close friend of Sir Joshua Reynolds, Dr Francklin succeeded Goldsmith as Honorary Professor of Ancient History to the Royal Academy in 1774. Though he was a popular preacher, Charlotte Burney, who attended a service given by him, was not impressed: 'I was not delighted with him. He has a hectoring manner—wants some new teeth, and has a bad voice' (*ED* ii. 296; see also *LCB* i. 299 and n. 3). See below, p. 195, for an explanation of his odd behaviour during this visit.

62 Edward Poore (*c*.1743–95), barrister, son of Edward Poore (d. 1780), MP. He was a not very popular member of the Burney circle. Charlotte Burney wrote about him in her journal, stressing his lack of affability. See *ED* ii. 296–7, 300, 305; Namier.

63 FB's journal to SEB of her 2nd extended visit to Streatham, 12–*c*.26 Sept.

another account and that a Solid & substantial One: I mean, because, it informed me of those numerous & powerful Friends, your own Genius & intrinsic Merit have raised you up—the prospect is now fair before You— it cannot but be bright when shone upon by such first rate Luminaries of Wit & Learning. Keep it in your Eye; & if you pursue your Path with resolution, not suffering yourself to be check'd by Indolence or diffidence, & an overstrain'd Modesty, I dare say, it will lead You on to the Temple of Fame, & perhaps to that of Fortune.

'Tis true; I have more than once, Fanny, whisper'd in Your Ear, a gentle Caution—that You have much to lose— Why is that?—because much you have gain'd—Now You have gone so far, & so rapidly, You will not be allowed to Slacken your pace—this is so far from being meant as a discouragement, that it is intended to animate you.—But it will explain what was in my head, when I threw out those (perhaps *useless*, perhaps *too officious*) hints—I plainly foresaw (what has since happen'd) that, as your next step, You would be Urg'd, strongly Urg'd, by your many Friends & Admirers, to undertake a Comedy.—I think You Capable, highly Capable of it; but in the Attempt there are great difficulties in the way; some more particularly, & individually in the way of a Fanny than of most people—I will instantly name these, lest You should Misapprehend. I need not Observe to *You*, that in most of Our successful comedies, there are frequent lively Freedoms (& waggeries that cannot be called licentious, neither) that give a strange animation, & Vig[our] to the same, & of which, if it were to be depriv'd, it would lose wonderfully of its Salt, & Spirit—I mean *such* Freedoms as Ladies of the strictest Character would make no scruple, openly, to laugh at, but at the same time, especially if they were Prudes, (And You know You are one) perhaps would *Shy* at being *known* to be the Authors of—Some Comic Characters would be deficient without strokes of this kind in Scenes, where Gay Men of the ᴵ World are got together, they are natural & expected, ʳ& I suppose perfect Characters are out of the Question in a Comedy, [xxxxx 2½ *lines*]ⁿ the business would be mighty apt to grow *fade* without them [xxxxx *2 lines*]

Of late Years (I can't tell why, unless from the great Purity of the Age) some very fine-Spun, all-delicate, Sentimental Comedies have been brought forth, on the English, & more particularly on the French Stage which, (in my Coarse way of thinking, at least,) are such sick things so Void Of blood & Spirits! that they may well be call'd *Comedies Larmoyantes!*—and I don't find that they have been greatly relished by the public in general, any more than by *my* vulgar Soul—moral, sublime to a degree!

We cannot blame, indeed,—but we may Sleep![64]

They put me in mind of a poor Girl, a Miss Peachy[65] (a real, & in the end, a melancholy Story)—she was a fine young Woman; but thinking herself too ruddy & blowsy,[66] it was her Custom to bleed herself (an Art she had learn'd on purpose) 3 or 4 times against the Rugby Races in order to appear more dainty & Lady-like at the balls, &c—poor thing!—She lost her Aim!—for when she came, She *appear'd like* a Ghost, & at last became one!—her Arm bled in the night, & in the morning She was past recovery!—I am afraid these fine performances are not pictures of real life & manners—I remember I sat next to a Frenchman at the play at Milan,[67] who preferr'd the French Theatre to the whole World, & as much dislik'd the English—when I ask'd his reason, he cried,

Ma foi, il faut pousser des beaux Sentiments![68]

---

[64] Pope, *Essay on Criticism*, l. 242.

[65] Not further identified.

[66] *OED* cites this sentence as containing the earliest instance of *blowsy* in the sense of 'having a bloated face; red and coarse-complexioned'.

[67] SC had resided in Italy from 1738 to 1740, and was at Milan in Dec. 1738 (A. Macnaghten, 'The Recluse of Chessington Hall', *Country Life* cxli (9 Mar. 1967), 534; SC to Mrs Sheppard, 8 Jan. 1739 NS, BL Add. MS. 47458, f. 74).

[68] A cliché traceable back to Corneille. SC's Frenchman may have been echoing Molière, *Les Précieuses ridicules*, sc. iv: 'Il faut qu'un amant, pour estre agreable, sçache debiter les beaux sentimens; pousser le doux, le tendre, & le passionné ... ' (ed. M. Cuénin (Geneva, 1973), p. 17). There was even a play, by Georges de Scudéry (1601–67), entitled *Le Pousseur de beaux sentiments* (ibid., n. 32).

Excuse these digressions—the sum total amounts to this—it appears to me extremely difficult, throughout a whole spirited Comedy to steer clear of those agreeable, frolicksome *jeux d'Esprit*, on the one hand; and languor & heaviness on the other—pray Observe, I only say *difficult* not *impracticable*—at least to your dexterity, & to that I leave it. |

I find myself forestall'd by the intelligent Mrs Montagu in another Observation I was going to make, & which she very justly & judiciously enforces by the instance she gives of Fielding, who tho' so eminent in Characters & descriptions, did by no means succeed in Comedy.[69]

'Tis certain, different Talents are requisite for the two species of Writing, tho' they are by no means incompatible;—I fear, however, the labouring oar lies on the Comic Author.

In these little entertaining, elegant Histories, the writer has his full Scope; as large a Range as he pleases to hunt in—to pick, cull, select, whatever he likes:—he takes his own time; he may be as minute as he pleases, & the more minute the better; provided, that Taste, a deep & penetrating knowledge of human Nature, & the World, accompany that minuteness.—When this is the Case, the very Soul, & all it's most secret recesses & workings, are develop'd, & laid as open to the View, as the blood Globules circulating in a frog's foot, when seen thro' a Microscope.—The exquisite touches such a Work is capable of (of which, Evelina is, without flattery, a glaring[70] instance) are truly charming.—But of these great advantages, these resources, YOU are strangely curtailed, the Moment You begin a Comedy: *There* every thing passes in Dialogue, all goes on rapidly;—Narration, & description, if not extremely Short, become intolerable.— The detail, which, in Fielding, Marivaux, Crebillon,[71] is so delightful, on the *Stage* would bear down all patience,— *There* all must be compress'd into Quintessence—The Moment the Scene ceases to move on briskly, & business

---

[69] See above, p. 162.

[70] The adjective here is, of course, without its modern pejorative connotation.

[71] Claude-Prosper Jolyot de Crébillon (1707–77), novelist.

seems to hang, Sighs & Groans are the Consequence!—
Oh dreadful Sound!—in a Word, if the plot, the Story of
the Comedy, does not open & unfold itself in the easy,
natural unconstrain'd flow of the Dialogue; if that Dialogue does not go on with Spirit, Wit, Variety, Fun,
Humour, Repartee &—& all in short into the Bargain—
Serviteur!—Good bye—t'ye!—

O⟨nc⟩e more, now, Fanny, don't imagine that I am
discouraging You from the Attempt; or that I am
retracting, or shirking back from what I have said above—
i.e. that I think You highly capable of it:—on the Contrary,
I *re*affirm it—I affirm that in common Conversation I
observe in You a ready Choice of words, with a quickness
& Conciseness that have often ǀ surpriz'd me: this is a
lucky Gift for a Comic writer, & not a very common one;
so that if You have not the united Talents I demand, I
don't know who has;—for if You have your *Familiar*, your
Sprite, for ever thus at your Elbow, without calling for,
surely it will not desert you, when in deep Conjuration
raising Your Genius in your Closet—

Crisp. 'Most likely, Fanny, this tedious Homily must
have tir'd You.'

Fanny. 'If You think so, why did You write it?'

Crisp. 'I don't know; it came into my head; & I told
You once before on a former Occasion, I have
no Notion of reserve among Friends.'

Fanny. 'You think, then, I have need of all this tutoring,
& that I can't see my way without *Your* old
Spectacles?'

Crisp. 'No, No, Fanny, I think no such thing.—
besides; You have other Sorts of Spectacles, at
Streatham to put on if You should want them.
But You know, Old Men, are much given to
Garrulity, & old Daddys particularly; that have
been long us'd to prate don't know how to give
over in time.

Fanny. 'Well, Well, prythee have done, now.'
[xxxxx *3–4 words*]

Crisp. 'ALLOWD! AGREED!—God bless You, Adieu'
Your loving Daddy S.C.

[St Martin's Street,
pmk 8 December 1778]
To Susanna Elizabeth Burney

AL fragment (Barrett), Dec. 1778
Single sheet folio, 1 p. *pmks* 8 DE FREE red wax seal
Addressed: To | Miss S. Burney | at Lady Hales's | Howlets | Canterbury
Annotated (*by FBA*): ✠
The address is written and the letter franked by 'Ant. Chamier',
i.e., Anthony Chamier (see below).

[*Mr. Seward.*][72] called here twice to Day,—&, as usual,
was very lively & agreeable. He has lent me Collins's
Poems[73] to read,—do you know them? I shall try to make
him find out something of Lusignano[74]—he is the most
likely person I know to get intelligence of it.

Mr. Chamier[75] has been here, but—which I much
regret, I missed seeing him by nursing a vile Cold. He
has sent me a most delectable Message,—viz,—that he
insists upon my sending to him for Franks whenever I
want them,—at all Times, & in all quantities, & not wait
for my Father's calling, &c—but send to him from myself.

Is not this charming? Just at our separation?—

Mrs. Lewis[76] called yesterday,—luckily I was at Hetty's,[77]
she was full of the Book,—asked a million of questions

---

[72] Supplied by FBA, presumably from a preceding leaf, which is missing.

[73] The 3rd edn. of *The Poetical Works* of William Collins (1721–59), first
published in 1765, had appeared in 1776.

[74] See above, p. 182.

[75] Anthony Chamier (1725–80) (see *EJL* ii. 173 n. 59). Chamier had been
returned MP for Tamworth in June 1778, which gave him the franking privilege
(see Namier).

[76] Charlotte, née Cotterell (d. 1796), of Richmond, Surrey, and Carmarthen-
shire, younger daughter of Admiral Charles Cotterell (d. 1754); m. Revd John
Lewis (*c.*1717–83), MA (Oxon.), 1741, Dean of Ossory, 1755; a friend of SJ
(*Piozzi Letters* i. 121 n. 11; *GM* xxiv (1754), 435).

[77] A 'Haryart [Harriet] Burney', probably an otherwise unrecorded infant
daughter of EBB and Charles Rousseau Burney, was buried at Chessington on
25 Dec. (Chessington burial registers, copy in Society of Genealogists, London).
Cf. *EJL* i. 192–3.

about it's writer, & seemed well informed of most of the particulars, & *monstrously* eager to hear others. I could have Capered for Joy that I was out.—Sweet Mrs. Thrale has sent me another invite[78]—but I cannot go till after Christmas.—My Father has been attacked about Evelina by Sir William Chambers,[79] & Mr. Franks,[80]—whom he met at the Academy of Painting. & Mr. Penneck[81] is *breaking his Heart* that the Author did not make her fortune by it!—Very generous the folks are!

Writ[e] [*rest of line and bottom of page cut away*]

69   [St Martin's Street,
                                post 10 December 1778]
To Susanna Elizabeth Burney

ALS (Diary MSS II, Berg), Dec. 1778
Single sheet 4to, 2 pp.
Annotated (by FBA): ✳· *Huddisford's Warley.*

My dearest Susy,

I have now an *opportunity* to Write a Folio to you,—but you would have little reason to thank me, were I to make use of it, since it would be sad *mawkish* stuff;—for I have such [a] fixed depression upon my spirits, that [I] cannot raise them to any decent [d]egree of Chearfulness,—when I have told [y]ou the Cause, I think *you*, at least, will [not] wonder at the Effect.

Last Thursday morning [10 Dec.], my mother, [af]ter having been out some Time, returned [wi]th a pamphlet in her Hand—'So ho! [Fa]nny!' she cried, ⌐with a loud & violent⌐ [laugh,] '*I* have a *rod* for you,—& a *Nosegay*

[78] Missing.

[79] Sir William Chambers (1726–96), architect. He had been the Burneys' neighbour in Poland St. and was appointed 1st treasurer of the Royal Academy upon its establishment in 1768.

[80] Naphtali Franks (1715–96), of Mortlake, Surrey; FRS (1764). A passionate amateur musician, he had befriended CB in 1747. CB heard the 8-year-old Mozart at a private concert in Franks' house in 1764 (*LCB* i. 91 n. 15).

[81] The Revd Richard Penneck. See *EJL* ii. 75.

[too]!—' Good God! my Heart sunk [with]in me,—I was *sure* of what was [the th]ing, & I turned so sick that I [could] hardly speak:— |

You well know how much & how fearfully I have dreaded the Publication of my Name,—& *now*—to have it lugged into a Pamphlet!—I can never express how extremely I was shocked—I was obliged to run away—& I had not patience to read the Line—& I have not, since, to ask for it.—indeed it has quite knocked me up, for I have been in a state of utter lowness [& vex]ation ever since.

This vile Poem is called Warley,⁸²—perha[ps] it may already have spread to Howlet[ts;] if it is, do pray *entreat* Lady Hales & Miss [C.] that it may not be *further* spread by their means,—that is, that they will neve[r] mention it.—

Adieu, my dearest Love,—I hope to send y[ou a] better Letter next Time: I have just heard [from] Aberdeen,⁸³ where all is well. Write as long Let[ters] as you can, & believe me most truly yours F.[B.]

70   [St Martin's Street,
                        ?20 December 1778]
To Susanna Elizabeth Burney

AJL (Diary MSS I, Berg, paginated 833–48, foliated 7–10), Dec. 1778
8 single sheets 4to, 16 pp.

⁸² *Warley: A Satire. Addressed to the First Artist in Europe* (Sir Joshua Reynolds), by George Huddesford (1749–1809). The poem appeared anonymously in 2 parts, published on 28 Oct. and 7 Dec. Part 2, entitled *The Second Part of Warley: A Satire*, contains (p. 28) the line referring to FB: 'Will your metre a Council engage or Attorney, / Or gain approbation from dear little Burney?' In this part of the satire Huddesford has *Reynolds* speak, condemning the doggerel verse thus addressed to him. By means of an asterisk FB is identified at the page's foot as 'The Authoress of Evelina.' See *The Poems of John Bampfylde*, ed. R. Lonsdale (Oxford, 1988), pp. 21–3.
⁸³ Presumably from CB Jr., who had gone there to enroll in King's College, Old Aberdeen, where he would take his MA degree in 1781. The letter is missing.

Annotated (by FBA): Warley. Mason. Humphreys. Mrs. Reynolds. Dr. Johnson. Mrs Thrale. Sir Joshua Reynolds

To be sure, I have been most plentifully Lectured of late!—&, to be sure, I have been most plentifully chagrined!—but there is but *one* Voice, & *that* goes against me! I must, therefore, give up the subject, & endeavour to forget the ideas it raised in me.

I *will* try, my dear Susy, to become somewhat more like *other folks*, if, as seems by their reasoning, I am now so different to them. All I can say for myself is,—that I have *always* feared discovery, *always* sought concealment, & *always* known that no success could counter-ballance the publishing my Name. However, what is inevitable *ought* not to torment long,—& after *such* counsel as I have received, from almost all my best friends, it becomes my *duty* to struggle against my refractory feelings.

And now, my love, let me thank you for your Letter;[84]— & let me try to send you one that may make some amends for my last.

I will recollect the most particular circumstances that have happened *Journal fashion*, according to the old plan.

This same pamphlet that has so much grieved me was brought Home, by my mother, on Thursday [10 Dec.].— But who says my Name is not ¹ at full length?—I wish to Heaven it were *not*!

At Night, my Father went to the Royal Academy, to hear Sir Joshua Reynolds' Discourse:[85]—& now for a *Bouquet* of uncommon fragrance,—Mr. Mason[86] came up to my Father, & wished him *joy*,—& said the finest things imaginable of the Book, & extolled the *Characters*, & talked it all over. You, who respect & admire Mr. Mason as much as I do, will be sure such praise was some Cordial to me. Mr. Humphreys, too, joined his Vote. My Father

---

[84] Missing.

[85] Reynolds' 8th discourse, 10 Dec. 1778, published as *A Discourse, Delivered to the Students of the Royal Academy, on the Distribution of the Prizes, December 10, 1778* (1779); for a modern edition collating the 1778 text, see Joshua Reynolds, *Discourses on Art*, ed. R. R. Wark (San Marino, 1959), pp. 143–65.

[86] William Mason (1724–97), poet. See *EJL* i. 147 n. 10.

himself has seemed more pleased with Mr. Mason's approbation, than with any body's since the Streathamites.

On Sunday [13 Dec.], Mr. Seward called, in his way to Mr. Thrale's,—but I was, yet, so terribly dispirited, that I could not speak a Word to him.

On Monday [14 Dec.],—to my great dissatisfaction,—Mrs. Reynolds came. I was somewhat better with her, but wofully *dumpish*. 'Pray, said she, after some Time, how does Miss Fanny do?—O no! not Miss Fanny,—Miss Sukey I mean!—*this*, I think, is Miss Fanny?—though *your* name, Ma'am, is swallowed up in another,—that of—of—of *Miss Burney*,—if not of—of—of—Lord! how odd in Dr. Franklin to ask if *that* was not your Name!'

To be sure I stared, & asked where she had her intelligence? I found from my Father himself.

'Well, continued she, what would not Mrs. Horneck & Mrs. Bunbury[87] give to see the Writer of—*that* Book! Lord! they say they would walk 100 & 60 miles only to *see* her, if that would do!'

'Why then, quoth I,—I would walk just as far to *avoid* them!'

'O no! don't say that! I *hope* you will have the goodness to consent to meet them!—But I think I have made out how Dr. Franklin came to say that odd thing; Lord, thought he, am I now in Company with the Writer of that celebrated Book?—Well, I *must* say some thing;—so then he became so embarrassed, that, in his confusion, he made the blunder.'

Now I think the only question is which was most infinitely absurd, the *Question*, or the *Comment*?

The next morning [15 Dec.], the Miss Palmer's called. They were cold & formal, & full of reproaches that I had been so unsociable; however, by degrees, their reserve wore off. They invited us very pressingly for Saturday Evening; I would fain have been excused, for I more than ever wished to shirk seeing Sir Joshua Reynolds, as I

[87] Hannah, née Triggs (*c*.1726–1803), daughter of Robert Triggs, mayor of Plymouth (1751–2), and widow of Kane William Horneck (*c*.1726–52); and her 2nd daughter Catherine (*c*.1753–98), who m. (1771) Henry William Bunbury (1750–1811), the caricaturist. See *JL* x. 511 n. 25.

could not but suppose *he* as well as myself must think of this vile Pamphlet upon our meeting: & as I must owe to his extreme ⎮ partiality to the Book, & talk of the Writer, the Line that mentions me: however, they obviated all possible objections,—& disregarded all offered excuses,— my Father was to be at the *opera*,—still *I* must come,—my mother engaged by expecting Miss Young,[88]—still *I* was not to be let off,—if I was *ill*, they vowed they would send a *Physician*,—&, in short, I was obliged to promise to wait on them,—though I said I must hope, at least, to find them *alone*.

On Thursday [17 Dec.], my dear Father *talked me over* quite seriously about my vexation,—&, to be brief, made me promise to *think no more of it*,—which, though I could not literally perform, I have done all that *in me lay*. On Friday [18 Dec.], *I* had a visit from Dr. Johnson! he came on *purpose* to reason with me about this pamphlet, which he had heard from my *Father* had so greatly disturbed me. Shall I not love him more than ever?—however, Miss Young was just arrived, & Mr. Bremner[89] spent the Evening here, & therefore he had the delicacy & goodness to forbear coming to the point. Yet he said several things that *I* understood, though they were unintelligible to all others.—& he was more kind, more good humoured, more flattering to me than ever. Indeed, my uneasiness upon this subject has met with more indulgence from *him* than from *any* body! ⎮ He repeatedly charged me not to *fret*; & bid me not repine at my ⌐story⌐, but think of Floretta, *in the Fairy Tale*,[90] who found sweetness & con- solation in hers sufficient to counter-ballance her scoffers & Libellers!! Indeed he was all good humour & kindness, & seemed quite bent upon giving me comfort.[91]

---

88 Dorothy ('Dolly') Young (*c*.1721–1805). See *EJL* i. 20 n. 54.

89 Robert Bremner (*c*.1713–89), music publisher. See *EJL* i. 181.

90 SJ's 'The Fountains: A Fairy Tale', included in Anna Williams' *Miscellanies in Prose and Verse* (1766), pp. 111–41. A copy in HLT's hand is in the John Rylands University Library, Manchester. Reprinted in *Rasselas and Other Tales*, ed. G. J. Kolb (New Haven, 1990), pp. 231–49 (*Yale Edition of the Works of Samuel Johnson*, vol. xvi).

91 SJ's behaviour shows his typically great solicitude for mental distress.

The Next Evening [19 Dec.], just as I was Dressed for my formidable visit at Sir Joshua's, I received a Letter from Mrs. Thrale:[92] the longest & most delightful she has ever written me; it contains, indeed, warm expostulations upon my uneasiness, & earnest remonstrances that I would overcome it; but that she should think me worth the trouble of reproof, & the *danger* of sincerity, flattered, soothed & cheared me inexpressibly: & she speaks so affectionately of her regard for me, that I feel more convinced of it than ever.

By the way, it is settled that I am not to make my visit to Streatham till your return to Town; our dear Father not chusing to have us both absent at once.[93] Never theless, Mrs. Thrale, whose invitations, upon that plea, are, with her usual good sense & propriety, dropt ¦ or, rather, deferred any further pressing till your return, said, in her charming Letter, that she *must* see me, if only for an Hour, & insisted that I should accompany my Father on his next *Lesson Day*. I could not persuade myself to go out, till I wrote an answer,[94] which I did in the fullness of my Heart, & without form, ceremony or study of any kind.

Now to this grand visit: which was become more tremendous than ever, from the Pamphlet Business, as I felt almost ashamed to see Sir Joshua, & could not but conclude *he* would think of it too.

My mother, who changed her mind, went also. My Father promised to come before the Opera was half over.[95]

We found the Miss Palmers alone. Sir Joshua Dined at Mr. Beauclerk's.[96] We were, for near an Hour, quite easy, chatty & comfortable, no pointed speech was made, & no *starer* entered. But, when I asked the Eldest Miss Palmer

---

[92] See below, p. 205.
[93] Presumably so that SEB could replace FB as CB's amanuensis.
[94] Missing.
[95] CB had already seen the piece, *Demofoonte*, on 28 Nov. (see *LS* 5 i. 222).
[96] Topham Beauclerk (1739–80), son of Ld. Sydney Beauclerk (1703–44) and grandson of Charles Beauclerk (1670–1726), 1st D. of St Alban's, son of Charles II by Nell Gwynn. Topham Beauclerk was an original member of the Club and is chiefly remembered today because of his friendship with SJ.

if she would allow me to look at some of her Drawings, she said 'Not unless You will let me see something of *yours.*' 'Of mine? quoth I, O, I have Nothing ‖ to shew.' 'O fie! I am sure you have; you *must* have.' 'No, indeed; I don't Draw at all.' 'Draw? no, but I mean some of your *Writing.*' 'O, I never write,—except Letters.' 'Letters? those are the very things I want to see.' 'O, not such as *you* mean!'—'Lord, now, don't say so; I am *sure* you are about something,—& if you would but shew me—' 'No, no, I am about nothing,—I am quite out of conceit with writing.'

I had my thoughts full of the vile Warley.

'*You* out of Conceit? exclaimed she,—nay, then, if *you* are, *who* should be otherwise!'

Just then, Mrs. & Miss *Horneck*[97] were announced. You may suppose I thought directly of the 160 miles! & may take it for granted I looked them very boldly in the Face. Mrs. Horneck seated herself by my mother,—Miss Palmer introduced me to her & her Daughter, who seated herself next me.—but not one Word past between us!

Mrs. Horneck, as I found in the course of the Evening, is an exceeding sensible, well bred Woman. Her Daughter is very beautiful, but was low spirited & silent the whole visit. She was, indeed, very unhappy, as Miss Palmer informed me, upon account of some ill news she had ‖ lately heard of the affairs of A Gentleman to whom she is shortly to be married.[98]

I have not a *great* many Bon Mots of my own to record, as, I think, I seldom opened my mouth above once in a quarter of an Hour.

---

[97] Mary Horneck (*c.*1749–1840), who m. (1779) Francis Edward Gwynn (d. 1821), army officer, later Equerry to George III. See *JL* x. 511 n. 25.

[98] Since 1775 Francis Gwynn had been major in the 16th regiment of light dragoons, commanded by Gen. John Burgoyne. Burgoyne, attacked by the government because of the defeat of his forces by the Americans at the Battle of Saratoga in Oct. 1777, had gone over to the Opposition and openly declared his support of American independence. Gwynn may have been in some way tarnished himself by Burgoyne's disgrace, or he may have felt himself unable to continue to serve under such a 'disloyal' commander (who in fact later resigned his regiment). If indeed Gwynn's difficulties were military or political, he soon resolved them, becoming Lt-Col. of the 20th light dragoons in May 1779. See *AL*, 1778, p. 44; 1781, p. 56; Namier.

Next came a Mr. Guatkin[99] of whom I have nothing to say, but that he was very talkative with Miss Offy Palmer, & very silent with every body else; & that, in their talk, which on his part was all in a low voice, I more than once heard my own Name, pronounced in a *questioning* voice. For this I thanked him not.

Not long after came a whole Troup,—consisting of Mr. Cholmondeley![1]—O perilous Name!—Miss Cholmondeley, & Miss Fanny Cholmondeley, his Daughters,[2] & Miss Forrest.[3] Mrs. Cholmondeley, I found, was engaged elsewhere, but soon expected.

Now here was a trick of Sir Joshua! to make me meet all these people!

Mr. Cholmondeley is a Clergyman.[4] Nothing shining either in Person or manners, but, rather, some what *grim* in the first, & *glum* in the last. Yet he appears to have humour himself, & to enjoy it much in others.

Miss Cholmondeley I saw too little of to mention.

Miss Fanny Cholmondeley is a rather pretty, I pale Girl, very young & inartificial &, though Tall & grown up, treated by her family as a Child, & seemingly well content to really think herself such. She followed me which ever

---

[99] Robert Lovell Gwatkin, who m. (1781) Theophila ('Offy') Palmer (see above, p. 138 n. 62).

[1] The Hon. Robert Cholmondeley (above, p. 35 n. 10).

[2] Henrietta Maria Cholmondeley (1754–1806) and Hester Frances Cholmondeley (1763–1844), who m. (1783) William Bellingham (*c*.1756–1826), cr. (1796) Bt.

[3] Probably Cecilia ('Cecy') Frederica Marina Forrest (1750–1824), 3rd daughter of Commodore Arthur Forrest (1702–70) and his wife (m. 1747) Juliana, née Lynch (d. 1802). In 1785 the statesman William Windham (1750–1810) wrote to his friend, the Cholmondeleys' son, George James Cholmondeley (1752–1830), reproaching him for his 'Conduct to *Cecy*', 'whose only weakness has been too fond an attachment to you ... . That you should prefer a life of vanity and voluptuousness to a connection with such a woman as Miss Forrest, is no very honourable mark of your choice of happiness ... ' Windham married her himself in 1798 (*Memoirs of William Hickey (1749–1775)*, ed. A. Spencer (3rd edn., 1919), p. 262; *The Windham Papers*, ed. E. of Rosebery (1913), i. 77–78, ii. 77 n. 2; A. R. Forrest, *The Pedigree of the Forrest, Lowther, and Monk Families* (Derby, 1864), pp. 3–5; *GM* lxxii[2] (1802), 787).

[4] Originally an army officer, Cholmondeley had been dismissed from the service for cowardice in 1747. Entering holy orders, he became rector of St Andrew's, Hertford (*YW* xxxvii. 277; xliii. 113).

way I turned, & though she was too modest to *stare*, never ceased watching me the whole Evening.

Miss Forrest is an *immensly* [*sic*] Tall & not handsome Young Woman. Further I know not.

But they all shewed pretty evidently they knew who they should meet, & were determined, also, to know me should we meet again, for most plentifully, indeed, had I my share of Eye play.

A Table was now formed for Loo, at which most of the Company assembled, either to play, or to look on. And then I paraded round the room to have a good view of the Pictures with which it is ornamented. They are very fine ones, but you have seen them, & therefore I shall not turn descriptive in the *virtuose* style.[5]

Next came my Father, all gaity & spirits.

Then, Mr. William Burke.[6]—!—He whose warm Commendations of Evelina I have repeatedly heard of from Dr. Johnson.

Soon after, Sir Joshua returned home. He paid his Compliments to every body & then brought a chair next mine,—& said 'So you were afraid ⌐ to come among us?—' I don't know if I wrote to you a speech to that purpose which I made to the Miss Palmers?—& which, I suppose, they had repeated to him. He went on, saying I might as well fear *Hob goblins*,—& that I had only to hold up my Head, to be above them all!—

After this address, his behaviour was exactly what I should myself have *dictated* to him, for my own ease & quietness; for he never once even alluded to my Book, ⌐nor paid any sort of compliments to me—nor treated me with any sort of particularity,⌐ but conversed rationally,

---

[5] I.e., in the manner of an art connoisseur. This passage is previously unpublished, and *virtuose* as an attributive in this sense is not in *OED*.

[6] William Burke (*c*.1729–98), of Beaconsfield, Bucks, sometime MP, close friend and possibly distant cousin of Edmund Burke. He and Edmund Burke were both old friends of Kane Horneck, who named them trustees of his daughter Catherine, later Mrs Bunbury (above), in his will. William was also a long-time crony of Reynolds, with whom he had visited Paris for 6 weeks in 1768 (Namier; *Correspondence of Edmund Burke*, gen. ed. T. W. Copeland (Cambridge, 1958–78), ii. 16, vii. 64 n. 3, and *passim*).

gayly, & *serenely*: & so I became more comfortable than I had been ever since the first entrance of Company.

Our subject was chiefly Dr. Johnson's Lives of the Poets;—we had both Read the same, & therefore could discuss them with equal pleasure,—& we both were charmed with them, & therefore could praise them with equal warmth,—& we both love & reverence the Writer, & therefore could mix observations on the *Book* with the *Author* with equal readiness.

By the way, I believe I did not mention that Miss Palmer told me all the World gave me to Dr. Johnson!—for that he spoke of *me* | as he spoke of hardly any body!—

Our confab was interrupted by the Entrance of Mr. King:[7] a Gentleman who is, it seems, for ever with the Burkes. And presently Lord Palmerston[8] was announced.

By a change of seats, I was now next to Mrs. Horneck; who, after some general conversation with me, said, in a low voice, 'I suppose, Miss Burney, I must not speak of Evelina to you?'

'Why, indeed, Ma'am, said I, I would rather you should speak of any thing else.'

'Well,—I must only beg leave to say *one* thing, which is, that *my* Daughters had the credit of the first introducing it into this set. Mrs. Bunbury was the very first among us who read it; she met it, accidentally, at a Booksellers,—& she could not leave it behind her; & when she had read it, she sent it to me, & wrote me Word she was *sure* I should read it, & read it *through*, though it was a *Novel*: for she knew Novels were not favourites with me; &, indeed, they are, generally, so bad, that they are not to be read. But I have seen nothing like this since Fielding. But *where*, | Miss Burney, *where* can, or could You pick up such Characters?—*where* find such variety of incidents, yet all so natural?'

[7] Presumably Walker King (1751–1827), protegé and disciple of Edmund Burke; he later entered holy orders and became Bishop of Rochester (1809) (Copeland, x. 367–8 and *passim*; IGI).

[8] Henry Temple (1739–1802), 2nd Visc. Palmerston (Ire.). Though he was an MP and currently a lord of the Treasury, his interests were much rather literary and artistic, as attested by his friendships with Reynolds and Garrick and by his membership later in SJ's Club (Namier).

'O, Ma'am! *any* body might *find*, who thought them worth *looking* for.'

'O no; experience shews the contrary. *I* then recommended it to Lady Carysfort,[9]—a *very* sensible Woman,—& she sat up the whole Night to read it. And then we prevailed with Sir Joshua to read it,—&, when he once began it,—he left it niether for sleep nor *food*, for, to own the truth, he took to it yet more passionately than all the rest of us!'

Many more fine things were added to these, but I have not more room for *this* batch.

After this, Miss Offy Palmer, Laughing, asked me if I was afraid of a monkey? 'No!' quoth I,—'Why then, said she, will you look at one?' Upon which, I followed her into the next Room, & Miss Forrest & Miss F. Cholmondeley went with us. The monkey, as he did not prove very diverting, I shall not enlarge upon; but I saw the Girls were all *dying* to utter some quotation, or make some merriment, on this subject: & Offy *did* say 'I suppose, Miss Burney, *your* monkey ⎮ was larger than this?'

'Mine?—O, I have none,' returned I; quite *innocently*, & proposed leaving the Gentleman to take his *natural rest*.

This was agreed to; &, just as we entered, Sir Joshua sent for a picture of Lord Harcourt,[10] which Lord Palmerston desired to see. We all got about it. Lord Palmerston, standing next me, asked if I thought it like? & other such sort of questions, ⌐&, in a manner⌐ so very civil & attentive, that I could not entertain a doubt but that he was of the *Evelina Committee*, for, otherwise, he would not have dreamt of ⌐taking so much, & a so *very* civil notice of me, as he did.⌐

---

[9] Probably the Dowager Lady Carysfort, Elizabeth, née Allen (1722–83), who m. (1750) John Proby (1720–72), cr. (1752) B. Carysfort (Ire.); possibly her daughter-in-law, the current Lady Carysfort, Elizabeth, née Osborne (d. 1783), who m. (1774) John Joshua Proby (1751–1828), 2nd B. Carysfort, cr. (1789) E. of Carysfort, (1801) B. Carysfort (UK).

[10] George Simon Harcourt (1736–1809), 2nd E. Harcourt (1777). Sir Joshua's ledgers list in Dec. 1777 a charge of 35 guineas for a portrait of Harcourt (M. Cormack, 'The Ledgers of Sir Joshua Reynolds', *Walpole Society* xlii (1970), 154).

Mr. King, too, spoke to me, by my name, as if we had been some time known to each other.

'Now tell me, said Sir Joshua, to me, *which* of these Pictures you prefer; & then I shall *judge of your morals*—that, (pointing to a Portrait of Rembrandt's) or this?'—pointing to his own of Lord Harcourt. Now was not this abominable? however, he Laughed as he spoke, as if certain I should not answer him; &, indeed, I told him I would sooner be questioned by him on *any* other topic. The Portrait by Rembrandt is a *darling* with him.[11]

Well, while this was going *forwards*, a violent rapping bespoke, I was *sure*, Mrs. Cholmondeley,—& I ran from the *standers*, &, turning my back against the Door, looked over Miss Palmer's Cards: for, you may well imagine, I was really in a *tremor* at a meeting [which][12] so long has been in agitation, & with the person who, of *all* Persons, has been *most* warm & enthusiastic for my Book.

She had not, however, been in the room *half* an instant, ere my Father came up to me, &, tapping me on the shoulder, said 'Fanny, here's a lady who wishes to speak to you.'

I courtsied, in silent *reverence*,—she, too, Courtsied, & fixed her Eyes full on my Face; & then, tapping me with her Fan, she cried 'Come, come, You must not look grave upon *me*!'

Upon this,—I *te-he'd*,—she now looked at me yet more earnestly,—&, after an odd silence, said, abruptly 'But is it *true*?'

'What—ma'am?'

'It can't be!—tell me, though, *is* it true?'

I could only *simper.*

'Why don't you tell me?—but it *can't* be,—I don't believe it!—no,—you are an *Impostor!*'

Sir Joshua & Lord Palmerston were both at her side; Oh how notably silly must I look! She again repeated her question of *is it true?*—& I again affected not to

---

[11] Reynolds owned a number of Rembrandt portraits, but he considered 'The Vision of Daniel' (which he also owned) to be the artist's finest work (Graves iv. 1631).

[12] Inserted by FBA.

understand her,—& then Sir Joshua, taking hold of her arm, attempted to pull her away saying 'Come, come, Mrs. Cholmondeley, I won't have her over-powered here!'

I love Sir Joshua much for this. But Mrs. Cholmondeley, turning to him, said with quickness & vehemence 'Why, Lord I a'n't going to *kill* her!—don't be afraid,—I sha'n't *compliment* her!—I *can't*, indeed!—' Then, taking my Hand, she led me through them all, to another part of the Room, where again, she examined my *Phiz*, & viewed & re-viewed my whole person!—'*Now*, said she, *do* tell me,—is it true?—'

'*What*, Ma'am?—I don't—I don't know *what*—'

'Lord *what*,—why you *know* what,—in short, *can* you read? & *can* you write?'

'N—o—ma'am!'

'I thought so! cried she; I have *suspected* it was a trick, some time,—& *now* I am sure of it! Lord, you are too young by half! it *can't* be!—'

I Laughed, & would have got away,—but she would not let me. 'No, cried she, one thing you must, at least, tell me;—are you very conceited?'

What a question! 'Come, answer me! continued she;—you won't?—Mrs. Burney,—Dr. Burney,—come here,—tell me if she is not *very* conceited? if she is not *Eat up* with conceit by this Time?'

They were both pleased to answer '*not half enough*'

'Well! exclaimed she, that is the most wonderful part of all! Why that is yet more extraordinary than writing the Book!'

I then got away from her, & again looked over Miss Palmer's Cards: but she was after me in a minute. 'Pray, Miss Burney, cried she, aloud, do You know any thing of this Game?'

'No, ma'am.' 'No? repeated she; *ma foi*, that's pity!' This raised *such* a Laugh![13] I was forced to move on,—yet every body seemed *afraid* to Laugh, too, & *studying* to be delicate, as if they had been *cautioned*: which, I have since found, was really the case, & by Sir Joshua himself.

---

[13] Because of the echo of Mme Duval.

Again, however, she was at my side. 'What Game *do* you like, Miss Burney?' cried she.

'I play at none, ma'am.'

'No?—*pardie,* I wonder at that!'

Did you ever know such a Toad? again I moved on, & got behind Mr. W. Burke, who, turning round to me, said 'This is not very politic in us, Miss Burney, to play at cards, & have *You* listen to our follies.'

There's for you! *I* am to pass for a censor*ess* now!

My Frank will hold no more,—adieu, my dearest Susan, make my respects to Lady Hales & Miss C. ⎸

[*Concluding the Journal for 1778 is the following ALS from HLT to FB (Berg), 2 single sheets 4to, 4 pp., which FBA has paginated 819– 22 with the annotation*: A spirited charming, & rational Remonstrance on the unavailing disturbance of F.B. at being proclaimed an *Author,* in a poetical Epistle of Mr. *Huddisford* to Sir Joshua Reynolds,—by the following line—speaking of what ought to be the aim of Sir Joshua—if he did so—or so "Will it gain approbation from *dear little Burney*" N.B. It was Dr. Johnson who first gave that *nomenclature* to F.B. at Streatham, to distinguish her from her Father, Dr. Burney. *FBA quotes the line incorrectly and also gets the context wrong (see above, p. 193, n. 82). HLT's letter was received the evening of 19 Dec. (above, p. 197).*]

Streatham

Instead of writing monitory Letters to Dick, I find I must now be a little serious with the great Evelina. Why will you, my lovely Friend, give Consequence to Trifles by thus putting your Peace in their Power? Is not the World full of severe Misfortunes, & real Calamities? & will you fret and look pale about such Nonsense as this? let me see you on Thursday next [24 Dec.] if but for an hour, and let me see you chearful I insist. Your looking dismal can only advertise the paltry Pamphlet[14] which I firmly believe no one out of your own Family has seen and which is now only lying like a dead Kitten on the ⎸ Surface of a dirty Horsepond—incapable of *scratching*

---

[14] i.e., *Warley.*

anyone who does not take pains to dirty their Fingers for it.—

But it has proclaimed you Authoress of Evelina! and is that an Injury? surely you are not yet to learn how highly that little sweet Book has been praised, admir'd, & esteem'd by People whose good Word should at least weigh with you against such a Wretch as I hear this is, who has mention'd your Name *irreverently*—for I do not perceive he has done anything else at last.

And So—as Mowbray the brutal says of Lovelace the gay—

'*We comforted and advised him.*'[15]

When will Miss Susan come home[16] that I may have you here to *brace your Fibres* and enable you to endure these direful Misfortunes?—but I see you saying—'Why this is Mrs *Selwyn* without her Wit;' | Very well Madam! dont you be *Lady Louisa* then—without her Quality.

Give my best Love and kindest Compliments to your amiable Household—You know if I love you, and may be sure I pity your Pain, but do not mean to soothe it. This World is a rough road, and those who mean to tread it many Years must not think of beginning their Journey in Buff Soles.

What hurts me most is lest you should like me the less for this Letter; yet I will be true to my own Sentiments & send it; you will think me coarse & indelicate:—I can't help it!—you are twenty Years old and I am past thirtysix[17] there's the true Difference. I have lost seven Children[18]

---

[15] 'And thus we comforted him, and advised him' (*Clarissa* (1747–1748), vol. vii, letter 62: Mowbray to John Belford). Earlier in the letter Mowbray says of Clarissa: 'I never heard of such a woman in my life. What great matters has she suffered, that grief should kill her thus?'

[16] From Howletts, Kent.

[17] FB was actually 26, and HLT would turn 38 in Jan.

[18] HLT had given birth to her 12th and, as it turned out, her last child (Henrietta Sophia), the previous June. Of these, 7 had already died, at ages ranging from 10 hours to 9 years. Henrietta would die in 1783, aged 4. Four of the Thrale children reached maturity: Hester Maria (Queeney) (1764–1857); Susanna Arabella (1770–1858); Sophia (1771–1824); and Cecilia Margaretta (1777–1857). See *TSP*, p. xii.

and been cheated out of two thousand a Year,[19] & I cannot, indeed I cannot, sigh & sorrow over Pamphlets & Paragraphs.—Did you never hear Johnson's Story of the man with his Paper and Packthread?[20]

Mr Pepys—my Master in Chancery as your Papa calls him[21]—says you should try at a Tragedy,—He is in Love with The Character of Maccartney; the Pistol Scene;[22] & the denouement with Sir John Belmont.[23]

Murphy is charmed with the Comic part, and thinks highly of the Writer: will these help to fill the Scale against our formidable Adversary—God knows who,—in the Garret?

Adieu till Thursday [24 Dec.] '*my own dear little Burney.*' and forgive the Sauciness of a truly Affectionate
and faithful Friend *Servant* &c.
H: L: Thrale.

I can't stay till Thursday to hear if you forgive me,—nor will Forgiveness do—You must not love me less for all this—it would vex *me* more than many a silly Couplet, which *you* mind more than your Friends. Once more Adieu!

---

[19] Upon the death of HLT's uncle Sir Thomas Salusbury (1708–73), his estate at Offley Place, Herts, passed into the hands of his widow, Sarah, née Burroughs, whom he had married as his second wife 10 years previously. Until her uncle's remarriage and a subsequent estrangement, Hester Salusbury (HLT) had been considered his heir. See *TSP*, pp. 6, 16; Clifford, pp. 53, 104, 106–8.

[20] This was a warehouse clerk who insisted on meeting with SJ to confess that he had been taking paper and packthread for his own use; his conscience continued to bother him even after his master told him to take as much as he pleased. HLT tells the story in her *Anecdotes of Johnson*, where she observes that 'Mr. Johnson had indeed a real abhorrence of a person that had ever before him treated a little thing like a great one: and he quoted this scrupulous gentleman with his packthread very often … ' (ed. A. Sherbo, (1974), pp. 135–6).

[21] To distinguish him playfully from her 'Master', Henry Thrale (her husband). See *EJL* ii. 202 n. 6.

[22] *Evelina*, vol. ii, letter 12.

[23] Vol. iii, letter 19. See above, p. 29 and n. 91.

71

[St Martin's Street,
late December 1778
or January 1779]

To Lady Hales

ALS, draft (Barrett), Dec. 1778—Jan. 1779
Single sheet 4to, 2 pp.
FB's draft is written on a detached address sheet of a letter 'To | Dr Burney | Queen Square | Ormond Street'. The original is missing. The text is that of her final version; her changes and deletions are indicated in the notes.

I am so much astonished, & so much confused, by the equally unexpected & undeserved mark of yr. Ladyship's goodness, which I have just received,[24] that I am wholly at a loss in what manner to express my sense of it. Indeed, if yr. Ladyship is so determined to overpower us with favours, We shall be lead [*sic*] on, like most[25] others who receive more kindnesses than they merit, to turn encroachers, & beg to have added to the rest of our obligations some Instructions how to acknowledge them as we ought. How to *feel* them, I have the vanity to think we shall not, even from yr. Ladyship, require any Lessons.

Will you, dear Madam, forgive me if I own myself yet more[26] grateful for the Letter you have done me the Honour to write,[27] as I am for the very elegant present[28] which it accompanied? Yet I am infinitely struck with the beauty, taste, Colours & Patern of the Chintz.[29]

24 Originally 'mark I have just received of yr. Ladyship's goodness'.
25 'unmeriting' deleted.
26 'yet more' substituted for 'quite as'.
27 Lady Hales to FB, 'Howletts Friday Evening.' (Barrett).
28 Originally just 'for the Chintz'.
29 Originally just 'beauty & taste of the Chintz'. Lady Hales, Miss Coussmaker and SEB had been 'to take a view of the Sea at Deal ... a sad Smuggling town', where they made 'some purchases in contraband goods', including the chintz sent to FB (Lady Hales to FB).

[30]I am extremely glad it was in my power to facilitate Susan's wishes in contributing my mite[31] towards lengthening her stay at Howlets;[32] I am sure she would be the most insensible of human Beings were she not to the highest degree grateful for the Honour of your Ladyship's solicitude [to] | make her happy.

I beg leave to present my best compliments to Miss Coussmaker, & to subscribe myself,

very respectfully, Dear Madam,

Your Ladyship's

most obed^t &

most obliged

h^{le} servant

F. B.

[30] Here FB originally began a new paragraph, 'I beg your Lad', stopped, deleted it, and continued with the following on a new line. Apparently she had begun her valediction (see next paragraph), and then thought to acknowledge Lady Hales' thanks (n. 32).

[31] 'my mite' inserted.

[32] Lady Hales wrote: 'I have entreated Miss Susan to make my comp^{ts} & thanks to you, for indulging me with the pleasure of her amusing company some time longer, at least contributing all in y^r power towards it!' FB obviously interceded with her father on SEB's behalf, though SEB's continued stay at Howletts meant the postponement of her own proposed long visit to Streatham.

72

[St Martin's Street,
*c.*7 January 1779]

To Samuel Crisp

AL incomplete (Diary MSS I, Berg, paginated 827–32, foliated 4–5), Jan. 1779
   3 single sheets 4to, 6 pp.
   Annotated (by FBA): ✱· ✕ Jany 1779 N° II upon the first knowledge of F.B. that her name had been discovered, & had been Printed, in *Warley,* In Mr. Huddisford's poetic epistle to Sir Joshua Reynolds
   The letter is dated by the reference to the Thrales' return to Streatham (below, p. 212).

Your patience, my dear Daddy, in being able to mention my Name without *invectives* as you have done in Your Letter to Hetty,[1] *forces* me to write, because it makes me eager to thank you for not having taken offence at me. Indeed your last most excellent Letter[2] ought to have had my acknowledgements long since; but the fact is,—I received it when I was most violently *out of sorts,* & really had not spirits to answer it. I *intended* to have kept from *You* the subject of my uneasiness, because I know you will only *scoff* it,—or, perhaps, think it should rather have *gratified,* than *dispirited* me;—&, in truth, I have been so plentifully Lectured already upon my Vexation, that I feel no *goust* for further lashing & slashing: & yet I *will* own to you the subject, because I had rather, of the two, you should think me a fool, than think I wanted gratitude

[1] SC to EBB, 24 Dec. 1778 (Barrett). The surviving MS is incomplete. On the remaining leaf SC has written: 'I have just read Evelina over again & if there is not more true Sterling genius in 3 pages of that book than in all Richarsons [*sic*] nineteen Volumes put together I do hereby in form acknowledge myself to be the most tasteless of Courteous or Uncourteous Readers' SC's letter is postmarked 25 Dec., the same day that 'Haryart Burney' was buried at Chessington (see above, p. 191 n. 77), and it is probable that SC wrote it mainly to inform EBB of the death of her infant daughter, who presumably had been sent to a wet nurse in Chessington. The beginning of the letter would have contained the bad news, the kind of news that FBA habitually destroyed.
[2] 8 Dec. 1778. See above, pp. 186–90.

sufficient to thank you for the many useful hints, the kind
& excellent advice you took the trouble to give me. In
short, not to spend my whole ⌐ Letter in enigmatical
preluding,—just as I received your Letter, I had had
information that my Name had got into print,—&, what
was yet worse, was printed in a new Pamphlet.

I cannot tell you, &, if I could, you would, perhaps, not
believe me, how greatly I was shocked, mortified, grieved
& confounded at this intelligence: I had always dreaded
as a real Evil my Name's getting into *Print*,—but to be
lug'd into a Pamphlet!—

I must, however, now I have gone so far, tell you how
it is, lest you should imagine matters worse. This vile
Pamphlet is called *Warley* a Satire: it is addressed to the
First artist in Europe,—who proves to be Sir Joshua
Reynolds. Probably it is to his unbounded partiality for
Evelina that I owe this most *disagreeable Compliment,*—for
he had been so eager to discover the Author, that, by
what I have had reason given me to conjecture,—I fancy
he has been not a little *Laughed at* since the discovery, for
divers *comique* sort of speeches which he had made ⌐before
me.⌐

So now the murder's out! but, dear Daddy, don't *bela-
bour* me for my weakness, though ⌐ I confess I was, for
more than a week, unable to Eat, Drink or sleep for
vehemence of vexation:—I am, now, got tolerably stout
again,—but I have been furiously Lectured for my *folly,*
(as, I see, *every body* thinks it,) by all who have known of
it. I have, therefore, struggled against it with all my might,
& am determined to *aim,* at least, at acquiring more
strength of mind.—Yet, after all, I feel very forcibly that
I *am* not—that I *have* not been—& that I never *shall* be
formed or fitted for any business with the *Public*—yet,
now, my best friends, & my Father at their Head, absolutely *prohibit* a retreat;—otherwise, I should be strongly
tempted to empty the whole contents of my Bureau into
the Fire, & to vow never again to fill it.— — —But, had
my *Name* never got abroad with my *Book,*—ere this, I
question not, I should again have tried *how the World stood
affected to me.* Now once again to your Letter.

Why, my dear Daddy, will you use so vile, so ill applied a Word as *officious*[3] when you are giving me advice?—Is it not, of all favours ∣ the most valuable you can confer on me? & don't I know that if you had not somewhat of a *sneaking kindness* for me, you would as soon *bite off your own Nose* [as the Irishman says][4] as take so much trouble about me? I do, most earnestly, seriously & solemnly entreat that you will continue to me this first, best, greatest proof of regard, & I do, with the utmost truth & & [*sic*] gratitude, assure you that it is more really flattering to me than all the flummery in the World. I only wish, with all my Heart, you would be more liberal of it.

Every word you have urged concerning the *salt & spirit* of gay, unrestrained freedom in Comedies, carries conviction along with it,—a conviction which I feel in trembling! should I ever venture in that walk publicly, perhaps the want of it might prove fatal to me: I do, indeed, think it most likely that such would be the Event, & my poor piece, though it might escape Cat calls & riots, would be fairly *slept off the stage*. I cannot, however, attempt to *avoid* this danger, though I *see* it, for I would a thousand Times rather forfeit my character as a *Writer*, ∣ than risk ridicule or censure as a *Female*. I have never set my Heart on Fame, & therefore would not if I *could* purchase it at the expence of all my own ideas of propriety. You who *know* me for a *Prude* will not be surprised, & I hope not offended at this avowal,—for I should deceive you were I not to make it. If I *should* try, I must e'en take my chance,—& all my own expectations may be pretty easily answered!

The Streathamites have been all re-assembled for these 6 weeks,[5] & I have had invitation upon invitation to join them, or, in Mrs. Thrale's Words, to *go Home*—but Susan is at Howletts, & I can by no means leave Town till her return. However, we correspond; & her [HLT's] kindness for me promises to be as steady as it is flattering &

---

[3] See above, p. 187.
[4] Inserted by FBA.
[5] The Thrales had returned to Streatham on 26 Nov. following an extended visit to Brighton (*TSP*, p. 213).

delightful to me; but I never knew how much in *earnest* & in *sincerity* she was my Friend till she heard of my infinite *frettation*[6] upon occasion of being Pamphleted;— & then, she took the trouble to write me a long *scolding* Letter,—& Dr. Johnson came to *talk* to me about it, & to *reason* with me;—& now, that I ⌐find⌐ they have sufficient regard ⌐for me⌐ to *find fault* with me, I do indeed hope that I am *well* with them.

Now as to the *Heads of Chapters* concerning other folks, that you have asked for, I will lead the way towards sending them to you, by giving you a list of their Names,— & you shall chuse from among them *3* at a Time to be enlarged upon. Of those whom I have *seen* since the *Blabbation*[7] of my scribbling, the following are all I can recollect.

Dr. King,[8] Mr. Hayes.[9] Mr. Hutton.[10] Miss Palmers. Mrs. Reynolds. Mrs. Williams. Dr. Francklyn. Sir Joshua Reynolds. Mr. W. Burke. Mrs. Horneck. Mrs. Cholmondeley. *Molly Richmond*.[11] Mr. Baretti. Mr. Lowndes. The Bogles.[12] My Uncle. Mrs. Nollekens.[13]

---

[6] FB's is the only instance of the word found by the *OED*'s editors. Presumably she coined it, though, as in other such cases of humorous wordplay, it may also have been invented by SEB or by Charlotte Burney, or even by a member of the Chessington set.

[7] Not in *OED*. The paragraph containing this word and the rest of the letter were omitted in previous editions.

[8] The Revd Dr John Glen King. See *EJL* i. 150 n. 25.

[9] John Hayes (*c.*1708–92). See *EJL* i. 93 n. 39.

[10] James Hutton (1715–95). See *EJL* ii. 26 n. 61.

[11] Presumably the 'Mary Richmond' mentioned by MAR in her letter to FB, 10 Sept. 1775 (Berg). She visited the Burneys in St Martin's St. in Dec. of this year (SEB to FB Dec. 1779, Barrett), and FB reports seeing her again in Dec. 1782: 'Molly Richmond was here the whole Time, looking very miserably poor & mean, but well content with herself, & as happy, I really believe, to be *seen* as to see' (*EJL* v). Though evidently a long-time acquaintance of the family, she has not been further identified.

[12] John Bogle (*c.*1746–1803), painter of miniature portraits, and his wife (m. 1769) Marion ('May' or 'Mennie') Bogle, née Wilson (d. 1823). Bogle, who exhibited at the Royal Academy from 1772 to 1794, painted a miniature of FB in 1783, reproduced as the frontispiece to *EJL* i. See also D. Foskett, *A Dictionary of British Miniature Painters* (1972), p. 169; idem, *Collecting Miniatures* (1979), pp. 203–4; *JL* i. 89 nn. 24–5.

[13] Wife of the sculptor. See *EJL* ii. 211 n. 33.

You find I write *promiscuously*, & without any respect to Persons.[14] Now of those of whose opinions I have *heard* some thing,—viz Mr. Greville.[15] Mrs. D°—Mr. & Mrs. Crewe.[16] Mr. Mason. Mr. Humphrey, the miniature painter,—Mrs. Ord. Mr. Murphy. Mr. Pepys. Dr. Jebb. Sir William Chambers. Mr. Birch.[17] Mr. Penneck. Mr. Poore. Mr. Boone.[18] Mrs. Crawley.[19] Duch[ss] Devonshire. Miss Coussmaker. Mr. Chamier. Mr. Wedderburne, Sol[r] Gen[l].[20] Mr. Cambridge.[21] Mrs. Lewis. Mrs. Raper,[22] Count Bruhl.[23] |

[*rest of letter missing*]

[14] i.e., she does not list them in order of social precedence.

[15] Fulke Greville, CB's former patron, and his wife, Frances Greville, FB's godmother. See *EJL* i. 31.

[16] John Crewe, later B. Crewe, and his wife Frances, the Grevilles' daughter. See ibid.

[17] Perhaps the 'Thomas Birch, Esq.,' who subscribed to *Hist. Mus.* This in turn may have been the Thomas Birch, English merchant at St Petersburg, who died there in 1794 (*GM* lxiv[1] (1794), 483); Birch presumably would have been an acquaintance of Dr King (above), who was chaplain to the English factory at St Petersburg.

[18] Charles Boone, MP. See *EJL* ii. 172.

[19] Probably Charles Boone's mother-in-law (mother of his late first wife) Theodosia née Gascoyne (1693–1782), who m. (1715) John Crowley (often spelled Crawley) (1689–1728), MP, of Barking Hall, Suffolk. It was through her daughter Theodosia (1723–65), m. (1762) Charles Boone, that Boone acquired his seat of Barking Hall. Mrs Crowley was also mother-in-law of Ld. Ashburnham (see *EJL* ii. 186; also, Sedgwick s.v. Crowley, John; Namier s.v. Boone, Charles; IGI).

[20] Alexander Wedderburn (1733–1805), MP, *cr.* (1780) B. Loughborough, and (1801) E. of Rosslyn. Wedderburn had relinquished the post of Solicitor-Gen. in June 1778 to take up the position of Attorney-Gen. He would later become lord chancellor.

[21] Richard Owen Cambridge (1717–1802), wit, author of *The Scribleriad* (1751). FB would later become romantically linked with his son George Owen Cambridge (see *EJL* v-vi).

[22] Catherine Shepherd (1735–1823), daughter of Samuel Shepherd, m. (1763) Henry Raper (1717–89), of Chelsea. Both she and her husband subscribed to *Hist. Mus.*, and CB, in a letter to HLT, 16 Oct. 1778 (Osborn), mentions his having 'dined with my Fr[ds] the Rapers' on Sun., 11 Oct., perhaps the occasion when Mrs Raper voiced her opinion of *Evelina*. Her son Charles Chamier Raper (1777–1842) would later (1807) marry Frances (Fanny) Phillips, daughter of SBP and Molesworth Phillips (*LCB* i. 207–9 and n. 1, 257–8; MS 'Genealogies. Families of Kingston Barrett Raper Philips' (Barrett); IGI).

[23] Hans Moritz, Graf von Brühl (1736–1809), Saxon Envoy Extraordinary to England, 1764–1809.

[St Martin's Street]
11 January [1779]
To Susanna Elizabeth Burney

AJL incomplete (Diary MSS I, Berg, paginated 849–78, foliated 11–23), Jan. 1779
15 single sheets 4to, 30 pp.

Jany 11th

Your repeated call, my dear Susan, makes me once more attempt to finish my Visit to Sir Joshua;[24] but I have very much forgotten where I left off, therefore if I am guilty of repetition or tautology, you must not much *marvel*.

Mrs. Cholmondeley hunted me quite round the Card Table, from Chair to Chair; repeating various speeches of Madame Duval; & when, at last, I got behind a sofa, out of her reach, she called out aloud 'Polly!—Lord Polly! only think! Miss has Danced with a Lord!'[25]

Some Time after, contriving to again get near me, she began flirting her Fan, & exclaiming 'Well, Miss, *I* have had a Beau, I assure you! ay, & a very pretty Beau, too, though I don't know if his *Lodgings* were so *prettily furnished*, & *every thing*!' [as Mr. Smith's!][26]

Then, applying to Mr. Cholmondeley, she said 'Pray, Sir, what is become of my Lottery Ticket?'

'I don't know.' answered he.

'*Pardi*, cried she, you *don't know nothing*!'

I had now again made off,—&, after much rambling, I at last seated myself near the ꟾ Card Table:—But Mrs. Cholmondeley was after me in a minute, & drew a chair next mine. I now found it impossible to escape, & therefore forced myself to sit still. Lord Palmerston & Sir Joshua in a few moments seated themselves by us.

---

[24] On 19 Dec. (above, pp. 197–205).
[25] *Evelina*, vol. ii, letter 23.
[26] Inserted by FBA.

I must now write Dialogue fashion, to avoid the enormous length of Mrs. C.'s Name.

Mrs. Chol. I have been very ill,—monstrous ill, indeed! or else I should have been at *your* House long ago.—Sir Joshua, pray how do do?—you know, I suppose, that I don't come to see *you*?

Sir Joshua could only Laugh; though this was her first address to him.

Mrs. Chol. Pray, *Miss*, what's your Name?

F:B. Frances, Ma'am.

Mrs. Chol. Fanny?—Well, *all* the Fanny's are excellent! & *yet*,—my Name is Mary!—Pray, Miss Palmers, how are you? though I hardly know if I shall speak to *you* to-night! Lord, I thought I should never have got here! I have been *so* out of humour with the People for keeping me. If You but *knew*, cried I, to *whom* I am going to Night! & *who* I shall see to Night!—you would not dare keep me *mu^r ss^n ing*[27] here!'

During all these pointed speeches, her penetrating Eyes were fixed upon me; & what could I do?—what, indeed, could *any* body do, but colour & simper? *all* the company watching us! though all, very delicately, avoided joining the confab.

Mrs. Chol. 'My Lord Palmerston, I was told to night that Nobody could see your Lordship for *me*, for that you supped at my House *every* Night?— — —Dear, bless me, no! cried I, not *every* night!—& I looked as confused as I was able,—but I am *afraid* I did not blush, though I tried hard for it.' Then again turning to me. 'That Mr. what d'ye call him, in Fleet Street, is a mighty silly fellow; — — —perhaps You don't know who I mean?—one T. Lowndes,—but may be you don't know such a person?

F:B. 'No, *indeed* I do not! *That* I can safely say.'

Mrs. Chol. 'I could get nothing from him: but I told him I hoped he gave a good *price*, & he answered me that he

---

[27] i.e., loitering aimlessly, hanging about. FBA emended the spelling to '*muzzing*', and the word thus spelled is cited by *OED* as the first instance of this meaning. *OED*'s earliest instance of *muss*, in the related sense of 'to busy oneself in a confused, unmethodical, and ineffective manner', dates from 1876.

always did things *genteel*. What trouble & tagging[28] we had! Mr.—(I cannot recollect the name she mentioned) laid a wager the Writer was a *man*,—*I* said I was sure it was a *Woman*,—but now we are *both* out, for it's a *Girl!*'

In this comical, queer, flighty, whimsical, manner she ran on, till we were summoned to supper,—for we were not allowed to break up before;—& then,—when Sir Joshua & almost every body was ¦ gone down stairs, she changed her tone, &, with a Face & voice both grave, said 'Well, Miss Burney, You *must* give me leave to say *one* thing to you,—yet perhaps you won't, niether,—will you?'

'What is it, Ma'am?'

'Why it is—that I admire you more than any human Being! & *that* I can't help!—'

Then, suddenly rising, she hurried down stairs.

Did you ever hear the like?—

While we were upon the stairs, I heard Miss Palmer say to Miss Fanny Cholmondeley 'Well, you don't find Miss Burney quite so *tremendous* a person as you expected?'

How ridiculous!

Sir Joshua made me sit next him at supper,—Mr. William Burke was at my other side.—though, afterwards, I lost the *knight of Plymton*,[29] who, as he Eats no suppers, made way for Mr. Guanton,[30] &, as the Table was Crowded, stood at the Fire himself. He was *extremely* polite & flattering in his manners towards me, & entirely avoided all mention or hint at Evelina the whole Evening; indeed, I think I have met with more scrupulous delicacy from Sir Joshua, than from any body,—although I have *heard* more of his approbation than of almost any Other persons. ¦

We had a good deal of talk about Devonshire, Sir Joshua's native County:—& we agreed perfectly in praise of Ting mouth & its environs.—indeed, he said, he was *sure* I must admire it, for no person of *Taste* could do

---

[28] Probably meaning that she was dogging his heels, trying to pump information from him. The *OED* cites this sentence.
[29] Sir Joshua was born in Plympton Erle, Devonshire.
[30] A slip for Robert Lovell Gwatkin (above, p. 199).

otherwise,—so, you see, we had a little touch of *gallantry*, as well as of *virtù.*

Mr. W. Burke was *immensely* attentive at Table;—but, lest he should be thought a *Mr. Smith* for his pains, he took care, who ever he helped, to add—'You know I am *all for the Ladies!*'[31]

I was glad I was not next Mrs. Cholmondeley, but she frequently, & very provokingly, addressed herself to me;—once she called out aloud 'Pray, Miss Burney, is there any thing *new* coming out?' And another Time, 'Well, I wish people who *can* entertain me, *would* entertain me!' These sort of pointed speeches are almost worse than direct attacks, for there is no knowing how to look, or what to say;—especially where the Eyes of a whole Company mark the object for whom they are meant.

To the last of these speeches, I made no sort of answer, but Sir Joshua, very good naturedly, turned it from *me,* by saying 'Well, let every one do what they can in their different ways,—do *you* begin yourself.'

'Lord I can't! cried she;—I have *tried,*—but I can't.'

'Do you think, then, answered he, that all the World is made only to entertain *You?*'

A very lively Dialogue ensued,—but I grow tired of writing,—one thing, however, I must mention, which, at the Time, frightened me wofully.—

'Pray, Sir Joshua, asked Lord Palmerston, what is this *Warley* that is just come out?'

Was not this a cruel question?—I felt in *such* a twitter!—

'Why, I don't know,—answered he,—but the Reviews, my Lord, speak very well of it.'[32]

Mrs. Chol. Who writ it?

Sir Joshua. Mr. Huddisford.

---

[31] See above, p. 70.

[32] e.g., the review of Part 1 in the *Monthly Review* lix (Nov. 1778), 394: 'None of the many imitations, that we have seen, of the Bath Guide, come so *near,* though not quite *up* to the jocund spirit, and easy strain of that celebrated piece of comic poetry.' The same review, however, objected to the 'general grossness' of Part 2 (ibid., lix (Dec. 1778), 473), and the *GM* reviewer (of Part 1 only) would condemn the 'nastiness' of Part 1 as well, observing that 'Swift and Anstey seem to have been our author's models; but he hobbles with very unequal paces after those two great masters ... ' (*GM* xlix (Jan. 1779), 36).

Mrs. Chol. O!—I don't like it at all, then!—*Huddisford!*—
what a Name!—Miss Burney, pray can you conceive any
thing of such a name as *Huddisford?*'

I could not speak a Word, & I dare say I looked *no
how*;—but was it not an unlucky reference—to *me?*

Sir Joshua attempted a kind of vindication of him,—
but Lord Palmerston said, drily 'I think, Sir Joshua, it is
Dedicated to *you?*'

'Yes, my Lord.' answered he. |

'O, your servant! is it so? cried Mrs. Chol.—then you
need say no more!'

Sir Joshua Laughed, & the subject to my great relief,
was dropt.

When we broke up to depart,—which was not till near
2 in the morning,—Mrs. Cholmondeley went up to my
mother, & begged her permission to visit in St. Martin's
Street.—Then, as she left the Room, she said to me,
with a droll sort of threatening look, 'You have not got
rid of me yet,—I have been forcing myself into your
House.'

I must own I was not at all displeased at this, as I had
very much, & very reasonably, feared that she would have
been, by then, as sick of me from disappointment, as she
was, before, eager for me from curiosity.

When we came away, Offy Palmer, laughing, said to
me 'I think this will be a *breaking in* to you!' 'Ah, cried I,
if I had *known* of your Party!—' 'You would have been
sick in Bed, I suppose?' I would not answer *no*,—yet I was
glad it was *over*. And so concludeth this memorable Evening. Yet I must tell you that I observed, with much
delight, that who-ever spoke of the *Thrales*, was | sure to
turn to *me*. Whence I conclude—since I am sure no puffs
of *mine* can have caused it—that her kindness towards me
has been published by herself.

I shall now skip to the Thursday following [24 Dec.],
when I accompanied my Father to Streatham. We had a
delightful ride, though the Day was horrible: but I should
have told you that, in the *intrim* [*sic*], I had another Letter
from Mrs. Thrale, in answer to mine,[33] & yet more kind
& more sweet than the former one.

[*See p. 220 for n. 33*]

We went immediately into the Music Room, where Miss Thrale was alone. Exactly according to my expectations was her behaviour,—c'est à dire civil, cold, & like that of a first meeting, though we had parted on the terms of the utmost intimacy. But her natural reserve is so prevalent, that an absence of even 3 Days would be sufficient to restore it to her in its full strength & power, however, *before* that absence, it might have been disolved, or even melted into kindness.

In 2 minutes, we were joined by Mr. Seward,—&, in 4, by Dr. Johnson. How different was the behaviour of *both* these! Mr. Seward, though himself a reserved & cold young man, has a Heart *open* to | friendship, & very *capable* of good nature & good will, though I believe it *abounds* not with them to all indiscriminately: but he *really* loves my Father, & *his* reserve *once*, is *always* conquered. He seemed heartily glad to see us both:—& the dear Dr. Johnson was more kind, more pleased, & more delightful than ever. Our several meetings in Town seem now to have quite *established* me in his favour, & I flatter myself that if he was *now* accused of loving me, he would *not* deny it, nor, as before, insist on waiting longer ere he went so far.[34]

'I hope, Dr. Burney, cried Mr. Seward, You are now come to *stay*?'

'No! cried my Father, shaking his Head, that is utterly out of my power at present.'

'Well but—this fair lady. (N.B. *fair & Brown* are *synonymous* terms in *conversation*, however opposite in *Looks*;— thus, Mr. Seward, in a Note to my Father,[35] desired his best Respects to Mrs. Burney & the *fair Evelina*,—so never marvel at the application of this Word in future.) I hope will stay?—'

'No, no, no!—' was the *response*;—& he came to me, & pressed the invitation very warmly,—but Dr. Johnson, going to the Window, called me from him. |

[33] Both letters are missing.
[34] See above, p. 155.
[35] Missing.

'Well, my dear, cried he, in a low voice, & how are you *now?* have you done *fretting?*—have You got over your *troubles?*'

'Ah, Sir, quoth I, I am sorry they told *you* of my folly,—yet I am *very* much obliged to you for bearing to hear of it with so much indulgence, for I had feared it would have made you hold me cheap ever after.'

'No, my dear, no! what should I hold you cheap for? it did not surprise *me* at all,—I thought it very natural but you must think no more of it.'

F.B. 'Why, Sir, to say the truth, I don't know, after all, whether I do not owe the affair, in *part*, to *you!*

Dr. J. 'To me?—how so?'

F.B. Why the appellation of *little Burney* I think must have come from you, for I know of nobody else that calls me so.'

This is a *fact*, Susy,—& the '*dear* little Burney' makes it still more suspicious, for I am sure Sir Joshua Reynolds would never speak of me so facetiously after *one* meeting.

Dr. Johnson seemed almost shocked, & warmly denied having been any way accessary.

'Why, Sir, cried I, they say the Pamphlet was written by a Mr. Huddisford,—now I never saw, never heard of him before,—how, therefore, should he know ¹ whether I am *little* or *Tall?*—he could not call me *little* by inspiration,—I might be a *patagonian*³⁶ for any thing *he* could tell.'

Dr. J. Pho,—fiddle faddle,—do you suppose your Book is so much talked of, & not yourself?—do you think your Readers will not ask questions, & inform themselves whether you are short or Tall, young or old? Why should you put it on *me?*'

After this, he made me follow him into the Library, that we might continue our confab. without interruption. And, just as we were seated, entered Mrs. Thrale.—I flew to her—& she received me with the sweetest cordiality.—they placed me between them, & we had a most delicious *Trio.*—

³⁶ See above, p. 153.

We talked over the visit at Sir Joshua's,—& Dr. Johnson told me that ⌐I ought to be very civil to⌐ Mrs. Cholmondeley, ⌐as she⌐ was the *first* person who publicly praised & recommended Evelina among the Wits: Mrs. Thrale told me that at Tunbridge & Brighthelmstone it was the *universal* topic;—& that Mrs. Montague had pronounced the *Dedication* to be *so* well written, that she could not but suppose it must be the *Doctor's*. 'She is very kind, quoth *I*, because she likes one part better than another to take it from me!' |

'You must not mind that, said Dr. Johnson, for these things are always said where Books are successful. There are 3 distinct kind of Judges upon all new Authors or productions;—the first, are those who know no rules, but pronounce entirely from their natural Taste & feelings; The 2ᵈ are those who *know*, & *judge* by *rules*; & the 3ᵈ are those who *know*, but are *above* the rules. These last are those you should wish to satisfy: *next* to them, rate the *natural* judges,—but ever despise those opinions that are formed by the *rules*.'³⁷

Soon after, we were joined by Mr. Seward,—&, during our conversation, Mr. Davenant³⁸ entered,—he said nothing, but looked for some thing on the Table, *leering* all the Time at your humble servant, & then retired. I was, afterwards, introduced to Mrs. Davenant. Mr. Thrale was out.

Mrs. Thrale wanted me much to stay all Night,—but it could not be; & she pressed me to come the next week, to be introduced to Miss Streatfield, who, she said, much wished *the same* but these wishes only serve to chill me, for I am sure I shall always disappoint them, & | therefore,

---

³⁷ SJ evidently places Mrs Montagu in this last category. For her disapproval of *Evelina*, see above, p. 162 n. 10, where SJ accuses her of jealousy. Her witticism that FB's 'Silver-Smiths are Pewterers ... & her Captains Boatswains' certainly exhibits a rigid and stereotyped view of class behaviour.

³⁸ Corbet D'Avenant (1753–1823), who assumed the surname of Corbet in 1783 and was cr. Bt in 1786; m. (1774) Hester ('Hetty') Salusbury D'Avenant, née Cotton (c.1748–1822), HLT's cousin, and godmother to Cecilia Margaretta Thrale (1777–1857), the Thrales' 11th child (*TSP*, pp. 92, 95, 176). Mr D'Avenant had attended a party in St Martin's St. in 1778, described in *ED* ii. 284–7 and *Mem.* ii. 101–14.

the minute I hear any body desires particularly to see me, —*I* desire particularly to avoid them! —don't scold, Susy, for I can't help it. The idea of being an object of any attention gives me a restraint equally unconquerable & uncomfortable. I therefore entirely defered repeating my visit till your return: for I only could have had *leave* for one Day.

When we came Home, we heard that Mrs. Cholmondeley had been at our House almost all the morning, asking questions innumerable about me, & asserting that she *must* come to *close quarters* with me, ere she could satisfy her mind fully that all those *Characters* could be my own! She said, more-over, that Lord Palmerston, hearing the Authoress of Evelina was to be at Sir Joshua's, had *begged* to be invited! so I might well be struck with his politeness to her! —but what was most charming, she said that my whole behaviour that Evening was *set upon* afterwards, & that the Jury brought in their verdict that it was strictly proper! —This, I will own, has relieved me from some very disagreeable apprehensions I had been full of, that I had certainly disappointed the whole party, & exposed myself to their ridicule.

She said a million of *handsome* things of the Book, you may suppose, & begged to see us very soon. She sat up a whole Night, with a large party, to read it! Madame Duval is, all to-gether, her greatest favourite among the Characters.

Last Week [the week of 28 Dec.], I called on Mrs. Williams, —& Dr. Johnson, who was just returned from Streatham, came down stairs to me—& was so kind! —I quite doat on him, —& I do really believe, that, take away Mr. Crisp, there is no man out of this House who has so real & affectionate a regard for me: & I am sure, take away the same person, I can with the utmost truth say the same thing in return.

I asked after all the Streathamites, —'Why, said he, we now only want *you*, —we have Miss Streatfield, Miss Brown, Murphy & Seward, —we only want *you*! —has Mrs. Thrale called on you lately?' 'Yes, Sir.' (N.B. She has called twice.) 'Ah, said he, [xxxxx *1 word*] *you* are such a darling!'

Mrs. Williams added a violent Compliment to this, but concluded with saying 'My only fear is lest she should put me in a Book!'

'Sir Joshua Reynolds, answered Dr. Johnson, ⌐ says that if he ⌐was⌐ conscious to himself of any trick, or any affectation, there is Nobody he should so much fear as this little Burney!'

This speech he told me once before, so that I find it has struck him much,—& so, I suppose it did Mr. *Huddisford*, who, probably, has heard one similar to it![39]

I made but a short visit, as Mrs. Williams was going out.—but finished the Day at my aunts very sociably & merrily. Did I tell you, in my last, that Cousin James is in Town? he is mighty well, & very gay; & I hope you will return among us ere he leaves Town.

The Sunday following [3 Jan.] Mr. Seward drank Tea, & Mr. Baretti supped here. The latter has been here frequently of late: & he has lent me the Prince of Abyssinia Translated into French by himself, & in manuscript.[40]

I had a great deal of conversation with Mr. Seward about Miss Streatfield: he thinks her a very pleasing Girl, but, notwithstanding her knowledge of what he calls 'the Crooked Letters',[41] he owned that he thought her niether bright nor *deep* ⌐in respect to *parts*⌐: & rather *too* tender Hearted, for that she had *Tears at Command*.[42] ⌐

---

[39] From Sir Joshua himself. Huddesford, son of a president of Trinity College, Oxford, studied painting as a young man and was Reynolds' pupil. About this time Reynolds completed a double portrait of him and J. C. Bampfylde (*The Poems of John Bampfylde*, ed. R. Lonsdale (Oxford, 1988), p. 21).

Despite SJ's disclaimer (above, p. 221), he undoubtedly *was* the ultimate source of the 'dear little Burney' in *Warley*. Reynolds probably repeated the phrase to Huddesford as illustrating SJ's fondness for FB.

[40] Baretti had made this translation years before at SJ's request. It would remain unpublished until 1970, when it appeared in an edition with the English original and Baretti's translation on facing pages (R. Carbonara, *Giuseppe Baretti e la sua traduzione del 'Rasselas' di S. Johnson* (Turin, 1970)). See also C. J. M. Lubbers-Van Der Brugge, *Johnson and Baretti* (Djakarta, 1951), pp. 86, 148; *Life* ii. 499–500.

[41] i.e., Greek.

[42] About this time HLT confided to her diary: 'Mr Thrale is fallen in Love *really* & *seriously* with Sophy Streatfield—but there is no wonder in that: She is very pretty, very gentle, soft & insinuating; hangs about him, dances round him, cries when She parts from him, squeezes his Hand slyly, & with her sweet

Miss Brown, though far less formed & less cultivated, he said had a *better* natural understanding: —but—she was coarse & rough!—

Of whom, I wonder, would Mr. Seward speak *really* well? I think, alltogether [*sic*], he is *more* difficult to please as to Persons than any body I know.

He was so facetious as to propose my Writing for Lady Miller's Vase[43] —& undertook to convey my verses to it. I thanked him *koindly*.[44]

He asked many questions of when I should go to Streatham, but said he was sure Miss Streatfield would not answer to me.

Baretti *worries* me about writing,—asks a million of questions of *how* much I have written, & so forth,—& when I say *nothing*, he raves & rants, & says he could beat me.

However, we had a very agreeable Evening,—Baretti was in very good humour, & Mr. Seward was extremely droll & entertaining. You know *les agremens* are all his own, when he chooses to ⌐exert¬ them.

And now, my dear Susan, to relate the affairs of an Evening *perhaps* the most important of my life.—to say *that*, is, I am sure, enough to interest you, my dearest Girl, in all I can tell you of it. |

Eyes full of Tears looks so fondly in his Face—& all for *Love of me* as She pretends; that I can hardly sometimes help laughing in her Face.

'A Man must not be a *Man* but an *It* to resist such Artillery ... ' (*Thraliana* i. 356, s.v. Dec. 1778).

[43] An antique vase, dug up at Frascati in 1769, belonging to Anna, née Riggs (1741–81), who m. (1765) John Miller (from *c.*1765, Riggs Miller), cr. (1778) Bt. The vase was the receptacle of verses composed by Lady Miller's guests at her villa in Batheaston. *Poetical Amusements at a Villa near Bath*, a collection of the best verses, was published in 1775. (Lord Palmerston (above) was a contributor.) Subsequent volumes appeared in 1776, 1777, and 1781. Horace Walpole wrote to Sir Horace Mann, 24 April 1776: 'They have instituted a poetic academy at Bath Easton, give out subjects and distribute prizes, publish the prize verses, and make themselves completely ridiculous' (*YW* xxiv. 197; see also xxxix. 240–2). FB would meet Lady Miller at Bath in 1780, and visit Batheaston shortly thereafter (*EJL* iv).

[44] Imitating the Irish accent of Lady Miller's husband. Lady Miller was herself of Irish descent, and widely ridiculed as a vulgar woman trying to be elegant.

On Monday last [4 Jan.], my Father sent a Note to Mrs. Cholmondeley to propose our waiting on her the Wednesday following [6 Jan.]: she was very *agreeable* to the proposal, &, accordingly, on Wednesday Evening, my Father, mother, & self went to Hertford Street.

I should have told you, that Mrs. Cholmondeley, when my Father, some Time ago, called on her, sent me a message[45] that, if I would go to see her, I should not again be stared at or worried.—O—& she acknowledged that my Visit at Sir Joshua's was a *formidable* one,—& that I was *watched* the whole Evening,—but that, upon the whole, the *company* behaved extremely well, for they only *ogled*!—

Well,—we were received by Mrs. Cholmondeley with great politeness, & in a manner that shewed she intended to entirely throw aside *Madame Duval*, & to conduct herself towards me in a new style. And, indeed, she succeeded, for her behaviour was quite *delicate*, to my infinite surprise, & she avoided *almost* all mention of my *little affair*. This, as it was very unexpected, gave me double pleasure, &, indeed, the whole Evening proved *delightful* to me.

Mr. & the Miss Cholmondeleys, & Miss Forrest were with her,—but who *else* think you?—Why Mrs. Sheridan![46]—I was absolutely *charmed* at the sight of her. I think her quite as beautiful as ever, & even *more* captivating, for she has, now, a look of ease & happiness that animates her whole Face.

Miss Linley[47] was with her. She is very handsome, but *nothing* near her sister: the *elegance* of Mrs. Sheridan's Beauty is unequaled by any I *ever* saw except Mrs. Crewes. I was pleased with her in *all* respects,—she is much more lively & agreeable than I had any idea of finding her; she was very gay, & very unaffected, & totally free from airs of *any* kind.

Miss Linley was very much out of spirits; she did not speak 3 words the whole Evening, & looked wholly

[45] Missing.

[46] Elizabeth Anne, née Linley, wife of Richard Brinsley Sheridan. See *EJL* i and ii.

[47] Mary Linley, later Mrs Tickell. See *EJL* i. 250 n. 67.

unmoved at all that past. Indeed she appeared to be heavy & inanimate.

Mrs. Cholmondeley sat next me. She is determined, I believe, to make me like her,—& she will, I believe, have full success, for she is *very* clever, *very* entertaining, & *very* much unlike any body else.

The first subject started was the Opera, & all joined in the praise of Pachierotti,—Mrs. Sheridan declared she could not hear him without Tears, & that he was the first Italian singer who ever affected her to such a degree.

They then talked of the intended marriage of the Duke of Dorset with Miss Cumberland,[48] & many ridiculous anecdotes were related: the conversation naturally fell upon *Mr.* Cumberland—& he was finely cut up!

'What a man is that! said Mrs. Cholmondeley!—I cannot bear him,—so querulous, so dissatisfied,—so determined to like nobody & no-thing but himself,—[49]

'What, Mr. Cumberland?' exclaimed I.

'Yes, answered she, I hope *you* don't like him?'

'I don't know him, Ma'am. I have only seen him once at Mrs. Ord's.'

'O, don't like him for your life!—I *charge* you not!—I hope you did not like his looks?'

'Why—quoth I laughing, I went prepared, & determined *to* like him,—but, perhaps, when I see him next, I may go prepared for the *contrary*.'

After this, Miss More was mentioned; & I was asked what I thought of *her*?

'I don't know her, Ma'am.'

'Don't be formal with *me*!—if you are,—I sha'n't like you!'

'I have no hope that you will *any* way!'

'O!—fie, fie!—but as to Miss More,—I don't like her at all;—that is, I detest her! She does nothing but flatter &

---

[48] The marriage did not materialize. Dorset m. (1790) Arabella Diana Cope (1769–1825), 1st daughter and coheir of Sir Charles Cope, 2nd Bt, of Bruern, Oxon. Elizabeth Cumberland m. (1782) Ld. Edward Charles Cavendish Bentinck.

[49] Later this year Sheridan would lampoon Cumberland as Sir Fretful Plagiary in his play, *The Critic* (see below, p. 444).

fawn: & then, she thinks ill of *nobody,*—don't you hate a person who thinks ill of nobody?—'

My Father then told what Dr. Johnson had said to her on the occasion of her praising him.[50]

'This rejoices, this does me good! cried she; I would have given the World to have heard that. O, there's no supporting the Company of professed Flatterers. She gives *me* such doses of it, that I cannot endure her; but I always sit still, & make no answer, but receive it as if *I* thought it my due: that is the only way to q[uie]t her. She is really detestable. I hope, Miss Burney, you don't think I admire *all* Geniusses?'

What a *Toad!*

'The only person *I* flatter, continued she, is Garrick,— & *he* likes it so much, that it pays one by the spirits it gives him.[51] *Other people* that I *like,* I *dare* not flatter.'

A *Tow row*[52] ensued, & the Earl of Harcourt was announced. When he had paid his Compliments to Mrs. Cholmondeley 'I *knew,* Ma'am, he said, that I should find you at Home.'

'I suppose, then, my Lord, said she, that you have seen Sir Joshua Reynolds, for he is engaged to be here.'

'I have, answered his Lordship,—& heard from him that I should be sure to find you.' & then he added some very fine compliment, but I have forgot it.

'O my Lord, cried she, You have the most discernment of any body!—his Lordship (turning another way) always says these things to *me,*—& yet he *never* flatters!'

Lord Harcourt, speaking of the Lady from whose House he was just come, but whose name I have forgotten,

---

[50] See above, p. 120.

[51] At the time of this letter Garrick was suffering from a severe attack of kidney disease that would prove fatal. The Burneys' great friend died of uremia at his house in the Adelphi on 20 Jan. He was buried in Westminster Abbey on 1 Feb. CB visited him on his deathbed on 18 Jan., and followed his hearse from the Adelphi to the Abbey in the same carriage (one of more than 50) with William Whitehead, the poet laureate, Topham Beauclerk, and Albany Wallis, one of Garrick's executors. Sheridan was the chief mourner. See Garrick, *Letters* iii. 1263–4; *Mem.* ii. 203; *GM* xlix (1779), 98.

[52] i.e., an uproar, noisy disturbance.

said Mrs. ____[53] is vastly agreeable,—but her fear of ceremony is really troublesome;—for her eagerness to break a Circle is such that she insists upon every body's sitting with their backs one to another! that is, the Chairs are drawn into little parties, of 3 together, in a confused manner, all over the Room.' |

'Why then, said my Father, they may have the pleasure of Caballing & Cutting up one-another, even in the same Room.'

'O I like the Notion of all things! cried Mrs. Chol. I shall certainly adopt it!' And then she drew her Chair into the middle of our Circle. Lord Harcourt turned his round, & his back to most of us,—& my Father did the same. You can't imagine a more absurd sight.

A *Rat Tat* instead of alarming, delighted them. Mrs. Chol. begged *me* to twirl round too,—but I could not bear to obey her upon the Entrance of Company; however, upon my resisting, she rose, & said 'O Miss Burney, you *must* be among us!' & *made* me turn round.

Just then,—the Door opened,—& Mr. Sheridan Entered.

Was I not in luck? not that I believe the meeting was *accidental*!—but I had more wished to meet him & his wife than any people I know not.

I could not endure my ridiculous situation, but replaced myself in an orderly manner immediately. Mr. Sheridan stared at them all, & Mrs. Chol. said she meant it as a hint for a *Comedy*.

Mr. Sheridan has a very fine figure, & a good, though I don't think a handsome Face. He is Tall & very upright, & his appearance & address are at once manly & fashionable, without the smallest tincture of foppery or modish graces. In short, I like him vastly,—& think | him every way worthy his beautiful Companion. And let me tell you, what I know will give *you* as much pleasure as it gave *me*, that by all I could observe in the course of the Evening,— & we stayed very late,—they are *extremely* happy in each

[53] FBA has written in 'Vesey' and deleted 'but whose name I have forgotten'. Elizabeth, née Vesey (*c*.1715–91), bluestocking hostess, m. 1 William Handcock; m. 2 (before 1746) Agmondesham Vesey (d. 1785), Irish MP.

other: he evidently adores her,—& she as evidently idolises him. The World has by no means done him justice.[54]

When he had paid his Compliments to all his acquaintance, he went behind the sofa on which Mrs. Sheridan & Miss Cholmondeley were seated, & entered into earnest conversation with them.

Upon Lord Harcourt's again paying Mrs. Cholmondeley some Compliment, she said 'Well, my Lord, after this I shall be quite sublime for some Days!—I sha'n't descend into common Life till—till—Saturday,—& then, I shall drop into the vulgar style,—I shall be in—the *ma foi* way.'[55]

I do really believe she could not *resist* this, for she had seemed *determined* to be quiet. Every body, very provokingly, heard this silently,—not a word was spoke for at least 2 minutes,—& to be sure *I* looked very wise mean Time!

When next there was a Rat-Tat,—Mrs. Cholmondeley & Lord Harcourt & my Father again, at the command of the former, moved into the middle of the Room:—And then Sir Joshua Reynolds & Dr. Wharton entered. No further Company came. You may imagine there was a general *war* at the *breaking of the Circle*,—&, when they got into order, Mr. Sheridan seated himself in the place Mrs. Cholmondeley had left, between my Father & myself.

And now I must tell you a little conversation which I did not hear myself till I came Home,—it was between Mr. Sheridan & my Father.

'Good God, Dr. Burney, cried the former, have you no *older* Daughters? can *this* possibly be the authoress of Evelina?—' & then he said abundance of fine things, & begged my Father to Introduce him to me! 'Why, it will

---

[54] Sheridan already had a reputation for a 'roving eye', and in the late 1780s and early 1790s would have a well-publicized affair with Lady Duncannon, younger sister of the Duchess of Devonshire. At this time he was suspected of romantic involvement with the beautiful Mrs Crewe, one of his many admirers among the ladies of fashion. See M. Bingham, *Sheridan: The Track of a Comet* (1972), pp. 159, 163–5; S. Ayling, *A Portrait of Sheridan* (1985), pp. 53–5, 106–7, 136–41, 143–5, 148.

[55] Echoing Mme Duval.

be a very formidable thing to her, answered he, to be introduced to *you*!' 'Well then,—by & by,—' returned he.

Some Time after this, my Eyes happening to meet his, he waved the Ceremony of introduction, &, in a low voice, said 'I have been telling Dr. Burney that I have long expected to see in Miss Burney a lady of the gravest appearance, with the quickest parts.'

I was never much more astonished than at this unexpected address, as, among all my numerous puffers, the Name of Sheridan has never reached me, & I did really imagine he had never deigned to look at my trash.

Of course I could make no *verbal* answer: & he proceeded then to speak of Evelina in terms of the highest praise, but I was in such a *ferment* from surprise (not to say pleasure) that I have no recollection of his expressions. I only remember telling him that I was much amazed he had spared Time to read it,—& that he repeatedly called it a most *surprising Book*. And, some Time after, he added 'But I hope, Miss Burney, you don't intend to throw away your Pen?'

'You should take care, Sir, said I, what you say,—for you know not what weight it may have.'

He wished it might have any, he said.—& soon after, turned again to my Father.

I protest, since the approbation of the Streathamites, I have met with none so *highly* flattering to me as this of Mr. Sheridan, & so *very* unexpected.

Sir Joshua, then, came up to me, &, after some general conversation, said 'Pray do you know any thing of the Sylph?'[56]—

This is a Novel, lately advertised by Lowndes. Mr. Hutton has already been with me to enquire if it was *mine*.

'No.' quoth I. 'Don't you upon your Honour?'

'Upon my Honour! did you suspect me?'

'Why a friend of mine sent for it upon suspicion.—'

'So did we, said Miss Linley, but I did not suspect after I had *read* it!'

---

[56] *The Sylph: a Novel*, in 2 vols., with the imprint date of 1779, was published on 4 Dec. 1778 by Thomas Lowndes (*Public Advertiser* 4 Dec. 1778).

'What is the reason, said Sir Joshua, that Lowndes always advertises it with Evelina?'[57]

'Indeed I know nothing about it.'

'Ma'am,' cried Mr. Sheridan, turning to me abruptly, you should send & order him *not*,—it is a take in, & ought to be forbid;—(&, with great vehemence he added) it is a most impudent thing in that fellow!'

I assure you I took it quite *koind*[58] in him to give me this advice. By the way, Mrs. Thrale has sent me a message to the same purpose.[59]

Sir Joshua went on with the Conversation. This, by the way, was the first Time he ever spoke to *me* of this so much honoured Book, but, now the subject was once started, he scrupled not to support it. He did not,

---

[57] *The Sylph* was advertised as 'Printed for T. Lowndes, No. 77, in Fleet-street. Where may be had, just published, in 3 Vols. Evelina, a Novel' (*Public Advertiser* 4 Dec. 1778 and subsequent issues, cited *LCB* i. 268 n. 2). On 28 Dec. the notice was revised to read: 'THE SYLPH, a Novel; and in three Volumes, Price 7s. 6d. sewed, EVELINA, a Novel' (ibid.).

[58] In imitation of Sheridan's Irish accent.

[59] HLT to FB, dated 'Decr 1778' by FBA (Berg): ' ... I cannot help writing just to express my Wishes that you would chide Lowndes for advertising his Novel called the *Sylph* in the Manner he does, for I find every body is falling apace into the Snare ... . this Morning's Post brought me a Letter from a Lady forty Miles off, from which I take Leave to copy for your use the following Paragraph. "I want your opinion of the Sylph, if as 'tis said it is written by *your* Miss Burney— ... "' HLT commented in *Thraliana* (i. 363), s.v. 20 Jan. 1779: ' ... her [FB's] Scoundrel Bookseller having advertised the Sylph along with it *Evelina*] lately, and endeavouring to make the World believe it *hers*; Mrs Leveson runs about the Town saying how clever Miss Burney must be! & what Knowledge of *Mankind* She must have! ... the Sylph is an obscene Novel, and more *Knowledge* of Mankind is indeed wanting to't than any *professed* Virgin should have.'

On 27 Jan. CB wrote to Lowndes (Comyn) complaining about the deception. Lowndes replied the same day (Barrett), promising that 'you shall approve of my future advertisement before Printed'. No mention is made of *The Sylph* in the advertisement for the 3rd edn. of *Evelina*, which first appeared in the *Public Advertiser* on 26 Feb. (*LCB* i. 267–8 and n. 3). The mischief, however, was irreversible: the *Public Advertiser*, 2 Apr. 1782, in wrongly attributing to FB 'the new Comedy of *Variety*', calls her 'the Authoress of Evelina, and the Sylph.'

The authorship of *The Sylph* has never been settled. It was widely attributed to the Duchess of Devonshire. Her recent biographer, Brian Masters, credits the attribution, further observing that Sheridan, a member of the Devonshire House set, 'must have been privy to the secret', though 'enjoined no doubt never to disclose his knowledge ... ' (*Georgiana Duchess of Devonshire* (1981), p. 70). But Lowndes wrote to CB (above) that 'The Sylph is wrote by an Es⟨sex⟩ Lady'.

however, begin any *formal* or *formidable Eloge*, but *dashed* his general Discourse with occasional civilities equally flattering & delicate.

Among other things, he said that 'Mr. Sheridan has declared he holds it *superior* to Fielding.'

'"God!"—impossible, impossible!'

'Nay, he has indeed,—& he must *really* think so, for he said it publicly at our Club.[60]—But I dare say he has been telling you so himself?'

F:B. No indeed;—but if he *had*, many things are said to *me* that are not to be believed.

Sir Joshua. But what is said at our *Club*, *is* to be believed. It is his real opinion.

F:B. Well,—I begin to think a Proclamation has been issued that all folks are to attack & try the strength of my poor Head!—& I fear they are determined Not to leave me short of Moorfields.'[61]

About this Time Mrs. Cholmondeley was making much sport by wishing for an Acrostic on her Name. She said she had several Times begged for one in vain, & began to entertain thoughts of writing one herself: 'For, said she, I am very famous for my *rhymes*, though I never made a line of *Poetry* in my life.'

'An Acrostic on *your* Name, said Mr. Sheridan, would be a formidable task;—it must be so long, that I think it should be divided into Cantos.'

'Miss Burney, cried Sir Joshua, who was now re-seated, are ˡ not you a writer of Verses?

F:B. No Sir!

Mrs. Chol. O don't believe her! *I* have made a resolution not to believe any thing she says.

Mr. Sheridan. I think a *lady* should not *write* verses, till she is past receiving them.

Mrs. Chol. (rising & stalking majestically towards him)— Mr. Sheridan! pray, Sir, what may you mean by this insinuation? did I not say *I* writ verses?

Mr. Sheridan. O—but you,—

---

[60] The Literary Club of SJ, founded by Reynolds in 1764. Sheridan was proposed by SJ himself for membership, and elected in 1777.

[61] i.e., Bethlehem (Bedlam) Hospital.

Mrs. Chol. Say no more, Sir! you have made your meaning but too plain already!—There, now,—I think that's a speech for a Tragedy!'

Some Time after, Sir Joshua, returning to his *standing* place, entered into *confab.* with Miss Linley & your slave upon various matters;—during which, Mr. Sheridan, joining us, said 'Sir Joshua I have been telling Miss Burney that she must not suffer her Pen to lie idle;—*ought* she?'

Sir Joshua No, indeed, ought she not.

Mr. Sheridan. —Do *you*, then, Sir Joshua, persuade her.—But perhaps you *have* begun some thing?—may we *ask?*—Will you answer a Question candidly?'

F:B. —I don't know,—but *as* candidly as *Mrs. Candour*[62] I think I certainly shall!

Mr. Sheridan. What, then, are you about now?

F:B. —Why—twirling my Fan, I think!'

Mr. Sheridan. No, no,—but what are you about *at Home?*—however,—it is not a fair Question, so I won't press it.' |

Yet he *looked* very inquisitive; but I was glad to get off without any *downright* answer.

Sir Joshua. *Any* thing in the *Dialogue* way, I think, she *must* succeed in,—& I am sure *invention* will not be wanting,—

Mr. Sheridan No, indeed;—I think, & say, she should write a *Comedy.*

Lord, Susy, I could not believe my own Ears! *This* from Mr. *Sheridan!*

Sir Joshua. I am sure *I* think so; & I hope she *will.*

I could only answer by *incredulous* exclamations.

'Consider, continued Sir Joshua, you have already had all the applause & fame you *can* have given you in the *Clozet,*—but the Acclamation of a *Theatre* will be *new* to you.'

And then he put down his Trumpet, & began a violent clapping of his Hands.

I actually shook from Head to foot! I felt myself already in Drury Lane, amidst the *Hub bub* of a first Night.

'O no! cried I, there *may* be a *Noise,*—but it will be just the *reverse,*—' And I returned his salute with a Hissing.

[62] Sheridan's character in *The School for Scandal.*

Mr. Sheridan joined Sir Joshua very warmly.

'O Sir! cried I, *you* should not run on so,—you don't know what mischief you may do!

Mr. Sheridan. I wish I *may*,—I shall be very glad to be accessory.

Sir Joshua. She has, certainly, something of a knack at Characters;—*where* she got it, I don't know,—& *how* she got it, I can't imagine,—but she certainly *has* it. And to throw it away is— — —

Mr. Sheridan. O she *won't*,—she will write a Comedy,—she has promised me she will!

F:B. O Good God!—if you both run on in this manner, I shall— — —

I was going to say *get under the Chair*, but Mr. Sheridan, interrupting me with a Laugh, said 'Set about one?—very well, that's right!'

'Ay, cried Sir Joshua, that's *very* right.—And *you*, (to Mr. Sheridan,) would *take* any thing of *Her's*,—would you not?—*Unsight unseen?*'

What a *point blank* Question! Who but Sir Joshua would have ventured it!

'*Yes*; answered Mr. Sheridan, with quickness,—& make her a Bow & my best Thanks into the Bargain!'

Now, my dear Susy, tell me, did you ever hear the *fellow* to such a speech as this!—it was all I could do to sit it.

'Good God, Mr. Sheridan, I exclaimed, are you not mocking me?'

'No, upon my Honour! this is what I have *meditated* to say to you the first Time I should·have the pleasure of seeing you.'

To be sure, as Mrs. Thrale says, if folks *are* to be spoilt,—there is nothing in the World so *pleasant* as spoiling![63] But I *never* was so much Astonished, & *seldom* have been so much delighted as by this attack of Mr. Sheridan. Afterwards he took my Father aside, & formally repeated his opinion that I should write for the stage, & his desire to see my Play,—with encomiums the most flattering of Evelina.

---

[63] See above, p. 154.

Consider Mr. Sheridan, as an *Author* & a *manager*,[64] &
really this conduct appears to me at once generous [xxxxx
1 word] & uncommon. As an *Author*, & one so high, & *now*
in his first Eclat, to be so lavish of his praise—is it not
[*rare*]?[65] As a *manager*, who must, of course, be *loaded* with
Pieces & recommendations, to *urge* me to write, & to
promise to *thank* me for my Writing, instead of making a
favour & a difficulty of even *looking* at it,—is it not truly
good-natured & liberal-minded?

And now, my dear Susy,—if I *should* attempt the stage,—
I think I may be fairly acquitted of presumption, &
however I may fail,—that I was strongly pressed to *try* by
Mrs. Thrale,—& by Mr. Sheridan,—the most successful
& powerful of all Dramatic living Authors,—will abun-
dantly excuse my temerity.

In short,—this Evening seems to have been *decisive*, my
many & encreasing scruples *all* give way to encouragement
so warm from so experienced a Judge, who is | himself
interested in not making such a request *par pure complai-
sance*.

Some Time after, Sir Joshua beckoned to Dr. Warton
to approach us, & said 'Give me leave, Miss Burney, to
introduce Dr. Warton to you.'

Not *me* to him!—We both made our reverences. & then
Sir Joshua,—who was now quite *facetious*, said, Laughing,
'Come, Dr. Warton, now give Miss Burney your opinion
of—*some thing*,—tell her what is your Opinion of—a certain Book.'

This was very provoking of Sir Joshua,—& Dr. Warton
seemed as much embarrassed as myself,—but, after a little
hesitation, very politely said 'I have no *opinion* to give,—I
can only join in the Voice of the *Public*.'

Sir Joshua is such an Enthusiast upon this subject, that
he seems eager to procure me *Homage* from all ⌐the
World.⌐

I have no more Time nor Room to go on, or I could
write you a *folio* of the Conversation at supper, when

---

[64] Of Drury Lane since 1776.
[65] Substituted by FBA for an unrecovered obliterated word.

every body was in spirits, & a thousand good things were
said: I sat between Sir Joshua & Miss Linley. Mrs. Cholmondeley addressed almost all her *Bon mots* & drolleries
to me,—& was flattering in her distinction to a *degree!*—
yet did not, as at our first meeting, *overpower* me. I like
[*rest of line and letter missing*] |

[*In the run of her journals in the Berg Collection FBA inserts the
following ALS from SC to FB, 19 Jan. 1779, 2 single sheets 4to, 3
pp., paginated 823–5:*]

Extract of a Letter from Gast, Dated Burford Jan. 12
1779

'— — —And am highly pleas'd Fanny is so deservedly
esteem'd, & in such high Vogue. I long to see her 2^d
Journal, but suppose it is not to be ventur'd to take a
Journey to Burford: therefore hope it need not be
return'd till I have read it, at Chesington. Nanny Leigh[66]
writes me there is a Book entitled Evelina, that all Bath
are mad after, said to be written by a Miss Burney,
Daughter to Dr Burney—that she fancies it must be M^r
Crisp's Favourite; & that she enjoys his Pleasure in the
Great Approbation it meets with.—[xxxxx *2 lines*]'

I long of all things, Fannikin, to see *Warley*, & [xxxxx
3 lines] the Continuation of your Journal (for I have
copied & will faithfully return by the first opportunity
your last)—if You answer me, You have not Continued
it, You are unpardonable & I advise You to set about it
immediately, as well as You can, while any traces of it rest
in your Memory—it will one day be the delight of your
old age—it will call back your Youth, your Spirits, your
Pleasures, your Friends, whom You formerly lov'd, & who
lov'd You. (at that time,—alas, probably, long gone off
the Stage) & lastly, when your own Scene is clos'd, remain
a valuable Treasure to those that come after You:—but I
will not *suppose* You have *not* Continued it—You *can't* be

---

[66] Anne ('Nanny') Leigh (*c.*1751–1830), daughter of the Revd Peter Leigh
of Lymm, Cheshire, m. (1780) Capt. John Frodsham (*c.*1737–91), RN. Nanny
Leigh was a cousin of SC and Mrs Gast. See W. H. Hutton, *Burford Papers*
(1905), pp. 15, 43, 52; *JL* i. 36 n. 89; IGI.

so wanting to yourself.—*this* is what I require:—the whole in all it's detail—not bits & Scraps of 3 Characters at a time, as You talk of[67]—that Won't satisfy my *Maw*.—As to your *vexations*, Child, I don't mind it of a Pin—Fram'd as You are, I know that must ⏐ come first, before You could be Easy.—People that are destin'd to live in the midst of the World, must & ought to be innoculated, before they can go about in safety—You talk of being *Slept off the Stage*[68]—Would You wish Your Book to die such a Death? there is no Alternative—if it lives, it's fate & yours are inseparable, & the Names of Evelina & Burney must & will go together, so that your discontent at what has happen'd, to me seems, strangely ill-founded; & your fantastic sickly Stomach is to recoil, forsooth, because You cannot compass impossibilities!

Well—I have been ruminating a good deal on the Obstacles & difficulties I mention'd in my last, that lye directly across *YOUR* Path (as a Prude): in the Walk of Comedy—on the most mature Consideration, I do by no means retract the general Principle that produc'd those observations; I will never allow You to sacrifice a *Grain* of female delicacy, for all the Wit of Congreve & Vanbrugh put together—the purchase would be too dear; but this much I will assert, & can prove by several instances; viz, that light principles may be display'd [xxxxx *1/2 line*] without *light Expressions*: And *that* is the Rock a Female must take Care to steer clear of—Vice must not talk *unlike itself*; but there is no necessity, it should Show all it's filth— a great deal of management & Dexterity will certainly be requisite to preserve, Spirit & Salt, & yet keep up Delicacy—but it *may* be done; & *You*, can do it, if any Body— Not but that [xxxxx *2 lines*]—Do You remember about a Dozen Years ago, how You Used to dance Nancy Dawson on the Grass plot,[69] with Your Cap on the Ground, & your long hair streaming down your Back, one shoe off, & throwing about your head like a mad thing?—now you are to dance Nancy Dawson with Fetters on—there is the

[67] See above, p. 213.
[68] See above, p. 212.
[69] See above, p. 34.

difference yet there is certainly a nameless Grace & Charm
in giving a loose to that Wildness & friskyness sometimes—
[xxxxx *4 lines*] I I am very glad You have secur'd M^rs
Montagu for your Friend—her Weight & Interest are
powerful; but there is one particular I do not relish; tho'
she means it as a mark of Favour & distinction—it is,
where she says—'If Miss Burney *does* write a play; I beg I
may know of it, &, (if she thinks proper) *see* it.'⁷⁰—[xxxxx
1 line] Now, Fanny, this same *seeing it* (in a profess'd
Female Wit, Authoress, & *Maecenas* into the Bargain) I
fear, implies too much *interference*—implies, *advising, cor-
recting, altering*, &c &c &c—not only so, but in so high a
Critic, the not submitting to such grand Authority, might
possibly give a secret, conceal'd lurking offence—Now
d'ye see, as I told You once before, I would have the
whole be *all your own—all of a Piece*—& to tell You the
truth, I would not give a pin for the advice of the ablest
Friend, who would not suffer me at last to follow *my own*
Judgment, without resentment—besides, let me whisper
in your Ear, the very Words Dr Johnson made Use of,
when Miss Streatfield's letter was mentioned—'She is—'
&c &c &c—'but my little B. writes a better Letter.'⁷¹ [xxxxx
6 lines] Adieu, send me a Vast Journal to Copy, containing
a full & true Account of all the Variety of Names you
have given me a List of, & what they have said of, & to
You—[xxxxx *1 line*]—may I send to Gast my Copy of
Your Journal, upon Condition of her letting Nobody see
it but Molly Lenthal?⁷² [xxxxx *1 line*] Shall we see You at
Ches. this summer? or are You to be *at home* at Streatham,

---

⁷⁰ See above, p. 162.
⁷¹ See above, p. 137.
⁷² SC wrote to Mrs Gast, 25 Jan. 1779: 'As to Fanny and her Journals; both
the first and second I have copied; and if I knew how to convey them to you,
I would do it, on Conditions nobody should see them but M. L. I have had a
long letter from her besides [FB to SC *c.*7 Jan. 1779, above, pp. 210–14]; as
she conceals nothing from me; she is not afraid of the imputation of Vanity,
by sending me a list of the first Rate people in the Kingdom, that have paid
such high honours to her Book as are hardly to be equalled' (Hutton,
pp. 25–6).

the whole Season & the old *homely home* quite forgotten?
Once more Adieu. Your loving Daddy, S.C. Ham & Kate
desire to be remembered.

　　Ches. Jany 19. 1779.

74　　　　　　　　　　　　　　　　　　　Streatham
　　　　　　　　　　　　　　　[*c*.16] February [1779]

To Susanna Elizabeth Burney

　　AJL (Diary MSS I, Berg, paginated 881–6, foliated 1–2), Feb. 1779
　　3 single sheets 4to, 6 pp.
　　Annotated (by FBA): Dr. Johnson and Sir Philip Clerke. ✻ ✻
　　FB appears to have gone to Streatham *circa* Tues., 2 Feb. The last
　　leaf is almost entirely blank. This circumstance, coupled with the lack
　　of a customary close or signature, suggests that she broke off abruptly
　　in order to catch the post or to take advantage of someone's return to
　　London.

　　　　　　　　　　　　　　　　　　　　Streatham, Feb.

I have been here so long, my dearest Sukey, without
writing a word, that now I hardly know where or how to
begin. But I will try to draw up a concise account of what
has past for this last fortnight, & then endeavour to be
more minute.

　　Mrs. Thrale & Dr. Johnson vied with each other in the
kindness of their reception of me: Miss Thrale was as
usual at *first*, cold & quiet. Nobody else was here.

　　The next Day Sir Philip Jennings Clerke[73] came. [H]e
is, at least, an *Elderly* man, not at all a man of *Letters*, but
extremely well bred, nay *elegant* in his manners, & sensible
& agreeable in his Conversation. He is a professed *minority*
man, & very active & zealous in the opposition. He has

---

[73] Sir Philip Jennings Clerke (1722–88), Bt, of Duddleston Hall, Salop, and
Lyndhurst, Hants; MP (Namier). He was a political and social crony of Henry
Thrale, and tried to court HLT after Thrale's death. Cf. HLT's character of
him at this time: 'Sir Philip has nothing particular to recommend him but good
plain sense & Manners highly polished ... . there is a total Absence of Literature,
& an Ignorance of common things in that way Which amazes one' (*Thraliana*
i. 372, s.v. 1 Mar. 1779). See below, *passim*; *EJL* iv–vi.

almost lived here lately, as he has some affairs of consequence to settle at Tooting, which is just by. He had,
when I came, a Bill in agitation, concerning *contractors*,—
too long a matter to explain on Paper,—but which was
levelled against Bribery & Corruption in the ministry; &
which he was to make a motion for in the House of
Commons the next Week.[74]

Men of such different principles as Dr. Johnson | & Sir
Philip, *you* may imagine, cannot have much simpathy or
cordiality in their political debates;—however, the *very*
superior abilities of the former, & the remarkable good
breeding of the latter, have kept both upon good terms,
though they have had several arguments, in which each
has exerted his utmost force for conquest.

The *Heads* of *one* of their debates, I must try to
remember, because I should be sorry to forget. Sir Philip
explained his *Bill*,—Dr. Johnson, at first, scoffed it;—Mr.
Thrale, (who was just come Home) Betted a Guinea the
motion would not pass;—& Sir Philip that he should
divide *150* upon it.

I am afraid, my dear Susy, you already tremble at this
political commencement,—but I will soon have done,—for
I know your Taste too well to enlarge upon this Theme.

Sir Philip, addressing himself to *Mrs.* Thrale, hoped
she would not suffer the *Tories* to warp *her* Judgement:—
& told *me* he hoped my Father had not tainted *my*
principles:—& then he further explained his Bill, &,
indeed, made it appear so equitable, that Mrs. Thrale
gave into it, & *wished* her Husband·to vote for it;—he still
hung back;—but, to our general surprise, Dr. Johnson,
having made more particular enquiries into it's merits, |
first *softened* towards it, & then declared it a very rational
& fair Bill, & joined with Mrs. Thrale in soliciting Mr.
Thrale's vote.

[74] On 13 Apr. 1778 Sir Philip had introduced a bill to 'restrain' members of
the House of Commons from 'being concerned' in any government contract
unless the contract 'be made at a public Bidding' (*CJ* xxxvi. 918). In his speech
he said that 'giving these contracts to Members ... did create a dangerous
influence in that House, which must operate much to the injury of the nation'
(Namier). The bill was defeated, but became a favourite Opposition point, and
was reintroduced by Sir Philip on 12 Feb. 1779.

Sir Philip was, & [with]⁷⁵ very good reason, quite delighted. He opened ⌐his⌐ politics more & freely declared his opinions,—which were so strongly against the Government, & so much bordering upon ⌐the⌐ republican principles, that Dr. Johnson took fire;—he called back his recantation,—begged Mr. Thrale *not* to vote for his Bill, & grew very animated against his antagonist.

'The Bill, said he, ought to be opposed by all honest men!—in *itself*, & considered *simply*, it is equitable, & I would forward it;—but when we find what a *Faction* it is to support & encourage, it ought not to be listened to. All men should oppose it, who do not wish well to sedition!'

These, & several other expressions yet more strong, he made use of, & had Sir Philip had less politeness, I believe they would have had a vehement Quarrel. He maintained his Ground, however, with calmness & steadiness, though he had niether argument nor wit at all equal to such an opponent.

Dr. Johnson pursued him with unabating vigour & dexterity,—&, at length,—though he could not convince, he so entirely baffled him, that Sir Philip was self-compelled to be quiet; which, with a very good grace, | he confessed. Dr. Johnson recollecting himself, & thinking, as he owned afterwards, that the dispute grew too serious, with a skill all his own, suddenly & unexpectedly turned it all to Burlesque,—taking Sir Philip by the Hand, ⌐just as they parted for⌐ the Night:—'Sir Philip, said he, you are too liberal a man for the Party to which you belong!—I shall have much pride in the Honour of converting you; for I really believe, if you were not spoilt by bad Company, the spirit of faction would not have possest you. Go then, Sir, to the House;—but make not your motion!—give up your Bill, & surprise the World by turning to the side of Truth & Reason. Rise, Sir, when they least expect you, & address your fellow Patriots to this purpose;—Gentlemen,—I have, for many a weary Day, been deceived & seduced by you;—I have now opened my Eyes,—I see that you are all scoundrels,—the subversion of all government

⁷⁵ Inserted by FBA.

is your aim;—Gentlemen, I will no longer herd among
Rascals in whose infamy my Name & Character must be
included;—I therefore renounce you all, as you deserve
to be renounced.' Then, shaking his Hand he added,
'Go, Sir, go to Bed,—meditate upon this recantation, &
rise in the morning ! a more honest man than you laid
down.'[76] !

75   [Streatham,
                              post 16] February [1779]
To Susanna Elizabeth Burney

AJL (Diary MSS I, Berg, paginated 887–94, foliated 6–9), Feb. 1779
4 single sheets 4to, 8 pp.
Annotated (by FBA): Murphy Streatham 1779
The foliation of this and the preceding item suggests that at least 2
leaves at the beginning of this letter have been destroyed. These leaves
probably contained the 'concise account' promised by FB (see above,
p. 240). As in the case of the preceding letter, this one ends abruptly
with the last leaf almost all blank.

Feb^y

Now, however, I must try to be rather more minute;—
on Thursday [?11 Feb.], while my dear Father was here,
who should be announced but Mr. Murphy.—the man of
all other *strangers* to me whom I most longed to see.
He is Tall & well made, has a very gentlemanlike
appearance, & a *quietness* of manner upon his first address
that, to me, is very pleasing. His Face looks sensible, &
his deportment is perfectly easy & polite.
When he had been welcomed by Mrs. Thrale, & had
gone through the Reception-salutations of Dr. Johnson &
my Father, Mrs. Thrale, advancing to me, said 'But here
is a lady I must introduce to you, Mr. Murphy,—here is
another *F:B.*'—

---

[76] Despite SJ's turnabout, Henry Thrale, though regularly classed as a 'friend'
of government, voted for Clerke's bill (Namier iii. 528). See below, p. 255.

'Indeed? cried he, taking my Hand, is this a sister of Miss Brown's [Frances Browne]?'

'No, no,—this is Miss Burney,—'

'What! cried he, staring, is this—is this—this is not the lady that—that—'

'Yes, but it is,'—answered she, Laughing.

'No?—you don't say so?—you don't mean the lady that—'

'Yes, yes, I do,—no less a lady, I assure you.'

He then said he was very glad of the Honour of seeing me, & I sneaked away.

When we came up stairs, Mrs. Thrale *charged* me to *make myself agreeable* to Mr. Murphy,—'He ¦ may be, of *use* to you, she said,—he knows stage Business so well,—& if you will but take a fancy to one another, he may be more able to serve you than all of us put together. *My* ambition is, that Johnson should write your Prologue, & Murphy your Epilogue;—*then* I shall be quite happy.'

Her Zeal in my "affairs" is really astonishing,—& I think if Mrs. Gast knew her, she would compare her with '*the amiable jumping Susette*,' whose warmth so much delighted her kind Heart.

At Tea Time, when I went into the Library, I found Dr. Johnson Reading, & Mrs. Thrale in close conference with Mr. Murphy.—'It *is* well, Miss Burney, said the latter, that you are come, for we were abusing you most vilely;— we were in the very act of pulling you to pieces.'

'Don't you think her very like her Father?' said Mrs. Thrale.

'Yes;—but what a sad man is Dr. Burney for running away so;—how long had he been here?'

Mrs. Thrale. = O but an Hour or 2. I often say Dr. Burney is the most of a male Coquet of any man I know, for he Only gives one enough of his Company to excite a desire for more.

Mr. Murphy. = Dr. Burney is, indeed, a most extraordinary man,—I think I don't know such another,—he is *at Home* upon *all* subjects,—& upon all so *agreeable*! he is a Wonderful man.

And now,—let me stop this Conversation, to go ¦ back to a similar one with Dr. Johnson, who, a few Days since, when Mrs. Thrale was singing our Father's praise, used this expression 'I love Burney,—my Heart *goes out* to meet him!'

'He is not ungrateful, Sir, cried I,—for most heartily does he love *you*.'

'Does he, Madam?—I am surprised at that.'

'Why, Sir?—Why should you doubt it?'

'Because, Madam, *Dr. Burney* is a man for *all the World* to love: it is but *natural* to love *him*.'

I could almost have cried with delight at this cordial, unlaboured éloge. Another Time, he said 'I much question if there is, in the World, such another man as Dr. Burney.'

But to return to the Tea Table.

'If I,—said Mr. Murphy, looking very archly, had written a certain Book,— — —a Book I won't name,—but a Book I have lately read,—I would *next* write a Comedy.'

'Good God, cried Mrs. Thrale, colouring with pleasure, do *you* think so, too?'

'Yes indeed; I thought so *while* I was reading it,—it struck me repeatedly.'

'Don't look at *me*, Miss Burney, cried Mrs. Thrale, for this is no doing of *mine*. Well, I do wonder what Miss Burney will do 20 years hence, when she can blush no more,—for now, she can never bear the Name of her Book. I

Mr. Murphy. = Nay, I name no Book,—at least no *author*,—how *can* I, for I don't *know* the author,—there is no name given to it; I only say, *whoever* writ that Book, ought to write a Comedy. *Dr. Johnson* might write it for ought I know!'

F.B. = O yes!—

Mr. Murphy. = Nay, I have often told *him* he does not know his own strength, or he would write a Comedy,—& so I think.

Dr. Johnson. = *Laughing*! Suppose Burney & I begin together?—

Mr. Murphy. = Ah, I wish to God you would!—I wish you would Beaumont & Fletcher us!

F:B. = My Father asked me this morning how my *Head* stood,—if he should have asked me this *Evening*, I don't know *what* answer I must have made!

Mr. Murphy. = I have no wish to turn any body's Head,—I speak what I really think;—*Comedy* is the *forte* of that Book,—I Laughed over it most violently;—I lent it to two young ladies, very sensible Girls, of my acquaintance, & they could not go to Bed while it was in reading, *that* seems to me as good a testimony as a Book can have. And if the Author—I won't say *who*.—(all the Time looking *away* from *me*) will write a *Comedy*, I will most readily, & with great pleasure, give any advice or assistance in my power.

'Well, now you are a *sweet* man! cried Mrs. Thrale, who looked ready to *kiss* him,—did not I tell you, Miss Burney, that Mr. Murphy was the man!—'

Mr. Murphy. = All I can do, I shall be very *happy* to do,—&, at least, I will undertake to say I can tell what the sovereigns of the upper Gallery will bear,—for they are the most formidable part of an Audience: I have had so much experience in this sort of Work, that I believe I can always tell what will be *Hissed* at least. And if Miss Burney will write, & will shew me— — —

Dr. Johnson. = Come, come, have done with this, now,—Why should you over power her?—Let's have no more of it. I don't mean to *dissent* from what you say,—I think well of it,—& approve of it,—but you have said *enough* of it.

Mr. Murphy, who equally loves & reverences Dr. Johnson, instantly changed the subject.

Am I not, my Susy, as Mrs. Thrale says, [an *amazing person*][77]—Think but of encouragement like this from so experienced a Judge as Mr. Murphy! how *amazing*, that this idea of a *Comedy* should strike so many! And how very kind is this offer of service!—Were I disposed to decline it, Mrs. Thrale would not suffer me,—Mr. Murphy is among her first favourites, & she has long quite set her Heart upon making him one of *mine*: but she has most

---

[77] Substituted by FBA for an obliterated phrase not recovered.

solemnly assured me she had never *hinted* to him the idea
of a Comedy.[78]

The rest of the Evening was delightful. Mr. Murphy
told abundance of most excellent stories,—Dr. Johnson
was in exceeding good humour, & Mrs. Thrale all chearfulness & sweetness. For *my* part, in spight of her injunctions, I *could not* speak,—I was in a kind of *consternation*;—
Mr. Murphy's speeches, flattering as they were, made me
tremble;—for I cannot get out of my Head the idea of
disgracing so many people!—And, after supper, Dr.
Johnson turned the Discourse upon *silent folks*,—whether
by way of *reflection* & reproof, or by *accident*, I know not,—
but I *do* know he is provoked with me for not talking
more;—& I was afraid he was *seriously* provoked,—but, a
little while ago, I went into the music Room where he was
Tête à Tête with Mrs. Thrale,—& calling me to him, he
took my Hand, & made me sit next him, in a manner that
seemed truly affectionate.

'Sir, cried I, I was much afraid I was going out of your
favour!'

'Why so? What should make you think so?'

'Why—I don't know,—my *silence*, I believe. I began to
fear you would give me up.'

'No, my Darling!—my dear little Burney, no;—when I
give *you* up,—'

'What then, Sir?' cried Mrs. Thrale.

'Why I don't know,—for who ever could give *her* up
would deserve worse than I can say,—I know not *what*
would be bad enough.'

---

[78] Sometime between 10 and 27 Feb. HLT confided to her diary the following
frank passage which contrasts rather interestingly with her public displays of
affection and solicitude for FB: 'Our Miss Burney is big with a Comedy for
next Season; I have not seen the *Ebauche*, but I wish it well: ... [She] is a
graceful looking Girl, but 'tis the Grace of an Actress not a Woman of Fashion—
how should it? (The Burneys are I believe a very low Race of Mortals.) her
Conversation would be more pleasing if She thought less of herself; but her
early Reputation embarrasses her Talk, & clouds her Mind with scruples about
Elegancies which either come uncalled for or will not come at all: I love her
more for her Father's sake than for her own, though her Merit cannot as a
Writer be controverted. The Play will be a good one too I doubt not—She is
a Girl of prodigious Parts—' (*Thraliana* i. 368).

So hitherto, thank Heaven, I have kept my Ground with him.

76   Streatham
                                    [?23] February [1779]
To Susanna Elizabeth Burney

AJL (Diary MSS I, Berg, paginated 895–902, foliated 1–4), Feb. 1779
4 single sheets 4to, 8 pp.
After writing the last letter, FB evidently returned to London and then came back to Streatham with her half-brother Richard Thomas Burney.

Streatham,—Tuesday, Feb^y

On my return hither, my dearest Susy, Mrs. Thrale received Dick with her usual kindness, & in the Evening we went to visit the Pitches. I have nothing new to tell you of that family, neither do I believe I *should* have, were I to visit them once a fortnight for a year:—but I must acquaint you that *another* report is spread, or *said* to be spread, concerning your *much abused* sister.

Miss Thrale, Miss Pitches & myself, after Tea, retired to have some Talk among ourselves,—which, of all things in the World, is most stupid with these sort of misses,—(I mean the P.'s—not Miss Thrale) & we took Dick with us, to make sport. Dick, proud of the office, played the Buffoon extremely well, & our Laughs reaching to the Company Room, We were followed by a Mr. Davis,[79] a

[79] The Revd Reynold Davies (1752–1820), BA (Oxon.), 1773, MA, 1816; Curate of St Leonard's, Streatham and later head of a boys' school there. FB exaggerates his 'half-wittedness', though HLT described him in 1793 as 'no *Extra* ordinary Man'. In 1798 she and her husband Piozzi entrusted to his care the education of Piozzi's nephew John Salusbury Piozzi Salusbury. Davies had instructed the Thrales' son Henry (1767–76) at the Loughborough House School for Boys, 2½ mi. from Streatham; Henry's schoolmate and friend John Thomas Stanley, later Ld. Stanley of Alderley, praised Davies as 'the master to whom I am most indebted for any advantage I gained during the time I was at the school'. See *Thraliana* ii. 853; *Piozzi Letters* i. 367 n. 2; *JL* vii. 122; *The Early Married Life of Maria Josepha Lady Stanley*, ed. J. H. Adeane (1899), pp. 3–4; *TSP*, pp. 128–9.

poor half witted Clergyman. Dick played his Tricks over again, &, mad with spirits, & the applauses of the young ladies, when he had done, he clapt Mr. Davis on the Back, & said 'Come, Sir, now do *you* do something to divert the Ladies.'

'No, Sir, no! I really can't.' answered he.

'What, sir! cried Dick, not if *the Ladies* request ⏐ you? Why then you'll never do for Mr. Smith!—you a'n't half so clever as Mr. Smith;—& I'm *sure* you'll never be a Sir Clement Willoughby!'

Did you ever hear the like? I was forced to turn myself quite away, & poor Mr. Davis was Thunder struck at the Boy's assurance.[80] When he recovered himself, he said to me 'Ma'am this is a very fine young Gentleman;—pray what Book is he in?

'Do you mean at school, Sir?'

'No, I mean what Books does he study at Home *besides* his Grammar?'

'Indeed I don't know; You must examine *him*.'

'No?—don't you know Latin, Ma'am?'

'No, indeed! not at all!'

'Really?—Well, I had heard you did.'

I wonder, my dear Susy, what *next* will be said of me! Yesterday, at Night, I told Dr. Johnson the enquiry, & added that I attributed it to my being at *Streatham*, & supposed the folks took it for granted nobody would be admitted there, without knowing *Latin* at least.

'No, my dear, no, answered he; the man thought it because you have written a Book; he concluded that a *Book* could not be written by one who ⏐ knew no Latin. And it is strange that it *should*, but perhaps you *do* know it,—for your shyness, & slyness, & pretending to know nothing, never took *me* in, whatever you may do with others. *I* always knew you for a *Toadling*!'

At our usual Time of *absconding*, he would not let us go, & was in high good humour;—& when, at last, Mrs.

---

[80] FB's complacency about (indeed, encouragement of) 'Dick's' rude behavior reflects the spoiling he generally received from his family and even friends of the family (including HLT), which no doubt contributed to the recklessness which eventually caused his exile to India (see *EJL* i. 183 n. 4).

Thrale absolutely refused to stay any longer, he took me by the Hand, & said 'Don't *you* mind her, my little Burney,—do *you* stay, whether she will or not.' So away went Mrs. Thrale, & left us to a Tête à Tête.

Now I had been considering that perhaps I *ought* to speak to him of my [new *Castle*,— — —][81] lest, hereafter, he should suspect that I *preferred* the counsel of Mr. Murphy: I therefore determined to take this opportunity, &, after some general nothings, I asked if he would permit me to take a great liberty with him? He assented with the most encouraging smile. And then, I said 'I believe, Sir, you heard part of what passed between Mr. Murphy & me the other Evening, concerning—a—a comedy,— now,—if I *should* make such an attempt,—would you be so good as to allow me,—any Time before Michaelmas, to put it in the Coach for you to look over as you go to Town?' | 'To be sure, my dear!—What, have you begun a Comedy, then?'

I told him how the affair stood.[82] He then gave me advice which just accorded with my wishes,—viz—not to make known that I had any such intention;—to keep my own Counsel,—not to *whisper* even the *Name* of it ⌐to my *Bedfellow*⌐,—to raise no expectations ⌐of it,⌐ which were *always* prejudicial, &, finally to have it *performed* while the Town knew nothing of whose it was.

I readily assured him of my hearty concurrence in his opinion; but he somewhat distressed me, when I told him that Mr. Murphy *must* be in my confidence, as he had *offered* his services, by desiring *he* might be the *last* to see it.

What I shall do, I know not, for he has, himself, begged to be the *first*. Mrs. Thrale, however, shall guide me between them. He spoke highly of Mr. Murphy, too, for he really loves him. He said he would not have it in the Coach, but that *I* should read it to him;—however, I could sooner drown or hang!—When I would have offered

---

[81] Substituted by FBA for an obliterated phrase not recovered.

[82] FB had already begun at least the '*Plan*' of a comedy (see below, p. 252), and may have been mulling it over as early as the preceding Aug. (see above, p. 110).

some apology for the attempt, he stopt me, & desired I would never make any, 'For, said he, if it succeeds, it makes it's *own* apology, if not,—' 'If *not*, quoth I,—I cannot do worse ¦ than Dr. Goldsmith, when *his* play failed,—*go home & Cry*!'[83]

He Laughed,—but told me, repeatedly, (I mean *twice*, which, for him, is very remarkable,) that I might depend upon all the service in his power; & has added it would be well to make Murphy the last Judge 'for *he* knows the stage, he said, & I am quite ignorant of it.' And afterwards, grasping my Hand, with the most affectionate warmth he said 'I *wish* you success! I *wish* you well! my dear little Burney!'

Indeed I am *sure* he does.

When, at length, I told him I could stay no longer, & bid him good Night, he said '*There is none like you*, my dear little Burney! *There is none like you!*—good night, my darling!'

You, my dearest Susy, who *know* so well how proud I am of his kindness, will, for that reason, think it not ill bestowed: but I very often, & very unaffectedly, wonder at it myself.

Yesterday morning Miss Brown made a visit here. Mrs. Thrale, unluckily, was gone to Town. But I am become quite intimate with her. She is a most good humoured, frank, unaffected, sociable Girl, & I like her very much. She ¦ stayed, I believe, 3 Hours. We had much talk of Mr. Murphy, whom she adores, & whose avowed preference of her to Miss Streatfield has quite won her Heart. We also talked much of Dr. Johnson, & she confessed to me that both she & Miss S. were in *fevers* in his presence,

[83] During the premiere performance of Goldsmith's *The Good Natured Man* (at Covent Garden on 29 Jan. 1768), the bailiffs' scene at the start of Act III was hissed by the audience. After the play Goldsmith joined members of the Club at the Turk's Head for a party in his honour. Convinced that the play was a failure, he burst into tears when alone with SJ after the others had left, and swore that he would never write again. Goldsmith astounded SJ by relating the story himself at the Chaplains' Table at St James's Palace 2 years later, where he and SJ were guests. HLT recorded the anecdote in *Thraliana* i. 83, s.v. June 1777, and later in her *Anecdotes of the Late Samuel Johnson* (1786) (ed. A. Sherbo (1974), p. 141). See also R. M. Wardle, *Oliver Goldsmith* (Lawrence, 1957), pp. 181–2.

from apprehensions. 'But, said she, a Lady of my acquaintance asked me, some Time ago, if I knew *you*;—& said no, for, then, I had not had the Honour of seeing you; well, said she, but I hear Dr. Johnson is quite devoted to her; they say that he is grown quite *polite*, & waits upon her, & gets her her Chair, & her Tea,—& pays her Compliments from morning to Night! Lord, I was quite glad to hear it,—for we agreed it would quite *Harmonize* him.'

It is well he did not take a *disgust* to me, for, if he had, *that*, too, would have spread abroad.

Miss Brown was excessively civil,—she regretted my not being of the Christmas party several Times, & said that she had *long* fancied herself acquainted with me, 'for, she continued, you have given me so much pleasure, & so many Hours entertainment, that I could not but *think* I knew you very well.' & much more to the ' same purpose.—

But I forgot to mention that, when I told Dr. Johnson Mr. Murphy's kind offer of examining my *Plan*, & of the several *rules* he gave me,—& owned that I had already gone too far to avail myself of his obliging intention,—he said 'Never mind, my dear,—ah! *you'll* do without, *you* want no rules!'

Tuesday night.—

3 Lines I must write ere I go to Bed,—to tell something that will make my Susan stare & start,—but not storm nor scold,—know then,—

That this Night,—*I* WON 1ˢ6ᵈ at Back gammon!—in a *pool* with Mrs. Thrale & Sir Philip Jennings Clerke!—

N.B. the first money I ever won in my Life. I think I shall Dedicate it towards raising a Temple to Fortune. '

77 [Streatham,
post 26 February 1779]
To Susanna Elizabeth Burney

AJL fragment (Diary MSS I, Berg), Feb. 1779
Single sheet 4to, 2 pp.
Both the beginning and end of the letter are missing. The remaining leaf has been cut in 2. The recto of the bottom cutting was originally pasted onto p. 901 (fo. 4) of the preceding letter, and the verso of the top cutting on p. 902 (which is blank).

[Mrs. Thrale has told me that, as soon as I left the][84] Drawing Room, they asked who I was;—& when they heard, Lady Westcoat[85] said. 'Why I was shewn another Lady at the Carmen Seculare,[86] who they told me was the Authoress of Evelina,—she was very young, & one of the prettiest Girls I ever saw.'

'Ay, said Mrs. Thrale, that was Charlotte Burney, *my* Miss Burney is not the *Beauty* of the Family.'

'But, said Lord Westcoat, she has done enough to make Beauty dispensed with.

'Lord, said Miss Lyttleton,[87] 'was that the Lady *that did* Evelina?—'

This was all Miss Lyttleton said during her visit,—she spoke *well*, you find, though not *much*!

84 Inserted by FBA at the top of the leaf; presumably copied from the end of the preceding leaf, which is missing and was probably destroyed by her.

85 Caroline née Bristow (*c*.1746–1809), who m. (1774, as his 2nd wife) William Henry Lyttelton (1724–1808), cr. (1776) B. Westcote (Ire.) and (1794) B. Lyttelton (UK). Ld. Westcote was at this time MP for Bewdley and a Ld. of the Treasury. A long-time friend of Thrale, he had accompanied him on the Grand Tour after the two left Oxford, and his portrait hung in the Streatham library (Clifford, pp. 35, 157).

86 The performance of a musical setting by François-André Danican Philidor of the *Carmen saeculare* of Horace (his major choral work, as it would prove), at the Freemasons' Hall, Great Queen Street, near Lincoln's Inn Fields. The first concert took place on 26 Feb., and the performance was repeated on 5 and 12 Mar. (*Public Advertiser* 26 Feb., 4 Mar., 12 Mar. 1779; see also *New Grove*).

87 Hester Lyttelton (1762–85), daughter of Ld. Westcote by his 1st wife Mary née Macartney (d. 1765). She m. (1783) Richard Colt Hoare (1758–1838), 2nd Bt (1787), of Stourhead, Wilts.

Mrs. Thrale sent to ask me to join them,—& when I came, I might have guessed what had past, by the curious looks, & simpering of Miss Lyttleton.

Before they went, Miss Streatfield came. Mrs. Thrale prevailed upon her to stay till the next Day.

I find her a very amiable Girl, & extremely handsome: not so *wise* as I expected, but *very well*: however, had she *not* chanced to have so uncommon an Education with respect to Literature, I believe she would not have made her way *among the Wits* by the force of her Natural parts.

Mr. Seward, You know, told me that she had *Tears at command*,—& I begin to think so too, for when Mrs. Thrale, who had previously told me I should see her Cry, began coaxing her to stay, & saying 'If you go, I shall know you don't love me so well as Lady Gresham,[88]—' she *did* cry,—not *loud*, indeed, nor *much*, but the Tears came into her Eyes, & rolled down her fine Cheeks.

'Come hither, Miss Burney, cried Mrs. Thrale, come & see Miss Streatfield cry!'

I thought it a mere *badinage*, so went to them,—but When I saw real Tears, I was shocked, & saying 'No, I won't look at her,' ran away, frightened lest she should think I Laughed at her,—which Mrs. Thrale did so openly, that, as I told her, had she served *me* so, I should have been affronted with her ever after.[89]

Miss Streatfield, however, whether from a sweetness not to be ruffled, or from not perceiving there was any room for taking offence, gently wiped her Eyes, & was perfectly composed.

Very strange!—

---

[88] Henrietta Maria née Clayton (1737–1804), m. (1765) Sir John Gresham (1735–1801), 6th Bt, of Titsey, Surrey (IGI). She was probably an object of general contempt amongst HLT's circle, ranking dead last in HLT's assessment of the character and accomplishments of 44 of her female friends and acquaintances (*Thraliana* i. 330–31). HLT gives Lady Gresham 10 points (on a scale of 0 to 20) for 'Good humour', but 0 for 'Conversation Powers', 'Person Mien & Manner', and 'Ornamental Knowlege'.

[89] HLT's open ridicule of Sophy Streatfeild no doubt reflects her resentment over Mr Thrale's having fallen in love with her (see above, p. 224 n. 42).

Now, Madam, for a little touch of politics: You start,—
but don't be frightened,—I shall only give you the marrow
of the matter.

Some Time ago,—Sir Philip Jennings Clerke came to
spend a few Days here,—as he does continually,—& was
in prodigious spirits—for his Bill had passed! he had
divided *more* than 150,[90]—so the wager [xxxxx *1 word*] |

78   Streatham
                              [*pmk* 11 March 1779]
To Samuel Crisp

ALS fragment (Diary MSS I, Berg, paginated 905–6), Mar. 1779
Single sheet 4to, 2 pp. *pmk* 11 MA red wafer
Addressed: S: Crisp Esqr, | at Mrs. Hamilton's, | Chesington, | near
Kingston | Surry.
Annotated (by FBA): Delightful Early intercourse with Dr. Johnson
and Mrs. Thrale. March 1779 Nº 3. ✵· ✵· × ✖
The beginning of the letter is missing.

[xxxxx *2 lines*]
The kindness & honours I meet with from this
charming Family are greater than I can mention,—sweet
Mrs. Thrale hardly suffers me to leave her, & Dr. Johnson
is another Daddy Crisp to me, for he has a partial
goodness ⌜to me⌝ that has made him sink the shortness
of our acquaintance, & treat & think of me as one who
had long laid claim to him.

If you knew these two *you* would love them, or I don't
know you so well as I think I do: Dr. Johnson [has][91]
more *fun*, & comical humour, & Laughable & [*tear in MS*]

[90] Sir Philip's bill about government contractors had been 'brought in' again
on 12 Feb. by a vote of 158 to 143, thus winning for Sir Philip the wager he
had made against Henry Thrale (see above, p. 241). It was, however, defeated
again on 11 March, on a motion to commit the bill to a Committee of the whole
House. The bill did not finally pass into law until 1782, upon the replacement
of the North ministry by the second Rockingham administration. See *CJ* xxxvii.
140, 219; *EJL* v.
[91] Inserted by FBA for a tear in the paper.

nonsense about him, than almost any body I ever saw: I
mean, ⌜though,⌝ when with those he likes; for otherwise,
he can be as severe & as bitter as Report relates of him.
Mrs. Thrale has all that gaity of disposition, & lightness
of Heart, which commonly belongs to 15. We are, therefore, *merry enough*, & I am frequently seized with the same
tittering & ridiculous fits as those with which I have so
often amazed & amused poor Kitty. | One thing let me
not omit of this charming Woman, which I believe will
weigh with you in her favour,—her *political Doctrine* is so
exactly like yours, that it is never started, but I exclaim
'dear Ma'am,—if my Daddy Crisp was here, I believe,
between you, you would croak me mad!—' And this
sympathy of *horrible foresight*[92] not a little contributes to
incline her to believe the *other parts of speech* with which I
regale her concerning you.—She wishes very much to
know you,—& I am sure you would *hit it off* comfortably,—
but I told her what a vile taste you had for shunning all
new acquaintance, & shirking *almost* all your old ones.—
that *I* may never be among the latter, heartily hopes my
dear Daddy's

ever affectionate & obliged F:B.
at Hen. Thrale's. Streatham, Surry.
a modest hint!—

Best Love to Mrs. Ham & dear Kitty. |

---

[92] SC shared HLT's grim forebodings about Britain's future. The year before
she had written, regarding the ineptness of the King and his ministers: 'See
him now ... Despised at home, ridiculed abroad; insulted by the French,
uncertain of Protection or Assistance from the English; his Colonies revolted
& declared Independent by foreign Powers; his own Subjects on the point of
Rebellion even in his Capital, his Navy out of Repair, his Army in Disgrace,
Public Credit a Jest, and a National Bankruptcy talked on as necessary, &
expected as irresistible' (*Thraliana* i. 241, s.v. 7 Mar. 1778; see also ibid. i. 391,
394–5). About SC, SEB later wrote to FB that he 'spends his life in perpetual
apprehension of terrible National Calamities' (Barrett, printed *ED* ii. 262).

79

Streatham,
[26] March [1779]

To Susanna Elizabeth Burney

AL incomplete (Barrett), Mar. 1779
Double sheet 4to, 4 pp.

Streatham, March
25th [*sic*]
Friday.

I thank you heartily, my dearest Girl, for your Journal,[93] &, in hopes you will continue it, I will try to collect a few scraps of anecdotes to send you in return.

Thursday [18 Mar.], after my Father left us, we spent the Day quite by ourselves, *cioè*[94] Mrs. & Miss Thrale & Ladies, your slave.—But why do I attempt *methodising* affairs, when I have Time to write so little?—I must dispense with that ceremony, & only mention the principal occurrences I can recollect.

Mr. Thrale & Sir Philip Jennings Clerke came hither last Saturday morning [20 Mar.], to stay till Monday [22 Mar.]. I keep immensely well with Sir Philip, as I hear from Mrs. Thrale, & he is so much concerned about my Cough, & my *starving system* as you *can't think*. Dr. Johnson came to Dinner, & to make the same stay with us.—& the first question he asked me was *when he should bring Mr. Mence*[95] *to see us again?*

---

[93] Missing.

[94] 'that is' (Ital.).

[95] Perhaps Samuel Mence (*c.*1743–86), son of Benjamin Mence of Worcester City; singer in the Chapel Royal, St James's Palace, and a lay vicar in Lichfield Cathedral. The conjunction of Worcester, Lichfield, and his being a singer suggest the possibility; no other mention of a '*Mr. Mence*' has been found in connection with the Burneys, the Thrales, or SJ and his circle (Highfill; *GM* lvi¹ (1786), 267; IGI).

A Mr. Berresford,[96] also, Dined here. He is a Young Clergyman who is Tutor to the Duke of Bedford, a very forward, bold, shallow, conceited young [Man.] ǀ And, that our party might be large enough, Mrs. Pitches & her 3 Eldest Daughters, & Mr. Embry, came to Tea.

When Cards were produced, Mr. Berresford came up to me, with a smile of ineffable complacency, said 'I hope, Ma'am, *You* never play at Cards?'

'I don't know why you *hope* it, quoth I, but I never do.'

'*Why*, Ma'am, I can't so well tell you,—but I was *sure* you did not,—I saw it in your Face,—indeed it would be scandalous that you should.'

And then he began talking about our Cousin Richard, who he knows very well, & admires *beyond expression*, & of the Barborne Family in general. & soon, to more common topics, interspersing all his speeches with complimentary hints that acquainted me he knew more of me than I did of him.

He endeavoured to draw out Dr. Johnson, but he got a *blow or two*, & then was fain to desist, declaring that the Dr. was *very unsociable*.[97]

Some Time after, this dear Doctor came to the back of my Chair; & I told him I hoped he was better than when I saw him last?—'Ah, cried he, you hope no such thing,— you hope nothing about the ǀ matter,—but have you seen the Print I have brought you?' 'No, where is it?—' 'In the

[96] The Revd Benjamin Beresford (*c*.1750–1819), son of James Beresford of Bewdley, Worcs. In 1772 he matriculated at St Mary Hall, Oxon., but did not take a degree. He subsequently became private tutor to Ld. Francis Russell (1765–1802), 5th D. of Bedford, 1771, who provided him with 2 livings at Bedford. In Nov. 1780 he created a sizeable scandal by eloping to Gretna Green with an Irish heiress, Sidney Hamilton (*c*.1766–1827). He later settled on the Continent, and was successively English tutor to Queen Louise of Prussia (1796), instructor of English at the Univ. of Dorpat (1803–6), British Chaplain at Moscow (*c*.1806–15), and instructor then professor of English at the Univ. of Berlin (1815–19). In 1801 he was awarded a Ph.D. by the Univ. of Halle for his translations of German songs into English, and because of these translations he has been called a 'pioneer literary intermediary between Germany and England' (P. A. Shelley, 'Benjamin Beresford, Literary Ambassador,' *PMLA* li (1936), 476 and *seq*.; see also *YW* xxxiii. 363–4 and nn. 36–40).

[97] Boswell reports Beresford as having dined with him and SJ at Edward Dilly, the bookseller's, on 15 Apr. 1778 (*Life* iii. 284; *Boswell in Extremes 1776–1778*, ed. C. McC. Weis and F. A. Pottle (New York, 1970), p. 282).

Library.' Up I *hoisted*, to make for it,—& Dr. Johnson, taking one of the Candles, said 'I'll light you.' & followed me.—To be sure the Pitches did not giggle,—nor Mr. Berresford stare,—& to be sure Sir Philip will never again be jocose about my sweet heart!

The Print is as like him as it can look,—& I am sure I shall ever value it among things most precious to me.[98]

When I had received & thanked him for it, he would not let me return to the Company, but desired me to stay where I was,—& so, most sociably, we seated ourselves to a very comfortable Tete à Tete, & talked over matters, things & Persons without *reserve or favour*.—& we stayed together till the Ladies & Mr. Berresford departed, & the rest of the Party came to Supper. [*4 lines cut away at bottom of page*]

My dear love a thousand thanks for your noble pacquet,—I will write more by the post, but now have not Time to add another word. Pray continue writing to me as you can; it makes me very comfortable to hear how you all go on: my Love to Charlotte, & tell her if she does not speedily send me a Letter, all the folks here will think her very *unnatural*, & suppose *she* is quite out of the scrape.[99] O—& let me beg, my dear Susy, that you w^d not *Page* your Journal till I return it you, for if *34b* should accidentally be spied, it would occasion very awkward questions.[1]

---

[98] The print given by SJ to FB is probably the line engraving executed by John Hall (1739–97) and published 1 Feb. 1779 by Thomas Cadell. This engraving, after the Reynolds portrait which SJ announced to HLT as 'finished' in Oct. 1778 and which from 1781 hung in the Streatham library, served as the frontispiece to the 9th edn. of *The Rambler* (1779). The Reynolds portrait, universally praised for its likeness to SJ, is now in the Tate Gallery. FBA's will contains no mention of the Johnson print, and the present whereabouts of her copy is not known. See the illustration and *Life* iv. 450–1, 460.

[99] No letters survive between Charlotte Burney and FB before 1780. 'Scrape' suggests some kind of altercation in the Burney home, probably between the Burney children and their stepmother.

[1] Probably from their stepmother. This sentence seems to suggest that SEB had interpolated a page not meant for EAB's eyes.

SAMUEL JOHNSON L.L.D.

5. Samuel Johnson. From a portrait by Sir Joshua Reynolds engraved by John Hall. Used as the frontispiece to the 9th edition of *The Rambler*, 1779.

Miss Thrale will be much obliged to you for the Notes to the Feather Song,[2] if you have them,—I think that Tenducci[3] gave them to you.

Adieu my dear Love: remember me to every body with proper propriety.

[*bottom of page cut away; end of letter missing*] |

[*On 28 Mar. SC wrote to Mrs Gast: 'As to Fanny Burney, she now in a manner lives at Streatham; and when she was, not long ago, at home for a week* [*c.*11–18 Mar.], *Mrs. Thrale wrote to her to come home* [the letter is missing]. *As you say, she is so taken up with these fine Folks, I imagine we shall see but little of her now. She is become so much the fashion, is so carried about, so fetéd from one fine house to another, that if she wished it, it is now really almost out of her power to see her old Friends, as she us'd to do. When I foretold her in my last letter* [missing], *that I expected this would be the Case, she disavow'd the thought* [perhaps in the missing start of the letter to SC, *pmk* 11 Mar.], *and said if the gain of new friends were to deprive her of the old ones, she should regret the Exchanges. I know Dr. Johnson, Mrs. Thrale, Mrs. Montagu and some of the Wits are driving hard at her to write a Comedy; and by a Hint from Hetty* (which must be a profound Secret to M[olly]. L[enthall]. *and all the World*) *I have reason to think she is actually at Work. Mrs. Montagu holds a grand house-warming and Festival on Easter Sunday* (or Monday rather [5 Apr.], *for she is a mighty good Woman*) *at her magnificent new-built house, which is then to be open'd for the first time for the Reception of Company. All the Wits and Genius's in London are invited, and Fanny among the rest, together with the Thrales and Dr. Johnson. I imagine she reserves an intended letter to me till that is over, when perhaps she may give me some account of it, tho' possibly I may flatter myself in vain, considering the Changes occasion'd by Change of Circumstance and Station; but Hetty told me she intended writing soon. However, I have not heard from her a long while; but Basta, things must be as they may, as ancient Pistol says'* (W. H. Hutton, Burford Papers (*1905*), *p. 29*).]

<hr>

[2] Presumably the anonymous piece, *The Feathers. A Favorite Masquerade Song*, published as a single sheet folio by Peter Hodgson, who was active in London from *c.*1776 to 1781 (*BUCEM*; Maxted).

[3] Giusto Ferdinando Tenducci (*c.*1735–90), Italian castrato soprano and composer (*New Grove*). He first came to London in 1758, and his acquaintance with the Burneys probably dated from 1760, when he sang in a concert in London featuring precocious young instrumentalists, one of whom was the 10-year-old EB, who played the harpsichord (Scholes i. 98).

80

To Samuel Crisp

AL incomplete (Diary MSS I, Berg, paginated 907–10), May 1779
2 single sheets 4to, 4 pp.
Annotated (by FBA): ✳· ✖ N*o* 6. confidential avowal of having written
a play, intended for Representation and requested by the Manager—
Mr Sheridan.—

Streatham,
May 4th

Oh! my dear Daddy—
Ah!—alas!—woe is me!—
In what terms may I venture to approach You?—I don't
know,—but the more I think of it, the more guilty I
feel.—I have a great mind, instead of tormenting *you* with
apologies, & worrying *myself* with devising them, to tell
you the plain, honest, literal Truth,—indeed, I have no
other way any *chance* of obtaining your forgiveness for
my long silence. Honestly, then, my Time has, ever since
the receipt of your last most excellent Letter,[4] been not
merely *occupied*, but *burthened* with much employment,—I
have Lived almost wholly at Streatham, & the little Time
I have spent at Home, has been divided between indis-
pensable Engagements, & *preparations* for returning
hither: but you will say there is no occasion to exert much
honesty in owning this much,—therefore now to the secret
of the disposal of my *private* Hours,—the long & the short
is,—I have devoted them to writing;—& I have finished a
Play.— | I must entreat you, my dearest Daddy, to keep
this communication to yourself; or, at least, if you own it
to Kitty, whose long friendship for me I am sure deserves

---

[4] Missing. SC had complained about FB to Mrs Gast in a letter of 9 Apr.
1779: 'I have not yet heard from her, and now begin not to expect it' (Hutton,
p. 31).

my confidence,—make her ⌐swear¬ not to reveal it to *any body* whatsoever.

This is no capricious request, as I will explain,—my own secret inclination leads me forcibly & involunt[arily] to desire concealment,—but that is not *all*,—for Dr. Johnson himself *enjoins* it,—he says that nothing can do so much mischief to a Dramatic Work as *previous expectation*; & that my wisest way will be to endeavour to have it *performed* before it is known, except to the managers, to be written.

Advice that so much corroborates with my wishes, you may easily imagine I readily promised to follow. I shall, therefore, make niether more nor fewer Confidents than my *own* Family, *this* Family, & *Yours*,—in which I will include Mrs. Gast, whose kindness I am too proud of to forfeit ⌐it¬ by reserve or distrust.[5]

Now though I dare not hope my confession has made my peace with You, yet I feel inwardly easier | for having got thus far,—for, in strictest truth, my Heart has long smote me for not thanking you for your last Letter.

I am extremely sorry you decline my 3 characters at a Time,[6] as I have nothing better to offer you. Journal I have kept none,—nor had any Time for such sort of Writing. In my absences from Susan, I have, indeed, occasionally made *essays* in that style,—but they are very imperfect, uncertain, & abrupt. However, such sketches as *she* has had, I will borrow of her for *you*,—if, after all my transgressions, you are not sick both of me & my affairs.

The Paragraph you saw in the papers concerning a *Lady's first attempt in the Dramatic walk*, meant a Miss

---

[5] SC wrote to Mrs Gast, 7 May 1779: 'Fanny (but *Mum*) has actually finished a Comedy, which I suppose will come out next Winter' (Hutton, p. 34). In a later letter, undated, he tells Mrs Gast that FB 'always remembers you; and in her Caution about Secrecy, she excepts you and says she is too proud of your Favor and Affection to desire you should be treated with reserve by her— there's a girl for you!' (ibid., p. 37).

[6] See above, p. 238.

Richardson, of Tower Hill, who has just brought out a play called the Double Deception.[7]

I wish with all my Heart it was in my power to take a Trip to Chesington for a few Days,—I have so *many* things I long to talk over, & I wish so sincerely to see you again.—The *homely-Home*, as you call it,[8] will *never* be forgotten while I keep aloof from my *last Home*. |

But I forgot to mention, that another, & a very great reason for *secresy* in regard to my new attempt, is what you have yourself mentioned—avoiding the interference of the various Macaenas's who would expect to be consulted,—of these, I could not confide in *one*, without disobliging all the rest;—& I could not confide in *all*, without having the play read all over the Town before it is acted. Mrs. Montagu, Mrs. Greville, Mrs. Crewe, Sir Joshua Reynolds, Mrs. Cholmondeley, & many inferior &cs, think they have an *equal* claim, one with the other, to my confidence: & the consequence of it all would be, that, instead of having it, in your words *all my own, & all of a piece*,[9] every body would have a stroke at it, & it would become a mere patchwork of all my acquaintance. The only way to avoid this, is to keep to myself that such a thing exists,—those to whom I have owned it seem all of the same opinion, & I am resolutely determined to own it to no more.

Evelina continues to sell in a most wonderful manner,—a 4th Edition is preparing, with Cuts, designed by Mortimer[10] just before he Died, & executed by Hall & Bartolozzi [xxxxx *1 line*] |

[*rest of letter missing*]

---

[7] *The Double Deception*, by Elizabeth Richardson, daughter of a London tradesman, opened at Drury Lane, 28 Apr. 1779, and ran for 4 nights. The reviewer for the *London Chronicle* (29 Apr. – 1 May 1779, s.v. 30 Apr.) described it as 'the first effort of a lady's dramatic muse.' It was also her last. At the head of an epilogue presumably written by her and printed in the *Town and Country Magazine* xi (May 1779), 269–70, she complained of '*a severe Illness*,' and she died of a consumption the following Oct. (*LS* 5 i. 251, 254, 257, 261, 314, 315; D. E. Baker, I. Reed, and S. Jones, *Biographia Dramatica* (1812), ii. 172).

[8] See above, p. 240.

[9] See above, p. 180.

[10] John Hamilton Mortimer (1740–79), painter and engraver. Mortimer had

81

Streatham
[*pmk* 20] May [1779]

To Samuel Crisp

ALS (Barrett), May 1779
Single sheet folio, 1 p. *pmk* 20 MA FREE
Addressed: To | Sam: Crisp Esqr | at Chessington | near Kingston |
Surry
Annotated (by FBA): ✵· ⊕ 20. May. 1779 This was the *Envellope* of
some Journal Letters to Miss Susan Burney, written at Streatham sent
for Mr Crisp to peruse.
The letter is franked 'H Free Thrale'.

Streatham
[20] May

My dear, dear Daddy!—your last sweet Letter[11] was the
most acceptable I almost ever received in my Life,—your
extreme kindness to me nearly equalled the Joy I had
from hearing you were getting better.[12] I do *long* to see
you most eagerly, & will, with my first power, contrive
it.—Indeed, I have made every body *here* long to see you
too, but I would not for any bribery be as little likely to
have *my* longing gratified as their's is.—Your exculpation
of me was like Yourself, liberal & unsuspicious,[13]—&

died on 4 Feb. The engravings, dated 24 Nov. 1779 in the published edition,
were by John Hall, Francesco Bartolozzi (1727–1815), and 'Walker' (probably
William Walker (1729–93)). The 4th edn., though with the imprint date 1779,
was not actually published until Feb. 1780 (Thieme; IGI; *London Evening Post*
15–17 Feb. 1780, s.v. 17 Feb.; *London Packet* 16–18 Feb. 1780, s.v. 18 Feb.).
Lowndes gave £73 for Mortimer's drawings (*DL* i. 214 n. 1).

[11] SC to FB 15 May 1779 (Barrett).

[12] SC was suffering from weakness, fever, insomnia, gout, and swelling of
the legs and ankles. FB, having heard of his illness by accident at Streatham,
had sent a messenger to Chessington to enquire after his health. SC reassured
her that, though he was still 'very weak', 'this last night has been much better,
& I have had more, & more comfortable refreshing Sleeps, than for Months
past—this is some Encouragement—'. See Hutton, p. 37.

[13] 'I do most entirely acquit You of all Symptoms of neglect—your self
accusations, & exculpations I had long before hand settled with myself—'.
Earlier in the letter SC had praised the goodness of FB's heart, and he wrote
to Mrs Gast: 'With all this sudden Change, her head is not turn'd. She does by
no means forget her Old Friends' (Hutton, p. 37).

indeed, my dear Daddy, my Heart was as unalterably &
gratefully attached to you as it *could* be, & so it must ever
remain,—for, for many, many years, you have been more
dear to me than *any* other person out of my immediate
Family in the whole World:—& this, though I believe I
never was so *gross* before as to say, to *you*, is a notorious
fact to all others,—& Mrs. Thrale is *contented* to come next
you, & to *know* she cannot get above you.—I am half
ashamed of this *un*delicacy,—but your Illness, & kindness
joined put me *off my guard*. However, I hope you will
make no *bad use* of my confession!

I enclose in the beginning of my scrawl to Susan while
she was at Howletts. I have enough for 2 or 3 Franks
more, & will send another in about a week,—but I shall
hope that my friend Kitty will again favour me with a few
Lines in the *Intrum* of intelligence concerning your
Health.[14] My best Love to her & Mrs. Ham.—a[g]ain, my
dearest Daddy,—I hope you will excuse the strange rig
me roll stuff I enclose, which, indeed, is not very well
prepared for inspection,—but it is open & unreserved, &
therefore proper for only kind Eyes.—Kitty may rd. it to
you.—& believe me,

ever & ever yours F.B.

82   Streatham and Brighton, [21–7] May [1779]

To Susanna Elizabeth Burney

AJLS (Berg, Diary MSS I, paginated 911–26, foliated 1–8), May
1779
    8 single sheets 4to, 16 pp. *pmk* 31 MA FREE red seal
Addressed: To | Miss S: Burney | St Martins Street | Leicester Fields |
London
    The journal is franked 'H Free Thrale'.

[14] Kitty Cooke's letters to FB do not survive. FB probably destroyed them
out of kindness to Kitty's memory, since they were no doubt full of semi-literate
oddities. '*Intrum*' presumably reproduces Kitty's spelling (and pronunciation) of
'interim'.

Streatham,
Friday, [21] May

Once more, my dearest Susy, I will attempt Journalising,
& endeavour, according to my promise, to keep up something of the kind during our absence, however brief &
curtailed.

We took up Sir Philip Jennings Clerke at some Coffee
House in our way, & 2 armed men met us at the Picadilly
Turnpike;—& so guarded,[15] we got Here very safe, but
not till past 1 in the morning [20 May]. Sir Philip left us
the next Day at Noon [20 May], but we shall see him
again when we return from Brighthelmstone.

To Day [21 May], while Mrs. Thrale was chatting with
me in my Room, we saw Mr. Murphy drive into the Court
Yard,—down stairs flew Mrs. Thrale but, in a few minutes,
up she flew again, crying 'Mr Murphy is crazy for your
play,—he won't let me rest for it,—do *pray* let me run
away with the 1ˢᵗ Act.—' Little as I like to have it seen in
this unfinished state, she was too urgent to be resisted,—
so off she made with it.

I did not shew my Phiz till I was summoned to Dinner;
Mr. Murphy,—probably out of *flumery*,[16]—made us wait
some minutes, &, when he *did* come, said 'I had much
ado not to keep you all longer, for I could hardly get
away from some new acquaintances I was just making.'

This was *pretty enough*; &, far from *boring* the subject,[17]
he did not any more even hint at it.

---

[15] Against highwaymen, of course. The *Daily Adv.* 19 May 1779 reported
that 'On Monday [17 May] as Mr. Latham was returning from Town to Bexley,
in Kent, where he lives, he was stopped near the Old Half-Way House, on the
Deptford Road, by a Footpad, who on stopping the Carriage, and demanding
Mr. Latham's Money, was by that Gentleman instantly shot dead.' On 8 May,
in London, at night, the Marquess of Granby, returning in his carriage from
the Duke of Rutland's, was stopped by a highwayman who threatened to 'blow
the Marquis's Brains out' if he did not deliver his money. The highwayman
was overpowered by one of the Marquess's footmen, who hustled him off to
Sir John Fielding (ibid. 11 May 1779).

[16] i.e., mere flattery or empty compliment.

[17] i.e., pushing the subject, with perhaps a pun on 'boring' the listeners. The
use of *bore* as a transitive verb in just this sense is not in the *OED*. This sentence
was omitted from the earlier editions, and thus appears here for the first time.

As he could not stay to sleep here, he had only Time, after Dinner, to finish the 1ˢᵗ Act. He was pleased | to commend it very liberally; he has pointed out 2 places where he thinks I might enlarge, but has not criticised one *Word*, on the contrary; the Dialogue he has honoured with high praise.[18]

So far is well,—what may be yet to come I know not. Further particulars I shall write to my dear Padre himself.[19]

O—but—shall I tell you something?—Yes, though you won't care a fig,—but I have had my first Lesson in Latin, [xxxxx *2 words*] Dr. Johnson tutored Miss Thrale while I was with you, & was set off for Litchfield before I came; but Mrs. Thrale attended the Lecture, & has told me every word of it she could recollect: so we must both be ready for him against his return. I heartily wish I rejoiced more sincerely in this *Classical plan*; but the truth is, I have more fear of the malignity which will follow it's being known, than delight in what advantages it may afford. All *my* delight, indeed, is that this great & good man should think me worthy his instructions.[20]

Mr. Berresford, I find, Dined here the Day I spent in Town [19 May]; asked, as usual, much about my Ladyship, &, in particular, whether I should be here the next Day? And, when Mrs. Thrale answered yes, he said 'Then, if you please, Ma'am, I shall be happy to wait upon you.'— 'A degree of Assurance,' said she, in telling this, 'that quite confounded me, so I only said *Sir, your servant!*' |

[18] Presumably the day before HLT had noted in her diary: 'Fanny Burney has read me her new Comedy; nobody else has seen it except her Father, who will not suffer his Partiality to overbiass his Judgment I am sure, and he likes it vastly.—but one has no Guess what will do on a Stage, at least I have none; Murphy must read an Act tomorrow, I wonder what he'll say to't. I like it very well for my own part, though none of the scribbling Ladies have a Right to admire its general Tendency' (*Thraliana* i. 381). To this entry she added the following note: 'Murphy liked it very well, but her confidential friend Mʳ Crisp advised her against bringing it on, for fear of displeasing the female Wits—a formidable Body, & called by those who ridicule them, the *Blue Stocking Club*' (ibid., n. 3). See below, *passim*.

[19] This letter does not survive.

[20] HLT wrote to SJ at Lichfield on 26 May: 'Miss Burney & Hester profess hard Study & steady Secresy ... ' (SJ, *Letters*, ed. R. W. Chapman (Oxford, 1952), ii. 288). See below, pp. 336, 452.

On Thursday [20 May], therefore, his friends the
Pitches, by whom he was originally introduced here, came
to Tea, & he accompanied them. I was up stairs when
they arrived, & stayed till summoned to Tea; when I
entered, he flew to get me a Chair,—but, pretending not
to observe him, I hastened to seat myself at the other end
of the Room,—& this little circumstance evidently
affronted him,—he muttered aloud something that I
would not *allow* him the honour of getting me a *Chair*,—
&, presently, placing himself next the pretty Peggy
Pitches, entered into close conference with her in a low
Voice.

Before the Evening was over, however, he glided, by
degrees, round to a seat between Sophy Pitches & me, &
we had some general conversation upon public places
& performers.

I should not be so extremely shy & distant to a man
who to *me* has said nothing but what might pass for
common gallantry, but that I am watched so much not
only by *this* family, but by all the Pitches, that I can niether
look at, speak to, or hear him, without exciting attention
& observation. And, indeed, I have always thought that
to repay particular partiality with a marked repugnance
is the most impertinent & insolent triumph of which
female Vanity can be guilty. But Mr. Berresford has laid
himself open to ¦ mortifications he has a natural right to
avoid, by his hasty & injudicious professions. He thought,
perhaps, that those who were *my* friends, would rather
promote his cultivating an acquaintance which he publicly
[de]clared might have serious Consequences;—but he
knew not that *their* partiality was so much greater than
his, that they liked not to see even a *possibility* of my being
so disposed of.

Brighthelmstone,
May 26th

I have not had a moment for writing, my dear Susy,
since I came hither, till now,—for we have been perpetually engaged either with *sights* or *Company*,—for notwith-

standing this is not the *season*, here are folks enough to fill up Time from morning to Evening.

The Road from Streatham²¹ hither is beautiful: Mr., Mrs. Miss Thrale, & Miss Susan Thrale & I Travelled in the Coach, with 4 Horses, & 2 of the servants in a chaise, besides two men on Horseback: so we were obliged to stop for some Time at 3 places on the Road.

Rhygate,²² the 1ˢᵗ Town, is a very old, half ruined Borough, in a most neglected condition: a high Hill, leading to it, afforded a very fine Prospect, of the *Malvern* Hill Nature, though inferior.²³ We amused ourselves, while we waited here, at a Bookseller's shop,²⁴ where Mrs. Thrale enquired if they had got the *Book* she had recommended ǀ to them? 'Yes, Ma'am, was the answer; & it's always *out*,—the Ladies like it vastly.'

I suppose I need not tell you what it was?

We went very near Epsom, before we came to this Town, & I made out dear Chesington with my Glass,—I sent off a Pacquet to my Daddy there before I left Streatham, & shall expect & few Lines to know how he goes on very soon.

Crawley,²⁵ our next resting place, offered no *prog—*

²¹ FB and the Thrales travelled to Brighton via the New Road. From Streatham, the distance to Brighton by this route was about 46 mi.

²² Reigate, a municipal borough and market town in Surrey, approximately 13 mi. from Streatham. 'A large number of the older buildings, the rents of which seldom ran to two figures and could have left no margin for repairs, showed evident signs of neglect and it was no doubt these that provoked Miss Burney's disparaging comment' (W. Hooper, *Reigate: Its Story Through the Ages* (Guildford, 1945), p. 154).

²³ Reigate Hill, 1½ mi. N. of the town, is 700 ft. high and commands an extensive view of the Weald. By comparison, the highest of the Malvern Hills, on the border between Worcs and Herefs, reaches an altitude of 1395 ft.

²⁴ Perhaps the shop of Mr Allingham, who took over the bookseller and stationer business of Thomas Pickstone 'at the Bible Opposite the Town Hall in Ryegate', *c.*1776 (H. R. Plomer, G. H. Bushnell, and E. R. McC. Dix, *Dictionary of the Printers and Booksellers ... in England, Scotland and Ireland from 1726 to 1775* (1932), p. 198; trade card of Pickstone, illustrated in Hooper, p. 155).

²⁵ A village in Sussex, 10 mi. S of Reigate. *Prog* means 'food' or 'provisions', but FB may also mean it figuratively as 'food for the mind', in which case her use of the term in this sense would antedate the earliest example in *OED* by 4 years, also from an FB letter (in Apr. 1783). This sentence is previously unpublished.

At Cuckfield,[26] which is in Sussex, & but 14 miles hence, we Dined. It is a clean & pretty Town, & we passed all the Time we *rescued* from Eating in the Church Yard, where I copied 4 Epitaphs in my Tablets,—& you shall have them.

I

Lord, thou hast pointed out my Life
In length much like a span;
My Age was nothing unto thee,
So Vain is every man.

The 2ᵈ was

An indulgent Husband, & Friend sincere,
And a Neighbourly man lies buried here.

The 3ᵈ was upon a Young Wife.

Not 12 months were past after our Wedding Day,
But Death in come, & from a loving Husband
took me away.

The 4ᵗʰ, upon a Young Couple who both died soon after marriage.

Repent in Time, make no delay,
We after each other were soon called away.

So, you see, the Dabler's have not been idle in the noble Town of Cuckfield.

The View of the South Downs from *that* place to *this* is very curious & singular. We got Home by about 9 o'clock [22 May]. Mr. Thrale's House is in West Street,[27] which is the *Court* end of the Town here as well as in London. 'Tis a neat, small House, & I have a snug comfortable Room to myself. The sea is not many Yards from our Windows. Our Journey was delightfully pleasant, the Day

---

[26] A market town in Sussex, 9 mi. S of Crawley and 14 mi. N. of Brighton.

[27] No. 64 West Street, according to E. Cobby, *The Brighthelmston Directory, for 1799* (Brighton, 1799), p. 28, which describes the house as having 2 parlors, 3 best bedrooms, and 6 servants' bedrooms. See also Clifford, p. 81.

being divine, the roads in fine order, the Prospects charming, & every body good humoured & chearful.

We found Sophy Thrale perfectly well, & the whooping Cough entirely gone. The next morning, Whitsunday [23 May], we went to the Brighthelmstone Church,[28]—&, entering, from the Carriage, a Door at the Top of a Hill, I was not a little surprised to find myself already in the Gallery, without ascending one step: but the Church is built by the side of a declivity which is made answer the purpose of stairs. It reminded me of the Houses in Brixham, Devonshire,[29] where they are so built by the sides of Hills, that the Top of them generally leads to a different part of the Town from the bottom: &, in the *upper* streets, they are ǀ entered from the Garrets. We had a sermon preached by Dr. Hinchcliffe,[30] Bishop of Peterborough;—a plain & sensible Discourse.

After Church, Miss Thrale & I proceeded to the Steyn,[31] which is the great public Walk:—the Parade, where the folks stroll, is *pretty enough*; open to the sea at one side, & bounded by high Hills on the other. She then took me to the Cliff, which has the best view of the sea, & sauntered about the Town with me till the heat drove us home.

The Sussex militia, of which the Duke of Richmond[32] is Colonel, is now here. Mr. Fuller,[33] a very intimate young friend of Mr. Thrale, who is Captain of a Company

[28] St Nicholas, the old parish church of Brighton, stands 158 ft. above sea level, almost on the Dyke Road ridge of the South Downs (E. W. Gilbert, *Brighton: Old Ocean's Bauble* (1954), p. 36). On the N. wall (E. end), near what used to be the Thrale pew, is a tablet recording that SJ used to worship there.

[29] See *EJL* i. 281–3.

[30] John Hinchliffe (1731–94); DD (Cantab.), 1764; Bp of Peterborough, 1769–94; Master of Trinity College, Cambridge, 1768–88; Dean of Durham, 1788–94.

[31] The Steine, 'a fine lawn on the Eastern part of the town' (*Universal British Directory* (1791–8), ii. 370).

[32] Charles Lennox (1735–1806), 3rd D. of Richmond; army officer; Field Marshal, 1796. Ld.-Lt. of Sussex since 1763, he became Col. of the Sussex Militia on 2 June 1778 (*ML* 1781, p. 61).

[33] John Fuller (1757–1834), of Rose Hill, Sussex, only son of the Revd Henry Fuller (b. 1712/13), Rector of South Stoneham, Hants; Capt., Sussex Militia, 15 June 1778; MP, 1780–84, 1801–12. HLT describes 'Jack' Fuller, who succeeded to his uncle Rose Fuller's estates at Rose Hill and in Jamaica in 1777, as 'wild, gay, rich, loud' (*Thraliana* i. 480). See Namier; Thorne; IGI; *ML* 1781, p. 61.

belonging to it, Dined ⌐here.⌐ He is a Young man of a very large Fortune, remarkably handsome, having a striking resemblance to Mrs. Crewe, & very gay, sensible, unaffected & agreeable. He is a Cousin to *Rose* Fuller, but, as this account may tell you, carries his relationship merely in his Name.

At Tea we had more Company; Major Holroyd,[34] his Lady, & Miss Firth,[35] who is on a visit at her House. The 1st of these is major of the militia, a very rich Sussex Gentleman, & *agreeable enough*, — | It was *he*, who, you may remember, Mrs. Thrale said told her he had Dined at Sir Joshua Reynold's with the Father of the *celebrated Lady who writ Evelina*, — & congratulated her about *knowing* me. I suppose he gave me a good stare, but as I did not, at the Time, recollect this circumstance, I did not heed him. His Lady is Tall, genteel, rather sensible, but terribly gossiping & full of the scandal of the place. Miss Firth is, in every thing, like her.

They took us to the Parade before Tea, to see the soldiers mustered, a ceremony the officers are obliged to go through every night. We then returned here, & had a chatty & comfortable Evening.

Monday [24 May] was a *Field Day*, & Captain Fuller invited us to Breakfast with him, before we proceeded to the Downs. We did so, — that is, Mrs. & Miss T. & I, for

[34] John Baker Holroyd (1735–1821), of Sheffield Place, in Fletching, Sussex, and Greave Hall, nr. Ferrybridge, Yorks; cr. (1781) B. Sheffield of Dunamore (Ire.), (1783) B. Sheffield of Roscommon (Ire.), (1802) B. Sheffield (UK), and (1816) E. of Sheffield (Ire.). He became a Major of the Sussex Militia on 4 June 1778 (*ML* 1779, p. 58), but later this year resigned his commission in order to raise his own army regiment, the 22nd Dragoons. A close friend of Edward Gibbon, he edited the historian's papers after his death. He m. 1 (1767) Abigail Way (1746–93), daughter of Lewis Way of Richmond, Surrey, and sister of Benjamin Way, MP. See below, p. 448; Namier; IGI.

[35] Miss Ann Firth, nicknamed 'Miss Huff' by the Holroyd family, had been companion to Mrs Holroyd since her marriage to Holroyd in 1767. In 1793 she retired to live at Doncaster, but continued to be the bosom friend of the Holroyds. She was still living in 1829 and survived to 100. She may have been the 'Anne Firth', daughter of Abraham Firth (?1694–1767), who was christened at Huddersfield, Yorks, in 1735; if so, this would date her death *c*.1835. See *The Letters of Edward Gibbon*, ed. J. E. Norton (1956), ii. 9, iii. 293, 413 and *passim*; *GM* xxxvii (1767), 479; IGI; *Letters of Lady Louisa Stuart to Miss Louisa Clinton*, ed. J. A. Home (Edinburgh, 1901–03), ii. 197 and portrait facing i. 356.

Mr. Thrale was not up in Time. Captain Fuller's apartments are on the Steyn, & he had his men all drawn out before the House, & *under arms*, against we came. He is a very pleasing young man, & I like him very much. He gave us *Eggs*, Tea & Chocolate for Break fast: he told us that *Eggs* made the fashionable *officer's Breakfast* at Brighthelmstone, as being *good for the Voice*, which they are obliged to exercise ¦ as much as their persons, in giving *the Word*, & so forth.

After this, Mrs. Holroyd called in her ⌐Coach⌐ to take us to the Downs; where was to be the *shew*. Captain Fuller escorted us on Foot. He belongs to the light Infantry, & was pretty well worked, I believe, with the heat & the exercise before he had done.

To be sure, after the Review I so lately saw at Blackheath,[36] *this* Field Day had nothing very surprising in it: but, alltogether, the morning was pleasant. Major Holroyd, who acted as the General, was extremely polite, & attentive, & came to us between every evolution, to explain & talk over the manoeuvres. Captain Fuller, too, whenever he was at liberty, favoured us with his Company,—so we were very grand, & very military.

On our return, we went to the Major's. His House is on the Steyn, & the best, I believe, in the Town, both for situation & fitting up. After this, Mrs. & Miss Thrale paraded me about the Town, & took me to the principal shops, *to see the World*.

When we came Home, Capt. Fuller called to excuse himself from Dining here, on account of Business with his men. He got into chat, however, & stayed more than [an][37] Hour. He wanted me violently to play to him,—but

---

[36] The windswept common S of Greenwich Park in London. The royal reviews for the summer commenced there on 10 May: 'Yesterday Morning [10 May] their Majesties, accompanied by the Prince of Wales and the Bishop of Osnaburgh, and attended by Lord Amherst, Lord Townshend, and several General Officers, went to Blackheath to see the Review of the four Troops of Horse and Horse-Grenadier Guards, in which they performed their whole Exercise with that Dexterity and Exactness that gave a general Satisfaction' (*Daily Adv.* 11 May 1779; see also *GM* xlix (1779), 267).

[37] Inserted by FBA.

I am less able than ever so to do, as I literally *never* touch a key, lest I should be heard.[38] |

We drank Tea & spent the Evening at Major Holroyd's. They took us to the Parade, to see the *muster*, & there we were joined by Capt. Fuller, who went with us to the Major's. There were, also, 3 other officers, Mr. Lucius Concanno[n],[39] an Irish Lieutenant, a staring, smiling man, of few words; Mr. Godfrey,[40] a very handsome, conceited Youth, & Mr. John Fuller,[41] (another Cousin of the Rosebud,) a heavy, *Sussex Headed* young man.

Captain Fuller was, again, quite vehement with me to play,—& I had great difficulty, indeed, to escape,—he said he would *watch* me the whole Time I remained here, & set *spys* to watch if I was not to be caught, privately, at the Piano Forte; 'And I have 75 servants here, he said, all in my Livery,—' meaning his *Company*, as you probably guess!—Mrs. Holroyd & Miss Thrale both performed,—& then I was assaulted, & re-assaulted, & the Major said he would Head a File of musqueteers against me—upon which, all the Officers arose, & came to me in a body, joining in the Petition,—I tried to *run* for it, but was stopt by a *detachment*,—Mrs. Thrale joined with them, till, taking my Hand, she found I actually *shook*, & then she got me off. [xxxxx *1 line*]

---

[38] For FB's aversion to playing the harpsichord or pianoforte, see also *EJL* i. 188–9, ii. 22–3.

[39] Lucius Concannon (*c.*1764–1823), Irish adventurer; possibly son of Luke Concannon, grocer, of Thomas St., Dublin. He became an ensign in the Sussex Militia on 24 Mar. 1779, and Lt., 4 Apr. 1780. Subsequently an ensign in the 40th Ft and cornet in the 17th Dragoons, he retired from the military on half-pay in 1783. In 1790 he married Sarah Anne Richmond, of St Marylebone, Middlesex, each having posed as wealthy to the other. Quickly undeceived, they moved to Paris and opened a fashionable gaming house there. Later they returned to London and opened another successful gaming house, in Grafton St. Eventually Concannon amassed enough wealth and influence to become an MP (for Appleby, 1818–20, and Winchelsea, 1820–23). See Thorne; *ML* 1780, p. 61; 1782, p. 61.

[40] George Godfrey, commissioned a Lt. in the Sussex Militia, 6 June 1778 (*ML* 1779, p. 58; 1782, p. 61). Not further traced.

[41] John Trayton Fuller (d. 1812), of Ashdown House, Sussex, son of Thomas Fuller (1715–80), London merchant; Lt., Sussex Militia, 11 June 1778, Capt., 2 Oct. 1779. He was actually the elder brother of Rose Fuller (1748–1821), and first cousin of Capt. John Fuller. See W. Berry, *Pedigrees of … Sussex* (1830), p. 279; *ML* 1779, p. 58; 1782, p. 61.

Tuesday [25 May] I accompanied Mrs. & Miss Thrale to Lewes, a Town about 8 miles from Brighthelmstone,[42] where we went to see Mrs. Shelley,[43] a Cousin of Mrs. Thrale. ¦ but found her not at Home. We then proceeded to Dr. Delap,[44] a clergyman, of whom I expect to have more to say in a Day or 2, as he is to visit us, & bring a M.S. *play* with him![45] — Mr. Shelley met us in our way, & invited us back to his House, — &, while we were returning, Captain Fuller came up to the Coach Door, & invited himself to Dine with us. He was at Lewes, with all the Sussex officers, to wait upon the Duke of Richmond; Mrs. Thrale offered him the vacant seat in the Coach, & we went on to the Shelleys.

They have a large & charming House in this Town; Mrs. Shelley is just a *good sort of Woman*, she has a great family, of very fine Children.[46] We spent all the morning with them, & then, with our Captain, came Home, & had a most agreeable Ride.

The Country about this place has a most singular appearance; there is not a Tree within several miles, but Hill rises above Hill in quantity innumerable. The sea is the great object from all parts.

In the Evening we had a large party, consisting of the Bishop of Peterborough, his Lady,[47] the Holroyds, Miss Firth, & our light Infantry Captain.

[42] The market town of Lewes in Sussex is 8 mi. NE of Brighton.

[43] Philadelphia Cotton (*c.*1738–1819), daughter of HLT's uncle Sir Lynch Salusbury Cotton, 4th Bt; m. (1763) Henry Shelley (1727–1805) of Lewes (J. Comber, *Sussex Genealogies: Lewes Centre* (Cambridge, 1933), p. 251).

[44] Revd John Delap (1725–1812), poet and dramatist; DD (Cantab.), 1762; Vicar of Iford and Kingston nr. Lewes, 1765; Vicar of Woolavington, W. Sussex, 1774. Delap lived in Lewes.

[45] *The Royal Suppliants.* Garrick had rejected the play in 1774, but it would finally be produced at Drury Lane in 1781, with a prologue supplied by HLT and an epilogue by Arthur Murphy. See below, *passim*; *EJL* iv; Garrick, *Letters*, iii. 932–3.

[46] Henry (1767–1811), later MP for Lewes; Thomas (1771–80); Philadelphia (1764–1818); Elizabeth (d. 1840); Cordelia (living 1828); and Eleanor (living 1824), m. (1806) George John Dalbiac (Comber, pp. 251–2; *GM* cix[2] (1840), 221).

[47] Elizabeth née Crewe (*c.*1744–1826), m. (1767) John Hinchliffe, Bp of Peterborough (*JL* v. 208 n. 5).

The Bishop is a man of very mild manners, & most courteous demeanour; his Lady is sister in Law to Mrs. Crewe:[48] she is pretty & lively. They, Mr. Thrale & Mrs. Holroyd, played at Cards from Tea to supper, & the rest of us formed into occasional little parties. |

Thursday, [27] May

We pass our Time here most delectably,—this dear & most sweet Family grow daily more kind to me, &, *all* of them, contrive to make me of so much consequence, that I can *now* no more help being *easy*, than, till lately, I could help being *embarrassed*. Mrs. Thrale has, indeed, from the first moment of our acquaintance, been to me all my Heart could wish, & now her Husband & Daughter get ground in my *good grace & favour*[49] *every* Day. They are, indeed, more obliging & good to me than any thing but *ocular demonstration* could give you a true idea of.

Yesterday morning [26 May] they shewed me the Rooms,—which are not, yet, opened. They are 2 *sets*, & really very fine, large, & well fitted up.[50] Thence we strolled to the Steyn, & were, by turns, joined by Major Holroyd, Mr. Concannon, & Capt. Fuller.

---

[48] Dr Hinchliffe had met the Crewe family through his position as an usher (under master) in the Westminster School (1755–62); he had had John Crewe as a pupil there and travelled with him in 1763. The connection, cemented by his marriage to Crewe's sister, proved useful to his career. FBA would remember her first meeting with the Hinchliffes in a French exercise written in 1802, in which she also reminisced about the Thrales and Arthur Murphy (*JL* v. 208–11).

[49] FB humorously alludes to her 'royal' status by employing a phrase ('*grace & favour*') normally reserved for the King and Queen. Cf. 'He ... was admitted by the grace and favour of Queen Margaret to her household and habitation' (J. R. Walbran, *Memorials of the Abbey of St. Mary of Fountains* (1863–78), i. 188, cited *OED* s.v. hospitate, *v. rare*, hospitation).

[50] Brighton possessed, at this time, 2 sets of Assembly Rooms. Those at the Castle Inn, designed by John Crunden (*c.*1745–1835), were erected in 1766. Those at the Old Ship Hotel, designed by Robert Golden (*c.*1738–1809), were commissioned in 1775. The Castle had 4 rooms including a ballroom and a card room, while the Old Ship had a ballroom and an adjoining card room or supper room. The principal balls and assemblies were held alternately in the two establishments under the regulation of a single Master of Ceremonies. See C. Musgrave, *Life in Brighton* (Hamden, 1970), pp. 73–6; H. Colvin, *Biographical Dictionary of British Architects 1660–1840* (1978), s.v. Crunden, Golden.

Just before we went to Dinner, a Chaise drove up to the Door,—& from it issued Mr. Murphy!—he met with a very joyful reception, & Mr. Thrale, for the *first* Time in his Life, said he was a *good fellow*;—for he makes it a sort of *rule* to salute him with the Title of *scoundrel or Rascal.* They are very old friends, & I question if Mr. Thrale loves any man so well.[51]

He made me many very flattering speeches of his eagerness to go on with my Play,—to know what became of the several Characters,—& to what place I should next conduct them, assuring me that the first Act ¦ had run in his Head ever since he had read it.

In the Evening, we all adjourned to Major Holroyd's, where, besides his own Family, we found Lord Mordaunt,[52] son to the Earl of Peterborough,—a pretty, languid, *tonnish* Young man;—Mr. Fisher,[53] who is said to be a *scholar*, but is nothing enchanting as a *Gentleman*;—young Fitzgerald,[54] as much *The Thing* as ever,—& Mr. Lucius Concannon.

Mr. Murphy was the life of the party,—he was in good spirits; & extremely entertaining: he told a million of stories, admirably well,—but stories won't do upon paper, therefore I shall not attempt to present you with them.

This morning [27 May], as soon as Breakfast was over, Mr. Murphy said 'I must now go to the seat by the sea

---

[51] Murphy and Thrale had been cronies since 1760 or earlier (J. P. Emery, *Arthur Murphy* (Philadelphia, 1946), p. 85).

[52] Charles Henry Mordaunt (1758–1814), styled Visc. Mordaunt, became the 5th E. of Peterborough on 1 Aug. of this year upon the death of his father Charles Mordaunt (1708–79), 4th E. In 1785 the *'tonnish'* young lord, who never married, was assessed £2,500 in damages for *crim. con.* with Lady Anne Foley, for which the two were lampooned in a pair of tête-à-tête portraits in the *Town and Country Magazine* (GEC, *Peerage*, x. 505 n. a).

[53] Probably the Revd John Fisher (1748–1825), Canon of Windsor, 1786; DD (Cantab.), 1789; Bishop of Exeter, 1803; Bishop of Salisbury, 1807. Fisher had appeared as tenth wrangler on taking his degree of BA in 1770, and was eminent for his classical attainments. FB later came to know him well at Windsor.

[54] Probably Keane Fitzgerald (1748–1831), son of Keane Fitzgerald (d. 1782), the Burneys' former neighbour and landlord in Poland St. In a letter to SC in 1776 FB had described the young Fitzgerald as 'half a Coxcomb' (*EJL* ii. 211; see also IGI s.v. London for Fitzgerald's date of christening).

side, with my *new set of acquaintance*, from whom I expect no little entertainment.'

'Ay, said Mrs. Thrale, & there you'll find us *all*!

—I believe this Rogue means *me* for Lady Smatter: but *Mrs. Voluble* must speak the Epilogue, Mr. Murphy.'[55]

'That must depend upon who performs the part, answered he.'

'Don't talk of it *now*, cried I, for Mr. Thrale knows nothing of it.'

'I think, cried Mr. Murphy, you might touch up *his* character in *Censor*?'

'Ay, cried Mr. Thrale, I *expect* a knock some Time or other,—but, when it comes, I'll carry all my Myrmidons to *cat call* it!' |

Mr. Murphy then made me fetch him the 2ᵈ Act, & ⌐made⌐ off with it.

As soon as he was gone, Major Holroyd called, & made a long & sociable visit. He improves upon further knowledge,—& his *Lady* does the contrary. He was full of the praises of Mr. Murphy, whose good natured readiness to *shew off* has won the Hearts of all our clan. He seems, indeed, as worthy admiration for his Temper as for his Talents.

We had a very grand Dinner, to Day, (though nothing to a Streatham Dinner,) at the Ship Tavern, where the officers mess; to which we were invited by the Major & Captain. All the officers I have mentioned, & 3 or 4 more, the Holroyds, Miss Firth, Lord Mordaunt, Messieurs Murphy, Fisher, Fitzgerald, Mr. Kipping,[56] a ridiculous

[55] Implying that Murphy will write the epilogue. Lady Smatter is a vain, pretentious, ignorant bluestocking, head of the literary circle FB dubs 'The Witlings'. She endlessly lards her conversation with misquotations from the standard authors. Mrs Voluble is landlady to Dabler, one of the witlings; she is meddling, sneaky, and, as her name suggests, talkative. Censor (below) is a benevolent cynic, satirical and resourceful.

[56] Henry Kipping (1726–85), apothecary and surgeon, who, along with Dr Lucas Pepys, had treated Ralph Thrale (1773–75) in his fatal illness. Kipping lived at 28 West St., near the Thrales' house. FB below calls him 'a prating, good humoured old Gossip' (p. 378). He was a respected practitioner, beloved by the Thrales, and in addition an expert swordsman who once disarmed an army officer who had insulted him. See *TSP*, pp. 122–3, 125; *Piozzi Letters* i. 136, 139 n. 32; P.J. and R.V. Wallis, *Eighteenth Century Medics* (Newcastle upon

apothecary, Dr. Delap & our own party, made an *immensely* formidable appearance.

Dr. Delap arrived in the morning, & is to stay 2 Days. He is too silent for me to form much judgment of his *companionable* Talents, & his appearance is snug & reserved. Mrs. Thrale is reading his play, & likes it much. It is to come out next season. It is droll enough that there should be, at this Time, a Tragedy & Comedy in exactly the same situation, placed so accidentally in the same House.

I was seated, at Dinner, between Mr. Fisher & Captain Fuller, which I liked well, as the latter is ⏐ the only Young man I have seen here who has more sense than affectation: indeed, of the latter quality he has not a grain.

We afterwards went on the Parade, where the soldiers were mustering, & found Capt. Fuller's men all [half intoxicated;][57] & Laughing so violently as we past by them, that they could hardly stand upright. The Captain storm'd at them most angrily, but, turning to us, said 'These poor fellows have just been paid their arrears, & it is so new to them to have a sixpence in their pockets, that they knew not how to keep it there.'

The Wind being extremely high, our Caps [&] Gowns were blown about most abominably; & this encreased the risibility of the merry light Infantry; Captain Fuller's desire to keep order made *me* Laugh as much as the men's incapacity to obey him: for, finding our *flying Drapery* provoked their mirth, he went up to the *biggest Grinner*, & shaking him violently by the shoulders, said 'What do [you][58] Laugh for, Sirrah? do you Laugh at the Ladies? &, as soon as he had given the reprimand, it struck him to be so ridiculous, that he was obliged to turn quick round, & commit the very fault he was attacking, by Laughing most furiously.

We drank Tea & spent the Evening at Home, where ⏐ we had almost as large a party as at the mess,—for though

Tyne, 1985), col. 646; T. W. Horsfield, *The History ... of Sussex* (Lewes, 1835), i. 142; Musgrave, p. 80.

⁵⁷ Substituted by FBA for an obliterated phrase not recovered.
⁵⁸ Inserted by FBA.

we *omitted* all the Officers but the Major, Captain, & Mr. Concannon, we *added* the Bishop of Peterborough & Mrs. Hinchcliffe,—the former of which is always very civil to me, & the latter *more* than civil, for she even *seeks* to confab with me, &, as she is very lively & good humoured, I am always *agreeable* to accept her advances.

Continual interruptions & entrance of Company made me lose the Post,—our return is now *posponed* [*sic*], for Mr. Thrale finds so much amusement here, he is unwilling to move: He will, however, *certainly* be in Town the *Birth Day*,[59] when I know more, I will write again. Just had y^rs [60] — 100 thanks—y^r F B |

83   West Street, Brighton,
                                    30 May — 1 June [1779]
To Susanna Elizabeth Burney

AJL (Berg, Diary MSS I, paginated 927–48, foliated 1–11), May 1779
11 single sheets 4to, 22 pp.

West Street—Brighthelmstone,
May 30th

To my no small concern, I am obliged to write upon this wrinkled paper,—having no other but what is *too good*,—you'll excuse me, Ma'am!—Now to a few Words upon Thursday [27 May].

I broke off where we were all assembled at this House,— which, by the way, is exactly opposite to the Inn in which Charles the 2^d hid himself, after the Battle of Worcester, previous to his escaping from the kingdom,—so I fail not to look at it with *loyal satisfaction*,—& his black Wig'd

[59] The King's Birthday, 4 June.
[60] Missing.

majesty has, from the Time of the Restoration, been its sign.[61]

After Tea, the Bishop, his Lady, Lord Mordaunt & Mrs. Holroyd seated themselves to play at Whist: & Mr. Murphy, coming up to me, said 'I have had no opportunity, Miss Burney, to tell you how much I have been entertained this morning,—but, I have a great deal to say to You about it,—I am extremely pleased with it indeed.'

'O yes, no doubt!' cried I, sideling off for fear of being heard.

'The Dialogue, said he, is charming, & the—'

'What's that? cried Mrs. Thrale,—Mr. Murphy always flirting with Miss Burney?—And *here*, too, where every body is watched!' And she cast her Eyes towards Mrs. Holroyd, who is as censorious a country Lady as ever locked up all her ideas in a Country Town. She has told us sneering anecdotes of every Woman, & every Officer in Brighthelmstone, &, in particular, has so tormented Captain Fuller with spreading | scandalous suggestions about him & a Mrs. Johnston,[62] a very beautiful Woman whose House he frequently visited during her residence here, that he quite sickens at the sight of her. He reminds me, in his manners & disposition, of Miss Kinnaird, for he has the same kind of openness & honesty that distinguished her Character;—&, therefore, you may imagine, when, to *such* a disposition, Youth, & Independance, & great spirit are joined, he does not without resentment receive what he regards as an injury;—so that he & Mrs. Holroyd are upon merely & barely civil terms. He makes no scruple of manifesting his dislike of her by total inattention & constant neglect;—& she, who is formality

[61] Cromwell's Parliamentary army smashed Charles II's Scottish forces at Worcester on 3 Sept. 1651. Following 6 weeks on the run, Charles slept the night of 14 Oct. at the George Inn at Brighton (afterwards renamed The King's Head), and early the next morning sailed for France aboard the *Surprise*, owned by Capt. Nicholas Tattersall of Brighton. See *Charles II's Escape from Worcester: A Collection of Narratives Assembled by Samuel Pepys*, ed. W. Matthews (Berkeley, 1966), pp. 70–72, 83, 142–43, 153, 154, 159–60, 176; R. Ollard, *The Escape of Charles II After the Battle of Worcester* (1966), pp. 113–15, 125–31.

[62] Perhaps Hester Maria Napier (1754–1819), daughter of Francis Napier (c.1702–73), 6th B. Napier, of Lewes, Sussex; m. (1774) Alexander Johnstone (b. 1750, d. by 1819) of Carnsalloch.

itself, & expects the utmost deference & respect, is so much provoked at his careless indifference, that she takes every opportunity of pointing it out, & endeavouring to put him to the blush. It is all, however, in vain, for, where [*sic*] she not the lady of his superior officer, I believe he would hardly answer her when she speaks to him.

Mr. Murphy, checked by Mrs. Thrale's exclamation, stopt the conversation, & said he must run away, but would return in half an Hour. 'Don't expect, however, Miss Burney, he said, that I shall bring with me what yo[u] are thinking of,—no, I can't part with it yet!—'

'What! at it again! cried Mrs. Thrale,—this flirting is incessant,—but it's all to Mr. Murphy's credit.' |

Now I am *forced* to come to the *good* paper!—monstrous provoking! Mrs. Thrale told me, afterwards, that she made these speeches to divert the attention of the Company from our *subject*, for that she found they were all upon the watch the moment Mr. Murphy addressed me, & that the Bishop & his Lady almost threw down their Cards from eagerness to discover what he meant.

I am, now, more able to give you some sketch of Dr. Delap, &, as he is coming into the World next Winter in my own *Walk*, &, like me, for the *first* Time of trying the stage,[63]—You may shake us together, when I have drawn him, & conjecture our fates.

He is, commonly & naturally, grave, silent & absent, but, when any subject is once begun upon which he has any thing to say, he works it threadbare,—yet hardly seems to know, when all is over, what, or whether any thing has past. He is a man, as I am told by those who know, of deep learning, but totally ignorant of Life & manners. As to his person & appearance, they are much in the John Trot[64] style of other great clergymen. He seems inclined to be

[63] In fact, Delap had had a tragedy, *Hecuba*, produced at Drury Lane in Dec. 1761-Jan. 1762; it received 4 performances (*LS* 4 ii. 907, 911).

[64] Defined as 'commonplace', 'ordinary' by Dobson (*DL* i. 222 n. 1). It is the name of Sir Fopling Flutter's one English servant in Etherege's *The Man of Mode*. The name also occurs in the writings of Steele, the elder Colman, Foote, etc., and is similarly used as an attributive by Charlotte Smith in *The Young Philosopher* (1798), i. 207: 'I have been tired of such John Trott sort of prosing since I was ten years old' (cited *OED* s.v. sort, *sb.*[2] 6. c.).

particularly civil to me, but not knowing how, according
to the general forms, he has only shewn his inclination
by | perpetual offers to help me at Dinner, & repeated
exclamations at my not Eating more profusely.

So much for my Brother Dramatist.

The supper was very gay; Mrs. Thrale was in high
spirits, & her Wit flashed with incessant brilliancy,—Mr.
Murphy told several stories with admirable humour,—&
the Bishop of Peterborough was a Worthy 3^d in contributing towards general entertainment. He turns out most
gaily sociable. We had not much of Capt. Fuller's Company, as he was obliged to see after his Drunken men, for
fear of riots: niether, indeed, does he talk much in large
Companies, but he listens to all that passes among *the
Wits*, with a most uncommon ardour, & enjoys their bon
mots & *flashes of merriment* beyond measure.

He out-stayed them all, & *told* me how much he was
delighted with the conversation, & how happy in an
opportunity of *picking up some thing* in such society. After
which, Mrs. Holroyd was discussed &, poor lady, not very
mercifully!—Mrs. Thrale openly declares her dislike of
her, for her want of entertainment, & for her suspicious
watching of her Husband, &, indeed, of every body else;—
& Capt. Fuller | has a very good *right* to censure her,—so,
between them, she was pretty well *done up*. Mrs. Thrale
said she Lived upon the Steyn for the pleasure of viewing,
all Day long, *who walked with who*, how often the same
persons were seen together, & what visits were made by
Gentlemen to Ladies, or Ladies to Gentlemen.

'She often tells me, said the Captain, of my men,—O,
she says, Captain Fuller, your men are really always after
the Ladies!—'

'Nay, cried Mrs. Thrale, I should have thought the
Officers might have contented her,—but if she takes in the
soldiers too, she must have business enough!'

'O she gets no satisfaction by her complaints, for I only
say 'Why Ma'am, we are all young!—all young & gay!—&
how can we do better than follow the Ladies?'

'After all, returned Mrs. Thrale, I believe she can talk
of nothing else, & therefore we must forgive her: for,

when she has made observations upon the people she sees, & drawn conjectures,—'

'O, interrupted the Captain, *conjectures* are not for every Day!—they are rather above *common* fare, & one, well worked, lasts 2 or 3 Days.'

Mr. Thrale says that this Captain is an admirable mimic, singer, story teller, & *what not?*—& we worried him to exhibit,—but he complained it was Bed Time, & ran away. ┃

Now for   Friday, May 28th

In the morning, before Breakfast, came Dr. Delap, & Mrs. Thrale, in ambiguous terms, complimented him upon his play, & expressed her wish that she might tell *me* of it,—upon which hint, he instantly took the manuscript from his Pocket, & presented it to me, begging me, at the same Time, to tell him of any faults that I might with it.

There, Susy—am I not grown a grand person,—not merely looked upon as a *Writer*, but addressed as a *Critic*,—upon my Word this is vast fine!

As this was, again, a Field Day, we all attended the militia. Mrs. Thrale, Mrs. Hinchcliffe, Mrs. Holroyd & I went in the former's Carriage, & poor Miss Thrale was obliged to go with Miss Firth & the Major's Children.[65] The Exercise was upon one of the Downs,—&, as before, the Major & the Captain made us frequent visits,—as did also Mr. Concannon, who is Mrs. Holroyd's *protegè*, for she says he is the only man in the Battallion who has even the civility to Hand a Lady from her Carriage, for the rest, she vows, are mere Brutes!—We have told Captain Fuller this heavy charge, but he likes her too little to value her opinion. By the way, it is really amazing the fatigue these militia officers go ┃ through, without compulsion or Interest to spur them,—Major Holroyd is a man of at

---

[65] Maria Josepha Holroyd (1771–1863), who m. (1796) John Thomas Stanley (1766–1850), cr. (1839) B. Stanley of Alderley, Cheshire; and Louisa Dorothea Holroyd (1776–1854), who m. (1797) Gen. Sir William Henry Clinton (1769–1846).

least £8000 a year, & has a Noble seat, called Sheffield place, in this County,—& quits ease, pleasure, retirement in the Country, & public diversions in London, to take the charge of the Sussex militia!—Captain Fuller, too, has an Estate of 4 or 5000 a year,—is but just of age,—has figure, understanding, Education, Vivacity & Independance,—& yet, voluntarily, devotes almost all his Time, & almost all his attention, to a Company of light Infantry!—Instances such as these, my dear Susy, ought to reconcile all the pennyless sons of toil & Industry to their cares & labours, since those whom affluence invites to all the luxuries of indolence, sicken of those very gifts which the others seem only to exist to procure.

Upon the Downs we met the Bishop, Lord Mordaunt & Mr. Fisher, but we were kept too much in motion, by the various evolutions which obliged us to whisk from place to place, to have any steady conversation.

As soon as we returned Home, I siezed Dr. Delap's play. It is called Macaria.[66]—Mr. Thrale, who frequently calls me Queen Dido from a notion that I resemble an Actress in France who performed that part,[67] & from a general idea of my Theatrical turn, was ¦ mightily diverted at this oddly timed confidence of Dr. Delap, & Tapping at my Door, called out 'Queen Dido, what, rehearsing still?—Why I think you should tip the Doctor the same Compliment!'

I could only read the 1st Act before Dinner. Mrs. Thrale came to me, while I was Dressing, & said 'Murphy is quite charmed with your second act,—he says he is sure it will do, & *more* than do,—he has been talking of you this half Hour,—he calls you a *sly, designing body*,—& says you look all the people through most wickedly. He watches You—& Vows he has caught you in the fact:—nobody & no

---

[66] An earlier title of *The Royal Suppliants*.

[67] Perhaps the famous French tragic actress Claire-Joseph Léris (1723–1803), called Mlle Clairon, whom Thrale may have seen during his travels on the Continent after leaving Oxford in 1745, and who would have been about FB's present age at that time. Like FB short of stature, she could also be construed (judging from portraits) as bearing a certain facial resemblance to her. See Clairon's remarks on the character of Dido in *Memoirs of Hyppolite Clairon* (1800; rpt. New York, 1971), i. 47–8.

thing, he says, escapes you, & you keep looking round for Characters all Day long. And Dr. Delap has been talking of you—'

'I hope he does not suspect the play?'

'Lord,—Why he would not tell!'

'O but I should be sorry to put it in his power!—'

'Why he's such an absent creature, that if he were to hear it to Day, he would forget it to-morrow.

'No, as he is engaged in the same pursuit himself at this very Time, I believe he would *remember* it.—

'Well,—it's too late, however, *now*,—for he knows it!—but I did not tell him,—Murphy did,—he broke out into praises of the second act before him.' |

I could only say I was sorry for it.

'But he'll tell nobody, depend upon it,—continued she; it only put him upon asking 100 questions about you, & singing your praise;—he has tiezed me all the morning about your *Family*, & how many sisters & Brothers you have, & if you were Dr. Burney's Daughter, & a million more enquiries.'

At Dinner we had a large party,—consisting of Mr. & Mrs. Shelley of Lewes, who are very civil, good sorts of people; 2 of their Daughters,[68] who, like most other Country misses, are immoveably silent before *the Elders*, &, rudely free before the *Youngsters*,—Mr. Murphy, Dr. Delap & Captain Fuller.

During Dinner, I observed that Mr. Murphy watched me almost incessantly, with such archness of Countenance that I could hardly look at him;—& Dr. Delap did the same, with an earnestness of gravity that was truly solemn!—Till Mr. Murphy, catching my Eye *full point* said 'We have been talking of you,—ask Mrs. Thrale what I say of you!—I have found out your schemes, sly as you are,—Dr. Delap, too, heard how I discovered You.—'

'O but Dr. Delap, answered Mrs. Thrale, is the best man in the World for discoveries,—for he'll forget every word by to-morrow,—sha'n't you, Dr. Delap?'

---

[68] See above, p. 276 n. 46.

'Not Miss Burney! cried the Doctor, gallantly,—I'm sure
I sha'n't forget Miss Burney!' ∣

When Mrs. Thrale gave the signal for our leaving the
Gentlemen, Dr. Delap, as I past him, said in a whisper
'Have you read it?'

'No,—not quite.'

'How do you like it?'

I *could* make but one answer;—how strangely ignorant
of the World is this good clergyman to ask such a question
so abruptly!

[xxxxx 7 *lines*]

We were engaged, as soon as the Shelleys left us, to
finish the Evening at Major Holroyd's, but as I feared
hurting Dr. Delap by any seeming indifference, I begged
Mrs. Thrale to let me stay at Home till I had read his
play, & therefore the rest of the party went before me.

I had, however, only 3 Acts in my possession; the story
is of the Daughter & Widow of Hercules;[69]—& indeed,
I liked the play much better than, from it's Author, I
expected to do. The story is such as renders his [xxxxx
1 word] ignorance of common Life & manners [xxxxx *2–
3 words*] not very material, since the Characters are of the
Heroick Age, & therefore require more ∣ classical than
Worldly knowledge, &, accordingly, it's only resemblance
is to the Tragedies of AEschylus & Sophocles,[70]—

When I had finished it, I went to the Majors, where the
party of the Night was The Bishop & his Lady, Lord
Mordaunt, Mr. Fitzgerald, Mr. Fisher, Captain Fuller, Mr.
Concannon, Mr. Murphy, Thrales, Holroyds, Miss Firth,
2 or 3 young officers, & myself.

When the Tea was over, Captain Fuller, who is passionately fond of music, again attacked me upon the subject,
though without much expectation of success, I believe,—
and I turned the Tables, by beginning an attack upon
him, to treat us with some of his mimicry, & other various
species of *fun*, which Mr. Thrale told us he performed
admirably. He would not, however, listen to us, but, when

---

[69] Macaria and Deianira.
[70] It is based on Aeschylus's *Suppliants* and Euripides' *Heraclidae*.

he found the matter urgent, quickly said 'There are *Times & seasons*, Sir;—what I can do one Day, I can't always do another,—this sort of stuff depends upon a man's spirits, it can't always be done when called for.' This was too true to be cavilled at, & every body gave him up, but me,—&, for more idle fun, I tiezed him on,—till he frankly said 'I should be very ready to do any thing that could give any diversion, if it was *proper* & *seasonable*,—but I don't much care to be looked upon as the Buffoon of the Company, who will exhibit at Command for the cure of the Vapours.'

'You are afraid, perhaps, of this *right reverend seignor*, but, I'm sure, he is as gay, & as ready for sport as any of us.'

'It won't do now, *indeed!*—'

'Well,—shall it do *another* Time?'

'Yes,—when we have only 2 or 3 people.'

'Well, but do you promise *I* shall be one? Before I go?'

'Yes,—in private.'

And then, Mrs. Thrale & some others coming up, he walked away, though I had, first, *generously* said *I* would plague him no more.

Some or other kind of nonsense occuring to me, I called him back;—he did not hear me, but Mrs. Thrale, who was in high spirits, called out aloud 'Mr. Fuller! this way!—Miss Burney calls you, Sir!' As I had really nothing to say worth hearing, I turned off, & he, thinking it was for further pressing, said in a low Voice, to Mrs. Thrale 'I have promised Miss Burney that I will exhibit to her one Time in private.'

This, though said with the utmost innocence, made Mrs. Thrale hallow aloud. 'O, this, is too great! cried she,—you'll exhibit to Miss Burney only in private. ⌐Very well, Captain!¬ And then she went, Laughing, with his speech to the card Table.

'O, cried he, ⌐half vexed,¬ & following her, this is *enough*, I suppose!—the *conjecturers* will want nothing more!' And he looked towards Mrs. Holroyd.[71]—but, whether from

---

[71] A rare instance of risqué comedy in FB's surviving journals. The paragraphs containing it are marked for deletion in the MS, and are previously

delicacy, pique, or accident, he spoke to me no more all the Evening, till Mr. Thrale's Coach was announced, to which he Handed me.

Lord Mordaunt, who was my neighbour at supper, was marvellous civil, in the languid & gentle way.

Saturday, May 29th

Early in the morning, the kind Mrs. Thrale brought me your Letter,[72]—saying 'Here,—here's news from Home, my master would have had me kept [*sic*] it till Breakfast, but I told him he did not love you so well as I did,—he vowed that was not true,—but it's plain it was, for *I* was in most haste to make you happy.'

Thus sweet & good & kind she always is.—

Your Letter, my dearest Girl, calls for my best thanks,— I am quite grieved at losing so much of my dear Bessy, Edward & Anna Maria,[73]—I will, however, contrive to get to Them & you immediately after we return from Brighthelmstone.

During Breakfast, the Miss Pitches, Peggy & Sophy, called. They are come, with their Father, to spend 2 Days here. Mr. & Mrs. Thrale, who have a great aversion to flirting & flaunting misses at a public place, are rather disconcerted at their arrival, & determined to see as little of them as is possible.

When they left us, Mrs. & Miss Thrale took me to Widget's,[74] the *milliner & Library Woman* on the *Steyn*; where we rummaged over a set of paltry Books,—among them, I saw the 2d Edition of Evelina.

---

unpublished; Fuller's 'innocent' remark has been scored over, but not heavily enough to count as an obliteration.

[72] Missing.

[73] FB's Worcester cousins Elizabeth Warren and Edward Francesco Burney, and her niece Hannah Maria Burney.

[74] Miss E. Widgett was proprietor of a library next to the post office on the south side of the Steine (both are illustrated in an engraving in the grangerized set of *DL* (i. 226) in the National Portrait Gallery Archive and Library, Lewisham). She was co-publisher of *A Description of Brighthelmston and the Adjacent Country; or, The New Guide for Ladies and Gentlemen Resorting to that Place of Health and Amusement.*

We were soon joined here by Mr. Concannon, who is always very civil, but never minded. After a little dawdling conversation, he took up a volume of Evelina,—I sat very snug,—but he never looked at me,—he read on for some Time with much earnestness, | & then, taking the privilege of being a subscriber to the shop, took another Volume, & walked away with both. This, I really believe, was all accidental, for he never looked towards me, nor seemed to have any idea that I saw what he was doing.

Soon after, Captain Fuller came in to have a little chat. He said he had just gone through a great operation— 'I have been, he said, cutting off the Hair of all my men.'

'Good God, why?'

'Why the Duke of Richmond ordered that it should be done, & the fellows swore they would not submit to it,— so I was forced to be the operator myself. I told them they would look as smart again when they had got on their Caps;—but it went much against them,—they vowed, at first, they would not bear such usage,—some said they would sooner be run through the body, & others that the Duke should as soon have their Heads. I told them I would soon try that, & fell to work myself with them.'

'And how did they bear it?'

'O, poor fellows, with great good nature, when they found *his Honour* was their Barber: but I thought proper to submit to hearing all their Oaths, & all their *Jokes*, for they had no other comfort, but to hope I should *have enough of* it, & such sort of Wit. 3 or 4 of them, however, escaped,—but I shall | find them out. I told them I had a good mind to cut my own Hair off too, & then they would have a *Captain Crop*. I shall sooth them to-morrow, with a present of New Feathers for all their Caps.'

Presently we were joined by Dr. Delap & Mr. Murphy. The latter, taking me aside, said 'Has Mrs. Thrale told You what I said?—' 'I don't know,—she has told me some odd sort of—*nonsence*, I was going to say.'

'But, do you know the Name I have settled to call you by?'

'No.—'

'Miss *Slyboots*!—that is exactly the thing!—O you are a wicked one!—I have found you out!'

'O to be sure!—but *pray*, now, don't tell such a name about,—for if *you* give it, it will soon spread.'

Then he began upon the 2ᵈ Act,—but I fear'd being suspected, & stole away from him.

A little while after, he again advanced to me, with a Book in his Hand, & a Face full of *waggery*, & said 'Look, Miss Burney,—do you know this?—what silly Book is it?— did you ever see it?'

It was the 3ᵈ volume of Evelina;—I twitched it from him, & walked off, for I saw Captain Fuller look very curious. I am not able to guess whether or not he is acquainted with that business, but I fancy *yes*, as I know the Holroyds & Miss Firth are violently fond of [*leaf torn*]

Different occupations, in a short Time, called away [all][75] | our Gentlemen, but Dr. Delap; & he, seating himself next me, began to Question me about his Tragedy. I soon said all I wanted to say upon the subject,—&, soon after, a great deal *more*,—but *not* soon after was he satisfied!—he recurred to the same thing a million of Times, asked the same Questions, exacted the same Compliments, & worked the same passages, till I almost fell asleep with the sound of the same words: And, at last, with what little animation was left me, I contrived to make Miss Thrale propose a walk on the Steyn, &, crawling out of the shop, I sought,—& found,—*revival* from the sea Breezes. Yet not before he had planed [*sic*] a meeting at Streatham, where a Council, composed of Dr. Johnson, Mr. Murphy & Mrs. Thrale, are to sit upon the Play, for *final* Judgement, & where, at his express desire, I am to make one. This is to take place some Time before the Spa Journey. By the way, my being of *that* party seems looked on as a thing of course,—& *nothing* can be half so desireable;— were I *not* included, I should die of mortification from the continual hearing of new plans & proposals to render it more & more delightful.[76]

---

[75] Inserted by FBA for a tear in the leaf.

[76] In an undated letter of about this time, SC wrote to Mrs Gast that FB, at 'the latter end of August', was to go with the Thrales 'and Dr. Johnson and Mrs. [*sic*] Murphy a Tour of pleasure through the Austrian Netherlands, and so on to Aix la Chapelle and the Spas. They are to be out about two months,

Upon the Steyn, we were again joined by Captain Fuller, & by the Miss Pitches. We strolled there some Time, &, on our return, found Mr. Murphy in the Parlour. He followed me out of it, when I was going up stairs to [dre]ss on purpose to say good natured & flattering things, [in a] dry, humourous, abusive way, of my 2^d Act. ⌐ Nothing can be more comfortable than his manner of honouring it with his approbation. He is, indeed, with all his fun & buffoonry, a most amiable man, & I find myself taking to him more & more every Day.

In the Evening, the grand meeting was at this House. The party the same as usual, only with the addition of the Miss Pitches, who *invited themselves*. The Bishop, Mrs. Hinchcliffe, Mrs. Holroyd & Dr. Delap went to Whist;— Mr. & Mrs. Thrale attended their Table, & the Major, Mr. Murphy, Mr. Concannon, Capt. Fuller, Miss Firth, the Miss Pitches, Miss Thrale & myself went to Commerce.

Peggy Pitches, who is the greatest little Coquet in Sussex, fixed her Eyes, & armed her dart, at Captain Fuller,—she smiled, tittered, lisped, languished, & *played pretty* all the Evening,—but the Captain was totally insensible,—he has, indeed, so little passion for flirtation, that he would rather listen to Mr. Murphy, the Bishop, or Mrs. Thrale, than either speak to, or look at, the most celebrated *Toast* in the kingdom. [xxxxx *2 lines*]

But Peggy, who thought a red Coat a certain prognostick of gallantry, was not easily to be discouraged: when she found her little graces not merely *ineffectual*, but wholly *unobserved*, she began to set down her cards, in a pretty, ⌐ affected, manner, protesting she did not know how to play, & begging his advice:—nothing, however, ensued from this, but that, by his inattention & indifference, I fancy he thought her a Fool.

When it came to her turn to deal, she mixed the cards, let them drop, tittered, & flung herself into sundry

---

travel with the greatest Ease and Luxury and Leisure, and live at the rate of ten thousand a year!' (W. H. Hutton, *Burford Papers* (1905), p. 37). The trip had to be cancelled because of the worsening war situation (see below, p. 339).

attitudes, & then begged the Captain to shuffle & deal for her.

Captain Fuller, to Ridicule, I believe, her affectation, took the contrary extreme; he put on an awkward, clownish Countenance, shuffled the Cards with a ludicrous clumsiness, & making various vulgar grimaces, *licked his Thumb* in order to deal!

This failing, her next attempt was more spirited; she looked over his Hand, &, declaring all cheating was allowable at Commerce, snatched one of his Cards to make her own Hand better.

The Captain, however, had so little gallantry, that instead of regarding this theft as a favour, & offering her her choice of what she pleased, he insisted upon having his Card returned!—& when she resisted, recovered it, in an easy manner, by exposing all her Hand, & then, very composedly, proceeded with the Game without comment.

This determined insensibility made her give him up,— she blushed, & sat quiet the rest of the Evening.

The supper, as usual, was all gaity, Wit & good humour.

When it was over, Captain Fuller asked who had commands to London, & said he was to go thither the next Day. Mrs. Thrale invited him to Streatham, & settled for a 3 Days visit from them to that sweet place for the 10th 11th & 12th of June, when he is to meet Miss Brown | & Miss Streatfield. We were all very sorry to lose him.

Sunday, May 30th

The Bishop preached again, & an excellent sermon. After Church, we all sauntered upon the Steyn, & then Miss Thrale & I went in the Coach to a place called the *Spa*, about half a mile from Brighthelmstone, where there is a well of mineral water.[77] I tasted it,—& repented so

---

[77] The chalybeate spring, St Ann's Well, at Wick, ½ mi. W of St Nicholas's Church. A Brighton physician, Dr Richard Henderson, described its taste as 'not unpleasant, something like that upon a knife after it has been used in cutting lemons' and claimed that its water 'had been found serviceable in several cases of general debility, crapulas, indigestion, atony of the stomach and fluor albus' (E. W. Gilbert, *Brighton: Old Ocean's Bauble* (1954), pp. 60, 61, 64–5). Perhaps FB was one of those described by another Brighton physician as

doing. Mr. Fuller called to take leave while we were out. Mr. Mitchel,[78] the Clergyman of the place, came to Dine with us. He is a gross, fat, paralytic glutton: very well as to knowledge & Learning, but such a sensualist, that I love not his sight.

Just as I was finishing my attire for Dinner, I saw Captain Fuller drive past in his Phaeton, & stop at the Door. He had not Time to alight,—I went down stairs as soon as I was ready, & found the 3 Thrales, Mr. Murphy & Mr. Mitchel crowding the Door to take leave of him. He kissed his Hand to me with a military air, & wishing me good morning, drove away.—I mention this, because it *comes into play* afterwards.

In the middle of the Dinner, Mr. Mitchell, who had scarce opened his mouth to me twice before, turned to me abruptly, & very gravely said 'Pray, Miss Burney, where is Captain Fuller going?'

'To London, I believe, Sir.'

'Lord, said Mrs. Thrale, how odd Mr. Mitchell is! What should make him ask Miss Burney?'

'Why, Ma'am, said he, a very obvious reason,—I thought her most likely to know.'

'And why should you think that, Sir?' quoth I.

'Because I observed he would not go till he had seen you. I *saw* very plainly!—he is a fine young man, & I think—'

'I think, cried Mrs. Thrale, he could not shew his Taste more! And he is so amiable & so sensible, that I wish niether Queeny nor Miss Burney nor Miss Brown *worse luck.*'

---

experiencing 'a degree of nausea and a sense of weight in the stomach' (ibid., p. 65).

[78] Revd Henry Michell (1714–89), of Lewes; MA (Cantab.), 1739; Rector of Maresfield, Sussex, 1739–89; Vicar of Brighton and Rector of W. Blatchington, 1744–89; classical scholar. At this time he had been suffering for more than 15 years from a 'paralytic affection' that rendered him incapable of writing, forcing him to use his children as amanuenses (Nichols, *Lit. Ill.* iv. 867 n.). There is a portrait of him in ibid. iv, facing p. 866; see also Nichols, *Lit. Anec.* iv. 447 n.

'It is presumed, Ma'am, said Mr Mitchell, that he is now gone to Town to wait upon Dr. Burney.,—such, at least, is the Brighthelmstone report.'

'Well, said Mrs. Thrale, but, *seriously* though, before You came down, when I said, remember you are engaged at Streatham for the 10th 11th & 12th, he said '*Will Miss Burney be there?*'

So this sort of rallery [*sic*] filled up the Dinner talk. Nor has it stopt here, for,—the next morning, Mrs. Thrale told *me* that the Children's Nurse[79] had told *her* that it was said in Brighthelmstone that Mrs. Thrale was Courting Mr. Fuller for her Daughter,—but that Miss Burney had stept in the way, & Mr. Fuller had fallen in Love with *her*!—

What strange & absurd rubbish serves to feed these vacant headed persons![80]

Sunday Evening we had only the Bishop, his Lady & Mr. Murphy, & we were most outrageously merry!

Dr. Delap is returned to Lewes;—"but it seems he" *bored* Mr. Murphy & Miss Thrale "to Death about *me*," asking so many Questions of *how* I came to write Evelina ǀ & *why* I writ it at all, & *what* set me on, & other such curious enquiries, that, at last, they almost lost all patience with him.

Monday, May 31st The Bishop & his Lady, Mrs. & Miss Thrale & I went to see Sheffield Place, the seat of Major Holroyd. It is a most delightful House,—large, superb, &

---

[79] Presumably the Thrale family's 'Old Nurse' Tibson ('Tibby'), of indeterminate age, who was fond of drinking brandy and who was later suspected of stealing from Streatham Place. After HLT's remarriage to Piozzi she stayed with Queeney Thrale, and FBA asked to be remembered to her in a letter to Queeney in 1801 (*TSP, passim*; FBA to Hester Maria Thrale, 24 Feb. 1801, Bowood).

[80] In early 1781 HLT wrote in *Thraliana* (i. 480): 'Queeney ... likes a more brilliant Character I think ... She doats on a *Flasher*. ... Jack Fuller seems her Favorite: Jack Fuller of all People! wild, gay, rich, loud, I wonder how a Girl of Delicacy can take a Fancy to Jack Fuller of Rose-hill? no proposal however has been made, nor do they often meet ... ' Her opinion of Fuller in the diary is characteristically more frank and acerbic than her public assertions. SJ, in the last corrected edn. of his *Dictionary* (1773), defines *flasher* as 'a man of more appearance of wit than reality'.

elegant. They have 63 Bed Chambers, & Dressing Rooms to almost every one. The Major & his Lady were there to receive us, & do the Honours of the House, pleasure Grounds, & Park. The greatest part of the mansion is new Built, & most beautifully fitted up. In Dooms Day Book it is recorded that it belonged to a Brother of the Conqueror.[81]

After passing our morning here very agreeably, we all went, accompanied by the Major & his Lady, to Lewes, to Dine at the Shelleys. I have nothing new to say of them. We spent the Evening at the Major's.

Tuesday, June 1st—the morning, as usual, was spent in sauntering & reading & Chatting,—& we concluded our Brighthelmstone Jaunt by supping in the Evening at the Bishop of Peterborough's, where we were regaled with most *excellent discourse.*

I have never mentioned sea Bathing,—but I have practised it, & I

[*FB abruptly ends the journal here, leaving the rest of the recto and the verso blank. She returned to London with Arthur Murphy, who on 8 June wrote to HLT at Streatham: 'I was much tempted to go off with Miss Burney, but as you entrusted her to me, I found myself restrained from such a flight. Ask her if I did not behave in the most composed manner all the way to Town, without once touching Her Knees, & calling a Blush of Surprize' (MS Rylands, quoted Emery, p. 144).*]

---

[81] Holroyd had bought the estate from John, E. De La Warr, in 1769, and had the house 'much improved, beautified, and enlarged' by the architect James Wyatt (W. Angus, *Seats of the Nobility and Gentry in Great Britain and Wales* (1787), Plate 26; J. P. Neale, *Views of the Seats of the Noblemen and Gentlemen in England, Wales, Scotland, and Ireland,* iv (1821), No. 48). An exactly contemporary illustration is in W. Watts, *The Seats of the Nobility and Gentry* (1779), Plate 3. According to the Domesday Book, in 1068 the manor was granted by William to his half-brother Robert (*c.*1031–90), Count of Mortain in Normandy and E. of Cornwall (Angus, loc. cit.; Neale, loc. cit.).)

84   Streatham,
                                                    15 June [1779]
To Susanna Elizabeth Burney

AJL (Berg, Diary MSS I, Barrett, paginated 959–72, foliated 1–8),
June 1779
8 single sheets 4to, 16 pp.

Streatham
June 15th

Now, my dear Susan, hard & fast let me write up to the
present Time.

I left you all, as you truly say, on Saturday [12 June],
in no very high spirits; Mrs. Thrale's visible uneasiness &
agitation quite alarmed me. I dared ask her no Questions,
but, soon after we drove off, Sir Philip Clerke, gently &
feelingly, led to the subject, &, in the course of our ride,
got from her all the particulars of poor Mr. Thrale's
dreadful & terrifying attack.

I find, with true concern, that it was undoubtedly a
paralytic stroke; he was taken ill at his sister's, Mrs.
Nesbitts,[82]—during Dinner; he did not absolutely fall, but
his Head sunk upon the Table,—&, as soon as he was
able to raise it, they found that his reason had left him!
He talked wildly, & seemed to know nobody; Mrs. Nesbit
brought him Home,—he was much better before Dr.

[82] Susanna Thrale (d. 1789), sister of Henry Thrale; m. (1758) Arnold
Nesbitt (c.1722–79), merchant and MP. Nesbitt had died on 7 Apr. On Tues.,
8 June, Thrale learned from the Nesbitts' solicitor that he was potentially liable
for the repayment of £220,000 for which he had co-signed a bond with Nesbitt
in 1760. He collapsed shortly after, whereupon Mrs Nesbitt, instead of calling
for a physician, brought the insensible Thrale back to Streatham. CB, who was
at Streatham, rushed back to London and sent Dr Bromfield, who arrived
2 hours later. HLT did not learn of this threat of bankruptcy to Thrale and
his heirs until 1791, and then was convinced that the 'sudden Shock & Terror'
of it had brought on the stroke and eventually his premature death 2 years
later. See *Thraliana* i. 389–90, ii. 803–4; *TSP*, pp. 219–20; *Autobiography, Letters
and Literary Remains of Mrs. Piozzi*, ed. A. Hayward (2nd edn., 1861), ii. 37–9;
Namier.

Bromfield could be fetched, yet, for 3 Days afterwards, his senses, at intervals, were frightfully impaired. Poor Mrs. Thrale had been in an Agony of horror & alarm almost incessantly from the Time of her seeing him.

The Saturday that I came, was the first Day that he had not once spoken incoherently,—no wonder, then, that Mrs. Thrale was so little like herself!

She spoke in terms of highest praise of Mr. Seward, who, indeed, has behaved upon this occasion in the most friendly & Zealous manner; & exerted his medicinal skill, which is very uncommon, with equal address & kindness.[83]

When she had unburthened her full & anxious Heart, she began, insensibly, to recover her spirits,—& told us that the party of company for the 3 settled Days still held good, for 'Mr. Thrale, she said, desires not to have any body suppose he has been ill, but, on the contrary, wants all his friends to *see* how well he is. I met your handsome Captain, Miss Burney, in the streets, & reminded him of his Engagement for to Day [12 June], Sunday & Monday, & he will certainly come,—but *how does Miss Burney do?* the rogue asked!—so *that* was uppermost in *his* Head.'

This drew on Sir Philip's rallery, & glad was I that my dear Mrs. Thrale was capable of attempting any thing like sport & gaity.

When we stopt here, Sir Philip immediately went to Mr. Thrale, but I ran past the Door, & up to my own Room, for I quite dreaded seeing him till I had prepared myself to meet him without any seeming concern, as I was told that he was extremely suspicious of being thought in any danger. I dawdled away about an Hour, & then, made Miss Thrale accompany me into the Parlour. Miss Thrale will do any thing for me.

Mr. Thrale was there, with Sir Philip, Mr. Seward & Captain Fuller. I endeavoured to enter & behave as if nothing had happened; I saw Mr. Thrale fix his Eyes

---

[83] HLT wrote on Fri., 11 June, that '*Seward* was the first to fly to our Assistance; fetch Physicians, carry Reports, turn out troublesome Enquirers, attend Mr Thrale in all his Operations'. She complained of Murphy and of CB's 'Indifference', but allowed that 'Mr Seward has supplied every body's neglect' by staying with her (*Thraliana* i. 390).

upon me, with an inquisitive & melancholy earnestness, as if to read my opinion: indeed his looks were vastly better than I expected, but his evident dejection quite shocked me. I did not dare go up to him, for if he had offered to shake Hands with me, I believe I should have been unable to have disguised my concern, for indeed he has, of late, made himself a daily encreasing interest in my regard & kind wishes. I therefore turned short from him, & pretending earnest talk with Miss Thrale went to one of the Windows.

Captain Fuller & Mr. Seward both followed us. They both made their Compliments with great civility.

'What, said Mr. Thrale, have not you two met before?'

'No, said the Captain, I saw nothing of Miss Burney in Town.'

'It was I, said Sir Philip, had the Honour of accompanying her hither with Mrs. Thrale, — &, indeed, I never see her without wishing myself 30 years younger.'

This was a wish not to be controverted!

Sir Philip & Mr. Thrale then entered into conversation with each other, & the 2 Beaus with Miss Thrale & me. Mr. Fuller's easy gaity & natural vivacity were very useful, — for they involuntarily enlivened us all. We had much discussion of the Brighthelmstone parties & people, but, in the midst of it, Mr. Seward gave me a very awkward sensation by saying 'Pray, Miss Burney, have You picked up any Characters at Brighthelmstone for *our Comedy?*'

Mr. Fuller stared, & I was forced to hasten to explain that it was only a *jocose proposal* of Mr. Seward. He is, indeed, so fond of the idea, that ever since, in his dry & droll way he started it, he has never seen me without making it the chief topic of his discourse to me. But, as my own *real* Comedy always occurs to me with the subject, I can't help feeling as if *detected*, or, at least, *suspected*, every time it is mentioned.

Mr. Murphy, by the way, has not been here since I came: if he had, I doubt not but he would have frightened me with his provoking hints as much as he did before Baretti, & perhaps, as then, have been molified into quietness with nothing less than seeing me kneel slyly behind some of their Chairs to supplicate his mercy! At present, however, I find Mr. Seward & Mr. Fuller are wholly without suspicion.

At Dinner every body tried to be chearful; but a dark & gloomy cloud hangs over the Head of poor Mr. Thrale which no flashes of merriment or beams of wit can pierce through: yet he seems pleased that every body should be gay, & desirous to be spoken to & of as usual.

At Tea, we had the Company of Dr. & Mrs. Parker.[84] I think I have mentioned them before. By chance I was about 10 minutes alone with the Doctor in the Parlour, who, with a formality that accompanies whatever he says, *slowly* observed 'So!—they are gone,—& I am now left alone with the Evelina!'

I instantly started some other subject, in order to stop him, but, with the same gravity, he, nevertheless, chose to continue.

'You have gained great esteem, great esteem, indeed, in the World, by that performance.—'

'The World, cried I, is sometimes, taken with a very kind fit,—I'm sure it has in regard to that poor Book.'

'No, not so,—only with a *judicious* fit.' And then he proceeded with formal Compliments till we were joined by the rest of the Company.

After Tea, the Parkers left us, & we walked round the Grounds: we now walk as much [as] possible in order to seduce Mr. Thrale to take exercise, which is not only the *best*, but the *only* thing for him.

While we were talking of our Brighthelmstone acquaintance, Mrs. Thrale told Mr. Fuller that I could imitate Mrs. Holroyd's voice & manner very exactly,—which, indeed, may soon be done, for they are only ridiculously monotonous. Mr. Fuller was highly diverted at the intelligence, for he hates her with all his Heart;—he flew *to* me, & *at* me, eagerly entreating me to exhibit:—I could, however, *so soon bite off my own Nose* as stand forth to perform, at

---

[84] The Revd Dr William Parker (1714–1802), DD (Oxon.), 1754, Chaplain in Ordinary to the King, 1771; and his wife (m. 1768) Mary, née Whitwell (1729–99) (*JL* i. 167 n. 60).

demand, any thing that I previously knew was to draw all Eyes upon me,—I therefore declared off instantly & seriously; but Captain Fuller was half crazy with earnestness & Mr. Seward, who had never, I dare ¹ answer, thought of me but as the quietest of creatures, was, for *him*, equally vehement,—so that they pestered me incessantly & furiously;—&, when I would have turned back, to escape from them, vowed they would follow where ever I went.

Captain Fuller, in order to draw me in, put on a fine *mawdlin* Face, crossing his Hands, & mincing his mouth, by way of representing a Lady who was to visit me as Mrs. Holroyd: 'And pray, pray Mrs. Holroyd, how do you find yourself? Is it not vastly entertaining to Live upon the Steyn? but then these militia officers,—I fear they are very sad fellows,—& there is one Captain Fuller,—what sort of fellow is he?—very troublesome & noisy, I'm afraid,—I'm sure the major has enough to do with such a set of riotous young fellows;—& then, at the mess, Ma'am, Lord! I suppose he can hardly keep them quiet,— always in some mischief or other,—one Day, a plate will be broke,—another Day, a Glass,—& then such flinging of knives & forks at one another's Heads!—' And, in this ridiculous manner, with a thousand affected grimaces, he ran on till our Walk was at an End. I had however, much pleasure in seeing that Mr. Thrale suffered himself to be entertained with his Buffoonery.

Miss Thrale & I, going together to the Drawing Room, were followed by Mr. Seward, who, shutting the Door, renewed his importunities with redoubled earnestness, saying 'Come, to me—now Nobody is by,—*pray*, Mrs. ¹ *Holroyd, pray* oblige me!'

I only Laughed at his mock eagerness, but, growing more urgent, he almost staggered me, at last, by catching both my Hands, & kneeling to me. I made him, however, rise almost immediately, & protested I really had no *power* to offer myself for a *spectacle*.

'Then I won't see you, cried he, I won't look at you,' & he bound a Handkerchief across his Eyes.

I would have made use of this absurd sport to have stolen away, but the Gentleman was not quite so well blinded as to suffer that, & kept me with continued importunity till the rest of the folks joined us.

Cards were, then, called for, & Mr. & Mrs. Thrale, Sir Philip & Mr. Seward went to whist. Mr. Fuller, who hates them [cards][85], stayed to Chat with Miss Thrale & me.

Poor Mrs. Holroyd was, again, our theme; but he did not again press me to take her off; he contented himself with discussing her Character, & telling me his reasons for disliking her. He thinks she has used him extremely ill, for she propagated reports to the prejudice of Mrs. Johnston that might have ruined her with her Husband, & have cost him or Mr. Johnston his Life. 'How she *dared*, said he, warmly, attack a woman of her Character with such scurility, I can not imagine,—however, I have only paid her with *contempt*, for she was *worth* no other resentment.'

And when he gave me a particular account of his acquaintance with Mrs. Johnston, from the first moment of his seeing her, & spoke of her with an ꞁ openness of praise so honest & unaffected, that if I *had* harboured any suspicions against her, I should have lost them instantly.

Sunday, June 13ᵗʰ After Church we all strolled round the Grounds,—& the topic of our Discourse was Miss Streatfield. Mrs. Thrale asserted that she had a power of captivation that was irresistable; that her beauty, joined to her softness, her caressing manners, her Tearful Eyes, & alluring looks, would insinuate her into the Heart of *any* man she thought worth attacking.[86]

Sir Philip declared himself of a totally different opinion, & quoted Dr. Johnson against her, who had told him that, taking away her *Greek*, she was *as ignorant as a Butterfly*.

Mr. Seward declared her *Greek* was all *against* her with *him*, for that, instead of reading Pope, Swift or the Spectator, Books from which she might derive useful knowledge & improvement, it had led her to devote all her reading Time to *the first 8 Books of Homer*.

---

[85] Substituted for 'them' by FBA.

[86] HLT was rationalizing to herself her husband's infatuation with Miss Streatfeild (see above, p. 224 n. 42).

'But, said Mrs. Thrale, her *Greek*, you must own, has made all her *celebrity*; you would have heard no more of her than of any *other* pretty Girl, but for that.'

'What *I* object to, said Sir Philip, is her *avowed* preference for this *parson*,[87]—surely it is very indelicate in any lady to let all the World know with whom she is in love?'

'The *Parson*, said the severe Mr. Seward, I suppose spoke *first*,—or she would as soon have been in love with you, or with me.'

You will easily believe I gave him no pleasant look. He wanted me to slacken my pace, & tell him *in confidence* my *private* opinion of her; but I told him, very truly, that as I knew her chiefly by *account*, not by *acquaintance*, I had not absolutely *formed* my opinion.

'Were I to Live with her 4 Days, said this odd man, I believe the 5th I should want to take her to Church.'

'You'd be devilish tired of her, though, said Sir Philip, in half a Year. A *crying* Wife will never do!'

'O yes, cried he, the pleasure of soothing her would make amends.'

'Ah, cried Mrs. Thrale, I would ⟨en⟩sure her power of Crying herself into *any* of your Hearts she pleased. I made her Cry to Miss Burney, to shew how beautiful she looked in Tears.'

'If I had seen her, said Mr. Seward, I would never have visited you again.'

'O but *she* liked it passionately, answered Mrs. T. for she knows how well she does it. Miss Burney would have run away,—but she came forward on *purpose* to shew herself. I would have done so by nobody else, but Sophy

---

[87] The Revd Dr William Vyse (1741–1816), DCL (Oxon.), 1774, Canon Residentiary of Lichfield, 1772, Rector of St Mary, Lambeth, and of Sundridge, Kent, 1777. Miss Streatfeild had been openly declaring her love for this learned divine since about 1775. It was perhaps later this year that she learned of his secret marriage early in his life to some lower class woman whom he had pensioned off (see below, p. 374). HLT's editor, Abraham Hayward, writes that Vyse 'was separated from his wife, of whom he hoped to get rid either by divorce or by her death, as she was reported to be in bad health' (*Autobiography ... of Mrs. Piozzi*, i. 118–19). By 1792 he had thrown Miss Streatfeild over, 'either in despair at his wife's longevity or from caprice' (ibid.). Miss Streatfeild never married, and at his death was bequeathed by him £500 'in testimony of my sincere regard' (*EJL* v; *JL* i. 164, xi. 416 and n. 20; *Thraliana* i. 378).

Streatfield is never happier than when the Tears trickle from her fine Eyes in Company.'

'Suppose, Miss Burney, said Mr. Seward, we make her the Heroine of our Comedy? And call it *Hearts have at ye all*!

'Excellent! cried I, it can't be better.'

'Tell me, then, what situations you will have?—But stay, I have another Name that I think will do very well for ¹a Comedy,—*Every Thing a bore*.'

'O, mighty well,—& *you* shall be the Hero!'

'Well said Miss Burney! cried Mrs. Thrale; & pray let his Name be Mr. Chagrin.'

Well, indeed, did she name him, for I think his *ennui*, his sickness of the World & its Inhabitants, grows more & more obvious & strong every Day. He is, indeed, a melancholy instance of the inefficacy of Fortune, Talents, Education, Wit & Benevolence united to render any man happy whose mind has not a native disposition of content.

At Dinner, we had 3 persons added to our Party;—my dear Father, Miss Streatfield & Miss Brown.

Well selected, gay, good humoured, & uncommonly agreeable as was the whole society, the Day failed of being happy,—for Mr. Thrale's extreme seriousness & lowness, & Mrs. Thrale's agitated & *struggling* chearfulness, spread a degree of gravity & discomfort over us, that, though they prevented not partial & occasional sallies, totally banished our accustomed general & continued gaity. [Miss Thrale, too, was inwardly, very uneasy.][88]

Miss Brown, however, as you may remember I foresaw, proved the Queen of the Day. Miss Streatfield requires longer *Time* to make conquests. She is, indeed, much more really beautiful than Fanny Brown, but Fanny Brown is more showy, & her open, good humoured, gay, Laughing Face inspires an almost immediate wish ¹ of conversing &

---

[88] Added by FBA, no doubt for the edification of Queeny (now Lady Keith), who would live to see the appearance of the *Diary and Letters*. Mrs Barrett, however, omitted the addition in the published volume. FBA here and elsewhere tries to mitigate the original portrait she gives of Queeny as for the most part a self-centered and unfeeling daughter, but her doctoring of the MS, once revealed, serves merely to underscore Queeny's coldness.

merry making with her. Indeed the 2 Days she spent here have raised her greatly in my regard; she is a charming Girl, & so natural & easy & sweet tempered that there is no being half an Hour in her Company without ardently wishing her well.

My handsome Captain, as Mrs. Thrale called him, was extremely pleased with her,—indeed, I wish he had been *seriously* struck, for I think there is some resemblance in their Characters, & know not how either of them could chuse more judiciously.

I had very little talk with my dear Father, & could not get a moment to write to you.

Mr. Seward, as you probably heard, went to Town with my Father. He said he was going, in 2 Days, to Cornwall. After they were gone, Miss Brown's singing, Mr. Fuller's & my disputes of *who* should exhibit, & general conversation closed the Day.

Monday, June 14th proved far more lively & comfortable. Mr. Thrale Daily looks some what better, & his sweet Wife's natural spirits & happiness insensibly, though not uniformly, return.

Miss Streatfield, Miss Brown & I slept in 3 Rooms leading one into another,—we all rose about 6 o'clock; &, the morning being lovely, we walked till Breakfast Time. So we are become *prodigious intimate*, & Fanny Brown & I shut ourselves up, the Night before, purposely to talk of Mr. Murphy, & *try* which could praise him most.—We really made a good Battle of it.—But I don't know which was Conqueror: *If* he had heard us!—

At Breakfast, our party was Sir Philip, Mr. Fuller, Miss Streatfield, Miss Brown, the Thrales & I.

The first office performed, was Dressing Miss Brown; she had put on bright Jonquil Ribbons,—Mrs. Thrale exclaimed against them immediately,—Mr. Fuller half joined her,—& away she went, & brought Green Ribbons of her own, which she made Miss Brown run up stairs with to put on. This she did with the utmost good humour;—but *Dress* is the last thing in which she excells, for she has Lived so much abroad, & so much with Foreigners at Home, that she never appears habited as an English Woman, nor as an high bred Foreigner, but rather as an Italian opera Dancer. And her wild, careless, giddy manner, her loud hearty Laugh, & general negligence of appearance, contribute to give her that air & look. I like her so much, that I am quite sorry she is not better advised, either by her own, or some friend's Judgement.[89]

Miss Brown, however, was *Queen* of the Breakfast, for though her giddiness made every body take liberties with her, her good humour made every body love her,—& her gaity made every body desirous to associate with her. Sir Philip *played* with her, as with a young & sportive kitten;— Mr. Fuller Laughed & chatted with her; & Mr. Seward [when here][90] tiezed & tormented her. The truth is, he cannot bear her, & she, in return, equally fears & dislikes him;—but still, she could not help attracting his Notice.

We then all Walked out, & had a very delightful stroll; but, in returning, one of the Dogs (we have 12, I believe, belonging to the House) was detected pursuing the sheep on the Common,—Miss Thrale sent one of the men after him, & he was siezed to be punished;—the poor Creatures Cries were so dreadful, that I took to my *Feet*, & ran away with the utmost swiftness in my power to the House,— but, to my great amazement, the tender S.S. stayed to look on during the whipping.[91]

When,—after all was over, they returned to the House, the saucy Captain Fuller, as soon as he saw me, exclaimed 'O!—some hartshorn! some hartshorn for Miss Burney!'

I instantly found he thought me guilty of affectation; & the drollery of his *manner* made it impossible to be affronted with his accusation; therefore I took the trouble to *try* to clear myself,—but know not how I succeeded. I assured him that if my staying could have answered any

---

[89] See also above, p. 98, for Fanny Browne's '*slovenly* way of Dressing', though HLT rated her a relatively high 14 (out of a possible 20) for 'Person Mien & Manner' (ibid. n. 77). Overall, HLT ranked her 5th (out of 45 women rated) for character and accomplishments, giving her 15 for 'Worth of Heart', 8 for 'Conversation Powers', 19 for 'Good humour', and 17 for 'Ornamental knowledge'. Of 'Useful Knowledge' she could give no opinion (*Thraliana* i. 331).

[90] Inserted by FBA.

[91] See also *EJL* i. 135, 290 for FB's sensitivity to the suffering of animals.

purpose, I would have *compelled* myself to hear the screams, & witness the corrections of the offending animal; but that, as that was *not* the ˡ case I saw no necessity for giving myself pain officiously.

'But I'll tell you, cried he, my *reason* for not liking that Ladies should run away from all disagreeable sights; I think that, if they are totally unused to them, whenever any accident happens, they are not only *helpless*, but *worse*, for they scream & rant, & get out of the way, when, if they were not so frightened, they might be of some service: I was with a lady the other Day, when a poor fellow was brought into her House half killed,—but, instead of doing him any good, she only shriekt, & called out, Oh! ⌜Christ Jesus! Lord have⌝ mercy on me! & ran away.'

There was an honesty so characteristic in this attack, that I took very serious pains to vindicate myself, & told him that, if I had any knowledge of myself, I could safely affirm that, in any case similar to what he mentioned, instead of running away, I should myself, if no abler person were at Hand, have undertaken not merely to *see*, but to *bind* the man's Wounds. Nor, indeed, can I doubt but I should.

The Bell now Ringing for the Children's Noonings, Captain Fuller proposed our all going to the House keeper's Room to partake of it; Miss Brown, Mrs. & Miss Thrale & I readily followed, but Miss Streatfield declined accompanying us. When we had Laughed ˡ

[*a leaf or leaves missing*]

Gormondised with equal avidity, we sent a message to the S.S. to *beg* her to join us; this, when she resisted, Captain Fuller said he would go & feed her, & then [g]et some Tart to take to her; but I proposed that we should carry her the whole of the Entertainment,—&, [i]n a moment, we all assailed her, Captain Fuller with [a] Leg of Lamb, Miss Thrale with a Dish of Peas, Miss Brown with a Jug of milk, & I with a Gooseberry Tart.

We found her conversing with Mr. Thrale upon the Lawn. Our *Joke*, however, did not take!—she looked half frightened, & gravely said *she was not hungry.* Mr. Fuller pursued her with his Leg of Lamb, but her seriousness soon repressed his *enjouement,*[92] & so back again we all went, [feeling][93] rather more foolish than we came.

Miss Brown was quite *downed*[94] & ashamed,—but Mr. Fuller & I both agreed that though the frolic had failed with the S.S., it had answered *our* purpose, since *we* had had our Diversion from it.

After this, we all went, in a *body*, c'est a dire Sir Philip (who is ever ready for sport) Mr. Thrale, Mr. Fuller, the S.S. Miss Brown, Miss Thrale & I to the Tattersals, to see the *place*. And very good amusement it afforded us,—but I have nothing new to tell you of it.[95] Miss Brown, Miss Thrale, Mr. Fuller & I made a party of our [o]wn all the morning, & were *so merry as ever you saw in your Life!* And, when we returned hither, we 4 strolled into the Drawing Room, while the rest continued walking.

A violent contest now ensued between Captain Fuller & me concerning our imitations;—but, at length, he was brought to compliance, & shewed some of his tricks, by taking off a whole Band of musicians performing the march in Motezuma.[96] This he did very comically, making himself, in rotation, Violin, Base, Flute, Bassoon, French Horn & Harpsichord.

But, when he had done, I thought I should have been devoured by his impetuousity to make *me* return the Compliment. He protested, & said he would take *his Bible Oath*, that I had promised at Brighthelmstone that, when *he* played the Fool to me, I would make him amends!— however, I never did. He got me a Chair, & another for himself, & personated a militia Officer visiting Mrs. Holroyd,—& persecuted me with a thousand ridiculous questions, all leading to such subjects as that lady treats of: & went on, with a comical absurdity, till he grew tired, &

---

[92] Sprightliness, playfulness.
[93] Inserted by FBA.
[94] A favorite expression of SJ. *OED* cites 2 examples from him (in 1778 and 1780), and SJ, in his *Dictionary*, quotes a line from Sidney: 'To *down* proud hearts that would not willing die.'
[95] See above, p. 84.
[96] The opera by Sacchini (see *EJL* ii. 78).

then, very seriously, he *begged*, as a *great favour* that I would oblige him.

I was upon the point of trying 50 Times, for he was so earnest that I was ashamed of refusing; but I have really no manner of command of my voice when I am not quite easy, & though I had run on in Mrs. Holroyd's way, to Mrs. Thrale for half an Hour together, it had been *accidentally*, & when some of her *Cackle* just *occurred* to me, not *deliberately*, & by *way* of exhibition.

I have just an opportunity to send to Town,—adieu, my dearest Girl. |

85   Streatham,
                        [*post* 15–?26] June [1779]

To Susanna Elizabeth Burney

AJL (Berg, Diary MSS I, Barrett, paginated [973]–90, foliated 9–18), June 1779
10 single sheets 4to, 20 pp.

Streatham,

The foolery with which I concluded my last pacquet, was put an End to by the Entrance of Sir Philip, & Mrs. Thrale. Some thing being said of the pleasantness & [q]uietness of this situation, Mrs. Thrale said 'Why yes, it's something better than a villa at Hampstead or Hygate, here you can see your Town House from your Country House, even though *George's*[97] is at Hampstead.' looking

---

[97] 'Soon after, the conversation turning upon public places, young Branghton asked if I had ever been to *George*'s at Hampstead? ... "I'll treat you there some Sunday soon"' (*Evelina*, ed. E. A. Bloom (1968), p. 187; vol. ii, letter 13). New Georgia, a two-storey wooden cottage and grounds in Turner's Wood, Hampstead, was built in 1737. 'The chief attractions were the number of mechanical oddities set in motion in the garden and in various little rooms into which the house was divided. London shopkeepers ... often made their way to the place on Sunday afternoons' (W. W. Wroth, *The London Pleasure Gardens* [1896], pp. 187–8, cited ibid., p. 429). Mr Smith dismisses the place as 'low' (*Evelina*, p. 187).

wickedly towards me. 'George's? cried Sir Philip, why *you* were never there?'

'Yes, I have been, answered she, & at White Conduit House[98] too,—Now Miss Burney's Face lightens up!—But, by the way, *George's* is spelt wrong,[99]—it's the *only* fault, I believe, in the Book, but—'

'Ah, dear Ma'am, cried I, let me hear of it some other Time!'

'Nay, I vow, I know no other fault in all the 3 Volumes.'

Mr. Fuller Laughed, but Sir Philip, lowering his voice, enquired Mrs. Thrale's meaning; however, the subject was [s]oon changed, for she went away. And then Sir Philip, Mr. Fuller, Miss Brown & I made a Quartetto for the rest of the morning, & we were so sociable & happy, that we never [re]collected Dressing or Dinner, till it was just 5 o'clock,—[w]hen Sir Philip, looking at his watch & giving the infor[m]ation, most effectually roused us,—We jumped up, & flew [ou]t of the Room as if we had been followed by Wild Beasts. Our subject of Discourse had been Dr. Johnson: Mr. Fuller has a passionate desire to see & know him, has, also, curiosity insatiable to hear of his Character & manners. |

While we were Dressing, Mr. Seward returned,—he ha[d] posponed [*sic*] his Journey to Cornwall,—&, before Dinner, Dr. Delap, just arrived from Lewes. |

I did not, therefore, want a Friend at *Table*, for, as us[ual,] he resumed his watchful attention & care of my *plate*, & hi[s] wondering & re-iterated exclamations at the little I Eat,—telling me, however, that, with or without Eating, I knew how to make myself immortal! So, you find, he has not lost his gallantry. Besides, when Painting

---

[98] A tavern located beside the White Conduit (which supplied water to the Charterhouse) on Islington Hill. It had a coffee and tea room, a fishpond, a cricket field, and 'pleasing walks prettily disposed' (the *Sunday Rambler*, 1774, quoted in *The London Encyclopaedia*, ed. B. Weinreb and C. Hibbert (Bethesda, Maryland, 1986), p. 954). Evelina spends an evening there with her grandmother and the Branghtons, but finds the people who frequent the place 'all smart and gaudy, and so pert and low-bred, that [she] could hardly endure being amongst them' (*Evelina*, p. 193; vol. ii, letter 14).

[99] i.e., it should be 'Georgia's'.

was talked of, he asked me if I could *draw*? *no*, quot[h] I,—'What, cried he, only Characters?'

And, soon after, 'I have brought you; he said, the rest of my Tragedy: you & Dr. Johnson & Murphy & Mrs. Thrale must sit in judgement on it. And pray tell me what you think of it,—you said some things about it tha[t] struck me a good deal,—I beg you'll tell me as you go o[n.']

I could only say he did me a *great deal* of Honour, & *all that.*

When he gave an account of the Company he had left at Brighthelmstone, he mentioned Mrs. Holroyd,—& instantly all our folks looked at *me*, & Captain Fuller in pa[r]ticular with a Laugh portending such mischief, that I was fain, with all the supplication I could put into my Phi[z,] to beg him to be quiet: for, really, I should ambition nothing so little as to have it further spread that [I] took off her, or any body.[1] However, Mr. Fuller did no[t,] like Mr. Murphy, continue his Threats till I *knelt* [to] him, but gave them up at my first fright.

Soon after Tea, Mr. Fuller left us, having first enquired of me what I thought of a Ranelagh Party for the Evening, & whether I would accompany him & Sir Philip thither which, after due deliberation, as I declined, they were obliged to go without me. I hope you admire my forbearance & prudence?

The rest of the Evening, one Party devoted to Cards, but Miss Brown, Miss Thrale & I to fun & nonsense. And, really, we made so much, that Mr. Seward, I believe, thought us crazy, & wished us confined.

Tuesday, June 15th As soon as Breakfast was over, we lost Miss Brown, who was obliged to return to Wimbledon, where her Father Lives. I was really sorry to part with her, &, but that I am so little in Town, would certainly have asked her to call on me.

---

[1] Cf. *EJL* i. 197, where FB calls 'the art of mimickry ... a dangerous talent', and ii. 161, where she mentions the 'abuse & ill will' Jenny Barsanti suffers because of it.

When she was gone, Mr. Seward's *ennui* coming under consideration, Mrs. Thrale asked us if he was not the Poco curante[2] in Candide? Not one of us had read it.

'What, cried Mr. Seward, have not *you*, Miss Burney?'

'No, never.'

'Well, said Mrs. Thrale, I am quite *amazed* at that!—I did not *expect* Dr. Delap or Sophy Streatfield to have read it, but how *You* missed it, I do wonder.'

'Miss Streatfield, said Mr. Seward, I dare say never reads but in *form*,—finishes one Book before she will *look* at another, & spreads a Green Cloth on her Table, & sits to it in earnest.'

'Perhaps, said Dr. Delap, Miss Burney, like Dr. Middleton,[3] is in a *course of Reading*, so goes on regularly—'

'No, no, cried Mrs. Thrale, that is not her way,—she is very desultory a Reader.' |

'I dare say she is, said Mr. Seward, & that makes her so clever.'

Candide was then produced, & Mrs. Thrale read aloud the part concerning Poco curante,—& really, the Cap fitted so well, that Mr. Seward could not attempt to dispute it.

At Dinner, we had the Company of the Bishop of Peterborough & Mrs. Hinchliffe, Sir Philip & my dear Father. It was not, however, like a *Brighthelmstone* meeting, for Mrs. Thrale's gaity was all forced, & the Bishop & his Lady seemed to suppose it necessary to be quiet & grave. The contrary, however, is the case, for poor Mr. Thrale *seeks* entertainment, & seems best pleased when others are most chearful.

At Night, when all our Company was gone except those who slept here, viz. Sir Philip, Dr. Delap, Miss Streatfield, & Mr. Seward, the latter, who absolutely refused playing Cards, entered into a droll sort of conversation with me,

[2] Lord Pococurante, i.e., 'small care', a Venetian nobleman who has everything but takes pleasure in nothing. See *Candide*, chap. 25.

[3] Presumably Conyers Middleton (1683–1750), DD, though no other mention has been found of his pursuing 'a *course of Reading*'. In 1723 he published a plan for arranging the books from Bishop Moore's library donated to Cambridge University.

concerning Miss Streatfield. I had heard her invite him to Dine at her House the next Day, to meet a Miss Boone,[4] a strange sort of person, whom he rather wished to see;— yet he talked to me of going the next Day to *Cornwall*. 'No, no, cried I, not to-morrow,—you'll go none to Cornwall to-morrow!—'

'If I don't, then, said he, I shall go to Windsor.'

'Not till after *Dinner*, then,' cried I, Laughing.

'Why so? cried he; do you think I mean to meet a *boon* Companion?'

'I think that's an excellent *pretence*,' quoth I.

'I believe it will be a great *bore*, said he; I don't think I shall go.' |

F:B. I would venture some Wager upon that!'

Mr. Seward. Why, what makes you think I shall go?'

F:B. Because I don't know how you can do better.'

Mr. Seward. O, but you know she's *engaged*.[5]

F:B. Yes, but you may like to *Dine* with her, for all that.

Mr. Seward. Yes, I like her *passing well*,—that's to say, *passablement bien*,—nothing more.'

Soon after, Miss Thrale joined us, & then he flung himself on a sofa to *ruminate*. I, who was in no very melancholic mood, began prating nonsense with Miss Thrale, who, though she has no great passion to ⟨utter it,⟩ has a Disposition not to be excelled for *enjoying* it, when made by any one she likes: but, in the midst of our Cackle, I perceived Mr. Seward had wound himself close to us, &, though pretending to *lollop*,[6] was listening with all attention. 'O, cried I, do pray go to the other sofa,— such stuff as we talk will distract you.'

'No, no, said he,—pray go on,—it will divert me.'

I was not good natured enough to consent to this, but told him if *he* would not go, *we* would;—he begged us to

---

[4] Ann Elizabeth Boone (1745–87), eldest daughter of Daniel Boone (1710–70), of Rook's Nest, Surrey, MP (half-brother of Charles Boone), and his wife (m. 1736) Anne, née Evelyn (1721–81) (Namier; *Miscellanea Geneologica et Heraldica* 2nd ser. iv (1892), 339). See below, p. 372.

[5] Alluding to Miss Streatfeild's '*avowed* preference' for Vyse.

[6] i.e., loll about.

keep still,—but we were in no *still* humour, so we moved off to another corner, & went on with our own Chit Chat.

Finding us very *merry*, though not very *wise*, in a few minutes he deigned to follow us, & desired to be admitted of our party; but I was inexorable, & bid him go away & *meditate* by himself,—'We shall only *Bore* you, I cried, so pray leave us,—our folly will I else overpower You.'

'O, now you are too bad!' said he, &, half piqued, went off. Afterwards, at supper, when some of them,—I forget which,—accused me of turning Mr. Seward away, I fairly said I was *afraid* of him, lest *our* nonsence should provoke his contempt, or *his* ennui should excite *mine*. And, indeed, one of these apprehensions must be almost always well grounded in his presence.

Wednesday, June 16ᵗʰ We had, at Breakfast, a scene of it's *sort*, the most curious I ever saw.

The *Persons* were Sir Philip, Mr. Seward, Dr. Delap, Miss Streatfield, Mrs. & Miss Thrale & I.

The Discourse turning, I know not how, upon Miss Streatfield's Tears, Mrs. Thrale said 'Ay, I made her Cry once for Miss Burney as pretty as could be;—but nobody *does* cry so pretty as the S.S.—I'm sure when she cried for Seward, I never saw her look half so lovely.'

'For Seward? cried Sir Philip, did she cry for Seward?— what a happy Dog!—I hope she'll never cry for *me*, for if she does, I won't answer for the consequences!'

'Seward, said Mrs. Thrale, had affronted Johnson, & then Johnson affronted Seward,—& then the S.S. cried—'

'O, cried Sir Philip, that I had but been here!'

'Nay, answered Mrs. Thrale, you'd only have seen how like 3 fools 3 sensible people behaved; for my part, I was quite sick of it,—& of them too.'

Sir Philip. But what did Seward do? was he not *melted*?

Mrs. Thrale. Not he; he was thinking only of his *own* affront, & taking fire at that. I

Mr. Seward. Why yes, I *did* take Fire, for I went & planted my back to it.

S.S. And Mrs. Thrale kept stuffing *me* with Toast & Water.

Sir Philip. But what did *Seward* do with himself? Was not he in *extacy*? what did he do or say?

Mr. Seward. O, I said pho, pho, don't let's have any more of this,—it's making it of too much consequence,—no more piping, pray.

Did you ever hear such a speech made before such a lady, in your Life? I actually put down my Tea, & held up my Hands in expression of wonder!—both at *his* making, & *her* enduring it.

Sir Philip. Well, I have heard so much of these Tears, that I would give the Universe to have a sight of them.

Mrs. Thrale. Lord, she shall Cry again if you like it.

S.S. No,—pray, Mrs. Thrale;—

Sir Philip. O pray do!—pray let *me* see a little of it!—

Mrs. Thrale Yes, *do* cry, a little, Sophy;—(in a wheedling Voice) *pray* do!—consider, now, you are going to Day,—& it's very hard if you won't *cry* a little;—indeed, S.S., you *ought* to cry—'

Now for the wonder of wonders,—when Mrs. Thrale, in a coaxing voice, suited to a Nurse soothing a Baby, had run on for some Time,—while all the rest of us, in Laughter, joined in the request,—two Crystal Tears came into the soft Eyes of the S.S.,—& rolled gently down her Cheeks!—such a sight I never saw before,[7] nor could I have believed;—she *offered* not to conceal, or dissipate them,—on the contrary, she really *contrived* to have them seen by every body. She looked, indeed, uncommonly handsome, for her *pretty Face* was not, like Chloes, *blubbered*,[8] it was smooth & elegant, & niether her Features or complexion were at all ruffled,—nay, indeed, she was *smiling* all the Time.

'Look, look! cried Mrs. Thrale, see if the Tears are not come already!'

Loud & rude bursts of Laughter broke from us all at once;—how, indeed, could they be restrained?—Yet we all stared, & looked & re-looked again & again 20 Times

---

[7] But see above, p. 254.

[8] FB alludes to Prior's 'A Better Answer', l. 1: 'Dear Cloe, how blubber'd is that pretty Face?' (Matthew Prior, *Literary Works*, ed. H. B. Wright and M. K. Spears (2nd edn., Oxford, 1971), i. 450).

ere we could believe our Eyes. Sir Philip I thought would have died in convulsions, for his Laughter & his politeness, struggling furiously with one another, made him almost black in the Face; Mr. Seward looked half vexed that her Crying for *him* was now so much lowered in its flattery, yet *Grinned* incessantly;—Miss Thrale Laughed as much as *contempt* would allow her;—Mrs. Thrale & I *rolled* on our Chairs;—but Dr. Delap seemed *petrified* with astonishment.

When the violence of our mirth abated, Sir Philip, colouring violently with his efforts to speak, said 'I thank you, Ma'am,—I'm much obliged to you.' But I really believe he spoke without knowing what he was saying.

'What a wonderful command, said Dr. Delap, very gravely, that Lady must have over herself!'

'She has certainly 2 Bags well stored next her Eyes,—' said Mr. Seward.

She now took out a Handkerchief, & wiped her Eyes.

'Sir Philip, cried Mr. Seward, how can you suffer her to dry her own Eyes?—You, who sit next her?'

'I dare not dry them for her, answered he, because I am not the *right man*,—'

'But if *I* sat next her, returned he, she should not | dry them herself.'

'I wish, cried Dr. Delap, I had a Bottle to put them in!—'tis a thousand pities they should be wasted.'

'There, now, said Mrs. Thrale, she looks for all the World as if nothing had happened,—for, you know, nothing *has* happened!'

'Would *you* cry, Miss Burney, said Sir Philip, if we ask'd you.'

'Lord, cried Mrs. Thrale, I would not do thus by Miss Burney for ten Worlds!—I dare say she would never speak to me again. I should think she'd be more likely to walk out of my House, than to *Cry* because I bid her.'

'I don't know how that is, said Sir Philip, but I'm sure she is gentle enough.'

'She *can* cry, I doubt not, said Mr. Seward, on any proper occasion.'

'But I must know, said I, what *for*.'

I did not say this loud enough for the S.S. to hear me;—but if I had, she would not have taken it for the reflection it *meant*; she seemed, the whole Time, totally insensible to the numerous strange, &, indeed, *impertinent* speeches which were made, & to be very well satisfied that she was only manifesting a tenderness of disposition that encreased her beauty of Countenance.

At least, *I* can put no other construction upon her conduct, which was, without exception, the strangest I ever saw! Without any *pretence* of affliction, to weep merely because she was *bid*, though *bid* in a manner to *forbid* any one else!—to be in good spirits all the Time,—to see the whole Company expiring of Laughter at her *Tears* without being at all offended,—&, at last, to dry them up, & go on with the same sort of Conversation she held before they started,—All this to do is too extraordinary for Comments.

What Sir Philip or Mr. Seward privately thought of this incident, I know not yet; but Dr. Delap has made me sick with Laughing, by his odd manner of speaking of it. 'Yes, he says, she has pretty blue Eyes,—very pretty, indeed,— she's quite a wonderful miss!—if it had not been for that little Gush I don't know what would have become of me! It was very good natured of her, really, for she charms & uncharms in a moment; she is a *bane & an antidote* at the same Time.'

Then, after considering it more deeply, 'I declare, he said, I was never so much surprised in my life! I should as soon have expected that the Dew would fall from Heaven because Mrs. Thrale called for it, as that that Miss what d'ye call her would have cried just because she was asked!—But the thing is, *did* she Cry?—I declare I don't believe it!—yet I think, at this moment, I saw it,— only I know it could not be,—something of a mist, I suppose, was before my Eyes.'

Miss Streatfield returned to Town at Noon; Mr. Seward, who had begged her to give him a seat in her Carriage, changed his mind, & went, before her, with Mr. Thrale. I believe, indeed, not from whim, but the friendly intention of accompanying him to Dr Heberdens,[9] for he knows

[*See opposite page for n. 9*]

so much of Physic, that Mrs. Thrale is never so happy as when her Husband is with him.

Before they went, Miss Streatfield condescended to again invite Mr. Seward to Dinner, & ask if he would not come? 'I don't know, cried he,—it will be just as it happens,—perhaps I may, perhaps not,—I can't promise.'

A pretty Gentleman to be invited by a Lady!

Soon after, coming up to say something to me, I told him I was sure I should *win* my wager, if I had laid it.

'No, cried he, I don't know that; I believe it will be too great a *bore*. But what will you lay?'

'O, with *You* nothing, because you may act accordingly.'

'Yes, yes, you *must*,—what shall it be?—suppose *Evelina*.'

'No, indeed;—I won't lay that, or any thing else with *you*.'

'Yes, yes,—we *must* have a wager, then I shall be sure of a *boon* at any rate.'

'Yes, but not such Trash as that!—you, who are making a Library, & very difficult in your choice,—Lord, I would not have you *contaminate* it with such stuff for the world!'

'What will you put against it?—the last Edition?—'

'What?—Why Tom Thumb, Jack Hickerthrift,[10] & Jack the Giant Killer.

'Pho, pho,—let's see,—do you love Poetry?—suppose we put Prior's Poems?[11]—'

'No, no,—nothing at all,—I will lay no wager—'

'Well, it's agreed, then; Evelina against Prior.'

'No, indeed, I don't say *done*,—I don't agree to it at all.—'

'I *insist* upon it;—it's a fair wager,—& I shall never speak to you again if you don't stand to it.'

[9] William Heberden (1710–1801); MD (Cantab.), 1739; scholar and one of the most eminent physicians of the century. The Thrales had summoned him during their son Harry's fatal illness (*TSP*, p. 152). In the present crisis Dr Bromfield sent for him after Thrale's attack (see above, p. 298 n. 82; *Thraliana* i. 389). After seeing Thrale again Heberden pronounced him 'now wholly out of Danger', but confided privately to Seward 'that he never would wholly recover' (ibid. i. 391, 399).

[10] Jack (or Tom) Hickathrift, a mythical labourer who slew a giant in Norfolk. Sterne refers to him in *Tristram Shandy*, vol. i, chap. 14.

[11] See below.

And then he made off. However, happen what may, I shall niether pay nor receive, though I expect a violent *fuss*,—unless, indeed, he forgets it ere we meet again. |

Sunday, June 20th

Dr. Delap stayed here till Yesterday, when he returned to Lewes. He attacked me, before he went, about my *Comedy*, & said he had some *claim* to see it,—however I escaped shewing it, though he vows he will come again, when he is able, on *purpose*;—but I hope we shall be set out for Spa.

Yesterday we had a great Dinner,—the Party, Lord & Lady Gage,[12] Sir Sampson & Lady Gideon,[13] Mr. & Mrs. D'Avenant.

Lord Gage is a very facetious man in the story telling way, & in *active Wit*, he is very entertaining.

Lady Gage is fat, smooth, soft, sweet & obliging. She did me the Honour to seat herself next me after Dinner, & talk with me till she went away, with great politeness & good nature.[14]

Sir Sampson Gideon is much such another character, & happened, before & during Dinner, to employ himself in the same civil way.

Lady Gideon is very pretty & very elegant, though tant soit peu affected.

Mr. & Mrs. D'Avenant are Mrs. Thrale's Cousins; a very agreeable, & remarkably happy Couple.

Sir Philip Clerke was also with us. And, at Tea Time, Mr. Beresford entered. He rather gains ground, I find, here, from the diversion his strange & assured manner

---

[12] William Hall Gage (1718–91), of Firle and Lewes, Sussex, and High Meadow, Glos; 2nd Visc. Gage (Ire.); cr. (1780) B. Gage of Firle (UK) and (1790) B. Gage of High Meadow (UK); MP; m. (1757) Elizabeth, née Gideon (*c.*1739–83), sister and co-heir of Sir Sampson Gideon. Ld. Gage was at this time Paymaster of Pensions.

[13] Sir Sampson Gideon (1745–1824), 1st Bt, of Spalding, Lincs; m. (1766) Maria-Marowe, née Wilmot (1743–94). Sir Sampson later took the name of Eardley instead of Gideon and was cr. (1789) B. Eardley (Ire.).

[14] HLT rated her 19 (out of a possible 20) for 'Good humour' (*Thraliana* i. 331).

occasions. He really does not at all want *parts*, however deficient he is in *address*.

The D'Avenants & Sir Philip are here still; so is my good friend Mr. Lort.

Poor Mr. Thrale, thank God, *does* get better, though he continues very low,—but the efforts he makes, against both *disease* & long *habit* to keep from sleeping in the afternoon, (which he has been prohibited indulging) & the patience with which he bears being *worried* to keep him awake, joined to his dejection, is so affecting that I [c]ould almost cry sometimes to look at him.

June 23^d

Mr. Thrale continues, I hope, to get better, though slowly.

2 Days ago, while I was sitting with him in the Library, Mr. Seward entered. What is become of his *Cornwall* scheme I know not. As soon as the first enquiries were over, 'Miss Burney, he said, I have lost my Wager.'

'It was no *Wager*, cried I; it was only an *opinion*.'

'Yes, indeed, it was; & I have ordered the Books. I shall have them very prettily Bound for you, & the last Edition.'

'I hope, then, you want them yourself? for I'm sure they will be nothing to *me*.'

Here, for the Time, the matter dropt.

The rest of the Day, he hardly ever spoke to me but about what he calls *our Comedy*, & he pressed & tiezed me to set about it. But he grew, in the Evening, so queer, so *loll*,[15] so ennuyé, that, in a fit of absurdity, I called him *Mr. Dry*; & the name took so with Mrs. Thrale, that I know not when he will lose it. Indeed, there is something in this Young man's alternate drollery & lassitude, entertaining qualities, & wearying complaints, that provoke me to more [pertness][16] than I practice to almost any body.

The Play, he said, should have the double Title of The Indifferent Man, or every thing a Bore;—& I protested

---

[15] i.e., droopy. This adjectival use of the word is not in *OED* (the word is omitted in *DL* i. 241).

[16] Substituted by FBA for an obliterated word not recovered.

Mr. *Dry* should be the Hero. And then we ran on, jointly, planning a succession of ridiculous scenes,—he lashing himself pretty freely, though not half *so* freely, or so much to the purpose as *I* lashed him,—for I attacked him, through the Channel of *Mr. Dry*, upon his *ennui*, his causeless melancholy, his complaining languors, his Yawning inattention, & his restless discontent. You may easily imagine I was in pretty high spirits to go so far,—in truth, nothing else could either have prompted or excused my facetiousness. And his own manners are so cavalier, that they always, with me, stimulate a ⌐saucy⌐ return.

He repeatedly begged me to go to Work, & commit the projected scenes to Paper; but I thought that might be carrying the Jest too far, for, as I was in no humour to spare him, *written* raillery might, perhaps, have been less to his Taste than Verbal.

He Challenged me to meet him the next morning [Tues., 22 June] before Breakfast in the Library, that we might work together at some scenes,—but I thought it as well to let the matter drop, & did not make my Entry till they were all assembled.

His mind, however, ran upon nothing else;—&, as soon as we happened to be left together, he again attacked me,—'Come, said he, have you nothing ready yet? I dare say you have half an Act in your pocket.'

'No, quoth I,—I have quite forgot the Whole business;—I was only in a humour for it last Night.'

'How shall it begin? cried he,—with *Mr. Dry* in his study?—his slippers just on,—his Hair about his Ears,—exclaiming what a bore is Life!—what is to be done next?'

'Next? cried I,—what, before he has done any thing at all?

'O, he has *Dressed* himself, You know.—Well, then he takes up a Book——'

'For Example, *this*,' cried I, giving him Clarendon's History.[17]

---

[17] *The History of the Rebellion and Civil Wars in England*, by Edward Hyde (1609–74), 1st E. of Clarendon. The work was first published at Oxford in 3 vols., 1702–04. The Streatham copy was a 3 vol.-in-6 8vo edn. which was sold

He took it up *in Character*, & flinging it away, cried 'No,—this will never do,—a History by a Party writer is odious.'

I then gave him Robertson's America.[18]

'This, cried he, is of all reading the most melancholy; an account of Possessions we have lost by our own folly.'

I then gave him Baretti's Spanish Travels.[19]

'Who, cried he, flinging it aside, can read Travels by a fellow who never speaks a Word of Truth?'

Then I gave him a Volume of Clarissa.[20]

'Pho! cried he,—a Novel writ by a Bookseller!—there is but one Novel now one can bear to read,—& that's written by a Young lady.'

I hastened to stop him with Dalrymple's Memoirs,[21] & then proceeded to give him various others, upon all which he made severe, splenetic, yet comical comments;—& we continued thus employed till he was summoned to accompany Mr. Thrale to Town.

He returned with him to Dinner. My dear Father also Dined here.

He took a very early opportunity of telling me he had brought his *Wager*,—I assured him I should not take it,—but, in the afternoon, he came up to me with the Books in his Hand. They are a large & new Edition, with 2 Prints by Bartolozzi.[22]

---

at the auction of HLT's library in 1816 (*Sale Catalogues of Libraries of Eminent Persons*, gen. ed. A. N. L. Munby (1971–75), v. 402).

[18] *The History of America*, 2 vols. 4to (1777), by William Robertson (1721–93) (ibid., v. 422).

[19] *A Journey from London to Genoa, through England, Portugal, Spain, and France*, 2 vols. 4to (1770), by Giuseppe Baretti (ibid.).

[20] From a 7-vol. 8vo edn. (ibid. v. 402), presumably the 4th edn. 8vo of 1751 (W. M. Sale, *Samuel Richardson: A Bibliographical Record of His Literary Career with Historical Notes* (New Haven, 1936), pp. 56–61).

[21] *Memoirs of Great Britain and Ireland*, 2 vols. 4to (1771, 1773), by Sir John Dalrymple, Bt (1726–1810). This was sold at a 2nd auction in 1823, after HLT's death (*Sale Catalogues*, v. 545).

[22] This must have been the recently published 2-vol. 8vo edn. (by Thomas Evans) of *The Poetical Works of Matthew Prior* (see Prior, *Literary Works*, i. pp. xxxviii, xlv-xlvii). However, there is only 1 illustration to this edn., a frontispiece engraving (publ. 20 Jan. 1779) of 'Henry and Emma' by J. K. Sherwin, after a design by Mortimer. No illustrations to Prior are identified by A. W. Tuer in his comprehensive 'List of Bartolozzi's Works', in *Bartolozzi and His Works* (1882),

I absolutely refused to accept them.

We had a violent Contest;—he insisted upon it that it was using him ill not to take them, & I insisted upon it that I had never agreed to the Wager,—which, indeed, ǀ is very true.

At last, applying to Miss Thrale, he begged her to put them in my Room. My remonstrances were vain,—but *Mrs.* Thrale interposed, & told her to let us settle the matter our own way.

He had a good mind, he said, to carry them there himself. In conclusion, we niether of us receded,—& the Books were left on the Reading Table.

The rest of the Evening, he was siezed with the *ennui*,— & as his splenetic fits rather excite my mirth than pity, I made my own Diversion out of him pretty freely. Indeed I am half sorry for, & half sick of his *dismal* humours, which, I am afraid, gain ground upon him.

How strange it is—that we never either see or hear from Mr. Murphy!—Mrs. Thrale writ him word of her Husband's situation, yet he has taken no manner of notice of her intelligence. I cannot but suppose her Letter miscarried, for it is impossible he can be so unfeeling, ungrateful, & inconsistent unlike all that he *seemed* ⌜to be⌝ as to be unconcerned at the danger of so old & so good a friend as Mr. Thrale.[23]

The next morning, Wednesday, June 22^d [23] I had some very serious talk with Mr. Seward,—& such as gave me no inclination for raillery, though it was concerning his *ennui*; on the contrary, I resolved, at the moment, never to rally him upon that subject again, for his account of himself filled me with compassion. He told me that he had never been well for Three Hours in a Day in his Life!—& that when he ǀ was thought only *tired*, he was really so ill that he believed scarce another man would

---

ii. 85–152. If FB is not mistaken about the Bartolozzi prints, these would have had to have been 2 otherwise unknown illustrations specially bound in by Seward.

    23 HLT complained in her diary that 'Murphy's a disippated Rogue, & loves his Friends while they can talk & hear' (*Thraliana* i. 390). But there would be no rift between him and the Thrales.

stay in Company. I was quite shocked at this account, & told him, honestly, that I had done him so little justice as to attribute all his *languors* to Affectation.[24]

When Mrs. Thrale joined us, he told us he had just seen Dr. Jebb,—Sir Richard, I mean,[25]—& that he had advised him to *marry*,—'No, cried Mrs. Thrale, *that* will do nothing for *You*,—but if you *should* marry, *I* have a Wife for you?

'Who? cried he,—the S.S.?'

'The S.S:—no?—she's the last person for you,—her extreme softness, & tenderness, & weeping, would add languor to languor, & irritate all your Disorder,—t'would be Drink to a Dropsical man.—'

'No, no,—it would sooth me,—'

'Not a Whit! it would only fatigue you.—The Wife for *You* is Lady Anne Lindsay,[26]—she has Birth, Wit & Beauty, she has no Fortune, so she'd readily accept you,—& she has such a spirit that she'd *animate* you I warrant you!— O she would trim[27] you well! You'd be all alive presently. She'd take all the care of the *money* affairs,—& allow you out of them Eighteen pence a Week!—That's the Wife for you!'

Mr. Seward was by no means *agreeable* to the proposal; he turned the Conversation upon the S.S., & gave us an account of 2 Visits he had made her, & spoke in favour of her manner of Living, Temper, & Character. When he

---

[24] *DNB* mentions Seward's 'pronounced tendency to hypochondria.' Aged 32 at this time, he died 20 years later 'of a dropsy', 'a lingering disorder' which suggests underlying heart or kidney disease (see *GM* lxix¹ (1799), 439). It is impossible to know, of course, whether his suffering in 1779 was of a physical or psychoneurotic nature, or both.

[25] Dr Jebb had been created Bt the previous Sept.

[26] Lady Anne Lindsay (1750–1825), eldest daughter of the 5th E. of Balcarres. She m. (1793) Andrew Barnard (d. 1807) (*EJL* ii. 85 nn. 61–2). Her lack of a fortune was due perhaps in part to her having 10 siblings; also, her father (d. 1768) had spent the last 23 years of his life improving the family estate. About this time HLT entered an example of her wit in *Thraliana* (i. 392, s.v. 5 July 1779): 'Says Lady Anne Lindsay when Fordyce the Banker sent her Sister a Haunch of stinking Venison during the Days of Courtship—have nothing to say to this Fellow good Margaret; he begins both with *Bribery* and *Corruption.*'

[27] i.e., scold (cf. above, pp. 154, 163, 165).

had run on in this strain ꞁ for some Time, Mrs. Thrale cried 'Well,—so you are grown very fond of her?'

'O dear no! answered he, drily, not at all!'

What a queer mortal he is!

'Why I began to think, said Mrs. Thrale, you intended to supplant the Parson.'

'No, I don't: I don't know what sort of an *old* woman she'd make; the *Tears* won't do then. Besides, I don't think her so sensible as I used to do.'

'But she's very *pleasing*, cried I, & very amiable.'

'Yes, she's *pleasing*,—that's certain: but I don't think she *reads* much,—the *Greek* has spoilt her.'

'Well, but you can *read* for yourself.'

'That's true; but does she *Work* well?'

'I believe she does; & that's a better thing.'

'Ay, so it is, said he saucily, for *Ladies*,—Ladies should rather *Write* than read.'

'But *Authors*, cried I, before they Write should read.—'28

'So I heard some *News*, returned he, Yesterday,—I heard that you did not write Evelina?—so you go about here, pluming yourself with borrowed Feathers.'

'Ay, well, I hope, then, they will find somebody else to own it.'

I know he meant nothing but a Letter from Mr. Bewley to my Father, which he shewed us yesterday, which contains a declaration of a Mr. Mordaunt's that he *won't* believe Evelina could be Written by a Young Woman, or, indeed, by any Woman.29

---

28 FB quotes Matthew Prior, 'Protogenes and Apelles', l. 47 (*Literary Works* i. 464). The editors thank Prof. Antonia Forster, Univ. of Akron, for her help in tracing this quotation.

29 William Bewley of Great Massingham, Norfolk, CB's friend and correspondent, wrote to him 29 May 1779 (Osborn): 'I know not whether Mr Mordaunt will have the good fortune to cast his eyes upon you: if he should, I know not whether the elegant discriminator of Men & Manners—the Author^ss of Evelyna—will be most gratified or mortified should he repeat, in town, his declaration that he means to read that work every 3 or 4 months, together with his firm persuasion—but this is *entre nous*—that no *young woman*, or even *woman*, could be the Author of it.' The Revd Charles Mordaunt (1736–1820), MA (Oxon.), 1760, was Rector of Little Massingham, Norfolk (IGI).

Returning again to the S:S. & being again rallied about her by Mrs. Thrale, who said she believed, at ˡ last, he would end there,—he said 'Why if I *must* marry,—if I was bid chuse between that & racking on the Wheel,—I believe I should go to her.'

We all Laughed at this exquisite Compliment, but, as he said, it *was* a Compliment, for though it proved no *passion* for *her*, it proved a *preference*.

'However, he continued, it won't do.'

'Upon my Word, exclaimed I, you settle it all your own way!—the *lady* would be ready at any rate!'

'O yes!—*any* man might marry Sophy Streatfield.'

I quite stopt to exclaim against him.

'I mean, said he, if he'd pay his Court to her.'

Are not these Lords of the Creation sweet modest Creatures?

When we broke up, I stole away Prior from the Table, & packed it up, intending to make him take it to Town with him; but *he* stole *himself* away, & went without speaking.

At Dinner, however, he returned!—He told me he was just come from an Old Gentleman who had been enquiring concerning Evelina of him,—'so you see, Ma'am, how your Fame spreads, both far & near!—he asked me if I could lend it to him, for he said he was told he *must* read it;—so *I* told him, too, & that I was just come from the young lady who writ it.'

And then, in his provoking way, he sat *grinning* at me. Now he has once broken the Ice again upon this subject, he is perpetually leading to it. ˡ

Thursday [24 June] I really have not leisure to write a Word about. Mr. Berresford was here.— — —

Friday morning [25 June] when I came down, Mr. Seward again attacked me about Prior. & hoped I had taken it into my Room. 'No, I cried, I have packed it up for you,' & I brought it forth.

'You *must* keep them, he cried,—I shall think you use me very ill else,—they are yours,—they are very pretty Books, & *ought* to be yours.'

'They are none of mine, indeed ˡ

[*FB breaks off abruptly here, with the remaining half of the MS page left blank. As in the past, she probably stopped to send her letter off by the post or by a private hand. FBA adds the following 'incomplete completion':* 'I am obliged to break off but I have forced the Books upon him, though he has really the air of being seriously affronted with me.—I can't help it—though I am sorry: but I cannot break into a system I have observed so regularly of never']

86   [Streatham,
                                       post 26 June 1779]

To Susanna Elizabeth Burney

AJL fragment (Berg, Diary MSS I, paginated 991–2, foliated 3), June 1779
1 single sheet 4to, 2 pp. and 1 5-line cutting from the middle of another sheet.
The foliation suggests that there were originally at least 3 sheets, or 6 pp. The beginning and conclusion of the letter are missing. The top of the 1st page is cut away.

And now I cannot resist telling you of a dispute which Dr. Johnson had with Mrs. Thrale the next morning [?26 June] concerning me, which that sweet woman had the honesty & good sense to tell me.

[*bottom of page and top of next page cut away*]

& my success—you was very affronting to my Goods, & I should have been very glad to have had them. I think of returning Home next Thursday, [1 July]—but, in case I am detained, so that Betty[30] may wash the Things as usual for Wednesday,

[*bottom of page cut away*]

Now, my dearest Susy, for the little dispute I promised you.

---

[30] Perhaps the Burney family's old servant, Betty Hutton (*EJL* i. 65 n. 45).

Mrs. Thrale told me that Dr. Johnson was talking to her & Sir Philip Jennings of the amazing progress made of late years in Literature by the Women. He said he was himself all astonished at it, & told them he well remembered that a Woman who could spell a common Letter was regarded as all accomplished,—but that *now*, they vied with the men in *every* thing.

'I think, Sir, said my friend Sir Philip, the young lady we have here is a very extraordinary proof of what you say.'

'*So* extraordinary, Sir, answered he, that I know none like her,—nor do I believe there *is*, or there ever *was* a *man* who could write *such* a Book so young.'

They both stared,—no wonder, I am sure!—& Sir Philip said 'What do you think of *Pope*, Sir? could not *Pope* have written such a one?'

'Nay, nay, cried Mrs. Thrale, there is no need to talk of *Pope*,—a Book may be a clever Book & | an excellent Book, & yet not want a *Pope* for it's Author. I suppose he was no older than Miss Burney when he writ Windsor Forest;[31] & I suppose *Windsor Forest* is not equal to Evelina!'

Windsor Forest, repeated Dr. Johnson, though so delightful a Poem, by no means required the knowledge of Life & manners, nor the accuracy of observation, nor the skill of penetration necessary for composing such a Work as Evelina: He who could *ever* write Windsor Forest, might as well write it Young as Old. Poetical abilities require not *age* to mature them; but Evelina seems a work that should result from long Experience & deep & intimate knowledge of the World; yet it has been written without either. Miss Burney is a real Wonder. What she is, she is intuitively. Dr. Burney told me she had had the fewest advantages of any of his Daughters, from some

---

[31] Pope claimed to have written the first part of the poem in 1704, when he was 16. He added to it and revised it until its publication in 1713. See Pope, *Pastoral Poetry and an Essay on Criticism*, ed. E. Audra and A. Williams (1961), pp. 125–31.

peculiar circumstances. And such has been her timidity, that he himself had not any suspicion of her powers.'[32]

'Her modesty,' said Mrs. Thrale—(as she told me) is really beyond bounds. It quite provokes me. And, in fact, I can never make out how the mind that could write that Book could be ignorant of its value.'

'That, Madam, is another Wonder, answered my dear— dear Dr. Johnson, 'for modesty with her is neither pretence nor decorum; 'Tis an ingredient of her Nature; for she who could part with such a Work for Twenty pounds, can know so little of it's worth, or of her own, as to leave no possible doubt of her native humility.'[33]

My kind Mrs. Thrale told me this with a pleasure that made me embrace her with gratitude: but the astonishment of Sir Philip Clerke at such an *eloge* from Dr. Johnson was quite, she says, comical. The Dispute |

[*rest of letter missing*]

---

[32] CB later recalled in his memoirs that 'My 2ᵈ daughter, Fanny ... was wholly unnoticed in the nursery for any talent or quickness of parts. Indeed at 8 years old she did not know her letters. ... Her mother & I ... began now to be uneasy at her backwardness; when, all at once, she read as if by intuition, nor did any of the family ever know how the talent was acquired' (CB *Mem.*, pp. 141–2). FBA continued in *Mem.* i. 168 (as '*Copied from a Memorandum-book of Dr. Burney's, written in the year 1808, at Bath*') that 'in company, or before strangers, she was silent, backward, and timid, even to sheepishness ... ' In 1764 CB sent EB and SEB to France to improve their French, but left FB at home, perhaps, says Joyce Hemlow, because 'her "tender veneration" for her Roman Catholic grandmother might easily turn to the Roman Catholic Church if she were in favourable surroundings', and also because he may have felt that his other 2 daughters were more promising (*HFB*, p. 15). Another plan, to send FB and her sister Charlotte to France after EB and SEB's return, was abandoned because of CB's 2nd marriage, in 1767.

[33] FB had tried to hold out for 30 guineas (not pounds), but had capitulated to her publisher Lowndes for 20 (see *EJL* ii. 286–7). FBA reports in *Mem.* ii. 151 that Lowndes gave her the extra 10 'pounds' after the 3rd edn., which appeared in Feb. 1779 (above, p. 232 n. 59).

Streatham,
5–20 July [1779]

To Susanna Elizabeth Burney

AJL (Berg, Diary MSS I, paginated 949–58), 5–20 July 1779
5 single sheets 4to, 10 pp.

Streatham, [Mon.] July 5th

I have hardly had any power to Write, my dear Susy, since I left you, for my Cold has encreased so much that I have hardly been able to do any thing but *lollop* for the Head ache.

Mr. Thrale I think is better, & he was chearful all the ride; we took up Mrs. Thrale at Harrop's,[34] & she made as much of me as if the 2 Days had been 2 months.

I was heartily glad to see Dr. Johnson, & I believe he was not sorry to see me: he had enquired very much after me, & very particularly of Mrs. Thrale whether she loved me as well as she used to do; Nay, (as she has told me,) he said 'I am very glad to see Queeny take so much to her, for it will be a great service to her;—she cannot but reap advantage from having such a mind as could Write Evelina poured into her Ears.'

So You see his 6 Weeks absence has not weakened his partiality to my *Bantling*.

He is better in Health than I have ever seen him before; his Journey[35] has been very serviceable to him, & he has taken very good resolutions to reform his Diet;—so has my Daddy Crisp,[36]—I wish I could *pit* them one against the other, & see the effect of their emulation.

---

[34] Probably the wholesale haberdashery warehouse of Josiah Harrop (1735–1808) at No. 4 George Yard, Lombard St. Harrop went bankrupt in 1788 (*GM* xxix (1759), 347; lviii¹ (1788), 373; lxxviii¹ (1808), 373; IGI; LDGL).
[35] To Lichfield and Ashbourne to visit his stepdaughter Lucy Porter (1715–86) and his friend Dr John Taylor (1711–88).
[36] Expressed in his letter to FB 28 May 1779 (Barrett).

I wished twenty Times to have transmitted to Paper the Conversation of the Evening, for Dr. Johnson was as brilliant as I have ever known him,—& that's saying *Something*;—but I was not very well, & could | only attend to him for present entertainment.

In the Evening we took the Tour round the Grounds, & were met on the Lawn by the Pitches Family; poor Sophy had not been well; she looked as pale as Death, & Peggy looked hardly any better:—yet little did I imagine the former had but one more Day to Live!—this was Friday Night [2 July], at about 9 o'clock, & she walked hither from Streatham Town;—& the next News I heard of her was on Sunday morning [4 July] that she was *Dying*,—& on Sunday Noon that she was Dead!—

Though I knew her very little, & had never cultivated any acquaintance with, or entertained any kindness for her,—yet the so sudden & unexpected Death of a Young, pretty & innocent Girl, with whom I had been walking & conversing but 2 Evenings before, both astonished & shocked me.

The cause of this fatal catastrophe cannot be ascertained.[37] She had not been quite well for some months, but had no Cough, nor any consumptive symptom;—she went to Bed on Friday Night early & more languid than usual; on Saturday she was siezed with Hysteric fits,—these grew stronger & stronger, & lasted all Day,—towards Night she was totally senseless;—on Sunday morning, Mrs. Thrale saw her,—she then in a burning Fever, speechless, insensible, & convulsed,—Mrs. Thrale sent instantly for Dr. Jebb,—she had had the Physicians here,—but finding her case desperate, the Apothecary ventured to give her some of James's Powders,[38]—the poor dying Girl had not | swallowed them 2 minutes, ere the fatal hyccough [*sic*] was heard, & she expired.

Is not this dreadful?—the surviving Relations are all in the most bitter affliction. There are 2 conjectures concerning the latent cause of her Death: the first & most

---

37 See below, p. 338.
38 The famous remedy devised by Robert James (1705–76), MD (*JL* i. 68 n. 2).

probable is Mrs. Thrale's, that she was a martyr to the *Worms*,³⁹—the 2ᵈ is the Apothecary's, that she was in love with Mr. Beresford,—ruined her Constitution with fasting & pining, & then Died of the Illness resulting from indigestion & deep grief.

Certain it is, that the first Time I saw Mr. Beresford, which was in Company with all the Pitches, he asked my opinion of the 3 sisters,—& when we discussed their several qualities, he said 'I *used* to like Sophy the best, & was always talking & prating with *her*,—& chatting nonsense, & so forth,—but I have quite done with her, for I found her so heavy that I grew quite tired of trying at her.'

If, therefore, this poor thing *had* any partiality for this man, she probably imagined he also had for her, &, when she found her mistake, & that he neglected her, she might possibly be cruelly disappointed & afflicted. However, I have not much, if any belief in this suggestion, though it is not incredible. |

[Sat.] July 10ᵗʰ

Since I writ last, I have been far from well,—but I am now my *own man again*—à peu pres.—

Very concise indeed must my Journal grow, for I have now hardly a moment in my *power* to give it; however I will keep up it's Chain, & mark, from Time to Time, the *general course of things*.

Sir Philip Jennings has spent 3 Days here, at the close of which he took leave of us for the summer, & set out for his seat in Hampshire. We were all sorry to lose him; he is a most *comfortable* man in society, for he is always the same, easy, good humoured, agreeable & well bred. He has made himself a favourite to the whole House, Dr. Johnson included, who almost always prefers the

---

³⁹ HLT wrote in *Thraliana* i. 393: 'On Sunday last I saw the Death of Miss Sophia Pitches, She was here on the Fryday Evening on a Visit—on Sunday Morning after prayers—

I saw, and kissed her in her Shroud!

I think She died of a Disorder common enough to young Women the Desire of Beauty; She had I fancy taken Quack Med'cines to prevent growing fat, or perhaps to repress Appetite … .'

Company of an intelligent man of the World to that of a scholar.

Lady Lade spent the Day here last Sunday [4 July]. Did I ever do her the justice to give you a sketch of her since I have been more acquainted with her than when I first did her that favour?[40]—I think not.

She is gay even to levity, wholly uncultivated as to Letters, but possesses a very good natural capacity, & a fund of humour & sport that makes her company far more entertaining than that of half the best educated women in the Kingdom: the pride I have mentioned never shews itself without some provocation; & where ever she meets with respect, she returns it with interest.

In the course of the Day, she said to me in a whisper 'I had a Gentleman with me Yesterday who is crazy to | see *you*,—& he tiezed me to bring him here with me,—but I told him I could not till I had paved the way.—'

I found, afterwards, that this Gentleman is Mr. Edmund Phipps,[41] a Younger Brother of Lord Mulgrave[42] & of the Harry Phipps Hetty[43] Danced with at Mr. Laluze's masquerade. Lady Lade appointed the next Tuesday to bring him to Dinner. As he is a particular favourite with Mrs. Thrale, her Ladyship had no difficulty in gaining him admittance.

I think Times are come to a *fine pass* if people are to come to *Streatham* with no better views.

Well,—on Tuesday [6 July] I was quite ill,—& obliged to be Blooded,—so I could not go down to Dinner!—

Mr. Seward accompanied Lady Lade & Mr. E. Phipps, & added to the provocation of my confinement.

---

[40] See above, p. 125.

[41] Hon. Edmund Phipps (1760–1837), 4th son of Constantine Phipps (1722–75), cr. (1767) B. Mulgrave (Ire.). Phipps, who in 1780 began a military career, became a Gen. in the army (1819) and Col. of the 60th (Royal American) Ft (1807).

[42] Constantine John Phipps (1744–92), 2nd B. Mulgrave (Ire.), 1775; cr. (1790) B. Mulgrave (UK); currently MP and a Ld. of Admiralty.

[43] FB originally wrote 'Hetty & I'. She does not mention dancing herself with Henry Phipps in her account of the Lalauze masquerade in 1770 (*EJL* i. 106, 118 n. 40).

I heard from Miss Thrale of Mr. Phipp's *eagerness* & disappointment,—which were almost comical: he asked a thousand questions about me, & gave a thousand praises to my Book,—& when, in the Evening, he heard that I was better, & preparing to come down, he quite clapped his Hands with joy.—How ridiculous!—

Lady Lade & Mrs. Thrale both persuaded me to make my appearance, &, as my Head grew much easier, I thought it better so to do, than to encrease a curiosity I was sure of disappointing, by any delay I had *power* to prevent. 'You will like him, I dare say, said Mrs. Thrale, for he is *very* like you;—' & then, with liberal partiality, she sung the *eloge* of us both.

I heard afterwards that, when they returned to the Parlour, Mr. Phipps, among other questions, asked 'Is she very pretty?—'

N.B.—I wish there was no such question in the Language.—

'Very pretty?—no, said Mrs. Thrale,—but she is very like *you*:—do you think *yourself* very handsome, Mr. Phipps?'

'Pho!—cried he,—I was in hopes she was like her own Evelina.—'

'No, no such thing, said Mrs. Thrale,—unless it is in timidity,—but niether in beauty, nor in ignorance of Life.'

I am very glad this passed before I came down,—for else, I think I should have struck him *all of a heap*,—

Now it's my turn to speak of him.

He is very Tall,—not *very* like me in *that*, you'll say;— very Brown,—not *very unlike* me in *that*, you'll say,—for the rest, however, the Compliment is all to *me*.

I saw but little of him, as they all went about an Hour after I came down: but I had Time to see that he is very sensible, very elegant in his manners, & very unaffected & easy.—And *so* watchful of me, that his Eyes never, but upon meeting mine, were withdrawn from me.

I am always glad when meetings of this sort are over.

Mr. Seward was not well, nor in spirits: but he seems to owe me no ill will for forcing back the Prior upon him.

Apropos to Books, I have not been able to read Wraxall's Memoirs[44] yet,—I wish Mrs. Ord had not lent them
me,—& now Lady Lade, too, has brought me 2 volumes,
called | Sketches from Nature,[45] & written by Mr. Keate,
what I have read of them repaid me nothing for the Time
they took up,—a mere, & paltry imitation of Stern's
Sentimental Journey!

[Tues.] July 20th

What a vile Journalist do I grow!—it is, however, all I
can do to keep it *at all going*,—for, to let you a little into
the Nature of things, You must know my *studies* occupy
almost every moment that I spend by myself;—Dr.
Johnson gives us a [Latin][46] Lesson *every* morning,—I
pique myself somewhat upon being ready for him,—so
that really, when the Copying my Play, & the Daily
returning occurrences of every fresh Day, are considered,
You will not wonder that I should find so little opportunity
for scrawling Letters.

What progress we may make in this most learned
scheme I know not, but, as I have always told you, I am
sure I fag more for fear of Disgrace than for hope of
profit; to devote so much Time to acquire something I
shall always dread to have known is really unpleasant
enough, considering how many things there are I might
employ myself in that would have no such draw back.—
However, on the other side, I am both pleased & flattered
that Dr. Johnson should think me worth *inviting* to be
his Pupil, & I shall always recollect with pride & with
pleasure the instructions he has the goodness to give
me:—so, since I cannot without *dishonour* alter matters,

---

[44] *Memoirs of the Kings of France of the Race of Valois* (1777), by Nathaniel
William Wraxall (1751–1831), traveller and memoirist; cr. (1813) Bt.

[45] *Sketches from Nature, taken and coloured in a Journey to Margate* (1779), by
George Keate (1730–97), writer. FB had met Keate in 1774, and was offended
by his conceit (*EJL* ii. 34–6).

[46] Inserted by FBA.

'tis as well to turn French woman, & take them in the *tant mieux* fashion.[47] |

I find, by the Papers, that Miss Kinnaird is married,—to a Mr. Wiggan,[48]—I hope, therefore, she is settled in England, &, that I may chance to see her again. I quite long to hear if she has met with a man at all deserving of her. I never had so much affection for a short acquaintance in my life as for this sweet Girl.—Ah how does the Word *affection* joined to *sweet Girl* remind me of our dear Barsanti![49]—I hope you sent my Letter,[50]—&, if you wished it, added some lines of your own. I am not sorry, now, that I never saw Mr. Lister,[51] since I could see him

[47] HLT commented in her diary: 'Doctor Johnson has undertaken to teach my eldest Daughter *Latin* and has actually undertaken & begun his Work. Fanny Burney, Author of Evelina is to learn with her of the same Master—Mr Thrale says it is better to each of them than a Thousand Pounds added to their Fortune. Dear Creatures! how earnestly do I wish them Success! they love one another and will improve by studying together—what a Master they have too! Happy Rogues!—' (*Thraliana* i. 393, s.v. July 1779). See below, p. 452.

[48] Thomas Wiggens (d. 1785), of Leigh, Kent; MP (Okehampton), 1784–5. They were married on 30 June in the Church of St James Piccadilly (Namier; IGI).

[49] Jane ('Jenny') Barsanti (d. 1795) (*EJL* i. 73 n. 63).

[50] Missing.

[51] John Richard Kirwan Lyster, scion of an ancient Irish family and close friend of the D. of Leinster, had secretly courted Barsanti and married her against his family's wishes on 9 June 1777 at St Martin-in-the-Fields, London. He died in Dublin on 13 Jan. 1779; had he outlived his father, he would have inherited an estate of £1500 a year, of which of course Jane received nothing. A daughter, Jane Kirwan Lyster, was born posthumously. She m. (1800) William Jameson (d. 1834), KC, of Dublin, and died in 1808.

In a letter to FB of 12 Aug. 1779, CB Jr. included verses (preserved as 'Part of a Letter to Miss Burney London Aug. 12. 1779', Osborn) in which he referred to Barsanti's 'hard ... Fate', mentioning her widowhood, her infant, and also her aged mother whom she had to care for, all necessitating her return to the stage (she had first acted in Dublin the winter of 1776–77). By 14 Sept. 1779 she had married Richard Daly (1758–1813), actor and later manager of the Smock Alley Theatre, Dublin. She apparently was swept off her feet by the handsome Daly, as she initially settled an income of £20 a week on him. For the rest of her life she had to endure the philanderings and financial extravagances of her husband, whose charming manner concealed a brutal nature. This passage contains FB's last known mention of Barsanti until 1824, when she writes that a daughter of Barsanti had appealed to her for financial aid; she adds that Barsanti (Mrs Daly) in later years grew very corpulent and had altogether 9 or 10 children. See Highfill; *JL* xi. 491–2 and n. 4; H. L. L. Denny, *Memorials of an Ancient House* (Edinburgh, 1913), pp. 105–6.

no more,—but pray, my Love, the moment any answer comes from poor Jenny, let it be *instantly* sent me.

A new light is, of late, thrown upon the Death of poor Sophy Pitches,—Dr. Hervey,[52] of Tooting, who attended her the Day before she expired, is of opinion that she killed herself by Quackery,—that is, by *cosmetics*, & preparations of lead or mercury, taken for her Complection, which, indeed, was almost unnaturally white:—he thinks, therefore, that this pernicious stuff got into her veins, & poisoned her!—Peggy Pitches, nearly as white as her sister, is suspected strongly of using the same beautifying methods of destroying herself;—however, as Mrs. Thrale has hinted this suspicion to her, & charged her to take care of herself, we hope she will be frightened & warned to her safety. Poor foolish Girls!—how dearly do they pay for the ambition of being fairer than their neighbours! I say *they*, for poor Peggy looks upon the point of Death already. |

Mr. Beresford has been here often lately. I find him so much what I have already told you of him, that I forbear to trouble you more *copiously* about him. I am, however, pleased to see that he ceases his particularity both of looks & manner to *me*, as, while it lasted, I was really embarrassed how to behave with civility to him, & not incur either rallery, or, at least, attract observation.

Yesterday Mrs. Vesey came hither to Tea. I'm sure if Anstey saw her he would make an exception to his assertion that 'he never should see an old woman again'[53]—for she has the most wrinkled, sallow, Time beaten Face I ever saw. She is an exceeding well bred woman, & of agreeable manners,—but all her Name in the *World* must, I think, have been acquired by her dexterity & skill in selecting Parties, & by her address in rendering them easy with one another.—An art, however, that seems to imply no mean understanding.

[52] Probably James Hervey (*c.*1751–1824); B.Med. (Oxon.), 1777; D.Med., 1781; FRCP, 1782.

[53] Christopher Anstey, *An Election Ball* (2nd edn., 1776), p. 41: 'As I never shall see an old Woman again', meaning that no woman will ever appear old again because of cosmetic arts.

The breaking up of our Spa Journey my Father has doubtless told you.—you, who knew the pleasure with which I looked forward to it will not wonder I should be disappointed;—however, I have driven it from my mind,—for, in the first-place, I have no right to *repine* at the loss of what I had no right to think my *due*, & in the second place, there comes no good of thinking of impossibilities, a wise maxim! pray hoard it.

The fears & dangers of being taken by the Enemy, which prevented our Journey, have proved to be but too well grounded, for Mrs. Vesey informed us that the Duchess of Leinster,[54] Lady F. Campbell,[55] & several others, were all actually taken by a French privateer in crossing the sea in order to proceed to Spa!—We have, however, heard that they are all safe & at liberty. But this accident will probably put a stop to all other attempts of a Continental visit during the War.[56]

88 [Streatham, 29]–30 July [1779]

To Samuel Crisp

ALS fragment (Berg, Diary MSS I, paginated 993–8), 30 July 1779
3 single sheets 4to, 6 pp. red wafer
Addressed: Samuel Crisp Esqr, | at Mrs. Hamilton's, | Chesington.

[54] Hon. Emilia Olivia St George (d. 1798), m. (1775) William Robert Fitzgerald (1749–1804), 2nd D. of Leinster (Ire.).

[55] Mary Meredith (*c.*1738–1807), who m. (1769) as her 2nd husband Ld. Frederick Campbell (1729–1816). However, the captured lady was in fact Sarah Izard (d. 1784), m. (1763) Ld. William Campbell (*c.*1732–78), Ld. Frederick's brother. The other passengers included Mrs Anne Seymour Damer, the sculptor and relation of Horace Walpole; Walpole comments on the adventure in letters to George Selwyn and Lady Ossory, both 20 July 1779. The incident occurred about 7 July, and news of it was published in the London papers on 17 July. The ladies were in a packet boat going from Dover to Ostend; they were set free at Dunkirk. See *YW* xxx. 270 and nn. 4, 6; xxxiii. 113 and nn. 2–3, 6; B. Fitzgerald, *Emily Duchess of Leinster 1731–1814* (1949), p. 160.

[56] The war situation had worsened for Britain on 16 June when Spain declared war on her, thus allying herself with America and France (*YW* xxiv. 482–5).

Annotated (by FBA): ⁕ ⚔ 1779—N° 12 on Mr Thrale's illness. Dr. Johnson's comic kindness, & a MS. Play.
    The beginning of the letter is missing.

Friday, July 30th

Now, my dear Daddy, let me attempt something more like an Answer to your two last most kind Letters[57] than what I writ last night.

In the first place, I have the pleasure to tell You that Mr. Thrale is as well as ever he was in *Health*,—though the alarming & terrible blow he so lately received had, I fear, given a damp to his *spirits* that will scarce ever be wholly conquered. Yet he grows Daily rather more chearful, but the shock was too rude & too cruel to be ever forgotten.

In regard to my own Health, I am now *perfectly* well. Your admonitions relating to *writing* I do & will keep in mind,—& I am sure you will be glad to hear that, at Streatham, I have a new Desk which Mr. Thrale was so kind as to order for me himself, & which, when placed upon a Table, is just a comfortable height, & prevents my stooping more than the nature of such an Employment actually requires. You are very good to interest yourself so much upon this subject, & I hardly ever take a Pen in my Hand without thinking of your charges. ⌐As I had no fever, I did not use saline[58] Draughts, but I shall certainly try them, according to your directions, when I am obliged to try their ⟨efficacy⟩.⌐ |

I am not half so well satisfied with your account of *yourself* as I hoped to have been,[59]—I fear you are not so steady in your intended reformation as to Diet & Exercise

---

[57] SC to FB *post* 20 June 1779 (Barrett) and 21 July 1779 (Barrett).

[58] 'Of medicines: Consisting of or based upon salts of the alkaline medicines or magnesium' (*OED* s.v. saline A.4.a). The recipe for 'Saline Mixture' in W. Buchan, *Domestic Medicine* (1790), p. 681, is to 'Dissolve a drachm of the salt of tartar in four ounces of boiling water' (cited ibid.).

[59] 'I suppose the immediately dangerous Symptoms that my good Friends suspected attended me, are in some measure pass'd; but uneasiness, sleeplessness, indigestion &c are pretty assiduous about me—' (SC to FB *post* 20 June 1779).

as you proposed being?—Dr. Johnson has made resolutions exactly similar to Yours, &c, in *general*, adheres to them with strictness, but the *old Adam*, as you say,[60] stands in *his* way, as well as in his Neighbour's. I wish I could *pit* you against each other, for the sake of both!—Yet he professes an aversion to *you*, because he says he is sure you are very much *in his way with me*,—however, I believe you would niether of you retain much *aversion* if you had a fair meeting.

I cannot tell you how kind I take your invitations to me,—I had half feared I was to be *left out of the scrape now*, & & am sure I should wish all my new Friends at Jericho, if their goodness to me procured coldness, neglect or suspicion from my old & deep-rooted ones. I will most certainly & thankfully contrive to accept your kind offer, &, if possible, when Mrs. Gast is with you, as that would be doubling my pleasure. But you, ⎸ my dear Daddy, must let me know what Time will be most convenient & comfortable to yourself for seeing me, & then I will manage matters as well as I can to conform to it.

⌐I know not, yet, my own destination for the Autumn, but when I do, I shall acquaint you with it directly.⌐

All you say of *the Times* made me shudder,[61]—yet I was sure such would be your sentiments, for all that has happened you actually fore saw, & represented to me in strong colours last spring: I mean in relation to the general decline of all Trade, opulence & prosperity.

This seems a strange unseasonable period for *my* undertaking, among the rest,—but yet, my dear Daddy, when

---

[60] 'I am continually making good resolutions of great Care & regularity of Diet & Exercise, but the old Adam in me, sometimes gets the better; for which I am sure to suffer–' (SC to FB 28 May 1779).

[61] SC was frightened about the possibility of a French-Spanish invasion and even conquest of Britain: 'I declare I had much rather be under ground, than stay behind, to see the insolent Bourbon trampling under foot this once happy Island, & insulting & oppressing its wretched inhabitants ... . I am prognosticating, *when Bourbon shall be all in all*' (SC to FB 21 July 1779; see *ED* ii. 261–2).

you have read my conversation with Mr. Sheridan,[62] I believe you will agree that I must have been wholly insensible, nay, almost *ungrateful*, to resist encouragement such as he gave me,—nay, *more* than encouragement, *entreaties*,—all of which, he warmly repeated to my Father.

Now as to the Play itself,—I own I had wished to have been the Bearer of it when I visit | Chesington,—but you seem so urgent, & my Father himself is so desirous to Carry it you, that I have given that plan up.

"To own the Truth, I had not given the *broad hint* in my last upon this subject, had I not secretly flattered myself that your silence about it was owing to the very ⟨reason⟩ you have assigned for it[63], [xxxxx *3 lines*]

You will find it of an enormous length, though half as short again as the *original*, but you must ⟨advise me as⟩ to what parts to curtail."

Oh my dear Daddy, *if* your next Letter were to contain your *real* opinion of it, how should I dread to open it!— Be, however, as honest as your good nature & delicacy will *allow* you to be, & assure yourself I shall be *very* certain that all criticisms will proceed from your earnest wishes to obviate those of others,—& that you would have much more *pleasure* in being my *panegyrist*.

As to Mrs. Gast,—I should be glad to know *what* I would refuse to a sister of yours that she *wished*;—make her therefore of your *Coterie*, if she is with | You while the piece is in your possession.[64]

---

[62] Sheridan had strongly encouraged FB to write a comedy the preceding Jan. (see above, pp. 234–36). SC wrote to Mrs Gast in an undated letter that 'Mr. Sheridan, the manager of all the playhouses and the operas, has been privately applied to about her play next winter, and says whatever comes from her he will receive with open arms, and as a great honour, let what will prior Engagements stand in his way' (W. H. Hutton, *Burford Papers* (1905), p. 37).

[63] 'I had with the utmost difficulty restraind my self from soliciting a sight of your newborn Babe ... & that from a Motive of delicacy & Self Denial, in Consequence of my own Advice, to be very reserv'd in communicating it to your Friends—' (SC to FB 21 July 1779). The '*broad hint*' seems to be in a missing letter to SC which he alludes to when he chides FB for taxing him with 'indifference!—neglect!—' (ibid.).

[64] 'If Gast should come here while it [the play] remains in my Possession, may I show it to her?' (ibid.).

And now let me tell you what *I wish* in regard to this affair.

I should like that your First reading should have nothing to do with *me*,—that you should go quick through it, or let my Father read it to you, forgetting all the Time, as much as you can, that *Fannikin* is the Writer, or even that it is a play in manuscript, & *capable* of alterations:— And then, when you have done, I should like to have 3 Lines, telling me, as nearly as you trust my candour, it's general effect.—

After that,—take it to your own Desk, & lash it at your leisure.

Adieu, My dear Daddy—I shall hope to hear from you *very* soon,—& pray believe me

Yours ever & ever
Frances Burney.

Let it fail *never so much*, the *manager* will have nothing to reproach me with: is not that some comfort?—[He would really listen to no denial.][65]

89   [St Martin's Street,]
                                            4 August [1779]

To Charles Burney

AL incomplete (Barrett), 4 Aug. 1779
Single sheet 4to, 2 pp.
Annotated (by FBA): ✕ 1779

4 Aug[st]

Your sweet Letter,[66] my dearest Sir, has quite *comforted my Bowels*,—your advice & admonitions & cautions I will attend to with all my power,—& pray make Daddy Crisp send me *his*: I have, indeed, but little hope of ever writing what you will both approve, but I should be a Beast & a

[65] Added by FBA.
[66] Missing.

monster not to do the best I can when I have two such Daddys for my Judges, & two such Friends for my Critics. But, as you bid me *wait till some thing comes*, I shall not, I am sure, at present do any thing,—for my Heart is too much occupied with feelings of its own for my Head to devise & contrive feelings for others.[67]

My dear Hetty is again much better to Night,—but our dear Mrs. Thrale is *worse*,[68]—so that I have been, & seem likely still to be, in a state of anxiety very ⌐ remote from the clearness of Intellect requisite for forming plans, connecting incidents, pourtraying characters, & selecting things *probable* from things *uncommon*. To Day Hetty has again tried the Bark,[69] & with more success: she is brisk & comfortable, &, if the Bark will but agree with her, I am sure you will see her very shortly. ⌐My letter to Mrs. Burney of yesterday[70] I fear must have alarmed you all. She was then much worse, & I thought would [xxxxx *2-3 words*] Dr. Bromfield says he thinks her Fever intermitting almost regularly, & therefore that the Bark now *must* take effect, & will very speedily ⟨cure⟩ her. He is the most comfortable, humane, considerate, & kind Physician I ever saw. He now absolutely refuses to be even ⟨paid⟩.[71]

If you have not already opened the letter to Mrs B., pray do, as it will shew how things were situated, & that I *must* go to Streatham to morrow.[72] However, the Doctor is so comfortable about Hetty, that, now that⌐ ⌐

[*rest of letter missing*]

---

[67] CB had gone to Chessington via Streatham on 31 July (SEB to FB 1–2 Aug. 1779 (Barrett); *ED* ii. 255, 260). On 2 Aug., SC, SEB, Charlotte Ann Burney, Mrs Gast, Kitty Cooke, and Mrs Hamilton listened to CB's reading of FB's play 'The Witlings' (SEB to FB 3–6 Aug. 1779 (Barrett)). CB evidently wrote to FB the evening of the 2nd or on the 3rd, advising her not to make any revisions to the play until she had heard further from himself and SC.

[68] FB was at home in St Martin's St. nursing her ailing sister. HLT had been experiencing a difficult pregnancy, and would deliver a stillborn son on 10 Aug. (*Thraliana* i. 399–401).

[69] Jesuits' or Peruvian bark: the bark of the cinchona tree, the source of quinine, ground into a powder.

[70] Missing.

[71] A conjectural reading, suggested by the perennial financial straits of EBB and her musician husband.

[*See opposite page for n. 72*]

[St Martin's Street,
*c.*13 August 1779]
To Charles Burney

ALS (Berg, Diary MSS I, paginated 999–1002), Aug. 1779
2 single sheets folio, 4 pp. red wafer
Addressed: Dr. Burney.
Annotated (by FBA): ✣ *1779* In answer to Dr. Burney's *critique* on a
MS. comedy called The Witlings, sent for his verdict to Chesington by
F.B. NB. The objections of Mr. Crisp to the MS. Play of the Witlings
was its resemblance to Moliere's *Femmes Scavantes*—& consequent
immense inferiority. It is, however, a curious fact, & to the author a
consolatory one, that she had literally never read the *Femmes Scavantes*
when she composed The Witlings.

The fatal knell then, is knolled! & down among the
Dead Men sink the poor Witlings,—for-ever & for-ever &
for-ever!—[73]

[72] In response to an urgent, though deferred, summons from HLT: ' ... the
Symptom which most *certainly* indicates an approaching miscarriage continues as
before. ... I will send for you *home* next Week, and be *heroick* in my Virtue no
longer. Poor dear Mrs Burney [EBB] has however the nearest Claim, & unless
I am worse than at present I feel myself, the Coach shall not fetch you till
Tuesday next. I will not tell you *how* glad I shall be to·see you then, lest you
should come sooner ... ' (HLT to FB, [early Aug. 1779], Berg).
HLT's brush with mortality led her to compose later this month 'Three
Dialogues on the Death of Hester Lynch Thrale', written on the plan of Swift's
verses on his death. She seems to reveal her husband's true feelings about the
Burney clan in the third dialogue, where she has him say, 'I don't want to see
any of the Burneys.' Lady Lade then comments: 'Well! but I've left off
wondering at any thing: I always thought Miss Burney a monstrous favourite
at Streatham: to be sure Miss Streatfield's a great deal handsomer, & has a
better Nose: but Lord, what's (*with a sneer*) Features where *Wit* is so much
concerned?' ('Three Dialogues by Hester Lynch Thrale', ed. M. Zamick, *Bulletin
of the John Rylands Library*, xvi (1932), 110).
[73] FB in quick succession echoes Shakespeare, John Dyer (*fl.* 1714), and
possibly Pope. 'And so his knell is knoll'd' are Old Siward's words on the death
of his son Young Siward, slain by Macbeth (*Macbeth*, V. ix. 16). 'Down among
the dead men let him lie' is the refrain of a familiar poem (*Toast: Here's a Health
to the King*) by Dyer (not to be confused with the author of *Grongar Hill*). And
'for-ever & for-ever & forever!' may be meant to suggest Belinda's lament for
her lost lock of hair (see *The Rape of the Lock* iii. 154). FB thus plays with the
theme of loss, using literary allusion to make light of her frustration over the
rejection of her play by her 'Daddys'.

I give a *sigh* whether I will or not to their memory, for, however worthless, they were *mes Enfans*, & *one must do one's Nature*, as Mr Crisp will tell you of the Dog.[74]

You, my dearest Sir, who enjoyed, I really think, even more than myself the astonishing success of my first attempt, would, I believe, even more than myself, be hurt at the failure of my second;—& I am sure I speak from the bottom of a very honest Heart when I most solemnly declare that upon *your* Account any disgrace would mortify & afflict me *more* than upon my own,—for what ever appears with your *knowledge*, will be naturally supposed to have met with your *approbation*, & perhaps with your *assistance*;—& therefore, though all *particular* censure would fall where it *ought*, upon *me*,—yet any *general* censure of the *whole*, & the *Plan*, would cruelly, but certainly, involve *you* in it's severity.

Of this I have been sensible from the moment my *Authorshipness* was discovered,—& therefore, from that moment, I determined to have no *opinion* of my own in regard to what I | should thenceforth part with out of my own Hands. I would, long since, have Burnt the 4th Act, upon your disapprobation of it,[75] but that I waited, & was by Mrs. Thrale so much *encouraged* to wait, for your finishing the Piece.

---

[74] Despite the Chessington audience's generally favourable reception of the play, CB and SC jointly decided to veto any staging of 'The Witlings'. Their main reason seems to have been a fear of offending the bluestockings, whose learning is satirized in the play as ignorant pretence and affectation. As CB wrote to FB on 29 Aug.: 'the objections all fall on the Stocking-Club-Party—as my chief & almost only quarrel was with its Members. As it is, not only the Whole Piece, but the *plot* had best be kept secret, from every body' (*LCB* i. 279). CB had had, however, no objections to the play until this point. Indeed, HLT had written in May: 'Fanny Burney has read me her new Comedy; nobody else has seen it except her Father ... and he likes it vastly' (*Thraliana* i. 381, cited above, p. 268 n. 18). Clearly, SC, whose inclination to paranoia was exacerbated by chronic ill health, convinced CB of the dangers of allowing it to be staged: the enmity of the Blues could threaten CB's career as well as the reputation of his daughter. HLT astutely summed up the affair in *Thraliana* and lay the blame where it belonged: 'Mr Crisp advised her against bringing it on, for fear of displeasing the female Wits—a formidible Body, & called by those who ridicule them, the *Blue Stocking Club*' (i. 381 n. 3, cited ibid.).

[75] SEB, writing to FB about the Chessington reading of her play, noted that 'the fourth act was upon the whole that wch seemed least to exhilarate or interest the Audience ... ' (SEB to FB, 3–6 Aug. 1779, Barrett).

You *have* finished it, now,—in *every* sense of the Word,— *partial* faults may be corrected, but what I most wished was to know the general effect of the Whole,—& as *that* has so terribly failed, all petty criticisms would be needless. I shall wipe it all from my memory, & endeavour never to recollect that I ever writ it.

You bid me open my Heart to you,—& so, my dearest Sir, I will,—for it is the greatest happiness of my life that I *dare* be sincere to you,—I expected many Objections to be raised, a thousand errors to be pointed out, & a million of alterations to be proposed;—but—the *suppression of the piece* were words I did *not* expect,—indeed, after the warm approbation of Mrs. Thrale, & the repeated commendations & flattery of Mr. Murphy, how could I?—

I do not, therefore, pretend to *wish* you should think the decision for which I was so little prepared has given me no disturbance;—for I must be a far more egregious Witling than any of those I tried to draw to imagine you could [|] ever credit that I writ without some remote hope of success *now*, though I literally did when I composed Evelina. But my mortification is not at throwing away the Characters, or the contrivance;—it is all at throwing away the *Time,*—which I with difficulty stole, & which I have Buried in the mere trouble of *writing*.

What my Daddy Crisp says, 'that it would be the best *policy*, but for pecuniary advantages, for me to write no more'—is exactly what I have always thought since Evelina was published;—but I will not *now* talk of putting it in practice,—for the best way I can take of shewing that I have a true & just sense of the *spirit* of your condemnation, is not to sink, sulky & dejected, under it, but to exert myself to the utmost of my power in endeavours to produce something less reprehensible. And this shall be the way I will pursue, as soon as my mind is more at ease about Hetty & Mrs. Thrale,—& as soon as I have *read* myself into a forgetfulness of my old Dramatis persona,— lest I should produce something else as *Witless* as the last.

Adieu, my dearest, kindest, truest, best *Friend,*—I will never proceed so *far* again without your counsel, & then I shall not only save *myself* [|] so much useless trouble, but *you*, who so reluctantly blame, the kind pain which I am sure must attend your disapprobation. The World will not always go well, as Mrs. Sap.[76] might say, & I am sure I have long thought I have had more than my share of success already.

I expect *another* disappointment to follow; i.e. that of the Spa Journey,—for I believe poor Mrs. Thrale will not be able to go any where[77].—but [xxxxx *3–4 words*]—I must get in practice with a little philosophy, & then make myself amends for all evils by a concerted notion of bearing them well.—

Once more, adieu, dearest Sir!—& never may my philosophy be put to the test of seeing any abatement of true kindness from *you*,—for *that* would never be decently endured by

Your own
Frances Burney

91   [St Martin's Street,
                              c.13 August 1779]

To Samuel Crisp

ALS (Berg, Diary MSS I, paginated 1003–6), Aug. 1779
2 single sheets folio, 4 pp.
Addressed: S. Crisp Esq[r]
Annotated (by FBA): ✳ ✳ ✕ 1779 N° 14. F.B.'s Answer to a severe criticism upon a MS. Comedy submitted to the perusal of her two dear Daddys—native & adopted: after the same play had been highly commended by Mrs. Thrale & M[r] Murphy.

[76] Mrs Sapient, one of the bluestocking characters in 'The Witlings', is a pretentious mouther of inanely obvious platitudes.
[77] Despite the fear of capture by privateers (see above, p. 339), the plan of a Spa trip had obviously been revived, probably by Mr Thrale, whose stubborn streak made it difficult for him to lay aside anything he had set his heart on.

Well!—God's above all!—& there are *plays* that *are* to be
saved, & *plays* that are *not* to be saved[78]!—so good Night
Mr. Dabler!—good Night Lady Smatter,—Mrs. Sapient,
Mrs. Voluble,—Mrs. Wheedle—Censor,—Cecilia—Beau-
fort,—& you, *you great Oaf*, Bobby![79] good Night! good
Night!—

And good *morning*, Miss Fanny Burney!—I hope, now,
You have opened your Eyes for some Time, & will not
close them in so drowsy a fit again—at least till the full of
the moon.—

I won't tell you I have been absolutely *ravi* with delight
at the fall of the Curtain,—but I intend to take the affair
in the *tant mieux* manner, & to console myself for your
Censure by this greatest proof I have ever received of the
sincerity, candour, &, let me add, *esteem* of my dear
Daddy.—And, as I happen to love *myself* rather more than
my *play*, this consolation is not a very trifling one.

As to all you say of my *rep.* & so forth, I perceive the
kindness of your endeavours to put me in humour with
myself, & prevent my taking *huff*,—which, if I did, I
should deserve to receive, upon any future trial, *hollow*
praise from *you*,—& the *rest* from the Public. ‖

As to the M.S. I am in no hurry for it.—Besides, it
ought not to come till I have prepared an *ovation*, & the
Honours of conquest for it.

The only bad thing in this affair,—is that I cannot take
the comfort of my poor friend Dabler, by calling you
a *crabbed fellow*,—because you write with almost more
kindness than ever;—niether can I, (though I try hard)

---

[78] Cf. *Othello* II. iii. 106–7 (see also above, p. 154). In the following succession
of 'good Nights' FB echoes the crazed Ophelia (*Hamlet* IV. v. 72); note the
reference to lunacy below.

[79] Bob is the son of Mrs Voluble, who constantly belittles him. She uses this
particular epithet in Acts III and V. Mr Dabler is one of the witlings, a vain
poetaster who pretends to extemporize verses he has already composed. Mrs
Wheedle is a milliner, one of FB's 'low' creations. Cecilia is the play's heroine,
a slightly absurd romantic who loses her fortune when her banker, Stipend,
fails. Beaufort is Cecilia's lover, like her, romantic and impractical. Among
other characters whom FB does not mention are Jack, half brother to Beaufort,
who exemplifies fashionable haste to no purpose; Codger, Jack's slow-witted
father; Miss Jenny, Mrs Wheedle's apprentice; and Betty, Mrs Voluble's maid.

persuade myself that you have not *a grain of Taste in your whole composition.*[80]

This, however, seriously, I do believe that, when my two Daddys put their Heads together to concert for me that Hissing, groaning, catcalling Epistle they sent me,[81] they felt as sorry for poor little Miss Bayes as she could possibly do for herself.

You see I do not attempt to repay your frankness with the art of pretended carelessness,—but though I am somewhat disconcerted just now, I will promise not to let my vexation Live out another Day. I shall not *browse* upon it,—but, on the contrary, drive it out of my thoughts by filling them up with things *almost* as good of other people's.

Our Hettina is much better,—but pray don't keep Mr. B. beyond Wednesday [18 Aug.],[82] for Mrs. | Thrale makes a *point* of my returning to Streatham on Tuesday [17 Aug.], unless, which God forbid, poor Hetty should be worse again.

Adieu, my dear Daddy,—I *won't* be mortified, & I won't be *downed*,—but I will be *proud* to find I have *out* of my own family, as well as in it, a Friend who loves me well enough to speak plain truth to me.

Always do thus,—& always you shall be *tried* by your much obliged

& most affectionate
Frances Burney.

I long very much for the *confab.* you talk of.—but I wish till we *do* meet, you would write copiously.

[*FBA here inserts the following ALS (Berg) from SC to FB,* post 29 Aug. 1779, 2 single sheets 4to, 4 pp., paginated 1007–1010, with the annotation: on a MS. Play of F.B.'s and ideas of Mr. Crisp for another]

---

[80] In Act IV, after Censor has dismissed verses by Dabler (which Dabler pretends to be by Gay) as 'Despicable beyond abuse', Dabler says of his critic (in an aside), 'What a Crabbed fellow! there is not an ounce of Taste in his whole composition.' In Act II Lady Smatter accuses Cecilia of not having 'a grain of Taste'.

[81] Missing.

[82] Charles Rousseau Burney was evidently on a visit to SC at Chessington.

My dear Fannikin

I have known half a letter filld up with recapitulating the tedious, very particular reasons, why and wherefore &c &c &c, it was not sent before—I dont like the Example, & shall not follow it—I will only tell you, that I have been far from well; [xxxxx *5 lines*]—I should not say thus much, but from an anxious Care lest a Fannikin should think I am [xxxxx *2 words*] Supine, in any thing that relates either to her interest or Fame—thus much for preface.

Your other Daddy (who hardly loves You better than I do) I understand, has ⌐wrote⌐ You his sentiments on the Subject of your last letter[83]—I cannot but be of the same opinion: & have too sincere a regard for You, not to declare it—this Sincerity I have smarted for, & severely too, ere now—& yet, happen what will, (where those I love are concern'd) I am determin'd never to part with it—All the World (if You will believe them) profess to expect it, to demand it, to take it kindly, thankfully, &c &c &c—And yet how few are generous enough to take it, as it is meant!—it is imputed to envy, ill-will, a desire of lowering, & certainly to a total want of Taste—is not this, by vehement importunity, to draw your very entrails from you, & then to give them a Stab?—in this Topic, I find I have, ere I was aware ⌐of it⌐ grown warm—but I have been a Sufferer—my plain-dealing (after the most earnest solicitations, professions, & protestations) irrecoverably lost me Garrick—but his Soul was little[84]—Greville for a while, became my Enemy, tho' afterwards thro' his constitutional Inconstancy, he became more attach'd than before; & since that time thro Absence, Whim, & various Accidents, all is, (I thank Fortune,) dwindled to nothing— how have I wander'd!—I should never have thought aloud in this manner, if I had not perfectly known the make & Frame of a Fannikin inmost Soul, & by this declaration I

[83] CB to FB 29 Aug. 1779 (*LCB* i. 278–80), in reply to a missing letter of FB, in which she suggested that she might write a new play for the winter. CB discouraged the idea, on the grounds that Britain's economic downturn and fears of a French-Spanish invasion would keep people from the theatre.

[84] Garrick, who had produced SC's tragedy *Virginia* in 1754, refused to revive it. In 1774 he wrote to William Shirley: 'M^r G: has been Accus'd of partiality for not reviving Mr Crisp's Virginia' (Garrick, *Letters*, iii. 940).

give her the most powerful proof I am capable of, how highly I think of her generosity & understanding.

Now then, to the point—I have considerd as well as I am able what You State as Mrs Thrale's *Idea*—of *new modelling the play*,[85] & [xxxxx *13 lines*]

I Observe what You say, that the pursuing *this project is the only Chance You have of bringing out any thing this Year— & that with hard fagging perhaps You might do that.* I agree with You, that for *this Year,* You say true—but, my dear Fanny, for God's sake, dont talk of *hard Fagging!* It was not *hard Fagging,* that produced such a Work as Evelina!— — —it was the Ebullition of true Sterling Genius! you wrote it, because you could not help it!—it came, & so You put it down on Paper!—leave *Fagging,* & Labour, to him

> — — — — — — —who high in Drury Lane,
> Lull'd by soft Zephyrs thro the broken pane,
> Rhymes ere he wakes, & prints before Term Ends,
> *Compell'd by Hunger & request of Friends.*[86]

Tis not sitting down to a Desk with Pen, Ink & Paper, that will command Inspiration.

Having now so frankly spoke my mind on the present production, concerning which I am sorry & asham'd to differ from much wiser heads than my own; I shall acquaint

---

[85] FB had returned to Streatham on 17 Aug. On 18 Aug., HLT wrote in *Thraliana*: 'Fanny Burney has pleased me today—She resolves to give up a Play likely to succeed; for fear it may bear hard upon some Respectable Characters' (i. 401). Sometime after that date, she evidently suggested that FB recast the play. Presumably the remodelling would have involved jettisoning the bluestocking satire and possibly playing up the sentimental love interest between Cecilia and Beaufort. FB's letter to SC on the subject is missing.

HLT commented on FB's return: 'Fanny Burney has been a long time from me, I was glad to see her again; yet She makes me miserable too in many Respects—so restlessly & apparently anxious lest I should give myself Airs of Patronage, or load her with Shackles of Dependance—I live with her always in a Degree of Pain that precludes Friendship—dare not ask her to buy me a Ribbon, dare not desire her to touch the Bell, lest She should think herself injured—lest she should forsooth appear in the Character of Miss Neville & I in that of the Widow Bromley [characters in Murphy's *Know Your Own Mind*]' (ibid. i. 400).

[86] Cf. Pope, *Epistle to Dr Arbuthnot*, ll. 41–4. The underscoring of the last line is SC's.

you with a Fancy of mine—Your Daddy Doctor related to
me something of an Account You had given him of a most
ridiculous Family in your present Neighbourhood, which
even in the imperfect manner he describ'd it, struck me
most forcibly—the *Pitches*—he says You gave it him with
so much humour, such painting, such description, such
fun, that in your Mouth it was a perfect Comedy—he describ'd (from You) some of the Characters, & a general Idea
of the act—I was quite animated—there seem'd to me an
inexhaustible Fund of Matter for You to worke on, & the
Follies of the Folks, of so general a Nature, as to furnish
You with a profusion of what You want ┃ to make out a
most spirited, witty, Moral, Useful Comedy without
descending to the invidious, & cruel Practice of pointing
out Individual Characters, & holding them up to public
Ridicule. Nothing can be more general than the reciprocal
Follies of Parents & Children—few Subjects more
Striking—they, if well drawn, will seize the attention, &
Interest the feelings of all Sorts, high & low—in Short I
was delighted with the Idea—[xxxxx *1–2 words*] the proceedings of this Family, as he gave them, seem'd so preposterous, so productive of bad Consequences, so
Ridiculous besides, that their whole Conduct might be
term'd, the Right Road to go wrong.

Yʳ Daddy Doctor talks of Mʳˢ Thrale's coming over to
this place to fetch back him & Madame[87]—cannot You
prevail on her to drop You here for a little while? I long
to have a *good Talk* with You, as the Cherokees call it.[88]—
I cannot by letter say my Say—*my Say*, look ye, Fanny, is
honest—& that is something; & I think is merit enough
in these evil days to incline You now & then to turn your
Ear my Way.

I am yʳ loving Daddy S.C

[87] CB and EAB had arrived at Chessington on Tues., 24 Aug. (SEB to FB,
25–6 Aug., Barrett). CB wrote to HLT, 29 Aug.: 'Aᵇᵗ to morrow 7 night, if
matters & things go well—what think you of taking a peep at the old Castle &
Philosopher of Chesington?' (*LCB* i. 277).

[88] Delegations of Cherokee chiefs had visited England a number of times,
most recently in 1765. SC may be referring, however, to the familiar 'pow-
wow', which is a Narragansett expression. See G. S. Woodward, *The Cherokees*
(Norman, 1963), pp. 64–6, 80–82; *YW* x. 36, xxx. 94; *AR* viii (1765), [65–6].

[*FB inserts the following ALS (Berg) from HLT to FB, 12 Sept. 1779, 2 single sheets 4to, 4 pp., paginated 1349-[1352], with the annotation*: Mr. Crisp—& the Chesington visit.]

Streatham
Saturday—I
mean Sunday.

My Dear Miss Burney

And so here comes your sweet Letter;[89] & so I pleased Mr Crisp did I?[90] and yet he never heard it seems the only *good Things* I said; which were very earnest, and very honest, and very pressing Invitations to see Streatham nearer than through the Telescope.[91] Now that he did *not* hear all this was your fault Mademoiselle, for you told me that Mr Crisp was old, & Mr Crisp was infirm, & if I had found *those things so*, I should have spoken louder, & concluded him to be *deaf*: but finding him very amiable & very elegant, & very polite to *me*; & very unlike an *old Man*; I never thought about his being deaf—& perhaps was a little *coquettish* too in my manner of making the Invitation.—I now repeat it however & give it *under my hand*, that I should consider such a Visit as a very, very great honour, & *so* would Mr Thrale.—

& now for dismal! |

I have been seriously ill ever since I saw You, & in such violent pain with my Face Ears & Teeth that there has been a furious Inflammation indeed, & Fever enough to require Catharticks, & Fomentations,[92] & a great Blister

[89] Missing.

[90] The Thrales, accompanied by FB, apparently visited Chessington and met SC for the 1st time on 6 Sept., to their evident mutual satisfaction (see *LCB* i. 277 and n. 13). FBA later wrote that 'what most, in this visit, surprised Mrs. Thrale with pleasure, was the elegance of Mr. Crisp in language and manners', while 'what most to Mr. Crisp caused a similar pleasure, was the courteous readiness, and unassuming good-humour, with which Mrs. Thrale received the inartificial civilities of Kitty Cooke, and the old-fashioned but cordial hospitality of Mrs. Hamilton' (*Mem.* ii. 184–5).

[91] Presumably from the top of the house, which afforded a view of the surrounding countryside 'sixteen miles in circumference' (ibid. ii. 186).

[92] 'The application to the surface of the body either of flannels, etc. soaked in hot water, whether simple or medicated, or of any other warm, soft, medicinal substance' (*OED* s.v. fomentation 1).

on my Back. Mrs Burney has been to me a kind & useful Friend; has suffered me to keep her here all this Time— is here still—would not go to Sir Joshua's 'tho she was asked—because I could not; and has been as obliging & as attentive and as good to me as possible; Dick is happy, & rides out with my Master; & his Mamma & I look at them out of the Dressing Room Window—so much for self.

In the midst of my own Misery I felt for my Dear Mrs Byron's;[93] but Chamier has relieved that anxiety by Assurances that the Adm^l behaved quite unexceptionably, & that as to *Honour* in the West Indies, all goes well. The Grenades are a heavy Loss indeed,[94] nor is it supposed possible for Byron to protect Barbadoes & Antigua:[95] Barrington[96] has acted a noble part, I he & Count D'Estaing remind one of the heroick Contentions of distant Times.[97] The Lyon, on our Side, commanded by a Welch man[98]—& the Languedoc,[99] on the Side of the French, fought with surprizing Fury & lost a great number

---

[93] Sophia Trevannion (d. 1790), m. (1748) Hon. John Byron (1723–86), Vice-Adm., 1778. HLT wrote in *Thraliana* (i. 407): 'Mrs Byron ... is Distressed just now—her Husband is supposed to have foreborne fighting in this last Affair, the Loss of the Grenada Islands.—& She is wild with Grief.' She added, however, s.v. 15 Sept. (ibid.): 'This however prov'd a false Alarm, for here is Barrington come over, & gives Byron the best of Characters.'

[94] Grenada, Britain's largest sugar island after Jamaica, had surrendered to the French on 4 July 1779. Two days later, the British West Indies fleet, commanded by Byron, was defeated by the French fleet, commander-in-chief Vice-Adm. Charles Henri Estaing (1729–94), Comte d'Estaing, in a battle off St George's. The British casualty lists showed 183 killed and 346 wounded while the official French report was 190 killed and 759 wounded. See *The Private Papers of John, Earl of Sandwich*, ed. G. R. Barnes and J. H. Owen (1932–8), ii. 122–4; *GM* xlix (1779), 468; *YW* xxiv. 515 nn. 2–3; xxxiii. 122 n. 3.

[95] The French took neither.

[96] Vice-Adm. Hon. Samuel Barrington (1729–1800), who was slightly wounded aboard the *Prince of Wales* and was praised by Byron in his dispatch to the Admiralty for his 'spirited example' (*GM* xlix (1779), 467.

[97] Horace Walpole made a similar observation in a letter to Henry Seymour Conway, 13 Sept. 1779: 'In the naval battle between Byron and D'Estaing, our captains were worthy of any age in our story' (*YW* xxxix. 339).

[98] The *Lion*, under Capt. Hon. William Cornwallis (1744–1819), later (1799) Adm., was badly damaged and had to run for Jamaica. Cornwallis was not a Welshman; his family had been established in Suffolk since the 14th century.

[99] D'Estaing's ship.

of Men; it was a glorious Day, tho' on our Side unfortunate.

D'Orvilliers has left our Channel after only cutting a few Ships out of Torbay & chasing Sr Charles to Spit head.[1] Many suppose the home Campaign quite over for this Year.

Poor dear Cecchina![2] I know not where she is scampered to; but a Woman who does not love her told the Story, so I don't believe all the aggravating Circumstances, nor will not. I wish she would write to me from his Quarters wherever they are: I hear he is a Gentleman & eminent for personal Beauty, deeply in Debt, a fashionable gay Fellow; probably worthless enough in every Sense of the Word.—[3]

[1] A combined French and Spanish fleet, commander-in-chief Adm. Louis Guillouet (1708-*c*.1792), Comte d'Orvilliers, and the British Channel fleet, commander-in-chief Adm. Sir Charles Hardy (*c*.1714–80), sighted each other off Land's End on 31 Aug. Sir Charles, in an effort to lure the larger combined fleet into the Channel, retreated all the way to Spithead, which he reached on 3 Sept. The slower combined fleet followed the British for 24 hours, whereupon, after losing sight of them and being distracted by a convoy of 15 Dutch merchantmen under an escort of warships, it turned back and returned to Ushant. Ravaged by sickness and suffering from a shortage of fresh water and provisions, the 'other armada' returned to Brest on 10–15 Sept. See A. T. Patterson, *The Other Armada: the Franco-Spanish Attempt to Invade Britain in 1779* (Manchester, 1960), pp. 194–215.

[2] The Streatham circle's nickname for Fanny Browne.

[3] Fanny Browne eloped with Thomas Gunter Browne (1756–1834), the 2nd son of Thomas Gunter Browne (1724–57) of St John's, Antigua, by Ann (m. 1753), daughter of William Dickinson, of Antigua. His grandfather, the Revd Dr Francis Browne, was a Canon of Windsor. Born in Antigua, he was sent to school at Westminster and admitted to Cambridge, but did not matriculate. In 1777 he became a cornet in the 3rd Dragoons, and on 28 July 1779 a Lt in the 37th Ft. He subsequently was Capt. in the 102nd Ft (1781) and in the 60th Ft (1781), retiring on half-pay in 1783.

Browne presumably met Fanny through her brother Lyde Browne (*c*.1759–1803), who also went to the Westminster School and was a cornet in the 3rd Dragoons. The *Whitehall Evening Post* 16–18 Sept. 1779, s.v. 16 Sept., announced their marriage 'a few days ago'. HLT commented on the elopement in *Thraliana* (i. 407): 'Fanny Brown is run away—scampered off with a Cornet of Horse; I do love that little Minx, & hope She may yet be happy, tho' She has vexed me by this Exploit a little too.—Poor silly Cecchina! or F: B: as we used to call her.—I wish She had a good Whipping & 10,000£.'

After her elopement Fanny Browne disappears from FB's journals, but she reappears in 1811 in a letter of Sarah Harriet Burney, who mentions her as living in London and lamenting the fate of her scapegrace son Brotherton (baptised Dec. 1781, in London), whom crushing debts had forced to flee to

Peggy Pitches[4] is dying of the Dropsy here at Croydon |
where She is forced to lye at a Friend's house coming up
from Brighthelmstone—Oh those poor innocent silly Parents! how I do pity'em!—

So you will not come *home* now, till you see how
monstrously ill things always do go when you are out of
the way; & then you will hurry home & lose your Amusement for the sake of shewing your true Love of your
Friend—I know you well enough & will not fetch you till
Saturday [18 Sept.]

to Your ever Affec^{te}
H:L:T.

My Pain is all gone Thanks to Heaven & Dr Bromfield
— — —but such a pale Face! Well! my last Conquest was
a gallant one,[5] & must content me till Xmas; for the next
three Months I mean to rival my Name sake[6]—not in
fairness but in paleness—

Give her & every body a thousand Com^s: it was a
charming Circle that it was! so Adieu! |

92   Brighton,

10 October [1779]

To Charles Burney

ALS (Berg), 10 Oct. 1779
Single sheet 4to, 4 pp. wafer
Addressed: Dr. Burney
Annotated (by FBA): ✣ — 79

India. As for Thomas Gunter Brown, he eventually settled in France and by
c.1800 was living with a Mrs Greene, who had left her husband for him. In
1795 he published at London *Hermes Unmasked*, a small book on linguistics of
sufficient interest to be reprinted by the Scolar Press in 1969. See *Thraliana* i.
407; *JL* vii. 358 n. 9; Sarah Harriet Burney to Charlotte Francis Barrett, 26
June 1811 (Berg), in L. Clark, 'The Letters of Sarah Harriet Burney: An
Edition' (Univ. of Toronto Ph.D. thesis 1989), pp. 165, 168 n. 5.

  [4] 'Afterward Countess of Coventry. This, however, proved a mistake' (HLT's
note).

  [5] Meaning SC.

  [6] 'Mrs. Burney Junr [EBB] Whose name is *Hester*' (HLT's note).

Brighthelmstone
[Sun.] Octr 10th

My dearest Sir,

Here we are, all safe & all well,—Mrs. Thrale excepted,
who is grievously tormented with the Tooth ache. We got
to Tunbridge on Tuesday Evening [5 Oct.], & left it on
Friday morning [8 Oct.]. The S.S. was there, & looked, I
think, more lovely than ever.[7] There, also, we saw the
Attorney General, & his Lady,[8]—the Flashers of the place
were Lady Margaret Fordyce[9] & Lady Anne Lindsay,
neither of which did we see. We strolled, however, upon
the *Pantiles*,[10]—where we saw the World & his Honour
Brudenel,[11] looking more stiff & Pokerish than ever, *what
we call the musical system* not being at Hand to soften &
harmonize him.[12]

But the chief entertainment I received at Tunbridge
was from a little Niece | of Mrs. Playdell's,[13]—a most

---

[7] The Thrales visited Tunbridge expressly so that Mr Thrale might see
Sophie Streatfeild again: 'Mr Thrale longs to see his S: S: *that* makes us go to
Tunbridge' (*Thraliana* i. 409). But the encounter failed to dissipate his gloom:
'I hoped the Sight of Miss Streatfield might rouze him, but they met with but
little eagerness on either Side, her Head was preoccupied with Care I believe,
& his with Disease—they met without Interest, & parted without Pain' (ibid.).

[8] Alexander Wedderburn (above, p. 214), m. (1767) Betty Anne Dawson
(*c*.1745–81), daughter of John Dawson, of Morley, Yorks.

[9] Lady Margaret Fordyce (*EJL* i. 200 n. 49, ii. 85) was noted for her beauty
and her sister Lady Anne Lindsay (above, p. 325) for her beauty and wit.
Hence 'the Flashers', meaning people of 'brilliant appearance or accomplish-
ment' (*OED* s.v. flasher 4).

[10] The Parade at Tunbridge Wells, so named for its paving tiles, erroneously
called 'pantiles' after a type of roofing tile (see *OED* s.v. pantile 1.c.).

[11] The Hon. James Brudenell, MP, later 5th E. of Cardigan (*EJL* ii. 172 n.
56).

[12] Brudenell sang and was an enthusiastic patron of the opera and ballet.
His wife was an amateur singer of note, and the two had attended a Burney
musical party in 1775 (ibid.; J. Wake, *The Brudenells of Deene* (1954), pp. 289–
90). '*What we call the musical system*' mocks the 'trite', 'tonish' speech of Rose
Fuller (below, p. 362).

[13] Mrs Elizabeth Playdell *or* Pleydell, née Holwell (d. by 1798) (*EJL* i. 67 n.
50). Her niece was Selina Fitzroy Birch (*c*.1769–1801), daughter of William
Birch (d. 1800), solicitor, by Sally Birch (living 1800), née Holwell. By his will
(PCC, dated 20 Mar., prob. 2 Apr. 1800) Miss Birch's father left her a sixth of
his estate. This bequest seems to have made possible her marriage a month
later (7 May 1800) to the Hon. John Cochrane (1750–1801), 5th son of Thomas
Cochrane (*c*.1691–1778), 8th E. of Dundonald. She died the following year

charming little Girl, who seems, in every particular, to have a strong resemblance to her Aunt. She sings, Dances, Laughs, Cries, plays, or reasons like a little Woman,—&, in a moment, can, as opportunity gives leave, convert her vivacity into tenderness, or her tenderness into vivacity.

Since we came hither, I have seen nobody that I know, & Mr. & Mrs. T. very few,—but we are in the *way* to *know*, soon, all that we *see*. The Cumberlands, I find, are here,— the Beauclerks,[14]—St. Johns,[15] Seftons,[16] Duchess of Ancaster, Lady Charlotte Bertie,[17] all the Potts Family,[18] & many more. Also *Single Speech* Hamilton.[19]

Mr. Thrale, who, the last 2 or 3 Days we were at Streatham, seemed so much dejected, low spirited, inanimate & indolent as to alarm us all greatly, & to frighten Mrs. Thrale to Death, is so much revived already that he seems a new man,—he is in good spirits, mixes without

with her infant son, and her husband died 2 months after. See *GM* lxx[1] (1800), 392; lxxi[2] (1801), 1059; IGI.

[14] Topham Beauclerk (above, p. 197 n. 96) and his wife Lady Diana née Spencer (1734–1808), daughter of Charles Spencer, 3rd D. of Marlborough. She m. (12 Mar. 1768) Beauclerk 2 days after she was divorced by Frederick St John (1734–87), 2nd Visc. Bolingbroke, for her adultery with Beauclerk.

[15] Probably the Hon. Henry St John (1738–1818), of Rockley, Wilts, MP, army officer, 2nd son of John (d. 1749), 2nd Visc. St John; and his wife (m. 1771) Barbara St John (b. *c*.1733), daughter of Thomas Bladen (?1698–1780), of Glastonbury, Somerset, MP (Namier; Sedgwick).

[16] Charles William Molyneux (1748–94), 8th Visc. Molyneux of Maryborough (Ire.), cr. (1771) E. of Sefton (Ire.); and his wife (m. 1768) Isabella née Stanhope (1748–1819), daughter of William Stanhope (1719–79), 2nd E. of Harrington.

[17] Probably Mary Bertie (d. 1793), daughter of Thomas Panton (*c*.1697–1782), Master of the King's Running Horses, 2nd wife (1750) of Peregrine Bertie (1714–78), 3rd D. of Ancaster; and her daughter Lady Georgiana Charlotte Bertie (1764–1838), who later m. (1791) George James Cholmondeley (1749–1827), 4th E. of Cholmondeley, cr. (1815) M. of Cholmondeley.

[18] Percivall Pott (1714–88), surgeon, had attended both Thrale and his son Ralph in 1775. He m. (1746) Sarah Cruttenden (d. 1811). The Potts' 8 children were Percivall (1749–1833), Sarah (1751–91), m. John Reeve Frye, Elizabeth (b. 1752), Mary (b. 1754), Robert (b. 1756, living 1788), Joseph Holden (1758–1847), Anna (b. 1760), and Edward Holden (b. 1766, living 1788). See IGI; *DNB*; *GM* lxi[2] (1791), 1065; ciii[1] (1833), 186; will of Sarah Pott, PCC, dated 20 Nov. 1803, prob. 22 Feb. 1811; *TSP*, pp. 115–16.

[19] William Gerard Hamilton (1729–96), of Hampton Court, Middlesex; MP, 1754–96. Although he acquired an early reputation as a parliamentary speaker, his contempt for English politicians caused him to remain silent in the Commons from *c*.1765 till the end of his life; hence the nickname 'Single Speech' (Namier).

murmuring with the Company in the place, & I think is more chearful than I have seen him since his first attack[20].

The chief Diversion for the morning here seems to be Raffling, & the chief object for the Raffles at present is Dr. Johnson's Lives of the Poets. Bowen,[21] a Bookseller just set up here, says they sell extremely well,—& he has always a set for Raffling. The Duchess of Cumberland[22] tried for them in the last Business of this sort, but Lady Charlotte Bertie has won them. |

I have written *my* long Letter to Charles, & taken what pains I could to show the imprudence of the request concerning a Commendatory Letter.[23] I have also told him of his permission to draw upon Mr Fuller,[24] &c.

Adieu, my dearest Sir, I hope to Heaven you are able to keep off any further return of the rheumatism,—& I am ever & ever

Most dutifully & most affectionately
your F. Burney

---

[20] HLT noted in *Thraliana* (i. 409): 'We went forward to Brighthelmstone where every body observed the Torpor that hung about him, it went away however gradually, but almost totally: he rode with Spirit, eat with Appetite, & his Friends observ'd a most agreeable Alteration in his Looks ... '

[21] Joseph Bowen, bookseller and stationer, had a store at 95, Strand, London, and had recently opened a shop and circulating library on the Steine, Brighton. He is listed as a bankrupt in the *GM* liv² (July 1784), 559. He perhaps re-established himself and was the 'Mr. Bowen, bookseller and printer, of Cockey-lane, Norwich', who died 21 Oct. 1790 (ibid. lx² (1790), 1053). See Maxted.

[22] Hon. Anne Luttrell (1743–1808), m. 2 (1771) Henry Frederick (1745–1790), D. of Cumberland, brother of George III.

[23] CB Jr. was at Aberdeen, whence he had gone to study classics (at King's College) on the long road to redemption from the disgrace of his dismissal from Cambridge for stealing books (see *EJL* ii. 289–90). CB had evidently himself written a long letter to CB Jr. about the ill-advised (and unexplained) 'Commendatory Letter', to which FB had added her own; they are both missing.

[24] Presumably Richard Fuller (c.1713–82), head of the banking firm at No. 84, Cornhill, who had been one of the witnesses at CB's wedding to EAB in 1767 (CB *Mem.* 152–3 and n. 3, 177 n. 5; LDGL).

93

Brighton,
12 October [1779]

To Susanna Elizabeth Burney

AJL (Berg, Diary MSS I, paginated 1015–40), 12 Oct. 1779
14 single sheets 4to, 28 pp.
This journal letter was sent in 2 'budgets', as indicated by FB's
heading ('Brighthelmstone. 2ᵈ Budget') at the top of p. 1027. Though
our practice is generally to publish items separately as actually sent
through the mail or by private hand (where this is ascertainable), for
ease of reading we publish this journal as a single item, since the first
installment ends and the second begins literally in mid-sentence ('but
as I | have since heard', below, p. 371).

Brighthelmstone.
Octʳ 12ᵗʰ

As you say you will accept *memorandums* in default of
Journals, my dearest Susy, I will scrawl down such things
as most readily recur to my remembrance, &, when I get
to the present Time, I will endeavour to be less remiss in
my accounts.

I left you, indeed, in a most uncomfortable hurry,—
unable to give you half the *Chaste Embraces* I wished to
do, or even to thank you for your most kind assistance,—
when we meet next, however, I am much mistaken if I
am so served again.—

We spent that afternoon [1 Oct.] quite alone. Dr. Johnson
left Streatham in the morning [2 Oct.]. Mr. Thrale who
had, again, been much indisposed, though, thank God, not
with another attack like his last, was much better.[25]

Sunday [3 Oct.]—we had Lady Lade. She did not leave
us till the next Day. She & I are grown most prodigious

[25] SJ, however, wrote to HLT, 4 Oct. 1779: 'I was alarmed by hearing, that
my Servant had told in the house, for servants never tell their Masters, his
opinion that for the two last days Mr. Thrale was visibly worse'. He entreated
her to take Thrale to see Dr Heberden before setting out for Brighton (*LSJ* iii.
184). HLT recorded in *Thraliana* that just before the Brighton trip, 'Mʳ Thrale
had looked particularly ill for two or three Days, ... but he was cupped by Dʳ
Heberden's advice and the Symptoms went off' (i. 409).

friends;—she is really so entertaining & lively with those she thinks well of, that it is not often possible to pass Time more gayly than in her Company. Mr. Stephen Fuller, the sensible but deaf old Gentleman I have formerly mentioned, Dined here also;—as did his Nephew, Rose, whose trite, settled, tonish emptiness of Discourse is a never failing source of Laughter & diversion.

'Well, I say, what, Miss Burney, so you had a very good Party last Tuesday [28 Sept.]?—what we call the ¹ *Family Party*, in that sort of way?—Pray who had you?'

'Mr. Chamier,—'

'Mr. Chamier?—ay,—give me leave to tell you, Miss Burney, that Mr. Chamier is what we call a very sensible man!—'

'Certainly. And Mr. Pepys—'

'Mr. Pepys?—ay, very good! very good, in that sort of way.—I'm quite sorry I could not be here,—but I was so much indisposed—quite what we call the *Nursing Party*.'

'I'm very sorry,—but I hope little Sharp is well?—'

'Ma'am your most humble!—you're a very good lady, indeed!—quite what we call a good lady,—little Sharp is perfectly well,—that sort of attention, & things of that sort—the Bow-wow system is perfectly well. But pray, Miss Burney, give me leave to ask, in that sort of way,—had you any body else?'

'Yes,—Lady Lade & Mr. Seward.'

'So, so!—quite the Family system!—Give me leave to tell you, Miss Burney, this commands attention!—what we call a respectable invitation!—I am sorry I could not come, indeed,—for we young men, Miss Burney, we make it what we call a sort of a rule to take Notice of this sort of attention,—but I was extremely indisposed, indeed,—what we call the Walnut system had quite—Pray what's the News, Miss Burney?—in that sort of way, is there any news?'

'None that I have heard. Have *you* heard any?'

'Why very bad! very bad, indeed! quite what we call ¹ poor old England!—I was told, in Town,—Fact!—Fact, I assure you!—that these Dons intend us an Invasion this month!—they & the Monsieurs intend us the respectable salute this very month,—the powder system, in that sort of way!—Give me leave to tell you, Miss Burney, this is what we call a disagreeable visit, in that sort of way!—'[26]

I think, if possible, his Language looks more absurd upon Paper even than it sounds in conversation, from the perpetual recurrence of the same words & Expressions.

Poor little Peggy Pitches called to take leave of us. She looks almost dying. Her Eldest sister, Jenny, is just married,—married not only contrary to the advice & approbation & exhortations of her Parents, but even without waiting to be out of her first mourning for her sister Sophy!—[27]

All Monday [4 Oct.] was appropriated to Packing, &c. Mr. Seward failed making his promised visit,—he is gone, perhaps, to *Cornwall* at last!

Tuesday, Oct[r] 5th Mr., Mrs., Miss Thrale & *yours, Ma'am, yours,* set out on their Expedition;—the Day was very pleasant, & the Journey delightful, but that which chiefly rendered it so was Mr. Thrale's being apparently the better for it.

I need not tell you how sweet a Country for Travelling is Kent, as you know it so well.[28] We stopt at Sevenoak,[29] which is a remarkably well situated | Town,—& here, while Dinner was preparing, my kind & sweet Friends took me to Knoll,[30]—though they had seen it repeatedly themselves.

---

[26] Rumours of an invasion were rampant at this time, fueled by the sighting off Plymouth on 16 Aug. of the armada consisting of the combined fleets of Spain and France (A. T. Patterson, *The Other Armada: the Franco-Spanish Attempt to Invade Britain in 1779* (Manchester, 1960), *passim*). In fact, in a council of war held at Brest on 3 Oct. it was decided to send the combined fleets into winter quarters. But the rumours persisted, and on 26 Oct. and 28–30 Oct., respectively, the *Daily Adv.* and the *London Chronicle* reported plans for an imminent invasion (*YW* xxiv. 519 n. 6, 525 n. 8; xxxiii. 131 n. 7).

[27] Sophia Pitches had died on 4 July (above, p. 332). Jane Pitches m. (29 Sept. 1779) William Boyce, a Lt in the 16th Dragoons (above, p. 123 n. 32). Boyce rose to be Lt-Col. of his regiment and eventually gained enough of the family's approbation to prove his father-in-law's will (will of Abraham Pitches, PCC, prob. 27 Apr. 1792).

[28] Because of her visits to Lady Hales and Miss Coussmaker at Howletts.

[29] Sevenoaks, Kent, a market town 23 mi. SE of London.

[30] Knole Park, 1 mi. E of Sevenoaks, seat of the D. of Dorset.

The Park, which, it seems, is 7 miles in circumference, & has, as the Game keeper told us, 700 Head of Deer in it, is laid out in a most beautiful manner,—nearly, I think, equal to Hagley,[31] as far as belongs to the Disposition of the Trees, Hills, Dales, &c,—though, in regard to Temples, Obelisks, or any sort of Buildings, it will bear *no* comparison to that sweet place,—since nothing is there of that sort.

The House, which is very old, has the appearance of an Antique Chapel, or rather Cathedral;—2 immense Gates, & 2 Court Yards precede the Entrance into the Dwelling part of the House. The Windows are all of the small old Casements, & the general Air of the place is monastic & gloomy. It was begun to be Built, as the Housekeeper told us, in the Reign of Harry the 2ᵈ,[32] by Thomas a Becket:[33] but the *modern* part was finished in the Time of Elizabeth![34]—

The Duke of Dorset was not there himself, but we were prevented seeing the Library, & 2 or 3 other modernised Rooms, because *Maᶫᶫᵉ Bacelli*[35] was not to be disturbed. The House, however, is so very magnificently large, that we only coveted to see ǀ that part of it which was Hung with Pictures:—3 state Rooms, however, were curious

[31] Hagley Park, Worcs, the seat of Thomas Lyttelton (1744 – 27 Nov. 1779), 2nd B. Lyttelton of Frankley. The park, which is celebrated in Thomson's *Spring*, included an artificial ruined castle, a rotunda, a Palladian bridge, and a Doric temple. See C. Hussey, *English Country Houses: Early Georgian 1715–1760* (1955), pp. 195–9.

[32] Henry II (1133–89), King of England, 1154–89.

[33] Thomas à Becket (c.1118–70), Archbishop of Canterbury; Saint.

[34] Elizabeth I (1533–1603), Queen of England, 1558–1603. The earliest mention of Knole is in a document dating from 1281, in the reign of Edward I. The modern building was largely the work of Thomas Bourchier (c.1404–86), Archbishop of Canterbury, who bought Knole in 1456. Henry VIII acquired Knole in 1538. In 1566 Elizabeth I gave the reversion of Knole to her 2nd cousin Thomas Sackville (d. 1608), B. of Buckhurst, cr. (1604) E. of Dorset, the co-author of *Gorboduc* (1561) and *The Mirror for Magistrates* (1563 edn.). He took possession of the manor in 1603. See C. J. Phillips, *History of the Sackville Family* (1929), ii. 382, 395 and *passim*.

[35] Giovanna Zanerini, called Baccelli (d. 1801), dancer. She was Dorset's mistress and lived at Knole until Dec. 1789, departing just before the Duke's marriage in Jan. 1790 (see above, p. 227 n. 48). Her suite of rooms there is commemorated as 'Shelley's Tower'. Both Reynolds and Gainsborough painted her. See Highfill; E. Einberg, *Gainsborough's Giovanna Baccelli* (1976).

enough;—one of them had been fitted up by an *Earle of Dorsete* for the Bed Chamber of King James the first, when upon a visit at Knoll.[36] It had all the gloomy grandeur, & solemn finery of that Time;—the second State Room, a later Earle had fitted up for James the 2^d[37]— — —The 2 Charles's[38] either never honoured Knoll with their presence, or else condescended to sleep in their Father & Grandfather's Bed;—well, this James the 2^d's Room was more superb than his predecessors, flaming with Velvet Tissue, Tapestry, & what not?— — —but the *third* state Room was magnificence itself!—it was fitted up for King William;[39]—the Bed—Curtains, Tester, Quilt, & Valens, were all of the richest Gold flowers worked upon a silver Ground,—it's value, even in those Days, was £7000!—The Table, a superb Cabinet, Frame of the looking Glass, & all the Ornaments, & I believe, all the *Furniture* in the Room, were of solid massy silver, curiously embossed!—Nothing could be more splendid.

---

[36] FB probably refers to the Spangled Bedroom, which contained the furniture 'presented by King James I [(1566–1625), King of England, 1603–25] to Lionel, earl of Middlesex, lord-treasurer, from whom it descended, through his daughter, who married the fifth earl of Dorset, to the Sackville family' (J. H. Brady, *The Visitor's Guide to Knole* (Sevenoaks, 1839), pp. 121–2). For the bedroom prepared for James I's visit, see below, n. 39.

[37] The Venetian Bedroom. 'It contains a very elegant state bed, said to have been prepared for the reception of King James II [(1633–1701), King of England, 1685–9]. The canopy is richly carved and gilt at the head-board, surmounted with the royal arms' (ibid., p. 131). The E. of Dorset during James II's reign was Charles Sackville (1638–1706), 6th E. of Dorset, 1677.

[38] Charles I (1600–49), King of England, 1625–49, and Charles II (1630–85), King of England, 1660–85.

[39] William III (1650–1702), King of England, 1689–1702. No other mention has been found of such a room prepared for this monarch. FB seems to be describing the King's Bedroom, or Silver Room, which had been built in the south tower erected by Bourchier. 'A tradition in the family is that this room was prepared for the reception of James I [(1566–1625), King of England, 1603–25] at an expense of £20,000, of which no less than £8,000 was for the bed alone' (Phillips, ii. 349). 'The bedstead is profusely ornamented, with a canopy-top; and the furniture ... is of gold and silver tissue, lined with rose-coloured satin, embroidered and fringed with gold and silver. About the room are several chairs and stools, covered to correspond with the furniture of the bed' (Brady, pp. 156–7). The Earls during James I's reign: Thomas Sackville, 1st E. of Dorset; Robert Sackville (1561–1609), 2nd E., 1608; Richard Sackville (1589–1624), 3rd E., 1609; and Edward Sackville (1590–1652), 4th E., 1624.

But to leave all this shew, & come to what is a thousand Times more interesting—the *Pictures,* of which there is, indeed, a curious Collection!—I could have spent a *Day* in looking at every Room, & yet have longed to see them again.—*I* can, however, give a very imperfect & lame account of them, as we were so hurried by the House-keeper from Room to Room, & I was so anxious to miss nothing, that the merely *glancing* over so many beautiful Paintings has only left a faint remembrance in my Head of each particular Picture, though a very strong & deep impression of the pleasure they at the Time afforded me.

Among such as just now occur to me were a Lucretia, with a Dagger, a large whole length by Guido[40],—*extremely beautiful;*—purchased by the present Duke, in Italy:—a madonna & Child, small size, by Raphael,[41] so lovely I could not turn from it till called repeatedly,—a virgin by Carlo Dolci[42] that was *irresistably* attractive,—a Raphael by himself that was Noble,[43]—Landscapes by Poussin,[44] & 1 or 2 by Claude Lauraine that were enchanting,[45]— — — But all this will be heavy reading, my dear Susy,—so I will say no more till I *say* it with my *voice,*—but that the

[40] Guido Reni (1575–1642). This painting, 'a studio copy of high quality', was acquired by Dorset at Rome in 1771. It passed by inheritance to the 5th E. of Plymouth at Hewell Grange. The autograph painting (1625–6) has been in the Neues Palais at Potsdam since 1773. See D. S. Pepper, *Guido Reni: A Complete Catalogue of His Works with an Introductory Text* (New York, 1984), p. 254 and Plate 130.

[41] Raphael Sanzio (1483–1520). Perhaps the picture described by Brady, p. 149, as 'Madonna and Child.—After *Raphael.*'

[42] Carlo Dolci (1616–86). Perhaps the Madonna and Child with 'an old label on the back [which] states: "The Virgin and Child purchased from Mr. F. Custens Carlo Dulci, J. F., Duke of Dorset, 1775"' (Phillips, ii. 429).

[43] The label on the back states: 'This picture painted by Raphael Urbin, supposed to be his own portrait, was purchased by his Grace the Duke of Dorset in Rome, 1770' (ibid., ii. 427).

[44] FB probably means the 2 landscapes in the Billiard Room attributed to Nicolas Poussin in Brady, p. 126. These are presumably the 'Landscape, with Rocks and Shipping' and the 'Landscape, with Coursing and Mountains in Background' listed in Phillips, ii. 429; the first is attributed there, probably incorrectly, to Salvator Rosa and the second has no attribution. A. Blunt, *The Paintings of Nicolas Poussin: A Critical Catalogue* (1966) notes no Poussins at Knole.

[45] M. Röthlisberger, *Claude Lorrain: The Paintings* (New Haven, 1961), identifies no Claudes at Knole, nor are any claimed in the descriptions of Knole examined.

Collection is *infinitely* superior indeed to any I had ever
before seen,—& that, equally for Portraits, Historical
Pieces, & Landscapes.

There are several Pictures of Sir Joshua Reynolds, &,
though mixed in with those of the best old Painters, they
are so bewitching, & finished in a style of Taste, ꟷ Colouring, & expression so like their Companions, that it is
not, at first view, easy to distinguish the New from the
Old. The celebrated Ugolino Family[46] is almost too horrible to be looked at,—yet I was glad to see it again;—
2 Beggar Boys make an exceedingly pleasing Picture;[47]—
the Duke himself,[48] by Sir Joshua, among the Portraits of
his own Family, in a state Room, is, I think, by no means
a likeness to flatter his Grace's vanity.—One Room is
appropriated to Artists,—& among them 3 are by Sir
Joshua,—Dr. Johnson,[49] Dr. Goldsmith,[50] & Sacchini:[51]—
all charmingly done, & the 2 I know,[52] extremely like.

One Noble Gallery is fitted up with Copies of Raphaels
Cartoons, by Romana[53]—done so delightfully, I could
have looked at them till now,— — —but I believe I shall

[46] *Count Hugolino and his Children in the Dungeon, as Described by Dante*, an
uncommissioned history painting exhibited at the Royal Academy in 1773 and
purchased by the D. in 1775. FB had evidently seen it before, either in
Reynolds' studio or in the Exhibition (Graves i. 257, iii. 1218; Phillips ii. 419;
Reynolds, ed. N. Penny (1986), pp. 251–3 and *passim*).

[47] *A Beggar Boy and His Sister*, exhibited at the Royal Academy in 1775 and
purchased that year by the D. (ibid., pp. 64, 265, 297; Graves iii. 1116, 1135).

[48] FB presumably means the whole-length portrait of the D. in peer's robes,
painted in 1769 upon his succession to the Dukedom. The D. also sat for a
head-size portrait several years later (ibid. i. 256; Phillips ii. 419).

[49] A profile portrait bought by the D. in 1769 (Penny, pp. 240–41; Graves
ii. 519; Phillips ii. 419).

[50] A half-length profile purchased by the D. in 1778 (ibid. ii. 420; Graves
i. 369).

[51] FB had seen this portrait in Reynolds' studio in 1775 (*EJL* ii. 67–8 and
illustration p. 69).

[52] SJ and Sacchini.

[53] Giulio Romano (1499–1546) was an outstanding pupil of Raphael. The
cartoons at Knole, however, are copies in oil by Daniel Mytens (b. *c.*1590, d.
ante 1648), painter to James I and Charles I (the latter of whom commissioned
the copies), of 6 of the 10 famous designs by Raphael (on subjects from the
Acts of the Apostles) commissioned by Pope Leo X for tapestries hung in the
Sistine Chapel. Charles I presented the copies to Lionel Cranfield, 1st E. of
Middlesex, whose daughter, Frances Cranfield, married the 5th E. of Dorset,
and so these cartoons came to Knole (Phillips i. 421–2; Thieme).

never tear myself away from this delicious Collection—I
have almost writ myself back to Knoll—but lest I should
have writ *you* to sleep— — —I *will* have done;—

We Dined very comfortably at Seven Oaks & thence
made but one stage to Tunbridge. It was so dark when
we went through the Town, that I could see it very
indistinctly;—the Wells, however, are about 7 miles yet
further, so that we saw that Night Nothing,—but, I assure
you, I *felt* that I was entering into a new Country pretty
roughly, | for the Roads were so *sidelum* & *Jumblum*, as
Miss Lockwood[54] called those of Tingmouth, that I
expected an overturn every minute. Safely, however, we
reached the Sussex Hôtel, at Tunbridge Wells, part of
which, it seems, is in Kent, & part in Sussex.

Having looked at our Rooms, & arranged our affairs,
we proceeded to Mount Ephraim, where Miss Streatfield
resides. We found her with only her mother, & spent the
Evening there.

Mrs. Streatfield[55] is very, very little, but perfectly well
made, thin, genteel & delicate; she has been quite beautiful, & has still so much of beauty left, that to call it only
the *remains* of a fine Face seems hardly doing her justice.
She is very lively, & an excellent mimic, & is, I think, as
much superior to her Daughter in *natural* Gifts, as her
Daughter is to her in *acquired* ones.—& how infinitely
preferable are parts without Education than Education
without parts!—[56]

The fair S.S. is really in higher Beauty than I have ever
yet seen her,—& she was so carressing, so soft, so amiable,

[54] A 'rich old maid' whom FB had met at Teignmouth in 1773 (see *EJL* i.
276 and n. 71). Her quaint expression is presumably a corruption of 'sidelong'
and 'jumbling', meaning 'sloping' and 'jolting'.

[55] Anne Sydney (1732–1812), natural daughter of Jocelyn Sydney (*c.*1692–
1743), 7th E. of Leicester, 1737; widow (m. 1752) of Henry Streatfeild (1706–
62), of Chiddingstone, Kent (IGI).

[56] Cf. FB's assessment of Omai and Philip Stanhope (*EJL* ii. 62–3). HLT
described Mrs Streatfeild in 1776 as 'a Widow, high in Fortune, & rather
eminent both for the Beauties of Person & Mind' (*Thraliana* i. 17). But in 1778
she commented that 'Sophy Streatfield is adored by her Mother but does not
return her Affection', adding in a note: 'How should she love a silly, drunken,
old painted Puss Cat? tho' the best Mother under heaven ... ' (ibid. i. 355 and
n. 3).

that I felt myself insensibly inclining to her with an affectionate regard;—if it was not for *that little Gush,* as Dr. Delap said,[57] I should certainly have taken a very great fancy to her,—but Tears so ready— ¦ O they *blot out* my fair opinion of her.—Yet, whenever, I am *with* her, I like—nay almost *love* her,—for her manners are exceedingly captivating;—but—when I *quit* her,—I do not find that she improves by being *thought over.*—no, nor *talked over,*—for Mrs. Thrale, who is always disposed to half adore her in her presence, can never *converse* about her, without exciting her own contempt by recapitulating what has passed. This, however, must always be *certain,* whatever may be *doubtful,*—that she is a Girl in no respect like any other.

But I have not, yet, done with the mother; I have told you of her vivacity & her mimicry,—but her Character is yet not half told,—she has a kind of whimsical conceit, & of odd affectation, that, joined to a very singular sort of humour, makes her always seem to be rehearsing some scene in a Comedy.—She takes off, if she mentions them, all her own Children &, though she quite adores them, renders them ridiculous with all her power; she Laughs at herself for her smallness & for her vagaries, just with the same ease & ridicule as if she was speaking of some other Person,—&, while perpetually hinting at being old & broken, she is continually frisking, flaunting, & playing tricks, like a young Coquet. ¦

When I was introduced to her, by Mrs. Thrale, who said 'Give me leave, Ma'am, to present to you a Friend of your Daughter's, Miss Burney,—' she advanced to me with a tripping pace, & taking one of my Fingers, said 'Allow me, Ma'am, will you? to create a little acquaintance with you?—'

And, indeed, I readily *entered into an alliance* with her, for I found nothing at Tunbridge half so entertaining,—except, indeed, Miss Birch, of whom hereafter.—

The next morning [6 Oct.] the S.S. Breakfasted with us;—& then they walked *all about,* to shew me the place.

---

[57] See above, p. 318.

The Sussex Hotel, where we Lived, is situated at the side of the Pantiles, or Public Walk,—so called, because paved with Pantiles;—it is called so also, like the long Room at Hampstead,[58] because it would be difficult to distinguish it by any other Name,—for it has no beauty in itself, & borrows none from *foreign aid*, as it has only common Houses at one side & little millinary & Tunbridge ware shops at the other, & at each end is choaked up by Buildings that intercept all Prospect. How such a place could first be made a fashionable *pleasure* Walk, everybody must wonder!—

Thence we went to *the Well*,[59] which is at ǀ the bottom of the Pantiles, & where I drank a Glass of the Water,— it is mighty disagreeable to my taste. We then took a View of the Grove, Mount Ephraim, Mount Pleasant, & the other principal places belonging to the Wells,—after which we returned to stroll upon the Pantiles & see the Company, & then went to Mount Ephraim to Dine with Mrs. Streatfield.

Tunbridge Wells is a place that, to me, appeared very singular: the Country is all Rock, & every part of it is either *up* or *down* Hill,—scarce 10 yards square being level Ground in the whole place:—The Houses, too, are scattered about in a strange wild manner, & look as if they had been dropt where they stand by accident,—for they form niether *streets* nor *squares*, but seem *strewed promiscussly* [*sic*],—except indeed, where the regular shop keepers Live, who have got 2 or 3 dirty little Lanes much like dirty little Lanes in other places.

Mrs. Streatfield & I increased our intimacy marvellous much,—but she gave me the Nick name of *the Dove*,—for what reason I cannot guess, except it be that the Dove has a sort of *greenish Grey* Eye, something like mine,—be that as it may, she called me nothing else while I stayed at Tunbridge.

In the Evening, we all went to the Rooms. *The Rooms*, as they are called, consisted, for this Evening, of only *one*

---

[58] A building in Hampstead Wells in which the Hampstead Assemblies were held. See *Evelina*, ed. E. A. Bloom (1968), p. 428.

[59] The chalybeate springs.

apartment, as there was not Company enough to make more necessary, — & a very plain, unadorned & ordinary Apartment that was. |

There were very few People, — but among them Mr. Wedderburne, the Attorney General, — you may believe I rather wished to *shrink* from him, if you recollect what Mrs. Thrale said of *Him*, among the rest of the Tunbridge Coterie *last* season, — who discussed *Evelina* regularly every Evening, — & that *he*, siding with Mrs. Montagu,[60] cut up the Branghtons, — & had, as well as Mrs. Montagu, almost a *Quarrel* with Mrs. Greville upon the subject, because *she* so warmly vindicated, or rather *applauded* them. — *Lady Louisa*, however, I remember he spoke of with *very* high praise, — as Mrs. Montagu did of the Dedication, — & if such folks can find *any* thing to praise, *I* find myself amply recompensed for their censures, — especially when they censure what I cannot regret writing, since it is the part *most* favoured by Dr. Johnson.

Mr. Wedderburne joined us immediately, — Mrs. Thrale presently said 'Mr. Wedderburne, I must present my daughter to you, — and Miss Burney, — ' I Courtsied mighty gravely, & shuffled to the other end of the Party, however, if he has any knack at *Drawing*, I fancy he need not wish me to *sit* to him, for if his memory in retaining objects is equal to his *greediness* of examining them, he will be able to give as accurate a description of me 10 years hence, as Another man could do at the moment he faced me. — I cannot say I much enjoyed being so curiously inspected, but as I | have since heard abundant civil observations which he made to Mrs. Thrale, I do not *bear him malice*. — Generous enough, you'll say! —

Amongst the Company, I was most struck with, the *Hon. Mrs. Wilson*,[61] — lately Miss *Townshend*, & Daughter to Lady Greenwich — she ran away with a Mr. *Wilson*, a

[60] See above, p. 162 n. 10.

[61] Anne née Townshend (1756–1825), daughter of Charles Townshend (1725–67), Chancellor of the Exchequer, and Caroline née Campbell (1717–94), daughter of the 1st D. of Greenwich, cr. (1767) Baroness of Greenwich.. She m. 1 (23 Mar. 1779) Richard Wilson (d. 1815), an Irish adventurer who later became MP for Barnstaple; m. 2 John Tempest (d.?1831), of Lincolnshire (Thorne; *GM* xcv² (1825), 381; ci² (1831), 379).

man nearly old enough to be her Father,[62]—& of most notorious bad character,—both as a sharper & a Libertine;—this Wretch was with her,—a most hackneyed, ill-looking, object as I ever saw;—& the foolish Girl, who seems scarce 16, & looks a raw school Girl, has an air of so much discontent, & seems in a state of such dismal melancholy, that it was not possible to look at her without compassionating a folly she has so many Years to Live regretting!—I would not wish a more striking warning to be given to other such forward, adventurous Damsels, than to place them before this miserable Runaway,—who has not only disgraced her Family & enraged her Friends, but rendered herself a repentant mourner for Life.—[63]

Thursday morning [7 Oct.] we had again The S.S.—again we strolled upon the Pantiles,—& again we Dined at Mrs. Streatfield's. Among the Faces here I have seen none I ever saw before except Mr. Brudenel's & Miss Ellerker's,[64]—but almost all the other Faces were more worth looking at.

We spent the whole afternoon & Evening at Mount [Ephraim,] | &, at Mrs. Thrale's request, Mrs. Streatfield invited *Miss Boone* to Tea, purposely that I might see her.

Miss Boone is the same Lady Mr. Seward was invited to see by the S.S.;[65]—you may want, therefore, to know what is her particular attraction,—why simply & merely

[62] The marriage license claims that he was only 23, or the same age as Miss Townshend (Thorne v. 603 n. 1).

[63] Both Wilson and his wife 'were incorrigible spendthrifts and of a neurotic tendency verging on insanity' (ibid. v. 601). According to Joseph Farington, Wilson had 'gained a fortune by being mistaken for another man' at Brighton of the same name. Miss Townshend had heard the praises of this other Mr Wilson; Richard Wilson 'saw the attention with which she regarded him, was introduced to her ... and in ten days or a fortnight ran away with and married her and got £10,000' (in fact £2,000) (cited ibid.). Wilson may have been the Richard Wilson who in 1789 seduced and absconded with Ld. Rodney's 17-year-old daughter. In 1795 'Mrs Wilson committed adultery, and ran off, with one John Thomson, a failed attorney living in a cottage on the [Wilsons'] Datchworth estate' (ibid.). Wilson instituted divorce proceedings against her, but the bill died after the committee stage in the House of Lords, probably because of allegations that he had 'exploited his wife financially, had habitually beaten her and had kept a mistress in or near the house' (ibid. v. 602).

[64] Elizabeth Ellerker (1751–1831) (see *EJL* i. 259 n. 9).

[65] See above, p. 314.

SIZE!—She is *so Tall*, so fat, so large, that she might be shewn for *the great Woman* at any Fair in England. But with all this grossness of size, she is very Young, & very handsome!— — —

In regard to *Character*, she is as much a Female Falstaff, as she is in regard to *Person*,—for she loves nothing so well as Eating & Drinking, & never of either seems to get enough, even when she empties every Dish & every Glass.—She is also very ingenious,—Draws, paints, takes likenesses, & cuts out Paper Figures & devices remarkably well. & though she was invited to divert me as some thing *strange & preposterous*, I found her so sensible & so intelligent, that the diversion she gave me was all such as redounded to her own Honour.

She is a Daughter of the late Governor Boone,[66] & a Niece of *our* Mr. Boone.[67] And her mother is one of those included in Walpole's Beauties.[68]

Mrs. Streatfield's 2 sons made up our Party. | The Eldest, Harry, is a very pretty sort of young man,—the Youngest, Richard, is somewhat *below par*.[69]

[66] She was actually a granddaughter of Charles Boone (c.1684–1735), of Rook's Nest, Surrey, governor of Bombay, 1715–22, and a director of the East India Co., 1729–35 (Sedgwick; *Miscellanea Geneologica et Heraldica* 2nd ser. iv (1892), 339).

[67] Charles Boone (c.1729–1819), MP (*EJL* ii. 172 n. 54; above, p. 214).

[68] Horace Walpole's *The Beauties. An Epistle to Eckardt, the Painter*, verses written by him in 1746 for Lady Caroline Fox and published anonymously soon after in 4 fol. sheets by M. Cooper (reprinted in Dodsley's *Collection*, 1748, in Walpole's *Fugitive Pieces*, 1758, and in his *Works*, 1770). 'Two beauteous nymphs here, painter, place / Lamenting o'er their sister Grace; / One, matron-like, with sober grief / Scarce gives her pious sighs relief' (*YW* xxx. 328–9). Walpole's note in his MS copy identifies the matronly mourner (of her sister, Mary Evelyn) as '[Ann] Evelyn, wife to Daniel Boone Esq.' (*YW* xxx. 99–100, 104 n. 2, 328–9 and nn. 27–8; *Horace Walpole's Fugitive Verses*, ed. W. S. Lewis (1931), pp. 27, 32–3).

HLT wrote of Miss Boone in *Thraliana* (i. 463), s.v. 22 Nov. 1780: 'Miss *Boone* keeps a Monkey; She is a strange Woman, fat, sensual & gross; tho' accomplished enough as to painting, Working, making Wax Models &c: and is amazingly handsome too, her immense Magnitude considered—the Men however as I am told now—call her *Baboon*.'

[69] Henry Streatfeild (1757–1829), of Chiddingstone, Kent, high sheriff for Kent, 1792; and Richard Thomas Streatfeild (1759–1813), of The Rocks, Sussex, high sheriff for Sussex, 1798.

When Mrs. Streatfield told me of Miss Boone's ingenuity in cutting Paper, & I expressed some desire to see
her perform, she very obligingly took out her scissars, &
desiring Harry Streatfield to sit sideways, she cut out his
Face,—& that *without* first Drawing it,—& though it was
not a striking likeness, it seemed extremely well done.
Afterwards, by memory, she cut out the Duchess of
Devonshire, in a riding Hat, & *very* like indeed.

She then expressed *her* desire to take *me*,—but though
she was pleased to ask it as a *favour*, I begged to be
excused, for I have no passionate inclination to propagate
my Profile,—lest it should make every body hate their
own!—!—!—

The Poor S.S. had a mortifying Tale to tell concerning
Dr. V.[70]—that affair being totally at an End.—I am very
sorry for her disappointment, but *Ladies* chusing openly
for themselves, never appeared to me a *right* thing,—nor
does it prove *prosperous.*—

Mrs. Thrale begged her to Write to her soon,—& let
her know how she went on;—saying 'Why when Miss
Burney & I are parted for 2 or 3 Days, we write a score
of Letters.—'

'O!—cried Miss Boone, *What* would I give to see them!'

'Ay, said Mrs. Streatfield, I should like to see my *little
Dove's* Letters.'

'Dove? repeated Miss Boone,—don't call her a | *Dove*,—
for I'm sure she has very near been my Death!—'

It was in vain I intreated an explanation of this accusation,—for she would give me none,—but, soon after, I
heard her whispering Mrs. Streatfield the danger she had
been put in by reading Evelina *en Chemise*, because she
could not put it down after she got into Bed, &c— — —

Some Time after, 'Ah! cried Mrs. Streatfield, how I see
those *little Dove's Eyes* reading us all!—what would I give
to know her real opinion of me!—She *glances* at me with
such *enquiring Eyes*, that I die to know what they will tell
her of me!—'

---

[70] Dr Vyse. It was perhaps at this time that Miss Streatfeild learned of his
secret marriage. See above, p. 304 n. 87.

She *might* have known without much displeasure, for I really took to her quite kindly.

The next morning [8 Oct.] we had the Company of 2 young Ladies at Break fast,—the S.S. & a Miss Birch,—a little Girl but 10 years old, who the S.S. invited, well foreseeing how much we should all be obliged to her.

This Miss Birch is a Niece of the charming Mrs. Playdel,—& *so* like her, that I should have taken her for her Daughter,—yet she is not, now, quite so handsome, but as she will soon know how to display her Beauty to the utmost advantage, I fancy in a few years she will yet more resemble her lovely & most bewitching Aunt. '*Every body*, she said, tells her how like she is to her Aunt ǀ Playdell.'

As you, therefore, have seen that sweet Woman, only imagine her Ten years old, & you will see her sweet Niece. Nor does the resemblance rest with the Person,—she *sings* like her, *Laughs* like her, *talks* like her, *Caresses* like her, & alternately softens & animates *just* like her.

Her Conversation is not merely like that of a *Woman* already, but like that of a most uncommonly *informed, cultivated,* & *sagacious* Woman,—&, at the same Time that her Understanding is thus wonderfully premature, she can, at pleasure, through [*sic*] off all this rationality, & make herself a mere playing, giddy, romping Child. One moment, with mingled gravity & sarcasm she discusses Characters, & the next with school-Girl spirits, she jumps round the Room;—then, suddenly, she asks 'Do you know such or such a song?' & instantly, with mixed grace & buffoonery, she singles out an object, & sings it:—& then, before there has been Time to applaud her, she runs into the middle of the Room, to try some new step in a Dance;—&, after all this, without waiting till her vagaries grow tiresome, she flings herself, with an affectionate air, upon somebody's Lap, & there, composed & thoughtful, she continues quiet, till she again enters into ǀ rational Conversation.

Her Voice is really charming,—infinitely the most powerful as well as sweet I ever heard at her Age,—were she well & constantly taught, she might, I should think, do *any thing*;—for 2 or 3 Italian songs which she learnt out of only 5 months teaching by Parsons,[71] she sung like a little angel, with respect to *Taste, feeling & Expression*,—but she now learns of Nobody, & is so fond of French songs, for the sake, she says, of the *sentiment*,—that I fear she will have her wonderful abilities all thrown away. O how I wish my Father had the charge of her!—

She has spent 4 years out of her little life in France, which has made her distractedly fond of the French Operas,—Rose et Colas,[72]—Annette et Lubin[73]—&c—& she told us the *story* quite through of several I never heard of, always singing the *sujet* when she came to the Airs,—& comically changing parts in the Duets. She speaks French with the same fluency as English, & every now & then, addressing herself to the S.S. she uttered some *tender cant*, such as 'Que je vous adore!—' Ah! permetter que je me mette à vos pieds!—&c with a *dying languor* that was equally *laughable & lovely*. When I found, by her *taught songs*, what a delightful singer she was capable of becoming, I really had not patience to hear her little French Airs,—& entreated her to give them up,—but the little Rogue instantly began *pestering* me with them, singing, one after another, with a comical sort of *malice*, & following me round the Room, when I said I would not *listen* to her, to say 'But is not *this* pretty?—& *this*?—& *this*?' singing away with all her might & main.

She sung without any accompaniment, as we had no Instrument,—but the S.S. says she *plays*, too, very well. Indeed I fancy she can do well whatever she pleases.

We hardly knew how to get away from her, when the Carriage was ready to take us from Tunbridge;—& Mrs. Thrale was so much enchanted with her, that she went on the Pantiles, & bought her a very beautiful Ink-stand— 'I don't mean, Miss Birch, she said, when she gave it her, to present you this Toy as to a *Child*, but merely to beg

---

[71] William Parsons (*c.*1746–1817), musician. See *EJL* i. 182.

[72] *Rose et Colas* (1764), music by Pierre-Alexandre Monsigny (1729–1817), libretto by Michel-Jean Sedaine (1719–97) (*New Grove*).

[73] *Annette et Lubin* (1762), music by Adolphe-Benoit Blaise (d. 1772), libretto by Charles-Simon Favart (1710–92) (ibid.).

you will do me the favour to accept something that may make you now & then remember us.'

She was much delighted with this Present, & told me in a whisper that she should put a *Drawing* of it in her *Journal!* —

So you see, Susy, *other* Children have had this Whim! — But something being said of *Novels*, the S.S. said 'Salina do you ever read them?' | &, with a *sigh*, the little Girl answered 'But too often! — I wish I did not! —'

The only thing I did not like in this seducing little Creature was our *leave-taking*; — the S:S: had, as we expected, her fine Eyes suffused with Tears, — — —& nothing would serve the little Salina, who admires the S.S. passionately, but that she, also, must weep! —& weep, therefore she did, & that in a manner as pretty to look at, as soft, as melting, & as little to her discomposure, As the weeping of her fair *Example-setter*! The *Child's* success in this pathetic Art made the Tears of *both appear*, to the whole party, to be lodged, as the English merchant says, '*very near the Eyes.* —'[74]

Doubtful as it is whether we shall ever see this sweet syren again, Nothing, as Mrs. Thrale said to her, can be more certain than that we shall *hear* of her again, let her go whither she will.

Charmed as we all were with her, we all agreed that to have the *care* of her would be *distraction*! —'She seems the Girl in the World, Mrs. Thrale wisely said, to attain the highest reach of human perfection as a man's *mistress*! — as *such*, she would be a 2^d Cleopatra, & have the World at her command.'

Poor Thing — I hope to Heaven she will escape | *such* sovereignty, & *such* Honours!

But it is high Time I should take leave of her, — the S.S. — & of Tunbridge.

---

[74] Apparently a variation of an old proverb. 'Their tears are near their eyes' is described as a Cornish proverb in *Notes and Queries* 3rd ser. vi (1864), 494 (cited in G. L. Apperson, *English Proverbs and Proverbial Phrases: A Historical Dictionary* (1929), p. 621).

We got, by Dinner Time, to our first stage, Ukfield,[75]—
which afforded me nothing to *record* except 2 lines of an
admirable[76] Epitaph which I picked up in the Church
Yard.

A Wife & 8 little Children had I—
And 2 at a Birth who never did cry.[77]

Our next Stage brought us to

Brighthelmstone

where I fancy we shall stay till the Parliament calls away
Mr. Thrale.

The morning after our arrival [9 Oct.] our first Visit
was from Mr. Kipping,[78] the Apothecary, a Character so
curious that Foote[79] designed him for his next Piece
before he knew he had already written his last,[80] a prating,
good humoured old Gossip, who runs on in as incoherent
& unconnected a style of Discourse as Rose Fuller, though
not so *tonish*.[81]

The rest of the morning we spent, as usual at this place,
upon the Steyn & in Bookseller's shops. Mrs. Thrale
entered all our Names at *Thomas*'s,[82] the fashionable

[75] Uckfield, Sussex, a small town about 14 mi. SW of Tunbridge Wells.
Brighton lies another 16 mi. to the SW.

[76] Amended in the MS to 'curious', seemingly in the hand of Mrs Barrett,
who may have wanted to eliminate the sarcasm, as the 2nd line of the epitaph
apparently refers to still-born twins.

[77] The *Uckfield Visitor's Guide* (n.d.), p. 18, mentions FB's recording of this
epitaph. In her evident search for the bathetic she missed the following 'gem',
on a black marble slab commemorating John Fuller (d. 1610): 'Now I am dead
and lyd in grave, / And that my bones are rotten, / By this shall I remember'd
be, / Or else I am forgotten!' (T. W. Horsfield, *The History ... of Sussex* (Lewes,
1835), i. 369).

[78] See above, p. 279 n. 56.

[79] Samuel Foote (1721–77), playwright.

[80] FB presumably alludes to Foote's declining health, which caused him
eventually to undertake a journey to the south of France. He died even before
crossing the Channel, at Dover.

[81] HLTP imitates Kipping's speech in a letter to Queeney Thrale, 22 Apr.
1785: 'Sophy tells me poor Kipping is sick; *God bless my Soul Ma'am, why now
these Things will sometimes—but if the D^r would come down indeed*, but then *the Time
o' Year & that—& besides now you know Ma'am the Dr God bless him—but he is just
the same as ever for the matter of that. &c*' (*The Queeney Letters*, ed. M. of Lansdowne
(1934), p. 200).

[*See opposite page for n. 82*]

Bookseller.—But we find he has now a Rival, situated also upon the Steyn, who seems to carry away all the custom & all the Company. This is a Mr. Bowen,[83] who I is just come from London, & who seems just the man to carry the World before him as a shop keeper. Extremely civil, attentive to watch opportunities of obliging, & assiduous to make use of them,—skilful in discovering the taste, or turn of mind, of his Customers, & adroit in putting in their way just such temptations as they are least able to withstand. Mrs. Thrale, at the same Time that she sees his management & contrivance, so much admires his sagacity & dexterity, that, though open-Eyed, she is as easily wrought upon to part with her money, as any of the many Dupes in this place whom he persuades to *require indispensably* whatever he shews them.

He did not, however, then at all suspect who *I* was, for he shewed me nothing but schemes for Raffles, & Books, Pocket Cases, &c, which were put up for those purposes. It is plain I can have no *Authoress* Air, since so discerning a *Bookseller* thought me a fine lady spend thrift, who only wanted *occasions* to get rid of money!

In the Evening we went to *the Rooms*, which, at this Time, are open every other Night at *Shergold's*[84], or the

---

[82] 'R. Thomas', bookseller at Brighton, had in 1777 published *The Pigs: their Pedigree and Panegyric; a Brighthelmston Rhapsody, Humbly Inscribed to the Misses.* In 1774 Thomas took over the establishment of Edmund Baker, a fashionable bookseller from Tunbridge Wells, after Baker's death. Visitors entering their names at Thomas's or Bowen's bookshop meant that the Brighton Master of Ceremonies, William Wade (see below, p. 385), would call upon them at their lodgings and put down their names for invitation to the assemblies. See J. Feather, *The Provincial Book Trade in Eighteenth-Century England* (Cambridge, 1985), p. 90; C. Musgrave, *Life in Brighton* (Hamden, 1970), pp. 75–7; O. Sitwell and M. Barton, *Brighton* (1935), pp. 59–61.

[83] See above, p. 360. SJ, in a letter to HLT at Brighton, 16 Oct. 1779, expressed his sympathy for Thomas, whose trade was being taken over by Bowen: 'I am sorry for poor Thomas, who was a decent and civil Man. It is hard that he should be overwhelmed by a new comer. But *Thou by some other shalt be laid as low.* Bowen's day may come' (*LSJ* iii. 188–9). Despite SJ's prognosis, Thomas continued to run his business 'for many years' (Musgrave, p. 77), while Bowen was a bankrupt by 1784. Thomas's Library was later owned by Dubot and Gregory, and it became famous in its later years as Donaldson's Library.

[84] Samuel Shergold (d. 1804) was proprietor of the Castle Inn, which he opened in 1755. Actually, his assembly rooms were the older (above, p. 277 n. 50; Musgrave, pp. 64, 75, 214; *GM* lxxiv[2] (1804), 987).

New Assembly Rooms,—& the alternate Nights at *Hick's*,[85] or the Ship Tavern. This Night they were at the latter. |

There was very little Company, & nobody that any of us knew, except 2 or 3 Gentlemen of Mr. Thrale's acquaintance: among whom was that celebrated Wit & Libertine Mr. Beauclerke,—& a Mr. Newnham,[86] a rich Counseller, *learned in the Law*, but, to me, a displeasing man.

Almost every body but ourselves went to Cards,—we found it, therefore, pretty stupid,—& I was very glad when we came Home.

Sunday morning [10 Oct.] as we came out of Church we saw Mrs. Cumberland,[87] one of her sons,[88] & both her Daughters,—Mrs. Thrale spoke to them, but I believe they did not recollect me. They are reckoned the Flashers of the place,—yet every body Laughs at them, for their Airs, affectations, & tonish graces & impertinences.

In the Evening Mrs. Dickens,[89] a Lady of Mrs. Thrale's acquaintance, invited us to Drink Tea at the Rooms with her, which we did,—& found them much more full & lively than the preceding Night.

Mrs. Dickens is, in Mrs. Thrale's phrase, a *sensible, hard Headed Woman*; & her Daughter, Miss Dickens,[90] who accompanied us, is a pretty Girl of 15, who is always

85 John Hicks (Musgrave, p. 75). See above, p. 277 n. 50.

86 Probably George Lewis Newnham (*c.*1733–1800), of Newtimber Place, Sussex; KC, 1772; MP, 1774–80. He was the eldest son of Nathaniel Newnham (1698–1778), a Director of the East India Co. and the South Sea Co., and succeeded to the rich Newtimber estate on the death of his mother in 1788. He was returned unopposed at Arundel in 1774 on the interest of Sir John Shelley (for whom see below, p. 391). Taylor White, brother of John White, MP, branded him 'the vainest empty fellow I ever met with' (Namier; IGI).

87 Elizabeth née Ridge (*ante* 1741 – 1801), daughter of George Ridge, of Kilmeston, Hants, m. (1759) Richard Cumberland (*GM* lxxi[2] (1801), 1058; lxxxi[1] (1811), 596).

88 The Cumberlands had 4 sons: Richard (*c.*1761–94), George (1762–80), Charles (1764–1835), and William (*c.*1765–1832). This was perhaps the eldest son Richard, whom Queeney Thrale names below ('*Master Dickey*', p. 392).

89 Sarah (Sally) née Scrase (b. 1743, living 1797), daughter of the Thrales' friend and legal adviser Charles Scrase (1709–92), of Brighton; m. Anthony Dickins (1734–94), Prothonotary of the Court of Common Pleas (*JL* i. 85 n. 8; *Piozzi Letters* i. 148 nn. 23–4; FBA to Hester Maria Thrale 9 July 1797, Bowood; IGI).

90 Sarah Dickins (*c.*1764–1848), m. (1785) John Sawyer (1762–1845), of Heywood Lodge, Berks; sheriff of Berks, 1819.

Laughing,—not, however, from folly, as she deserves the same Epithet I have given her mother, but from Youthful good humour,—& from having from Nature, as Mr. Thrale comically said to her, after examining her some minutes, *a good merry face of her own.* |

We had, also, of our Tea Drinking Party, the Mr. Newnham I have mentioned, who,—though he did not seem to *see* me the Evening before, now *Miss Burney'd* me as if we had been old acquaintance,—was glad to have *me* of his opinion,—applied to me often, &c in short, as the Rose bud[91] would say, paid me *what we call the respectable attention.*

Pretty *smokeable* the change!

The folks of most consequence with respect to rank who were at the Rooms this Night were Lady Pembroke[92] & Lady Dye Beauclerk, both of whom have still very pleasing remains of the beauty for which they have been so much admired: but the *present* Beauty, whose *remains* our Children (i.e, *Nieces*) may talk of, is a Mrs. Musters,[93]

---

[91] Rose Fuller.

[92] Elizabeth (1737–1831), daughter of Charles Spenser (1706–58), 3rd D. of Marlborough; m. (1756) Henry Herbert (1734–94), 10th E. of Pembroke. Lady Diana Beauclerk was her elder sister.

[93] Sophia Catherine Heywood (*c.*1758–1819), eldest daughter and co-heir of James Modyford Heywood, of Maristow, Devon; m. (1776) John Musters (1753–1827), of Colwick Hall, Notts. Her portrait was painted by Reynolds, Hoppner, and Romney. Her reign as a beauty at Brighton was interrupted in 1786 when she returned home to Colwick and her husband confronted her with her infidelities with the P. of Wales. He threw her out, and even had the painter George Stubbs come back to Colwick to remove her image from two panels he had executed (one showing her on horseback with her husband and another of her and a family friend). Mrs Musters returned to Brighton to live out her days there on her considerable income. When she died her husband, in a spirit of forgiveness or to inter with her the memory of her transgressions, brought her body home for burial at Colwick, and erected a monument to her in Colwick Church.

Mrs Barrett tells an anecdote 'related by a gentleman still living at Brighton [1842]. He remembers meeting Mrs. Musters at the ball mentioned by Miss Burney, and being requested to give her a glass of water, it was turbid and chalky; upon which she said, as she drank it, "*Chalk is thought to be a cure for the heart-burn:—I wonder whether it will cure the heart-ache?*"' See *Diary and Letters of Madame d'Arblay* (1842–6), i. 435; W. P. W. Phillimore, *County Pedigrees: Nottinghamshire, Volume I* (1910), pp. 191–2; B. Sewell, 'The Strange Case of an Absent Wife', *Sunday Times Magazine*, 8 Dec. 1974, pp. 44–6.

an exceeding pretty woman, who is the reigning Toast of the season.

While Mrs. Thrale, Mrs. Dickens & I were walking about after Tea, we were joined by a Mr. Cure,[94] a Gentleman of the formers acquaintance—to whom, in the course of the Evening, he said 'Ma'am I think if you were to turn round the other way, when you come to the End of the Room, *your* Train & *Miss Thrale's* Train would both be less incommoded.'

Now as Miss Thrale was then walking with Miss Dickens, & at some distance, Mrs. Thrale only stared at him, & presently he added 'Miss Thrale is ᶦ very much grown since she was here last year,—& besides, I think she's vastly altered.'

'Do you, Sir? cried she;—I can't say I think so.'

'O vastly!—but young ladies at that Age are always altering. To tell you the truth I did not know her at all.'

This, for a little while, passed quietly;—but soon after, he exclaimed 'Ma'am, do you know I have not yet Read Evelina?'

'Have not you so, Sir'—cried She, Laughing.—

'No,—& I think I never shall,—for there's no getting it—the Bookseller's say they never can keep it a moment,—& the folks that hire it keep lending it from one to another in such a manner that it is never returned to the Library. It's very provoking.'

'Well, so it is, to be sure!—but *we* can't lend it you, I assure you,—for we have really & actually no set of it with us.'

'O no,—I was not thinking of that.'

'Then, for God's sake, Mr. Cure, what did you mention it for?'

'Why because I think it's the greatest praise that can be given to the Book.'

'But what makes you exclaim about it so to *me* in this odd manner?'

---

94 Possibly George Cure (1743–?98), BCL (Oxon.), 1768 (IGI; *GM* lxviii¹ (1798), 87).

'Why because, if you recollect, the last thing you said to me when we parted last year was ¦ be sure you read Evelina:—besides, don't you remember how it was all the talk last season?—every body, you know, was full of it.'

'So we begin, then, *this* year, just where we left off *last* year!—'

'Why yes, so as soon as I saw you I recollected it all again. But I wish Miss Thrale would turn more this way.—'

'Why what do you *mean*, Mr. Cure?—do you know Miss Thrale *now?*'

'Yes, to be sure, answered he, looking full at *me* 'though I protest I should not have *guessed* at her had I seen her with any body but you.'

'O ho!—cried Mrs. Thrale, Laughing, so you mean *Miss Burney* all this Time?—'

'What?—how?—hay?—why is that—is not that Miss Thrale?—is not that your Daughter?'

'No to be sure it is not,—I wish she was! I'm glad, however, to have had the *credit* of her.—'

'Ah, Ma'am, cried I, who but *you* would not have been *shocked* at the mistake!'

'No, believe me,—I wish nothing so much as that it was *no* mistake.—'

Mr. Cure, mean Time, looked *aghast*,—Mrs. Dickens laughed aloud,—& I, the whole Time, had been obliged to turn my Head another way that my *sniggering* might not sooner make him see ¦ his mistake.

As soon, I suppose, as he was *able*, Mr. Cure, in a low Voice, repeated '*Miss Burney!*—so then that lady is the *Authoress* of Evelina all this Time?—'

And, rather abruptly, he left us, & joined another party. Was it not a comical conversation?

I have much reason to believe he told his story to as many as he talked to, for, in a short Time, I found myself so violently stared at that I could hardly look any way without being put quite [out] of Countenance. Particularly by young Mr. Cumberland,[95] a handsome, *soft looking* Youth, who fixed his Eyes upon me incessantly, though,

[See p. 384 for n. 95]

but the Evening before, when I saw him at Hicks, he looked as if it would have been a diminution of his dignity to have regarded me twice.

This little ridiculous circumstance will, however, prevent any *more* mistakes of the same kind, I believe, as my *Authorshipness* seems now pretty well known & spread about Brighthelmstone;—the very next morning, Monday [11 Oct.], as Miss Thrale & I entered Bowen's shop, where we were appointed to meet Mrs. Thrale, I heard her saying to him, as they were both in serious & deep *confabulation*, 'So you have picked up all this, Mr. Bowen, have you?' then, seeing me, 'O ho,—she cried,—so one never ¹ is to speak of any body at Brighthelmstone, but they are to be at one's Elbow!—'

'I presume, quoth I, you were hardly speaking of me?—'

'No, but I was *hearing* of you, from Mr. Bowen.—'

And, when we left the shop, she told me that he had said to her, with a great many apologies, 'Pray—Ma'am, was that *charming lady* who came here with you on Saturday, the Authoress of Evelina?—'

Did I not tell you he was an admirable Bookseller.—

'O Ma'am, he continued, what a Book thrown away was that!—all the Trade cry shame on Lowneds, [*sic*]—not, Ma'am, that I *expected* he could have known its worth, because that's out of the question,—but when it's *profits* told him what it was, it's quite scandalous that he should have done nothing!—quite ungentlemanlike indeed!'

There's a Bookseller for you, Susy!—& much more, it seems, he added—& praised *me*, & my *Book*, till Mrs. Thrale was so well pleased, that as soon as I parted from her, she went to him again!—to have, she said, the *talk out*, that I had interrupted!—

My next Business was to go to the milliners, & prepare finery for a Ball in the Evening,—with which I purpose beginning my next Pacquet,—so adieu, my dearest Susy, for the present. ¹

---

⁹⁵ Perhaps Richard Cumberland. See above, p. 380 n. 88.

94

Brighton,
[*post* 12]–25 October [1779]

To Susanna Elizabeth Burney

AJL (Berg, Diary MSS I, paginated 1041–54), Oct. 1779
10 single sheets 4to, 20 pp.

3^d Budget. Brighthelmstone

And now,—if by the mention of a *Ball* I have raised in you any expectations of adventures,—which with *Charlotte*, at least, I doubt not has been the case,—I am sorry to be obliged to blast them all by confessing that none at all happen'd. We went in Company with Mrs. & Miss Dickens, but as all our Party were previously determined not to Dance, & all *kept* to the determination, the Ball, as all Balls to *spectators* must, proved but an irksome & tedious affair.

The most flashy among the Dancers were the Miss Cumberlands,—the Eldest is reckoned the best foot-performer in the place, but she is too violent & too *rampant* to suit *my* taste. That super-fine *delicacy* with which she sickened us at Mrs. Ords, has now given place to the contrary extreme, & she thinks proper to be all Life, spirit, & activity.

Almost immediately, upon our Entrance, Mr. Wade,[96] the master of the Ceremonies, enquired of Miss Thrale, Miss Dickens & me whether we chose to Dance?—for it is all *his* affair to assign the Ladies' Partners:—but, from the same motive, i.e *shyness*, we all declined his assistance.

---

[96] William Wade (d. 1809), who at first called himself Capt. Wade, came to Brighton from Bath, whence he had been driven for showing some letters sent to him by a lovestruck admirer (*Autobiography, Letters and Literary Remains of Mrs. Piozzi*, ed. A. Hayward (2nd edn., 1861), ii. 83). From about 1770 he held the office of Master of Ceremonies, the duties of which were to call upon visitors, to invite them to the assemblies, and to provide introductions and dancing partners. See Musgrave, pp. 75–6; *GM* lxxix[1] (1809), 285.

Lady Sefton, who continues extremely handsome, began the Country Dances,—Lord Gage & Sir Sampson Gideon came from Ferle,[97] about 16 miles off, ∣ to be at this Assembly.—they had just the same good nature & civility as at Streatham,—& I believe they have it so unaffectedly, that it would be equally shewn in the Drawing Room. Lord Gage Danced with the Eldest Miss Beauclerk,[98] a Girl about 13,—merely, no doubt, to please Lady Di,—& Sir Sampson with a Miss[99]

One thing, however, proved quite disagreeable to me,—& that was the whole behaviour of the whole Tribe of the Cumberlands,—which I must explain.

Mr. Cumberland, when he saw Mrs. Thrale, flew with eagerness to her, & made her take his seat,—& he talked to her with great friendliness & intimacy, as he has been always accustomed to do,—& enquired very particularly concerning her Daughter, expressing an earnest desire to see her;—but when, some Time after, Mrs. Thrale said, 'O,—there *is* my Daughter,—with Miss Burney.—' he changed the Discourse abruptly,—never came near Miss Thrale, & niether then, nor since, when he has met Mrs. T., has again mentioned her name: &, the whole Evening, he seemed determined to avoid us both!—

Mrs. Cumberland contented herself with only *looking* at me, as at a Person she had no reason or business to know.—

The 2 Daughters, but especially the Eldest, as well ∣ as the *son*, were by no means so quiet; they stared at me every Time I came near them as if I had been a thing for a *shew*, surveyed me from top to bottom,[1] & then, *again & again & again* returned to my *Face* with so determined

---

[97] Ld. Gage's country seat was at Firle, Sussex.

[98] Mary Beauclerk (1766–1851), m. (*c.*1795) Graf Franz von Jenison zu Walworth. Before her marriage she eloped (in 1789) with her married half-brother Ld. Bolingbroke after bearing him 2 illegitimate children (*YW* xxix. 71 n. 22, xxxiv. 56 and nn. 10, 13).

[99] FB apparently meant to supply 'Miss''s name before dispatching her letter, but failed to do so.

[1] FBA changed this phrase to 'from head to foot', showing again the almost absurd prudishness of her old age.

& so unabating a curiosity, that it really made me uncomfortable.

All the folks here impute the whole of this conduct to it's having transpired that I am to bring out a *Play* this season,—for Mr. Cumberland, though in all other respects an Agreeable & a good man, is so notorious for hating & envying & *spiting* all *authors of the Dramatic line*, that he is hardly decent in his behaviour towards them.

He has little reason, at present, at least, to bear *me* any ill will,—but if he is *capable* of such weakness & malignity as to have taken an aversion to me merely because I can make use of Pen & Ink, he deserves not to hear of my having suppressed my play, or of anything else that can gratify so illiberal & contemptible a Disposition.

Dr. Johnson, Mrs. Cholmondeley, Mr. & Mrs. Thrale have all repeatedly said to me 'Cumberland no doubt hates you heartily by this Time,'—but it always appeared to me a speech of mingled *fun* & *flattery*, & I never Dreamed of it's being *possible* to be true. However,— perhaps yet all this may be accidental,—so I will discuss the point no longer.[2] |

Tuesday morning [12 Oct.] the News-monger, Mr. Kipping, called to tell us there was to be a ship launched at Shoreham;—instantly the Coach & 4 was ordered, & we 3 Females set out: Mr. Thrale spends all his mornings here in Hunting.

Shoreham is a small Town 6 miles off.

We got there an Hour before the expected operation,— & Mrs. Thrale, half by accident, half *not*, fairly *Jockied* the Duchess of Ancaster & Lady Charlotte Bertie, her Daughter, out of the best place for seeing the shew.— This was a Room, that looked on to the sea, immediately opposite to the ship,—& which Room we entered just as we perceived the Duchess & her Party come out of it;— Mrs. Thrale then spoke to the man to whom it belonged, & asked leave for making use of his Window,—this being granted, the Post was, thus far, fairly our own:—but, in

---

[2] SJ wrote to HLT at Brighton, 21 Oct. 1779: 'What makes Cumberland hate Burney? Delap is indeed a rival, and can upon occasion *provoke a bugle*, but what has Burney done? Dos [*sic*] he not like her book?' (*LSJ* iii. 196).

about half an Hour, the Party returned, & one of the Ladies exclaimed 'O Duchess, your place is gone!'—'I thought some body was to have kept it.' said her Grace. And Lady Charlotte, who is a pretty, sullen looking Girl, made such glouty,[3] discontented Faces, as gave me no very favourable idea of her Temper.

Miss Thrale & I both retreated from our places to make way for them; but Mrs. Thrale, sheltered from *seeing* them by a large Calash,[4] pretended not to *hear* them, & kept her place very composedly. The Duchess now came to *one* ¦ side of her, to peep at the ship, & Lady Charlotte at the other,—& while they were both peering, Mrs. Thrale, very *tranquilly*, said 'How comfortable it is to stand here at *one's own* Window!'

This was a *finisher*!—the Duchess retired, calling her Daughter who, with much reluctance, & a thousand wry Faces, followed her.

When we talked this over, afterwards, Mrs. Thrale Laughed & said 'O, I never give way to folks because they are people of Quality,—I never got any thing from *them*, so why should they from *me*?'

In the Evening, we all went to the play, which was Mr. Colman's Suicide.[5] But that it was so ill performed that to judge of it would be very unfair; I should be tempted to speak hardly enough of it. The best part of our Entertainment was from a certain Tom Willet,[6] a poor crazy fellow, who Lives here, & who, being not in his senses, yet not bad enough for a mad House, wanders about the Town, & amuses himself with making signs & Grimaces to the Company of the Place. As Mr. Thrale, who has known him many years, encourages him some times by a Nod or a smile, he is certain to begin his *Gambols* as soon

---

[3] i.e., frowning, scowling (see *OED* s.v. glout, *v.*). This episode is previously unpublished, and *OED* does not give this form; it is given in the *EDD*.

[4] 'A woman's hood made of silk, supported with whalebone or cane hoops and projecting beyond the face' (*OED* s.v. calash, *sb.* 3).

[5] *The Suicide*, by George Colman the elder, performed in the North Street Theatre. It had opened in July 1778 at the Theatre Royal, Haymarket (*LS* 5 i. 184; Musgrave, pp. 98–9).

[6] Perhaps the Thomas Willett, son of John Willett and Anne, christened 13 Oct. 1745 at Cowfold, 14 m. NW of Brighton (IGI).

as he sees any of his Family: he was this Night in the
Pit,—& smiled, & shook his first Finger & his Head at us,
as often as any of I us looked at him; but his attention to
us was not sufficiently entertaining to himself to suffice
for his Evening's amusement, & therefore he made his
observations upon the Play aloud, commending, disap-
proving or adding at his pleasure: but though this was
diverting enough to *us*, the Players by no means approved
of it; & in the 2ᵈ Act, one of the Women, who had to say
'A servant should be Deaf & Dumb,' upon his adding
aloud 'Ay, & blind too!' said to her fellow Comedian 'That
man puts me out so, I don't know how to go on.' And
then this fellow Comedian, coming forward, said 'Upon
my word, Sir, if you talk so I can't recollect one word of
my part!'

Poor Tom Willet, nodding at them, said 'Well, well, I
won't!—' And again directed his chief attention to us.
When the first act was over, he got into the orchestra to
look over the music Books at his leisure; but the Fidlers,
not being ambitious of his Company, turned him out. He
then made a motion to come into our Box,—& being
prevented, threw in a Letter:—which, as it is short, I will
Copy

> *To Lord Robert Manners.*[7]
> My Lord, I happy *ham* to think I am I

[top half of page cut away]

We have had a Visit from Dr. Delap,—who as he Lives
at Lewes, always comes to Brighton when the Thrale
Family are there. He is in great concern about his play,
which he expects will soon appear: he asked me a million
of Questions about *mine*,—& when I told him I had
determined not to try it, was all amazement, & concluded
that Mr. Sheridan had disapproved it,—so, I suppose, for
my comfort, will *every body*,—however, I assured him that
I had never let him even *read* it,—having absolutely

---

[7] There *was* a well-known contemporary Ld. Robert Manners (*c.*1718–82),
Gen. and MP (Namier).

determined not to risk it. He blamed me, & advised me by all means to *shew* it, at least, & then abide by the manager's decision, which, at last, could not be more severe than my own. However, I told him I was not *Coqueting*, & therefore did not *wish* to be persuaded to try it. |

[*top half of page cut away*]

the first Course, he was very quiet;—but in the 2^d, being desired by Mrs. Garrick, to cut up a Pheasant, he said 'Ma'am, shall I have the honour to help your Ladyship to some of this?'—The lady, who was talking, did not hear him,—&, rather less civilly, he repeated his request— 'Ma'am, shall I help you to some of this?—' but still, unfortunately, the lady did not attend to him,—when, betrayed by impatience into his common Language, to the utter consternation of her Ladyship, & confusion of Mr. & Mrs. Garrick, he cried out 'G.— — —D.— — — you, Madam, shall I help you or not?'

'O Miss Burney, continued Dr. Delap, how I wish You were to see him!—you'd put him in a Book directly:—he can't speak for 2 minutes without 4 Oaths,— | I'd advise you very much, indeed, to go some Day to Chelsea & Dine with him,—you'd make a Folio of him!'[8]

Was not this Characteristic?—first to suppose a Female can go & Dine with any body she has a wish to see,—& 2dly to suppose I would *fill a Folio* with oaths, & swearing stories!—Do read this to my dear Father, who knows Dr. Delap well enough to be diverted with it.

His absence of mind is equal to his ignorance of the World;—in conversing once with Mr. Thrale, he so entirely forgot to whom he was talking, that, by way of

---

[8] The reference to Chelsea suggests that the profane speaker may have been William Kenrick, the notoriously scurrilous miscellaneous writer who had once been friendly with Garrick before turning on him. Kenrick, who lived in Chelsea, had died the preceding June, but Delap may have told this story to FB the previous May, when they first met; Kenrick had published a favorable review of *Evelina*, which FB mentions above, p. 14. The 'Ladyship' at the dinner party was perhaps the Garricks' close friend Lady Spencer, i.e., Margaret Georgiana Poyntz (1737–1814), m. (1755) Hon. John Spencer, cr. (1765) E. Spencer.

confirmation of something he asserted, he said 'I assure you it happened to me as I was going to Town once with Thrale.'

During his stay at Brighton, he called here one morning, & said 'I have lost 3 things this morning,—I went to the Steyn before Breakfast to take a Walk,—but I popt into Bowen's shop for a Book, & so forgot to Walk,—& just while I was there, a young lady came up to me, & said How di do, Dr. Delap?—but I did not know who it was,—however, she was a fine young Girl,—so I thought it was Miss Thrale,—but when she found I did not know her, she went off,—& then I recollected 'twas Miss Dickens;—so I thought for a minute whether I should call her back, or let her go tell her mother I did not know her,—but I did not call her,—so she went & told her ' mother I did not know her;—but all this made me forget my Book,—& so I came Home to Breakfast,—but first I went to the Beach, to look for the French Fleet,—however, I could not see them.—'9

A few Days since we Drank Tea at Mrs. Dickens, where, with other Company, we met Sir John & Lady Shelley.10 Sir John prides himself in being a Courtier of the last Age,—he is abominably ugly, & a prodigious *Puffer*,—now of his Fortune—now of his Family, & now of his Courtly connections & feats. & Lady Shelley is a beautiful Woman,—tall, genteel, & elegant in her Person, with regular Features, & a fine Complection. For the rest, she is well bred, gentle & amiable.11

She invited us all to Tea at her House the next Evening, addressing herself with particular civility to me, as I had never seen her before, though she had called here twice:

---

9 See above, p. 363 and n. 26.

10 Sir John Shelley (*c*.1730–83), 5th Bt, of Mitchelgrove, Sussex; former MP; Keeper of the Records in the Tower of London, 1755–83; Clerk of the Pipe in the Exchequer, 1758–83; and his 2nd wife (m. 1775) Elizabeth (1748–1808), daughter of Edward Woodcock, of Lincoln's Inn. She m. 2 (1790) John Stewart, MD (IGI).

11 Edward Gibbon later commented that 'Shipwrecks ... must soon, with the society of Ham. [William Gerard Hamilton] and Lady Shelly become the only pleasures of Brighton' (letter to Ld. Sheffield, 13 Nov. 1781, *The Letters of Edward Gibbon*, ed. J. E. Norton (1956), ii. 284).

nor did her politeness rest here;—she apologised to Mrs. Thrale for not having left me a *Card*, but said she would *wait on me* the next morning;—which she accordingly did,—to beg, she said, *the Honour of seeing me in the Evening,*—an Honour I condescendingly granted, nay more, as I found her so polite, I excused the boldness of her Visit, & received her with something like affability!!

At her House, the following Evening, we therefore went,—where we met Lady Pembroke, whose Character as far as it appears, seems exactly the same as Lady Shelley's. But the chief employment of the Evening was listening to Sir John's *Bragadocios* of what the old King[12] said to him,—which of the Ladies of Quality were his Cousins,—how many Acres of Land he enjoyed in Sussex,—& other such modest discourse.[13]

After Tea, we all went to the Rooms,—Lady Pembroke having first retired. There was a great deal of Company & among them the Cumberlands: the Eldest of the Girls, who was walking with Mrs. Musters, quite turned round her whole Person every Time we approached to keep me in sight, & stare at me as long as possible,—so did her Brother,[14]—I never saw any thing so ill bred & impertinent,—I protest I was ready to quit the Rooms to avoid them: till, at last, *Miss* Thrale, catching Miss Cumberland's Eye, gave her so full, determined, & *downing* a stare, that whether cured by *shame* or by *resentment*, she forebore from that Time, to look at either of us. Miss Thrale, with a sort of good natured dryness, said 'when ever you are disturbed by any of these starers, apply to *me*,—I'll warrant I'll cure them!—I dare say the Girl hates me for it,—but what shall I be the worse for that?—I would have served *Master Dickey* so too, only I could not for my Life catch his Eye.'

---

12 George II.
13 Commiserating with Lady Shelley and referring to Sir John's red face, HLT wrote: ' ... tis hard upon that poor delicate woman his Wife, to endure a bloody Face upon her Pillow, for the sake of bearing a bloody hand in her Coat of Arms' (HLT to FB, 5 July [1780], Berg).
14 Richard Cumberland, Jr.

Mr. Cumberland spoke with Mrs. Thrale some Time, not when *I* was with her!—I am really very sorry for all this foolish stuff,—though Mrs. Thrale says I ought to be *flattered* by it,—but I niether do, nor ever did, ambition the Honour & Glory of being hated & avoided by either the sons or Daughters of Parnassus.

In looking over the subscription Books, which are always open upon the Table at the End of the Room, I perceived my own Name,—written in Mr. Thrale's Hand,—& when I expostulated upon this ill usuage, — — —for I never knew when it was done, & so not only was prevented paying the subscription, but even making an *Oration*,—I found Mr. Thrale had not only made thus free with me at Hicks,—but also at Shergold, Bowens, & Thomas's!—You may imagine I resented this affront with becoming dignity!—though, really, I have *such* affronts so continually heaped upon me, that it requires no little Fortitude to sustain them.

Octr 20th

Last Tuesday [19 Oct.], at the request of Lady Shelly, who Patronised a poor Actor, we all went again to the Play,—which was *Dryden's Tempest*,[15]—& a worse perform-ance have I seldom seen;—*Shakespeare's* Tempest, which for Fancy, Invention & Originality is at the Head of beautiful improbabilities, is rendered, by the additions of Dryden, a childish Chaos of absurdity & obscurity: & the grossness & awkwardness of these poor unskilful Actors rendered all that ought to have been *obscure* so shockingly *glaring*, that there was no attending to them without disgust. Lady Shelly, whose Box we sat in, & who is modesty itself, was quite in pain during the whole repre-sentation;—Mrs. Thrale & Mrs. Dickens made themselves good diversion the whole Time,—Miss Thrale looked perfectly unmoved,—but All that afforded *me* any enter-tainment was looking at *Mr.* Thrale, who turned up his

---

[15] An adaptation of Shakespeare's play, by John Dryden (1631–1700) and Sir William D'Avenant (1606–68), first performed in 1667 in Lincoln's Inn Fields (*LS 1*, p. 123).

Nose with an expression of contempt at the *beginning* of the Performance, & never suffered it to return to it's usual place till it was *ended!*

The Play was ordered by Mrs. Cumberland. These poor Actors never have any Company in the Boxes unless they can prevail upon some lady to bespeak a Play, & desire her Acquaintance to go to it. But we all agreed we should not have been very proud to have had our names at the Head of a Play Bill of *Dryden's Tempest.*

By the way, Mrs. Cumberland has never once waited on Mrs. Thrale since our arrival,—though, till now, she always seemed proud enough of the acquaintance. Very strange!—*Mr.* Cumberland, after a Week's consideration & delay, called at last,—& chatted with Mr. & Mrs. Thrale very sociably & agreeably. I happened to be up stairs, & felt no great desire, you may believe, to go down,—& Mrs. Thrale archly ⌐ enough said afterwards 'I would have sent to you, but Hang it, thought I, if I only name her this man will snatch his Hat & make off!'

The other morning, the 2 misses came into Thomas's shop while we were there,—& the Eldest, as usual, gave me, it seems, the Honour of employing her Eyes the whole Time she stayed,—but this I was *told*, for I was too well prepared to *expect* her examination to look for it, & so never once lifted my Eyes from Moore's Fables for Females,[16] which I was reading, till they went. One would imagine by this insatiate curiosity, that they expected to read in my Face all the Characters in my Book.

We afterwards met them on the Steyn & they Courtsied to Mrs. Thrale, who stopt & enquired after their Father,—& then a dawdling Conversation took place—'How were you entertained at the play, Ma'am?— — —did you ever see any thing so full?—'O, cried Mrs. Thrale, the Ladies were all dying of it!—such holding up of Fans!—' 'O,—because it was so *hot*? cried Miss Cumberland, entirely misunderstanding her,—it was monstrous hot, indeed!—' And then we parted.—But the next Time I meet them, I

---

[16] *Fables for the Female Sex* (1744), by Edward Moore (1712–57). The latest edn. had been published in 1777.

intend to try if I can stop this their *staring system* by Courtsiing to them immediately. I think it will be impossible, if I claim them as *Acquaintance*, that they can thus rudely fasten their Eyes upon me. |

Monday *Oct^r* 25th

Our Time, since I writ Last, has been spent between the Shellys & Dickens, who are the only *Families* at whose Houses we have Visited.—but now for Yesterday.

Dr. Delap, as soon as his Duty was done at Lewes, came hither again: he is such a passionate admirer both of Miss Thrale & me, that, but for the *division* we make in his Heart, I know not what would become of it.

In the Evening he accompanied us to the Rooms, where we had appointed to Drink Tea with Mrs. & Miss Dickens: & there, by his simplicity & oddity, he made me Laugh till I was almost ashamed of myself. But he is quite angry with me for *condemning* my Play unheard,—& gave me *broad hints* of his desire to read it: I would not, however, understand him, but took an opportunity of letting him know I had it not here: which is a fact. He told me he had another Tragedy, & that I should have it to read.[17]

He was very curious to see Mr. Cumberland who, it seems, has given evident marks of aversion to his Name, whenever Mrs. Thrale has mentioned it,—that poor man is so wonderfully narrow-minded in his *Authorship* Capacity, though otherwise good, humane & generous, that he changes Countenance at either seeing or hearing of any Writer whatsoever. Mrs. Thrale, with whom, this *foible* excepted, he is a great favourite, is so *enraged* with him for | his *littleness* of soul in this respect, that, merely to plague him, she vowed at the Rooms she would walk all the Evening between Dr. Delap & me:—however, I wish so little to encrease his unpleasant feelings, that I determined to keep with Miss Thrale & Miss Dickens entirely: one Time, though, Mrs. Thrale, when she was sitting by Dr. Delap, called me suddenly to her, & when I was

---

[17] Perhaps 'Panthea', which had been rejected by Garrick and which would never be acted or printed (Garrick, *Letters* iii. 933 n. 3).

seated, said 'Now let's see if Mr. Cumberland will come & speak to me!—' However, he always turns resolutely another way, when he sees her with either of us:—though, at all other Times, he is particularly fond of her Company!

'It would actually serve him right, says she, to make Dr. Delap & you strut at each side of me, one with a Dagger, & the other with a mask, as *Tragedy* & *Comedy*.'

'I think, Miss Burney, said the Dr., you & I seem to stand in the same *predicament*,—what shall we do for the poor man?—suppose we burn a Play a piece?'

'Depend upon it, said Mrs. Thrale, he has heard, in Town, that you are both to bring one out this season, & perhaps one of his own may be deferred on that account.'

'Well, he's a fine man! cried the Doctor,—pray, Miss Burney, shew me him when you see him.'

'I hardly know him myself, answered I,—I never saw him but once, at Mrs. Ord's,—for *here* I have never *looked* at him,—so his aversion for me cannot well be *personal*, thank God!' |

'You are very near sighted, I think?'

'Yes.'

'How far can you see?'

'O—I don't know—as *far* as other people, but not *distinctly*.'

'Can you see, now, as far as the Fire?'

We were then about *2 yards* from it!—but these strange Questions come from him eternally.

At Tea we had the Company of Lady Poole[18] & her 2 Nieces.[19] Lady Poole has been a celebrated Brighton *sparkler* for some Years: she is very pretty, & seems sensible

---

[18] Charlotte White (1749–86), daughter of William White (1704–64), of Horsham, Sussex, m. (1772) Sir Ferdinando Poole (*c*.1731–1804), 4th Bt, of Poole, Cheshire, and Lewes, Sussex (J. Comber, *Sussex Genealogies: Horsham Centre* (Cambridge, 1931), p. 371).

[19] Elizabeth Pilfold (1762–1846), m. (1791) Timothy Shelley (1753–1844), of Field Place, Warnham, Sussex, 2d Bt, 1815, mother of Percy Bysshe Shelley; and Charlotte Pilfold (b. 1764), m. (1782) Thomas Grove; daughters of Lady Poole's sister Bethia (1739–79), m. (1762) Charles Pilfold (1727–90) of Effingham, Surrey (ibid.; Thorne, s.v. Shelley, Timothy; *GM* cxvi[2] (1846), 441). Their mother had died the previous June.

& shrewd, though not totally free from *tonish* affectation. Her Nieces are both pretty.

When they were all accomodated, Mrs. Thrale said 'Your Ladyship remembers Dr. Burney?—your admirer 2 years ago?—'

'Certainly.'

'This, Ma'am, is his Daughter.—'

She rose very civilly & looked at me with a flattering sort of curiosity:—& then we *confabed*.—& as soon as we parted to walk, she indulged Mrs. Thrale with saying most obliging things of me & my Book:—& *hoped* I was writing on,—*especially* a *Play*,—she should *dote* on seeing a *Play* by me—'Ah! said Mrs. Thrale, in telling me this, what would I have given that Cumberland had heard her!'

As soon as the Miss Cumberlands came into the Room, the Youngest, as she passed, Courtsied to me,—I had made an *inclination* of that kind in passing by their Pew in the morning:—but the Eldest had ¹ not yet done with *staring*,—& another vile trick she has, which is to make whoever joins her stare too,—& this Evening Lord Sefton, who, I believe, makes much more use of his Eyes than his Brains, while he was walking with her, turned himself quite round to stare at & after me every Time I passed him,—so that I was obliged to beg assistance of Miss Dickens to screen me from his rude curiosity: as to Miss Thrale, she thinks it very *good fun* & wonders I do not rejoice at it, because 'tis so *creditable*.

Some Time after, when we were sitting down, Mr. *Cure* approached us, &, with a most obsequious Bow, seated himself next me. He seemed, for some moments, to ponder upon what he should say—& then, not without hesitation, came out with 'I doubt not,—Miss Burney,—but you—you spend your Time here very—*profitably*.'

Meaning, as I found by his manner, that I *turned to account* all I saw & observed. I did not, however, chuse to understand him, & simply answered 'I don't know for *profitably*,—but *pleasantly* enough.'

'What I mean, Ma'am, said he, stammering,—is—is—is that you—that—that with *walking*—&—& *music*—for I have heard much of your musical talents—

'O no!—I have a *sister*, indeed—'

'But certainly you must study it a *little*,—& then with *reading—reading*, I am sure, you must delight in,—& with—with—with these sort of things—' |

I found he was dying to say with *writing*,—but I interrupted him, & said "Yes, we pass our Time very agreeably because, as Mr. Thrale comes to make some stay, he does not think it necessary to be always in Public, & therefore we spend nearly as much Time at Home & alone, as if we were not at a Public Place.'

'Certainly,. Ma'am,—to *you* that must be very desireable—you who so well know *how* to spend your Time. But I suppose, Ma'am, when you have spent your *mornings* well,—that is, to your liking—I suppose you give your *Evenings* to your—to—to—society?'

Here we were interrupted by the announcing of the Carriage, & we went into the next Room for our *Cloaks*,—where Mrs. Thrale & Mr. Cumberland were in deep conversation;—'O, *here's Miss Burney*,' said Mrs. Thrale, aloud,—Mr. Cumberland turned round, but withdrew his Eyes instantly & I, determined not to interrupt them, made Miss Thrale walk away with me.—In about 10 minutes, she left him, & we all came Home.

As soon as we were in the Carriage, 'It has been, said Mrs. Thrale warmly, all I could do not to affront Mr. Cumberland to Night!—'

'O I hope not, cried I,—I would not have you for the World.'—

'Why I *have* refrained,—but with great difficulty.—'

And then she told me the Conversation she had just had with him. As soon as I made off, he said, with a *spiteful* tone of voice 'O,—that young lady is an Author, I hear!'—'Yes, answered Mrs. Thrale, Author of Evelina.' 'Hump,—I am told it has some humour—' | 'Ay, indeed!—Johnson says nothing like it has appeared for years.' 'So! cried he, biting his lips, & waving uneasily in his Chair,—so! so!'—'Yes, continued she,—& Sir Joshua Reynolds told Mr. Thrale he would give 50 pounds to know the Author.' 'So! so!—O, vastly well!—' cried he, putting his Hand on his Forehead.—'Nay, added she,—Burke himself sat up all Night to finish it!'—This seemed quite too much for him,—he put both his Hands to his Face, & waving backwards & forwards, said 'O—vastly well!—this will do for any thing!'—with a tone as much as to say *pray no more!*—& then Mrs. Thrale bid him Good Night,—*longing*, she said, to call *Miss Thrale* first, & say 'so you won't speak to my Daughter?—why *she* is no Author!'—

I much rejoice that she did not,—& I have most earnestly entreated her not to tell this anecdote to any body here,—for I really am much concerned to have ever *encountered* this *sore* man—who, if already he thus burns with envy at the success of my Book, will, should he find his narrowness of mind resented by me, or related by my Friends, not only wish me ill, but do me every ill office here after in his power. Indeed I am quite shocked to find how he avoids & determines to dislike me: for, hitherto, I have always been willing & *able* to hope that I had not one real Enemy or ill wisher in the World;— I shall still, however, hope if I can but keep *Mrs. Thrale's* ⌐very great⌐ warmth of friendship within bounds, to some what conciliate matters, & prevent any *open enmity*, which authorises all ill Deeds, from taking place. All *Authorship Contention* I shudder to think of! |

95   Brighton,
        [25] October – 3 November [1779]

To Susanna Elizabeth Burney

AJL (Berg, Diary MSS I, paginated 1055–73), Oct.-Nov. 1779
10 single sheets 4to, 20 pp.

4ᵗʰ Pacquet. Brighthelmstone

I forgot, I find, *one* part of the Conversation;—which was Mrs. Thrale's saying 'I think there can be no greater testimony of it's worth, than that it went through 2 Editions in the first year,—nay, I believe I do it injustice, for I think it was 3.—'[20] '*I*, answered he, have done it *greater* injustice,—for I never read it.'—

Are you not *surprised*, Susy, that the Author of the *West Indian* can be so pitifully jealous, & meanly spiteful?—[21]

Oct[r] 28th—

Monday morning [25 Oct.] we spent in sauntering at the Booksellers, & upon the Steyn,—& at Bowen's we met the Miss Cumberlands who had a little Boy with them,—I went up to the Child, & admired his Hair, which was remarkably fine,—& then they both, with a courtesie that surprised me; began talking with me:—& that with as much readiness as if they had only waited for *me* to begin!—however, I am glad this has passed, as I hope it will occasion a change in their behaviour.

After this, I heard prodigious fine things said by Lady Hesketh,[22] a very handsome Baronet's widow, but *bien passée*,—who talked over every Character in Evelina with Mrs. Thrale & told her she was quite happy in having such an opportunity of seeing *it's author*.—So I assure you Mr. Cumberland has not *infected* the place with ill will!—on the contrary I am prodigiously *in Fashion*, & *hear* of Compliments & fine speeches almost Daily,—though I now grow tired of writing them, except when from *select folks*, or accompanied by odd circumstances. |

And now I must have the Honour to present to you a new Acquaintance, who this Day Dined here. Mr. Blakeney.[23]—An Irish Gentleman, late a Commissary in

---

[20] Actually 3 in the 1st 13 months, to be precise.

[21] The highest value in Cumberland's highly successful sentimental comedy (1771) is, of course, a good heart.

[22] Harriot Cowper (1733–1807), daughter of Ashley Cowper (d. 1788), m. Sir Thomas Hesketh (1727–78), cr. Bt, 1761. She was a 1st cousin and correspondent of William Cowper (1731–1800), the poet.

[*See opposite page for n. 23*]

Germany. He is between 60 & 70, but means to pass for about 30,—gallant, complaisant, obsequious & humble to the *Fair sex*, for whom he has an aweful reverence,—but, when not immediately addressing them, swaggering, blustering, puffing & domineering. These are his 2 *apparent* Characters,—but the *real* man is worthy, moral, religious,—*empty*, conceited & parading.

He is as fond of Quotations as my poor Lady Smatter,[24]—& like her, knows little beyond a *song*, & always blunders about the *Author* of that. His Language greatly resembles Rose Fuller's, &, as Miss Thrale well says, Rosy, when as old, will be much such another Personage. His whole Conversation consists in little French phrases, picked up during his residence Abroad, & in anecdotes & story telling, which are sure to be retold Daily, & Daily in the same words.

Having given you this general sketch, I will endeavour to illustrate it by some specimens,—but you must excuse their being unconnected, & only such as I can readily recollect.

Speaking of the Ball in the Evening, to which we were all going,—'Ah, Madam! said he to Mrs. ¦ Thrale,—there was a Time when—*tol de rol*!—tol de rol (rising & Dancing & singing) tol de rol—I could Dance with the best of them!—but now—a man forty & upwards, as my Lord Ligonier[25] used to say,—but—tol de rol,—there *was* a Time!—'

'Ay, so there was, Mr. Blakeney, said Mrs. Thrale, & I think you & I together made a very venerable appearance.'

'Ah! Madam,—I remember once at Bath,—I was called out to Dance with one of the finest young Ladies I ever

---

[23] Edward Blakeney (d. 1799) of Newman St., London, eldest son of Thomas Blakeney (d. 1762) of Feigh, co. Galway. HLT calls him 'Old Beau Blakeney a foolish Fellow enough' (ibid. i. 156). No information has been found about his being a commissary in Germany. He was the British consul at Nice, 1757–c.1762; the termination of his consulship seems to coincide with his inheriting his father's estate. For further biographical details about him, see below and notes.

[24] See above, p. 279 n. 55.

[25] John Louis Ligonier (1680–1770), cr. (1757) Visc. Ligonier (Ire.), (1766) E. Ligonier (UK); field marshal and commander-in-chief of the British Army. Blakeney implies that he personally knew this famous soldier.

saw,—I was just preparing to do my best,—when a Gentleman of my Acquaintance was so cruel as to whisper me Blakeney!—The Eyes of all Europe are upon you!—for that was the phrase of the Times,—Blakeney! says he, the Eyes of all Europe are upon you!—I vow to God, Ma'am, enough to make a man tremble!—tol de rol,—tol de rol,— (Dancing) the Eyes of all Europe are upon you!—I declare, Ma'am, enough to put a man out of Countenance!—'

Dr. Delap who was here, some Time after, in his ⌐gay⌐ way said 'Miss Burney, I could not find you any where this morning;—I went to the Steyn,—& to both the Bookseller's,—to look for you,—but I could see nothing of you;—so I picked up a Book.— — —' & then he repeated, to Mrs. Thrale, some Lines of Horace,—I have looked for them,—& *these are they,*— ┃ in English,— — —

> My Laligen I still will Love
> Who *softly speaks, & sweetly smiles.*[26]

He said them in *Latin.*— — —

'Horace, continued he, certainly saw Miss Burney in a Vision when he writ those Lines;—they are exactly prophetic of her.—'

'Well, cried Mrs. Thrale, I have often heard Horace was *inspired,* but I never before knew he was a prophet.'

'Ah, Madam, cried Mr. Blakeney, this Latin,—things of that kind,—we waste our Youth, Ma'am, in these vain studies,—for my part, I wish I had spent mine in studying French & Spanish,—more *useful,* Ma'am,—but, Lord bless me, Ma'am, what Time have I had for that kind of thing?—Travelling here, over the ocean,—Hills & Dales, Ma'am!—Reading the great Book of the World!—Poor ignorant mortals, Ma'am!—no Time to do any thing!—'

'Ay, Mr. Blakeney, said Mrs. Thrale, I remember how you downed Beauclerk & Hamilton,[27] *the Wits,* once at our House,—when they talked of *Ghosts.*'

'Ah, Ma'am,—give me a Brace of Pistols, & I warrant I'll manage a *Ghost* for you!—Not but Providence may

---

[26] *Carmina* I. xxii. 23–4: '*dulce ridentem Lalagen amabo, / dulce loquentem*'.
[27] Topham Beauclerk and William Gerard Hamilton.

please to send little spirits,—Guardian angels, Ma'am,—
to watch us,—*that* I can't speak about,—it would be presumptuous,—Good God, Ma'am, what can a poor ignorant
mortal know?—'

'Ay, so you told Beauclerk & Hamilton.—'

'Lord, yes, Ma'am!—poor Human Beings!—can't
account for any thing!—& all themselves Esprits forts!—I
vow to God, presumptuous, Ma'am!—Esprits forts,
indeed!—they can see no farther than their Noses!—poor
ignorant mortals!—Here's an admiral,—& here's a
Prince—& here's a General,—& here's a Dipper, & poor
Smoker the Bather,[28]—Lord, Ma'am, what's all this?—
strutting about—& that kind of thing—& then they can't
account for a blade of Grass!—'

After this, Dr. Johnson being mentioned,—'Ay, said he,
I'm sorry he did not come down with you,—I liked him
better than those others,—not much of a fine Gentleman,
indeed, but a clever fellow,—a deal of knowledge,—got a
d——d good understanding!'—

Dr. Delap, rather abruptly, asked my Christian Name,—
Mrs. Thrale answered,—& Mr. Blakeney *tenderly* repeated
'*Fanny*!—a prodigious pretty Name!—& a pretty Lady
that bears it,—Fanny!—ah, how beautiful is that song of
Swifts—

> When Fanny blooming fair
> First caught my ravish'd sight,
> Struck with her mien & air—

'Her *Face* & air, interrupted Mrs. Thrale,—for *mien* & air
we hold to be much the same thing.'[29]

'Right, Ma'am, right!—you, Madam,—Lord, Ma'am,
you know every thing!—but as to me,—to be sure I *began*

---

[28] Blakeney seems to mean the same thing by 'Dipper' and 'Bather', i.e.,
an assistant who helps someone to dip or bathe in the sea at Brighton, perhaps
in one of those submersible vehicles which were pushed or pulled into the
water (see below, p. 427). 'Smoker' was possibly a 'Bather' at Brighton who
smoked (?).

[29] Actually, 'her shape and air'. This popular song was not by Swift. Attributed to Ld. Chesterfield (see below), it is more probably by Thomas Philips (d.
1739). The subject of the song is Lady Frances Shirley (*c*.1706–78), daughter
of the 1st E. Ferrers (*YW* xxiv. 401 n. 14, xxviii. 412 n. 3).

with studying,—the old Greek & Latin, Ma'am,—but then Travelling, Ma'am,—going through Germany | & then France,—& Spain, Ma'am,—& dipping at Brighthelmstone,—over Hills & Dales,—reading the great Book of the World,— — —ay,—a little Poetry now & then to be sure I have picked up,—

> My Phoebe & I
> O'er Hills & o'er Dales & o'er Valleys will fly,
> And Love shall be by,[30]—

But, as you say, Ma'am,

> Struck with her Face & Air,
> I felt a strange delight,—

How pretty that is!—how *progressive* from the first sight of her!—Ah, Swift was a fine man!

'Why, Sir, I don't think it's Printed in his Works? said Dr. Delap.—

'No, said Mrs. Thrale, because 'tis Chesterfield's.'

'Ay, right! right, Ma'am! so it is!'— —

Now if I had heard all this *before* I writ my Play, would you not have thought I had borrowed the hint of my Witlings from Mr. Blakeney?—

'I am glad, Mr. Thrale, continued this Hero,—you have got your Fire place altered,—Lord God, Ma'am, there used to be such a wind there was no sitting here;—admirable Dinners,—excellent Company,—*tres bon* fare, —& all the Time *Signor Vento* coming down the Chimney!—Do you remember, Miss Thrale, how one Day at Dinner, you burst out a Laughing, because I said a *tres bon* Goose—' |

But if I have not now given you some idea of Mr. Blakeney's Conversation, I *never* can,—for I have written almost as many words as he ever uses,—& given you *almost* as many *ideas* as he ever starts!—And as he almost *Lives* here, it is fitting I let you know some thing of him.

---

[30] Not traced.

Well,—in the Evening we all went to the Ball, where we had appointed to meet Lady Shelly, Mrs. Dickens, & Mr. Mrs. & the Miss Shellys of Lewes.

We were there first; Mr. Wade saw us to our seats;—& began talking of the Dancing; 'Ay, said Mrs. Thrale, there are some Dancing misses coming presently, that will be glad enough to be taken care of by you,—as for *my* misses,—they seem determined to keep quiet.'

'That, said Mr. Wade, must be because they can do so much better things.'

'Why ay,—answered she,—I presume they both hold that they shine rather more in *Conversation*.'

'Yes, said he, glancing archly towards me,—they come here, I suppose, to comment upon others!—'

Such a speech as this would have determined me *to* Dance, but that it is so long since I have Exhibited, that I am a Poltroon;—besides, I see plainly *I* should be Watched & *commented* upon in a most scrutinizing manner,—for *that*, I have some reason to believe I am *without* Dance- ǀ -ing,—& therefore I think I am most safe—& know I am most easy—in resting a quiet spectator.

We were soon after joined by our party.—the Miss Shelly's both Danced;—Mr. Wade again came to Miss Thrale who, from the natural shyness & reserve of her Temper declines Dancing,—& then on to me,—& when I again told him I did not chuse to Dance, he seemed unwilling to believe me, & had the civility to repeat his Question twice,—however, my answer was the same.

All that did not Dance soon retired into the Card Room, except Miss Thrale & me,—& Mr. Shelly begged us to keep still, that his Daughters might occasionally join us;—this was very fatiguing, as they are *abominably* ignorant, flippant & conceited Girls,—however, when I found it impossible to get rid of them, I solaced myself by making sport from talking nonsense to them. Yet so little were they aware that I *meant* any sport, that they took every thing *à la Lettre*,—to the mutual diversion of Miss Thrale & myself.

The Eldest Miss Shelly had for a Partner one of the young Finch's,[31]—a most odiously vulgar young man,—

[*See p. 406 for n. 31*]

short, thick, & totally underbred; 'I, wonder, said she to me, between one of the Dances, what my Partner's Name is,—do you know?'— |

'I am not sure, quoth I, but I fancy Mr. Squab.'

'Mr. Squab? repeated she,—well, I don't like him at all.—Pray do you know who that Gentleman is that jumps so?' pointing to Mr. Cure.—

'Yes, answered I,—'tis a Mr. Kill.'

'Well, cried she, I don't like his Dancing at all. I wonder who that officer is?'—pointing to a fat, coarse sort of a man, who stooped immoderately.

'Captain Slouch, quoth I.'

'Lord, said she, I think the people here have very odd Names!—'

And thus, though the Names I gave them were merely & markingly Descriptive of their Persons, did this little Noodle & her sister instantly believe them,—though I Laughed myself sick all the Time.

When the Dancing was over, & we walked about, Mr. Cure, with his usual obsequiousness, came to speak to me, &, for a while joined us:—& these Girls, who Penned me between them, Tittered, & pinched me, & whispered observations upon *Mr. Kill*, till I was obliged to assume the most steady gravity to prevent his discovering how free I had made with him.

Just before we came away, Mr. Shelly came up to his Daughter, & said 'Pray, my dear, who was the Gentleman you Danced with?'

'Mr. Squab, Papa.' answered she.

'A good tight young man, said Mr. Shelley,—I must | go & make a Bow to him before we go.'—

Did you ever know such *innocents?*—to hear such a Name without suspicion, or any emotion?—I did not think it worth while to undeceive them,—though poor Mr. Finch must have been rather surprised if Mr. Shelly accosted him with 'your servant, Mr. Squab!'—however, I am pretty sure they did not meet.

---

[31] Presumably one of the 6 younger brothers of Heneage Finch (1751–1812), 4th E. of Aylesford.

All the Cumberlands were there. *Mr.* Cumberland avoids *Miss Thrale* as much as he does *me*,—merely, I suppose, because she is commonly with me!—However, if such is his humour, he was not made too happy this Night—for, Mrs. Thrale told me that while she was seated next him, as he was playing at Cards, Dr. Delap came to her, & began singing *my* Eloge,—& saying how I should be *adored* in *France*,—that *that* was the Paradise of *Lady Wits*,—& that, for his part, if he had not known I was Dr. Burney's Daughter, he thought I had so much a French Face & look, that he should have guessed me for a Daughter of *Voltaire's*;—& other such speeches,—All of which, I fear, were so many torments to him,—'But, said Mrs. Thrale, *let* him be tormented, if *such* things can torment him!—for *my* part, '*I'd have a starling taught to hallow Evelina*'[32]— |

Oct[r] 29th—

I am absolutely almost sick with Laughing,—this Mr. Blakeney half Convulses me,—yet I cannot make *you* Laugh by Writing his speeches, because it is the manner which accompanies them that, more than the matter, renders them so peculiarly ridiculous. His extreme pomposity,—the solemn stiffness of his Person,—the conceited twinkling of his little old Eyes,—& the quaint importance of his delivery,—are so much more like some Pragmatical[33] old Coxcomb represented on the stage, than like any thing in real & common Life, that I think, were I a man, I should sometimes be betrayed into *Clapping* him for acting so well!—As it is, I am sure no Character in any Comedy I ever saw has made me Laugh more extravagantly.

He Dines & spends the Evening here constantly, to my great satisfaction.—

At Dinner, when Mrs. Thrale offers him a seat next her, he regularly says 'But where are *les Charmantes?*—

---

[32] Cf. *1 Henry IV* I. iii. 224–5.
[33] Conceited, self-important (*OED* s.v. pragmatical 4.b).

(meaning Miss T. & me) I can do nothing till they are accommodated.'

And whenever he Drinks a Glass of wine, he never fails to touch either Mrs. Thrale's or my Glass, with '*Est il permis?*'—

But at the same Time that he is so courteous, he is proud to a most sublime excess,—& thinks ╵ every Person to whom he speaks Honoured beyond measure by his Notice,—nay, he does not even *look* at any body, without evidently displaying that such Notice is more the effect of his benign condescendsion, than of any pretention on their part to deserve such a mark of his perceiving their existence. But you will think me mad about this man.

Our society has been very agreeably enlarged lately by the addition of Mr. Selwyn,[34]—a Gentleman of Family & Fortune, who was formerly a Banker in Paris,—[xxxxx *1 line*] & he appears to be a worthy, amiable, benevolent man,—He, as well as *the General*, i.e, Mr. Blakeney's nick name,[35]—always *Lives* with Mr. Thrale when at Brighthelmstone:—c'est à dire, Dines here every Day, & only departs at Bed Time. He brought me a message of kind Compliments from Mrs. Ord. She told him he would find me here. We are making a *pretty acquaintance* together, for every night when the rest go to Cards, we 2 are set to Back Gammon.

I have had the pleasure, once, of seeing the Holroyds,— they came over from Sheffield for a morning,—& we talked of nothing but our happiness last May.—We are all violently invited to pass some Time with them before we leave Sussex. ╵

We have also made acquaintance with Mrs. Chamier,[36] & the little mulatto she has the care of: Mrs. Chamier

---

[34] Charles Selwin *or* Selwyn (1715–94), of Down Hall, Essex. He had been a banker at Paris from *c.*1740 to *c.*1763 (*The Piozzi Letters* i. 102 n. 3; *YW* xiii. 239 n. 12).

[35] Blakeney had never been in the military, unless one counts his service as private secretary to his famous cousin Lt-Gen. William Blakeney when the latter was Lt-Gov. of Minorca (see below). The nickname was probably in allusion to this relationship and to his self-importance.

[36] Dorothy Wilson (d. 1799), daughter and co-heiress of Robert Wilson, merchant, of Woodford, Essex, m. (1753) Anthony Chamier (*EJL* ii. 173 n. 59).

looks by no means superior to what the *Housekeeper* of such a man as her Husband ought to look,—but she is good natured & merry, & serves to help *Steyn Chat* in a morning.[37] The little Girl, who is called Emily Jess, is a charming Creature,—none of the Fairest, to be sure, but otherwise really handsome, & so well mannered & agreeable, that we only wish ever to see Mrs. Chamier for *her* sake.[37]

Another of our *Steyn Chatters* is Lady Hesketh, to whom Mrs. Thrale has taken a great fancy;—she is an exceedingly handsome Woman, though *passée*, more than *non pas*—has Travelled a great deal, knows the World well, & is sensible & intelligent.[39]

Mr. Concannon is also just arrived here,—but as I never formerly thought him worth much more Room than is taken for his *Name*, I shall not now begin to shew him any more civility.

One of the most constant of our Steyn *Beaus* is Mr. Woodcock,[40] a Nephew of Lady Shelly,—&, like her, very handsome, & very gentle & obliging.

[37] Her husband seems to have despised her understanding. The following year, when he was dying, HLT wrote of her: 'She is a strange Creature, I used to make Fun by mimicking her; yet tis more dismal than comic to see Aversion continued to the very Confines of Life, against the Woman he had been tied to for 27 Years' (*Thraliana* i. 458–9).

[38] HLT, in a letter to CB, 9 Nov. 1779 (Hyde), calls the little girl 'Mr Chamier's Indian Miss'. The Chamiers had no children of their own. The girl was Amelia (or Emily) Harrison Jesse, the natural daughter of Chamier's late friend John Jesse, Esq., of the East India Co., Sumatra. Chamier, upon his death in 1780, left her £2,000 in trust. She m. (9 June 1792, at Bromley, Kent), William Ceely Trevillyan (*or* Trevillian) (1758–1843), of Exeter and of Middleney, Somerset, then a Capt. in the 11th Dragoons. Mrs Chamier, upon her decease (in 1799) left her £500 and her furniture, plate, etc. She d. in 1831 (wills of Anthony Chamier, PCC, dated 9 Oct., prob. 24 Oct. 1780, and Dorothy Chamier, PCC, dated 7 Nov. 1795, prob. 23 Mar. 1799 (information kindly supplied by Mrs John R. G. Comyn); *GM* lxii¹ (1792), 575; ci² (1831), 652; cxiii¹ (1843), 223; IGI).

[39] HLT describes her thus in 1781: 'Dear Lady Hesketh! and how like a Naples Washball She is: so round, so sweet, so plump, so polished; so red, so white ... with more Beauty than almost any body, as much Wit as many a body; and six Times the Quantity of polite Literature ... . I never can find out what that Woman does to keep the people from adoring her' (*Thraliana* i. 478).

[40] Edward Whitfield Woodcock (b. 1758), son of Lady Shelley's brother Edward Woodcock (1734–92), LL.D (Cantab.), 1771, Vicar of Watford, Herts, 1762–92, by Hannah (m. 1755, d. 1796), daughter of Thomas Whitfield, of

But the far best among our men acquaintance here, & him who, next to Mr. Selwin, I like the best, is a Mr. Tidy,[41]—you will probably suspect, | as Lady Hesketh did, last Night, when she met him here, that this is a *nick-Name* only,—where as he hath not, Heaven knows, a better in the World!—He *appears* a grave, reserved, quiet man,— but he *is* a sarcastic, observing, & *ridiculing* man,—no trusting to appearances! no, not even to *Wigs*!—for a meaner, more sneaking & pitiful Wig,—a Wig that less bespeaks a man worth two pence in his Pocket, or two ideas in his Head, did I never see than that of Mr. Tidy.

Novr 1st— — —

Yet warm as June!— — —pleasant & delightful is the Weather, & I Bathe almost Daily.—

Sunday Evening [31 Oct.] we went to the Rooms, attended by Mr. Blakeney & Mr. Selwin,—& there, for the *last Time this season*, we saw the Cumberlands[42]. The 2 misses lately, have Courtsied & smiled whenever I have met them,—but the Father has steadily & resolutely avoided me,—& upon my account, I fear, all *but* avoided Mrs. Thrale,—for he has called here only once,—& never spoken to or looked at her when I have been with her.—

Does he, if the success of Evelina has been painful to him, does he [*sic*] think that his shunning me will occasion one set the less to be bought, | or, one set the less to be Read?—

We have lost the Dickens, & miss them very much;— they are gone to Town,—& have pressed me very earnestly

Watford Place, Herts. He had matriculated at Cambridge in 1776 but did not take a degree (IGI; *GM* lxvi^1 (1796), 526).

[41] Richard Tidy (1719–88), of Brighton. HLT calls him 'dear Mr Tidy' in a letter to Mr Thrale and Queeney in 1780; like Mr Thrale, he was a brewer, being assessed in 1757 for a dwelling house, malt house and warehouse in Black Lion Street. He had been a widower for almost 20 years, his wife Mary (b. *c.*1732) having died in Feb. 1760 (*The Queeney Letters*, ed. M. of Lansdowne (1934), p. 133; J. G. Bishop, *A Peep into the Past: Brighton in 1744–61* (Brighton, 1895), p. 35; T. W. Horsfield, *The History ... of Sussex* (Lewes, 1835), i. 142; IGI).

[42] FB satirizes the farcical pride of Cumberland and ostentation of his daughters by employing the stock phrase for a closing performance.

to visit them,—particularly when I am at *Chesington*, where, they say, they have often heard of my being, as they have a house at Ewel, which they assure me will be but a pleasant Walk for me.[43]—Mrs. Chamier, also, has given me much invitation to call upon her at *Epsom* from Chesington,—but I am so little there, that I wish nothing less than making appointments of any sort to rob me of the little Time I am able to spend with my dear Daddy. Besides, I fancy he would like nothing less himself than my making Chesington so *popular*:—would you, Daddy?—for Ten to one but you get at this Pacquet, sooner or later?—

Mr. Cure took the first opportunity of a vacancy at my side, to join us, & to *sift* into some of my opinions,—for *that* I can plainly perceive, is his meaning & endeavour: however, I believe he finds in them nothing sufficiently *marvellous* to repay his curiosity.

But the most agreeable part of the Evening was the Time I spent with Mr. Selwin, who I have taken a prodigious fancy to,—& a very *odd* one, you will say, if you enquire the *Peticklers*,—for it is neither for brilliancy, Talents, Wit, Person or Youth,—since he is possessed of none of these,—but the fact is he appears to me *uncommonly good*,—full of humanity, generosity, delicacy & benevolence.

One Time, while Mrs. & Miss Thrale & I were parading up & down, he came to us, Laughing, & said 'A Gentleman has this moment been asking Lord Sefton who is the Lady in the *Hat* (N.B. I only had one)—& What!—answered his Lordship,—did you never read— — —' He stopt, & bit his Lips,—& *I* bit mine, & whisked to the other side.

I wonder if *ever* I shall cease feeling awkward at the first attack of every *fresh* attacker upon this subject.

Well but—do you know I have been writing to Dr. Johnson!—I tremble to *mention* it.—but he sent a message in a Letter to Mrs. Thrale to *wonder* why his Pupils did

---

[43] Ewell, Surrey, is 2½ mi. E of Chessington.

not write to him, & to hope they did not forget him:[44]
Miss Thrale therefore scrawled a Letter immediately,—&
I added only this little Post script:

P:S: Dr. Johnson's *other* Pupil a little longs to add a few
Lines to this Letter,—but knows too well that all she has
to say might be comprised in signing herself his obliged
& most obed^t serv^t

F: B. ▯

so that's better than a long *rig mi rol* about nothing.—[45]

Novr 3^d.

This moment come Home from the Steyn, where we
have been strolling the whole morning with all the Shelley
Family, Lady Gage, Sir Sampson Gideon, & some others.
All the Shellys, except *the Lady par excellence*, are most
tiresome & stupid People indeed!—& the *young Ladies*
wear me to Death,—I can never escape from them,—they
lug hold of me, & torment me to talk with them in a
manner so vulgar & disagreeable, that, when I am not in
the humour to make my own Diversion by ratling all sort
of Nonsense, I am so much fatigued by them that I feel
as drowsy as if it was 2 o'clock in the morning.

I believe I never mentioned that Lord & Lady Gage &
Sir Sampson Gideon have been here on a Visit?—I have,
however, nothing new to say of them, so the mention is
not of much consequence;—Lady Gage & Sir Sampson,
her Brother, are *always* what they appear at first, soft,

---

[44] 'The two younglings; what hinders them from writing to me. I hope they
do not forget me' (SJ to HLT, 28 Oct. 1779, *LSJ* iii. 202). Queeney Thrale's
letter to SJ and the original of FB's postscript are missing.

[45] FB's postscript annoyed SJ: 'Queeney sent me a pretty letter, to which
⟨Burney⟩ added a silly short note, in such a silly white hand, that I was glad it
was no longer' (SJ to HLT, 4 Nov. 1779, ibid. ii. 318). After Queeney sent him
a second letter, SJ replied, thanking her for her kindness and noting that at a
dinner party at Mr Vesey's, 'The talk was for a while about Burney's book, and
the old objection to the Captain's [Mirvan's] grossness being mentioned, Lady
Edgcombe said that she had known such a captain.' 'Do not tell this to Burney
for it will please her, and she takes no care to please me' (SJ to Hester Maria
Thrale, 11 Nov. 1779, ibid. ii. 324). FB made amends by writing to SJ on 16
Nov. (below, pp. 435–37). For Mrs Montagu's criticism of the Captain's grossness, see above, p. 162 n. 10.

gentle & obliging,—& though Lord Gage has a great deal of humour & fun, & tells comical stories, niether his humour, fun, or stories will bear *writing*, as they owe all their spirit & effect to the looks, gestures & manners with which he accompanies them. | Lady Gage is very earnest for us all to visit her at Ferle for a Day or 2 before we leave Sussex,—but I doubt Mr. Thrale will not consent to give up a Day's Hunting;—he is amazingly better, thank Heaven,—both in Health & spirits.

Last Monday [1 Nov.] we went again to the Ball,—Mr. Wade was quite urgent with us all to Dance, & Mrs. Thrale, to satisfy him, said she had no objection to *our* Dancing, if *he* would do us the honour to take us out:—for you must know at these sort of Places the most *honourable* thing for the Ladies is reckoned Dancing with the Master of the Ceremonies,—who, since we came, has only taken out Lady Sefton & the Miss Beauclerkes.[46]

I instantly declared that I did not chuse to Dance at all,—I have already told you my reasons, which I think are stronger than the pleasure I could have would obviate:—Mr. Wade opened the Ball with a Miss Benson,[47] a Lady who is on a Visit to Lady Shelly,—& then took out Miss Thrale,—who, as Mr. Selwin said, Danced *very much like a Gentlewoman*, & then he again came to me, & almost *made* me break my resolution,—but not *quite*, & so I again dismissed him. I love Dancing well enough to be half sorry, but yet I am glad I kept quiet.

Mr. Blakeney, who was there, & seated himself next to Lady Pembroke, at the Top of the Room, looked most sublimely happy!—He continues still to afford me the | *highest diversion*,—Rose Fuller was never *half* so enter-

---

[46] Mary Beauclerk and her younger sister Elizabeth (*c.*1767–93), m. (1787) George Augustus Herbert (1759–1827), styled B. Herbert; 11th E. of Pembroke and 8th E. of Montgomery, 1794.

[47] FB describes her below as 'very musical' and a close friend of the Harrises of Salisbury. She seems to have never married and was apparently living with Louisa Harris in Feb. 1809, when CB addressed a letter to the two of them (Osborn). HLT said that 'She has a large Fortune', but 'I believe She is of very mean Birth' (*Thraliana* i. 455). She was perhaps a Benson of Salisbury and cousin of James Harris's protégé William Benson Earle, but has not been further traced (see *EJL* ii. 130 n. 52; *GM* cv² (1835), 329).

taining!—& Mr. Selwin, who has long known him, & has all his stories & sayings by Heart, *studies* to recollect all his favourite topics, & tells me beforehand what he will say upon the subjects he prepares me for leading him to. Indeed, between him & Mrs. Thrale, almost all he has to say is already exhausted.

As he is notorious for his contempt of all *Artists*, whom he looks upon with little more respect than upon Day Labourers the other Day, when *Painting* was discussed, he *downed* Sir Joshua Reynolds as if he had been upon a level with a Carpenter or Farrier!—

'Did you ever, said Mrs. Thrale, see his Nativity?'[48]—

'No, Madam:—but I know his Pictures very well; I knew him many Years ago, in Minorca,—he Drew my Picture there,—& then he knew how to take a moderate Price,[49]—but now,—I vow to God, Ma'am, 'tis scandalous!—scandalous indeed!—to pay a fellow here 70 Guineas for scratching out a Head!—'[50]

'Sir, cried Dr. Delap, (who is here perpetually,) you must not run down Sir Joshua Reynolds, because he is Miss Burney's Friend.—'

'Sir, answered he, I don't want to run the man down;—I like him well enough, in his proper place,—he is as decent as any man of that sort I ever knew,—but for all that, Sir, his Prices are shameful!—Why he would not—

[48] 'The infant lying in a manger surrounded by the Virgin, St. Joseph, the shepherds, and four angels'. The Virgin was a portrait of Mrs Sheridan. Exhibited at the Royal Academy in 1779 (No. 245), the painting was almost entirely redone by Sir Joshua after its return. The D. of Rutland paid £1,200 for it. It was burnt at Belvoir Castle in 1816 (Graves iii. 1179).

[49] Reynolds had been in Minorca from Aug. 1749 until Jan. 1750, his visit being extended by a riding accident which badly damaged his face. Blakeney at that time was private secretary to his 2nd cousin (once removed) Lt-Gen. William Blakeney (1672–1761), cr. (1756) B. Blakeney of Castle Blakeney, Ireland, Lt-Gov. of Minorca since 1748, who became famous for his gallant defense of that island against the French in 1756. Reynolds, who was indeed charging low prices for his paintings, painted approximately 25 to 30 portraits, including almost all the officers of the garrison at Port Mahon, during his stay on the island. See D. Hudson, *Sir Joshua Reynolds: A Personal Study* (1958), pp. 27–30.

[50] In 1777 Sir Joshua's charges were 35 guineas for a head, and 70 guineas for a half-length (M. Cormack, 'The Ledgers of Sir Joshua Reynolds,' *Walpole Society*, xlii (1970), 105).

(looking at the poor Doctor with an enraged contempt) he would not do *your* Head, under 70 Guineas!'

'Well, said Mrs. Thrale, he had *one* Portrait at the last Exhibition, that I think hardly *could* be paid enough for,—it was of a Mr. Stuart,[51]—I had never done admiring it.' |

'What stuff is this, Ma'am! cried Mr. Blakeney, how can 2 or 3 Dabs of Paint ever be worth such a sum as that!'—

'Sir, said Mr. Selwyn, (always willing to draw him out,) you know not how much he is improved since you knew him in Minorca; he is now the finest Painter, perhaps, in the World.'

'Pho, pho,—Sir,—cried he, how can *you* talk so?—you, Mr. Selwyn, who have seen so many capital Pictures abroad?—'

'Come, come, Sir, said the ever odd Dr. Delap, you must not go on so undervaluing him, for, I tell you, he is a Friend of Miss Burneys.

'Sir, said Mr. Blakeney, I tell you again I have no objection to the man,—I have Dined in his Company 2 or 3 Times,—a very decent man he is,—fit to keep Company with Gentlemen;—but, Lord God, Ma'am!—what are all your modern Dablers put together to one ancient?—Nothing!—a set of—Not a Rubens[52] among them!—I vow to God, Ma'am, not a Rubens among them!'— — —

How flattered would Sir Joshua be by such commendation, *fit Company for a Gentleman—a decent man.*—but perhaps this his contempt of Dr. Delap's plea that he was *my* Friend, may make you suppose I am not in his good graces,—whereas I assure you, 'tis not so,—for the other Evening, when they were all at Cards, I left the Room for some Time,—&, on my return, Mr. Selwin said 'Miss Burney do not your Cheeks *Tingle?*—' 'No, quoth I,—why should they?—' 'From the conversation that has just passed,' answered he;—& afterwards, I heard from Mrs. Thrale that Mr. Blakeney had been singing my praises, & pronouncing me *a dear little Charmante.*

[51] A half-length portrait of Andrew Stuart (1725–1801), MP and a Ld. of Trade, exhibited at the Royal Academy in 1779 (No. 255) as 'Portrait of a Gentleman' (Graves iii. 943; Namier).

[52] Peter Paul Rubens (1577–1640), painter.

Adieu, my dear Love,—send all that relates to Mr.
Blakeney to my dear Father, if he has patience to hear
it,—Let me hear from you *very* soon & *very* frequently,—
but *inclose*,—Charlotte forget that—but *n'importe* for I
never think I pay too much for a Letter from Home.[53]

96   Brighton,
                       [*post* 3]–8 November [1779]
To Susanna Elizabeth Burney

AJL (Berg, Diary MSS I, paginated 1073.B-1084), Nov. 1779
8 single sheets 4to, 16 pp.

Brighthelmstone

To go on with the subject left off with in my last, my
favourite subject you will think it, Mr. Blakeney,—I must
inform you that his commendation was more astonishing
to me than any body's could be, as I had really taken it
for granted he had hardly noticed my existence;—but he
has also spoken very well of Dr. Delap, that is to say, in a
very *condescending* manner,—'That Dr. Delap, said he,
seems a good sort of man,—I wish all the Cloth were like
him,—but, lack a day!—'tis no such thing,—the Clergy in
general,—God d____d odd Dogs!—'
    Whenever *Plays* are mentioned, we have also a *regular*
speech about them,—'I never, he says, go to a Tragedy,—
it's too affecting,—Tragedy enough in real Life,—Tragedies are only fit for fair Females;—for my part, I cannot
bear to see Othello tearing about in that violent manner,—
& fair little Desdemona—Lord God, Ma'am, 'tis too
affecting!—to see your Kings & your Princesses,—tearing
their pretty Locks,—O there's no standing it!—*a straw
Crown'd monarch*—what is that, Mrs. Thrale?—
    a straw Crown'd monarch, in mock majesty,—

---

[53] This last seems written a bit hurriedly. FB appears to be saying, in effect,
'never mind, Charlotte, send me a separate letter, I don't mind paying for it.'

I can't recollect, now, where that is,[54]—but, for my part, I really cannot bear to see such sights,—& then out come the white Handkerchiefs,—& all the pretty Eyes are wiping,—& then comes poison, & Daggers,—& all that kind of thing,—O Lord, Ma'am!—'tis too much,—but yet the fair tender Hearts—the pretty little Females all like it.'

This speech, word for word, I have already heard from ⎮ him *literally* 4 Times.

When Mr. *Garrick* was mentioned, he honoured him with much the same style of Compliment as he had done Sir Joshua Reynolds. 'Ay, ay, said he, that Garrick was another of those fellows that people run mad about,—Lord God, Ma'am, 'tis a shame to think of such things!—an Actor Living like a Person of Quality!—scandalous!—I vow to God, scandalous!—'

'Well,—commend me to Mr. Blakeney! cried Mrs. Thrale, for he is your only man to down all the people that every body else sets up!—'

'Why, Ma'am, answered he, I like all these people very well in their proper place;—but to see such a set of poor Beings Living like Persons of Quality!—'tis preposterous!—common sense, Madam, common sense is against that kind of thing;—as to Garrick, he was a very good mimic,—an entertaining fellow enough, & all that kind of thing,—but for an Actor to Live like a Person of Quality!—O scandalous!—'

Some Time after, the *musical Tribe* was mentioned, when, as I fully expected, a *bob*[55] was given to *them*: He was at Cards, at the Time, with Mr. Selwyn, Dr. Delap & Mr. Thrale,—while we *fair females*, as he always calls us, were speaking of Agujari;—he constrained himself from flying out as long as he was able,—but upon our mentioning her having ⎮ £50 a song,[56] he suddenly, in a great

---

[54] The line is from *Manners: a Satire* (first publ. 1739), by Paul Whitehead (1710–74): 'Midst the mad Mansions of *Moor-fields*, I'd be / A straw-crown'd Monarch, in mock Majesty' (ll. 3–4) (*Satires Written by Mr. Whitehead* (1748; rpt. Los Angeles, 1984), p. 5).

[55] See above, p. 72.

[56] Lucrezia Agujari's fee at the Pantheon (*EJL* ii. 75).

rage, called out '*Catgut & Rosen!*—Lord God, Ma'am, 'tis scandalous!'—

We all Laughed,—& Mr. Selwyn, to provoke him on, said 'Why, Sir, how shall we part with our money better?'

'O fie! fie! cried he, I have not patience to hear of such folly,—Common sense, Sir, common sense is against it;—why now there was one of these fellows at Bath last season,—a *Mr. Rozzini*,[57]—I vow to God I longed to Cane him every Day!—such a Work made with him!—all the fair Females sighing for him!—Jesus! enough to make a man sick!—'

Another Time, when we were all at Dinner, it became Mr. *Selwin's* turn to be downed,—for he said 'What quantities of Bankers there are now!—Lord, I remember when there were only about 6!—but now the whole kingdom is filled with them,—we have nothing but Bankers, musicians & Dentists in all quarters.'

Did you ever hear the like?—*Clubbing* us with *Dentists*. I am surprised he omitted to mention *Barbers*, too!—

I think I have told you that the Cumberland's are gone.

Novr 8th

I have not writ some Time,—but *n'importe*, You are still a pacquet in *arrear*, & therefore my Conscience is well at ease.

On Wednesday [3 Nov.], just before Dinner, Dr. Delap arrived again from Lewes, &, in the Evening, ¦ he, Mr. Selwin & Mr. Tidy accompanied us to Sir John Shelly's. The *General* was otherwise engaged.

We found there only Sir John, his fair Lady, Mr. Woodcock, her Nephew, & a Miss Benson, a very *dark* & plain Young Woman, but shrewd & clever.

Dr. Delap, who always seats himself next me when he possibly can, began, in his abrupt way, to talk to me of his Play,—& told me he could not make Sheridan answer his Letters;—he had, when last here, asked my advice

---

[57] Venanzio Rauzzini had taken up residence in Bath in 1777, where with the violinist Lamotte he managed concerts at the New Assembly Rooms. He eventually settled there permanently (*New Grove*).

very earnestly what to do, & I told him I thought he had best write to the *Father*, as he acted as manager,[58]—this he had not only done, but made me dictate *what* he should write,—which was a very short *Billet*, merely to enquire of Mr. Sheridan Sen[r] how the parts were cast in his Play, & when it was to come out:—to this, however, he has received no answer;—how terribly negligent & inattentive these managers are!—I was very sorry for poor Dr. Delap, who is quite harassed with suspence & doubts:—but I was *not* sorry when he was called to the Whist Table, because I am afraid lest the occasional *fragments* of our Conversations that may be picked up, should make people imagine we are talking of some Theatrical Piece of *mine*.

Miss Benson, who cut out the first Rubber, immediately advanced to me, & entered into Conversation. I found she was very musical,—knew all the singers & Players, & was very intimate with the Harris Family,—with the Eldest Miss Harris[59] she corresponds at present. She also talked of my Father & of Hetty & Mr. Burney,—& so we did not want for *subjects*,[60]—yet I was glad when she was called to the Card Table, for though she is sensible & intelligent, there is a *hardness* in her Countenance, & a sort of *inflexibility* in her manner, that took off from all the *agrement* of Conversation.[61]

The next morning [4 Nov.] Mrs. & Miss Thrale & I went to Lewes, to visit the Shellys,—&, as usual, I was

[58] Richard Brinsley Sheridan, manager of the Drury Lane Theatre since 1776, had hired his father Thomas Sheridan (1719–88) in Sept. 1778 to help him with the management, at an annual salary of £600 (E. K. Sheldon, *Thomas Sheridan of Smock-Alley* (Princeton, 1967), pp. 284–6).

[59] Katherine Gertrude Harris (1750–1834), m. (1785) Hon. Frederick Robinson (1746–92) (C. T. Probyn, *The Sociable Humanist: The Life and Works of James Harris 1709–1780* (Oxford, 1991), p. xv).

[60] Miss Benson's passion for music was apparently so great that it influenced her love life. HLT described her in 1780 as 'being attached by Sentiment to Dick Cox', a banker who 'is Musick-mad' (*Thraliana* i. 455). This was Richard Cox (1719–1803). Since Cox was married, HLT supposed, correctly, that Miss Benson will 'never marry' (ibid.; see also *GM* xvii (1747), 296, lxxiii[2] (1803), 887, letter of Richard Cox, 21 Nov. 1791, Osborn).

[61] 'Miss Benson is a very sensible Woman, and I think a very good Woman. but course in her Person & her Mind, with an external Smoothness too—bad Wood with Varnish of Speenham Land, gives one some Idea of Miss Benson' (*Thraliana* i. 455).

obliged to have recourse to all my *powers of rhapsody* to prevent *succumbing* beneath the weight of the Miss Shelly's flippant *silliness,—folly* is really too respectable a word for them.

At Dinner we had 5 Gentlemen,—Mr. Shelly of Lewes, Mr. Tidy, Dr. Delap, &c, as usual, Mr. Selwyn & Mr. Blakeney.

I have always, at Dinner, the good fortune to sit next the *General,*—for I am sure if I had not I could not avoid offending him, because I am so eternally upon the *titter* when he speaks, that if I faced him, he *must* see my merriment was not merely at his *humour,* but excited by his ᐧ *Countenance,* his *Language,* his *winking,* & the very tone of his *Voice.* Indeed, even though he does *not* see the full effect of his power over my muscles, I have more than once feared affronting him;—but a little circumstance I will tell you, has lately made me easy upon that subject.

Mr. Selwin, who, as I have already hinted, indulges my enjoyment of Mr. Blakeney's Conversation by always trying to draw him out upon such topics as he most shews off in, told me, some Days since, that he feared I had now exhausted all his stories, & heard him discuss all his *shining* subjects of discourse;—but, afterwards, recollecting himself, he added that there was *yet* one in reserve, which was *Ladies learning Greek,*—upon which he had, last year, flourished very copiously.—The *occasion* was Miss Streatfield's knowledge of that Language, & the *General,* who wants 2 or 3 phrases of Latin to make him pass for a man of Learning, (as he fails not Daily to repeat his whole stock,) was so much incensed that a *fair Female* should presume to study *Greek,* that he used to be quite outrageous upon the subject. Mr. Selwyn, therefore, promised to treat me with hearing his Dissertation, which he assured me would Afford me no little Diversion. ᐧ

Accordingly, the next Time we all met, Mr. Selwin, very *innocently,* mentioned Miss Streatfield,—then enquired what *Greek* she knew,—& then proceeded to other similar Questions,—but all in vain!—the *General* preserved a profound silence.

Another,—& another Time, he made the same attempt,—but, another & another Time, was in the same manner defeated.

After these repeated Disappointments, Mr. Selwyn, one morning when he called here, (which he does *every* morning) expressed his surprise at his failure, & at the *General's* obstinate silence upon a matter he had formerly been so fond of.

'Why,—cried Mr. Thrale,—'tis on Miss Burney's account,—he takes it for granted *she*, too, is a Grecian.'

Every one agreed to this,—& thus I found that I was tolerably well with him, since he paid me so much deference as to forbear spouting a flourish *ready made, cut & dry*, & fit *at all points* for use, merely to avoid giving me uneasiness.—*You* may think this a small matter,—but *I*, who see how little he values who he offends, & how happy he is at every offered opportunity of pouring forth his set speeches & settled Harangues,—do thence infer that the *dear little Charmante* is extremely well in his good graces.

Mr. Selwyn, however, yet promises that, if I ⎸ will publicly disclaim all knowledge of Greek, & all inclination to know it, he will still ensure my hearing Mr. Blakeney's sentiments *la dessus*.

To return, however, to Thursday [4 Nov.].

I really begin to wish Dr. Delap came less to Brighthelmstone, for though, in his way, I like him vastly well, I am half ashamed of being so eternally engaged by him in private discourse;—it is true, our *subject*,—which is always his Play, gives me not any reason to shirk him,—but as it is a matter that, in delicacy to *him*, I am obliged to answer in the same low voice he speaks to me in,—& as nobody here can possibly guess our *theme*,—I cannot say I am thoroughly pleased with it.

I was, however, attacked this Day about *another* Quarter;—while we were waiting for Dinner, Mr. Selwyn came up to me, & entered into Conversation concerning Miss Benson—she seemed, he said, very sensible, & he wished much to have heard the Conversation which passed between us,—*but*, he rather severely added, there was something in her *look* so far from *captivating*, that he had not the courage—or indeed, inclination,—to address her.

Now I have seen, as I told him *en reponse*, a hundred Faces more *ugly*,—but the truth is, Miss | Benson's *character* of Countenance, which is hard & determined, Constitutes the forbidding part of her Visage, much more than any real defect in the Visage itself.

We both agreed, however, that we had a thousand Times rather converse with Lady Shelly, who has not half Miss Benson's strength of parts, merely because her *manner* was so infinitely more attractive.

While we were thus *communeing*, Mrs. Thrale, who was talking with Dr. Delap, suddenly turned round to us, &, very drily, said 'O—there's Mr. Selwyn flirting with Miss Burney!—there's a very good flirtation going forward there!—however, (again turning from us) I don't *look*,—that I may know nothing of it!'—

I leave you to guess whether, after this, the Conversation was *continued*.

During Dinner, Dr. Delap, in his abrupt way, suddenly called across the Table to ask where I Lived?—when I said in St. Martin's Street, he endeavoured to direct himself to it from the Mews,[62]—& Mr. Blakeney, to *help* him, led him to St. Martin's *Lane*, & I could not satisfy him it was a different place:—Mr. Tidy tried to make it out better for them,—Dr. Delap puzzled himself with turning from the right to the left, & the left to the Right till I was almost sore with Laughing,—but when | Mr. *Selwyn* said he knew the *House*, as well as street, from formerly visiting a Gentleman who Lived in it,[63]—Mrs. Thrale, very

---

[62] The Royal Mews, nr. Buckingham Palace.

[63] According to the rate books, the residents between Sir Isaac Newton and CB were: Paul Docmenique, Esq., 1728–35; Robert Crosby, 1736–59; and Archibald Murray, 1760–74 (*Survey of London* xx. 108). The first was probably Paul Docminique (1643–1735), an eminent London merchant of Huguenot origin and an MP (see Sedgwick), who may have helped the young Selwin become established in the banking business at Paris (though this last is pure conjecture). A second, perhaps more likely speculation, is that Selwin visited Murray for some reason after his retirement from banking in Paris and his return to England *c.*1763. A visit to Crosby is the least probable, as Selwin was mostly at Paris during Crosby's residence.

sarcastically, said 'No doubt, Sir, you'll soon *renew* your acquaintance with it!'—

Niether has her raillery stopt here;—for the next morning [5 Nov.] at Breakfast, not only she, but *Mr. & Miss* Thrale, gave *me* a *point blank* attack upon this subject,—& they all pretended that the *Cards were in my own Hands,*—Mr. Thrale gravely asked me if I would *accept* the offer?—& said, *he* should much approve of it, & would give *his consent* most willingly;—Miss Thrale, as seriously, pronounced *her* approbation;—but *Mrs.* Thrale vowed she should withhold *her's,* on account of the disproportion of our Ages.[64] She has, I know, in a most extraordinary manner, set her Heart upon my becoming *Lady Lade,*— &, wild as the wish may seem, I find it grows stronger & stronger, & it is with difficulty I can lead her from the subject whenever she has started it:—I am sure I heartily wish Sir John was married, for I am tired of his Name,— & God forbid I should ever, to speak seriously, so entirely change all my *present* inside as to be Bribed by ANY Fortune to connect myself with a man | of *profligate manners & weak Intellect?*—Great as is the honour this dear & partial Family (for *Mr.* Thrale joins in the wish) does me in desiring my alliance with them, I begin to half sicken whenever I hear the proposal,—it is so totally repugnant both to my principles & Inclinations. I am heartily glad he never visits here.

In regard to Mr. Selwyn,—as I am sure he thinks no more about me than about Miss Thrale, Miss Ord, or any other miss who is rather agreeable to him than *dis*agreeable, I niether thought it requisite to play the tender *Bergere* in accepting, or the haughty *Princesse* in refusing him.

Well,—to go on,—at Dinner we had our *3* Gentlemen,— for Dr. Delap was still here,—&, in the Evening, we had 2 Ladies, Mrs. & Miss Augusta Byron.[65]—

[64] Selwin was 37 years older than FB.

[65] Sophia née Trevannion (d. 1790), m. (1748) John Byron (1723–86), later Vice-Adm.; grandmother of Ld. Byron, the poet; and her daughter Augusta Barbara Charlotte Byron (*c.*1763–1824), later m. Christopher Parker (1761–1804), afterwards Vice-Adm. (*JL* i. 36 n. 88; *Piozzi Letters* i. 240 n. 16).

Mrs. Byron has much resemblance to Mrs. Strange;[66]—
thin, rather Tall, with sharp, piercing, penetrating Eyes,
a ready wit, a voluble Tongue, a Heart warm with Friendship, or passionate with enmity, & a manner quick, fiery
& alarming, though affectionate.

Augusta is not quite 17,—very Tall, not handsome, but
pleasing & agreeable in Face & Person,—modest, obliging,
soft, & amiable. She was *Dying* with impatience to see *me*,
because she *idolizes* Evelina,—& therefore I have not had
much trouble in making her my Friend,—*Friend*, indeed,
I cannot already call her,—but she is an *Enthusiast* about
me,—she I *looks* at me as if it was an ⌐*heaven*⌐ to see me,
Addresses me as if it was an *Honour* to speak to me, & *listens*
to me as if it was an *improvement* to hear me!—she quite
bores every body with my praise,—& her mother says 'tis
well if she does not hire a Chaise & run away with me.—
In short, she has just such a youthful & mad enthusiasm
about me as you & I, at her Age, should have had about
Richardson.— —

Mrs. Byron, too, honours me with the most distin-
guishing kindness,—& they both seem quite earnest to
continue the acquaintance in Town.—

We *Fair sex* had all the Conversation to ourselves after
Tea, as the 4 Gentlemen went to Whist: which, indeed, I
was very glad of, for Dr. Delap was so much disposed for
private talk, & so eternally engaging me in it,—though I
have not now one thing left to say about his Play, that he
has not heard repeatedly,—that he made me half ashamed
of his attention,—for, in a place such as this, nothing is
so easily settled as a *good intelligence* between any 2 people
who are often together.

Saturday morning [6 Nov.], to my great relief, he
returned to Lewes.

In the Evening we had Lady Shelly, Miss Benson & Mr.
Woodcock. All our Gentlemen Dined out;—& Mr. Thrale
vowed he would come Home as late as possible, that he I
might avoid seeing Miss Benson, to whose *bel viso* he has

---

[66] Mrs Isabella Strange, wife of Robert Strange the engraver, who with her
husband and children had been living in Paris since 1775. They were close
friends of the Burneys (*EJL* i. 55 n. 17, ii. 112 n. 23 and *passim*).

taken a most insuperable aversion! Did you ever hear the like of the airs of these men fellows—for Mr. Selwin gives the same reason for not *talking* with her!—He, however, did not avoid the House on her account, for at Mrs. Thrale's request, he stole from his Party as soon as Dinner was over, & came & joined ours,—which he did not quit till Bed Time: for, when our Ladies & their Beau retired, we had a long—& a *sad*—political Conversation.—He is among those I hate to hear *Croak*, because he is much in the way of knowing too well *why*,—as he has a large Correspondance Abroad, & an extensive acquaintance among ministers & Court People at Home:—& my Daddy Crisp himself thinks not more dismally of the state of our affairs!—

Miss Benson, I find, passes for a fine Harpsichord Player,—& when Lady Shelly announced her abilities with strong commendation, she looked *as though* the praise was all too little!—but I found it all *puff*,—she attempted Schobert & Boccherini,[67]—& played them much as Miss Coussmaker would have done.—[68]

When she was gone, Mr. Selwin dryly said to me 'Surely she was *excellent*—by that *air decidée* with which she performed!'—She is, indeed, by no means oppressed with humility,—but, let alone *that*, her Conversation is lively & agreeable enough— |

Well but,—I think I have not touched upon Mr. Blakeney, & therefore you cannot object to having a little more of his Conversation.

The other Day, at Dinner, the subject was, *married Life*,—& among various Husbands & Wives, Lord Longville[69] being mentioned, Mr. Blakeney pronounced his panegyric, & called him his Friend.—

---

[67] Johann Schobert (*c.*1735–67) and Luigi Boccherini (1743–1805), composers (*EJL* ii. 131–2 nn. 60–61).

[68] SEB thought Miss Benson to be a student of Charles Rousseau Burney (SEB to FB Nov. 1779, Barrett).

[69] Hon. Henry Yelverton (1728–99), 7th Bt; 3rd E. of Sussex, 4th Visc. de Longueville, and 18th Ld. Grey of Ruthin, 1758. This is the only possible identification, though it seems odd that he should be called 'Lord Longville' in 1779.

Mr. Selwin, though with much gentleness, differed from him in opinion, & declared he could not think well of him, as he knew his lady,[70] who was an amiable Woman, was used very ill by him.

'*How*, Sir?'—cried Mr. Blakeney.

'I have known him, answered Mr. Selwyn, frequently *pinch* her, till she has been ready to Cry with pain, though she has endeavoured to prevent it's being observed.'

'And I, said Mrs. Thrale, know that he pulled her Nose, in his frantic brutality, till he broke some of the vessels of it,—&, when she was *dying* she still found the torture he had given her by it so great, that it was one of her last Complaints.'[71]

The *General*,—who is all for Love & Gallantry—far from attempting to vindicate his Friend, quite *swelled* with indignation at this account, &, after a Pause big with anger, exclaimed 'Wretched Doings! Sir, wretched Doings!'

Did you ever hear such a term before for such barbarous meanness?

'Nay, I have known him, added Mr. Selwin, insist upon Handing her to her Carriage,—& then, with an affected kindness, pretend to kiss her Hand,—instead of which, he has almost bit a piece out of it!'

'Pitiful!—pitiful! Sir, cried the *General*,—I know nothing more shabby!—'

'He was equally inhuman to his Daughter,[72] said Mrs. Thrale, for, in one of his rages, he almost throttled her.'

'Wretched Doings! again exclaimed Mr. Blakeney, who glowed with passion,[73]—what! cruel to a fair Female!— Oh fie! fie! fie!—a fellow who can be cruel to Females &

---

[70] Hester Hall (*c.*1736–77), daughter of John Hall, of Mansfield Woodhouse, Notts, whom he married in 1757.

[71] According to HLT, he also used to horsewhip her, whereupon she would send for her brother to beat him (HLT to FB Dec. 1781, Berg). She died on 11 Jan. 1777, and her husband remarried on 29 Jan. 1778 (to Mary, daughter of John Vaughan, of Bristol, d. 1796).

[72] Lady Barbara Yelverton (1760–81). Perhaps in reaction to her father's treatment, she eloped, when age 15, to Gretna Green with Edward Thoroton Gould.

[73] '"*Wretched doings Ma'am!*" as old Blakeney says; "*Wretched doings!*"' (HLT to FB 19 Aug. 1781, Berg).

Children or Animals, must be a pitiful fellow indeed!—I wish we had had him here in the sea!—I should like to have had him stripp'd, & that kind of thing, & been well Banged by 10 of our Dippers here with a Cat o'nine Tails:—Cruel to a fair Female?—O fie! fie! fie!—'

I know not how this may *read*, but I assure you it's *sound* was too ludicrous to be borne decently.

However, I have never yet told you his most favourite story, though we have regularly heard it 3 or 4 Times a Day!—And this is about his *Health*.

'Some years ago, he says,—let's see, how many?—in the year 71.—ay, 71, 72,—thereabouts, I was taken very ill,—&, by d—d ill luck, I was persuaded to ask advice of one of these Dr. Gallipots,[74]—O how I hate them all!—Sir, they are the vilest pick-pockets,—know nothing, Sir!—nothing in the World!—poor ignorant mortals!—& then they pretend—Lord, Sir, I hate them all!—I have suffered so much by them, Sir,—lost 4 years of the happiness of my life,—let's see, 71—72—73—74—ay, 4 years, Sir!—mistook my Case, Sir!—& all ' that kind of thing,—why, Sir, my feet swelled as big as two Horses Heads!—I vow to God I'll never consult one of those Dr. Gallipots while I live again!—lost me, Sir, 4 Years of the happiness of my Life!—Why I grew quite an object!—You would hardly have known me!—lost all the Calves of my Legs!—had not an ounce of Flesh left, & as to the *Rouge*—why my Face was the Colour of that Candle!—Those deuced Gallipot fellows!—why they rob'd me of 4 years—let me see, ay,—71—72—&c—'

And then it all goes over again!

This story is almost *always* Apropos;—if *Health* is mentioned, it is Instanced to shew it's precariousness;—if *Life*,—to bewail what he has lost of it;—if *pain*—to relate what he has suffered;—if *pleasure*, to recapitulate what he has been deprived of;—but—if a *Physician* is hinted at—eagerly indeed is the opportunity siezed of inveighing against the whole Faculty. '

---

[74] A contemptuous term for apothecaries, after a kind of earthen glazed pot used by them for ointments and medicines (*OED*). Blakeney seems to mean both apothecaries and physicians (see below, p. 433).

97

To Susanna Elizabeth Burney

AJL fragment (Berg, Diary MSS I, paginated 1085–92), Nov. 1779
4 single sheets 4to, 8 pp.
Annotated (by FBA): Brighthelmstone. 5th Pacquet.
The first line (in brackets) has been written in a small hand by FBA
at the top of the page, and was probably copied from the conclusion
of an earlier leaf which has been destroyed.

[We keep to our Time of return.]
Now to go back to a little Journalising.
Sunday, Novʳ 7th — ⌐After Church⌐ Miss Thrale & I took
Miss Jess, the little mulatto, with us to the Steyn, — in our
way we met Mr. Selwin, who joined & walked with us
almost all the morning, & so fine was the Weather & so
mild & soft the sea Breezes, that had it been the 1st of
June we could not more have enjoyed ourselves.

In the Evening, we all went to the Rooms, where by
appointment, we Drank Tea with Mrs. & Miss Byron. We
met there all the folks we know here, & had a sociable &
agreeable Evening.

I was much surprised, while we were standing in the
Tea Room, at being suddenly addressed by Mrs.
Peachell,[75] a Lady who I have seen here some Time, —
she enquired after my Father & mother & *you*, — & then
began talking of Miss Coussmaker & Lady Hales, — this
led me to recollect having heard of her in that Family; —
& I think you have told me she was a sister of Sir Thomas
Hales.

Monday Evening [8 Nov.] we went to Mrs. Byrons. She
is really a charming Woman. Augusta was never tired of

---

[75] Margaretta née Hales (d.?1807), daughter of Sir Thomas Hales (*c.*1694–
1762), 3rd Bt, sister of Sir Thomas Pym Hales (*c.*1726–73), 4th Bt; m. (1769)
Samuel Pechell (d. 1782), of Richmond, Surrey, a Master in Chancery (his will,
PCC, dated 16 May 1778, prob. 18 May 1782; *GM* lii (1782), 207, lxxvii² (1807),
1084).

entreating me to visit them in Town,—which, with very great pleasure, I shall certainly do, *con permissione*.

Tuesday [9 Nov.] was a very agreeable Day, indeed, & I am sure a *merry* one to me: but it was all owing to the *General*, & I do not think you seem to have a true taste for him,—so I shall give you but ' a brief account of my entertainment from him.

We had a large party of Gentlemen to Dinner, who were—Mr. Hamilton, commonly called *single speech Hamilton*, from having made *one* remarkable speech in the House of Commons against Government, & receiving some douceur to be silent ever after.[76]—This Mr. Hamilton is extremely Tall, & handsome,—has an air of haughty & fashionable superiority, is intelligent, dry, sarcastic & clever. I should have received much pleasure from his Conversation powers, had I not previously been prejudiced against him by hearing that he is infinitely artful, double & crafty.

Captain Webster[77] accompanied him; he is in the Sussex militia, a Baronet's son, & a Tall handsome young man. He seems sensible & knowing, but talked so much of his own Detts [*sic*] & extravagance that I liked him not.[78]

Mr. Bateson[79] was also of their Party; a civil, quiet, sensible & well behaved young man.

The shrewd Mr. Tidy,—our ever solemn *General*, & our gentle, well bred, & good Mr. Selwin bring up the Rear.

The Dinner Conversation was too general to be well remembered;—niether, indeed, shall I attempt more than *partial scraps*, relating to *my Hero*, of what passed when we *adjourned to Tea*.

Mr. Hamilton, Mr. Selwin, Mr. Tidy & Mr. Thrale seated themselves to Whist. The rest looked on;—but the

[76] See above, p. 359 n. 19.

[77] Godfrey Webster (1748–1800), son of Sir Godfrey Webster (*c.*1695–1780), 3rd Bt, of Battle Abbey, Sussex; Capt., Sussex Militia, 10 June 1778 (*ML* 1779, p. 58; 1781, p. 61). He succeeded his father as the 4th Bt the following May.

[78] A prominent figure in the reform movement in Sussex, Webster was also a notorious rake, spendthrift and gambler cursed with an almost insanely violent temper, and he finally shot himself (Namier).

[79] Perhaps Thomas Bateson (b. *c.*1753), of Middlesex, matr. (Cantab.), 1773.

General, as he *always* does, took up the News Paper, with various *comments* made *aloud* as he went ǀ on reading to himself, diverted the whole Company. Now he would cry 'Strange! strange! that!' presently—'What stuff! I don't believe a Word of it!'—a little after 'O Mr. Bate![80] I wish your Ears were Cropt!'——then, 'Ha! Ha! Ha!—*Funnibus*![81] *Funnibus*, indeed!' And, at last, in a great rage he exclaimed 'What a fellow is this! to presume to arraign the conduct of persons of Quality!'

Having diverted himself & us in this manner till he had read every Column methodically through, he began all over again: & presently called out 'Ha! Ha!—here's a pretty thing,—' & then, in a plaintive voice, languished out some wretched verses.

Although the only mark of approbation with which they favoured these Lines was Laughing at them, he presently found some thing else equally bad, which he also praised,—also read—& also raised a Laugh at. Then 'Here's a Paragraph, he cries, I must read you about Ireland,—' & he *waded* through a long deal of uninteresting stuff, to which Nobody even *pretended* [to] listen, but went on either with Cards or Conversation as coolly as if he had read to himself. Having finished it, he looked about him, & exclaimed '*Quel Histoire!*'

A few minutes after, he began puffing & blowing with rising indignation, & at last Cried out 'what a fellow is this!—I should not be at all surprised if General Burgoyne Cut off both his Ears![82]

[80] Presumably the Revd Henry Bate (1745–1824), later (1781) Bate Dudley, cr. (1813) Bt. Bate was editor of the *Morning Post*, the organ of the Court party. His pugnacious articles sometimes got him into duels, which caused him to be known as the 'Fighting Parson'. Blakeney's reference to Bate suggests that he was reading the *Morning Post*, but the combination of items FB mentions is not in any of the issues of 2–9 Nov. 1779, nor has it been found in any other newspaper of that week scanned by the editors.

[81] Blakeney presumably garbles some Latin term.

[82] Gen. John Burgoyne had been under attack by the Government ever since his defeat at Saratoga in 1777 (see above, p. 198 n. 98). He responded by going over to the Opposition, and had just recently resigned both his regiment and his governorship of Fort William.

'You have great variety there,' cried Mr. Hamilton, drily, ⏐ but I think, Mr. Blakeney, You have read us nothing to Day about the Analeptic Pills.'[83]

Though we all *burst* at this, the General, unconscious of any Joke, gravely answered 'No, Sir,—I have not seen them yet,—but I dare say I shall find them by & by.'

And, by the Time the next Game was finished, he called out—'No,—I see nothing of the Analeptic Pills to Day,— but here's some Samaritan Drops.—'!!![84]

This insensibility excited a general *Grin*.

Soon after, he began to rage about some Baronet whose Title began *Sir Carnaby*[85]—'Jesus! he cried, what names people do think of!—here's another, now,—Sir Oenesiphorus Paul![86]—why now what a Name is that!—poor human Beings here inventing such a Name as that:—I can't imagine where they met with it!—it is not in the Bible.'

'There you are a little mistaken,' said Mr. Hamilton, coolly.

'Is it?—well I protest,—Oenesiphoras!—ha! ha!—'

'But you don't exactly pronounce it right, returned Mr. Hamilton,—it is Oenesiphor*us*—not *As*,—as you say it.'[87]

Mr. Blakeney made no answer, but went on reading the News Paper to himself.

'Is there nothing entertaining You can favour us with, Sir?' cried Mr. Selwin, who, with all his goodness & his quietness, enjoys the General as much as any *Tiezer* among us. Mr. Blakeney in a few minutes found some other Paragraph about his own Ireland,—Nobody, however, listened. Mr. Selwin, soon after, called upon him again,—

---

[83] 'Dr. James's Analeptic Pills', 'for Rheumatisms, &c.' is advertised, e.g., in the *London Chronicle* 4–6 Nov. 1779, s.v. 5 Nov. (xlvi. 435). 'Analeptic', a characteristic bit of contemporary medical jargon, means restorative or strengthening (*OED*).

[84] 'The UNIVERSAL BALSAMICK, called SAMARITAN WATER. ... 1. For strains, bruises, and injuries from blows or falls. 2. For fresh wounds of every kind. 3. For old sores and ulcers, even of the very worst nature." (and 7 other complaints) (*Morning Chronicle* 8 Nov. 1779).

[85] Sir Carnaby Haggerston (1756–1831), 5th Bt, of Haggerston Castle, Northumb.

[86] Sir Onesiphorus Paul (1746–1820), 2nd Bt, of Rodborough, Glos.

[87] See 2 Timothy 1: 16.

but he had now discovered the determined inattention of the Company, & therefore, very angrily, answered 'No, Sir,—no,—there's no going on so,—you're all [so] busy at your Cards, & all that kind of thing,—that there's no End to it!'—

Soon after, the Conversation [turned] upon Mrs. Thornhill,[88] |

[*top of page cut away*]

at her Table, & attends her regularly to the Rooms. This subject being pretty freely discussed, several very severe things were said by *every* body but Mr. Selwin, who was concerned for his *Cousin*,[89] & Mr. Blakeney, who happened to be a Friend of Mr. Lyon.[90] No respect, however, was paid either to Relationship or Friendship, & the satire went bitterly round,—till at last Mr. Selwin, shrugging his shoulders, half Laughing, & half vexed, cried out 'Alas for my poor Cousin!'—

'Nay, said Captain Webster, don't pity him,—I'm sure he's a *very* happy man,—I should think myself so in such a situation,—he has got a very pretty woman—'

'And a very *young* one,' said Mr. Bateson.

'And he's got a very good *Estate*, said Mr. Blakeney, & all that kind of thing.'[91]

'And he *seems*, said Mr. Hamilton, gravely,—in a fair way to go to Heaven.'

This Cutting sneer, closed the subject,—for what could be added to it?[92] Some Time after, Colds & Rheumatisms

---

[88] Perhaps Jane Gould (?1754–1827), daughter of Edward Gould, of Mansfield Woodhouse, Notts; m. (24 Apr. 1779) Bache Thornhill (1747–1830), Esq., of Stanton, Derbyshire (IGI). She was sister of the Edward Thoroton Gould who had eloped with Lady Barbara Yelverton, whose mother also came from Mansfield Woodhouse and whom Selwin seems to have known personally (above, pp. 425–26 and nn. 69–72). Bache Thornhill, like Mr Blakeney, who visits Mr Thornhill below, p. 438, later subscribed to *Camilla*.

[89] Mr Thornhill.

[90] Not identified.

[91] Bache Thornhill had inherited the estate of Stanton upon the death of his father in 1761.

[92] The sneer is presumably aimed at Mr Thornhill for countenancing Mr Lyon's attentions to Mrs Thornhill. If our identification of the Thornhills is correct, then the conduct of Lyon and Mrs Thornhill was all the more

being mentioned, Mr. Selwin asserted that the Ladies of England destroyed themselves by their slight Covering, & added that the French Ladies escaped a thousand Complaints to which *we* were all prone, merely by the warmth of their Cloathing.

'Ah, Ladies, cried Mr. Blakeney, if you would but Dress like |

[top of page cut away]

Mr. Hamilton, who had now given his Place at the Whist Table to Mr. Bateson, related to us a very extraordinary cure performed by a Physician, who would not *write* his Prescriptions, 'Because, said he, they should not *appear* against him, as his advice was out of rule:⁹³ but the Cure was performed, & *I* much honour, & would willingly employ such a man.'

'How? Exclaimed Mr. Blakeney, who always fires at the very name of a Physician, 'What! let one of those fellows try his *Experiments* upon you?—For *my* part, I'll never employ one again as long as I Live!—I've suffered too much by them!—lost me 5 years of the happiness of my Life!—ever since the year—let's see,—71—72—'

'Mrs. Thrale, interrupted Mr. Hamilton, I was in some hopes Dr. Johnson would have come hither with you.'

Mrs. Thrale answered him,—but Mr. Blakeney went on.

'One of those Dr. Gallipots, now,—Heberdeen,—attended a poor fellow I knew,—O, says he, he'll do vastly well!—& so, & so on,—& all that kind of thing,—but the next morning when he called,—the poor Gentleman was Dead!—there's your *Mr. Heberdeen* for you!—Lord God, Sir,—O fie!—fie!—'

'What will you do without them?' said Mr. Hamilton.

'Do?—Jesus! Sir,—Why Live like men!—who wants a pack of their d_____d Nostrums?—I'll never employ one again while I Live!—they mistook my case,—& Lord God,

---

scandalous, as Mrs Thornhill had been married less than 7 months, and was 7 months pregnant with the Thornhills' first child, Henry, b. 7 Jan. 1780.

⁹³ Contrary to custom (*OED* s.v. rule, *sb.* 3.c).

Sir, they played the very Devil with ⏐ me, & all that kind
of thing. — Sir they robbed me; of 5 years of the happiness
of my Life. — 71 — 72 — '

'What, interrupted Mr. Hamilton, are you 72?'

The *unmoved* contempt with which he asked this set the
whole Company in a roar, — Mr. Blakeney angrily
answered 'No, sir, no, — no such thing, — but I say —'

& then he went on with his story, — *no calves to his Legs —
mistook his case — Feet swelled as big as Horses' Heads — not an
ounce of Flesh —* & all the old phrases were repeated with
so sad a solemnity, — & attended to by Mr. Hamilton with
so contemptuous a *frigidity*, — that I was obliged to take up
a news paper, to hide ⌜the absolutely *convulsive* motions⌝
of my Face! — ⌜as to⌝ Miss Thrale, ⌜she burst out aloud,
&⌝ ran out of the Room, — Mr. Selwin Laughed till he
could hardly hold his Cards, — Captain Webster hallowed
quite indecently, — & Mr. Tidy *shook* all over as if he was
in an Ague. — I never, hardly, saw a whole party so merrily
disposed, — & yet the General never found it out! —

But how this subject runs away with me! — I *must* break
off some Time, — so adieu now.

Novr 15th

I have kept no Journal lately, — & am in no humour to
methodize, — but to keep up *the Chain*, I'll just tell the
Heads of the Chapters.

We have been to Ferle, — the seat of Lord Gage, — &
there we were very graciously received by his Lordship &
his Lordship's Lady, — & Sir Sampson Gideon, who is
there, — & they shewed me the House, — Lady Gage ⏐ &
every body attending me *as though* it had been the first
visit of *no small person*, — but indeed the civilities & kindness
I meet with from all Quarters — now the Cumberlands are
gone! — are amazing, — but especially from Mrs. Byron,
Lady Shelly, & Lady Hesketh, who, in their several ways,
have quite *subdued* me with Honours.

Lady Hesketh has been here 2 or 3 Times, — & we like
her much. To practical knowledge of the World she adds
a good Understanding, &, though rather formal, is well
bred & Agreeable.

The Shellys we have also visited & been visited by: & Miss Benson niether rises nor falls with me.

Poor Mrs. Byron is ill, & we have seen but little of her,—however Mrs. Thrale, good, friendly & zealous, attends her Daily.

Mr. Murphy has writ to Mrs. Thrale, & made honourable mention of *me*,—calling me '*Dr. Burney's 10th muse.*'

Mr. Hamilton Drank Tea here on Sunday [14 Nov.], & was, in his sarcastic way, extremely entertaining.

Mr. Tidy, too, has repeated his Visits,—but though we seem to *look kindly* enough at each other, I believe we are each too much upon the watch for *the other*,—for we niether of us *shew off.*

Well—what else have I to say?—nothing, but that I feel this *Influenza* advancing fast upon me,—& that Mr. Selwin has been a little *gallant* about it,—for when Mr. Hamilton was making his Entrance on Sunday, I began to Cough,—& Mr. Selwin, advancing to *me*, while the others were bowing & Courtsiing to *Mr. Hamilton*, said 'What makes Miss Burney Cough so?—' & took hold of my Hand to add *how ill he liked to hear me*;—You may believe I was not slow in withdrawing it,—but though I say *gallant*, I do not seriously mean it,—for if he likes me, or likes not my Cough, it is in a style very much *removed* from *gallantry*, & which does me much more honour, for it seems *bordering*, at least, upon Esteem, good opinion, & friendly regard. |

98   Brighton,
                                             16 November [1779]

To Samuel Johnson

ALS (National Library of Wales, MS 11103D), 16 Nov. 1779
Double sheet 4to, 3 pp.
Addressed (by Henry Thrale): To | Doctor S: Johnson | Bolt Court | Fleet Street | London
pmk: 17 NO BRIGHTHELMSTONE seal *franked*: Hfreethrale

Brighthelmstone,
Novr 16th

And so—while I am studying to avoid the contempt, or ridicule, of Dr. Johnson by forbearing to Write to him, I incur his displeasure by my silence![94]—

Well, Dear Sir, I must own I am too much 'pleas'd with the rebuke'[95] to complain of it,—& if you will condescend to receive such nothings as I can present You with, I shall have more happiness & more pride than You would bear to hear of in being allowed to send them.

If I have appeared less eager to accept your invitation of now & then reminding You of my Existence than might be expected, it has proceeded from nothing less than not caring for the ⎸permission;—but, to own the truth, I had an horror of Writing to You when I knew I had nothing to say,—for how could I Live so much at Streatham, & not perceive your cruelty to Letter scriblers? have I not again & again seen Irony gathering in your Eyes, & Laughter trembling upon your Lips as You have glanced over their unfortunate productions?—Ah Sir—Who was it called me a spy?—& how could I execute my Office without secretly resolving to profit by my observations?[96]

So much in my own vindication,—which, now I have written, I half fear to send,—for though I cannot now read my own Doom,—as I have ⎸that of others,—in your Countenance, yet I cannot help fancying I see You smiling at my self-importance, & hear you exclaiming 'A silly little Baggage! who cares whether she Writes or no?'

Now really, Sir, as Mr. Tyers[97] says, this is a *difficult solution!*—I will however, send off thus much, come of it

---

[94] See above, p. 412 n. 45.

[95] 'I own, I'm pleas'd with this rebuke' (Swift and Pope, *Imitation of the Sixth Satire of the Second Book of Horace*, l. 60). The imitation was written by Swift in 1714, published in 1727, and reprinted with additions by Pope in 1738. The line is Swift's (Pope, *Imitations of Horace*, ed. J. Butt (1961), pp. 248, 253).

[96] Much as she liked SJ, FB here clearly demonstrates how intimidated she was by him, claiming that she has 'nothing to say' to him while sending her sister scores of pages of scintillating character sketches, just the kind that SJ would have loved to receive.

[97] Thomas ('Tom') Tyers (1726–87), joint manager of Vauxhall Gardens (which his father founded) and friend of SJ. Boswell reports that he amused everybody 'by his desultory conversation' (*Life* iii. 308).

what may,—& if, in your next Letter to our dear mistress,
You will but send me a kind Word, I will either Write or
be quiet as you shall please to direct,—only *do* let it be a
kind Word for the sake of the very sincere Respect with
which I am,

Dear Sir,

Your obedient & obliged *Pupil*

Frances Burney.[98]

99   [Brighton,

16–?18] November [1779]

To Susanna Elizabeth Burney

AL incomplete (Barrett, Berg, paginated 1093–4), Nov. 1779
4 single sheets 4to, 8 pp.

Tuesday morn,

Nov[r] [16][99]

I am a little vexed, my dear Susy,—& so I will [tr]y to
*un*vex myself by writing to you,—

I have already told you the opinion of all [my] dear
Friends here with respect to Mr. Selwin's thoughts [of]
me,—& I have also told you *my* opinion of their mistake;—
Well, since that Time, the subject has never been mentioned *plumply*[1] till yesterday—but Mrs Thrale, who has
quite set her whole Heart against the Notion, has taken—
or rather *made*, Daily opportunities of telling Mr. Selwin
her aversion of marriages with a disproportion of age, &
has, almost every Time he has been here, either inveighed

---

[98] 'My Father has been to D[r] Johnson's this morn[g]— ... he bid my Father tell
us he had had *a rare Letter* from you—& seemed mightily pleased with your
having written.' (SEB to FB 18 Nov. 1779, Barrett). 'Pray tell my Queeny
how I love her for her letters, and tell Burney that now she is a good girl, I
can love her again' (SJ to HLT, 20 Nov. 1779, *LSJ* iii. 219).

[99] FB incorrectly wrote '17th'.

[1] Antedates the earliest example (also by FB) in *OED* by 7 years; this letter
is previously unpublished.

against them with serious energy, or Laughed them to scorn with all her powers of ridicule.

Mr. Selwyn, all this Time, constantly & readily has joined in her opinion,—& has so frequently, & so willing declared that he has *given the thing up,* that *all is over* with him, & that for the future he shall be a mere *spectator* of the World, that Mrs. Thrale's suspicions died away, &, insensibly, the subject has, of late, appeared less pointed.

I must, however, acknowledge that, during all this, he has by no means seemed piqued or offended [in] his behaviour to *me,*—on the contrary, to own the truth, I am inclined to think he likes me *very* well,—for though he has never once made me the least trifling Compliment, or ever made use of any particularly civil expression, his attention to me is more than commonly well bred, & his Eyes are almost perpetually directed my way.

Don't let this, however, mislead you into a notion that I regard Mr. Selwin as a *Conquest,* because I really do not,—his *kindness* towards me has in it no mixture of *gallantry,* & I am fully persuaded he has as resolutely settled to end his Days a Bachelor as if he were a French abbé, & *obliged* so to do.

This being my real opinion, *my* behaviour to *him* has been very unaffected, & as all I have seen of him has led me to both esteem & like him, I have never been backward to converse & associate with him.

Thus much preface;—now to yesterday [Mon., 15 Nov.].

We Dined quite alone, as Mr. Selwin & the General were engaged at Mr. Thornhill's. Mrs. Thrale, after Dinner, speaking of the uncommon favour in which I stood with the Brighthelmstoners in general, added 'Ay, Sussex is the place for Miss Burney,—all the folks here are never tired with admiring her,—she must have one of our Sussex Baronets at las[t.]'

She meant, I know, Sir John Lade, who has an Estate [here.][2]

'No, said Mr. Thrale, she shall have little Selwyn, that, *I* think, will do extremely well.'

[2] At Warbleton.

'So do not I! exclaimed Mrs. Thrale, what! marry a man old enough to be her Father!'

'Lord, cried I, Laughing, I dare say he will Live ᐧ full as long as I shall, however much older he may be.'

'So much the *worse*,' said Mrs. Thrale, & very firmly she discussed the cause.

Mr. Thrale, whose opinion is very different, declared, heatedly, & very seriously, that he should not be at all surprised at the proposal, which, indeed, he fully expects.

I was *much* surprised to hear him say this, after the many *disclaiming* speeches Mr. Selwin has made;—as to *Mrs.* Thrale, she is so amazingly partial [to] me, that I wonder not, now, at any expectations of *her's*, because she thinks the *World is my own*,—but *Mr.* Thrale, far less sanguine, & not at all romantic or flighty in his Notions, both surprises & perplexes me by adhering to this assertion.

Mrs. Thrale was, however, I believe quite alarmed [by] it,—& resolved, I fancy, to *strike a stroke* against [it] with all speed.

As yet, you will wonder why I should be *vexed*,—so now I come to *that* part of the story.

This morning [16 Nov.], at Breakfast, Mrs. Thrale declared herself very eager for Mr. Selwin to call,—which, as he constantly does, he did before Eleven. Miss Thrale [&] I have both of us violent Colds, & Mrs. Thrale, having hastily talked over that, fell, I know not how, but very abruptly, upon the subject of marriage, [&] with all her strength of argument, & all her [capac]ity of raillery, she *downed* disproportioned matches ᐧ with an earnestness that shewed her whole Heart was in her subject.

Mr. Thrale tried to *look* her silent,—but she only went on more warmly;—he then looked at *me* as if to see how *I* took it,—*Mrs.* Thrale most expressively did the same,—& *Miss* Thrale did nothing else,—except, indeed, that she Laughed!—

I understood them, as you may imagine, easily enough from the beginning,—but when they all thus assailed *me* with their Eyes, as well as Mr. Selwin, I felt so conscious of their meaning, that in spite of my utmost efforts to

seem to take the Conversation as *general*, I presently felt
my whole Face on Fire!—Nobody, I believe, has so *very*
little command of Countenance as myself!—

Mr. Selwyn, I am certain, also well understood them,—
but he did not, as hitherto, declare his own opinion the
same;—the attack, I believe, was so strong as to surprise
him.

Mrs. Thrale, to finish all, at last said 'But perhaps I
should not say all this to *you*, Mr Selwin, as you are now
on your preferment.'[3]

Mr. Selwin made a kind of embarrassed Laugh & said
something—but so like *nothing* that it could not be understood. Whether *her* earnestness, [or] *my* Colouring, which
I fear he could not but see, robbed him of his usual
disclaiming readiness I know not I but certain it is that we
were both of us horribly embarrassed. This dear Mrs.
Thrale is the most unguarded of all human Beings, &
though with my whole soul I most affectionately & most
truly Love her as she *is*, I cannot help Daily wishing she
would a *little* more guide herself like other folks.

The power there is in an *attack* to make an appearance
of *guilt* is astonishing;—ill founded as are Mrs. Thrale's
apprehensions, niether Mr. Selwin nor I could have
looked much more confused had we each been as full of
Design as I am satisfied we were of innocence. But I am
actually *shocked* that I should thus tacitly have marked *my*
consciousness of their meaning by that vile Colouring:
but though I could have heard all their *speeches* placidly
enough, the being so *looked* at would have made me
ashamed had the Object in question been as much *out* of
the Question as Mr. Burney-Holt.[4]

I think I saw that he was hurt,—he took hardly any
kind of notice of me while he stayed,—& seemed half-

---

[3] HLT perhaps means that Selwin was now living on an inheritance which
he might have been denied had his father remarried a much younger woman.

[4] FB's half-cousin Thomas Burney (b. 1738), who had taken the additional
name of Holt at the request of an uncle, *c.*1770, but who had evidently
relinquished the additional name (after his uncle's demise?) by the time of his
death, in 1799 (*EJL* i. 92 n. 38, 110 and n. 20; his will, PCC, prob. 26 Feb.
1799). FB described him as 'very deficient both in good Temper & good
breeding' (*EJL* i. 110).

inclined, as he quitted the Room, to avoid making me, as usual, a separate Bow;—probably he thinks it impertinent enough to seem thus, in a manner, *rejected* where he never Dreamt of offering himself to be *accepted*.

I have written all this *schotffe* [*sic*][5] in Intervals of a nefarious Headache, which accompanies a bad Cold that I has made me beg leave to decline going down to Dinner. I am better, however, & shall make my appearance at Tea.— —

I have just been interrupted by Mrs. Thrale—it is almost *charming* to be ill where she is,—her kindness, sweetness, & affectionate attention would make amends for much more pain than I suffer at present.

Dr. Delap is just come from Lewes, to pass the Week at Brighton, & is below with the General & Mr. Selwyn. They have all, she says, at the motion of the General, been Drinking my Health,—'He enquired, she added, for *the Charmante*, as soon as Dinner appeared,—& commended you much, & said you were really a very pretty sort of a little Female;—& Dr. Delap said you were the charmingest Girl in the World for a Girl who was so near being *nothing*, & they all agreed nobody ever had so little a shape before, & that a Gust of Wind would blow you quite away.—But Mr. Selwin is *very* sorry indeed,—& says nothing,—I begin to think he is half in love in good earnest,—well, after all, he is a *very* good Creature—But the General enquired when you *Bathed*, & says he is sure you were not properly *dipped*,—Hey day, cried Dr. Delap, do you think the sea is not big enough to dip Miss Burney?—why I am sure I could Bathe her in a Bason of Water!—so they are all talking of you,—but Mr. Selwin is afraid sadly lest you I should be *neglected*,—& asks if you should not *have* something,—well, I love him for it, I declare,—that I *do*.'

I am sure if he or any body saw how I am *attended*, they would be almost *ashamed*, for this most sweet woman waits upon me as if I was the *hopes* of *her House*.

---

[5] See above, p. 41 n. 17.

Nov^r [18th]^6

When I went down stairs, I found them all assembled
to Tea, — Dr. Delap approached me full speed, & enquired
how I did, & rejoiced at my coming down, with his usual
abruptness, —

'Here, cried Mr. Blakeney, here comes Mademoiselle, —
[he] then came & solemnly congratulated me on being
able to quit my Room.

But Mr. Selwin said not a word! — Mrs. Thrale has really
made him afraid of looking within a mile of me, which
he hardly did all the Evening. Indeed had you heard how
pointed & how *bitter* her speeches were, you would not
wonder. He was grave & silent the whole Evening.

Dr. Delap talked for Every body! — he was in prodigious
spirits; — he has heard, at last, that his Tragedy is preparing for the stage. He asked me 100 Times what [I]
would advise him to do concerning casting the parts! [*Go*]*d*
bless him! he has very little occasion to trouble [his] Head
about *that* for, far from waiting for *his* [*permis*]*sion*, the
managers will not even take the pains [to] tell him their
own actual determination.

The next Day [17 Nov.] we had the very same Party; —
Mr. [Selw]in began the Day with the same reserve he
finished the last, — a reserve which however it might
indeed, I saw it *did*, quiet *Mrs. Thrale*, struck *me* in another
manner.

Dr. Delap rejoiced very good-naturedly in seeing me so
much better; — Mr. Blakeney pressed me to *Eat & Drink*
with much solemnity of kindness, — 'Why, Ma^{lle}, you Eat
nothing! — it's all very fine, & delicate, & all that kind of
thing, — but then you'll be no *substance*, — & so & so on, —
& then we [will] lose you! —'

'Miss Burney thinks she can be no smaller, said Dr.
Delap, so she thinks it hardly worth while to Eat at all
[—] only loss of Time: I suppose a Chicken would feed
her a month.

'O fie! fie! fie!' exclaimed the General, —

---

^{6} Conjecturally supplied; the page is torn.

'Ay, continued the Dr.—I assure you, Miss Burney, Mr. Blakeney has been murmuring very much about your not Eating. He is the first Person I ever heard find fault with Miss Burney,—I believe nobody ever *did* before.'

Dr. Delap, I assure you, makes me speeches such as these.—

In leaving the Dining Parlour, I happened to drop one of [my] gloves under the Table, but, to avoid a *fuss*, I took no notice of it, but got another Pair from up stairs. When the men were summoned to Tea, Mr. Selwin came first,—& holding my Glove in his Hand, called out 'Has nobody lost any thing?'

I claimed it immediately,—he pretended he had a right [to] put it *on*,—& he pulled off the new one which I was just Drawing on before I was aware of his Design,—however I made him stop *there*,—but he managed to press my Hand between both his before I could recover my *Property*.

This sort of *Badinage*, however, may always pass for [no]thing,—but I am going, my dear Susy, to confess to you what I do *not* think passes for Nothing,—charging you to let [*no*] *human Being* but Charlotte see the same,—& Charlotte [is] as discreet as she is affectionate,—I would trust her with my [life.]

When I told you my total disbelief of the suggestions of [Mr.] Selwin's opinion of me, I told you what I really thought, [but] since that morning's hard attack, I have changed my notio[ns.] |

[*rest of the letter missing*]

100   Streatham,
                                    [27 November 1779]

To Charles Burney

ALS (Berg, paginated 1333–35), Nov. 1779
Double sheet 4to, 3 pp.   red wafer
Addressed: Dr. Burney—
Annotated (by FBA): Credo 79 80 ✳

Streatham,⁷ Sat. mornᵍ [27 Nov.],
2 O'Clock.

My dearest Sir,

We have this moment finished the Critic;⁸—I have been extremely well entertained with it indeed,—the first Act seems as full of wit, satire & spirit as it is of Lines;—for the rest, I have not sufficiently attended to the plays of *these degenerate Days* to half enjoy or understand the censure & ridicule meant to be *lavished* on them;—however, I could *take in* enough to be greatly diverted at the flighty absurdities so well—though so severely pointed out.—

If you mean to let Mrs. Crewe⁹ know of this indulgence, I am sure you will tell her how much I am obliged to her for allowing it, *comme il faut, & all that kind of thing.*¹⁰—

Our dear master came Home to Day quite as well as you saw him Yesterday. He is in good spirits & good humour, but I think he looks sadly.—So does our Mrs. T.—who agitates herself into an almost perpetual Fever.—¹¹

Adieu, my dearest Sir,—a thousand thanks for this Treat,—Dr. Johnson is very gay & sociable & comfortable, & quite as kind to me as ever,—& he says the Bodlein [*sic*] Librarian has *but done his Duty*,¹²—& that when he goes to Oxford, he will write *my* Name in the Books, & my Age when I writ them; & sign it with his *own*,—'& then, he says, the World may know that we

⁷ FB had returned with the Thrales to Streatham from Brighton on 23 Nov. (*Thraliana* i. 410; below, p. 450).

⁸ Sheridan's comedy, lampooning Richard Cumberland as Sir Fretful Plagiary, had been first performed 30 Oct. 1779 at Drury Lane (*LS 5* i. 292).

⁹ Sheridan, who was rumoured to be in love with Mrs Crewe, had lent her a MS copy of the play, which she in turn gave to CB on 18 Nov. (SEB to FB, 3–27 Nov. 1779 (Barrett)). CB visited Streatham with SJ on 25 Nov., and left the copy for FB and HLT to read. FBA incorrectly noted on this letter: 'Sheridan's Critic, printed at this time, but unpublished'. The play in fact was not printed until 1781, at which time Sheridan dedicated it to Mrs Greville, Mrs Crewe's mother and FB's godmother.

¹⁰ FB is imitating Mr Blakeney.

¹¹ Mr Thrale had suffered a second stroke while returning from Brighton. See below, p. 451.

¹² FBA noted: 'The Bodlein Librarian had placed Evelina in his noble Library—to the author's astonished delight.' The Bodleian Librarian at this time was John Price (*c.*1735–1813), M.A. (Oxon.), 1760, B.D., 1768.

so mix'd our studies, & so join'd our Fame—[13]

for we shall go down Hand in Hand to Posterity!—'[14] |

Mrs. T. sends her best love,—I don't know when I can leave her, – but not, unless you desire it, till Mr. T. seems better established in Health, or till Mrs. D'Avenant can come hither.

Mr. Seward is now here. Once more, Dearest Sir, *Good Night* says

Your Dutiful
& most affectionate
F.B.[15] |

101 [Streatham,
4 December 1779]

With Hester Lynch Thrale
to Charles Burney

AL and ALS (Boston Public Library, Ch.I.1.14–15), Dec. 1779
Single sheet 4to, 2 pp.
Annotated (by FBA):—79
HLT begins the letter, which was taken to town by Mr Selwin and presumably delivered by his servant (below, p. 453).

Your Daughter Dear Sir is no longer *better* but *well.* She will eat her boil'd Chicken today, & I hope find an Appetite for it; she slept sweetly, I saw her twice in the Night, & all the Symptoms of Fever are gone today. What an efficacious Remedy is James's Powders!—She took a 3:ᵈ again last Night—only think! 24 Grains in all, a whole Paper, has that dear Girl swallow'd; & ⌐though we did not expect it⌐, we have a perfect Cure.—Yesterday there

---

[13] Cf. Pope, *Epistle to Mr. Jervas*, ll. 9–10: 'And reading wish, like theirs, our fate and fame, / So mix'd our studies, and so joined our name.'

[14] There is no evidence in any of the Bodleian copies of *Evelina* that SJ carried out his intention (*LCB* i. 293 n. 8). He may of course have simply been joking. He visited Oxford again in 1781, 1782 and 1784 (*Life* iii. 454).

[15] For CB's reply to this letter, written the same day, see *LCB* i. 292–3.

was Headach & Lassitude, but today all is well—& she shall say so herself.

My poor Master droops miserably, but has no visible Illness: We must do as well as we can.

[*FB continues:*]

Instead, my dearest Sir, of adding a few lines about *myself*, I can only tell you about *Mrs. Thrale*—she has been quite a *slave*—as well as both *physician* & *Nurse* to me ever since Thursday Even^g [2 Dec.]—& I have ˡ not taken any thing but out of her own Hand,—so I hope you will thank her a little, for she's quite *past me*.[16]—I am this morning fit for a *Country Dance*, had we not rather a lack of Partners,—so, hoping with you for a Merry Christmas,— I am most dear Sir!—Your FB—
My best love to all.—
& that kind of thing—

102   Streatham,
                        6–[9] December [1779]
To Susanna Elizabeth Burney

AJL (Berg, paginated 1317-[28]), Dec. 1779
6 single sheets 4to, 12 pp.   wafer
Addressed: Miss Susan Burney

Streatham, Monday, Dec. 6—

As I am now well enough to employ myself my own way, though not to go down stairs, I will take this first opportunity I have had since my return hither to again

---

[16] 'Fanny Burney has kept her Room here in my house seven Days with a Fever, or something that She called a Fever: I gave her every Medcine [*sic*], and every Slop with my own hand; took away her dirty Cups, Spoons, &c. moved her Tables, in short was Doctor & Nurse, & Maid—for I did not like the Servants should have additional Trouble lest they should hate her for't— and now—with the true Gratitude of a Wit, She tells me, that the *World thinks the better of me* for my Civilities to her. It does! does it?' (*Thraliana* i. 413).

write to my dearest Susan. Your letters, my love, have been more than usually welcome to me of late,—their Contents have been very entertaining & satisfactory, & their arrival has been particularly seasonable,[17]—not on account of my *illness*—that alone never yet lowered my spirits as they are *now* lowered, because I knew I must ere long, in all probability, be again well,—but oh Susy I am— I have been—& I fear must always be alarmed indeed for Mr Thrale—& the more I see & know him, the *more* alarmed, because the more I love & dread to lose him—

I am not much in cue[18] for Journalising—but I am yet less inclined for any thing else, as writing to my own Susy commonly lightens my Heart,—so I'll e'en set about recollecting the *good* as well as *bad* that has past since I writ last,—for *else* I were too selfish—I cannot remember where I left off.—but to go back to the last few Days we spent at Brighthelmstone I must tell you that on the last Friday [19 Nov.]—But I cannot recollect *anecdotes*, nor write them if I did,—& so I will only draw up an *Exit* for the Characters to which I had endeavoured to Introduce you.

Lady Hesketh made us a very long, sociable & friendly Visit before our departure, in which she appeared to much advantage, with respect to conversation abilities, good breeding, & good *goust* for us all,—I saw that she ¦ became quite enchanted with Mrs. Thrale,—& she told *her* I know not what fine things of *me*,—she *made* me talk away with her very copiously, by looking at me, in a former Visit, when she was remarking that Nothing was so formidable as to be in Company with *silent observers*;— where upon I gathered courage, & boldly entered the Lists,—& her Ladyship has enquired my Direction of Mrs. Thrale, & told her that the Acquaintance should not drop at Brighton, for she was determined to *wait upon me in Town*. So I entered not the Lists to be *disgraced*, which is a very good thing.

[17] FB had presumably just received SEB's AJL to her of 30 Nov. – 4 Dec. 1779 (Barrett), delivered by HLT's servant, whom HLT was dispatching to town frequently as a messenger.

[18] Mood, disposition, humour, frame of mind (*OED* s.v. cue, *sb.*² 4).

We saw, latterly, a great deal of the Holroyds,—the *Colonel*—for he has given up his *majorship* in the militia & is raising a Company for himself,[19] appeared to us just as before, sensible, good humoured & pleasant,—& just as before also persued his Lady,—tittle-tattling, monotonous & tiresome.

They had a *Miss Cooke*[20] with them,—who I only mention because her name was also *Kitty*—& because her resemblance to *our* Kitty did not stop there, for she was always gay & always good humoured.

Lady Shelley was as civil to me as Lady Hesketh. Indeed I have good reason to like Sussex!—as my Cold prevented my waiting upon her with Mrs. Thrale to take leave, she was so good as to come to *me*. I am rather sorry she never comes to Town, for she is a sweet woman, & *very* handsome.

Miss Benson called upon us several Times,—& I abide exactly by what I have already said of her.

Dr. Delap was with us till the Friday Night [19 Nov.] preceding our departure;—he has asked me, in his unaccountable way, *if I will make him a dish of Tea in St. Martin's Street?*—

We had, also, made an acquaintance that we occasionally saw with a Miss Sto⟨w⟩ that I have never had Time to mention,—little Girl she is, just 7 years old, & plays on the Harpsichord so well that she made me very fond of her;—she Lived with a mother & Aunt niether of whom I liked,—but she expressed so much desire to *see Dr.*

[19] Holroyd, a Major in the Sussex Militia, resigned in order to raise his own regiment, the 22nd (or Sussex) Regiment of (Light) Dragoons, of which he took command with the rank of Lt-Col., 14 Dec. 1779 (*AL*, 1780, p. 58; above, p. 273 n. 34). 'Colonel Holroyd's Light Dragoons are reported to the War-office as complete. They have considerably more than their number. It is said there is not a finer corps in the whole army' (*Morning Post* 5 Nov. 1779).

[20] Presumably the 'Miss Cooke' whom Edward Gibbon asks Holroyd to 'respectfully salute' in a letter to Holroyd, 6 Oct. 1779 (*The Letters of Edward Gibbon*, ed. J. E. Norton (1956), ii. 228). J. E. Norton, referring to FB's passage (publ. *DL* i. 445), conjectures (op. cit. n. 3) that this was a sister of Mrs Holroyd's sister-in-law Mrs Benjamin Way, i.e., one of the daughters of William Cooke (1711–97), Provost of King's College, Cambridge. William Cooke's daughter Catherine, however, had m. (Oct. 1775) Samuel Hallifax, later Bishop successively of Gloucester and St Asaph; this 'Kitty' Cooke, therefore, was perhaps a cousin and namesake.

Burney, & is so clever & forward & quick & ingenious a Child, that I could not forbear giving her my Direction in Town, which she received very gladly, & will, I am sure, find me out as soon as she leaves Brighton.[21]

Miss Thrale & I paid visits of *congée* to Mrs. Chamier & Miss Emily Jess,—what you tell me of that little Girl's opinion of Miss Thrale I am very sorry to say seemed, by all I have heard, to be the *general* opinion of her.[22]—She follows so exactly the bent of her humour, regardless whether she pleases or offends, that I find—& I love her well enough to find it with concern, she is very generally disliked.

We went together, also, to Miss Byron,—but she was invisible with this *Influenza*;—the mother, however, admitted us,—& spent almost the whole 2 Hours she kept us in *exhorting* me most kindly to visit her, & promising to Introduce me to the Admiral,—which I find is a *great thing*, as he always avoids seeing any of her Female Friends, even Mrs. Thrale, from some odd peculiarity of Disposition.

On Monday [22 Nov.], at our last Dinner, we had Mr. Tidy, Mr. Blakeney & Mr. Selwin.—& in the Evening came Mrs. Byron.—

Mr. Tidy I liked better & better,—he reminded me of *Mr. Crisp*,—he has not so good a Face, but it is that *sort* of Face, & his *Laugh* is the very same!—for it first puts every Feature in comical motion, & then fairly shakes his whole Frame,—so that there are tokens of thorough enjoyment

---

[21] Such a visit is not recorded. This was presumably the same Miss Stow (or Stowe) who, with her mother and younger sister, visited Mrs Delany in St James's Place in May 1781. Mrs Delany commented: 'My company last Tuesday were, Mrs. Stow and her 2 daughters the youngest but 6 and plays several minuets and cotillions, in most exact time and perfectly *clean*, so she bids fair to be as *early* a *wonder* as her sister! ... The little *demi semi quaver* played a minuet in such good time without any hesitation that y[r] daughter [Miss Port] and the eldest Miss Stowe danced to it!' (Mrs Delany to Mrs Port, 6–8 May 1781, *Delany Corr.* vi. 20). The talented little girls and their mother and aunt have not been further identified; their family no doubt destined them to bring their musical gifts to the relative obscurity of genteel marriages.

[22] 'Tuesday Eve[g] [16 Nov.] M[r] Chamier called ... —He said his little Emily had written him word she had *seen Miss Burney*, & *liked her vastly*, but *did not like Miss Thrale at all!*' (SEB to FB, 3–27 Nov. 1779 (Barrett)).

from Head to Foot!—He & I should have been very good Friends, I am sure, if we had seen much of each other,— as it was, we were *both* upon the watch, drolly enough.—

Mr. Blakeney, though, till very lately, I have almost *Lived* upon him, I shall not *bore* you with more than naming—for I find you make no *defence* to my hint of having given you too much of him,—& I am at least glad you are so sincere.

With respect to Mr. Selwyn,—as my last Pacquet was finished but the very Night before we set off, ᛁ I have already told you every thing concerning him:—yet I should not be a faithful Narratoress[23] if I asserted that the easy & unaffected manner in which he had, when I then finished my account, conducted himself towards me was to the *last* the same,—for 2 or 3 Times he seemed again *wavering* into more particularity,—one Time, while he was at Cards he missed Deal, & told me he was thinking of the *Herring Bone* I had swallowed at Dinner (which had, indeed, been very troublesome to me) & another Time, he took my Hand, though it was crossed formally before me, between both his—without either Rhyme or reason of pretence for so doing.—

& of Mrs. Byron I have nothing more to add.

Tuesday morning [23 Nov.], before we set out, Mrs. Thrale & I took a stroll by the sea side, *pour prendre congée* of that sole *ornament* & *support* & *cause* of the Town of Brighthelmstone. In our way we again saw Mr. Selwyn, who was just returning Home from his sea plunge.—He expressed much anxiety to hear News of Mr. Thrale,—& Mrs. Thrale readily promised to write to him soon:— upon which, turning round to me, he said 'I had been thinking of begging Miss Burney to write,—*only a line*— *only a Note*—' he added with quickness, as if fearful he had said wrong.—But Mrs. Thrale did not hear—& I did not answer him. ᛁ

And now my dear Susy to Tragedy—for all I have yet writ is *Farce* to what I must now add—but I will be brief for your sake as well as my own,—

---

[23] This form not in *OED*; paragraph previously unpublished.

Poor Mr. Thrale had had this vile Influenza for 2 Days before we set out,—but then seemed better,—we got on to Crawley all well,—he then ordered 2 of the servants to go on to Rhygate & prepare Dinner,—mean Time he suffered dreadfully from the Coldness of the Weather, he shook from Head to Foot, & his Teeth *chattered* aloud very frightfully: when we got again into the Coach, by degrees he grew warm & tolerably comfortable:—but when we stopt at Rhygate,—his speech grew inarticulate, & he said one word for another,—I hoped it was accident,—& Mrs. Thrale, by some strange infatuation, thought he was *joking*,—but Miss Thrale saw how it was from the first;—by very cruel ill luck, too tedious to relate, his precaution proved useless, for we had not only no *Dinner* ready, but no *Fire*, & were shewn into a large & comfortless Room,—The Town is filled with militia.— Here the cold returned dreadfully,—& here, in short, it was but too plain to *all* his Faculties were lost by it!—Poor Mrs. Thrale worked like a *servant*,—she lighted the Fire with her own Hands,—took the Bellows, & made such a one as might have roasted an ox in 10 minutes,—but I will not dwell on particulars,—after Dinner Mr. T. grew better,—& for the rest of our Journey was sleepy, & mostly silent!—It was late in the Night I when we got to Streatham,—Mrs. Thrale consulted me what to do,—I was for a physician immediately,—but Miss Thrale opposed that, thinking it would do harm to alarm her Father by such a step;—however Mrs. Thrale ordered the Butler to set off by 6 the next morning for Dr. Heberden & Mr. Seward.

The next morning, however, he was greatly better,—& when they arrived he was very angry,—but I am sure it was right;—Dr. Heberden ordered nothing but *Cupping*.[24]—

[24] Cf. HLT's account of the episode: 'On Monday last the 22: of Nov[r] he complain'd of the headache, eat no Dinner & looked most dreadfully ... We ... set out yesterday Tuesday 23: ... and the Weather was very Cold. M[r] Thrale said his head ached, but when we got to *Cookfield* [HLT adds in a note 'I mean *Rye Gate* where we were to dine'] he had such a shivering & Torpor came on as shocked me, & set poor Miss Burney o' crying—his Wits were quite unsettled, & his Articulation almost wholly lost; Dinner revived him a little, but the

Mr. Seward was very good & friendly,—& spent 5 Days here,—during all which Mr. Thrale grew better.

Dr. Johnson, you know, came with my dear Father the Thursday [25 Nov.] after our return. You cannot, I think, have been surprised that I gave up my plan of going to Town immediately,—indeed I had no Heart to leave either *Mr.* Thrale in a state so precarious, or his dear wife in an agitation of mind hardly short of a Fever.—

Things now went tolerably smooth,—*very* tolerably, though Miss Thrale & I renewed our Latin Exercises with Dr. Johnson, & with great *eclat* of praise:[25]—at another Time [I] could have written much of *him* & of *Mr. Seward*, for many very good Conversations past,—but now I have almost forgot all about them.

The Tuesday following [30 Nov.] I received your kind Letter, & *Instances* to return on Thursday [2 Dec.] with my Father,[26]—but [I] determined to take no measures either way till I saw how matters went at the last.

Wednesday morning [1 Dec.], while Miss Thrale & I were taking our Lessons of Dr. Johnson, Mr. Selwin was suddenly announced, & entered the Library. Mrs. Thrale had kept her ˡ promise, & acquainted him of the melancholy state of the House, & he was so impatient for further intelligence, that he was now only on his *road* from Brighton, for he could not go on to Town before he had been to Streatham. For Benevolence & friendliness I believe he will yield to none. Unfortunately niether our master or our mistress were at Home;—he stayed with us about half an Hour, & then ran away because his Carriage & Brighton Luggage &c were waiting.

Evening & the Night he was comatose, & I called in Heberden in the Morning. he ordered Cupping which restored him so far that we are now just as we were before this last Attack.—' (*Thraliana* i. 410).

[25] FB's misgivings about these lessons were confirmed when her father eventually disapproved of them. Two years later HLT noted that 'Dʳ Burney did not like his Daughter should learn Latin even of *Johnson* who offered to teach her for Friendship, because then She would have been as wise as himself forsooth, & Latin was too Masculine for Misses—' (*Thraliana* i. 502). Queeney went on (SJ, *Letters* ii. 311 n. 4).

[26] 'Thursday ... we all hope to see you return home in the Eveᵍ wᵗʰ my Father—' (SEB to FB, 3–27 Nov. 1779, s.v. 27 Nov. (Barrett)).

The next Day [2 Dec.] I was far from well, as my dear Father must have told you,—& I got worse & worse, & could not go down to Dinner,—but in the Evening being rather better, I just popt down to play one Rubber with dear Mr. Thrale, whose Health I have truly at Heart, & who is only to be kept from a heavy & profound sleep by Cards,—& then I was glad to come back, being again worse:—but let me add I had *insisted* on performing this feat.

I took 8 grains of James' Powder,—for I felt too ill to take less, & had a miserable Night, but in the morning [3 Dec.] grew more easy,—I kept my Bed all Day, & my ever sweet Mrs. Thrale Nursed me most tenderly, letting me take nothing but from herself,—the next Night was better,—& the next morning [4 Dec.] Mr. Selwin came again,—he had heard, the preceding Evening, by some Lady who had seen my mother, that I was ill,—& before Breakfast he was here.—That Lady, I suppose, was Mrs. Denoyer.[27] |

He heard a good account of me,—& the Note you had that Day, Saturday [4 Dec.], from Mrs. Thrale, he took to Town, &, I suppose, sent by his servant.

I will say no more about the Illness, but that it was short though rather violent. Mr. Thrale has visited me every Day very affectionately;—his Daughter is, I believe, no happier for my confinement;—on Saturday [4 Dec.], as I got into Mrs. Thrale's Dressing Room to Dinner, Dr. Johnson also visited me:—on Sunday [5 Dec.] Mr. Murphy

[27] Sophia Sallier (*c*.1733–1810), m. 1 (1757) Philip Denoyer (d. 1788), a dancing master to the Royal Family; m. 2 (1789) Simon Wilson, Esq. The Denoyers may at this time have been neighbors of the Burneys in Leicester Fields, since Denoyer's will (PCC, dated 6 Nov. 1784, prob. 19 May 1788) mentions 'my Leashould Messuage in Leicester Fields in which I did live' (Highfill; *YW* ix. 29 n. 29; *GM* lviii[1] (1788), 468, lvix[1] (1789), 572, lxxx[1] (1810), 189; IGI).
Mrs Denoyer, an intimate friend of Mr Selwin, had visited St Martin's St. on Sat. morning and mentioned to FB's stepmother his visit to Streatham on Wed., which caused EAB subsequently to 'ask a thousand questions ab^t him' (SEB to FB, 5 Dec. 1779 (Barrett)). Her husband had recently been captured (and presumably shortly after released) by the French while crossing the Channel (*George III, Later Correspondence*, ed. A. Aspinall (Cambridge, 1962–70), v. 660).

came to Dinner:—&, in the Evening, begged that he might be admitted to ask me how I did. I was rather *Bundled* up, to be sure, with Cloaks, &c, but could not well refuse,—so he & Mr. Thrale, *Lady* & *Daughter*, all came together.

He appeared in *high flash*—took my Hand & insisted on kissing it,—& made me use all my strength to get it from him after even *repeating* that operation,—& then he entered into a mighty gay, lively, droll & agreeable Conversation,—Vowing *how often* he should have been in St. Martin's Street had he not known *I* was such a Rambler,—& running on in flighty Compliments, highly seasoned with Wit, till he diverted & put us all into spirits:—but Mrs. Thrale, who was fearful I should be fatigued, found no little difficulty to get him away;—he vowed he would *not* go,—said *she* might, & all of them, but for *his* part, he desired not [|] to Budge,—&, at last, when, by repeated remonstrances he was made retreat, he Vowed he *would* come again.

As soon as their Tea was over below stairs, Dr. Johnson came to make me a visit,—& while he was with me, I heard Mr. Murphy's step about the adjoining Rooms, not knowing well his way—& soon after, in he bolted, crying out 'They would fain have stopt me, but here I am!—'

However, I have no Time to write what passed: except that he *vowed* when he came next he would read the rest of my Play,—however, I shall bring it with me to Town, & *hide* it.

The next Day, Monday [6 Dec.], he left us,—& Lady Lade came,—she sat up stairs with me the whole morning, & she has been saying such shocking things of her apprehensions for my dear Mr. Thrale, that they have quite overset me, being already weaker by the Fever:—& just now, unluckily, Mrs. Thrale came in suddenly, & found me in so low spirited a situation that she insisted on knowing the cause,—I could not tell her, but hinted that Lady Lade, who was just gone down, had been talking dismally, & she immediately concluded it was concerning *Sir John*,—I am sure she wondered at my [|] prodigious *susceptibility*, as she well might—but I preferred passing for half an Idiot to telling her what I cannot tell *you* of Lady Lade's shocking & terrifying speeches.

Thursday [9 Dec.]—

My dearest Susanna—I shall return Home on Saturday [11 Dec.] to *stay*—probably all Winter. I will now only *name names* & have done. Tuesday morning [7 Dec.] I went down stairs,—Mr. Selwin was in the Library,—he had called to know how we all did,—every thing is just as it *should be* with respect to him at present, for he again behaves very unaffectedly—the Thrale's are all quieted, & he has for me only so much kindness as I hope he will not give up, since it is equally inoffensive to us both.

Mr. Seward came the same Day—& he is but this minute gone; he, too, is *extremely* yet very *comfortably* civil to me,— more so than *ever*, but quite without *airs* or *gallantry*, & therefore I was in better humour with him than ever,—

God bless—

yours

103   St Martin's Street,
14 December [1779]

To Hester Lynch Thrale

AL (Berg, Diary MSS I, paginated 1341–[4]), 14 Dec. 1779
Single sheet 4to, 2 pp. *pmk* ⟨PENNY⟩ POST PAID W TU wafer
Addressed: Mrs. Thrale | Streatham, | Surry.
Annotated (by FBA): 1780 [*sic*]

Decr 14th
St. Martin's Street.

Three Days only have I left dear Streatham—& I feel as if I had niether seen or heard of it as many months— Gratify me, Dearest Madam, with a few lines to tell me how You all do, for I am half uneasy—& *quite* impatient for intelligence. Does the *Card system* flourish?—does Dr.

Johnson continue gay & good humoured, & *'valuing Nobody'* in a morning?—is Miss Thrale steady in asserting that all will do perfectly well?—but most I wish to hear whether our Dear master is any better in spirits?—& whether my sweet *Dottoressa*[28] perseveres in supporting & exerting her own?—

I never returned to my own Home so little merrily disposed as this last Time,—when I parted with my master, I wished much to [have thanked him][29] for all the kindness [he has so constantly shewn me, but I][30] | found myself too grave for the purpose—however, I meant, when I parted with *You*, to make myself amends by making a speech long enough for *both*,—but then I was yet *less* able,—& thus it is that some or other cross accident for ever frustrates my Rhetorical designs!

I hope You found Mrs. Byron better,—I wish much to wait upon her, but this eternal Naso[31] of mine continues *indisposed*, & my Father will not suffer me to leave the House a moment.

Adieu, my dearest Madam,—pray give my affectionate Respects to Mr. Thrale & Dr. Johnson, my Love to Miss Thrale, & Comp^ts to your *Doves*,—& pray believe me

ever & ever[32]

---

28 'Woman doctor' (It.), i.e., HLT.
29 Supplied by FBA for 1½ lines cut away at bottom of leaf.
30 Also supplied for cut-away portion.
31 'Nose' (It.).
32 Close of valediction cut away, presumably for the signature.

APPENDIX 1

DR CHARLES BURNEY AND
GREGG'S COFFEE HOUSE

A SET of circumstantial evidence strongly suggests that Fanny Burney's father was proprietor of Gregg's Coffee House, York Street, Covent Garden, from about 1769 to 1784.

The shadowy 'Cousin', Mrs Gregg, to whom Burney addresses a verse letter in the first volume of this edition (Aug. 1768, 'At her House, York Street, Covent Garden', *EJL* i. 28–31), is identified in a Burney family pedigree belonging to Dr Burney's descendant Mr John R. G. Comyn as 'Mrs. E. Gregg', first cousin twice removed of Fanny Burney and first cousin of her paternal grandmother Mrs Ann (Cooper) Burney (who with her spinster daughters Ann and Rebecca was living with Mrs Gregg in 1768). The initial 'E.' in her name supports the conjecture (ibid., n. 74) that Mrs Gregg was the 'Elizabeth Gregg, Widow,' who was buried in St Paul's Churchyard, Covent Garden, 11 Dec. 1768. Rebecca Burney is listed as paying the poor rate from 1769 through 1783–84, when the house fell temporarily vacant (Rate Books for York Street, Covent Garden, Westminster Reference Library). But it is probable that her brother, Dr Burney, male head of the London Burneys, inherited the house upon Mrs Gregg's death; in his will he mentions (writing in 1807) 'my house in York Street, Covent Garden' (Scholes ii. 263), and bequeaths the rent to Rebecca, who had moved elsewhere. (Ann and Grandmother Burney had long since died.)

The rate books show a 'Francis Gregg', presumably Mrs Gregg's husband, living in York Street from 1730 to 1742 and again from 1749. (His name is still given in the books for 1768, though he had evidently died by that time.) In a notice in the *General Advertiser* for 10 Feb. 1752 occurs the earliest known mention of 'Gregg's Coffee-House, in York street, Covent Garden' (see B. Lillywhite, *London Coffee Houses* (1963), p. 247). In 1763 Dr Burney gave his business address there in *Mortimer's Universal Director*. In her Journal for 1778 Burney mentions a parcel left for her at '⌐Gregg's⌐ Coffee House. ⌐York street⌐', of which she had been informed by her aunts (p. 2), and in June she writes to her publisher Lowndes that 'I sent to Gregg's to enquire if any parcel had been left there for Mr

Grafton' (p. 33). The inference to be drawn from the foregoing evidence clearly is that the coffee house and the house of Mrs Gregg, Grandmother Burney and Rebecca and Ann Burney were one and the same. The rate books indicate that about late 1751 Francis Gregg acquired the house next door from an 'Elizabeth Lucas', and the sudden jump in the poor rate from £18 to £30 suggests that he enlarged and renovated it, presumably to open the Coffee House on the premises. (He sold his old house the following year.) It is possible that he acquired the new house (and the initial capital for the renovation) by marriage to Elizabeth Lucas, his erstwhile next-door neighbor. (The Burney family pedigree does not give Mrs Gregg's maiden name or any prior married name.)

Conclusive proof that Ann and Rebecca Burney were actively associated with the Coffee House comes in a letter from Samuel Crisp to Burney's younger sister Charlotte, 4 Aug. 1782 (Berg). Crisp asks her to help him find certain letters in a newspaper and observes, ' ... if your Aunts keep the Papers at the Coffee House, fil'd as they are done with, the letters wanted may be hunted out amongst them'. In conjunction with the other evidence, it requires no large leap of faith to assume that the aunts actually lived at the Coffee House (presumably in the original section of the house above or behind) and that they managed it for Dr Burney.

As mentioned above, the house in York Street fell temporarily vacant in 1783–84. After that date, a succession of unfamiliar names are listed as paying the rates. One name, however, Mr 'Hernon', is probably the 'Mr John Hanon' whom Dr Burney identifies as the tenant in York Street in 1807. There is apparently no other mention anywhere of the coffee house after the reference in Crisp's letter of 1782, which suggests that the establishment was closed in 1783–84, and the house simply let as a residence after that date.

The Coffee House, falling into his lap as it were, was probably welcomed at the start by Dr Burney as an additional source of income; he was often hard-pressed to sustain his genteel style of life. By 1783–84 perhaps business was falling off, or his aging sisters no longer felt capable of running the establishment for him. In any case he undoubtedly kept his ownership of the business a close family secret, it being 'beneath the dignity' of an aspiring man of letters hobnobbing with the aristocracy to be involved in such a lowly trade. His daughter Fanny obviously also felt it a duty to keep his ownership a secret, as she tried in her later years to edit out any direct mentions of the coffee house. (The only untouched naming of it is in the letter to Lowndes in June 1778, which she did not have in her possession.) In the Journal for 1778 she attempted to obliterate 'Gregg's' and 'York street' (in 'Gregg's Coffee House. York street'), substituting 'the Orange' for Gregg's. (She had previously used the Orange Coffee House in the Haymarket as the rendezvous for delivering *Evelina* to the publisher.)

It is interesting to note that the newspapers in Gregg's Coffee House, mentioned by Samuel Crisp in his letter to Charlotte Burney, probably formed the nucleus of the famous Burney Collection of Early English Newspapers in the British Library, bequeathed to that institution by Fanny's brother Charles upon his death in 1817. Charles probably began the collection upon his return to London after obtaining an MA degree from Aberdeen University in 1781. (For this suggestion we are indebted to Prof. Betty Rizzo, City College of New York.)

APPENDIX 2

CHARLES BURNEY JUNIOR'S
LINES ON *EVELINA*

THIS 'Sonnet' is in CB Jr.'s MS 'Poetical Trifles', in the Osborn
Collection. Another version, entitled 'Sonnet written in a blank
leaf of Evelina', ending 'An *Orville* love thee, & the world
admire', and signed 'Charles Burney. DD. October, 1778', is
copied into Charlotte Burney (Francis) Broome's Commonplace
Book of Verses (MS Eng 926) in the Houghton Library.

Sonnet, written in Evelina, and addressed to the Ladies.

> Ah! beauteous Nymph, who e'er thou art,
> Who shalt peruse this hapless Virgin's tale,
> When pleasure fires thy gentle heart,
> By Fancy led, and fan'd by Rapture's gale,
> Expand thy mind—receive the proffer'd joy—
> The fruit of genuine wit can never cloy.
>
> If tears of sympathy should flow,
> Check not the offspring of a generous mind:
> Who hears unmov'd another's woe,
> No soothing friend in misery shall find:
> The tender bosom claims a sweet relief,
> When virtue lulls to rest the social grief.
>
> O grave the Moral on thy breast,
> See saintlike innocence, superiour rise:
> See Fashion's glittering slaves deprest—
> See—and those lures of Idleness despise!
> So to distinguish'd joys thou mayst aspire—
> The Virtues love thee, and the World admire.

INDEX

This is an index of all proper names in Fanny Burney's text and of selected names in the introduction, annotations, and appendices. In general, women are given under their married names unless they first appear under their maiden names. Similarly, peers are given under their titles unless they are first mentioned before their elevation. For the most part, works are cited under the author (translator, editor), composer, or artist. Main biographical notes are indicated in boldface.